Mike Holt's Illustrated Guide to

UNDERSTANDING NEC® REQUIREMENTS F

BONDING AND GROUNDING

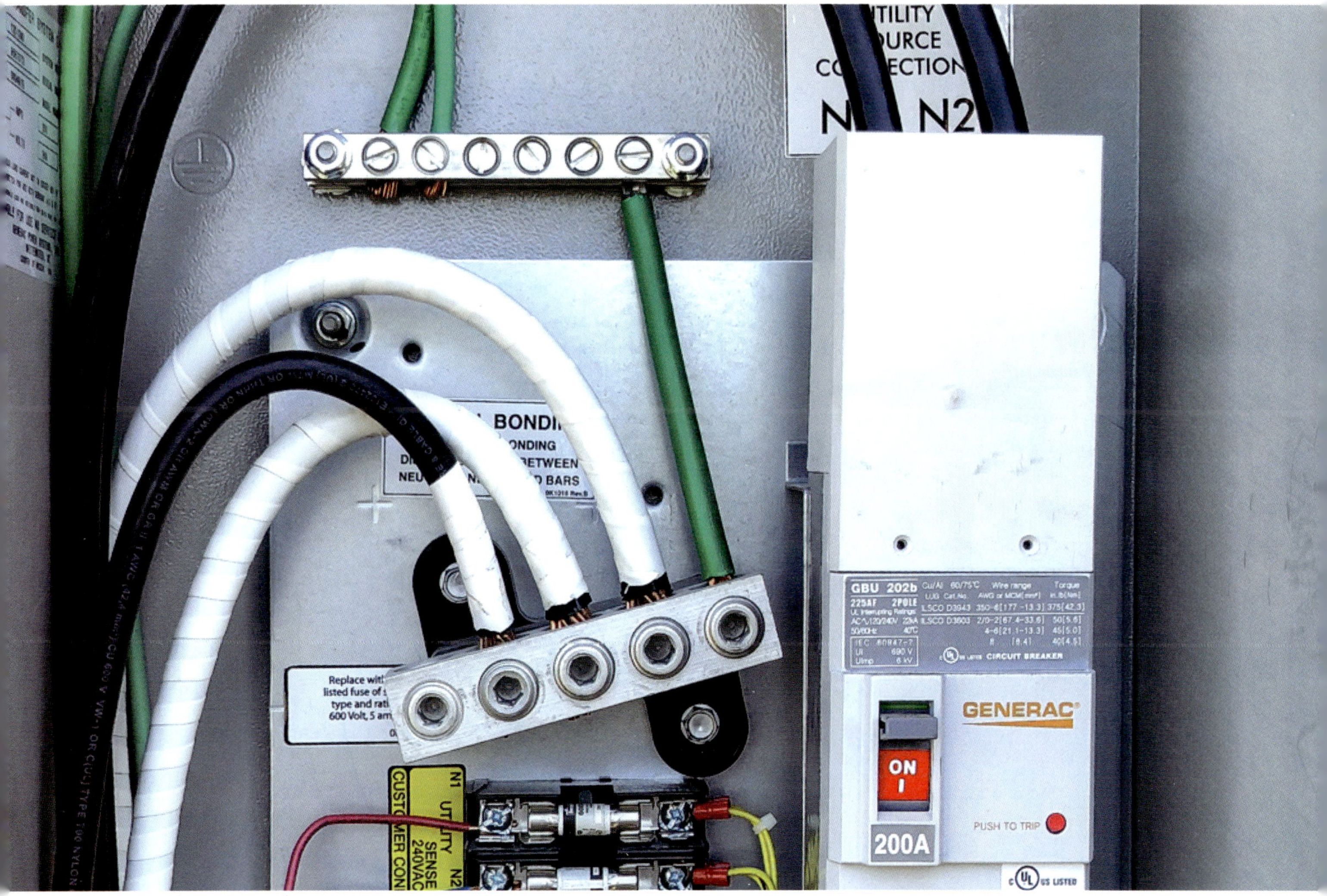

BASED ON THE

2023 NEC®

Mike Holt Enterprises
MikeHolt.com • 888.632.2633

NOTICE TO THE READER

The text and commentary in this book is the author's interpretation of the 2023 Edition of NFPA 70®, *National Electrical Code*®. It shall not be considered an endorsement of or the official position of the NFPA® or any of its committees, nor relied upon as a formal interpretation of the meaning or intent of any specific provision or provisions of the 2023 edition of NFPA 70, *National Electrical Code*.

The publisher does not warrant or guarantee any of the products described herein or perform any independent analysis in connection with any of the product information contained herein. The publisher does not assume, and expressly disclaims, any obligation to obtain and include information other than that provided to it by the manufacturer.

The reader is expressly warned to consider and adopt all safety precautions and applicable federal, state, and local laws and regulations. By following the instructions contained herein, the reader willingly assumes all risks in connection with such instructions.

Mike Holt Enterprises disclaims liability for any personal injury, property or other damages of any nature whatsoever, whether special, indirect, consequential or compensatory, directly or indirectly resulting from the use of this material. The reader is responsible for relying on his or her personal independent judgment in determining safety and appropriate actions in all circumstances.

The publisher makes no representation or warranties of any kind, including but not limited to, the warranties of fitness for particular purpose or merchantability, nor are any such representations implied with respect to the material set forth herein, and the publisher takes no responsibility with respect to such material. The publisher shall not be liable for any special, consequential, or exemplary damages resulting, in whole or part, from the reader's use of, or reliance upon, this material.

Mike Holt's Illustrated Guide to Understanding NEC® Requirements for Bonding and Grounding, based on the 2023 NEC®

First Printing: January 2023
Author: Mike Holt
Technical Illustrator: Mike Culbreath
Cover Design: Bryan Burch
Layout Design and Typesetting: Cathleen Kwas

ISBN 978-1-950431-74-8

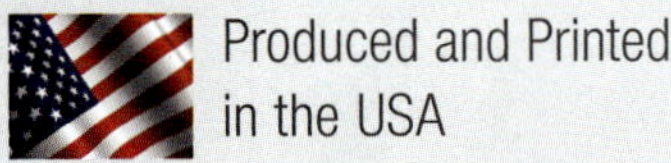

Produced and Printed in the USA

This logo is a registered trademark of Mike Holt Enterprises, Inc.

NFPA

nec
NFPA

NEC®, NFPA 70®, NFPA 70E® and *National Electrical Code*® are registered trademarks of the National Fire Protection Association.

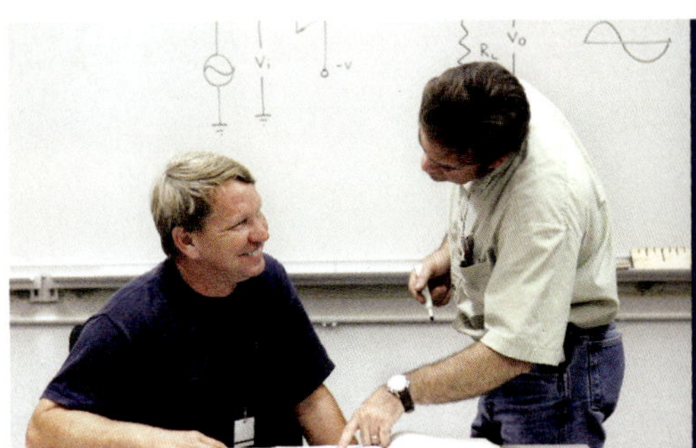

I dedicate this book to the

Lord Jesus Christ, *my mentor and teacher.*

Proverbs 16:3

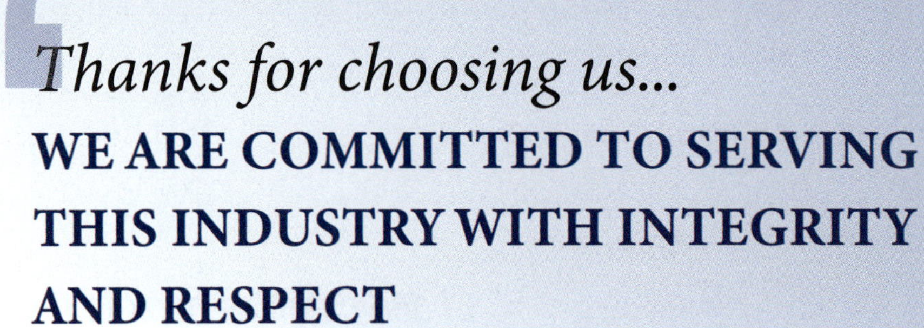

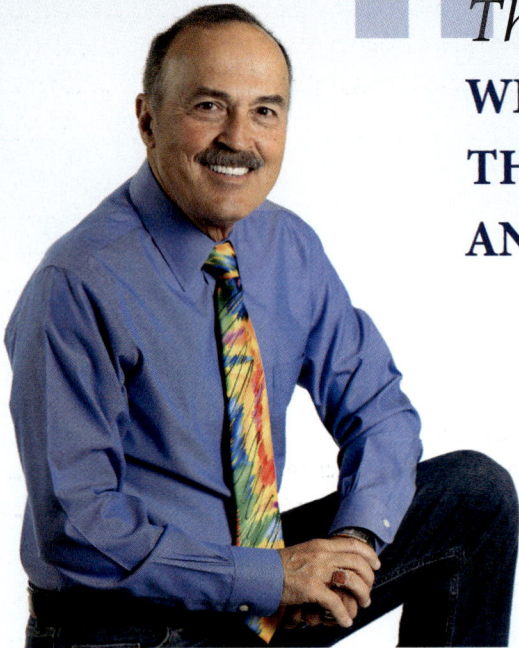

Thanks for choosing us...

WE ARE COMMITTED TO SERVING THIS INDUSTRY WITH INTEGRITY AND RESPECT

Since 1975, we have worked hard to develop products that get results, and to help individuals in their pursuit of success in this exciting industry.

From the very beginning we have been committed to the idea that customers come first. Everyone on my team will do everything they possibly can to help you succeed. I want you to know that we value you and are honored that you have chosen us to be your partner in training.

You are the future of this industry and we know that it is you who will make the difference in the years to come. My goal is to share with you everything that I know and to encourage you to pursue your education on a continuous basis. I hope that not only will you learn theory, *Code*, calculations, or how to pass an exam, but that in the process, you will become the expert in the field and the person others know to trust.

To put it simply, we genuinely care about your success and will do everything that we can to help you take your skills to the next level!

We are happy to partner with you on your educational journey.

God bless and much success,

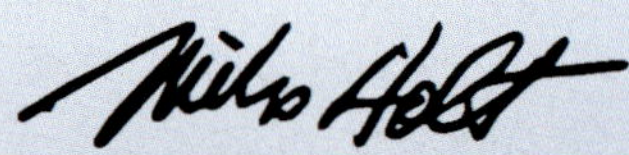

TABLE OF CONTENTS

ABOUT THIS TEXTBOOK

Mike Holt's Illustrated Guide to Understanding NEC Requirements for Bonding and Grounding, based on the 2023 NEC

What's the difference between grounded and bonded? Is there a difference? Did you know that many in our industry confuse and mis-use these terms? This textbook will help you understand those differences and the essential function of each in electrical systems. It is the first in the series of Mike Holt textbooks that focuses on a single topic—Bonding and Grounding.

This textbook isn't just about Article 250; it is about the bigger picture of constructing an essentially safe electrical system. It spans the length of the entire *NEC®* and assumes that you understand Electrical Theory, the application of *NEC* rules, and basic *NEC* calculations. To fully benefit from this content, it's suggested that you have completed Mike Holt's Understanding Electrical Theory and both Volume 1 and Volume 2 of Mike's Understanding the *National Electrical Code®* series.

This textbook covers the application of the *NEC* rules relating to bonding and grounding so that you understand how and why electrical systems must be built to fail safely. The textbook was designed to be used along with the associated video series in which Mike and a panel of experts expand on the rules, analyze them, and give them context by discussing their practical application in real-world settings. Your journey through this topic will explore subjects that include:

- how electrical shock, electrocution, and fire happen
- the difference between grounding and bonding
- the purpose of the effective ground fault current path
- how Overcurrent, GFCI, and AFCI devices work

Mike's writing style is informative, practical, easy to understand, and applicable for today's electrical professional. Just like all of Mike Holt's textbooks, this one is built around hundreds of full-color illustrations and photographs that show the requirements of the *National Electrical Code* in practical use. The images provide a visual representation of the information being discussed, helping you better understand just how the *Code* rules are applied.

Keeping up with requirements of the *Code* should be the goal of everyone involved in electrical safety—whether you're an installer, contractor, inspector, engineer, or instructor. This textbook is the perfect tool to help you enhance your understanding of one of the most important, and possibly least understood, areas of the *Code*.

The Scope of This Textbook

This textbook, *Mike Holt's Illustrated Guide to Understanding NEC Requirements for Bonding and Grounding, based on the 2023 NEC*, covers those installation requirements that we consider to be important and is based on the following conditions:

1. Power Systems and Voltage. All power-supply systems are assumed to be one of the following nominal voltages or "voltage class," unless identified otherwise:

- 2-wire, single-phase, 120V
- 3-wire, single-phase, 120/240V
- 4-wire, three-phase, 120/240V Delta High-Leg
- 4-wire, three-phase, 208YY120V or 480Y/277V Wye

2. Electrical Calculations. Unless the question or example specifies three-phase, they're based on a single-phase power supply. In addition, all amperage calculations resulting in a decimal fraction 0.50 of an ampere or higher are rounded to the nearest whole number in accordance with Section 220.5(B).

3. Conductor Material/Insulation. The conductor material and insulation are copper THWN-2, unless otherwise indicated.

4. Conductor Sizing.

Circuits Rated 100A or Less. Conductors are sized to the 60°C column of Table 310.16 [110.14(C)(1)(a)(2)]. Where equipment is listed and identified for use with conductors having at least a 75°C temperature rating, the conductors can be sized to the 75°C column of Table 310.16 [110.14(C)(1)(a)(3)].

Circuits Rated Over 100A. Conductors are sized to the 75°C column of Table 310.16 [110.14(C)(1)(b)(2)].

5. Overcurrent Protective Device. The term "overcurrent protective device" refers to a molded-case circuit breaker, unless specified otherwise. Where a fuse is specified, it's a single-element type fuse, also known as a "onetime fuse," unless the text specifies otherwise.

How to Use This Textbook

This textbook is to be used along with the *NEC* and not as a replacement for it. Be sure to have a copy of the 2023 *National Electrical Code* handy. You'll notice that we've paraphrased a great deal of the *NEC* wording, and some of the article and section titles appear different from the text in the actual *Code* book. We believe doing so makes it easier to understand the intent of the rule.

Always compare what's being explained in this textbook to what the *Code* book says. Get with others who are knowledgeable about the *NEC* to discuss any topics that you find difficult to understand.

We carefully select what is covered in Mike Holt's textbooks to include content that represents the most common installations. This textbook follows the *NEC* format, but it doesn't cover every *Code* requirement. For example, it doesn't include every article, section, subsection, exception, or Informational Note. So, don't be concerned if you see that the textbook contains Exception 1 and Exception 3, but not Exception 2.

Cross-References. *NEC* cross-references to other related *Code* requirements are included to help you develop a better understanding of how the *NEC* rules relate to one another. These cross-references are indicated by *Code* section numbers in brackets, an example of which is "[90.4]."

Informational Notes. Informational Notes contained in the *NEC* will be identified in this textbook as "Note."

Exceptions. Exceptions contained in this textbook will be identified as "Ex" and not spelled out.

As you read through this textbook, allow yourself sufficient time to review the text along with the outstanding graphics and examples, which will be invaluable to your understanding of the *NEC*.

Answer Keys

If you ordered your textbook directly through Mike Holt Enterprises, your digital answer key can be found in your online account. Go to MikeHolt.com/MyAccount and log in to your account, or create one if you haven't already done so. If you are not currently a Mike Holt customer, you can access an answer key at MikeHolt.com/MyAK23BG.

Watch the Videos That Accompany This Textbook

Mike, along with an expert panel, recorded videos to accompany this textbook. Watching these videos will complete your learning experience. The videos contain explanations and additional commentary that expand on the topics covered in the textbook. Mike and the panel discuss the nuances behind the rules, give them context, and explain their practical application in the field.

To watch a few video clips, scan this QR *Code* with a smartphone app or visit www.MikeHolt.com/23BGvideos for a sample selection. To get the complete video library that accompanies this book, call 888.632.2633 and let them know you want to add the videos, or visit MikeHolt.com/upgrade23BG.

Technical Questions

As you progress through this textbook, you might find that you don't understand every explanation, example, calculation, or comment. If you find some topics difficult to understand, they are discussed in detail in the videos that correlate to this book. We recommend that you review *Mike's Understanding the National Electrical Code Volumes 1 and 2* textbooks, as well as *Understanding Electrical Theory*. You may also find it helpful to discuss your questions with instructors, co-workers, other students, or your supervisor—they might have a perspective that will help you understand more clearly. Don't become frustrated, and don't get down on yourself. If you have additional questions that aren't covered in this material, visit MikeHolt.com/Forum, and post your question on the Code Forum for help.

Textbook Errors and Corrections

We're committed to providing you the finest product with the fewest errors and take great care to ensure our textbooks are correct. But we're realistic and know that errors might be found after printing. If you believe that there's an error of any kind (typographical, grammatical, technical, etc.) in this textbook or in the Answer Key, please visit MikeHolt.com/Corrections and complete the online Correction Form.

Textbook Format

The layout and design of this textbook incorporate special features and symbols that were designed for Mike Holt textbooks to help you easily navigate through the material, and to enhance your understanding of the content.

Formulas

$$P = I \times E$$

Formulas are easily identifiable in green text on a gray bar.

Modular Color-Coded Page Layout

Chapters are color-coded and modular to make it easy to navigate through each section of the textbook.

According to Article 100

Throughout the textbook, Mike references definitions that are easily identified by colored text "**According to Article 100,**" at the start of the paragraph.

Additional Background Information Boxes

Where the author believes that information unrelated to the specific rule will help you understand the concept being taught, he includes these topics, easily identified in boxes that are shaded gray.

> **Dangers of Objectionable Current**
>
> Objectionable neutral current on metal parts can cause electric shock, fires, and the improper operation of electronic equipment and overcurrent protective devices such as GFPEs, GFCIs, SPGFCIs, and AFCIs.

Caution, Danger, and Warning Icons

These icons highlight areas of concern.

Caution

CAUTION: An explanation of possible damage to property or equipment.

Danger

DANGER: An explanation of possible severe injury or death.

Warning

WARNING: An explanation of possible severe property damage or personal injury.

Key Features

Detailed full-color educational graphics illustrate the change in a real-world application.

Each first level subsection of each *Code* rule is highlighted in yellow to help you navigate through the text.

Underlined text denotes changes to the *Code* for the 2023 *NEC*.

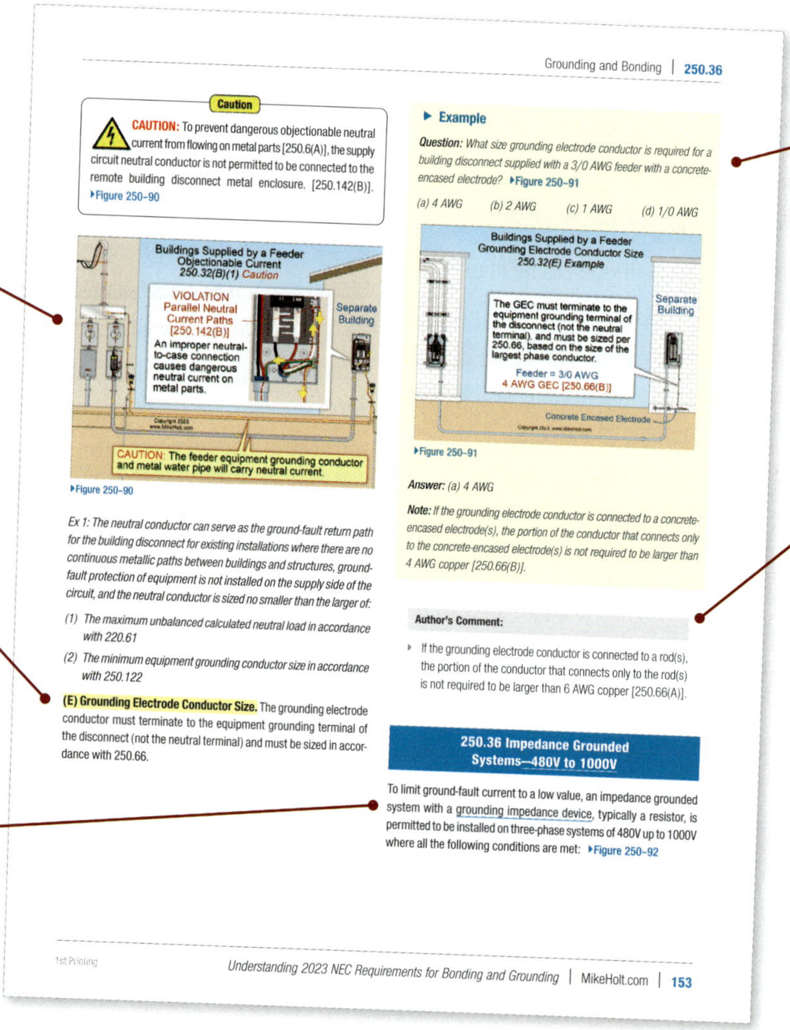

Examples and practical application questions and answers are contained in yellow boxes.

Author's Comments provide additional information to help you understand the context.

If you see an ellipsis (• • •) at the bottom right corner of a page or example box, it is continued on the following page.

ADDITIONAL PRODUCTS TO HELP YOU LEARN

Upgrade Your Textbook with the Bonding and Grounding Videos, based on the 2023 *NEC*

One of the best ways to get the most out of this textbook is to use it in conjunction with the corresponding videos. These videos showcase dynamic discussions as Mike and his video team of industry experts deep-dive into the topics in this book. They analyze each rule, its purpose, and its application in the field.

Whether you're a visual or an auditory learner, watching the videos as you work through the textbook will enhance your knowledge and provide additional in-depth insight into each topic. Upgrade your program today, and you will broaden your understanding of the rules and their impact on your work. All upgrade purchases include the corresponding videos plus a digital copy of the textbook.

UPGRADE PACKAGE INCLUDES:

- *2023 Bonding and Grounding streaming videos*

Digital answer key

Plus! A digital version of the textbook

Ready to get started? To add the videos that accompany this textbook, scan the QR code, call our office at 888.632.2633, or visit MikeHolt.com/upgrade23BG.

Have questions? You can e-mail info@MikeHolt.com.

Product Code: [23BGUPGRADEVI]

Understanding the *NEC* Complete Video Library

Do you want a comprehensive understanding of the *Code*? Then you need Mike's best-selling Understanding the *NEC* Complete Video Library. This program has helped thousands of electricians learn the *Code* because of its easy-to-use format. Mike guides students through the most utilized rules and breaks them down in a complete and thorough way. The full-color instructional graphics in the textbooks help students visualize and understand the concepts being taught; the videos provide additional reinforcement with Mike and the panel discussing each article, its meaning and its application in the real world. When you need to know the *Code*, this program is the best tool you can use to start building your knowledge—there's no other product quite like it.

PROGRAM INCLUDES:

Understanding the National Electrical Code—Volume 1 Textbook

- *Understanding the NEC Volume 1 streaming videos*

Understanding the National Electrical Code—Volume 2 Textbook

- *Understanding the NEC Volume 2 streaming videos*

Bonding and Grounding Textbook

- *Bonding and Grounding streaming videos*

Understanding the National Electrical Code Workbook (Articles 90-480)

Digital answer keys

Plus! A digital version of each textbook

Product Code: [23UNDLIBMM]

To order the additional products that complete this library, please call our office at 888.632.2633.

2023 Changes to the *NEC* Video Program

Don't let the scale of the changes to the *Code* intimidate you. This package will get you up to speed on the most essential 2023 *NEC* changes. The textbook is well-organized, easy to follow, and the full-color illustrations and photos bring the material to life. The videos bring together a group of experts from the field to discuss the changes and how they apply in the real world.

PROGRAM INCLUDES:

Changes to the 2023 NEC Textbook

- *Changes to the 2023 NEC streaming videos*

Digital answer key

Plus! A digital version of the textbook

Product Code: [23CCMM]

2023 *Code* Books and Tabs

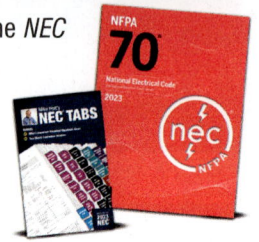

The easiest way to use your copy of the *NEC* correctly is to tab it for quick reference. Mike's best-selling tabs make organizing your *Code* book easy. Please note that if you're using it for an exam, you'll need to confirm with your testing authority that a tabbed *Code* book is allowed into the exam room.

To order your *Code* book and tabs, visit MikeHolt.com/Code.

Product Code: [23NECB]

To order visit MikeHolt.com/Code, or call 888.632.2633.

HOW TO USE THE *NATIONAL ELECTRICAL CODE*

The original *NEC* document was developed in 1897 as a result of the united efforts of various insurance, electrical, architectural, and other cooperative interests. The National Fire Protection Association (NFPA) has sponsored the *National Electrical Code* since 1911.

The purpose of the *Code* is the practical safeguarding of persons and property from hazards arising from the use of electricity. It isn't intended as a design specification or an instruction manual for untrained persons. It is, in fact, a standard that contains the minimum requirements for an electrical installation that's essentially free from hazard. Learning to understand and use the *Code* is critical to you working safely; whether you're training to become an electrician, or are already an electrician, electrical contractor, inspector, engineer, designer, or instructor.

The *NEC* was written for qualified persons; those who understand electrical terms, theory, safety procedures, and electrical trade practices. Learning to use the *Code* is a lengthy process and can be frustrating if you don't approach it the right way. First, you'll need to understand electrical theory and if you don't have theory as a background when you get into the *NEC*, you're going to struggle. Take one step back if necessary and learn electrical theory. You must also understand the concepts and terms in the *Code* and know grammar and punctuation in order to understand the complex structure of the rules and their intended purpose(s). The *NEC* is written in a formal outline which many of us haven't seen or used since high school or college so it's important for you to pay particular attention to this format. Our goal for the next few pages is to give you some guidelines and suggestions on using your *Code* book to help you understand that standard, and assist you in what you're trying to accomplish and, ultimately, your personal success as an electrical professional!

Language Considerations for the *NEC*

Terms and Concepts

The *NEC* contains many technical terms, and it's crucial for *Code* users to understand their meanings and applications. If you don't understand a term used in a rule, it will be impossible to properly apply the *NEC* requirement. Article 100 defines those that are used generally in two or more articles throughout the *Code*; for example, the term "Dwelling Unit" is found in many articles. If you don't know the *NEC* definition for a "dwelling unit" you can't properly identify its *Code* requirements. Another example worth mentioning is the term "Outlet." For many people it has always meant a receptacle—not so in the *NEC*!

Article 100 contains the definitions of terms used throughout the *Code*. Where a definition is unique to a specific article, the article number is indicated at the end of the definition in parenthesis (xxx). For example, the definition of "Pool" is specific to Article 680 and ends with (680) because it applies ONLY to that article. Definitions of standard terms, such as volt, voltage drop, ampere, impedance, and resistance are not contained in Article 100. If the *NEC* does not define a term, then a dictionary or building code acceptable to the authority having jurisdiction should be consulted.

Small Words, Grammar, and Punctuation

Technical words aren't the only ones that require close attention. Even simple words can make a big difference to the application of a rule. Is there a comma? Does it use "or," "and," "other than," "greater than," or "smaller than"? The word "or" can imply alternate choices for wiring methods. A word like "or" gives us choices while the word "and" can mean an additional requirement must be met.

An example of the important role small words play in the *NEC* is found in 110.26(C)(2), where it says equipment containing overcurrent, switching, "or" control devices that are 1,200A or more "and" over 6 ft wide require a means of egress at each end of the working space. In this section, the word "or" clarifies that equipment containing any of the three types of devices listed must follow this rule. The word "and" clarifies that 110.26(C)(2) only applies if the equipment is both 1,200A or more and over 6 ft wide.

Grammar and punctuation play an important role in establishing the meaning of a rule. The location of a comma can dramatically change the requirement of a rule such as in 250.28(A), where it says a main bonding jumper shall be a wire, bus, screw, or similar suitable conductor. If the comma between "bus" and "screw" was removed, only a "bus screw" could be used. That comma makes a big change in the requirements of the rule.

Slang Terms or Technical Jargon

Trade-related professionals in different areas of the country often use local "slang" terms that aren't shared by all. This can make it difficult to communicate if it isn't clear what the meaning of those slang terms are. Use the proper terms by finding out what their definitions and applications are before you use them. For example, the term "pigtail" is often used to describe the short piece of conductor used to connect a device to a splice, but a "pigtail" is also used for a rubberized light socket with pre-terminated conductors. Although the term is the same, the meaning is very different and could cause confusion. The words "splice" and "tap" are examples of terms often interchanged in the field but are two entirely different things! The uniformity and consistency of the terminology used in the *Code*, makes it so everyone says and means the same thing regardless of geographical location.

NEC Style and Layout

It's important to understand the structure and writing style of the *Code* if you want to use it effectively. The *National Electrical Code* is organized using twelve major components.

1. Table of Contents
2. Chapters—Chapters 1 through 9 (major categories)
3. Articles—Chapter subdivisions that cover specific subjects
4. Parts—Divisions used to organize article subject matter
5. Sections—Divisions used to further organize article subject matter
6. Tables and Figures—Represent the mandatory requirements of a rule
7. Exceptions—Alternatives to the main *Code* rule
8. Informational Notes—Explanatory material for a specific rule (not a requirement)
9. Tables—Applicable as referenced in the *NEC*
10. Annexes—Additional explanatory information such as tables and references (not a requirement)
11. Index
12. Changes to the *Code* from the previous edition

1. Table of Contents. The Table of Contents displays the layout of the chapters, articles, and parts as well as the page numbers. It's an excellent resource and should be referred to periodically to observe the interrelationship of the various *NEC* components. When attempting to locate the rules for a specific situation, knowledgeable *Code* users often go first to the Table of Contents to quickly find the specific *NEC* rule that applies.

2. Chapters. There are nine chapters, each of which is divided into articles. The articles fall into one of four groupings: General Requirements (Chapters 1 through 4), Specific Requirements (Chapters 5 through 7), Communications Systems (Chapter 8), and Tables (Chapter 9).

Chapter 1—General
Chapter 2—Wiring and Protection
Chapter 3—Wiring Methods and Materials
Chapter 4—Equipment for General Use
Chapter 5—Special Occupancies
Chapter 6—Special Equipment
Chapter 7—Special Conditions
Chapter 8—Communications Systems (Telephone, Data, Satellite, Cable TV, and Broadband)
Chapter 9—Tables-Conductor and Raceway Specifications

3. Articles. The *NEC* contains approximately 160 articles, each of which covers a specific subject. It begins with Article 90, the introduction to the *Code* which contains the purpose of the *NEC*, what is covered and isn't covered, along with how the *Code* is arranged. It also gives information on enforcement, how mandatory and permissive rules are written, and how explanatory material is included. Article 90 also includes information on formal interpretations, examination of equipment for safety, wiring planning, and information about formatting units of measurement. Here are some other examples of articles you'll find in the *NEC*:

Article 110—General Requirements for Electrical Installations
Article 250—Grounding and Bonding
Article 300—General Requirements for Wiring Methods and Materials
Article 430—Motors, Motor Circuits, and Motor Controllers
Article 500—Hazardous (Classified) Locations
Article 680—Swimming Pools, Fountains, and Similar Installations
Article 725—Class 2 and Class 3 Power-Limited Circuits
Article 800—General Requirements for Communications Systems

4. Parts. Larger articles are subdivided into parts. Because the parts of a *Code* article aren't included in the section numbers, we tend to forget to what "part" an *NEC* rule is relating. For example, Table 110.34(A) contains working space clearances for electrical equipment. If we aren't careful, we might think this table applies to all electrical installations, but Table 110.34(A) is in Part III, which only contains requirements for "Over 1,000 Volts, Nominal" installations. The rules for working clearances for electrical equipment for systems 1,000V, nominal, or less are contained in Table 110.26(A)(1), which is in Part II—1,000 Volts, Nominal, or Less.

5. Sections. Each *NEC* rule is called a "*Code* Section." A *Code* section may be broken down into subdivisions; first level subdivision will be in parentheses like (A), (B),..., the next will be second level subdivisions in parentheses like (1), (2),..., and third level subdivisions in lowercase letters such as (a), (b), and so on.

For example, the rule requiring all receptacles in a dwelling unit bathroom to be GFCI protected is contained in Section 210.8(A)(1) which is in Chapter 2, Article 210, Section 8, first level subdivision (A), and second level subdivision (1).

Note: According to the *NEC Style Manual*, first and second level subdivisions are required to have titles. A title for a third level subdivision is permitted but not required.

Many in the industry incorrectly use the term "Article" when referring to a *Code* section. For example, they say "Article 210.8," when they should say "Section 210.8." Section numbers in this textbook are shown without the word "Section," unless they're at the beginning of a sentence. For example, Section 210.8(A) is shown as simply 210.8(A).

6. Tables and Figures. Many *NEC* requirements are contained within tables, which are lists of *Code* rules placed in a systematic arrangement. The titles of the tables are extremely important; you must read them carefully in order to understand the contents, applications, and limitations of each one. Notes are often provided in or below a table; be sure to read them as well since they're also part of the requirement. For example, Note 1 for Table 300.5(A) explains how to measure the cover when burying cables and raceways and Note 5 explains what to do if solid rock is encountered.

7. Exceptions. Exceptions are *NEC* requirements or permissions that provide an alternative method to a specific rule. There are two types of exceptions—mandatory and permissive. When a rule has several exceptions, those exceptions with mandatory requirements are listed before the permissive exceptions.

Mandatory Exceptions. A mandatory exception uses the words "shall" or "shall not." The word "shall" in an exception means that if you're using the exception, you're required to do it in a specific way. The phrase "shall not" means it isn't permitted.

Permissive Exceptions. A permissive exception uses words such as "shall be permitted," which means it's acceptable (but not mandatory) to do it in this way.

8. Informational Notes. An Informational Note contains explanatory material intended to clarify a rule or give assistance, but it isn't a *Code* requirement.

9. Tables. Chapter 9 consists of tables applicable as referenced in the *NEC*. They're used to calculate raceway sizing, conductor fill, the radius of raceway bends, and conductor voltage drop.

10. Informative Annexes. Annexes aren't a part of the *Code* requirements and are included for informational purposes only.

Annex A. Product Safety Standards
Annex B. Application Information for Ampacity Calculation
Annex C. Conduit, Tubing, and Cable Tray Fill Tables for Conductors and Fixture Wires of the Same Size
Annex D. Examples
Annex E. Types of Construction
Annex F. Availability and Reliability for Critical Operations Power Systems (COPS), and Development and Implementation of Functional Performance Tests (FPTs) for Critical Operations Power Systems
Annex G. Supervisory Control and Data Acquisition (SCADA)
Annex H. Administration and Enforcement
Annex I. Recommended Tightening Torque Tables from UL Standard 486A-486B
Annex J. ADA Standards for Accessible Design
Annex K. Use of Medical Electrical Equipment in Dwellings and Residential Board-and-Care Occupancies

11. Index. The Index at the back of the *NEC* is helpful in locating a specific rule using pertinent keywords to assist in your search.

12. Changes to the *Code*. Changes in the *NEC* are indicated as follows:

- Rules that were changed since the previous edition are identified by shading the revised text.
- New rules aren't shaded like a change, instead they have a shaded "N" in the margin to the left of the section number.
- Relocated rules are treated like new rules with a shaded "N" in the left margin by the section number.

- Deleted rules are indicated by a bullet symbol "•" located in the left margin where the rule was in the previous edition. Unlike older editions the bullet symbol is only used where one or more complete paragraphs have been deleted.
- A "Δ" represents partial text deletions and or figure/table revisions somewhere in the text. There's no specific indication of which word, group of words, or a sentence was deleted.

How to Locate a Specific Requirement

How to go about finding what you're looking for in the *Code* book depends, to some degree, on your experience with the *NEC*. Experts typically know the requirements so well that they just go to the correct rule. Very experienced people might only need the Table of Contents to locate the requirement for which they're looking. On the other hand, average users should use all the tools at their disposal, including the Table of Contents, the Index, and the search feature on electronic versions of the *Code* book.

Let's work through a simple example: What *NEC* rule specifies the maximum number of disconnects permitted for a service?

Using the Table of Contents. If you're an experienced *Code* user, you might use the Table of Contents. You'll know Article 230 applies to "Services," and because this article is so large, it's divided up into multiple parts (eight parts to be exact). With this knowledge, you can quickly go to the Table of Contents and see it lists the Service Equipment Disconnecting Means requirements in Part VI.

Author's Comment:

- The number "70" precedes all page numbers in this standard because the *NEC* is NFPA Standard Number 70.

Using the Index. If you use the Index (which lists subjects in alphabetical order) to look up the term "service disconnect," you'll see there's no listing. If you try "disconnecting means," then "services," you'll find that the Index indicates the rule is in Article 230, Part VI. Because the *NEC* doesn't give a page number in the Index, you'll need to use the Table of Contents to find it, or flip through the *Code* book to Article 230, then continue to flip through pages until you find Part VI.

Many people complain that the *NEC* only confuses them by taking them in circles. Once you gain experience in using the *Code* and deepen your understanding of words, terms, principles, and practices, you'll find it much easier to understand and use than you originally thought.

With enough exposure in the use of the *NEC*, you'll discover that some words and terms are often specific to certain articles. The word "solar" for example will immediately send experienced *Code* book users to Article 690–Solar Photovoltaic (PV) Systems. The word "marina" suggests what you seek might be in Article 555. There are times when a main article will send you to a specific requirement in another one in which compliance is required in which case it will say (for example), "in accordance with 230.xx." Don't think of these situations as a "circle," but rather a map directing you to exactly where you need to be.

Customizing Your *Code* Book

One way to increase your comfort level with your *Code* book is to customize it to meet your needs. You can do this by highlighting and underlining important *NEC* requirements. Preprinted adhesive tabs are also an excellent aid to quickly find important articles and sections that are regularly referenced. However, understand that if you're using your *Code* book to prepare to take an exam, some exam centers don't allow markings of any type. For more information about tabs for your *Code* book, visit MikeHolt.com/Tabs.

Highlighting. As you read through or find answers to your questions, be sure you highlight those requirements in the *NEC* that are the most important or relevant to you. Use one color, like yellow, for general interest and a different one for important requirements you want to find quickly. Be sure to highlight terms in the Index and the Table of Contents as you use them.

Underlining. Underline or circle key words and phrases in the *Code* with a red or blue pen (not a lead pencil) using a short ruler or other straightedge to keep lines straight and neat. This is a very handy way to make important requirements stand out. A short ruler or other straightedge also comes in handy for locating the correct information in a table.

Interpretations

Industry professionals often enjoy the challenge of discussing, and at times debating, the *Code* requirements. These types of discussions are important to the process of better understanding the *NEC* requirements and applications. However, if you decide you're going to participate in one of these discussions, don't spout out what you think without having the actual *Code* book in your hand. The professional way of discussing a requirement is by referring to a specific section rather than talking in vague generalities. This will help everyone involved clearly understand the point and become better educated. In fact, you may become so well educated about the *NEC* that you might even decide to participate in the change process and help to make it even better!

Become Involved in the *NEC* Process

The actual process of changing the *Code* takes about two years and involves hundreds of individuals trying to make the *NEC* as current and accurate as possible. As you advance in your studies and understanding of the *Code*, you might begin to find it very interesting, enjoy it more, and realize that you can also be a part of the process. Rather than sitting back and allowing others to take the lead, you can participate by making proposals and being a part of its development. For the 2023 cycle, there were over 4,000 Public Inputs and 1,956 Public Comments. This resulted in several new articles and a wide array of revised rules to keep the *NEC* up to date with new technologies and pave the way to a safer and more efficient electrical future.

Here's how the process works:

STEP 1—Public Input Stage

Public Input. The revision cycle begins with the acceptance of Public Input (PI) which is the public notice asking for anyone interested to submit input on an existing standard or a committee-approved new draft standard. Following the closing date, the committee conducts a First Draft Meeting to respond to all Public Inputs.

First Draft Meeting. At the First Draft (FD) Meeting, the Technical Committee considers and provides a response to all Public Input. The Technical Committee may use the input to develop First Revisions to the standard. The First Draft documents consist of the initial meeting consensus of the committee by simple majority. However, the final position of the Technical Committee must be established by a ballot which follows.

Committee Ballot on First Draft. The First Draft developed at the First Draft Meeting is balloted. In order to appear in the First Draft, a revision must be approved by at least two-thirds of the Technical Committee.

First Draft Report Posted. First revisions which pass ballot are ultimately compiled and published as the First Draft Report on the document's NFPA web page. This report serves as documentation for the Input Stage and is published for review and comment. The public may review the First Draft Report to determine whether to submit Public Comments on the First Draft.

STEP 2—Public Comment Stage

Public Comment. Once the First Draft Report becomes available, there's a Public Comment period during which anyone can submit a Public Comment on the First Draft. After the Public Comment closing date, the Technical Committee conducts/holds their Second Draft Meeting.

Second Draft Meeting. After the Public Comment closing date, if Public Comments are received or the committee has additional proposed revisions, a Second Draft Meeting is held. At the Second Draft Meeting, the Technical Committee reviews the First Draft and may make additional revisions to the draft Standard. All Public Comments are considered, and the Technical Committee provides an action and response to each Public Comment. These actions result in the Second Draft.

Committee Ballot on Second Draft. The Second Revisions developed at the Second Draft Meeting are balloted. To appear in the Second Draft, a revision must be approved by at least two-thirds of the Technical Committee.

Second Draft Report Posted. Second Revisions which pass ballot are ultimately compiled and published as the Second Draft Report on the document's NFPA website. This report serves as documentation of the Comment Stage and is published for public review.

Once published, the public can review the Second Draft Report to decide whether to submit a Notice of Intent to Make a Motion (NITMAM) for further consideration.

STEP 3—NFPA Technical Meeting (Tech Session)

Following completion of the Public Input and Public Comment stages, there's further opportunity for debate and discussion of issues through the NFPA Technical Meeting that takes place at the NFPA Conference & Expo®. These motions are attempts to change the resulting final Standard from the committee's recommendations published as the Second Draft.

STEP 4—Council Appeals and Issuance of Standard

Issuance of Standards. When the Standards Council convenes to issue an NFPA standard, it also hears any related appeals. Appeals are an important part of assuring that all NFPA rules have been followed and that due process and fairness have continued throughout the standards development process. The Standards Council considers appeals based on the written record and by conducting live hearings during which all interested parties can participate. Appeals are decided on the entire record of the process, as well as all submissions and statements presented.

After deciding all appeals related to a standard, the Standards Council, if appropriate, proceeds to issue the Standard as an official NFPA Standard. The decision of the Standards Council is final subject only to limited review by the NFPA Board of Directors. The new NFPA standard becomes effective twenty days following the Standards Council's action of issuance.

Temporary Interim Amendment—(TIA)

Sometimes, a change to the *NEC* is of an emergency nature. Perhaps an editing mistake was made that can affect an electrical installation to the extent it may create a hazard. Maybe an occurrence in the field created a condition that needs to be addressed immediately and can't wait for the normal *Code* cycle and next edition of the standard. When these circumstances warrant it, a TIA or "Temporary Interim Amendment" can be submitted for consideration.

The NFPA defines a TIA as, "tentative because it has not been processed through the entire standards-making procedures. It is interim because it is effective only between editions of the standard. A TIA automatically becomes a Public Input of the proponent for the next edition of the standard; as such, it then is subject to all of the procedures of the standards-making process."

Author's Comment:

- Proposals, comments, and TIAs can be submitted for consideration online at the NFPA website, www.nfpa.org. From the homepage, look for "Codes & Standards," then find "Standards Development," and click on "How the Process Works." If you'd like to see something changed in the *Code*, you're encouraged to participate in the process.

SECTION
I

ELECTRICAL THEORY

Introduction to Section I—Electrical Theory

In order to understand the bonding and grounding of electrical systems, you need to understand how and why electricity does what it does. The material covered in this section is extracted from our *Mike Holt's Understanding Electrical Theory for NEC Applications* textbook, and is a short review of the core principles of electricity. It should be considered a vital component of being a successful electrical professional.

If you find these concepts unfamiliar, please take the time to review electrical theory, so that you can understand and correctly apply the *NEC* rules for bonding and grounding. Visit MikeHolt.com/Theory.

Note: The unit numbers and style format in this section correspond to the *Understanding Electrical Theory for NEC Applications* textbook. You will notice that not all sections are included. For example, there is a Unit 4 and a Unit 6, but not a Unit 5. To see the complete content related to Electrical Theory, visit MikeHolt.com/Theory.

UNIT
1

ATOMIC STRUCTURE

1.1 Introduction

To understand electricity, you must first understand the physics that apply to electricity. The foundation of electricity begins with the structure of an atom which includes protons, neutrons, and electrons and how they interact with each other. In this unit you will learn:

- The atomic structure of an atom
- The law of electrical charges
- About static charge and static electricity
- What lightning is and how lightning protection works

1.2 Atomic Theory

An atom contains three types of subatomic particles: protons, neutrons, and electrons. The center of an atom is referred to as the "nucleus" and contains protons and neutrons. Electrons orbit around the nucleus of an atom. ▶Figure 1–1

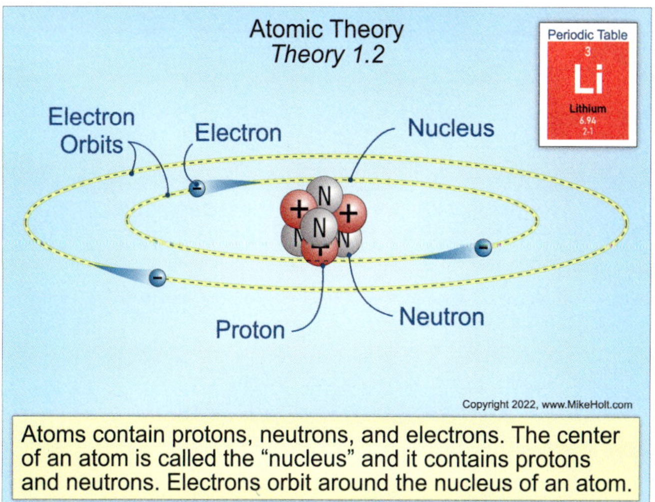
Atomic Theory
Theory 1.2
Periodic Table
3
Li
Lithium
Electron Orbits
Electron
Nucleus
Proton
Neutron
Copyright 2022, www.MikeHolt.com
Atoms contain protons, neutrons, and electrons. The center of an atom is called the "nucleus" and it contains protons and neutrons. Electrons orbit around the nucleus of an atom.

▶Figure 1–1

(A) Protons. Protons have a positive charge with lines of force going straight out in all directions. ▶Figure 1–2

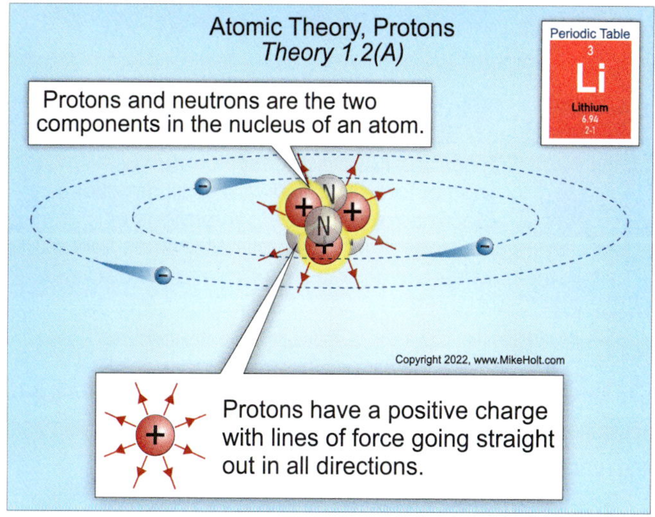
Atomic Theory, Protons
Theory 1.2(A)
Periodic Table
3
Li
Lithium
Protons and neutrons are the two components in the nucleus of an atom.
Copyright 2022, www.MikeHolt.com
Protons have a positive charge with lines of force going straight out in all directions.

▶Figure 1–2

(B) Neutrons. Neutrons have no charge and therefore no lines of force. ▶Figure 1–3

(C) Electrons. Electrons have a negative charge with lines of force going inward in all directions. Electrons are smaller than protons or neutrons and about 1,800 times lighter. Electrons actively participate in the transfer of energy. ▶Figure 1–4

Atomic Theory, Neutrons
Theory 1.2(B)
Periodic Table
3
Li
Lithium
6.94
2-1
Copyright 2022, www.MikeHolt.com
Neutrons have no charge; therefore, no lines of force.

▸Figure 1–3

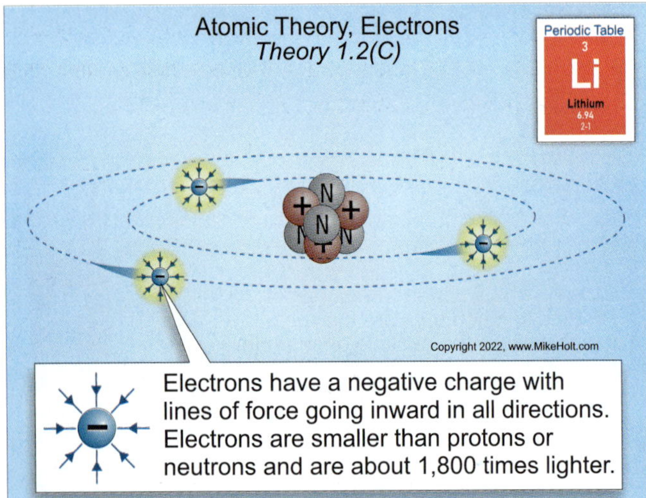
Atomic Theory, Electrons
Theory 1.2(C)
Periodic Table
3
Li
Lithium
6.94
2-1
Copyright 2022, www.MikeHolt.com
Electrons have a negative charge with lines of force going inward in all directions. Electrons are smaller than protons or neutrons and are about 1,800 times lighter.

▸Figure 1–4

(D) Nucleus. The nucleus of an atom only contains protons and neutrons. They are about the same size, have nearly the same mass, and remain in the center of an atom. ▸Figure 1–5

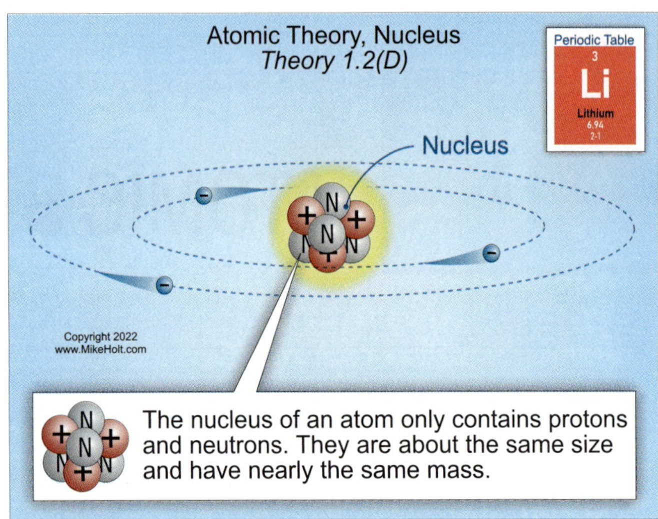
Atomic Theory, Nucleus
Theory 1.2(D)
Periodic Table
3
Li
Lithium
6.94
2-1
Nucleus
Copyright 2022
www.MikeHolt.com
The nucleus of an atom only contains protons and neutrons. They are about the same size and have nearly the same mass.

▸Figure 1–5

1.3 Electrostatic Field

Subatomic particles that attract or repel other subatomic particles follow Coulomb's Law which states that, "Particles with like electrostatic charges repel each other, and particles with unlike electrostatic charges attract each other."

The negative charges of electrons repel the negative charges of electrons; the positive charges of protons repel the positive charges of protons; while the negative charges of electrons and positive charges of protons attract each other. ▸Figure 1–6, ▸Figure 1–7, and ▸Figure 1–8

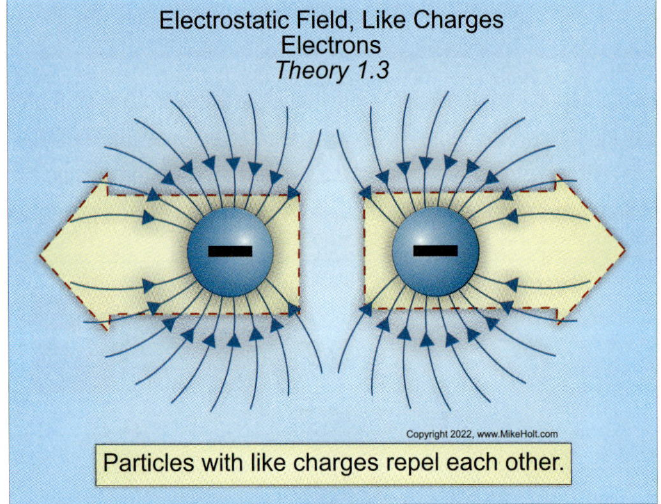
Electrostatic Field, Like Charges
Electrons
Theory 1.3
Copyright 2022, www.MikeHolt.com
Particles with like charges repel each other.

▸Figure 1–6

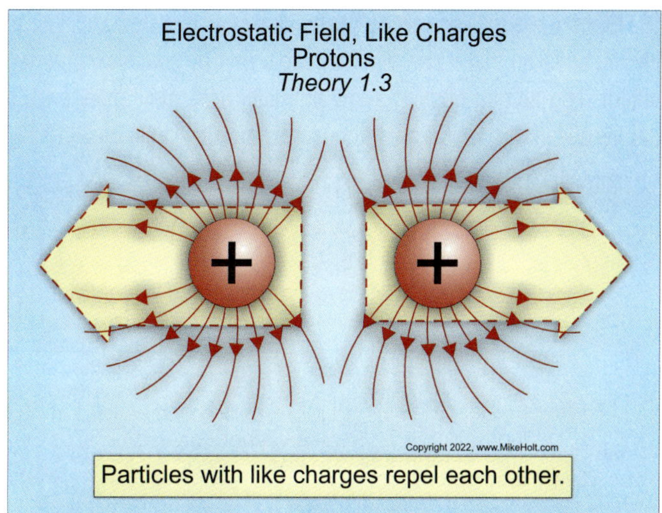
Electrostatic Field, Like Charges
Protons
Theory 1.3
Copyright 2022, www.MikeHolt.com
Particles with like charges repel each other.

▶Figure 1–7

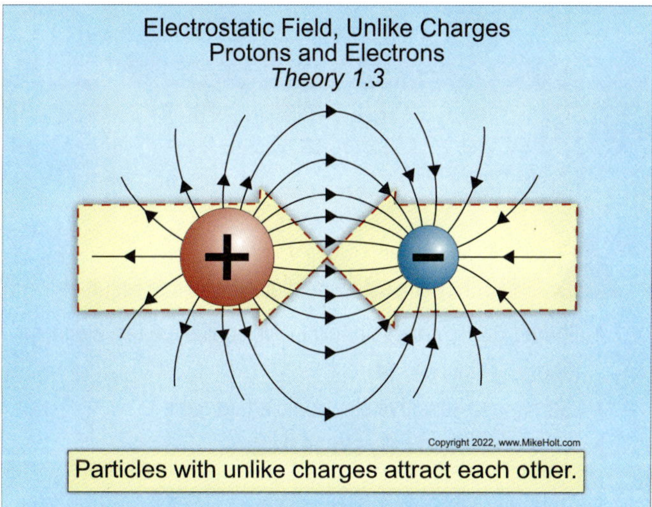
Electrostatic Field, Unlike Charges
Protons and Electrons
Theory 1.3
Copyright 2022, www.MikeHolt.com
Particles with unlike charges attract each other.

▶Figure 1–8

1.4 Atomic Charge of an Atom

The atomic electrostatic charge of an atom is either balanced, negative, or positive depending on the number of electrons compared to the number of protons.

(A) Balanced Atomic Charge. When an atom's charge is balanced, it means there are an equal number of positive and negative charges within the atom. Under this balanced atomic charge condition, the number of electrons is equal to the number of protons. ▶Figure 1–9

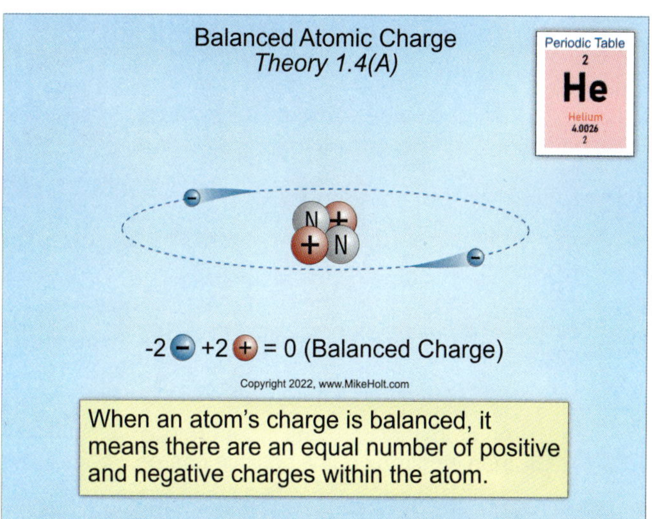
Balanced Atomic Charge
Theory 1.4(A)
Periodic Table
2
He
Helium
4.0026
2
-2 ⊖ +2 ⊕ = 0 (Balanced Charge)
Copyright 2022, www.MikeHolt.com
When an atom's charge is balanced, it means there are an equal number of positive and negative charges within the atom.

▶Figure 1–9

(B) Negative Atomic Charge. An atom that contains more electrons than protons has a negative charge. This happens when an atom gains an extra electron(s) in its electron cloud. ▶Figure 1–10

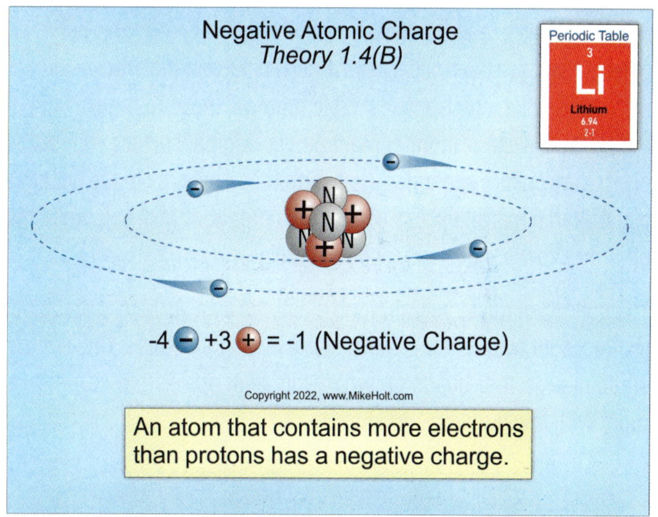
Negative Atomic Charge
Theory 1.4(B)
Periodic Table
3
Li
Lithium
6.94
2-1
-4 ⊖ +3 ⊕ = -1 (Negative Charge)
Copyright 2022, www.MikeHolt.com
An atom that contains more electrons than protons has a negative charge.

▶Figure 1–10

(C) Positive Atomic Charge. An atom that contains more protons than electrons has a positive charge. This happens when an atom loses an electron(s) from its electron cloud. ▶Figure 1–11

Author's Comment:

- There are a few "atomic models" that represent atomic structures. For simplicity, this material uses Bohr's model showing the electrons, protons, and neutrons.

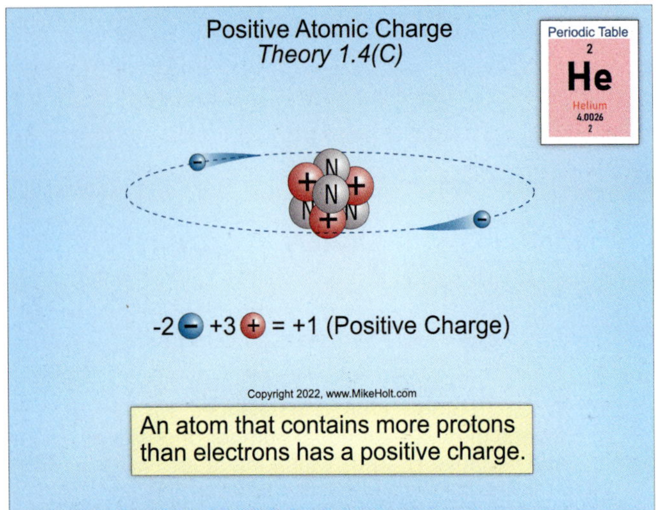
Positive Atomic Charge
Theory 1.4(C)
Periodic Table
2
He
Helium
4.0026
2
-2 +3 = +1 (Positive Charge)
Copyright 2022, www.MikeHolt.com
An atom that contains more protons than electrons has a positive charge.

▸Figure 1–11

1.5 Electrostatic Charge and Discharge

(A) Electrostatic Charge. Electrostatic charge is a condition that exists when there is an excess or deficiency of electrons between objects that have been separated. When unlike materials are in contact with each other, electrons from one material move to the surface of the other, but the protons remain on the original surface. When the objects are quickly separated, both materials display a charge because one material has an excess of electrons (negative charge), while the other has fewer electrons (positive charge).

The buildup of negatively charged electrons on a surface of an object produces an electrostatic charge. One example of this is the electrostatic charge that builds up when you walk across the carpet in a room with low humidity. ▸Figure 1–12

Electrostatic Charge
Theory 1.5(A)
The buildup of negatively charged electrons on a surface of an object produces an electrostatic charge. One example of the buildup of electrostatic charge occurs when you walk across the carpet in a low humidity room.
Copyright 2022, www.MikeHolt.com

▸Figure 1–12

(B) Electrostatic Discharge. The buildup of an electrostatic charge can be so large that it can discharge to a nearby positively charged object. The human body in a low humidity area may experience a dangerous static discharge of thousands of volts. ▸Figure 1–13

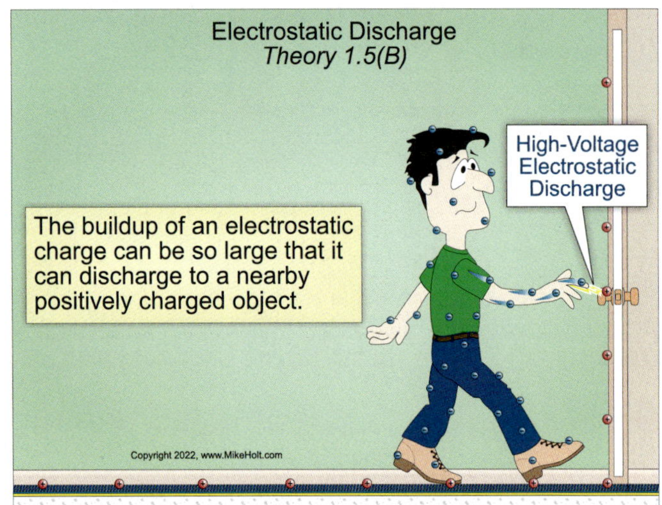
Electrostatic Discharge
Theory 1.5(B)
High-Voltage Electrostatic Discharge
The buildup of an electrostatic charge can be so large that it can discharge to a nearby positively charged object.
Copyright 2022, www.MikeHolt.com

▸Figure 1–13

Danger

DANGER: An electrostatic discharge can result in:

- Ignition of flammable or explosive liquids, gases, dusts, or fibers. ▸Figure 1–14
- Damage to sensitive electronic equipment.
- Loss of electronically stored data.

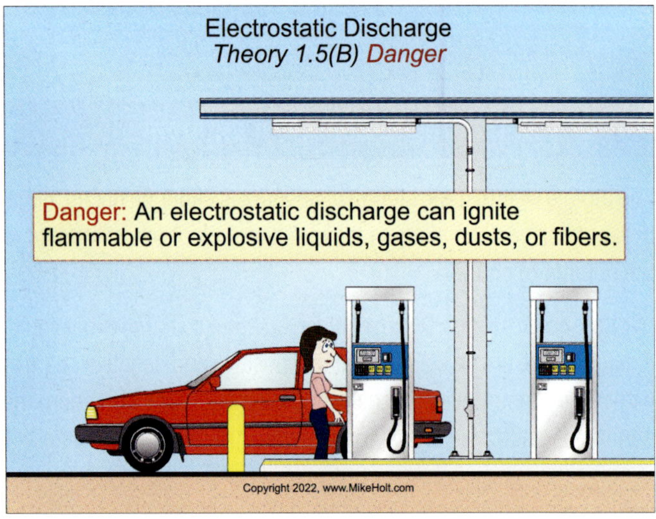
Electrostatic Discharge
Theory 1.5(B) Danger
Danger: An electrostatic discharge can ignite flammable or explosive liquids, gases, dusts, or fibers.
Copyright 2022, www.MikeHolt.com

▸Figure 1–14

1.6 Lightning

(A) Electrostatic Charge. Lightning is the discharging of high-voltage cells of electrostatic charge within clouds to and from the Earth—and sometimes to space. The electrostatic charge in a cloud is the result of friction caused by air movement within the cloud. ▸Figure 1–15

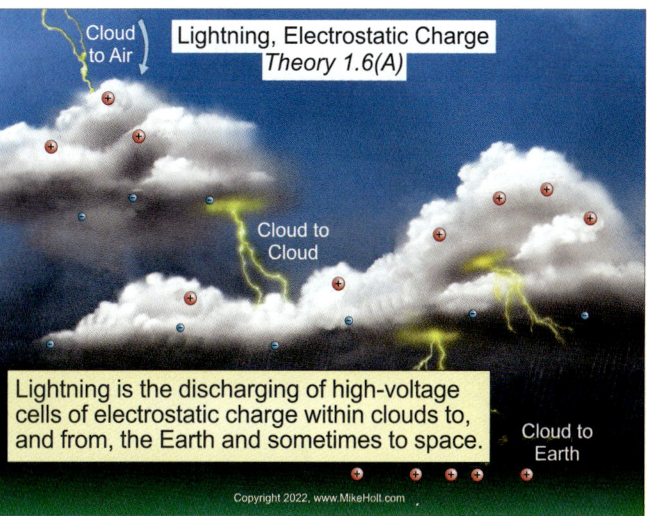
Lightning, Electrostatic Charge
Theory 1.6(A)
Cloud to Air
Cloud to Cloud
Lightning is the discharging of high-voltage cells of electrostatic charge within clouds to, and from, the Earth and sometimes to space.
Cloud to Earth
Copyright 2022, www.MikeHolt.com

▸Figure 1–15

(B) Discharge. Negative electrostatic charges in clouds are attracted to positive electrostatic charges in other clouds, the Earth, or space.

(1) Step-Down Leader. As a cloud's electrostatic charge builds up, it creates an ionized path from the cloud toward the Earth. This ionized path is referred to as a "stepped-down leader." ▸Figure 1–16

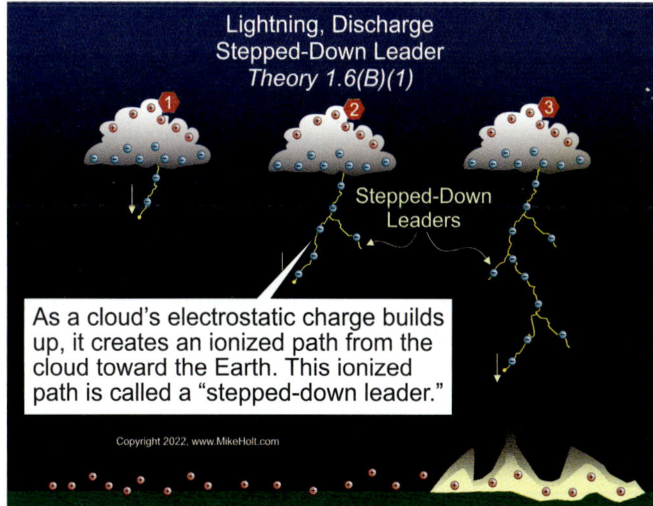
Lightning, Discharge
Stepped-Down Leader
Theory 1.6(B)(1)
Stepped-Down Leaders
As a cloud's electrostatic charge builds up, it creates an ionized path from the cloud toward the Earth. This ionized path is called a "stepped-down leader."
Copyright 2022, www.MikeHolt.com

▸Figure 1–16

(2) Step-Up Streamer. At the same time the stepped-down leader originates, a similar ionized path referred to as a "stepped-up streamer" rises from the Earth or other positively charged object. When the ionized path of the stepped leader and streamer connect, an electrostatic discharge (lightning strike) occurs. ▸Figure 1–17

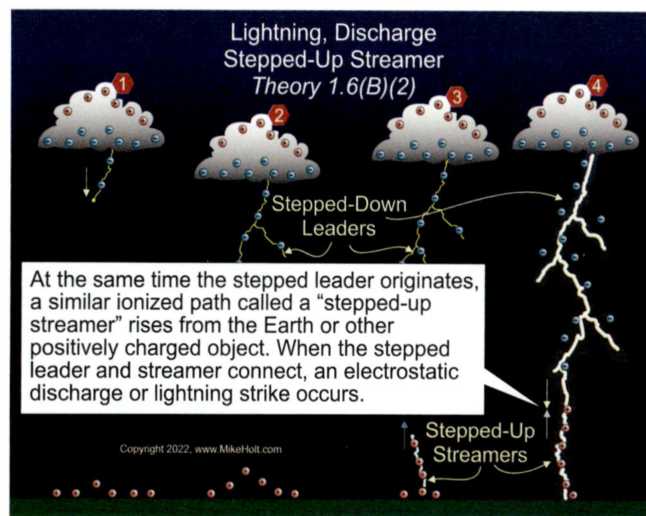
Lightning, Discharge
Stepped-Up Streamer
Theory 1.6(B)(2)
Stepped-Down Leaders
At the same time the stepped leader originates, a similar ionized path called a "stepped-up streamer" rises from the Earth or other positively charged object. When the stepped leader and streamer connect, an electrostatic discharge or lightning strike occurs.
Stepped-Up Streamers
Copyright 2022, www.MikeHolt.com

▸Figure 1–17

(3) Electrostatic Discharge. An electrostatic discharge (lightning strike) neutralizes the positive and negative electrostatic charges between the stepped-down leader and stepped-up streamer. ▸Figure 1–18

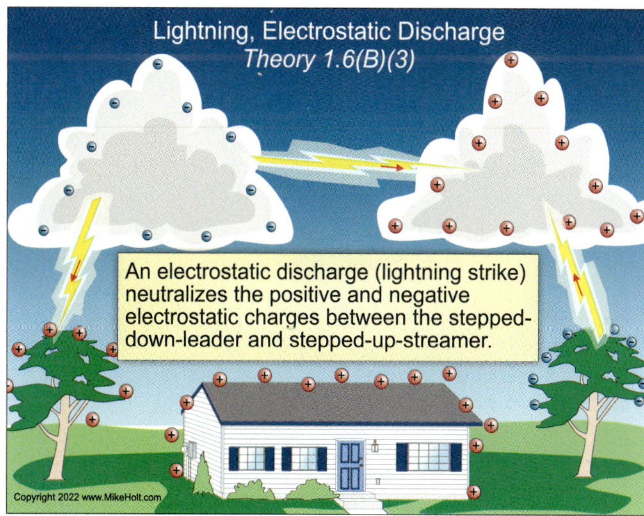
Lightning, Electrostatic Discharge
Theory 1.6(B)(3)
An electrostatic discharge (lightning strike) neutralizes the positive and negative electrostatic charges between the stepped-down-leader and stepped-up-streamer.
Copyright 2022 www.MikeHolt.com

▸Figure 1–18

Caution

CAUTION: Lightning generally strikes a point of higher elevation such as trees, buildings, or transmission lines. But lightning can strike an object at a lower elevation like a person in an open field.

(C) Death, Injuries, and Property Damage. Each year lightning causes deaths, injuries, and billions of dollars in property damage. When lightning strikes a nonconductive object, it will produce a high temperature at the strike point resulting in cracked concrete or the ignition of combustible materials. ▸Figure 1–19

Lightning
Death, Injuries, and Property Damage
Theory 1.6(C)
Copyright 2022
www.MikeHolt.com
Each year lightning causes deaths, injuries, and billions of dollars in property damage. When lightning strikes a nonconductive object, it will produce a high temperature at the strike point resulting in cracked concrete or the ignition of combustible materials.

▸Figure 1–19

1.7 Lightning Protection System

A lightning protection system is designed to protect property and persons against a direct lightning strike. The lightning protection system intercepts a lightning strike and provides a safe path for it to discharge to the Earth.

Lightning protection systems consist of a strike termination device, referred to as an "air terminal" or "lightning rod," placed on top of the structure to be protected. These devices are connected by large wires and then connected to the Earth. ▸Figure 1–20

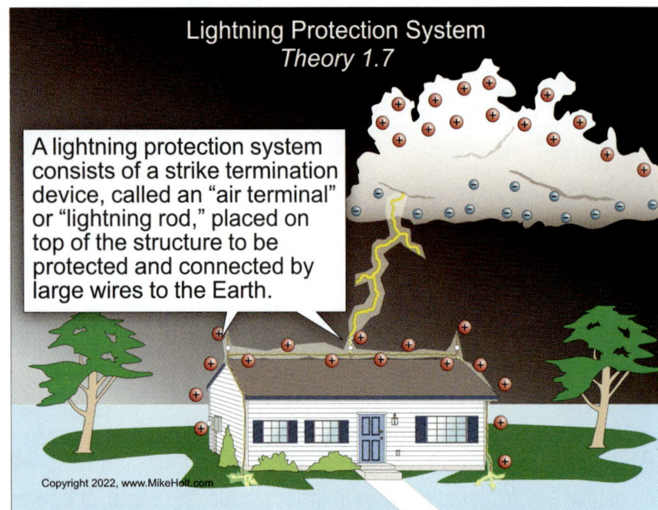
Lightning Protection System
Theory 1.7
A lightning protection system consists of a strike termination device, called an "air terminal" or "lightning rod," placed on top of the structure to be protected and connected by large wires to the Earth.
Copyright 2022, www.MikeHolt.com

▸Figure 1–20

Author's Comment:

- To adequately protect property from lighting, lightning protection systems should be installed in accordance with the requirements contained in NFPA 780, *Installation of Lightning Protection Systems.*

UNIT 1

REVIEW QUESTIONS

1.2 Atomic Theory

1. Atoms contain three types of subatomic particles: electrons, protons, and neutrons. The _____ orbit around the nucleus of an atom.

   (a) electrons
   (b) protons
   (c) neutrons
   (d) nucleus

2. _____ do not participate in the flow of energy and they have a positive electrical charge with lines of force going straight out in all directions.

   (a) Electrons
   (b) Protons
   (c) Neutrons
   (d) Nuclei

3. _____ have no charge and therefore have no lines of force.

   (a) Electrons
   (b) Protons
   (c) Neutrons
   (d) Nuclei

4. Because of their light weight, _____ actively participate in the transfer of energy and have lines of force going inward in all directions.

   (a) electrons
   (b) protons
   (c) neutrons
   (d) nuclei

5. The _____ of an atom only contains protons and neutrons.

   (a) electrons
   (b) protons
   (c) neutrons
   (d) nucleus

1.3 Electrostatic Field

6. Coulomb's Law states that, "Particles with _____ charges repel each other."

   (a) balanced
   (b) charged
   (c) unlike
   (d) like

7. Coulomb's Law states that, "Particles with _____ charges attract each other."

   (a) balanced
   (b) charged
   (c) unlike
   (d) like

1.4 Atomic Charge of an Atom

8. The atomic charge of an atom is _____ depending on the number of electrons compared to the number of protons.

   (a) balanced
   (b) positive
   (c) negative
   (d) all of these

9. If an atom contains an equal number of electrons and protons, the atom has a _____ atomic charge.

   (a) balanced
   (b) positive
   (c) negative
   (d) none of these

10. If an atom contains more electrons than protons, the atom has a _____ atomic charge.

    (a) balanced
    (b) positive
    (c) negative
    (d) none of these

11. If an atom contains more protons than electrons, the atom has a _____ atomic charge.

    (a) balanced
    (b) positive
    (c) negative
    (d) none of these

1.5 Electrostatic Charge and Discharge

12. When unlike materials are in contact with each other, electrons from one material move to the surface of the other, but the protons remain on the _____ surface.

    (a) first
    (b) original
    (c) last
    (d) none of these

13. When objects are quickly separated, both materials display a charge because one material has an excess of electrons while the other has _____ electrons.

    (a) no
    (b) fewer
    (c) more
    (d) extra

14. The human body in a low-humidity area may have a dangerous static discharge of several _____ volts.

    (a) hundred
    (b) thousand
    (c) million
    (d) billion

1.6 Lightning

15. Lightning is the _____ of high-voltage cells within clouds to, and from, the Earth and sometimes to space.

    (a) buildup
    (b) charging
    (c) discharging
    (d) neutralizing

16. As a cloud's electrostatic charge builds up, it creates an ionized path from the cloud toward the Earth; this ionized path is called a "_____."

    (a) stepped-down leader
    (b) streamer
    (c) ray
    (d) bolt

17. At the same time the stepped leader originates, a similar ionized path called a "_____" rises from the Earth or another positively charged object.

    (a) stepped leader
    (b) stepped-up streamer
    (c) ray
    (d) bolt

18. An electrostatic discharge (lightning strike) _____ the positive and negative electrostatic charges between the stepped leader and streamer.

    (a) disrupts
    (b) interrupts
    (c) neutralizes
    (d) equalizes

19. When lightning strikes a _____ object, it will produce a high temperature at the strike point resulting in cracked concrete or the ignition of combustible materials.

    (a) conductive
    (b) nonconductive
    (c) plastic
    (d) metal

1.7 Lightning Protection System

20. The lightning protection system intercepts the lightning strike and provides a safe path for it to_____ the Earth.

    (a) discharge to
    (b) neutralize within
    (c) dissipate to
    (d) charge particles in

UNIT 2

ELECTRON THEORY AND CHEMICAL BONDING

2.1 Introduction

Once atomic structure is understood, applying the concepts of electron theory and chemical bonding is next. In this unit you will learn:

- How the negative charge of electron movement participates in the creation of electricity
- The differences between conductors, semiconductors, and insulators
- What chemical bonding is and how it can change the electrical characteristic of an atom

2.2 Electron Orbitals

Electron orbitals represent the paths around the atom's nucleus that contain electrons. The negative charge of an electron is attracted to the positive charge of a proton. This attraction between electrons and protons is what keeps them together in the atom. ▶Figure 2–1

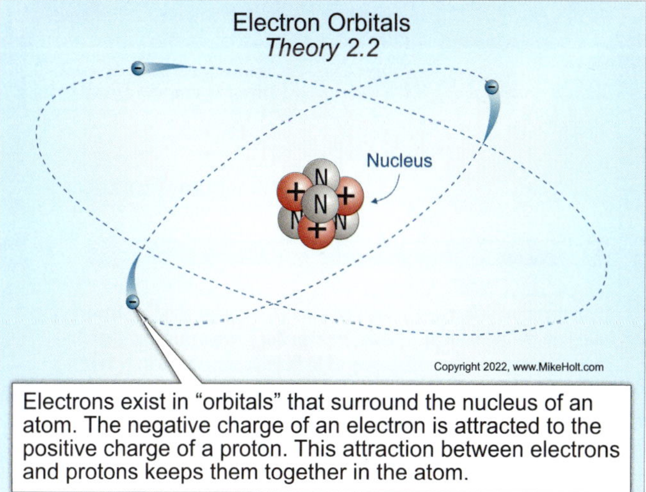

Electron Orbitals
Theory 2.2
Nucleus
Copyright 2022, www.MikeHolt.com
Electrons exist in "orbitals" that surround the nucleus of an atom. The negative charge of an electron is attracted to the positive charge of a proton. This attraction between electrons and protons keeps them together in the atom.

▶Figure 2–1

2.3 Valence Electrons

The outermost electron orbital of an atom is referred to as the "valence shell." Electrons in the valence shell are referred to as "valence electrons." ▶Figure 2–2

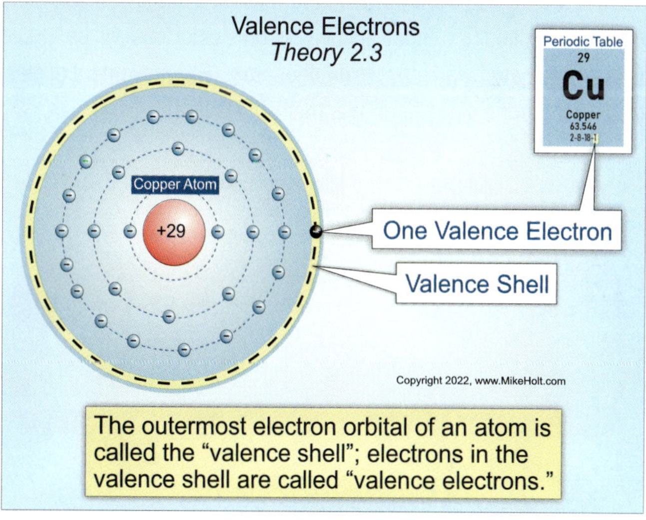

Valence Electrons
Theory 2.3
Periodic Table
29
Cu
Copper
Copper Atom
+29
One Valence Electron
Valence Shell
Copyright 2022, www.MikeHolt.com
The outermost electron orbital of an atom is called the "valence shell"; electrons in the valence shell are called "valence electrons."

▶Figure 2–2

2.4 Freeing Valence Electron(s) from an Atom

(A) Coulomb's Law. According to Coulomb's Law, the strength of the electrostatic field between protons and electrons decreases as the distance of the electrons from the nucleus increases. This means that the valence electrons farthest away from the nucleus are more easily separated from the atom. ▸Figure 2–3

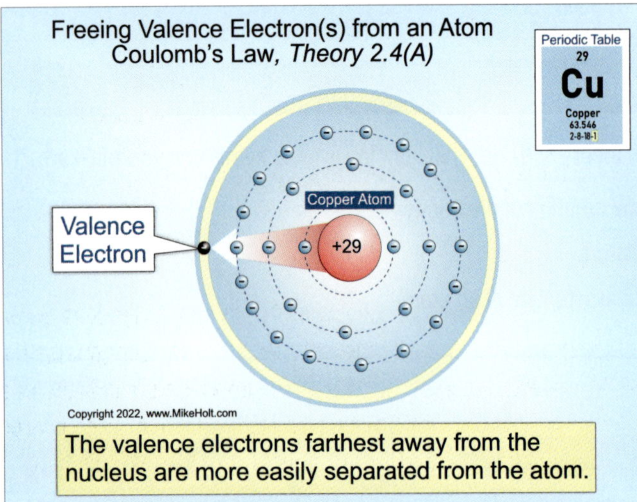
Freeing Valence Electron(s) from an Atom
Coulomb's Law, Theory 2.4(A)
Periodic Table
29
Cu
Copper
63.546
2-8-18-1
Copper Atom
+29
Valence Electron
Copyright 2022, www.MikeHolt.com
The valence electrons farthest away from the nucleus are more easily separated from the atom.

▸Figure 2–3

(B) Movement of Valence Electrons. Energy that is applied to an atom is distributed evenly among the valence electrons. If sufficient energy is applied to valence electrons, some electrons will be forced to leave their atom and move to another atom. This movement of electrons is the principle behind "electricity." ▸Figure 2–4

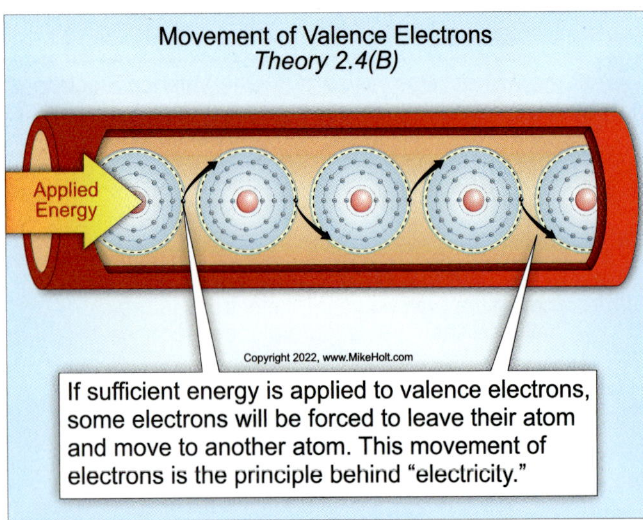
Movement of Valence Electrons
Theory 2.4(B)
Applied Energy
Copyright 2022, www.MikeHolt.com
If sufficient energy is applied to valence electrons, some electrons will be forced to leave their atom and move to another atom. This movement of electrons is the principle behind "electricity."

▸Figure 2–4

2.5 Conductance

(A) General. Conductance is how easily an object permits the movement of valence electrons from their atom. Conductive elements are made of atoms that contain one, two, or three valence electrons. Copper and aluminum are the two most common conductive elements used for electrical wiring. ▸Figure 2–5 and ▸Figure 2–6

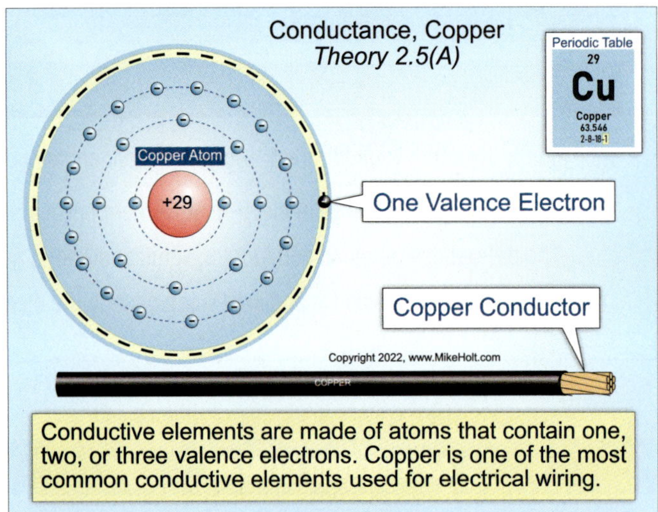
Conductance, Copper
Theory 2.5(A)
Periodic Table
29
Cu
Copper
63.546
2-8-18-1
Copper Atom
+29
One Valence Electron
Copper Conductor
Copyright 2022, www.MikeHolt.com
COPPER
Conductive elements are made of atoms that contain one, two, or three valence electrons. Copper is one of the most common conductive elements used for electrical wiring.

▸Figure 2–5

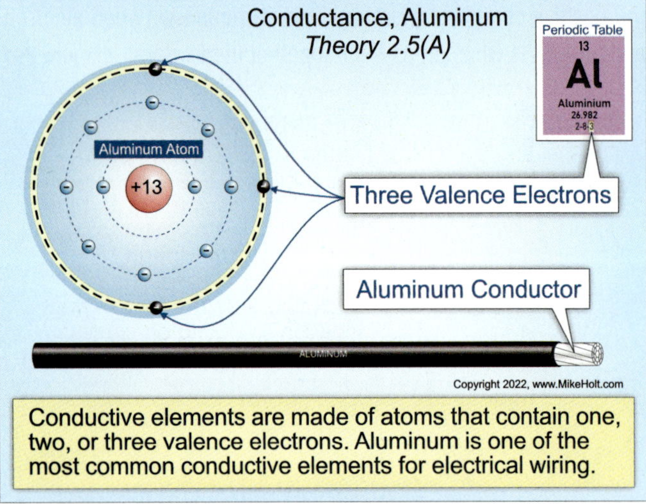
Conductance, Aluminum
Theory 2.5(A)
Periodic Table
13
Al
Aluminium
26.982
2-8-3
Aluminum Atom
+13
Three Valence Electrons
Aluminum Conductor
ALUMINUM
Copyright 2022, www.MikeHolt.com
Conductive elements are made of atoms that contain one, two, or three valence electrons. Aluminum is one of the most common conductive elements for electrical wiring.

▸Figure 2–6

(B) Conductivity. The most conductive elements in order of conductivity are silver, copper, gold, and aluminum. Silver is 106 percent more conductive than copper; gold is 71 percent as conductive as copper; and aluminum is 65 percent as conductive as copper. ▸Figure 2–7

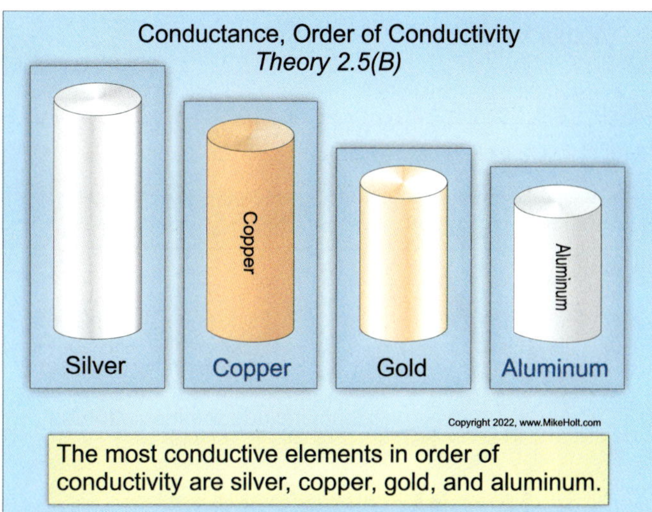
Conductance, Order of Conductivity
Theory 2.5(B)
Silver
Copper
Copper
Gold
Aluminum
Aluminum
Copyright 2022, www.MikeHolt.com
The most conductive elements in order of conductivity are silver, copper, gold, and aluminum.

▶Figure 2–7

Author's Comment:

- Silver and gold are better conductors than aluminum and will not corrode, but their cost makes them impractical for electrical wiring. Connectors for electronic circuits sometimes use gold or silver plating on copper terminals to prevent corrosion and ensure a reliable connection. ▶Figure 2–8

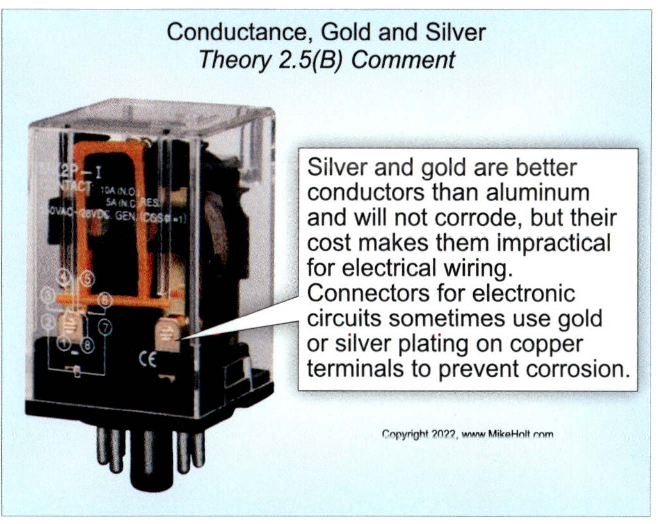
Conductance, Gold and Silver
Theory 2.5(B) Comment
Silver and gold are better conductors than aluminum and will not corrode, but their cost makes them impractical for electrical wiring. Connectors for electronic circuits sometimes use gold or silver plating on copper terminals to prevent corrosion.
Copyright 2022, www.MikeHolt.com

▶Figure 2–8

(C) Copper. Copper atoms have one valence electron. When energy is applied to the atom's valence electron, the electron can easily be forced to leave its orbit. ▶Figure 2–9

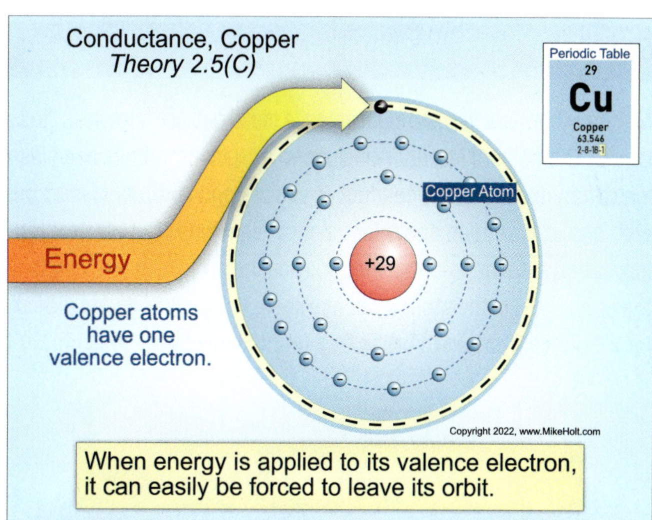
Conductance, Copper
Theory 2.5(C)
Periodic Table
29
Cu
Copper
63.546
2-8-18-1
Copper Atom
Energy
+29
Copper atoms have one valence electron.
Copyright 2022, www.MikeHolt.com
When energy is applied to its valence electron, it can easily be forced to leave its orbit.

▶Figure 2–9

(D) Aluminum. Aluminum atoms have three valence electrons. When energy is applied to the atom's valence electrons, the energy is distributed between the three electrons. This makes it more difficult for a valence electron to break free from an aluminum atom as compared to a copper atom with the same amount of energy. ▶Figure 2–10

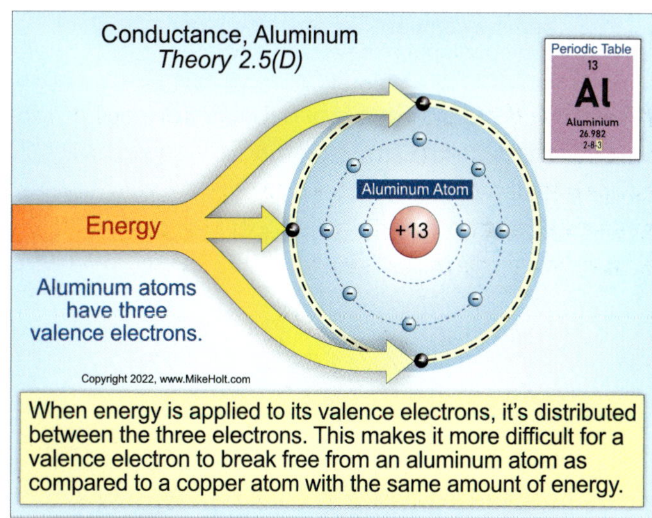
Conductance, Aluminum
Theory 2.5(D)
Periodic Table
13
Al
Aluminium
26.982
2-8-3
Aluminum Atom
Energy
+13
Aluminum atoms have three valence electrons.
Copyright 2022, www.MikeHolt.com
When energy is applied to its valence electrons, it's distributed between the three electrons. This makes it more difficult for a valence electron to break free from an aluminum atom as compared to a copper atom with the same amount of energy.

▶Figure 2–10

2.6 Insulators

Materials containing six to eight valence electrons are known as "insulators." Examples of insulators include wood, plastic, rubber, and glass. Insulators do not readily conduct electricity and composed of atoms with one or two open spots for valence electrons. The electrostatic forces between the valence electrons and the protons actively try to fill the opening(s) in the atom's valence shell. This makes it very difficult for a valence electron to break free from an insulator. ▶Figure 2–11

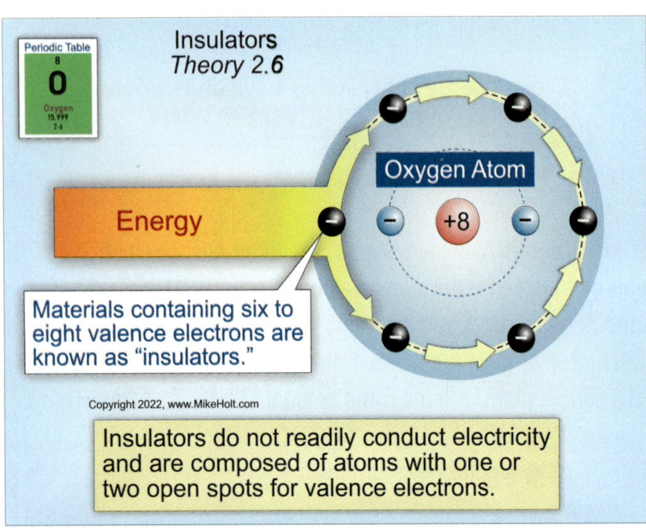
Insulators
Theory 2.6
Periodic Table
8
O
Oxygen Atom
Energy
+8
Materials containing six to eight valence electrons are known as "insulators."
Copyright 2022, www.MikeHolt.com
Insulators do not readily conduct electricity and are composed of atoms with one or two open spots for valence electrons.

▶Figure 2–11

Author's Comment:

- Examples of insulators in the electrical industry include the insulation on electrical wire and cables. ▶Figure 2–12

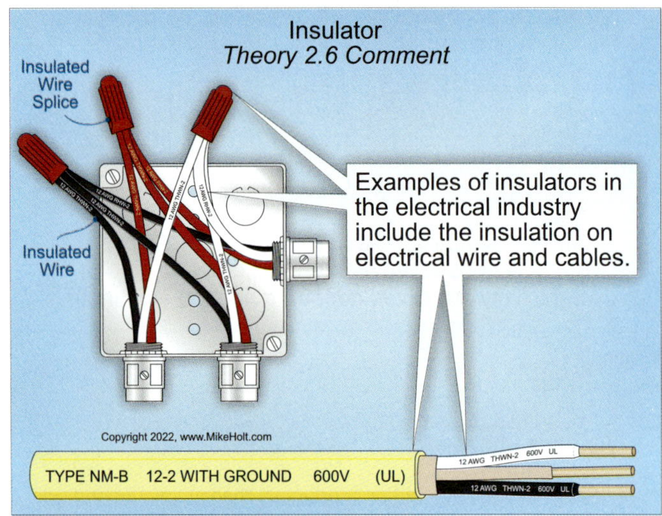
Insulator
Theory 2.6 Comment
Insulated Wire Splice
Insulated Wire
Examples of insulators in the electrical industry include the insulation on electrical wire and cables.
Copyright 2022, www.MikeHolt.com
TYPE NM-B 12-2 WITH GROUND 600V (UL)

▶Figure 2–12

UNIT 2

REVIEW QUESTIONS

2.2 Electron Orbitals

1. The _____ between the positive charge of the protons and negative charge of electrons keeps them together in the atom.

   (a) attraction
   (b) distinction
   (c) relationship
   (d) balance

2.3 Valence Electrons

2. The outermost electron orbital of an atom is called the "valence shell" and electrons in this shell are called "_____ electrons."

   (a) negative
   (b) positive
   (c) valance
   (d) special

2.4 Freeing Valance Electron(s) from an Atom

3. According to Coulomb's Law, the strength of the electrostatic field between protons and electrons _____ as the distance of the electrons from the nucleus increases.

   (a) increases
   (b) decreases
   (c) equalizes
   (d) strengthens

4. Energy that is applied to an atom is distributed _____ among all the valence electrons.

   (a) evenly
   (b) disproportionally
   (c) unequally
   (d) unevenly

2.5 Conductance

5. Conductance is how easily an object permits the ______ of valence electrons from their atom.

   (a) resistance
   (b) water
   (c) movement
   (d) none of these

6. Conductive elements are made of one, two, or three valence electrons. Copper and aluminum are the two most common _____ elements used for electrical wiring.

   (a) insulative
   (b) conductive
   (c) expensive
   (d) light weight

7. The best conductive elements in order of their conductivity are: _____.

   (a) gold, silver, copper, and aluminum
   (b) gold, copper, silver, and aluminum
   (c) silver, gold, copper, and aluminum
   (d) silver, copper, gold, and aluminum

8. Copper atoms have _____ valence electron(s). When energy is applied to the valance electron(s), the electron(s) can easily be forced to leave the orbit.

   (a) one
   (b) two
   (c) four
   (d) six

9. Aluminum atoms have _____ valence electrons. When energy is applied to the valence electrons, the energy is distributed between the electrons.

   (a) two
   (b) three
   (c) four
   (d) eight

2.6 Insulators

10. Materials containing six to _____ valance electrons are known as "insulators."

    (a) eight
    (b) ten
    (c) twelve
    (d) fourteen

1st Printing

UNIT 3

ELECTRICAL CIRCUITS AND POWER SOURCES

3.1 Introduction

A power source provides the energy necessary for electrons to move through a closed-loop path known as an "electrical circuit." In this unit you will learn:

- What an electrical circuit is
- What components make up an electrical circuit
- The two theories of electron current flow
- The different types of power sources that force electrons to move

3.2 The Electrical Circuit

An electrical circuit contains a power source that pushes and pulls electrons through the electrical circuit. This is known as "electricity." In an electrical circuit, the electrons leave the power source on a conductive path traveling toward a load and then return to the power source. ▸Figure 3–1

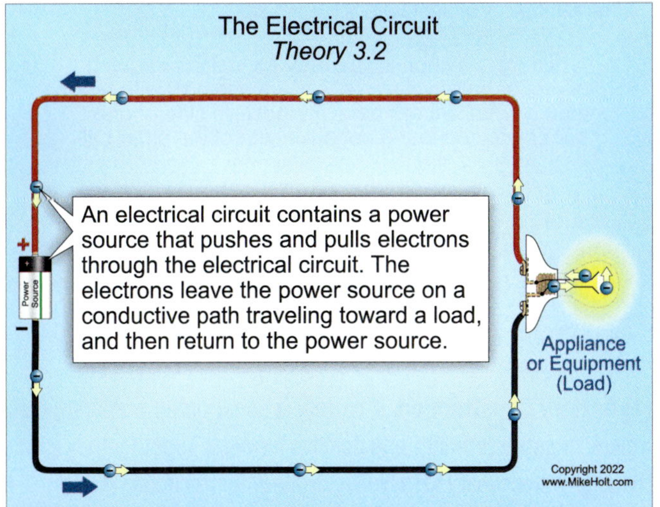

The Electrical Circuit
Theory 3.2
An electrical circuit contains a power source that pushes and pulls electrons through the electrical circuit. The electrons leave the power source on a conductive path traveling toward a load, and then return to the power source.
Power Source
Appliance or Equipment (Load)
Copyright 2022 www.MikeHolt.com

▸Figure 3–1

3.3 Electric Current Flow (Electricity)

The direction of current flow (electricity) is explained by one of two theories–the "Conventional Current Flow Theory" or the "Electron Current Flow Theory."

(A) Conventional Current Flow Theory, Franklin. During an experiment in 1752, Benjamin Franklin discovered that an electric charge from static electricity could move from one object to another. He theorized that current flowed from a positive charge to a negative charge. This theory became known as the "Conventional Current Flow Theory." ▸Figure 3–2

(B) Electron Current Flow Theory, Thompson. In 1897, Joseph J. Thompson explored the properties of cathode rays and discovered that current flow (movement of electrons) was actually the movement of negatively charged particles (electrons) from the negative terminal of the source toward the positive terminal of the source. Based on his discovery, Thompson developed the theory known as the "Electron Current Flow Theory." ▸Figure 3–3

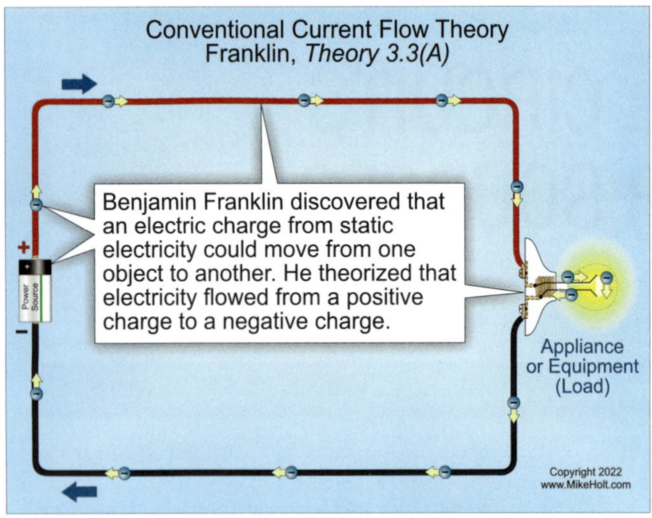
Conventional Current Flow Theory
Franklin, Theory 3.3(A)
Benjamin Franklin discovered that an electric charge from static electricity could move from one object to another. He theorized that electricity flowed from a positive charge to a negative charge.
Power Source
Appliance or Equipment (Load)
Copyright 2022 www.MikeHolt.com

▸Figure 3–2

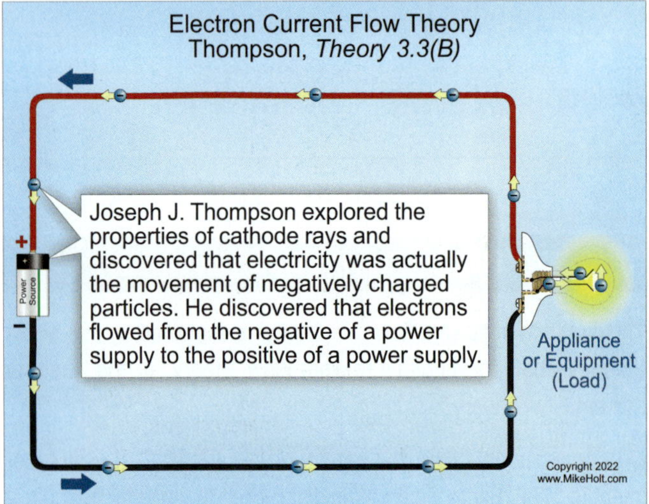
Electron Current Flow Theory
Thompson, Theory 3.3(B)
Joseph J. Thompson explored the properties of cathode rays and discovered that electricity was actually the movement of negatively charged particles. He discovered that electrons flowed from the negative of a power supply to the positive of a power supply.
Power Source
Appliance or Equipment (Load)
Copyright 2022 www.MikeHolt.com

▸Figure 3–3

Author's Comment:

- In this material we use Thompson's Electron Current Flow Theory because it accurately represents the direction of current flow.

3.4 Electrical Power Sources

To create current flow in an electrical circuit, a power source is placed in the circuit to supply the energy needed to cause electrons to leave their atom and move to other atoms through the circuit. The energy to move electrons can come from chemical activity, electromagnetism, photovoltaics, heat, or pressure. ▸Figure 3–4

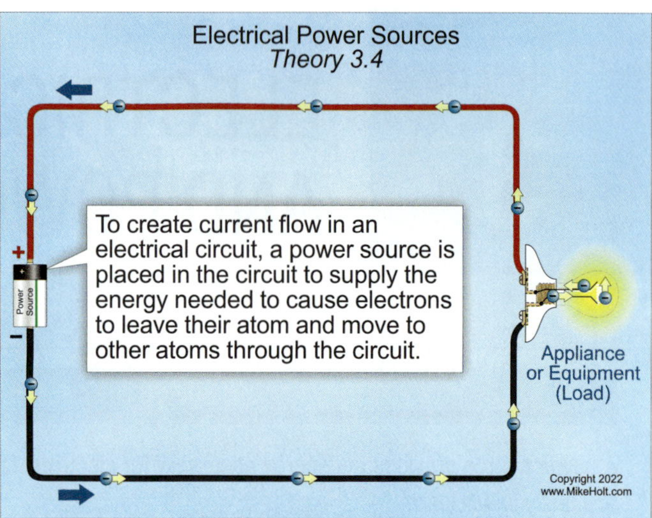
Electrical Power Sources
Theory 3.4
To create current flow in an electrical circuit, a power source is placed in the circuit to supply the energy needed to cause electrons to leave their atom and move to other atoms through the circuit.
Power Source
Appliance or Equipment (Load)
Copyright 2022 www.MikeHolt.com

▸Figure 3–4

(A) Chemical Activity. A battery is a chemical energy source constructed of one or more voltaic cells. Batteries built with more than one voltaic cell have the positive side of one cell connected to the negative side of the other cell. ▸Figure 3–5

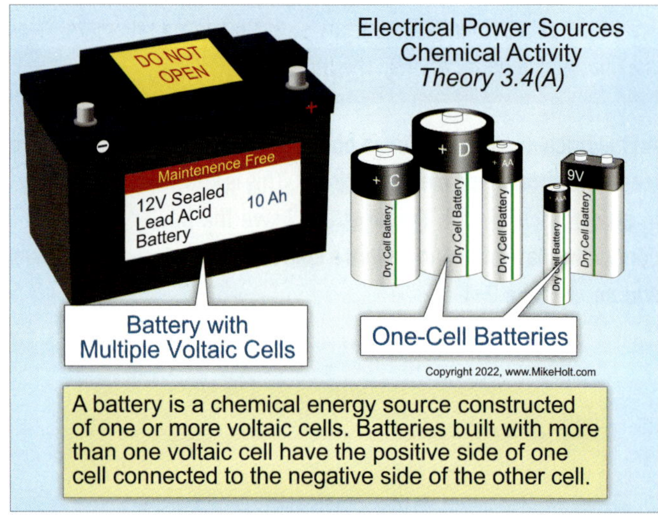
Electrical Power Sources
Chemical Activity
Theory 3.4(A)
DO NOT OPEN
Maintenence Free
12V Sealed Lead Acid Battery
10 Ah
Dry Cell Battery
9V
Battery with Multiple Voltaic Cells
One-Cell Batteries
Copyright 2022, www.MikeHolt.com
A battery is a chemical energy source constructed of one or more voltaic cells. Batteries built with more than one voltaic cell have the positive side of one cell connected to the negative side of the other cell.

▸Figure 3–5

Author's Comment:

- In 1800, Alessandro Volta invented the voltaic cell.

(1) Battery Construction. A battery is constructed with a(an) electrolyte, negative terminal, and positive terminal. Together they create the energy necessary to move electrons within a circuit. ▸Figure 3–6

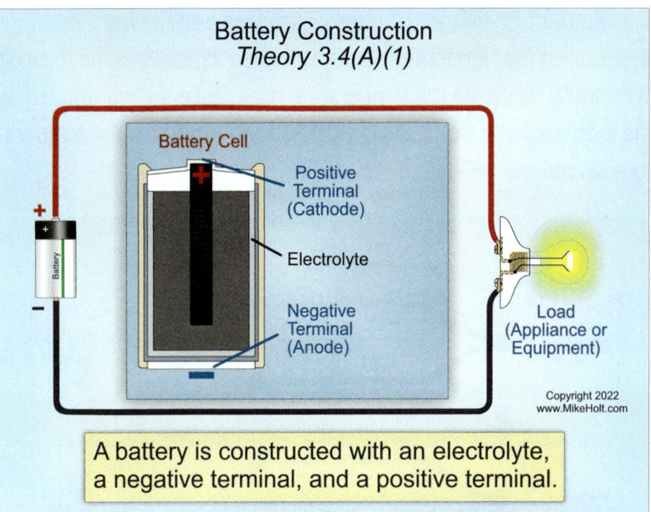
Battery Construction
Theory 3.4(A)(1)
Battery Cell
Positive Terminal (Cathode)
Electrolyte
Negative Terminal (Anode)
Load (Appliance or Equipment)
Copyright 2022 www.MikeHolt.com
A battery is constructed with an electrolyte, a negative terminal, and a positive terminal.

▸Figure 3–6

(2) Electrical Pressure in a Battery. Chemical activity in a battery causes a buildup of electrons at the negative terminal, creating the energy necessary to move electrons within a circuit. The electron buildup creates electrical pressure between the negative and positive terminals of the battery. The negative charge on the battery's negative terminal will flow to the battery's positive terminal where there is a conductive path between the terminals. ▸Figure 3–7

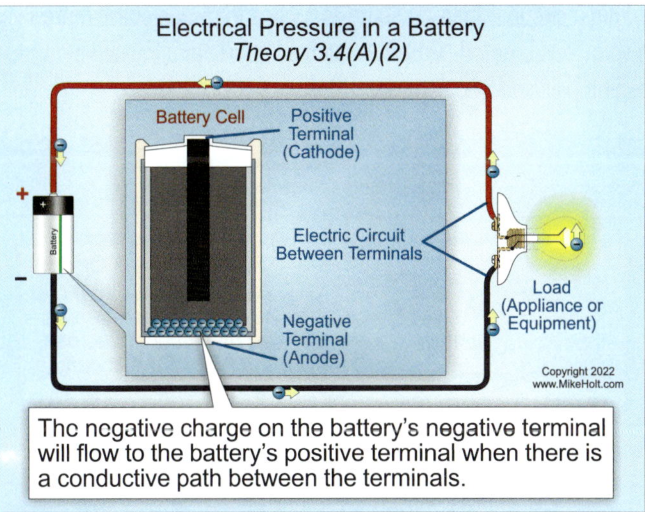
Electrical Pressure in a Battery
Theory 3.4(A)(2)
Battery Cell
Positive Terminal (Cathode)
Electric Circuit Between Terminals
Negative Terminal (Anode)
Load (Appliance or Equipment)
Copyright 2022 www.MikeHolt.com
The negative charge on the battery's negative terminal will flow to the battery's positive terminal when there is a conductive path between the terminals.

▸Figure 3–7

(3) Direct-Current Flow. Electrons in a battery leave the negative terminal and return to the positive terminal—always traveling in the same direction. This is known as "direct current" (dc). ▸Figure 3–8

(B) Electromagnetism. Most electrical energy is generated using electromagnetism, which creates the power necessary to move electrons within a circuit. ▸Figure 3–9

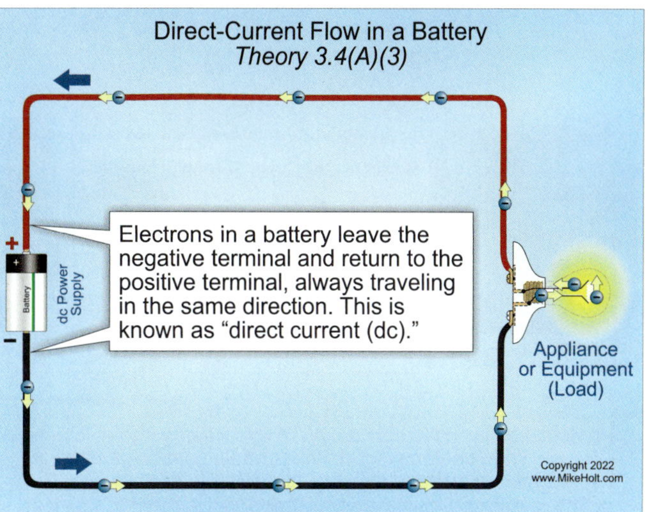
Direct-Current Flow in a Battery
Theory 3.4(A)(3)
dc Power Supply
Electrons in a battery leave the negative terminal and return to the positive terminal, always traveling in the same direction. This is known as "direct current (dc)."
Appliance or Equipment (Load)
Copyright 2022 www.MikeHolt.com

▸Figure 3–8

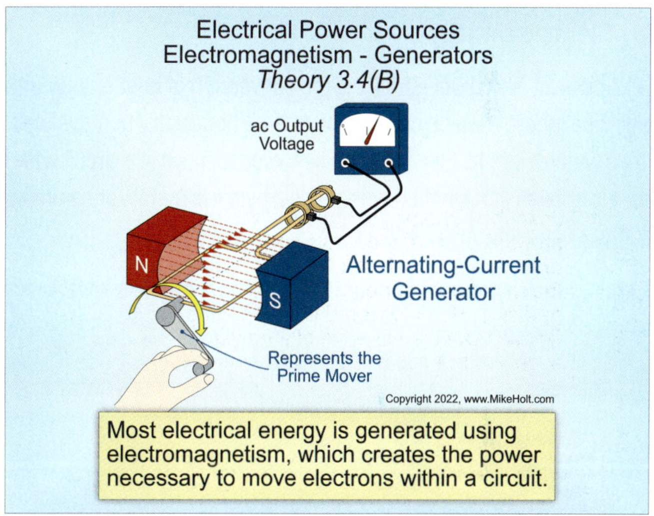
Electrical Power Sources
Electromagnetism - Generators
Theory 3.4(B)
ac Output Voltage
N
S
Alternating-Current Generator
Represents the Prime Mover
Copyright 2022, www.MikeHolt.com
Most electrical energy is generated using electromagnetism, which creates the power necessary to move electrons within a circuit.

▸Figure 3–9

(C) Photoelectricity. Photoelectricity is the conversion of light energy into electrical energy, which creates the power necessary to move electrons within a circuit. When photons (light) strike semiconductor plates, they cause electrons to flow from one semiconductor plate to another. ▸Figure 3–10

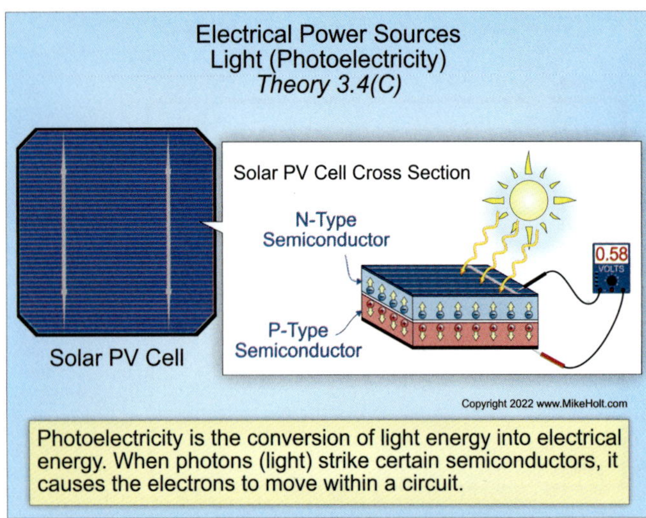
Electrical Power Sources
Light (Photoelectricity)
Theory 3.4(C)
Solar PV Cell Cross Section
N-Type Semiconductor
P-Type Semiconductor
0.58
VOLTS
Solar PV Cell
Copyright 2022 www.MikeHolt.com
Photoelectricity is the conversion of light energy into electrical energy. When photons (light) strike certain semiconductors, it causes the electrons to move within a circuit.

▸Figure 3–10

(D) Thermoelectricity.

(1) General. Thermoelectricity is the conversion of heat energy into electrical energy, which creates the energy necessary to move electrons within a circuit. Electrons can be forced to move in a circuit when heat is applied at a junction where two dissimilar metals or semiconductors connect. ▸Figure 3–11

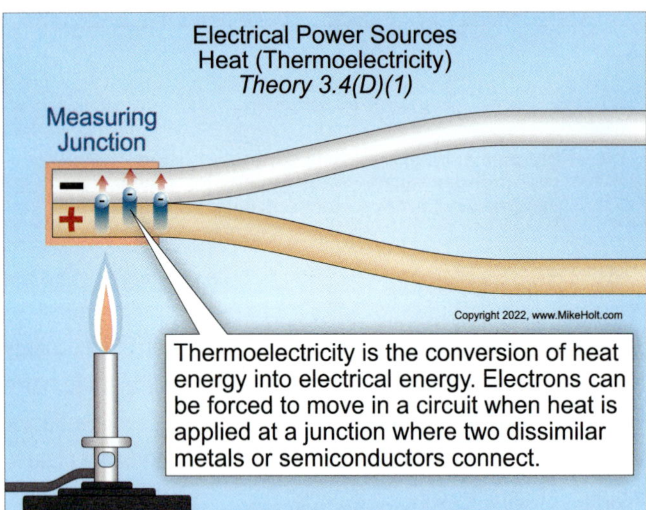
Electrical Power Sources
Heat (Thermoelectricity)
Theory 3.4(D)(1)
Measuring Junction
Copyright 2022, www.MikeHolt.com
Thermoelectricity is the conversion of heat energy into electrical energy. Electrons can be forced to move in a circuit when heat is applied at a junction where two dissimilar metals or semiconductors connect.

▸Figure 3–11

(2) Voltage. A common application of thermal electricity is a "thermocouple," which is a sensor that measures temperature. It consists of two different types of metals joined together at one end. When the junction of the two metals is heated or cooled, a voltage is created that can be correlated back to the temperature.

The amount of electrical energy produced by a thermocouple depends on the temperature at the junction, typically in the millivolt (1/1,000V) range. As the temperature rises, the energy produced by the thermocouple increases, and the opposite is true if the temperature decreases. ▸Figure 3–12

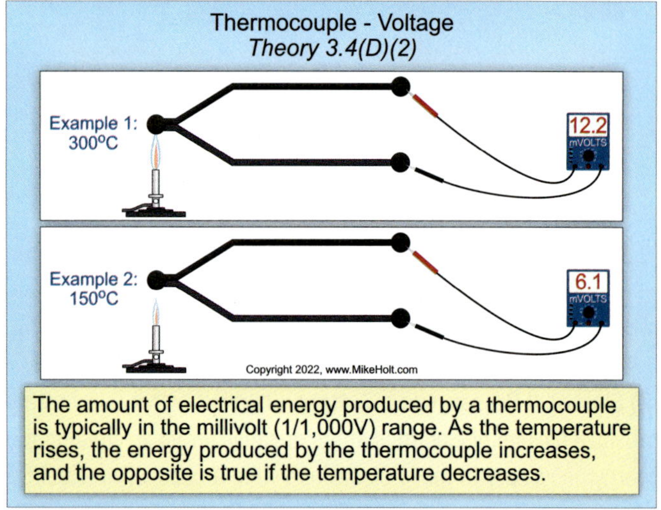
Thermocouple - Voltage
Theory 3.4(D)(2)
Example 1: 300°C
12.2
mVOLTS
Example 2: 150°C
6.1
mVOLTS
Copyright 2022, www.MikeHolt.com
The amount of electrical energy produced by a thermocouple is typically in the millivolt (1/1,000V) range. As the temperature rises, the energy produced by the thermocouple increases, and the opposite is true if the temperature decreases.

▸Figure 3–12

(E) Piezoelectricity. Piezoelectricity is the conversion of pressure or vibration into the electrical energy necessary to move electrons within a circuit. When pressure is applied to piezoelectric materials, a voltage is created. Materials such as quartz and certain ceramics exhibit piezoelectric behavior. ▸Figure 3–13

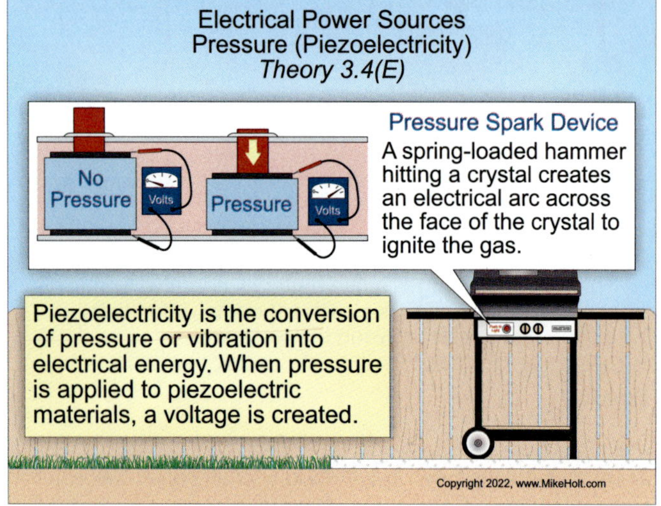
Electrical Power Sources
Pressure (Piezoelectricity)
Theory 3.4(E)
No Pressure
Volts
Pressure
Volts
Pressure Spark Device
A spring-loaded hammer hitting a crystal creates an electrical arc across the face of the crystal to ignite the gas.
Piezoelectricity is the conversion of pressure or vibration into electrical energy. When pressure is applied to piezoelectric materials, a voltage is created.
Copyright 2022, www.MikeHolt.com

▸Figure 3–13

Author's Comment:

- Uses of piezoelectricity include:
  - piezoelectric beepers in digital watches and electronics
  - piezoelectric tweeters in stereo speakers
  - sound-generating arrays for sonar, fish finders, and ultrasound devices
  - grill igniters

1st Printing

UNIT
3

REVIEW QUESTIONS

3.2 The Electrical Circuit

1. In an electrical circuit, the electrons leave the power source on a(an) _____ path traveling toward a load, and then return to the power source.

   (a) conductive
   (b) insulative
   (c) single
   (d) varying

3.3 Electric Current Flow (Electricity)

2. The direction of _____ flow is explained by one of two theories—the "Conventional Current Flow Theory" or the "Electron Current Flow Theory."

   (a) current
   (b) power
   (c) resistance
   (d) voltage

3. According to the _____ Current Flow Theory, Benjamin Franklin discovered that electricity flows from a positive charge to a negative charge.

   (a) Conventional
   (b) Electron
   (c) Maxwell
   (d) Tesla

4. According to the Conventional Current Flow Theory, Benjamin Franklin theorized that electric current flowed out of the ______ terminal, through the circuit and into the ______ terminal of the source.

   (a) positive, negative
   (b) negative, positive
   (c) negative, negative
   (d) positive, positive

5. According to the _____ Current Flow Theory, Joseph J Thompson discovered that electrons flowed from the negative terminal of the source toward the positive terminal of the source.

   (a) Conventional
   (b) Electron
   (c) Maxwell
   (d) Tesla

6. According to the Electron Current Flow Theory, Joseph J. Thompson discovered electrons flowed from the _____ terminal of the source toward the _____ terminal of the source.

   (a) positive, negative
   (b) negative, positive
   (c) negative, negative
   (d) positive, positive

3.4 Electrical Power Sources

7. To create current flow in an electrical circuit, a(an) _____ is placed in the circuit to supply the energy needed to cause electrons to leave their atom and move to other atoms through the circuit.

   (a) conductor
   (b) insulator
   (c) power source
   (d) wheel

8. A battery is a _____ energy source constructed of one or more voltaic cells.

   (a) chemical
   (b) solar
   (c) heat
   (d) magnetic

9. A _____ is constructed with an electrolyte, a negative terminal, and a positive terminal.

   (a) wind turbine
   (b) generator
   (c) solar cell
   (d) battery

10. Chemical activity in the _____ causes a buildup of electrons at the negative terminal, creating the energy necessary to move electrons within a circuit.

    (a) battery
    (b) generator
    (c) solar cell
    (d) wind turbine

11. Electrons in a battery leave the negative terminal and return to the positive terminal, always traveling in the same direction, this is known as "_____ current."

    (a) alternating
    (b) direct
    (c) straight
    (d) varying

12. Most electrical energy is generated using _____, which creates the energy necessary to move electrons within a circuit.

    (a) electromagnetism
    (b) photovoltaics
    (c) chemical activity
    (d) heat

13. Photoelectricity is the conversion of _____ energy into electrical energy, which creates the energy necessary to move electrons within a circuit.

    (a) light
    (b) magnetic
    (c) chemical
    (d) heat

14. Thermoelectricity is the conversion of _____ energy into electrical energy, which creates the energy necessary to move electrons within a circuit.

    (a) light
    (b) magnetic
    (c) chemical
    (d) heat

15. A common application of thermoelectricity is a "_____," which is a sensor that measures temperature.

    (a) thermostat
    (b) compass
    (c) heater
    (d) thermocouple

16. Piezoelectricity is the conversion of _____ or vibration into electrical energy necessary to move electrons within a circuit.

    (a) static electricity
    (b) pressure
    (c) magnetism
    (d) light

UNIT
4

THE ELECTRICAL SYSTEM

4.1 Introduction

The electrical system typically begins at the utility generating plant. Knowing how electricity gets from there to a building provides a better sense of "the big picture." In this unit you will learn:

- How electricity is generated at the utility generating plant
- About transmission and distribution voltages
- How electricity gets to a customer's premises

4.2 Source of Electrical Generation

The primary energy sources used to generate electricity include fossil fuels (coal, natural gas, and petroleum), nuclear energy, and renewable energy sources. Most electricity is generated with steam turbines using fossil fuels and nuclear power. Other electricity generation sources include gas turbines, hydro turbines, wind turbines, and solar photovoltaics. ▶Figure 4–1

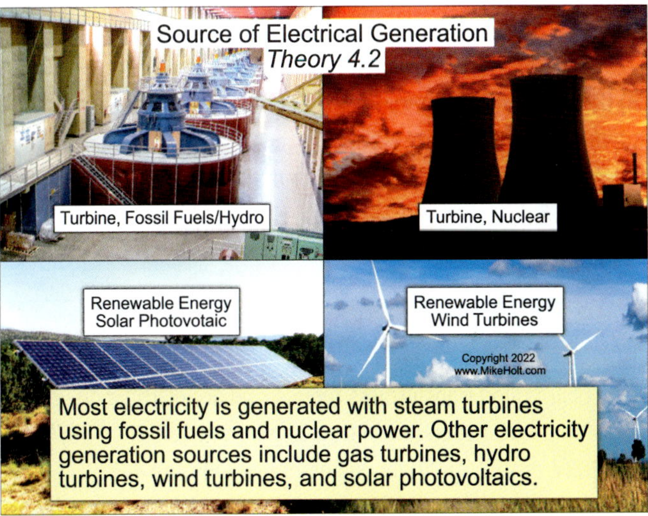
Source of Electrical Generation
Theory 4.2
Turbine, Fossil Fuels/Hydro
Turbine, Nuclear
Renewable Energy
Solar Photovotaic
Renewable Energy
Wind Turbines
Copyright 2022
www.MikeHolt.com
Most electricity is generated with steam turbines using fossil fuels and nuclear power. Other electricity generation sources include gas turbines, hydro turbines, wind turbines, and solar photovoltaics.

▶Figure 4–1

4.3 Step-Up Transmission Voltage

Once the utility has produced electrical energy, the voltage from the generating facility must be "stepped up" to be transmitted as efficiently as possible to where it is needed. Transformers at the utility generating facility "step-up" voltage for transmission distribution to between 69 kV and 765 kV. ▶Figure 4–2

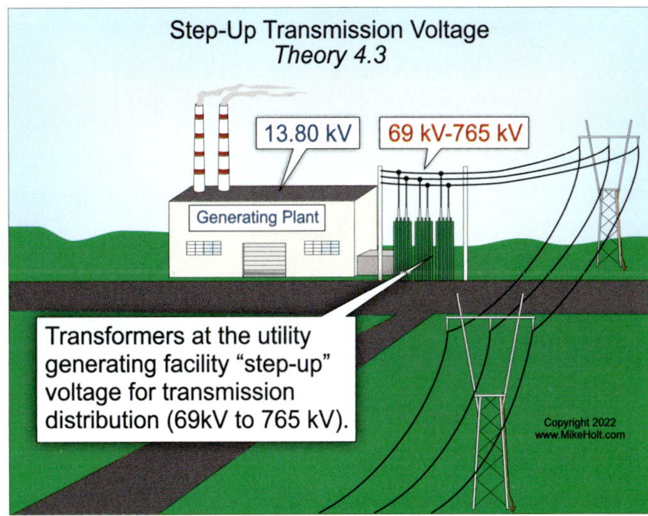
Step-Up Transmission Voltage
Theory 4.3
13.80 kV
69 kV-765 kV
Generating Plant
Transformers at the utility generating facility "step-up" voltage for transmission distribution (69kV to 765 kV).
Copyright 2022
www.MikeHolt.com

▶Figure 4–2

4.4 High-Voltage Transmission Lines

The most economical way to move electrical energy from the generating facility over long distances is to transmit the electrical energy at high voltages to distribution "step-down" substations. ▸Figure 4–3

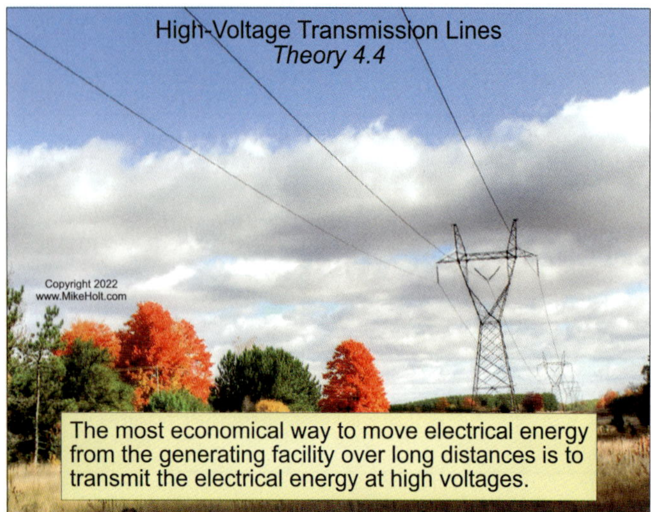
High-Voltage Transmission Lines
Theory 4.4
Copyright 2022 www.MikeHolt.com
The most economical way to move electrical energy from the generating facility over long distances is to transmit the electrical energy at high voltages.

▸Figure 4–3

Author's Comment:

- The most effective way to reduce voltage drop and power loss is to lower the current flowing through the transmission lines. This is accomplished by increasing the transmission voltage.

4.5 Primary Distribution Voltage

Once high-voltage transmission distribution power reaches the "step-down" substation, the voltage is stepped down from transmission voltage (69 kV to 765 kV) to primary distribution voltage which is between 13 kV and 34.50 kV. ▸Figure 4–4

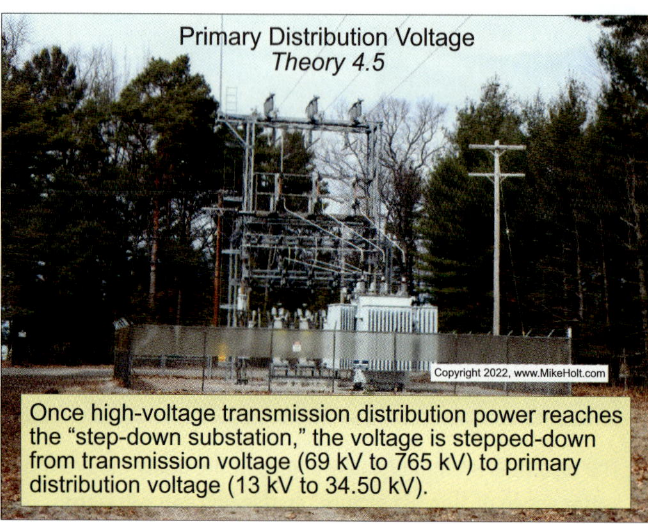
Primary Distribution Voltage
Theory 4.5
Copyright 2022, www.MikeHolt.com
Once high-voltage transmission distribution power reaches the "step-down substation," the voltage is stepped-down from transmission voltage (69 kV to 765 kV) to primary distribution voltage (13 kV to 34.50 kV).

▸Figure 4–4

4.6 Primary Distribution Wires

"Primary distribution wires" are run from the step-down substation to "distribution transformers."

(A) Overhead Primary Distribution Wires. Overhead utility primary distribution wires provide power to "distribution transformers" mounted on poles next to the building or structure served. ▸Figure 4–5

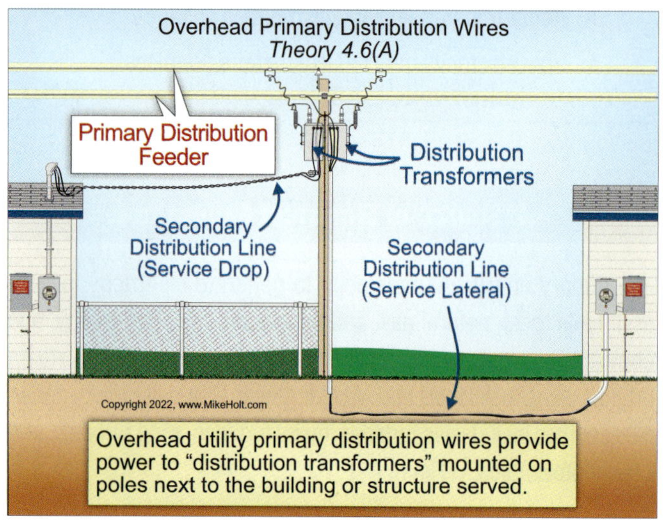
Overhead Primary Distribution Wires
Theory 4.6(A)
Primary Distribution Feeder
Distribution Transformers
Secondary Distribution Line (Service Drop)
Secondary Distribution Line (Service Lateral)
Copyright 2022, www.MikeHolt.com
Overhead utility primary distribution wires provide power to "distribution transformers" mounted on poles next to the building or structure served.

▸Figure 4–5

(B) Underground Primary Distribution Wires. Underground utility primary distribution wires provide power to pad-mounted distribution transformers located on the ground near the building or structure served. ▸Figure 4–6

4.7 Secondary Distribution Voltage

Utility distribution transformers reduce primary distribution voltage (13 kV to 34.50 kV) to secondary distribution voltage (120/240V, 120/208V, or 277/480V) for customer use. ▸Figure 4–7

 1st Printing

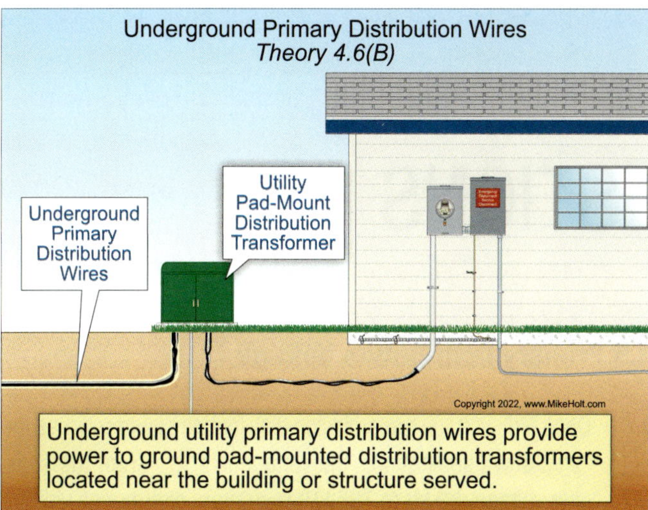
Underground Primary Distribution Wires
Theory 4.6(B)
Underground Primary Distribution Wires
Utility Pad-Mount Distribution Transformer
Copyright 2022, www.MikeHolt.com
Underground utility primary distribution wires provide power to ground pad-mounted distribution transformers located near the building or structure served.
▸Figure 4–6

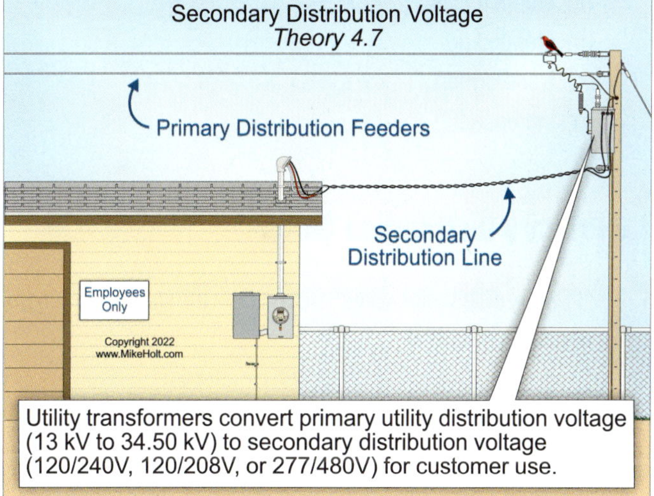
Secondary Distribution Voltage
Theory 4.7
Primary Distribution Feeders
Secondary Distribution Line
Employees Only
Copyright 2022 www.MikeHolt.com
Utility transformers convert primary utility distribution voltage (13 kV to 34.50 kV) to secondary distribution voltage (120/240V, 120/208V, or 277/480V) for customer use.
▸Figure 4–7

4.8 Service Drop and Service Lateral

Power from utility distribution transformers is delivered to the customer by utility overhead or underground wiring.

(A) Service Drop. Overhead wires from the utility primary distribution transformer to the premises are referred to as the "utility service drop." ▸Figure 4–8

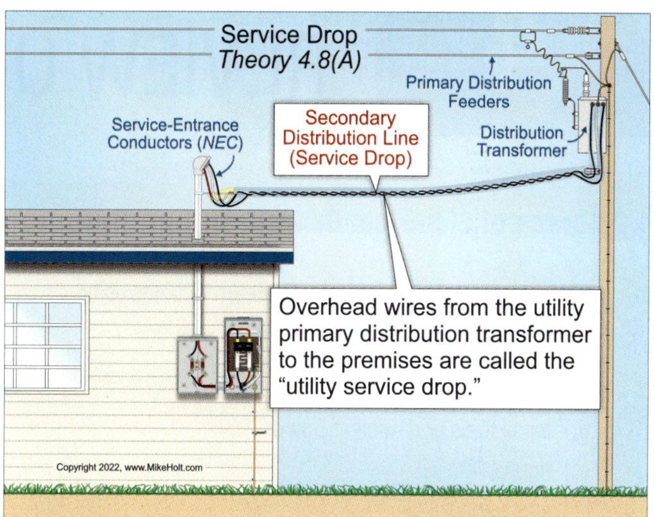
Service Drop
Theory 4.8(A)
Primary Distribution Feeders
Service-Entrance Conductors (NEC)
Secondary Distribution Line (Service Drop)
Distribution Transformer
Overhead wires from the utility primary distribution transformer to the premises are called the "utility service drop."
Copyright 2022, www.MikeHolt.com
▸Figure 4–8

(B) Service Lateral. Underground wires from the utility primary distribution transformer to the premises are referred to as "utility service lateral." ▸Figure 4–9

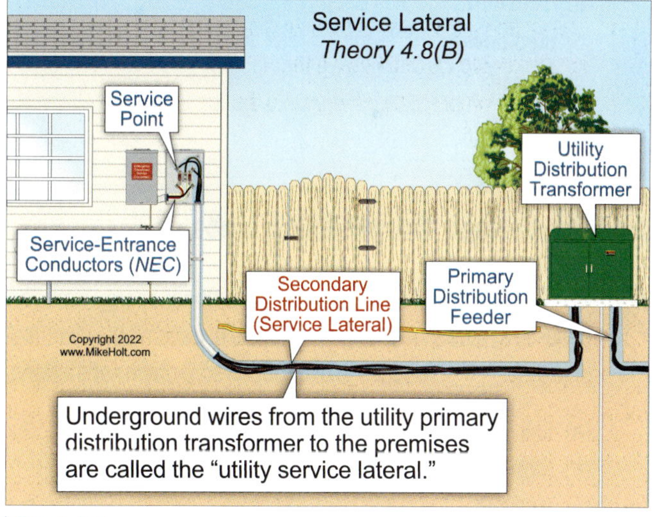
Service Lateral
Theory 4.8(B)
Service Point
Utility Distribution Transformer
Service-Entrance Conductors (NEC)
Secondary Distribution Line (Service Lateral)
Primary Distribution Feeder
Copyright 2022 www.MikeHolt.com
Underground wires from the utility primary distribution transformer to the premises are called the "utility service lateral."
▸Figure 4–9

UNIT
4

REVIEW QUESTIONS

4.2 Source of Electrical Generation

1. Most electricity is generated with steam turbines using _____.

   (a) fossil fuels
   (b) nuclear power
   (c) fossil fuels and nuclear power
   (d) none of these

4.3 Step-Up Transmission Voltage

2. Transformers at the utility generating facility "_____" voltage for transmission distribution to between 69kV and 765 kV.

   (a) transform
   (b) step-down
   (c) step-up
   (d) reduce

4.4 High-Voltage Transmission Lines

3. The most economical way to move electrical energy from the generating facility over long distances is to transmit the electrical energy at _____ voltages to distribution step-down substations.

   (a) low
   (b) high
   (c) medium
   (d) special

4.5 Primary Distribution Voltage

4. Once high-voltage transmission distribution power reaches the "step-down substation," the voltage is _____ from transmission voltage (69 kV to 765 kV) to primary distribution voltage which is between 13 kV and 34.50 kV.

   (a) stepped down
   (b) stepped up
   (c) transformed
   (d) increased

4.6 Primary Distribution Wires

5. "Primary distribution wires" are run from the step-down substation to "distribution _____."

   (a) wires
   (b) motors
   (c) generators
   (d) transformers

6. _____ utility primary distribution wires provide power to "distribution transformers" mounted on poles next to the building or structure served.

   (a) Overhead
   (b) Underground
   (c) Open
   (d) Enclosed

7. _____ utility primary distribution wires provide power to pad-mounted distribution transformers located near the building or structure served.

(a) Overhead
(b) Underground
(c) Open
(d) Enclosed

4.7 Secondary Distribution Voltage

8. Utility distribution transformers _____ the primary distribution voltage (13 kV to 34.50 kV) to secondary distribution voltage (120/240V, 120/208V, or 277/480V) for customer use.

(a) increase
(b) reduce
(c) step-up
(d) raise

4.8 Service Drop and Service Lateral

9. Power from utility distribution transformers is delivered to the customer by utility _____wiring.

(a) overhead
(b) underground
(c) overhead or underground
(d) none of these

10. Overhead wires from the utility primary distribution transformer to the premises are called the "utility _____."

(a) service drop
(b) service lateral
(c) service drop or service lateral
(d) none of these

11. Underground wires from the utility primary distribution transformer to the premises are called the "utility _____."

(a) service drop
(b) service lateral
(c) service drop or service lateral
(d) none of these

Notes

UNIT
6

DANGERS OF ELECTRICITY

6.1 Introduction

People working in the electrical industry are responsible for ensuring electrical installations are as safe as possible. In this unit you will learn:

- The purpose of the *National Electrical Code*
- How electrical fires are created
- What electric shock and electrocution are
- What arc flashes and arc blasts are

6.2 *National Electrical Code (NEC)*

To ensure the practical safeguarding of persons and property from the use of electricity, all wiring must be installed in accordance with NFPA 70, *National Electrical Code*. Installing electrical systems in accordance with the *NEC* and providing proper maintenance should result in an installation that is essentially free from fire, electric shock, electrocution, arc flash, and arc blast events.

6.3 Electrical Fire

Each year, fires from electrical failures result in the loss of lives and billions in property damage. The primary cause of an electrical fire is excessive heat when wires are not terminated correctly, not properly sized, or the loads exceed the circuits' rating. ▸Figure 6–1

Dangers of Electricity
Electrical Fire
Theory 6.3
Copyright 2022, www.MikeHolt.com
The primary cause of an electrical fire is excessive heat when wires are not terminated correctly, not properly sized, and/or the loads exceed the circuits' rating.

▸Figure 6–1

Author's Comment:

- Electrical installations typically fail at the terminations. Wire terminations must be properly tightened in accordance with the manufacturers' torque values. Loose wire terminations can lead to "glowing contacts" (a high resistive point between a wire and wire terminal), which can cause enough heat for a fire to start. ▸Figure 6–2

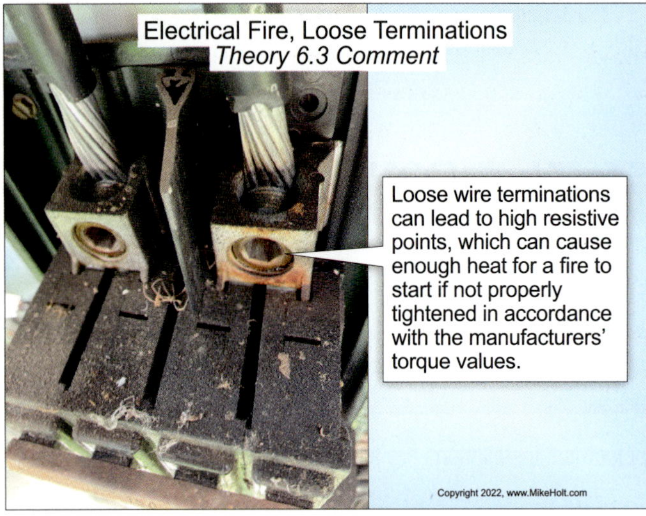

Electrical Fire, Loose Terminations
Theory 6.3 Comment
Loose wire terminations can lead to high resistive points, which can cause enough heat for a fire to start if not properly tightened in accordance with the manufacturers' torque values.
Copyright 2022, www.MikeHolt.com

▸Figure 6–2

6.4 Electric Shock

(A) General. The National Safety Council estimates that approximately 300 people in the United States die each year because of an electric shock from 120V and 277V circuits. For electrical current to flow, there must be a power source and a path for electrons to leave that power source, and then return to the same power source. People and animals can be shocked or electrocuted when electrons flow through their bodies, especially when those electrons flow through their hearts. ▸Figure 6–3

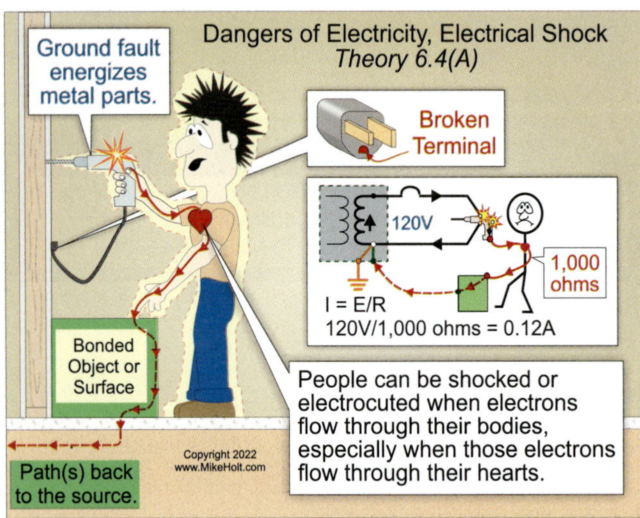

Dangers of Electricity, Electrical Shock
Theory 6.4(A)
Ground fault energizes metal parts.
Broken Terminal
120V
1,000 ohms
I = E/R
120V/1,000 ohms = 0.12A
Bonded Object or Surface
People can be shocked or electrocuted when electrons flow through their bodies, especially when those electrons flow through their hearts.
Path(s) back to the source.
Copyright 2022 www.MikeHolt.com

▸Figure 6–3

(B) Electric Shock or Electrocution. In less than a second, an individual can go into atrial fibrillation from electrical current when as little as 50/1,000 of an ampere connects with them. An electric shock disrupts the heart's electrical signal. When that occurs, the heart goes into a rapid, ineffective heartbeat of over 350 beats per minute. This is referred to as "atrial fibrillation" and prevents blood from circulating through the body. Death can result in a matter of minutes (electrocution), particularly when blood circulation to the brain is hindered. Cardiopulmonary resuscitation (CPR) can provide extra time, but defibrillation is essential for surviving atrial fibrillation. ▸Figure 6–4

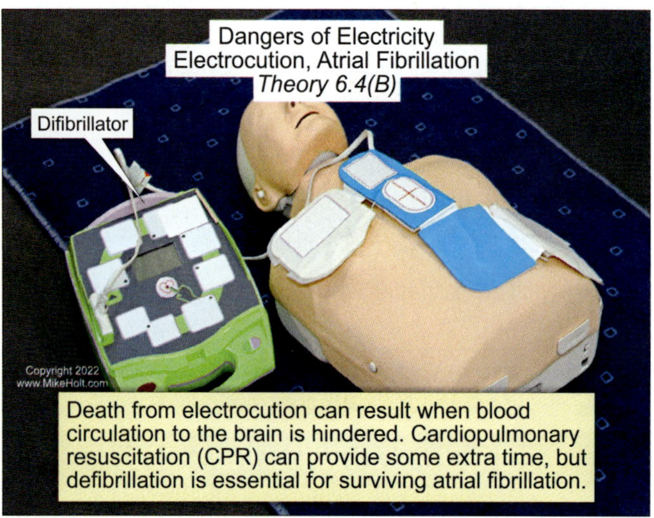

Dangers of Electricity
Electrocution, Atrial Fibrillation
Theory 6.4(B)
Difibrillator
Copyright 2022 www.MikeHolt.com
Death from electrocution can result when blood circulation to the brain is hindered. Cardiopulmonary resuscitation (CPR) can provide some extra time, but defibrillation is essential for surviving atrial fibrillation.

▸Figure 6–4

(C) Severity of Electric Shock. A shock from as little as 30V alternating current for as little as one second can disrupt the heart's electrical circuitry, causing it to go into ventricular fibrillation. The severity of an electric shock depends on the amount of current flowing through the body. This is determined by the electromotive force measured in volts and the contact resistance measured in ohms. The effects of 60 Hz alternating current on an average human include: ▸Figure 6–5

- ***Electrical Sensation.*** Tingle sensation occurs at about 0.30 mA for an adult female and 0.40 mA for an adult male.
- ***Perception Let-Go.*** Current over 0.70 mA is very uncomfortable to both genders.
- ***Maximum Let-Go Level.*** The "let-go threshold" is the current level where we lose control of our muscles, and the electricity causes muscles to contract until the current is removed. In other words, at this point we cannot let go of an energized circuit. The top let-go threshold level for a female is approximately 10 mA, and about 16 mA for a male.

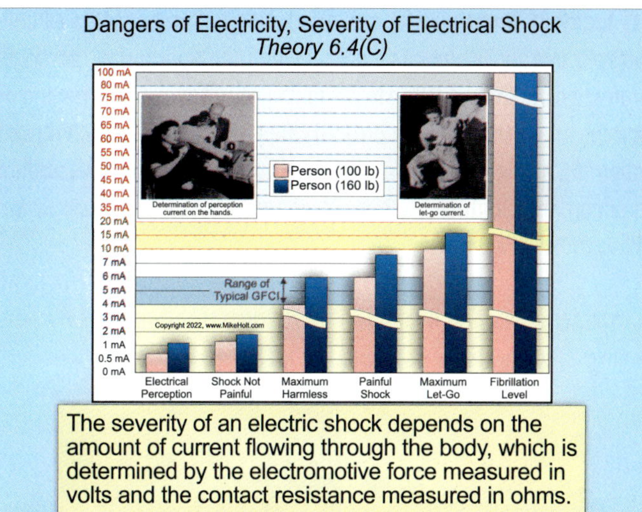
Dangers of Electricity, Severity of Electrical Shock
Theory 6.4(C)
Person (100 lb)
Person (160 lb)
Determination of perception current on the hands.
Determination of let-go current.
Range of Typical GFCI
Copyright 2022, www.MikeHolt.com
Electrical Perception
Shock Not Painful
Maximum Harmless
Painful Shock
Maximum Let-Go
Fibrillation Level
The severity of an electric shock depends on the amount of current flowing through the body, which is determined by the electromotive force measured in volts and the contact resistance measured in ohms.

▸Figure 6–5

- ***Fibrillation Level.*** 50 mA for 0.20 seconds (female) and 75 mA for 0.50 seconds (male).

6.5 Electric Arc Flash and Arc Blast

(A) General. In addition to electric shock, accidental contact of conductive metal objects with energized parts can result in a phase-to-phase or ground fault. These faults can cause a severe arc flash and arc blast. ▸Figure 6–6

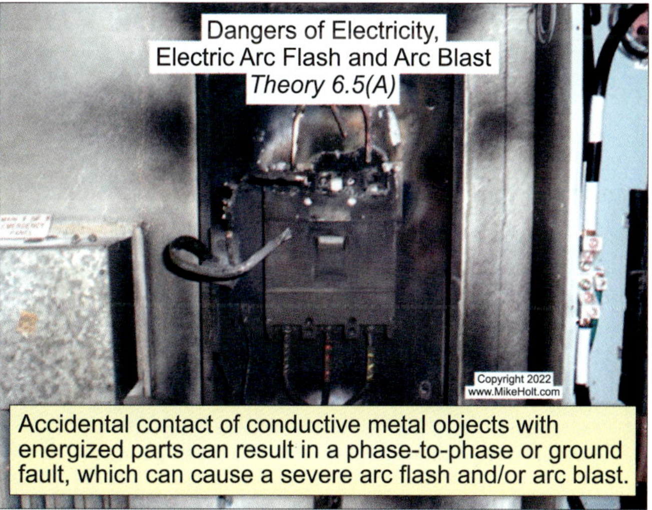
Dangers of Electricity,
Electric Arc Flash and Arc Blast
Theory 6.5(A)
Copyright 2022
www.MikeHolt.com
Accidental contact of conductive metal objects with energized parts can result in a phase-to-phase or ground fault, which can cause a severe arc flash and/or arc blast.

▸Figure 6–6

(B) Arc Flash. During an arcing fault, electrical energy is converted into various other forms of energy. Electrical energy can vaporize metal, which can change from a solid state to a vapor. When copper vaporizes, it expands in volume and creates a superheated plasma. Dangerous arc flashes (explosions of spewing molten metal) are possible when equipment and safeguards are not properly installed and used. An arc flash can cause temperatures approaching 35,000°F to vaporize anything within its immediate vicinity. ▸Figure 6–7

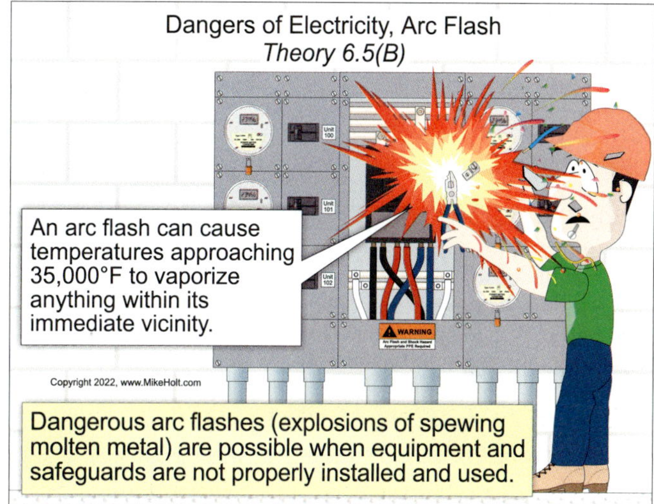
Dangers of Electricity, Arc Flash
Theory 6.5(B)
An arc flash can cause temperatures approaching 35,000°F to vaporize anything within its immediate vicinity.
Copyright 2022, www.MikeHolt.com
Dangerous arc flashes (explosions of spewing molten metal) are possible when equipment and safeguards are not properly installed and used.

▸Figure 6–7

Author's Comment:

- As an electrician it, is important for you to understand the information on an arc flash label to determine what level of personal protective equipment (PPE) to wear. ▸Figure 6–8

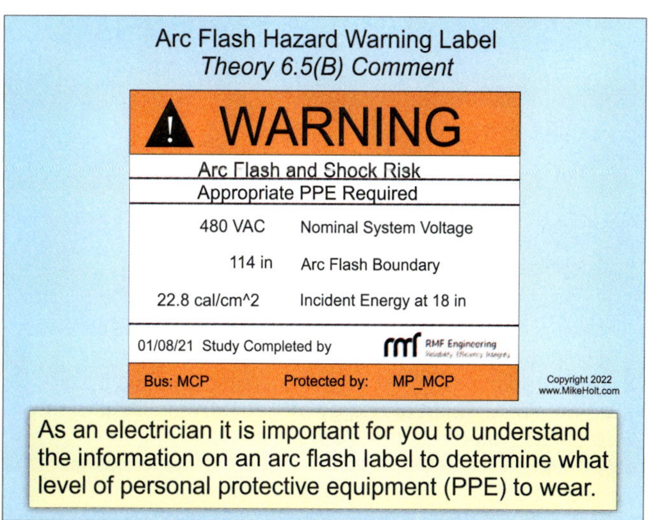
Arc Flash Hazard Warning Label
Theory 6.5(B) Comment
WARNING
Arc Flash and Shock Risk
Appropriate PPE Required
480 VAC Nominal System Voltage
114 in Arc Flash Boundary
22.8 cal/cm^2 Incident Energy at 18 in
01/08/21 Study Completed by
RMF Engineering
Bus: MCP Protected by: MP_MCP
Copyright 2022
www.MikeHolt.com
As an electrician it is important for you to understand the information on an arc flash label to determine what level of personal protective equipment (PPE) to wear.

▸Figure 6–8

(C) Arc Blast. In addition to an arc flash, an arcing fault can generate an arc blast. The strength of an arc blast creates an explosive pressure wave that can eject shrapnel, molten metal, plastic, and paint across a room. This arc blast can cause severe injuries or death to those who are close. There is no protection against an arc blast! ▸Figure 6–9

Dangers of Electricity, Arc Blast
Theory 6.5(C)
Copyright 2022
www.MikeHolt.com
An arcing fault can generate an arc blast. The strength of an arc blast creates an explosive pressure wave that can eject shrapnel, molten metal, plastic, and paint across a room and cause severe injuries or death to those who are close to the blast.

▸Figure 6–9

6.6 Arc Flash Incident Energy

(A) General. Incident energy is the amount of thermal energy measured in cal/cm^2 at a given working distance from an arc flash. Thermal energy of 1.20 cal/cm^2 is sufficient to cause second-degree burns to exposed skin. ▸Figure 6–10

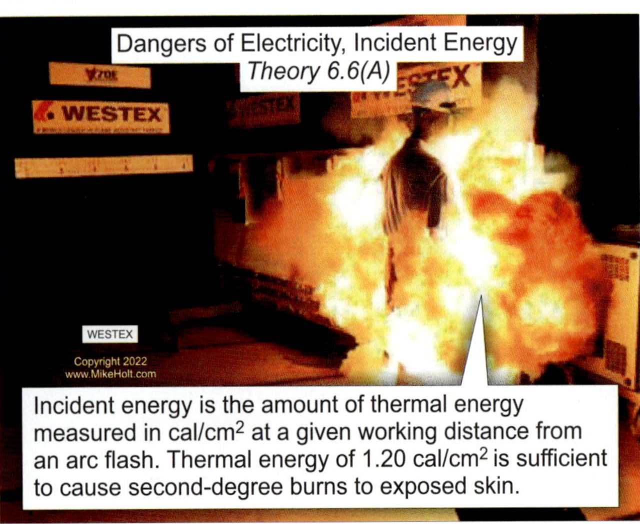
Dangers of Electricity, Incident Energy
Theory 6.6(A)
WESTEX
WESTEX
Copyright 2022
www.MikeHolt.com
Incident energy is the amount of thermal energy measured in cal/cm^2 at a given working distance from an arc flash. Thermal energy of 1.20 cal/cm^2 is sufficient to cause second-degree burns to exposed skin.

▸Figure 6–10

(1) Incident Energy Analysis. Predicting the amount of available incident energy is crucial when selecting the appropriate personal protective equipment (PPE) to prevent injury from clothing melting or burning due to the use of incorrectly rated PPE. Arc-rated clothing and other PPE associated with exposure to an arc flash must be selected in accordance with NFPA 70E, *Standard for Electrical Safety in the Workplace.* ▸Figure 6–11

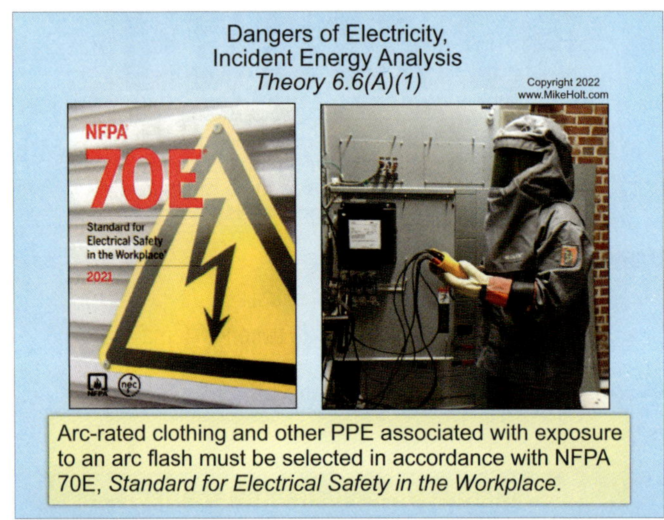
Dangers of Electricity,
Incident Energy Analysis
Theory 6.6(A)(1)
Copyright 2022
www.MikeHolt.com
NFPA
70E
Standard for Electrical Safety in the Workplace
2021
Arc-rated clothing and other PPE associated with exposure to an arc flash must be selected in accordance with NFPA 70E, *Standard for Electrical Safety in the Workplace.*

▸Figure 6–11

(B) Incident Energy Calculation. Determining the incident energy at a given point in the electrical system requires software that uses the values of short-circuit current and the time it takes for the circuit overcurrent protective device to clear. ▸Figure 6–12

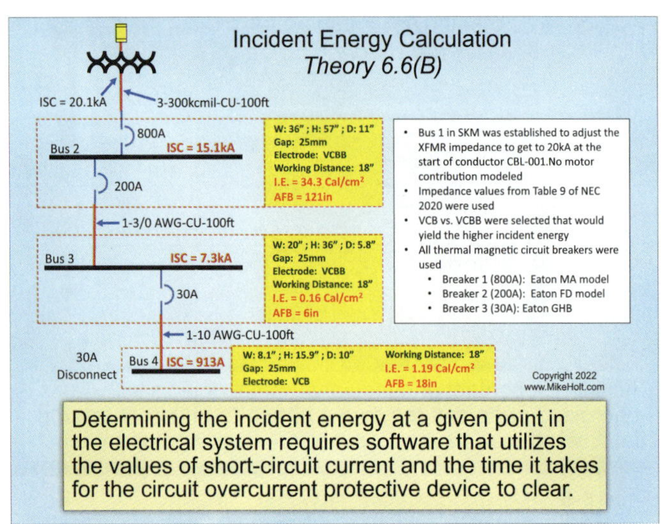
Incident Energy Calculation
Theory 6.6(B)
ISC = 20.1kA
3-300kcmil-CU-100ft
800A
Bus 2
ISC = 15.1kA
200A
W: 36" ; H: 57" ; D: 11"
Gap: 25mm
Electrode: VCBB
Working Distance: 18"
I.E. = 34.3 Cal/cm^2
AFB = 121in
1-3/0 AWG-CU-100ft
Bus 3
ISC = 7.3kA
30A
W: 20" ; H: 36" ; D: 5.8"
Gap: 25mm
Electrode: VCBB
Working Distance: 18"
I.E. = 0.16 Cal/cm^2
AFB = 6in
1-10 AWG-CU-100ft
30A Disconnect
Bus 4
ISC = 913A
W: 8.1" ; H: 15.9" ; D: 10"
Gap: 25mm
Electrode: VCB
Working Distance: 18"
I.E. = 1.19 Cal/cm^2
AFB = 18in
• Bus 1 in SKM was established to adjust the XFMR impedance to get to 20kA at the start of conductor CBL-001.No motor contribution modeled
• Impedance values from Table 9 of NEC 2020 were used
• VCB vs. VCBB were selected that would yield the higher incident energy
• All thermal magnetic circuit breakers were used
• Breaker 1 (800A): Eaton MA model
• Breaker 2 (200A): Eaton FD model
• Breaker 3 (30A): Eaton GHB
Copyright 2022
www.MikeHolt.com
Determining the incident energy at a given point in the electrical system requires software that utilizes the values of short-circuit current and the time it takes for the circuit overcurrent protective device to clear.

▸Figure 6–12

(C) Arc-Flash Boundary. The arc-flash boundary separates an area in which a person is likely to be exposed to second-degree burns. Where a body part is within the arc-flash boundary, the selected PPE must be rated for the anticipated available incident energy. ▸Figure 6–13

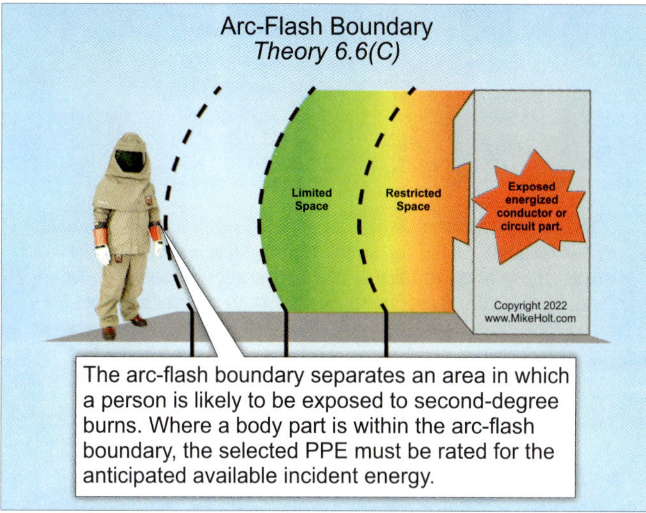
Arc-Flash Boundary
Theory 6.6(C)
Limited Space
Restricted Space
Exposed energized conductor or circuit part.
Copyright 2022 www.MikeHolt.com
The arc-flash boundary separates an area in which a person is likely to be exposed to second-degree burns. Where a body part is within the arc-flash boundary, the selected PPE must be rated for the anticipated available incident energy.

▸Figure 6–13

Author's Comment:

- The limited approach boundary and the restricted approach boundary are for shock protection only—not for arc-flash protection! ▸Figure 6–14

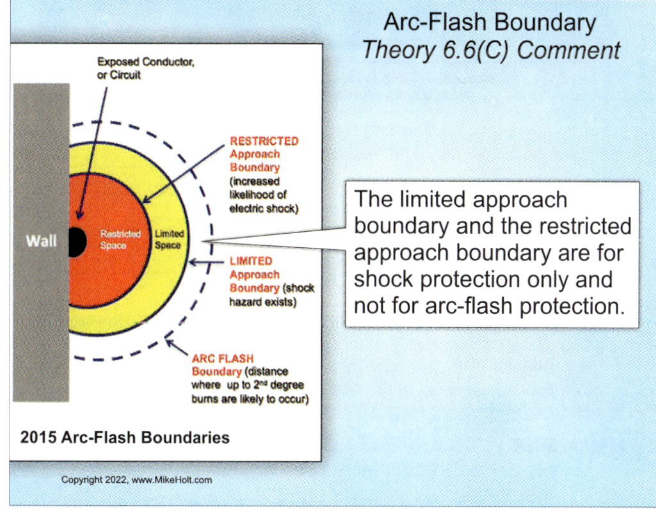
Arc-Flash Boundary
Theory 6.6(C) Comment
Exposed Conductor, or Circuit
RESTRICTED Approach Boundary (increased likelihood of electric shock)
Wall
Restricted Space
Limited Space
LIMITED Approach Boundary (shock hazard exists)
ARC FLASH Boundary (distance where up to 2nd degree burns are likely to occur)
2015 Arc-Flash Boundaries
Copyright 2022, www.MikeHolt.com
The limited approach boundary and the restricted approach boundary are for shock protection only and not for arc-flash protection.

▸Figure 6–14

6.7 Electrically Safe Work Condition

(A) General. Electrical work should never be performed while electrical equipment is energized. An electrically safe work condition is when electrical circuits have been de-energized, locked out/tagged out, and verification the circuit is completely de-energized.

(B) Absence of Voltage Test. In order to de-energize electrical equipment, an absence of voltage test must be performed wearing adequate PPE as required by NFPA 70E, *Standard for Electrical Safety in the Workplace*. ▸Figure 6–15

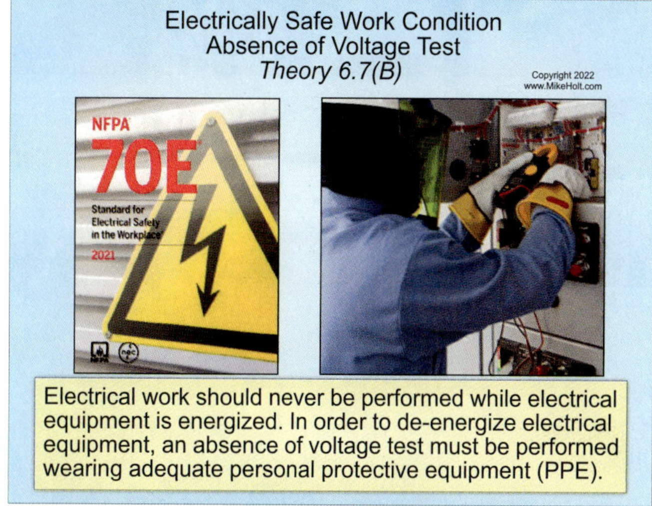
Electrically Safe Work Condition
Absence of Voltage Test
Theory 6.7(B)
Copyright 2022 www.MikeHolt.com
NFPA
70E
Standard for Electrical Safety in the Workplace
2021
Electrical work should never be performed while electrical equipment is energized. In order to de-energize electrical equipment, an absence of voltage test must be performed wearing adequate personal protective equipment (PPE).

▸Figure 6–15

(C) Lockout/Tagout. The lockout/tagout process is intended to shut off all sources of energy to equipment by preventing the operation of the disconnecting means. After a disconnect has been opened and the lockout device has been attached, a tag is placed on the disconnect to warn others not to operate the disconnect. ▸Figure 6–16

6.8 Personal Protective Equipment (PPE)

(A) General. Personal Protective Equipment (PPE) is intended to minimize the severity of an injury so it is survivable. PPE is designed to protect the body from a particular electrical hazard. When properly selected, it can protect against other electrical hazards. For example, rubber insulated gloves or leather protectors provide shock protection for hands or forearms and provides arc-flash protection. ▸Figure 6–17

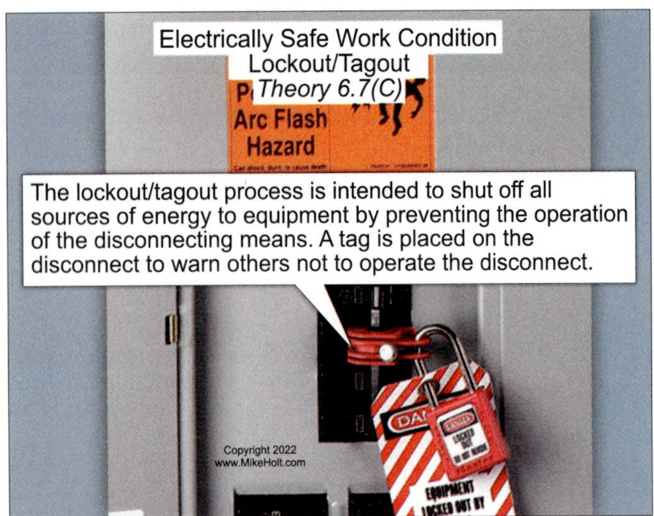
Electrically Safe Work Condition
Lockout/Tagout
Theory 6.7(C)
Arc Flash
Hazard
The lockout/tagout process is intended to shut off all sources of energy to equipment by preventing the operation of the disconnecting means. A tag is placed on the disconnect to warn others not to operate the disconnect.
Copyright 2022
www.MikeHolt.com

▶Figure 6–16

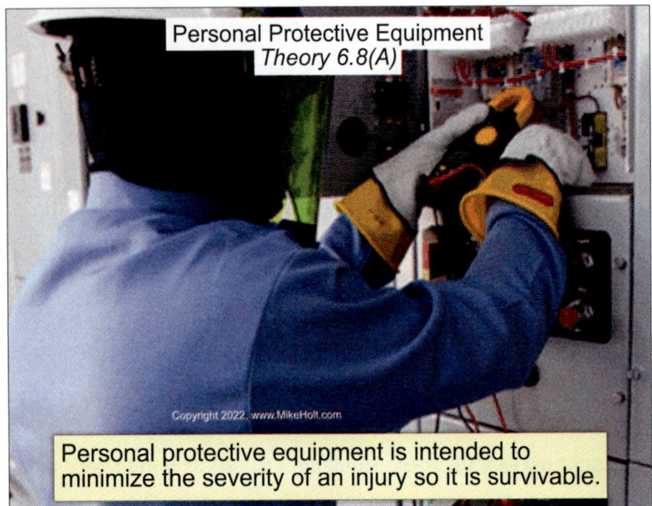
Personal Protective Equipment
Theory 6.8(A)
Copyright 2022, www.MikeHolt.com
Personal protective equipment is intended to minimize the severity of an injury so it is survivable.

▶Figure 6–17

(B) PPE Selection. When selecting the proper PPE for shock and arc-flash protection, the areas of the body to take into consideration include the head, face, neck, chin, eyes, ears, body, hands, arms, and feet. In addition, the protective clothing or gear must allow for movement and visibility. ▶Figure 6–18

(C) Arc-Flash PPE Category Method. The Arc-Flash PPE Category Table is used to determine the need for an appropriate level of arc flash PPE and the arc-flash boundary if the following is known:

- nominal system voltage
- calculated short-circuit current
- overcurrent protective device clearing time (0.03 seconds or 2 cycles)
- minimum working distance (18 in.)

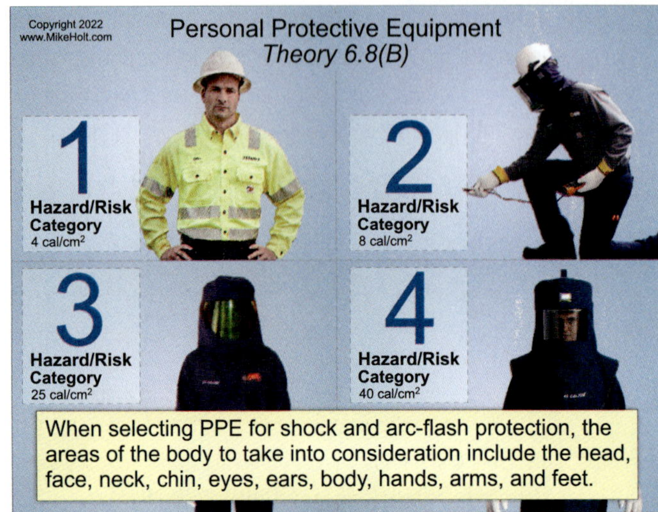
Copyright 2022
www.MikeHolt.com
Personal Protective Equipment
Theory 6.8(B)
1
Hazard/Risk
Category
4 cal/cm2
2
Hazard/Risk
Category
8 cal/cm2
3
Hazard/Risk
Category
25 cal/cm2
4
Hazard/Risk
Category
40 cal/cm2
When selecting PPE for shock and arc-flash protection, the areas of the body to take into consideration include the head, face, neck, chin, eyes, ears, body, hands, arms, and feet.

▶Figure 6–18

▶ Arc-Flash PPE Category Method Example

Question: *What level of PPE category and arc-flash boundary is required for a 480V, three-phase panelboard with a short-circuit current of 7000A, a working distance of 18 in., and a 200A circuit breaker with a clearing time of 0.03 seconds (2 cycles)?* ▶Figure 6–19

(a) Category 1, 19 in. *(b) Category 2, 36 in.*
(c) Category 3, 60 in. *(d) Category 4, 240 in.*

Arc-Flash PPE Category Method
Theory 6.8(C) Example

Table 130.7(C)(15)(a) Arc-Flash PPE Category and Boundary for Alternating-Current Systems

Equipment	Category	Boundary
Power 25 kVA or less, 240V or less; molded case circuit breaker	1	19 in.
Power 25 kVA or less, 480V or less; molded case circuit breaker	2	36 In.
Power 25 kVA or less, 480V or less; current-limiting fuse or circuit breaker	1	36 In.
Power 65 kVA or less, 480V or less; molded case circuit breaker	2	60 in.
Power 65 kVA or less, 480V or less; current-limiting fuse or circuit breaker	1	60 in.

For other conditions see Table 130.7(C)(15) in NFPA 70E.

Copyright 2022, www.MikeHolt.com

The Arc-Flash PPE Category Table is used to determine the need for an appropriate level of arc flash PPE and the arc-flash boundary.

▶Figure 6–19

Answer: *(b) Category 2, 36 in.*

UNIT 6

REVIEW QUESTIONS

6.2 National Electrical Code (NEC)

1. To ensure the minimum practical safeguarding of persons and property from the use of _____, all wiring must be installed in accordance with the *National Electrical Code* (*NEC*).

   (a) magnetism
   (b) electricity
   (c) heating
   (d) welding

6.3 Electrical Fire

2. The primary causes of an electrical _____ is excessive heat when wires are not terminated correctly, not properly sized, and the loads exceed the circuit wires' ampacity rating.

   (a) fire
   (b) overload
   (c) short circuit
   (d) fault

6.4 Electric Shock

3. The National Safety Council estimates that approximately _____ people in the United States die each year because of an electric shock from 120V and 277V circuits.

   (a) 100
   (b) 200
   (c) 300
   (d) 400

4. People and animals can be _____ or electrocuted when electrons flow through their bodies, especially when those electrons flow through their hearts.

   (a) knocked out
   (b) shocked
   (c) startled
   (d) injured

5. An electric shock disrupts the heart's electrical signal, and when that occurs, the heart goes into a rapid, ineffective heartbeat of over 350 beats per minute. This is called "_____ fibrillation" and prevents blood from circulating through the body.

   (a) atrial
   (b) ventricular
   (c) pressure
   (d) none of these

6. The severity of an electric shock is dependent on the amount of current flowing through the body, which is impacted by circuit voltage and _____ resistance.

   (a) contact
   (b) the Earth's
   (c) the body's
   (d) circuit

6.5 Electric Arc Flash and Arc Blast

7. In addition to electric shock, accidental contact of conductive metal objects with energized parts can result in a phase-to-phase or ground fault. These faults can cause a severe ______.

   (a) arc flash
   (b) arc blast
   (c) arc flash and/or arc blast
   (d) none of these

8. An electric arc flash can cause temperatures approaching _____ to vaporize anything within its immediate vicinity.

(a) 10,000°F
(b) 15,000°F
(c) 25,000°F
(d) 35,000°F

9. The strength of an arc _____ creates an explosive pressure wave that can eject shrapnel, molten metal, plastic, and paint across a room and cause severe injuries or death.

(a) flash
(b) blast
(c) fault
(d) fire

6.6 Arc Flash Incident Energy

10. _____ energy is the amount of thermal energy measured in cal/cm^2 at a given working distance during an electric arc flash event.

(a) Flash
(b) Blast
(c) Fault
(d) Incident

11. Predicting the amount of available incident energy is crucial when selecting the appropriate _____ to prevent injury from clothing melting or burning.

(a) personal protective equipment
(b) long-sleeved shirt
(c) helmet
(d) gloves

12. Determining the incident energy at a given point in the electrical system requires _____ that utilizes the values of short-circuit current and the time it takes for the circuit overcurrent protective device to open.

(a) PPE
(b) software
(c) an app
(d) a calculator

13. The arc-flash _____ separates an area in which a person is likely to be exposed to second-degree burns.

(a) zone
(b) perimeter
(c) boundary
(d) area

6.7 Electrically Safe Work Condition

14. A(An) _____ safe work condition is where electrical circuits have been de-energized, locked out/tagged out, and tested to verify that the circuit is de-energized.

(a) arc
(b) PPE
(c) mechanically
(d) electrically

15. In order to de-energize electrical equipment, a(an) _____ of voltage test must be performed wearing the adequate personal protective equipment (PPE) as required by NFPA 70E, *Standard for Electrical Safety in the Workplace*.

(a) absence
(b) missing
(c) confirmation
(d) diagnosis

16. The intent of the _____ is to shut off all sources of energy by operating the applicable disconnecting means.

(a) lockout/tagout process
(b) safety program
(c) employee handbook
(d) safety meeting

6.8 Personal Protective Equipment

17. Personal protective equipment (PPE) is intended to _____ the severity of an injury so it is survivable.

(a) eliminate
(b) maximize
(c) minimize
(d) deflect

18. The protective clothing or gear must allow for _____.

    (a) movement
    (b) visibility
    (c) movement and visibility
    (d) none of these

Notes

UNIT 25 OVERCURRENT PROTECTION

25.1 Introduction

Overcurrent protection is a complex subject because different types of overcurrent protective devices serve different purposes. In this unit you will learn the:

- Role of circuit overcurrent protection
- Difference between a circuit breaker and a fuse
- Fundamentals of time-current curves and selective coordination
- Difference between interrupting ratings and short-circuit current ratings ▸Figure 25–1

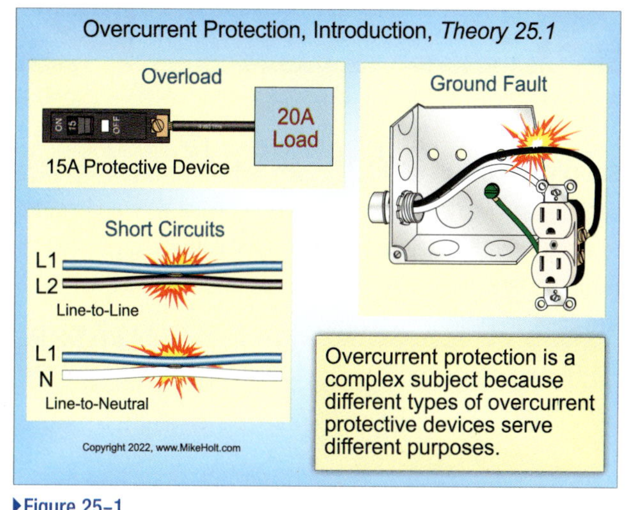
Overcurrent Protection, Introduction, *Theory 25.1*
Overload
20A Load
15A Protective Device
Ground Fault
Short Circuits
L1
L2
Line-to-Line
L1
N
Line-to-Neutral
Overcurrent protection is a complex subject because different types of overcurrent protective devices serve different purposes.
Copyright 2022, www.MikeHolt.com

▸Figure 25–1

25.2 Overcurrent Protection

(A) Purpose. The purpose of overcurrent protection is to protect wires and equipment against high temperatures caused by currents that exceed the equipment ampere rating or the ampacity of the wire. Current that exceeds the equipment ampere rating or the ampacity of the wire is referred to as "overcurrent." Overcurrent is caused by an overload, short-circuit, or ground-fault event. ▸Figure 25–2

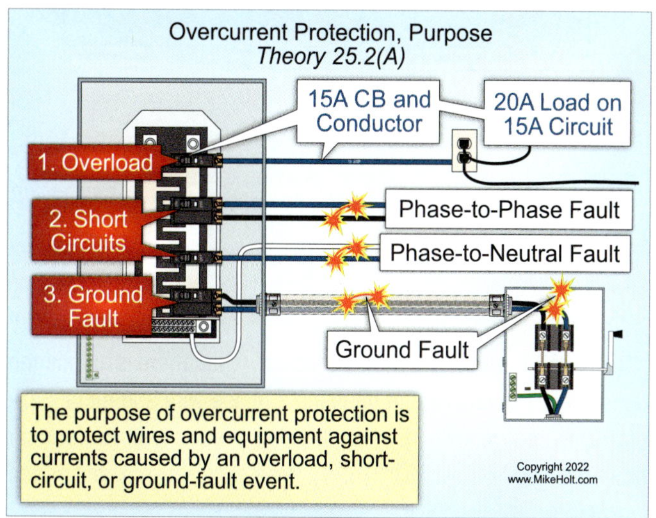
Overcurrent Protection, Purpose
Theory 25.2(A)
15A CB and Conductor
20A Load on 15A Circuit
1. Overload
2. Short Circuits
3. Ground Fault
Phase-to-Phase Fault
Phase-to-Neutral Fault
Ground Fault
The purpose of overcurrent protection is to protect wires and equipment against currents caused by an overload, short-circuit, or ground-fault event.
Copyright 2022 www.MikeHolt.com

▸Figure 25–2

(1) Overload.

(a) Equipment. An equipment overload is a condition when the current exceeds the equipment's ampere rating. Equipment overloads can occur because of undervoltage, undersized equipment for the load, or damages to equipment components such as a faulty motor bearing.

(b) Wires. An overload on a wire occurs when the load exceeds the ampacity of the wire. ▸Figure 25–3

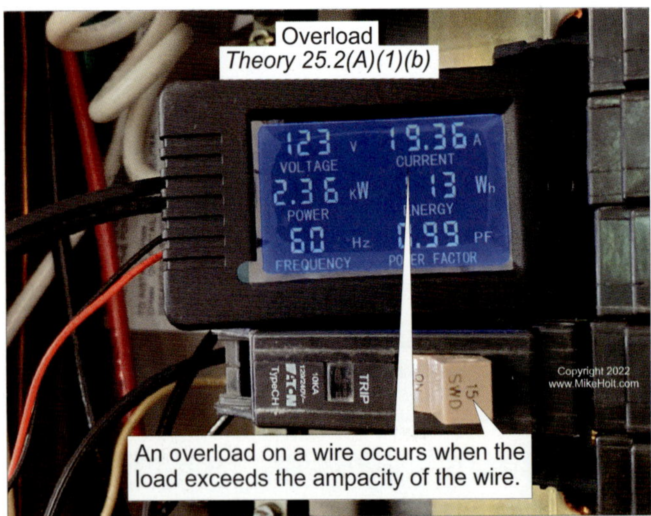
Overload
Theory 25.2(A)(1)(b)
An overload on a wire occurs when the load exceeds the ampacity of the wire.
Copyright 2022 www.MikeHolt.com

▸Figure 25–3

(2) Short Circuit. A short circuit occurs when there is an electrical connection between two phase wires or a phase wire and neutral wire. During a short-circuit event, short-circuit current can exceed ten times the ampere rating of the circuit overcurrent protective device. ▸Figure 25–4

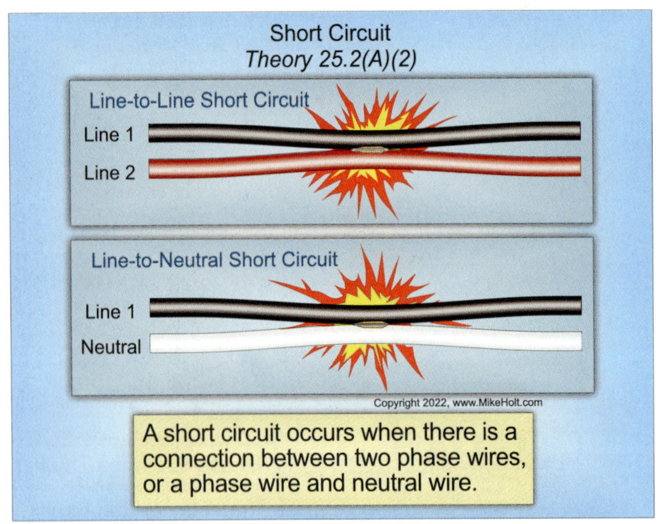
Short Circuit
Theory 25.2(A)(2)
Line-to-Line Short Circuit
Line 1
Line 2
Line-to-Neutral Short Circuit
Line 1
Neutral
Copyright 2022, www.MikeHolt.com
A short circuit occurs when there is a connection between two phase wires, or a phase wire and neutral wire.

▸Figure 25–4

(3) Ground Fault. A ground fault occurs when there is an unintentional electrical connection between a phase wire and metal parts of enclosures, raceways, or equipment. Ground-fault current can exceed ten times the ampere rating of the circuit overcurrent protective device. ▸Figure 25–5

(B) Overcurrent Protective Devices. Overcurrent protection is typically provided by fuses or circuit breakers. ▸Figure 25–6

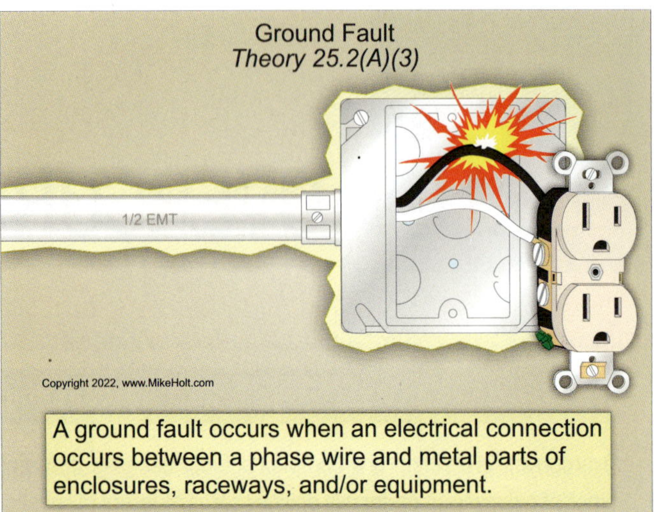
Ground Fault
Theory 25.2(A)(3)
1/2 EMT
Copyright 2022, www.MikeHolt.com
A ground fault occurs when an electrical connection occurs between a phase wire and metal parts of enclosures, raceways, and/or equipment.

▸Figure 25–5

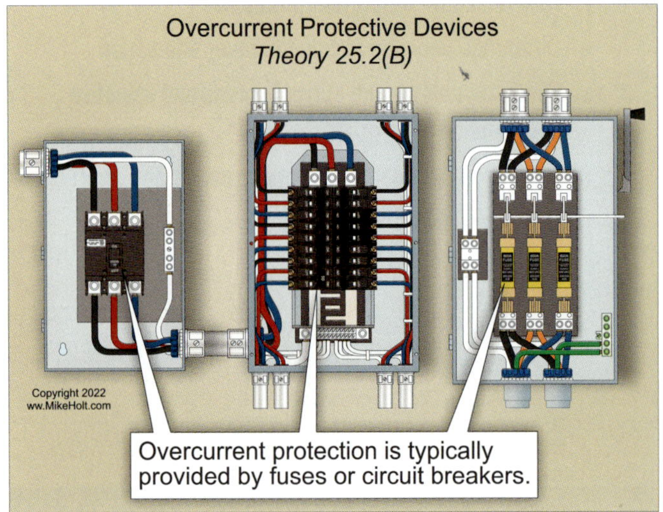
Overcurrent Protective Devices
Theory 25.2(B)
Copyright 2022 ww.MikeHolt.com
Overcurrent protection is typically provided by fuses or circuit breakers.

▸Figure 25–6

(C) Standard Sizes. Fuses and circuit breakers are available in a variety of ampere, voltage, and amperes interrupting capacity (AIC) ratings. The standard ampere ratings for overcurrent protective devices for electrical installations are listed in the *National Electrical Code*. ▸Figure 25–7

25.3 Fuses

(A) Fuse Elements. Fuses have an overload element and a short-circuit element within the fuse body which are designed to melt and open during an overload, short-circuit, or ground-fault event. ▸Figure 25–8

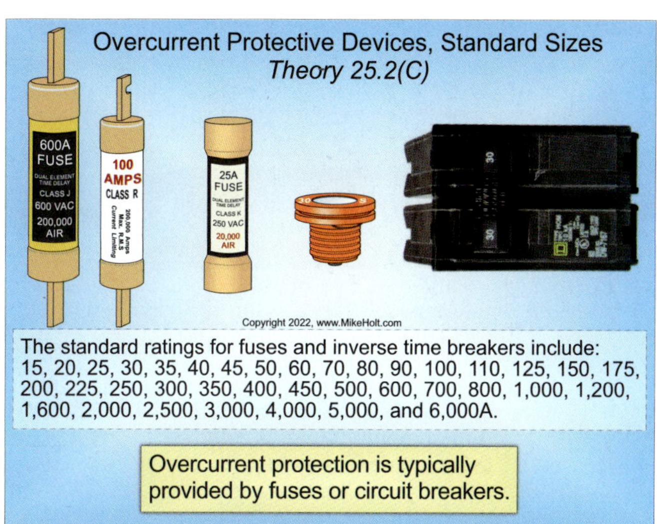
Overcurrent Protective Devices, Standard Sizes
Theory 25.2(C)
600A FUSE
100 AMPS CLASS R
25A FUSE
Copyright 2022, www.MikeHolt.com
The standard ratings for fuses and inverse time breakers include: 15, 20, 25, 30, 35, 40, 45, 50, 60, 70, 80, 90, 100, 110, 125, 150, 175, 200, 225, 250, 300, 350, 400, 450, 500, 600, 700, 800, 1,000, 1,200, 1,600, 2,000, 2,500, 3,000, 4,000, 5,000, and 6,000A.
Overcurrent protection is typically provided by fuses or circuit breakers.

▸Figure 25–7

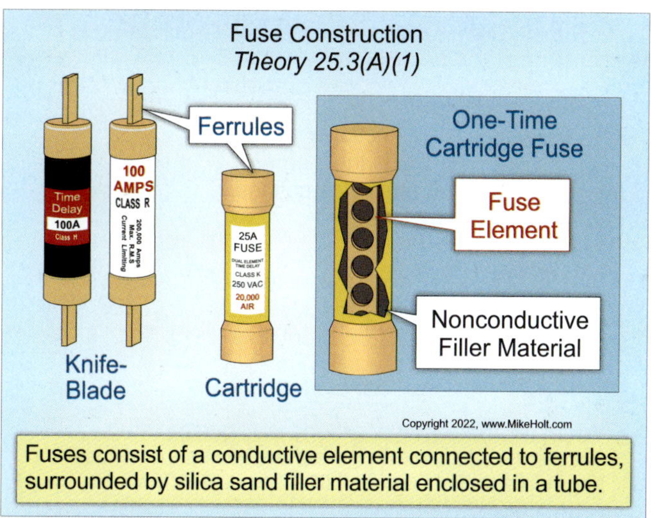
Fuse Construction
Theory 25.3(A)(1)
Ferrules
One-Time Cartridge Fuse
Fuse Element
Nonconductive Filler Material
Knife-Blade
Cartridge
Copyright 2022, www.MikeHolt.com
Fuses consist of a conductive element connected to ferrules, surrounded by silica sand filler material enclosed in a tube.

▸Figure 25–9

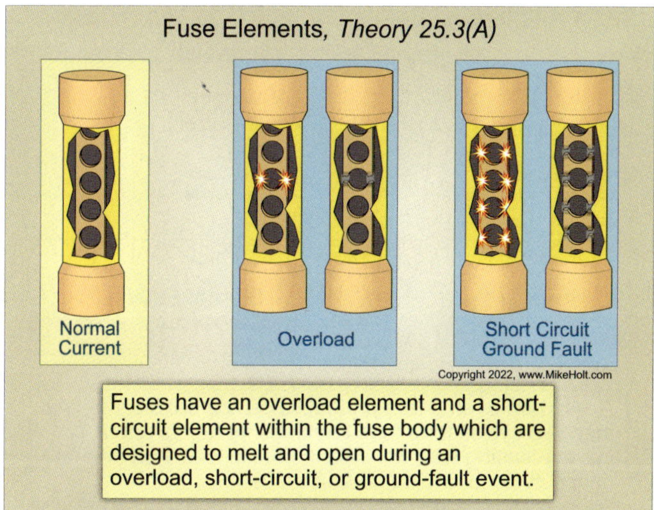
Fuse Elements, Theory 25.3(A)
Normal Current
Overload
Short Circuit Ground Fault
Copyright 2022, www.MikeHolt.com
Fuses have an overload element and a short-circuit element within the fuse body which are designed to melt and open during an overload, short-circuit, or ground-fault event.

▸Figure 25–8

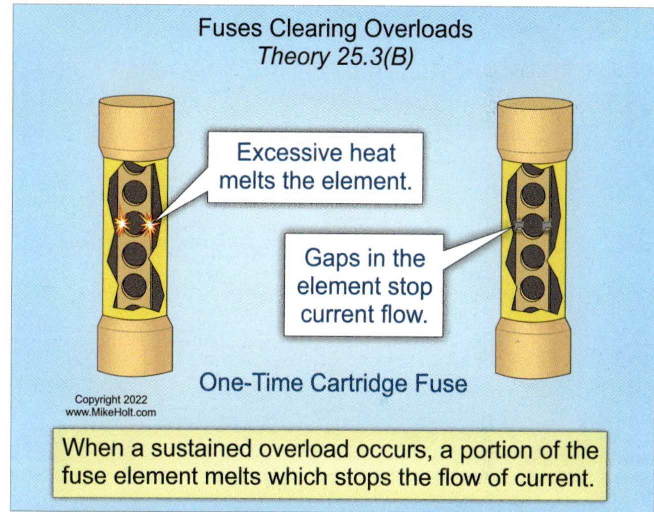
Fuses Clearing Overloads
Theory 25.3(B)
Excessive heat melts the element.
Gaps in the element stop current flow.
One-Time Cartridge Fuse
Copyright 2022 www.MikeHolt.com
When a sustained overload occurs, a portion of the fuse element melts which stops the flow of current.

▸Figure 25–10

(1) Fuse Construction. Fuses consist of a conductive element connected to end blades or caps, surrounded by silica sand filler material enclosed in a tube. ▸Figure 25–9

(B) Clearing Overloads. When current flows through the element of a fuse, it generates heat. During normal operation, the silica sand absorbs this heat. When a sustained overload occurs, the heat is not able to dissipate. A part of the fuse element melts which stops the current flow. The time it takes to melt the fuse element from an overload is dependent on the magnitude of the overload. ▸Figure 25–10

(C) Clearing Short Circuits and Ground Faults. When a short circuit or ground fault occurs, the fault current can be in the thousands of amperes. The high fault current causes the heat in the element to rise to a point where multiple conductive segments in the fuse melt and stops electrical current flow. ▸Figure 25–11

(D) Types of Fuses. The three most common types of fuses are single-element, dual-element, and current-limiting.

(1) Single-Element Fuse. A single-element fuse is referred to as a nontime delay fuse and is the least expensive type. ▸Figure 25–12

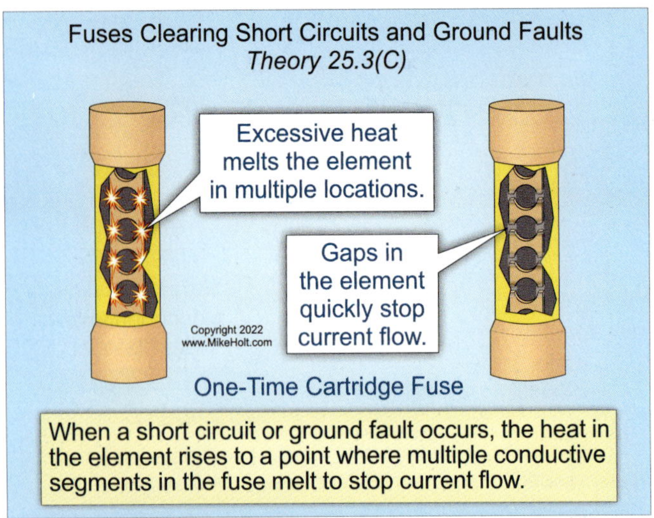
Fuses Clearing Short Circuits and Ground Faults
Theory 25.3(C)
Excessive heat melts the element in multiple locations.
Gaps in the element quickly stop current flow.
Copyright 2022 www.MikeHolt.com
One-Time Cartridge Fuse
When a short circuit or ground fault occurs, the heat in the element rises to a point where multiple conductive segments in the fuse melt to stop current flow.

▸Figure 25–11

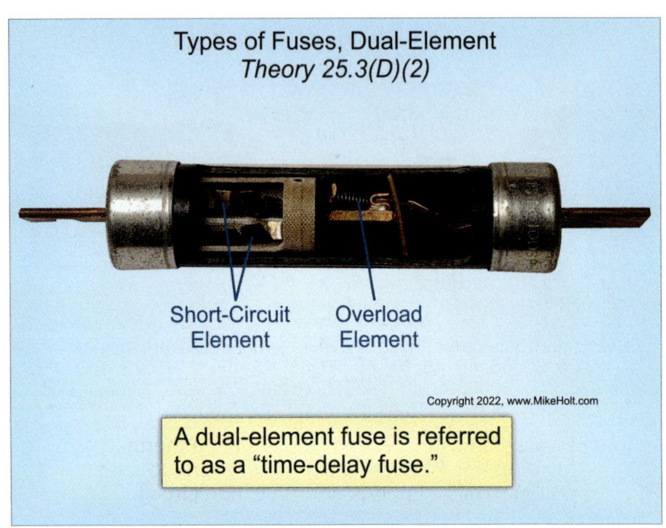
Types of Fuses, Dual-Element
Theory 25.3(D)(2)
Short-Circuit Element
Overload Element
Copyright 2022, www.MikeHolt.com
A dual-element fuse is referred to as a "time-delay fuse."

▸Figure 25–13

Types of Fuses, Single-Element
Theory 25.3(D)(1)
COOPER Bussmann
114 Old State Road
Ellisville, MO 63021-5942
Made in U.S.A.
A single-element fuse is referred to as a nontime delay fuse and is the least expensive type.

▸Figure 25–12

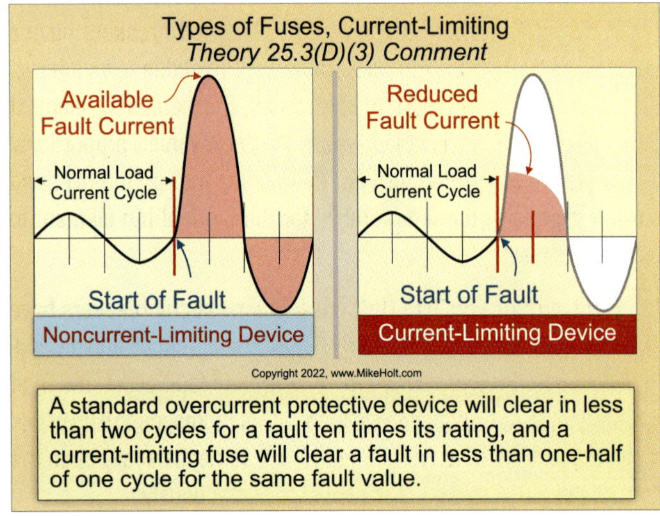
Types of Fuses, Current-Limiting
Theory 25.3(D)(3) Comment
Available Fault Current
Normal Load Current Cycle
Start of Fault
Noncurrent-Limiting Device
Reduced Fault Current
Normal Load Current Cycle
Start of Fault
Current-Limiting Device
Copyright 2022, www.MikeHolt.com
A standard overcurrent protective device will clear in less than two cycles for a fault ten times its rating, and a current-limiting fuse will clear a fault in less than one-half of one cycle for the same fault value.

▸Figure 25–14

(2) Dual-Element Fuse. A dual-element fuse is often referred to as a "time-delay fuse." ▸Figure 25–13

(3) Current-Limiting Fuses. A current-limiting fuse is designed to clear a short circuit or ground fault in less than one-half of one cycle. Current-limiting fuses limit the peak current to a value much less than a most circuit breakers or fuses.

Author's Comment:

- A standard overcurrent protective device will clear in less than two cycles for a fault ten times its rating. A current-limiting fuse will clear a fault in less than one-half of one cycle for the same fault value. ▸Figure 25–14

25.4 Circuit Breakers

A circuit breaker is capable of being opened and closed manually, and it automatically opens during an overcurrent condition. Circuit breakers are available in different configurations, such as inverse time, instantaneous trip, and adjustable trip.

(A) Inverse Time Circuit Breaker. Inverse time circuit breakers are the most common type used. They operate on the principle that as the current increases, the time it takes for the device to open decreases. This breaker contains a thermal trip element to open during an overload and an electromagnetic trip element to open during a short circuit or ground fault. ▸Figure 25–15

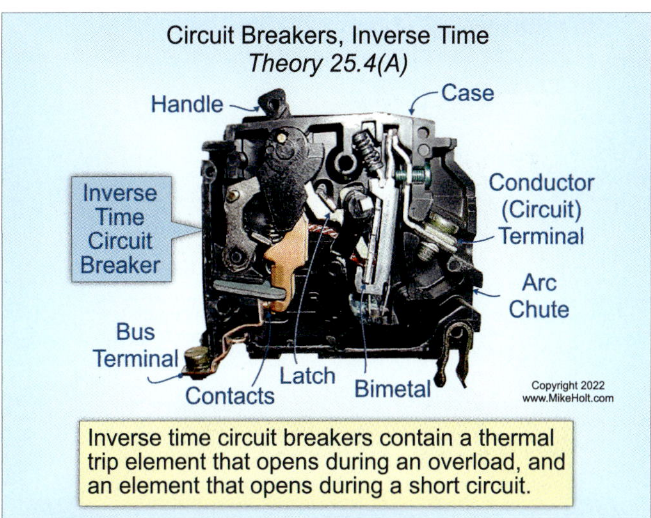
Circuit Breakers, Inverse Time
Theory 25.4(A)
Handle
Case
Inverse Time Circuit Breaker
Conductor (Circuit) Terminal
Arc Chute
Bus Terminal
Contacts
Latch
Bimetal
Copyright 2022 www.MikeHolt.com
Inverse time circuit breakers contain a thermal trip element that opens during an overload, and an element that opens during a short circuit.

▸Figure 25–15

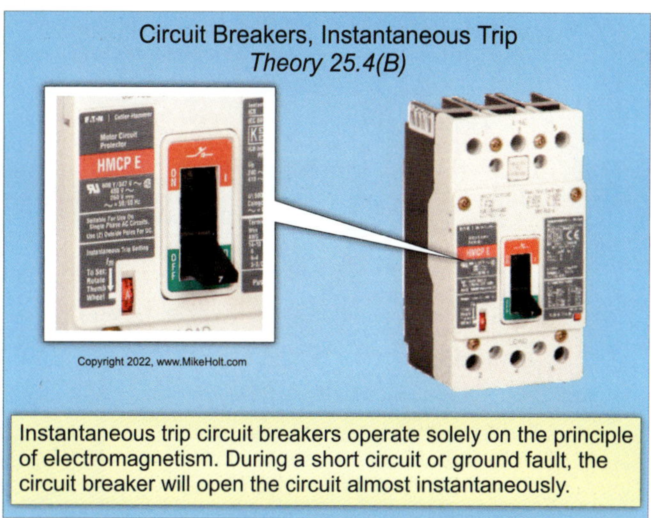
Circuit Breakers, Instantaneous Trip
Theory 25.4(B)
HMCP E
Copyright 2022, www.MikeHolt.com
Instantaneous trip circuit breakers operate solely on the principle of electromagnetism. During a short circuit or ground fault, the circuit breaker will open the circuit almost instantaneously.

▸Figure 25–16

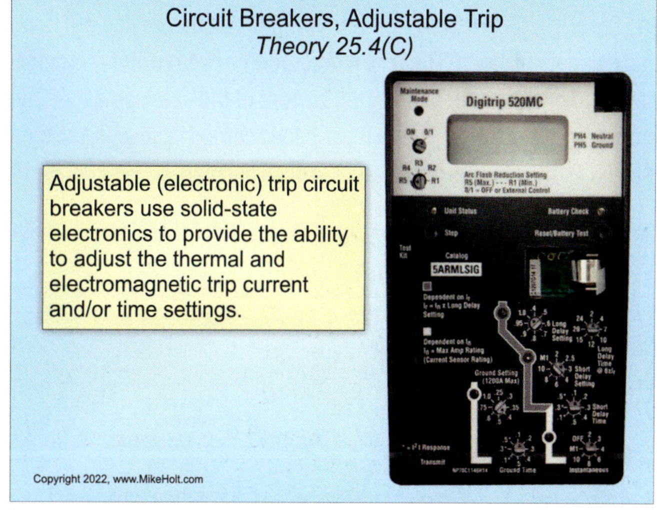
Circuit Breakers, Adjustable Trip
Theory 25.4(C)
Digitrip 520MC
Adjustable (electronic) trip circuit breakers use solid-state electronics to provide the ability to adjust the thermal and electromagnetic trip current and/or time settings.
Copyright 2022, www.MikeHolt.com

▸Figure 25–17

(1) Thermal Trip Element. Inverse time circuit breakers have a mechanical trip mechanism that opens the circuit due to an internal temperature rise from an overload condition. The thermal trip element operates on the time-current principle of being inversely proportional to the magnitude of the current. This means that as the overload current increases, the time it takes for the thermal trip element to open decreases.

(2) Electromagnetic Trip Unit. Inverse time circuit breakers have an electromagnetic trip unit that responds to short-circuit and ground-fault currents. During a short-circuit or ground-fault event, the fault current can be high enough to generate an electromagnetic field within the circuit breaker that is sufficient to electromechanically open the contacts of the circuit breaker almost instantaneously.

(B) Instantaneous Trip Circuit Breaker. Magnetic trip breakers without thermal elements are commonly referred to as "instantaneous trip circuit breakers" or "motor circuit protectors." Instantaneous trip circuit breakers operate solely on the principle of electromagnetism. The electromagnetic trip unit responds to short-circuit and ground-fault currents. During a short circuit or ground fault, the fault current will be approximately ten times (or more) the ampere rating of the circuit breaker. This high fault current value will generate a substantial electromagnetic field within the circuit breaker to mechanically activate its electromagnetic mechanism and open the circuit almost instantaneously. ▸Figure 25–16

(C) Adjustable (Electronic) Trip Circuit Breaker. Adjustable (electronic) trip circuit breakers use solid-state electronics to provide the ability to adjust the thermal and electromagnetic trip current and time settings to provide the user with flexibility for specific applications. ▸Figure 25–17

25.5 Overcurrent Protective Devices, Time-Current Curves

To protect against electric shock or prevent a fire, a dangerous overload, short circuit, or ground fault must quickly be removed by opening the circuit's overcurrent protective device. The time it takes for an overcurrent protective device to open is plotted on a time-current curve (TCC) chart. This chart has a vertical side that shows the time in seconds it will take the device to open relative to the current in amperes as shown on the bottom of the chart. ▸Figure 25–18

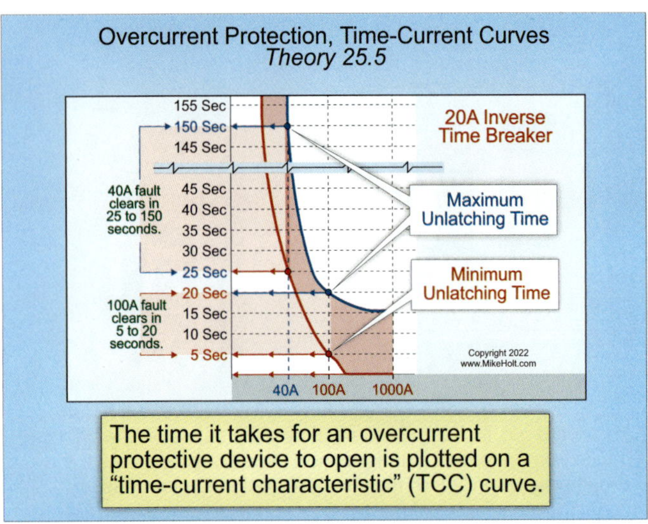
Overcurrent Protection, Time-Current Curves
Theory 25.5
155 Sec
150 Sec
145 Sec
40A fault clears in 25 to 150 seconds.
45 Sec
40 Sec
35 Sec
30 Sec
25 Sec
20 Sec
100A fault clears in 5 to 20 seconds.
15 Sec
10 Sec
5 Sec
40A 100A 1000A
20A Inverse Time Breaker
Maximum Unlatching Time
Minimum Unlatching Time
Copyright 2022 www.MikeHolt.com
The time it takes for an overcurrent protective device to open is plotted on a "time-current characteristic" (TCC) curve.

▸Figure 25–18

(A) Clearing Overloads. An overcurrent protective device will open and clear an overload. The time it takes for the overcurrent protective device to open is a function of the current of the overload above the ampere rating of the device. As the overload current increases, the time it takes for the thermal trip element to open decreases. ▸Figure 25–19

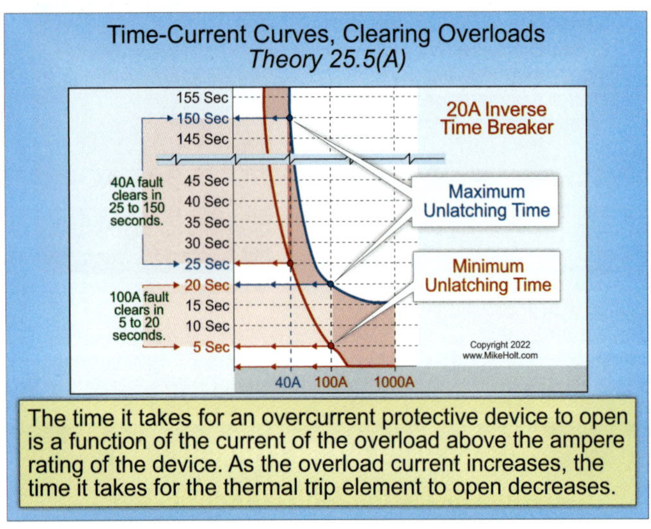
Time-Current Curves, Clearing Overloads
Theory 25.5(A)
155 Sec
150 Sec
145 Sec
40A fault clears in 25 to 150 seconds.
45 Sec
40 Sec
35 Sec
30 Sec
25 Sec
20 Sec
100A fault clears in 5 to 20 seconds.
15 Sec
10 Sec
5 Sec
40A 100A 1000A
20A Inverse Time Breaker
Maximum Unlatching Time
Minimum Unlatching Time
Copyright 2022 www.MikeHolt.com
The time it takes for an overcurrent protective device to open is a function of the current of the overload above the ampere rating of the device. As the overload current increases, the time it takes for the thermal trip element to open decreases.

▸Figure 25–19

(B) Clearing Short Circuits. To quickly clear a short circuit, the short-circuit current needs to rise to a level between ten and twenty times the rating of the circuit overcurrent protective device. Once the current reaches that level, the short circuit will clear almost immediately. ▸Figure 25–20

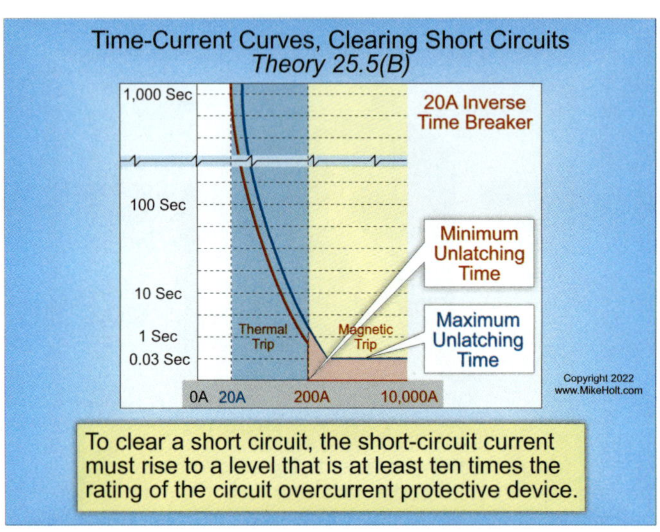
Time-Current Curves, Clearing Short Circuits
Theory 25.5(B)
1,000 Sec
100 Sec
10 Sec
1 Sec
0.03 Sec
Thermal Trip
Magnetic Trip
0A 20A 200A 10,000A
20A Inverse Time Breaker
Minimum Unlatching Time
Maximum Unlatching Time
Copyright 2022 www.MikeHolt.com
To clear a short circuit, the short-circuit current must rise to a level that is at least ten times the rating of the circuit overcurrent protective device.

▸Figure 25–20

(C) Clearing Ground-Faults.

(1) General. To quickly clear a ground fault, the ground-fault current needs to rise to a level between ten and twenty times the rating of the circuit overcurrent protective device. ▸Figure 25–21

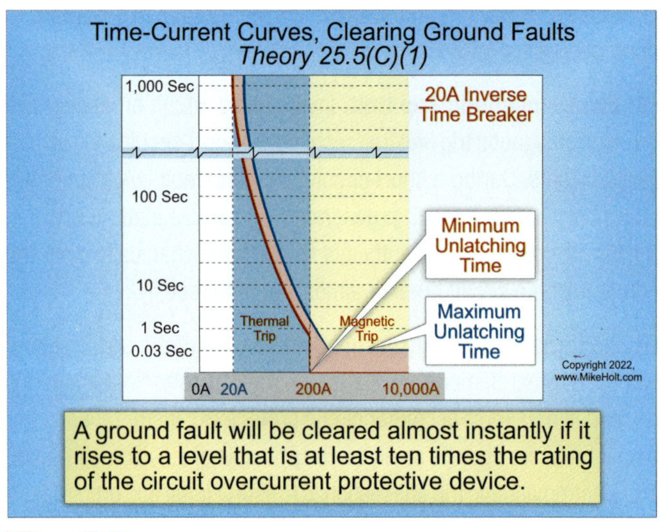
Time-Current Curves, Clearing Ground Faults
Theory 25.5(C)(1)
1,000 Sec
100 Sec
10 Sec
1 Sec
0.03 Sec
Thermal Trip
Magnetic Trip
0A 20A 200A 10,000A
20A Inverse Time Breaker
Minimum Unlatching Time
Maximum Unlatching Time
Copyright 2022, www.MikeHolt.com
A ground fault will be cleared almost instantly if it rises to a level that is at least ten times the rating of the circuit overcurrent protective device.

▸Figure 25–21

(2) Low-Impedance Ground-Fault Current Path. To remove dangerous touch voltage on metal parts produced by a ground fault, the fault-current path must have low enough impedance to allow the fault current to quickly rise to open the protection device. ▸Figure 25–22

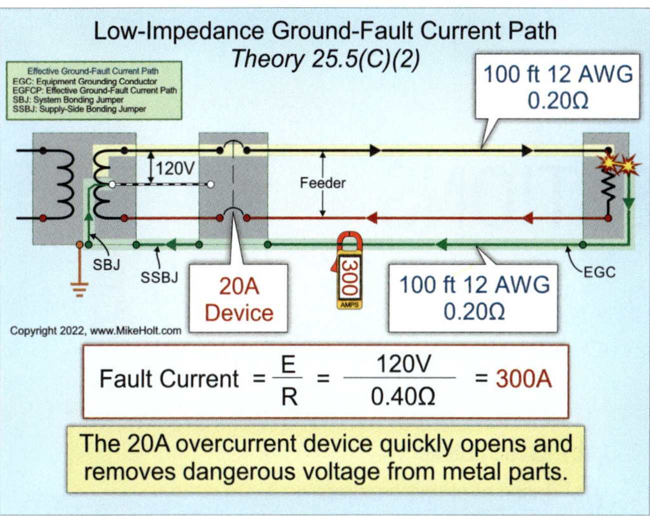
Low-Impedance Ground-Fault Current Path
Theory 25.5(C)(2)
100 ft 12 AWG
0.20Ω
120V
Feeder
SBJ
SSBJ
20A
Device
300
100 ft 12 AWG
0.20Ω
EGC
Copyright 2022, www.MikeHolt.com
Fault Current = E/R = 120V/0.40Ω = 300A
The 20A overcurrent device quickly opens and removes dangerous voltage from metal parts.

▶Figure 25–22

UNIT
25 REVIEW QUESTIONS

25.2 Overcurrent Protection

1. Overcurrent is current in excess of the equipment ampere rating or ampacity of the wires. It may result from a(an) _____.

   (a) overload
   (b) short circuit
   (c) ground fault
   (d) any of these

2. A(An)_____ is the operation of equipment or wires in excess of their rated ampacity.

   (a) overload
   (b) short circuit
   (c) ground fault
   (d) all of these

3. A(An) _____ is an electrical connection between any two phase wires, or a phase wire and neutral wire.

   (a) overload
   (b) short circuit
   (c) ground fault
   (d) all of these

4. A(An) _____ occurs when an unintentional electrical connection occurs between a phase wire and metal parts of enclosures, raceways, and/or equipment.

   (a) overload
   (b) short circuit
   (c) ground fault
   (d) all of these

5. Overcurrent protection is typically provided by _____.

   (a) fuses
   (b) circuit breakers
   (c) fuses or circuit breakers
   (d) none of these

25.3 Fuses

6. Fuses consist of a _____ element connected to end blades or caps, surrounded by silica sand filler material enclosed in a tube.

   (a) conductive
   (b) foam
   (c) light
   (d) nonconductive

7. When a sustained overload occurs through the element(s) of a fuse, the heat melts _____, stopping the flow of current.

   (a) several elements
   (b) all of the elements
   (c) a portion of the element
   (d) none of these

8. When a short circuit or ground fault occurs through the element of a fuse, the heat in the element rises to a point where _____ in the fuse melt to stop electrical current flow.

   (a) multiple conductive segments
   (b) a small portion of the segment
   (c) all of the segments
   (d) none of these

9. A _____ fuse is referred to as a nontime-delay fuse and is the least expensive type.

   (a) single-element
   (b) dual-element
   (c) current-limiting
   (d) all of these

10. A _____ fuse is often called a "time-delay fuse."

   (a) single-element
   (b) dual-element
   (c) current-limiting
   (d) all of these

11. A _____ fuse is designed to clear a short circuit or ground fault in less than one-half a cycle.

   (a) one-time fuses
   (b) dual-element fuses
   (c) special trip fuses
   (d) current-limiting

25.4 Circuit Breakers

12. A _____ is capable of being opened and closed manually and automatically opens during an overcurrent condition.

   (a) fuse
   (b) circuit breaker
   (c) motor starter
   (d) disconnect

13. _____ circuit breakers operate on the principle that as the current increases, the time it takes for the device to open decreases.

   (a) Inverse time
   (b) Adjustable trip
   (c) Instantaneous trip
   (d) all of these

14. The _____ trip element of a circuit breaker operates on the time-current principle of being inversely proportional to the magnitude of the current, which means that as the overload current increases, the time it takes for the trip element to open decreases.

   (a) magnetic
   (b) electronic
   (c) thermal
   (d) none of these

15. Inverse time circuit breakers have a(an) _____ trip unit that responds to short-circuit and ground-fault currents.

   (a) adjustable
   (b) instantaneous
   (c) electromagnetic
   (d) none of these

16. _____ circuit breakers operate on the principle of electromagnetism only and are commonly known as motor circuit protectors.

   (a) Inverse time
   (b) Adjustable trip
   (c) Instantaneous trip
   (d) all of these

17. _____ circuit breakers permit the thermal and electromagnetic trip current and/or time settings to be adjusted to provide the user with flexibility for specific applications.

   (a) Inverse time
   (b) Adjustable trip
   (c) Instantaneous trip
   (d) all of these

25.5 Overcurrent Protective Devices, Time-Current Curves

18. The time it takes for an overcurrent protective device to open is plotted on a _____ curve chart.

   (a) time-current characteristics
   (b) bar graph
   (c) pie chart
   (d) none of these

19. As the overload current _____, the time it takes for the thermal trip element to open decreases.

    (a) increases
    (b) decreases
    (c) remains the same
    (d) none of these

20. To quickly clear a short circuit, the short-circuit _____ must rise to a level that is between ten and twenty times the rating of the circuit overcurrent protective device.

    (a) voltage
    (b) current
    (c) resistance
    (d) power

21. To quickly clear a(an) _____, the ground-fault current needs to rise to a level between ten and twenty times the rating of the circuit overcurrent protective device.

    (a) overload
    (b) arcing fault
    (c) ground fault
    (d) none of these

22. To remove dangerous touch voltage on metal parts produced by a ground fault, the fault-current path must have _____ to allow the fault current to quickly rise to facilitate the opening of the protection device.

    (a) high impedance
    (b) low impedance
    (c) high voltage
    (d) low voltage

SECTION
II

NEC RULES FOR BONDING AND GROUNDING

Introduction to Section II—*NEC* Rules for Bonding and Grounding

Now that you have a better understanding of the "how and why" electricity does what it does, you're prepared to understand the *NEC* rules related to Bonding and Grounding. Section II of this book covers Article 250—Grounding and Bonding with a complete examination and explanation of not only every concept contained within Article 250, but also the rules for bonding throughout the other articles of the *NEC*.

From the pertinent definitions in Article 100 all the way to the bonding of communication systems in Chapter 8, the rules for (and differences between) bonding and grounding are explained in depth, all in an effort to ensure that electrical installations achieve the number one priority; and that is an "effective ground-fault current path" to maintain as safe an installation as possible!

ARTICLE 90 INTRODUCTION TO THE *NATIONAL ELECTRICAL CODE*

Introduction to Article 90—Introduction to the *National Electrical Code*

Article 90 describes the purpose of the *NEC*, when it applies, when it does not, who enforces the *Code*, and the arrangement of the different chapters. Although the information is valuable, this article contains no actual requirements. It only serves to provide the reader with the scope of the *National Electrical Code*.

This article stands alone outside of the chapter structure of the rest of the *Code* and has no parts because it contains no requirements. Take the time to become familiar with all nine sections of Article 90 before you begin your journey through the *NEC*. Doing so will help you better understand when and how to apply the *Code*.

90.1 Scope

Article 90 covers the use, application, arrangement, and enforcement of this *Code*. It also covers how mandatory, permissive, and nonmandatory text is expressed and provides guidance on the examination of equipment, planning wiring, and specifies the use and expression of measurements.

90.2 Use and Application of the *NEC*

(A) Purpose of the *NEC*.

Protect People and Property. The purpose of the *National Electrical Code* is to ensure electrical systems are installed in a manner that protects people and property by minimizing the risks associated with the use of electricity. ▸Figure 90–1

Purpose of the NEC
Protect People and Property
90.2(A)
Copyright 2023, MikeHolt.com
The purpose of the National Electrical Code is to ensure electrical systems are installed in a manner that protects people and property by minimizing the risks associated with the use of electricity.

▸Figure 90–1

NEC Not a Specification or Instruction Manual. The *NEC* is not a design specification standard, nor is it an instruction manual for the untrained. ▸Figure 90–2

Author's Comment:

- The *Code* is intended to be used by those who are skilled and knowledgeable in electrical theory, electrical systems, building and electrical construction, and the installation and operation of electrical equipment.

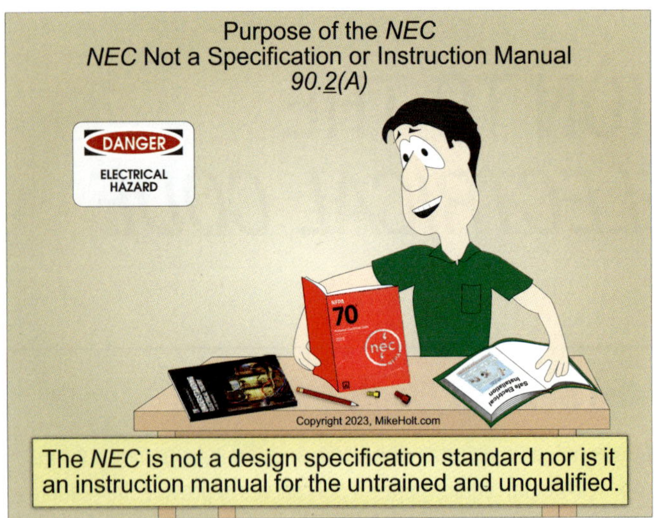

Purpose of the NEC
NEC Not a Specification or Instruction Manual
90.2(A)
DANGER
ELECTRICAL HAZARD
70
Copyright 2023, MikeHolt.com
The NEC is not a design specification standard nor is it an instruction manual for the untrained and unqualified.

▶Figure 90–2

(B) Essentially Safe Installation.

Considered Safe. The *NEC* contains the requirements considered necessary for safety.

Essentially Free from Hazards. Installations complying with the *Code* and properly maintained are considered essentially free from electrical hazards. ▶**Figure 90–3**

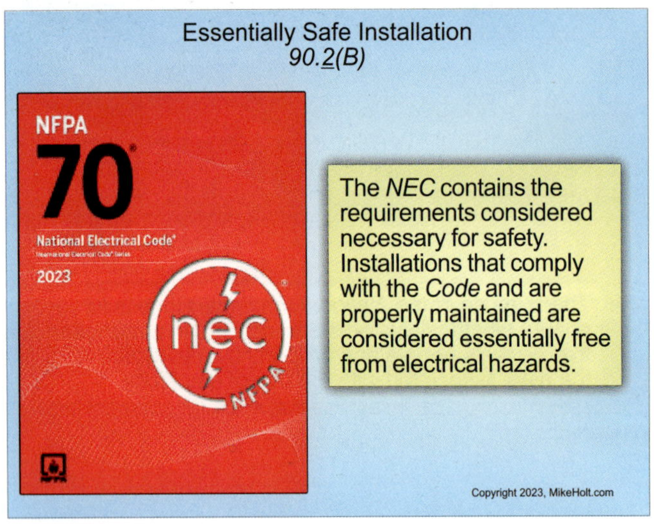

Essentially Safe Installation
90.2(B)
NFPA
70
National Electrical Code
2023
nec
NFPA
The NEC contains the requirements considered necessary for safety. Installations that comply with the Code and are properly maintained are considered essentially free from electrical hazards.
Copyright 2023, MikeHolt.com

▶Figure 90–3

NEC Rules not Intended. The requirements contained in the *NEC* are not intended to ensure an electrical installation will be efficient, convenient, adequate for good service, or suitable for future expansion. ▶**Figure 90–4**

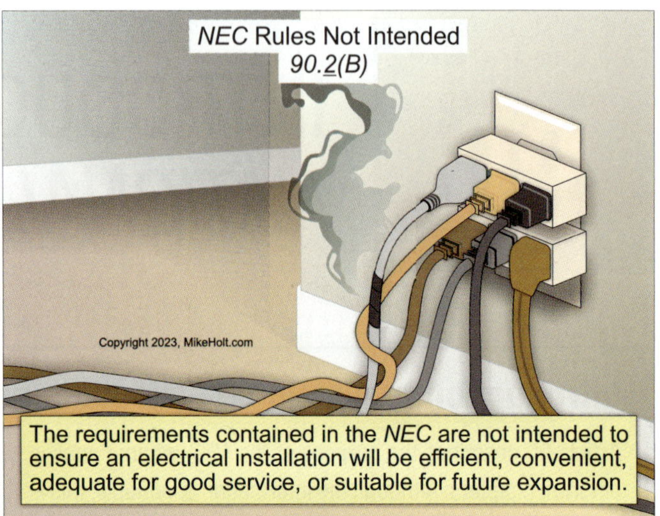

NEC Rules Not Intended
90.2(B)
Copyright 2023, MikeHolt.com
The requirements contained in the NEC are not intended to ensure an electrical installation will be efficient, convenient, adequate for good service, or suitable for future expansion.

▶Figure 90–4

Note: Hazards often occur because the initial wiring did not provide for increases in the use of electricity resulting in wiring systems becoming overloaded. ▶**Figure 90–5**

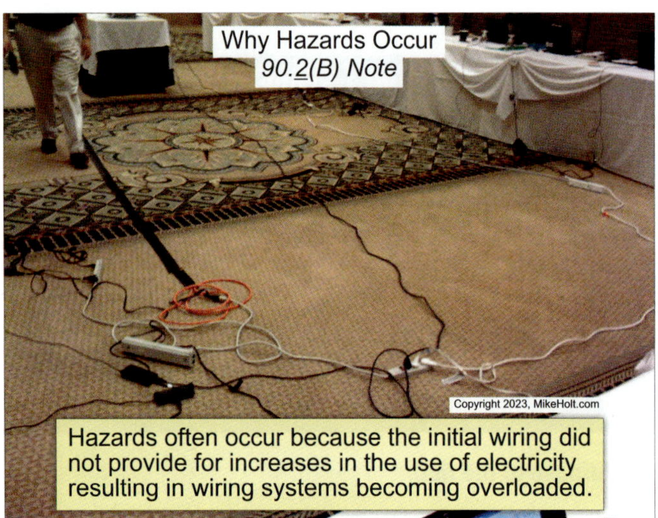

Why Hazards Occur
90.2(B) Note
Copyright 2023, MikeHolt.com
Hazards often occur because the initial wiring did not provide for increases in the use of electricity resulting in wiring systems becoming overloaded.

▶Figure 90–5

Author's Comment:

- The *NEC* does not require electrical systems to be designed or installed to accommodate future loads. However, consideration should be given not only to ensuring electrical safety (*Code* compliance), but also that the electrical system meets the customers' needs—both for today and in the coming years.

(C) Installations Covered by the *NEC*. The *Code* covers the installation and removal of electrical conductors, equipment, and raceways. It also covers limited-energy and communications conductors, equipment, and raceways, plus optical fiber cables for the following: ▶**Figure 90–6**

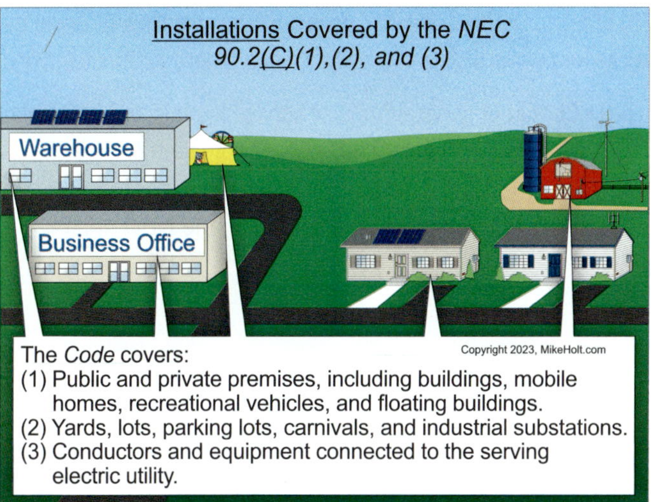
Installations Covered by the NEC
90.2(C)(1),(2), and (3)
Warehouse
Business Office
The Code covers:
(1) Public and private premises, including buildings, mobile homes, recreational vehicles, and floating buildings.
(2) Yards, lots, parking lots, carnivals, and industrial substations.
(3) Conductors and equipment connected to the serving electric utility.
Copyright 2023, MikeHolt.com

▶**Figure 90–6**

(1) Public and private premises including buildings, mobile homes, recreational vehicles, and floating buildings

(2) Yards, lots, parking lots, carnivals, and industrial substations

(3) Conductors and equipment connected to the serving electric utility

(4) Installations used by a serving electric utility such as office buildings, warehouses, garages, machine shops, recreational buildings, and other electric utility buildings that are not an integral part of a utility's generating plant, substation, or control center ▶**Figure 90–7**

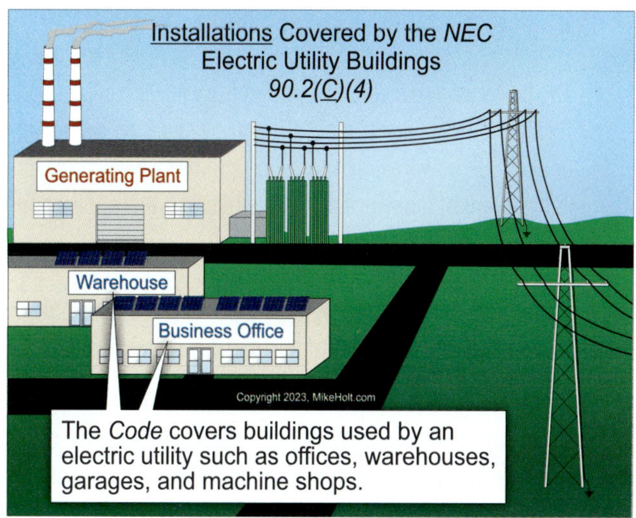
Installations Covered by the NEC
Electric Utility Buildings
90.2(C)(4)
Generating Plant
Warehouse
Business Office
Copyright 2023, MikeHolt.com
The Code covers buildings used by an electric utility such as offices, warehouses, garages, and machine shops.

▶**Figure 90–7**

(5) Installations supplying shore power to ships and watercraft in marinas and boatyards, including monitoring of leakage current ▶**Figure 90–8**

Installations Covered by the NEC
Marina Shore Power
90.2(C)(5)
Copyright 2023, MikeHolt.com
The NEC covers installations supplying shore power to ships and watercraft in marinas and boatyards, including monitoring of leakage current.

▶**Figure 90–8**

Author's Comment:

- The text in 555.35(B) requires leakage detection equipment to detect leakage current from boats and applies to the load side of the supplying receptacle.

(6) Installations used to export power from vehicles to premises wiring or for bidirectional current flow ▶**Figure 90–9**

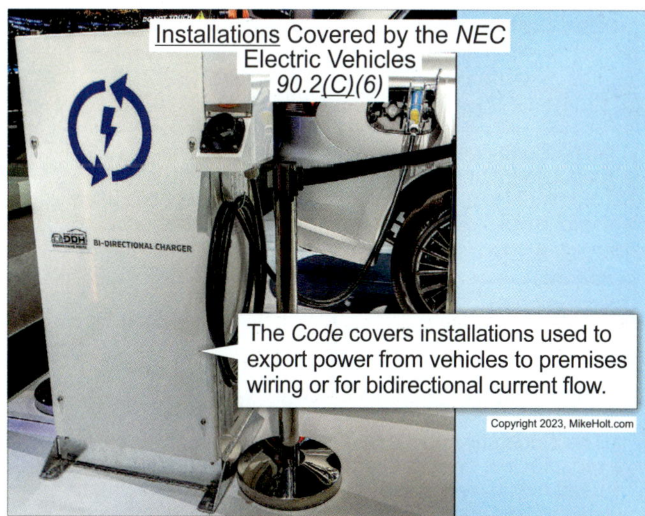
Installations Covered by the NEC
Electric Vehicles
90.2(C)(6)
BI-DIRECTIONAL CHARGER
The Code covers installations used to export power from vehicles to premises wiring or for bidirectional current flow.
Copyright 2023, MikeHolt.com

▶**Figure 90–9**

Author's Comment:

- The battery power supply of an electric vehicle can be used "bidirectionally" which means it can be used as a backup or alternate power source to supply premises wiring circuits in the event of a power failure. The rules for this application can be found in Article 625.

(D) Installations Not Covered by the *NEC*. The *Code* does not cover installations of electrical or communications systems for:

(1) Transportation Vehicles. The *NEC* does not cover installations in ships, watercraft (other than floating buildings), aircraft, or automotive vehicles (other than mobile homes and recreational vehicles).

Author's Comment:

- An automotive vehicle is any vehicle that may be transported upon a public highway. The wiring of food trucks is not required to comply with the *NEC*, since they are considered automotive vehicles.

(2) Mining Equipment. The *Code* does not cover installations in underground mines or self-propelled mobile surface mining machinery and its attendant electrical trailing cables.

(3) Railways. The *NEC* does not cover installations for railway power, energy storage, and communications wiring.

(4) Communications Utilities. The *Code* does not cover installations of communications equipment under the exclusive control of the communications utility located outdoors or in building spaces used exclusively for these purposes. ▸Figure 90–10

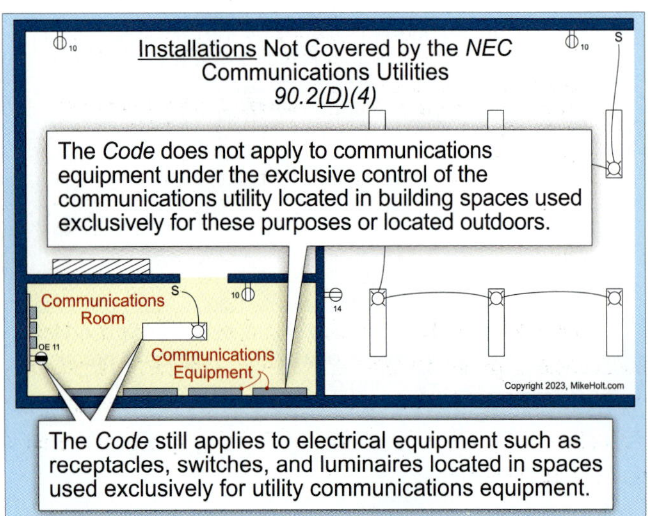
Installations Not Covered by the NEC
Communications Utilities
90.2(D)(4)
The Code does not apply to communications equipment under the exclusive control of the communications utility located in building spaces used exclusively for these purposes or located outdoors.
Communications Room
Communications Equipment
Copyright 2023, MikeHolt.com
The Code still applies to electrical equipment such as receptacles, switches, and luminaires located in spaces used exclusively for utility communications equipment.

▸Figure 90–10

Author's Comment:

- The *Code* still applies to electrical equipment such as receptacles, switches, and luminaires located in spaces used exclusively for utility communications equipment.

(5) Electric Utilities. The *NEC* does not cover installations under the exclusive control of a serving electric utility where such installations:

a. Consist of service drops or service laterals and associated metering. ▸Figure 90–11 and ▸Figure 90–12

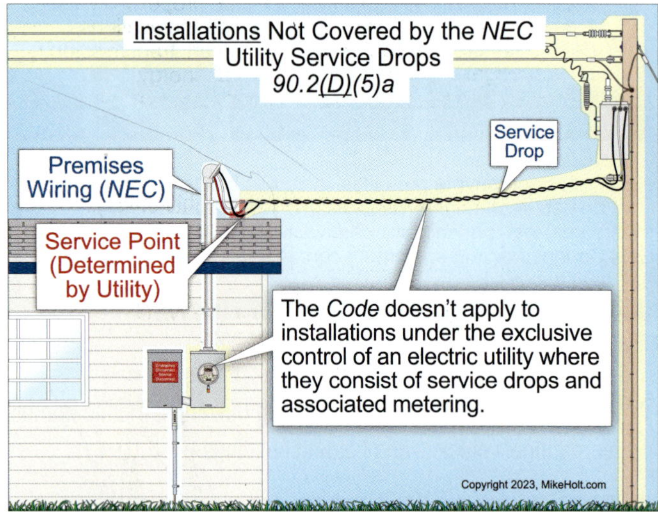
Installations Not Covered by the NEC
Utility Service Drops
90.2(D)(5)a
Service Drop
Premises Wiring (NEC)
Service Point (Determined by Utility)
The Code doesn't apply to installations under the exclusive control of an electric utility where they consist of service drops and associated metering.
Copyright 2023, MikeHolt.com

▸Figure 90–11

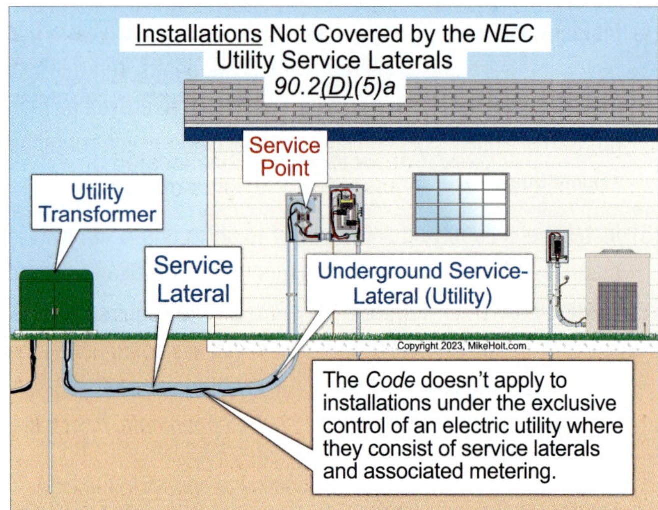
Installations Not Covered by the NEC
Utility Service Laterals
90.2(D)(5)a
Service Point
Utility Transformer
Service Lateral
Underground Service-Lateral (Utility)
Copyright 2023, MikeHolt.com
The Code doesn't apply to installations under the exclusive control of an electric utility where they consist of service laterals and associated metering.

▸Figure 90–12

b. Are on property owned or leased by the utility for the purpose of communications, metering, generation, control, transformation, transmission, energy storage, or distribution of electrical energy. ▸Figure 90–13

Installations Not Covered by the NEC
Utility Generation and Transmission
90.2(D)(5)b
Copyright 2023, MikeHolt.com
The Code doesn't apply to installations on property owned or leased by a utility for the purpose of communications, metering, generation, control, transformation, transmission, energy storage, or distribution of electrical energy.

▸Figure 90–13

c. Are in legally established easements or rights-of-way. ▸**Figure 90–14**

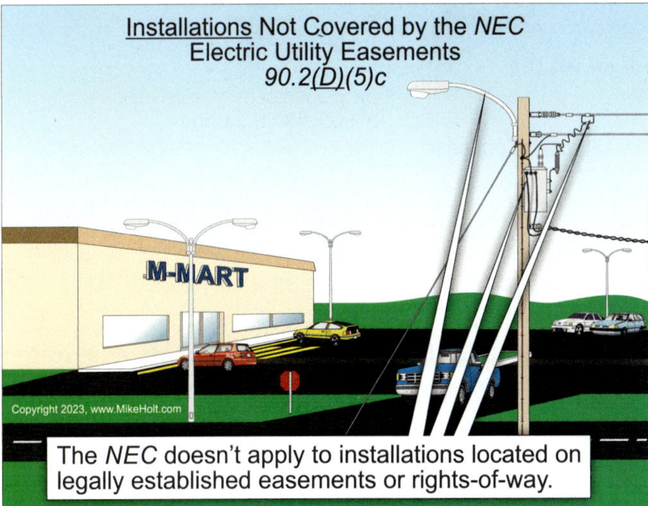
Installations Not Covered by the NEC
Electric Utility Easements
90.2(D)(5)c
M-MART
Copyright 2023, www.MikeHolt.com
The NEC doesn't apply to installations located on legally established easements or rights-of-way.

▸Figure 90–14

(E) Relation to International Standards. The requirements of the *NEC* address the fundamental safety principles contained in the International Electrotechnical Commission (IEC) Standard IEC 60364-1, *Low-Voltage Electrical Installations—Part 1: Fundamental Principles, Assessment of General Characteristics, Definitions.*

Note: IEC 60364-1, *Low-Voltage Electrical Installations—Part 1: Fundamental Principles, Assessment of General Characteristics, Definitions, Section 131*, contains fundamental principles of protection for safety that encompass protection against electric shock, thermal effects, overcurrent, fault currents, and overvoltage. All these potential hazards are addressed by the requirements in this *Code*. ▸**Figure 90–15**

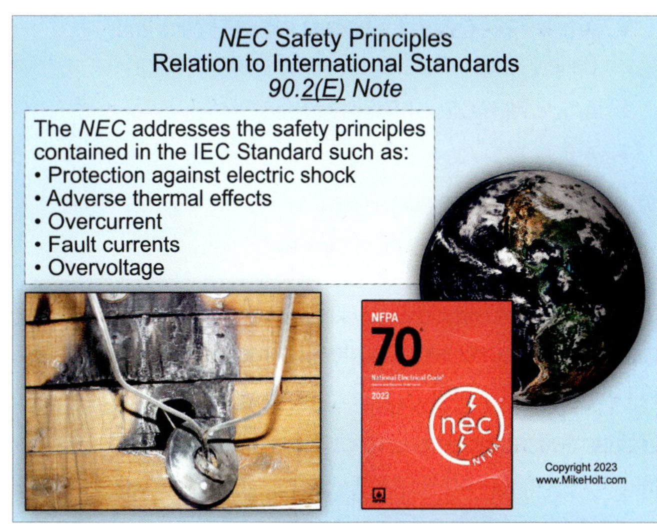
NEC Safety Principles
Relation to International Standards
90.2(E) Note
The NEC addresses the safety principles contained in the IEC Standard such as:
• Protection against electric shock
• Adverse thermal effects
• Overcurrent
• Fault currents
• Overvoltage
NFPA
70
2023
nec
Copyright 2023
www.MikeHolt.com

▸Figure 90–15

90.3 *Code* Arrangement

General Requirements. The *NEC* consists of an introduction and nine chapters followed by informative annexes. The requirements contained in Chapters 1, 2, 3, and 4 apply generally to all electrical installations. ▸**Figure 90–16**

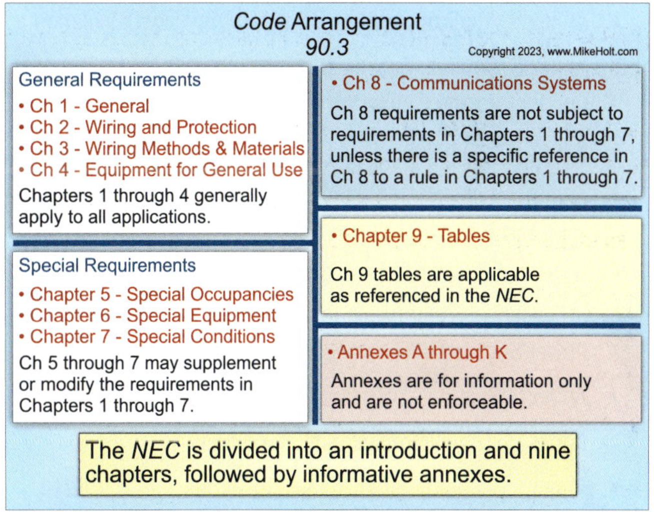
Code Arrangement
90.3
Copyright 2023, www.MikeHolt.com
General Requirements
• Ch 1 - General
• Ch 2 - Wiring and Protection
• Ch 3 - Wiring Methods & Materials
• Ch 4 - Equipment for General Use
Chapters 1 through 4 generally apply to all applications.
Special Requirements
• Chapter 5 - Special Occupancies
• Chapter 6 - Special Equipment
• Chapter 7 - Special Conditions
Ch 5 through 7 may supplement or modify the requirements in Chapters 1 through 7.
• Ch 8 - Communications Systems
Ch 8 requirements are not subject to requirements in Chapters 1 through 7, unless there is a specific reference in Ch 8 to a rule in Chapters 1 through 7.
• Chapter 9 - Tables
Ch 9 tables are applicable as referenced in the NEC.
• Annexes A through K
Annexes are for information only and are not enforceable.
The NEC is divided into an introduction and nine chapters, followed by informative annexes.

▸Figure 90–16

The requirements contained in Chapters 5, 6, and 7 apply to special occupancies, special equipment, or special conditions, which may supplement or modify the requirements contained in Chapters 1 through 7—but not Chapter 8. Chapter 7 wiring systems covered in this material include:

- Article 722—Cables for Power-Limited Circuits and Optical Fiber
- Article 724—Class 1 Power-Limited Circuits
- Article 725—Class 2 Power-Limited Circuits
- Article 760—Fire Alarm Circuits
- Article 770—Optical Fiber Circuits

Chapter 8 covers communications systems and is not subject to the requirements contained in Chapters 1 through 7, unless specifically referenced in Chapter 8.

Chapter 8 wiring systems covered in this material include:

- Article 800—General Requirements for Communications Systems
- Article 810—Radio and Television Antennas

Chapter 9 consists of tables that apply as referenced in the *NEC*. The tables are used to calculate raceway sizing, conductor fill, the radius of raceway bends, and conductor voltage drop.

Annexes are not part of the requirements of the *Code,* but are included for informational purposes only. There are eleven annexes:

- Annex A. Product Safety Standards
- Annex B. Application Information for Ampacity Calculation
- Annex C. Conduit, Tubing, and Cable Tray Fill Tables for Conductors and Fixture Wires of the Same Size
- Annex D. Examples
- Annex E. Types of Construction
- Annex F. Availability and Reliability for Critical Operations Power Systems (COPS), and Development and Implementation of Functional Performance Tests (FPTs) for Critical Operations Power Systems
- Annex G. Supervisory Control and Data Acquisition (SCADA)
- Annex H. Administration and Enforcement
- Annex I. Recommended Tightening Torque Tables from UL Standard 486A-486B
- Annex J. ADA Standards for Accessible Design
- Annex K. Use of Medical Electrical Equipment in Dwellings and Residential Board-and-Care Occupancies

90.4 *NEC* Enforcement

(A) Suitable for Adoption. The *NEC* is intended to be adopted for mandatory application by governmental bodies that exercise legal jurisdiction over electrical installations. ▸**Figure 90–17**

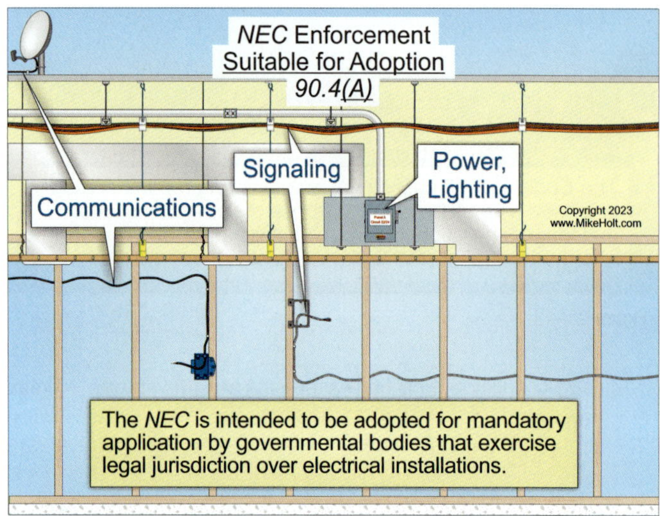
NEC Enforcement
Suitable for Adoption
90.4(A)
Communications
Signaling
Power, Lighting
Copyright 2023
www.MikeHolt.com
The *NEC* is intended to be adopted for mandatory application by governmental bodies that exercise legal jurisdiction over electrical installations.

▸**Figure 90–17**

Author's Comment:

- Once adopted (in part, wholly, or amended), the *National Electrical Code* becomes statutory law for the adopting jurisdiction and is thereby considered a legal document.

(B) AHJ Responsibility. The enforcement of the *NEC* is the responsibility of the "authority having jurisdiction" who is responsible for interpreting *Code* requirements, approving equipment and materials, and granting special permission. ▸**Figure 90–18**

According to Article 100, "Authority Having Jurisdiction" is defined as the organization, office, or individual responsible for approving equipment, materials, an installation, or a procedure. See 90.4 and 90.7 for more information.

"Approved" is acceptable to the authority having jurisdiction, usually the electrical inspector.

(C) Waiving Requirements and Alternate Methods. By special permission, the authority having jurisdiction may waive *NEC* requirements or approve alternate methods where equivalent safety can be achieved and maintained. ▸**Figure 90–19**

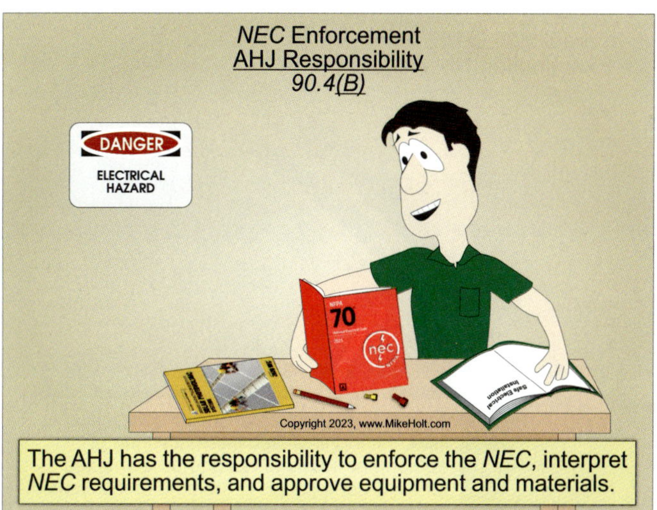
NEC Enforcement
AHJ Responsibility
90.4(B)
DANGER
ELECTRICAL HAZARD
Copyright 2023, www.MikeHolt.com
The AHJ has the responsibility to enforce the NEC, interpret NEC requirements, and approve equipment and materials.

▸Figure 90–18

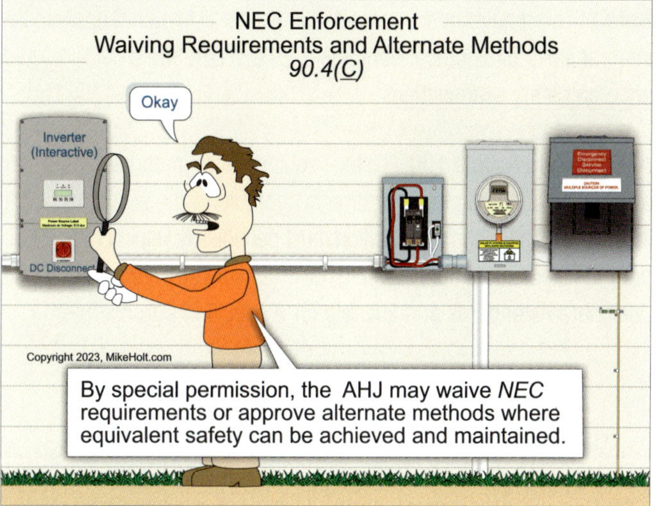
NEC Enforcement
Waiving Requirements and Alternate Methods
90.4(C)
Okay
Inverter (Interactive)
Copyright 2023, MikeHolt.com
By special permission, the AHJ may waive NEC requirements or approve alternate methods where equivalent safety can be achieved and maintained.

▸Figure 90–19

According to Article 100, "Special Permission" is defined as the written consent of the AHJ.

Author's Comment:

- According to 90.4(B), the authority having jurisdiction determines the approval of equipment. This means he/she can reject an installation of listed equipment and approve the use of unlisted equipment. Given our highly litigious society, approval of unlisted equipment is becoming increasingly difficult to obtain.

(D) Waiver of Product Requirements. If the *Code* requires products, constructions, or materials that are not yet available at the time the *NEC* is adopted, the authority having jurisdiction can allow products that were acceptable in the previous *Code* that was adopted in the jurisdiction to continue to be used.

Author's Comment:

- Typically, the AHJ will approve equipment listed by a product testing organization such as Underwriters Laboratories, Inc. (UL). The *NEC* does not require all equipment to be listed, but many state and local authorities having jurisdictions do. See 90.7, 110.2, and 110.3 and the definitions for "Approved," "Identified," "Labeled," and "Listed" in Article 100.
- Sometimes it takes years for testing laboratories to establish product standards for new *NEC* product requirements. It takes time before manufacturers can design, manufacture, and distribute those products to the marketplace.

90.5 Mandatory Requirements and Explanatory Material

(A) Mandatory Requirements. The words "shall" or "shall not" indicate a mandatory requirement.

Author's Comment:

- For greater ease in reading this material, we will use the word "must" instead of "shall," and "must not" will be used instead of "shall not."

(B) Permissive Requirements. The phrases "shall be permitted" or "shall not be required" indicate the action is permitted, but not required, or there are other options or alternatives permitted.

Author's Comment:

- For greater ease in reading, the phrase "shall be permitted" (as used in the *NEC*) has been replaced in this material with "is permitted" or "are permitted."

(C) Explanatory Material. Explanatory material referencing other standards, referencing related sections to an *NEC* rule, or just providing information related to a rule, is included in this *Code* in the form of informational notes or informative annexes. These are not enforceable as *NEC* requirements, unless the standard reference includes a date, the reference is to be considered as the latest edition of the standard.

Author's Comment:

- For convenience and ease in reading this material, "Informational Notes" will simply be identified as "Note."
- A Note, while not enforceable itself, may reference an enforceable *Code* rule elsewhere in the *NEC*.

Caution

CAUTION: Informational Notes are not enforceable, but notes to tables are. Within this material, we will call notes contained in a table a "Table Note."

(D) Informative Annexes. Nonmandatory information relative to the use of the *Code* is provided in informative annexes. These annexes are not enforceable as requirements of the *NEC, but* are included for informational purposes only.

90.7 Examination of Equipment for Safety

Product evaluation for *Code* compliance, approval, and safety is typically performed by a qualified electrical testing laboratory (QETL) in accordance with the listing standards.

Except to detect alterations or damage, listed factory-installed internal wiring of equipment does not need to be inspected for *NEC* compliance at the time of installation. ▸Figure 90-20

Internal Wiring of Equipment
Examination Not Required
90.7
GENE
Copyright 2023, MikeHolt.com
Except to detect alterations or damage, listed factory-installed internal wiring of equipment does not need to be inspected for NEC compliance at the time of installation.

▸Figure 90–20

Note 1: The requirements contained in Article 300 do not apply to the integral parts of electrical equipment [300.1(B)]. See 110.3 for guidance on safety examinations.

According to Article 100, "Listed" equipment or materials included in a list published by an organization acceptable to the authority having jurisdiction. The listing organization must periodically inspect the production of listed equipment or material to ensure it meets appropriate designated standards and suitable for a specified purpose.

ARTICLE
90

REVIEW QUESTIONS

NFPA
70
nec
NFPA

Please use the 2023 *Code* book to answer the following questions.

Article 90—Introduction to the *National Electrical Code*

1. Article _____ covers use and application, arrangement, and enforcement of the *National Electrical Code*.

   (a) 90
   (b) 110
   (c) 200
   (d) 300

2. The purpose of the *NEC* is for _____.

   (a) it to be used as a design manual
   (b) use as an instruction guide for untrained persons
   (c) the practical safeguarding of persons and property
   (d) interacting with inspectors

3. Compliance with the *Code* and proper maintenance result in an installation that is _____.

   (a) essentially free from hazard
   (b) not necessarily efficient or convenient
   (c) not necessarily adequate for good service or future expansion
   (d) all of these

4. Electrical hazards often occur because the initial _____ did not provide for increases in the use of electricity.

   (a) inspection
   (b) owner
   (c) wiring
   (d) builder

5. The *NEC* covers the installation and removal of _____.

   (a) electrical conductors, equipment, and raceways
   (b) signaling and communications conductors, equipment, and raceways
   (c) optical fiber cables
   (d) all of these

6. Installations supplying _____ power to ships and watercraft in marinas and boatyards are covered by the *NEC*.

   (a) shore
   (b) primary
   (c) secondary
   (d) auxiliary

7. Installations used to export electric power from vehicles to premises wiring or for _____ current flow is covered by the *NEC*.

   (a) emergency
   (b) primary
   (c) bidirectional
   (d) secondary

8. The *NEC* does not cover installations in _____.

   (a) ships and watercraft
   (b) mobile homes
   (c) recreational vehicles
   (d) any of these

9. The *Code* does not cover underground mine installations, or self-propelled mobile surface _____ machinery and its attendant electrical trailing cable.

    (a) paving
    (b) mining
    (c) harvesting
    (d) excavating

10. Installations of communications equipment under the exclusive control of communications utilities located outdoors or in building spaces used exclusively for such installations _____ covered by the *NEC*.

    (a) are
    (b) are sometimes
    (c) are not
    (d) may be

11. The *Code* does not cover installations under the exclusive control of an electric utility such as _____.

    (a) service drops or service laterals
    (b) electric utility office buildings
    (c) electric utility warehouses
    (d) electric utility garages

12. Chapters 1, 2, 3, and 4 of the *NEC* apply _____.

    (a) generally to all electrical installations
    (b) only to special occupancies and conditions
    (c) only to special equipment and material
    (d) all of these

13. Chapters 5, 6, and 7 of the *NEC* apply to _____ and may supplement or modify the requirements contained in Chapters 1 through 7.

    (a) special occupancies
    (b) special equipment
    (c) special conditions
    (d) all of these

14. Chapter 8 covers _____ systems and is not subject to the requirements of Chapters 1 through 7 unless specifically referenced in Chapter 8.

    (a) communications
    (b) fire alarm
    (c) emergency standby
    (d) sustainable energy

15. Annexes are not part of the requirements of this *Code* but are included for _____ purposes only.

    (a) informational
    (b) reference
    (c) supplemental enforcement
    (d) educational

16. The enforcement of the *NEC* is the responsibility of the authority having jurisdiction, who is responsible for _____.

    (a) making interpretations of rules
    (b) approval of equipment and materials
    (c) granting special permission
    (d) all of these

17. By special permission, the authority having jurisdiction may waive *NEC* requirements or approve alternative methods where equivalent _____ can be achieved and maintained.

    (a) safety
    (b) workmanship
    (c) installations
    (d) job progress

18. If the *Code* requires new products that may not yet be available at the time the *NEC* is adopted, the _____ can allow products that comply with the most recent previous edition of the *Code* adopted by the jurisdiction.

    (a) electrical engineer
    (b) master electrician
    (c) authority having jurisdiction
    (d) none of these

19. In the *NEC*, the word(s) "_____" indicate a mandatory requirement.

    (a) shall
    (b) shall not
    (c) shall be permitted
    (d) shall or shall not

20. When the *Code* uses "_____," it indicates the actions are allowed but not required.

    (a) shall or shall not
    (b) shall not be permitted
    (c) shall be permitted
    (d) none of these

21. Explanatory material, such as references to other standards, references to related sections of this *Code*, or information related to a *Code* rule, is included in this *Code* in the form of _____.

    (a) informational notes
    (b) footnotes
    (c) table notes
    (d) italicized text

22. Nonmandatory information relative to the use of the *NEC* is provided in informative annexes and are _____.

    (a) included for information purposes only
    (b) not enforceable requirements of the *Code*
    (c) enforceable as a requirement of the *Code*
    (d) included for information purposes only and are not enforceable requirements of the *Code*

23. Except to detect alterations or damage, qualified electrical testing laboratory listed factory-installed _____ wiring of equipment does not need to be inspected for *NEC* compliance at the time of installation.

    (a) external
    (b) associated
    (c) internal
    (d) all of these

Notes

CHAPTER
1

GENERAL RULES

Introduction to Chapter 1—General Rules

Chapter 1 of the *NEC* is divided into two articles. The first contains the definitions of important terms used throughout the *Code*, and the second provides the general requirements for all electrical installations. The definitions and rules in this chapter apply to all electrical installations covered by the *NEC*.

Chapter 1 is often overlooked because the rules are very broad and do not clearly apply to specific situations. Be sure you understand the rules, concepts, definitions, and requirements in Chapter 1 as doing so will make a difficult rule(s) much easier to apply. Chapter 1 articles covered by this material are:

- **Article 100—Definitions.** Article 100 contains the definitions essential to the application of this *Code.* Where terms are not defined in Article 100, the *NEC Style Manual* directs us to use *Webster's Collegiate Dictionary*, or to consult with the authority having jurisdiction.
- **Article 110—General Requirements for Electrical Installations.** This article covers the general requirements for the examination and approval, installation and use, and access to spaces around electrical equipment.

ARTICLE 100 DEFINITIONS

Introduction to Article 100—Definitions

Have you ever had a conversation with someone only to discover that what you meant and what they understood were completely different? This often happens when people have different interpretations of the words being used, and that is why the definitions of key *NEC* terms are located at the beginning of the *Code*. Definitions used out of context are a leading cause of misinterpretations of rules by people such as electricians, engineers, and inspectors. Because the *NEC* exists to protect people and property, it is important to be able to convey and comprehend the language used. Review and reference Article 100 whenever there is a possibility of an inaccurate (or incorrect) definition of a term being used in a rule.

100 Definitions

Scope. This article contains definitions essential to the application of this *Code*. Definitions of standard terms, such as volt, voltage drop, ampere, impedance, and resistance are not contained in Article 100. If the *NEC* does not define a term, then a dictionary or building code acceptable to the authority having jurisdiction should be consulted.

The *Code* does not include general or technical terms from other codes and standards. An article number in parentheses following the definition indicates that the definition only applies to that article.

Author's Comment:

- In this material, the Article 100 definitions that only apply to a specific article can also be found in that specific article.

Accessible (as applied to wiring methods). Capable of being removed or exposed without damaging the building structure or finish. They also cannot be permanently closed in or blocked by the building structure, other electrical equipment, other building systems (piping, ducts, drains, or other mechanical systems), or the building finish. ▶Figure 100–1

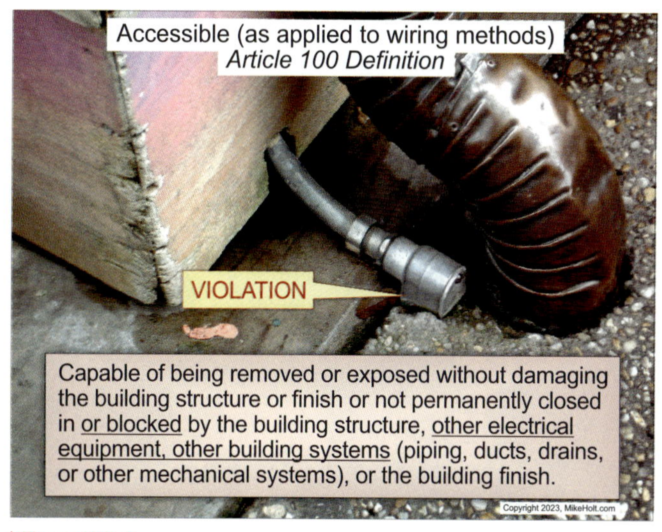
Accessible (as applied to wiring methods)
Article 100 Definition
VIOLATION
Capable of being removed or exposed without damaging the building structure or finish or not permanently closed in or blocked by the building structure, other electrical equipment, other building systems (piping, ducts, drains, or other mechanical systems), or the building finish.
Copyright 2023, MikeHolt.com
▶Figure 100–1

Author's Comment:

- Wiring methods above a suspended ceiling or below a raised floor with removable panels designed to permit access are examples of accessible as applied to wiring methods.
- A junction box above a suspended ceiling blocked by mechanical duct work is an example of a violation of this requirement.

Approved. Acceptable to the authority having jurisdiction (AHJ), usually the electrical inspector. ▶Figure 100–2

Approved
Article 100 Definition
Okay
Inverter (Interactive)
DC Disconnect
Acceptable to the authority having jurisdiction (AHJ), usually the electrical inspector.
Copyright 2023, MikeHolt.com

▸Figure 100–2

Author's Comment:

- Product listing does not mean the product is approved, but it can be a basis for approval. See 90.4, 90.7, and 110.2 and the definitions in this article for "Authority Having Jurisdiction," "Identified," "Labeled," and "Listed."

Attachment Plug (Plug Cap). A wiring device at the end of a flexible cord intended to be inserted into a receptacle to make an electrical connection. ▸Figure 100–3

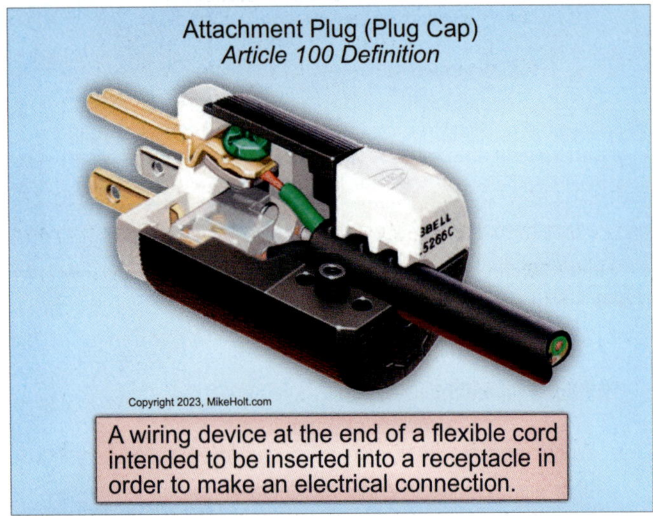
Attachment Plug (Plug Cap)
Article 100 Definition
Copyright 2023, MikeHolt.com
A wiring device at the end of a flexible cord intended to be inserted into a receptacle in order to make an electrical connection.

▸Figure 100–3

Authority Having Jurisdiction (AHJ). The organization, office, or individual responsible for approving equipment, materials, or installation. See 90.4 and 90.7 for more information. ▸Figure 100–4

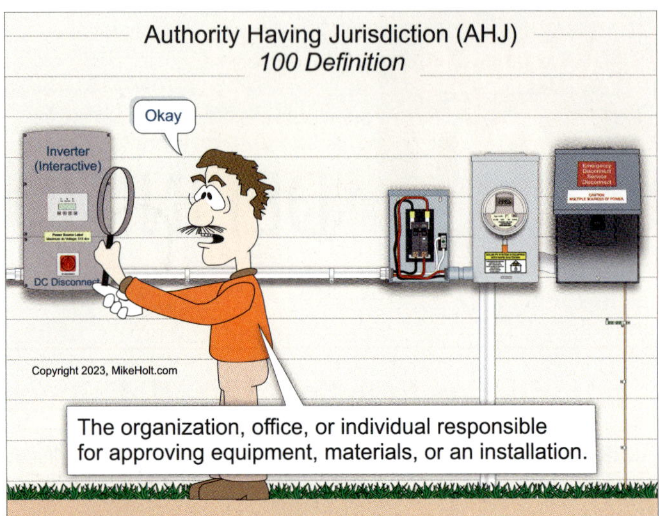
Authority Having Jurisdiction (AHJ)
100 Definition
Okay
Inverter (Interactive)
DC Disconnect
Copyright 2023, MikeHolt.com
The organization, office, or individual responsible for approving equipment, materials, or an installation.

▸Figure 100–4

Note: The authority having jurisdiction (AHJ) may be a federal, state, or local government department or individual such as a fire chief, fire marshal, chief of a fire prevention bureau, labor or health department, a building official, electrical inspector, or others having statutory authority. The utility company can also be an AHJ. In some circumstances, the property owner or his/her agent assumes the role, and at government installations, the commanding officer, or departmental official may be the AHJ.

Author's Comment:

- The AHJ is typically the electrical inspector who has legal statutory authority. In the absence of federal, state, or local regulations, the operator of the facility or his/her agent (such as an architect or engineer of the facility) can assume the role.
- Most expect the AHJ to have at least some prior experience in the electrical field, such as having studied electrical engineering or having obtained an electrical contractor's license. In a few states this is a legal requirement. Memberships, certifications, and active participation in electrical organizations such as the International Association of Electrical Inspectors (IAEI) speak to an individual's qualifications. Visit www.IAEI.org for more information about that organization.

Bonded (Bonding). Connected to establish electrical continuity and conductivity. ▸Figure 100–5

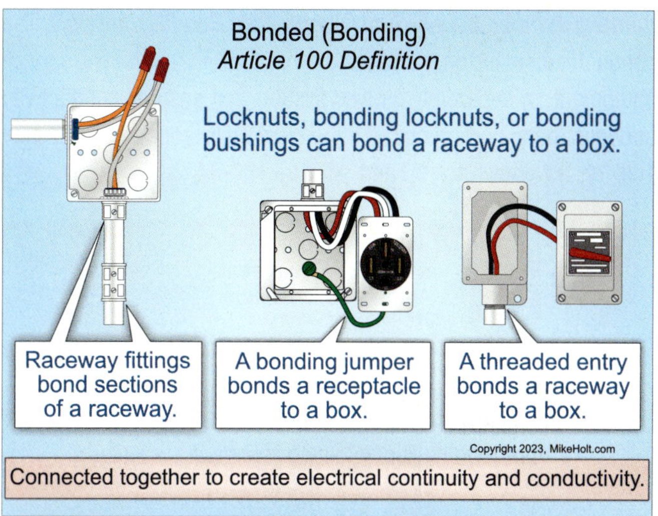
Bonded (Bonding)
Article 100 Definition
Locknuts, bonding locknuts, or bonding bushings can bond a raceway to a box.
Raceway fittings bond sections of a raceway.
A bonding jumper bonds a receptacle to a box.
A threaded entry bonds a raceway to a box.
Copyright 2023, MikeHolt.com
Connected together to create electrical continuity and conductivity.

▸Figure 100–5

Author's Comment:

- Bonding electrical equipment in accordance with 250.4(A)(3) and bonding metal parts in accordance with 250.4(A)(4) creates an effective path for ground-fault current to return to the supply source and open the overcurrent protective device.

Bonding Conductor (Bonding Jumper). A conductor that ensures electrical conductivity by connecting metal parts of equipment together. ▸Figure 100–6

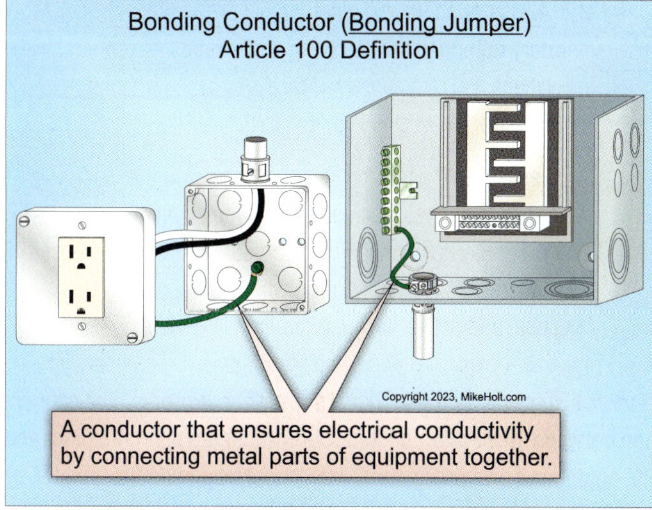
Bonding Conductor (Bonding Jumper)
Article 100 Definition
Copyright 2023, MikeHolt.com
A conductor that ensures electrical conductivity by connecting metal parts of equipment together.

▸Figure 100–6

Bonding Jumper, Equipment (Equipment Bonding Jumper). A connection to ensure electrical continuity between two or more portions of the equipment grounding conductor. ▸Figure 100–7 and ▸Figure 100–8

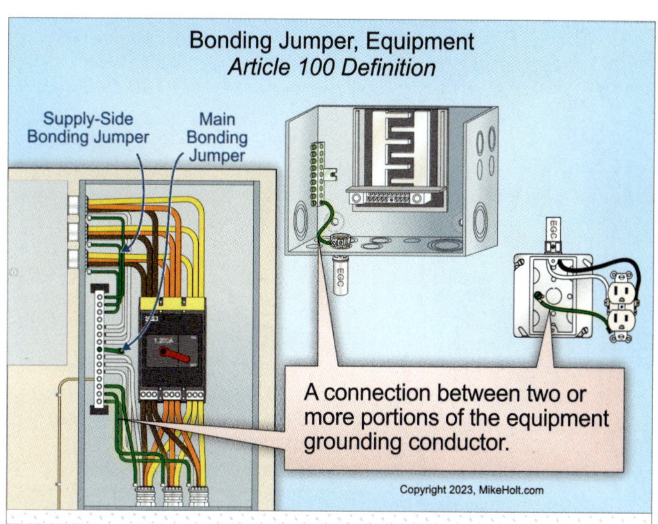
Bonding Jumper, Equipment
Article 100 Definition
Supply-Side Bonding Jumper
Main Bonding Jumper
EGC
A connection between two or more portions of the equipment grounding conductor.
Copyright 2023, MikeHolt.com

▸Figure 100–7

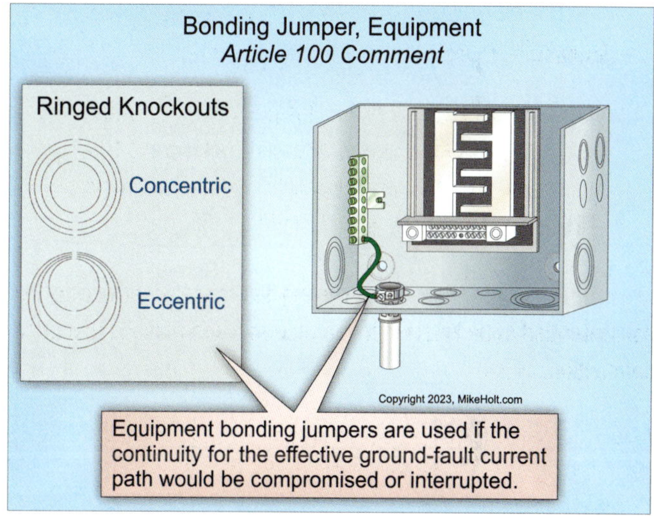
Bonding Jumper, Equipment
Article 100 Comment
Ringed Knockouts
Concentric
Eccentric
Copyright 2023, MikeHolt.com
Equipment bonding jumpers are used if the continuity for the effective ground-fault current path would be compromised or interrupted.

▸Figure 100–8

Bonding Jumper, Main (Main Bonding Jumper). A wire, screw, or busbar used to connect the service neutral conductor to the equipment grounding conductor at the service disconnect enclosure. ▸Figure 100–9, ▸Figure 100–10, and ▸Figure 100–11

Author's Comment:

- The main bonding jumper can be a wire, busbar, or screw [250.28(A)]. Connection to the service equipment enclosure must be in accordance with 250.8(A) and 250.24(C).

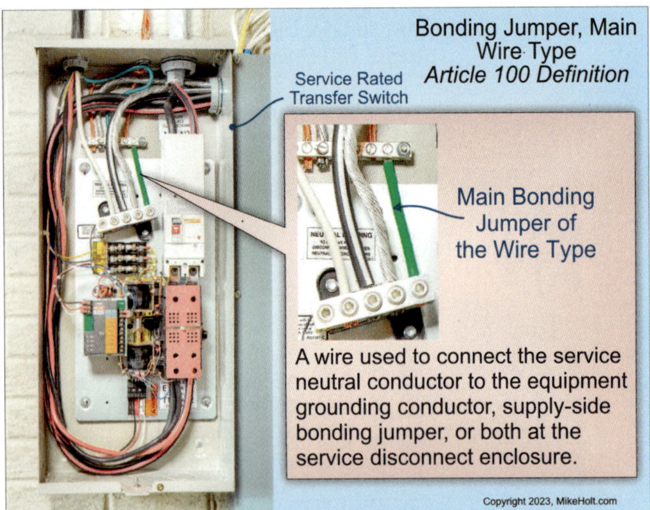
Bonding Jumper, Main
Wire Type
Article 100 Definition
Service Rated
Transfer Switch
Main Bonding
Jumper of
the Wire Type
A wire used to connect the service neutral conductor to the equipment grounding conductor, supply-side bonding jumper, or both at the service disconnect enclosure.
Copyright 2023, MikeHolt.com

▸Figure 100–9

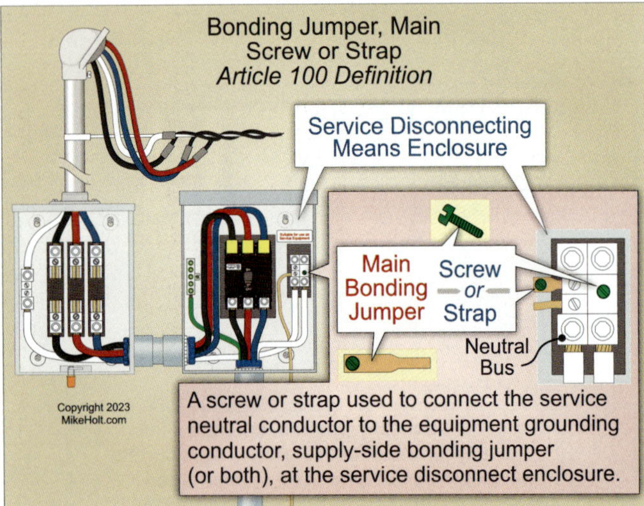
Bonding Jumper, Main
Screw or Strap
Article 100 Definition
Service Disconnecting
Means Enclosure
Main
Bonding
Jumper
Screw
or
Strap
Neutral
Bus
A screw or strap used to connect the service neutral conductor to the equipment grounding conductor, supply-side bonding jumper (or both), at the service disconnect enclosure.
Copyright 2023
MikeHolt.com

▸Figure 100–10

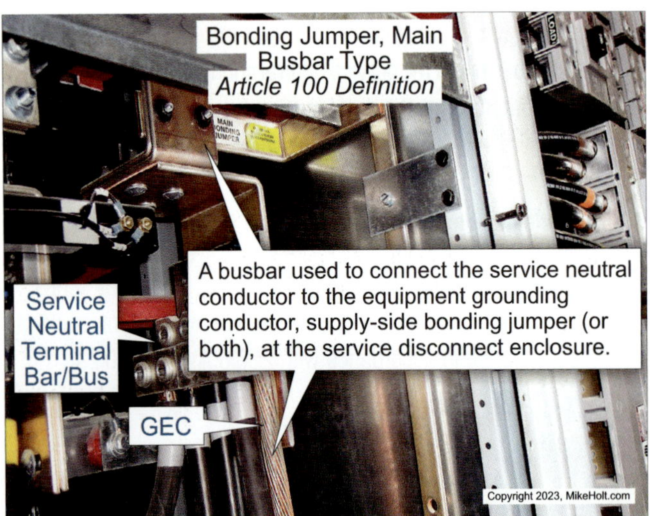
Bonding Jumper, Main
Busbar Type
Article 100 Definition
A busbar used to connect the service neutral conductor to the equipment grounding conductor, supply-side bonding jumper (or both), at the service disconnect enclosure.
Service
Neutral
Terminal
Bar/Bus
GEC
Copyright 2023, MikeHolt.com

▸Figure 100–11

Bonding Jumper, Supply-Side (Supply-Side Bonding Jumper). The conductor installed on the supply side of a service, within the service equipment, or separately derived system that ensures conductivity between metal parts required to be electrically connected. ▸Figure 100–12, ▸Figure 100–13, and ▸Figure 100–14

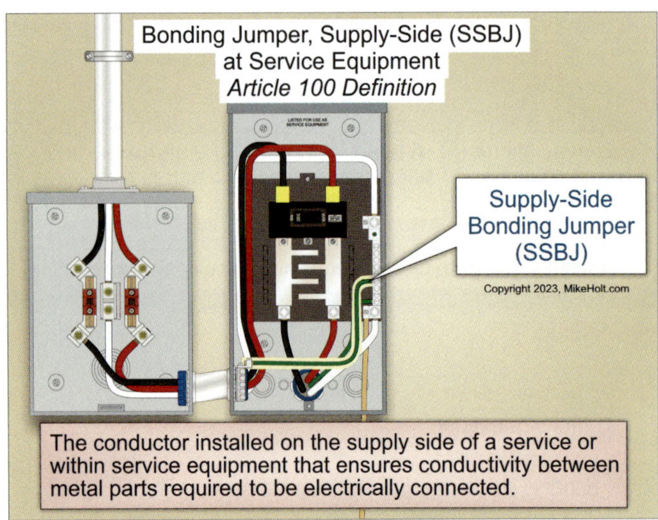
Bonding Jumper, Supply-Side (SSBJ)
at Service Equipment
Article 100 Definition
Supply-Side
Bonding Jumper
(SSBJ)
Copyright 2023, MikeHolt.com
The conductor installed on the supply side of a service or within service equipment that ensures conductivity between metal parts required to be electrically connected.

▸Figure 100–12

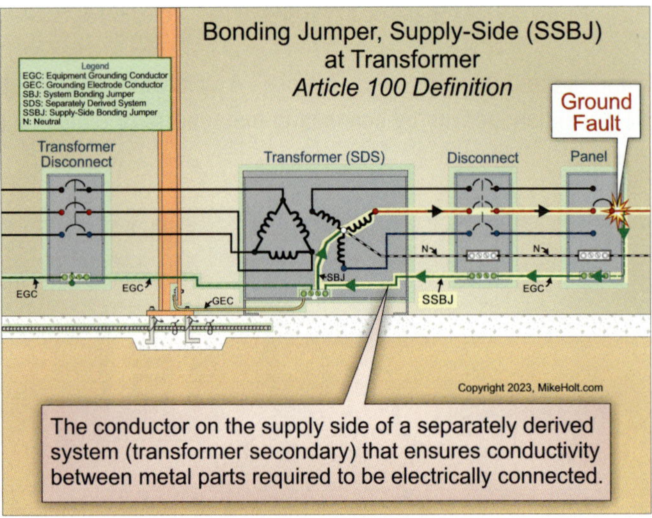
Bonding Jumper, Supply-Side (SSBJ)
at Transformer
Article 100 Definition
Legend
EGC: Equipment Grounding Conductor
GEC: Grounding Electrode Conductor
SBJ: System Bonding Jumper
SDS: Separately Derived System
SSBJ: Supply-Side Bonding Jumper
N: Neutral
Ground
Fault
Transformer
Disconnect
Transformer (SDS)
Disconnect
Panel
N
N
SBJ
EGC
EGC
GEC
SSBJ
EGC
Copyright 2023, MikeHolt.com
The conductor on the supply side of a separately derived system (transformer secondary) that ensures conductivity between metal parts required to be electrically connected.

▸Figure 100–13

Bonding Jumper, System (System Bonding Jumper). The connection between the neutral conductor or grounded-phase conductor and the equipment grounding conductor, supply-side bonding jumper, or both at a separately derived system, such as a transformer or generator. ▸Figure 100–15 and ▸Figure 100–16

Branch Circuit. The conductors between the final overcurrent protective device and the receptacle outlets, lighting outlets, or other outlets. ▸Figure 100–17

1st Printing

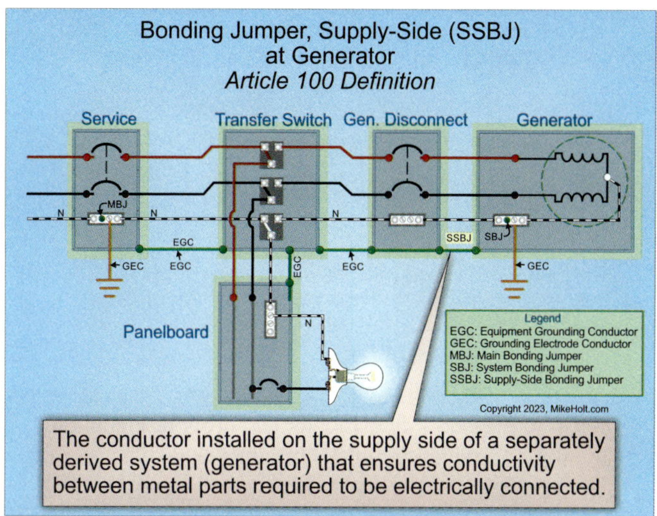
Bonding Jumper, Supply-Side (SSBJ)
at Generator
Article 100 Definition
Service
Transfer Switch
Gen. Disconnect
Generator
Panelboard
Legend
EGC: Equipment Grounding Conductor
GEC: Grounding Electrode Conductor
MBJ: Main Bonding Jumper
SBJ: System Bonding Jumper
SSBJ: Supply-Side Bonding Jumper
Copyright 2023, MikeHolt.com
The conductor installed on the supply side of a separately derived system (generator) that ensures conductivity between metal parts required to be electrically connected.

▸Figure 100–14

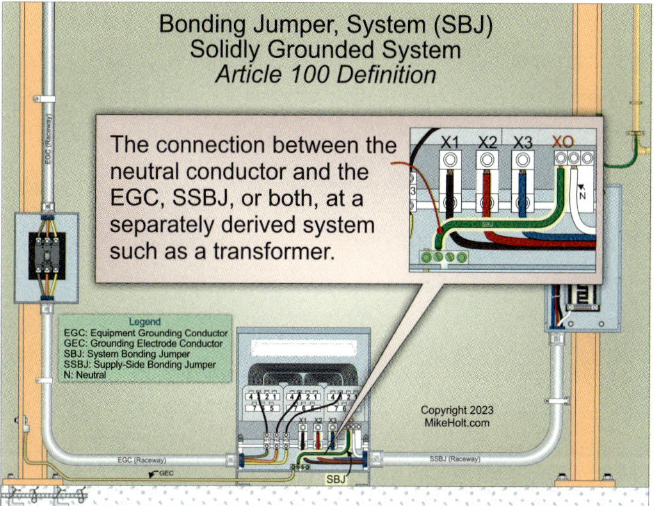
Bonding Jumper, System (SBJ)
Solidly Grounded System
Article 100 Definition
The connection between the neutral conductor and the EGC, SSBJ, or both, at a separately derived system such as a transformer.
Legend
EGC: Equipment Grounding Conductor
GEC: Grounding Electrode Conductor
SBJ: System Bonding Jumper
SSBJ: Supply-Side Bonding Jumper
N: Neutral
Copyright 2023
MikeHolt.com

▸Figure 100–15

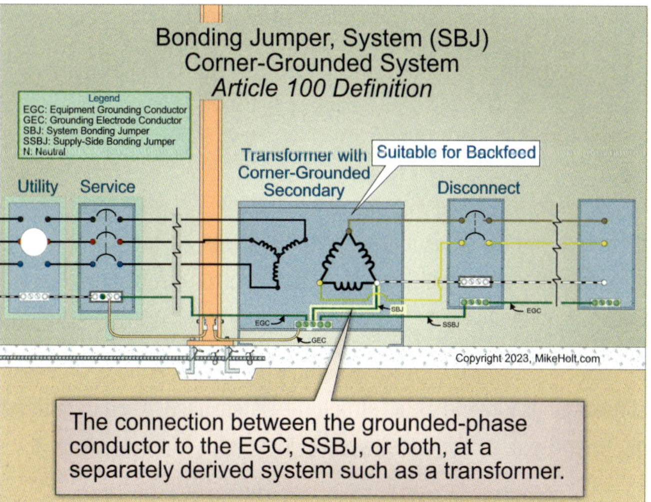
Bonding Jumper, System (SBJ)
Corner-Grounded System
Article 100 Definition
Legend
EGC: Equipment Grounding Conductor
GEC: Grounding Electrode Conductor
SBJ: System Bonding Jumper
SSBJ: Supply-Side Bonding Jumper
N: Neutral
Transformer with Corner-Grounded Secondary
Suitable for Backfeed
Utility
Service
Disconnect
Copyright 2023, MikeHolt.com
The connection between the grounded-phase conductor to the EGC, SSBJ, or both, at a separately derived system such as a transformer.

▸Figure 100–16

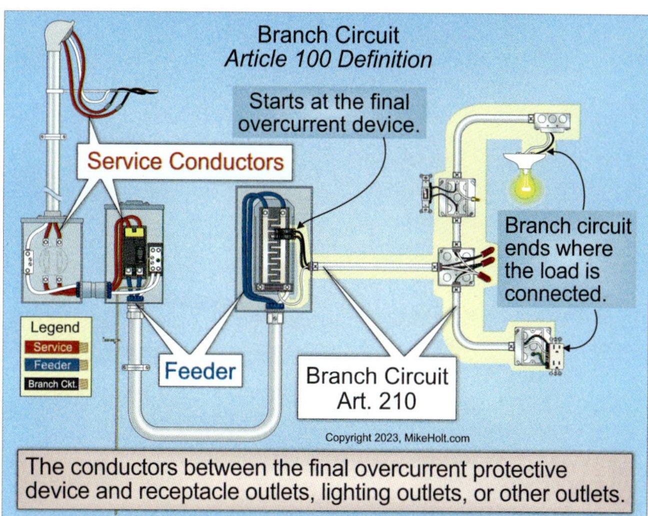
Branch Circuit
Article 100 Definition
Starts at the final overcurrent device.
Service Conductors
Branch circuit ends where the load is connected.
Legend
Service
Feeder
Branch Ckt.
Feeder
Branch Circuit
Art. 210
Copyright 2023, MikeHolt.com
The conductors between the final overcurrent protective device and receptacle outlets, lighting outlets, or other outlets.

▸Figure 100–17

Building. A structure that stands alone or is separated from adjoining structures by fire walls. ▸Figure 100–18

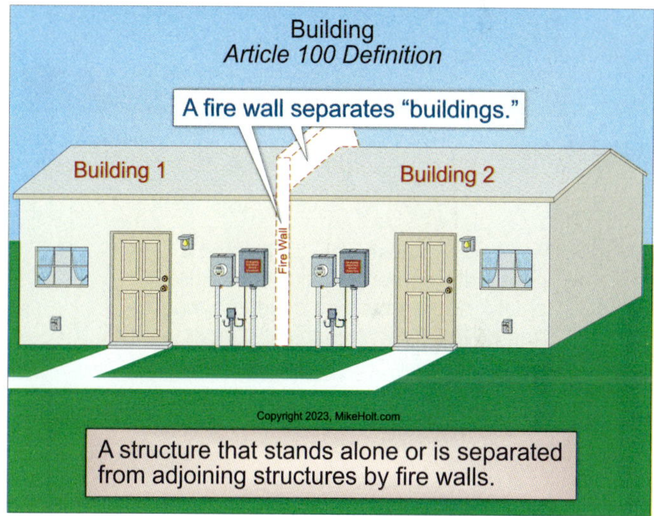
Building
Article 100 Definition
A fire wall separates "buildings."
Building 1
Building 2
Fire Wall
Copyright 2023, MikeHolt.com
A structure that stands alone or is separated from adjoining structures by fire walls.

▸Figure 100–18

Cable, Armored (Type AC). A fabricated assembly of conductors in a flexible interlocked metallic armor with an internal bonding strip in intimate contact with the armor for its entire length. ▸Figure 100–19

Cable, Coaxial (Coaxial Cable). A cylindrical assembly containing a conductor centered inside a metallic shield, separated by a dielectric material, and covered by an insulating jacket. ▸Figure 100–20

Cable, Metal-Clad (Type MC). A factory assembly of one or more insulated circuit conductors (with or without optical fiber members) enclosed in an armor of interlocking metal tape, or a smooth or corrugated metallic sheath. ▸Figure 100–21

Cable, Nonmetallic-Sheathed (Type NM). A wiring method that encloses two or more insulated conductors within an outer nonmetallic jacket. ▸Figure 100–22

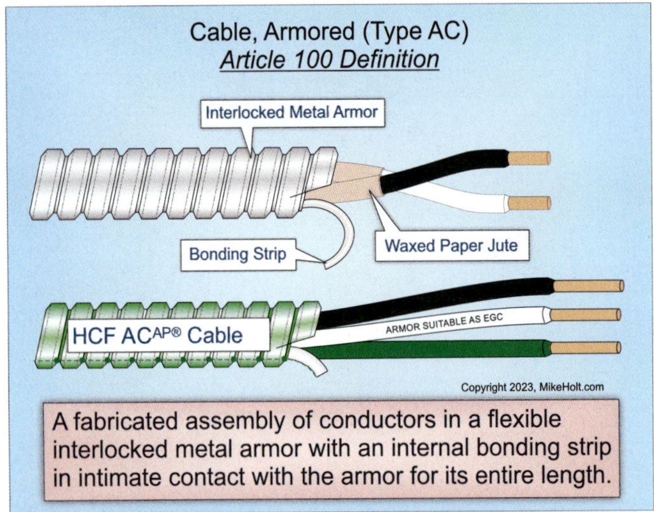
Cable, Armored (Type AC)
Article 100 Definition
Interlocked Metal Armor
Bonding Strip
Waxed Paper Jute
HCF ACAP® Cable
ARMOR SUITABLE AS EGC
Copyright 2023, MikeHolt.com
A fabricated assembly of conductors in a flexible interlocked metal armor with an internal bonding strip in intimate contact with the armor for its entire length.

▸Figure 100–19

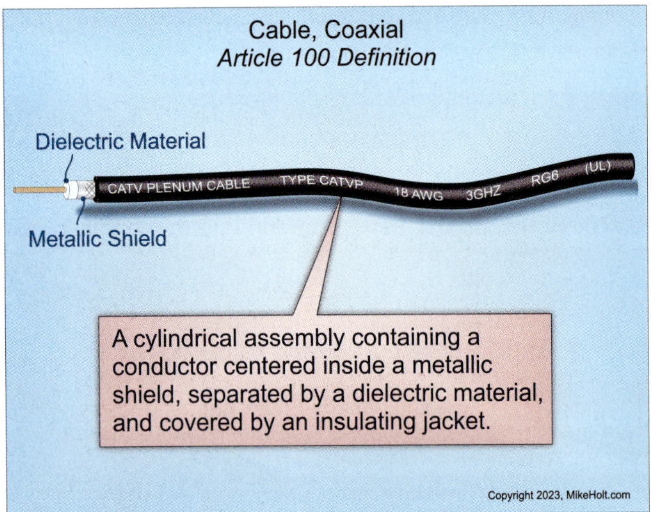
Cable, Coaxial
Article 100 Definition
Dielectric Material
CATV PLENUM CABLE TYPE CATVP 18 AWG 3GHZ RG6 (UL)
Metallic Shield
A cylindrical assembly containing a conductor centered inside a metallic shield, separated by a dielectric material, and covered by an insulating jacket.
Copyright 2023, MikeHolt.com

▸Figure 100–20

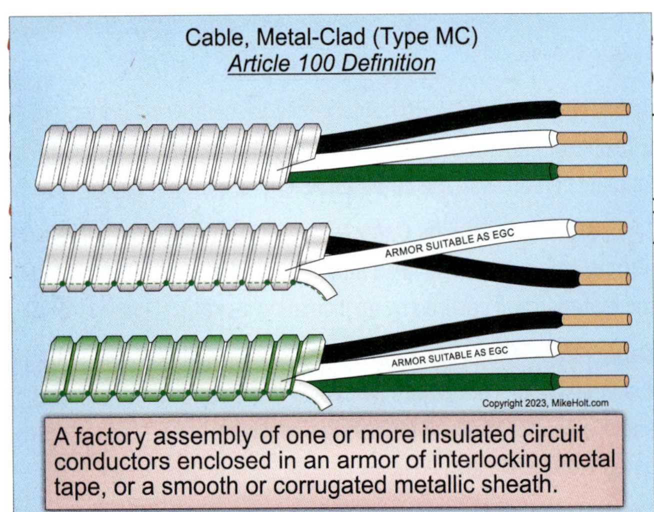
Cable, Metal-Clad (Type MC)
Article 100 Definition
ARMOR SUITABLE AS EGC
ARMOR SUITABLE AS EGC
Copyright 2023, MikeHolt.com
A factory assembly of one or more insulated circuit conductors enclosed in an armor of interlocking metal tape, or a smooth or corrugated metallic sheath.

▸Figure 100–21

Cable, Nonmetallic-Sheathed (Type NM)
Article 100 Definition
NON-METALLIC SHEATHED CABLE
CME
300722
1000 ft
A wiring method that encloses two or more insulated conductors within an outer nonmetallic jacket.
Copyright 2023, MikeHolt.com

▸Figure 100–22

Cable, Power and Control Tray (Type TC). A factory assembly of two or more insulated conductors (with or without associated bare or covered equipment grounding conductors) under a nonmetallic jacket. ▸Figure 100–23

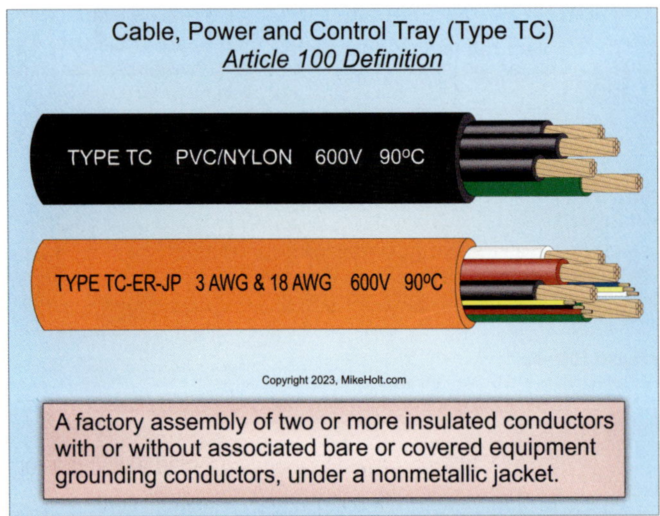
Cable, Power and Control Tray (Type TC)
Article 100 Definition
TYPE TC PVC/NYLON 600V 90°C
TYPE TC-ER-JP 3 AWG & 18 AWG 600V 90°C
Copyright 2023, MikeHolt.com
A factory assembly of two or more insulated conductors with or without associated bare or covered equipment grounding conductors, under a nonmetallic jacket.

▸Figure 100–23

Cable, Underground Feeder and Branch-Circuit (Type UF). A factory assembly of insulated conductors with an integral or overall covering of nonmetallic material suitable for direct burial in the Earth. ▸Figure 100–24

Cable Tray System. A unit or assembly of units or sections with associated fittings forming a rigid structural system used to securely fasten or support cables and raceways. ▸Figure 100–25

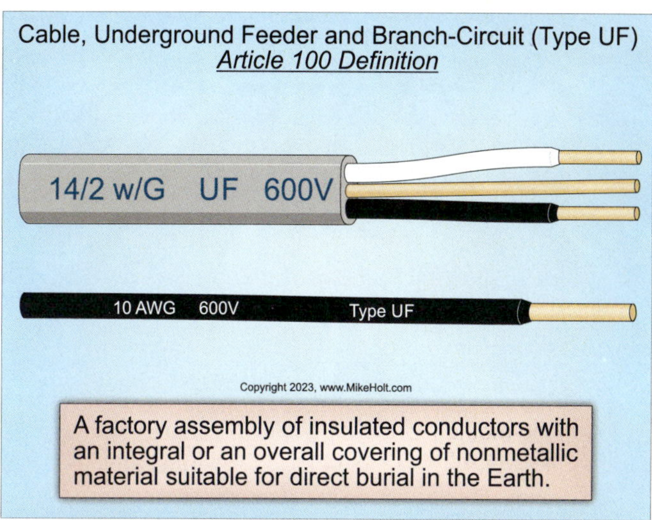
Cable, Underground Feeder and Branch-Circuit (Type UF)
Article 100 Definition
14/2 w/G UF 600V
10 AWG 600V Type UF
Copyright 2023, www.MikeHolt.com
A factory assembly of insulated conductors with an integral or an overall covering of nonmetallic material suitable for direct burial in the Earth.

▶Figure 100–24

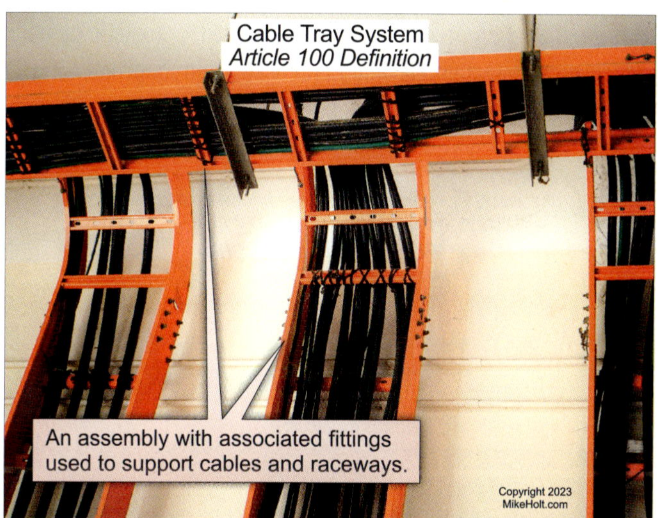
Cable Tray System
Article 100 Definition
An assembly with associated fittings used to support cables and raceways.
Copyright 2023 MikeHolt.com

▶Figure 100–25

Conductor, Copper-Clad Aluminum (Copper-Clad Aluminum Conductor). Conductors drawn from a copper-clad aluminum rod, with the copper metallurgically bonded to an aluminum core. ▶Figure 100–26

Conduit, Flexible Metal (FMC). A raceway of circular cross section made of a helically wound, formed, interlocked metal strip, and listed for the installation of electrical conductors. ▶Figure 100–27

Conduit, Intermediate Metal (IMC). A steel raceway of circular cross section that can be threaded with integral or associated couplings, and listed for the installation of electrical conductors. ▶Figure 100–28

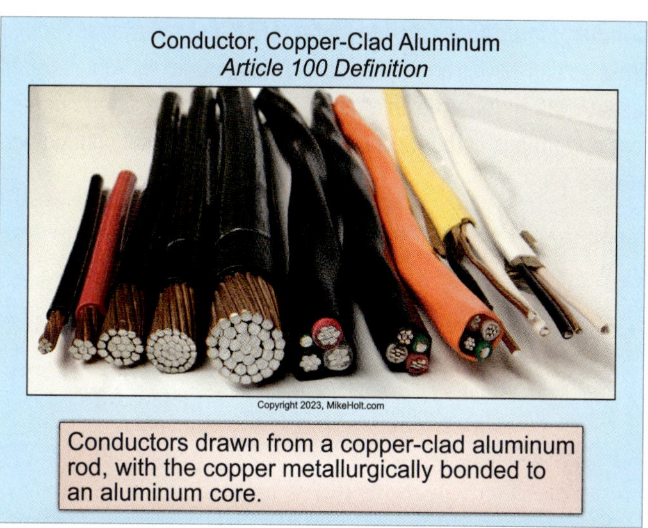
Conductor, Copper-Clad Aluminum
Article 100 Definition
Copyright 2023, MikeHolt.com
Conductors drawn from a copper-clad aluminum rod, with the copper metallurgically bonded to an aluminum core.

▶Figure 100–26

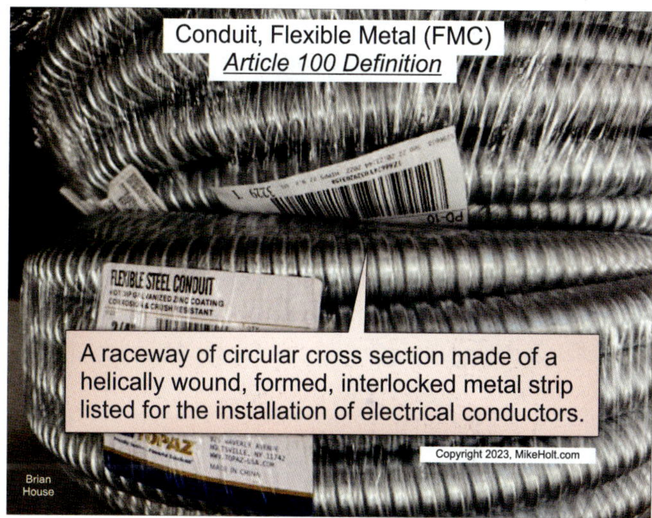
Conduit, Flexible Metal (FMC)
Article 100 Definition
FLEXIBLE STEEL CONDUIT
A raceway of circular cross section made of a helically wound, formed, interlocked metal strip listed for the installation of electrical conductors.
Copyright 2023, MikeHolt.com
Brian House

▶Figure 100–27

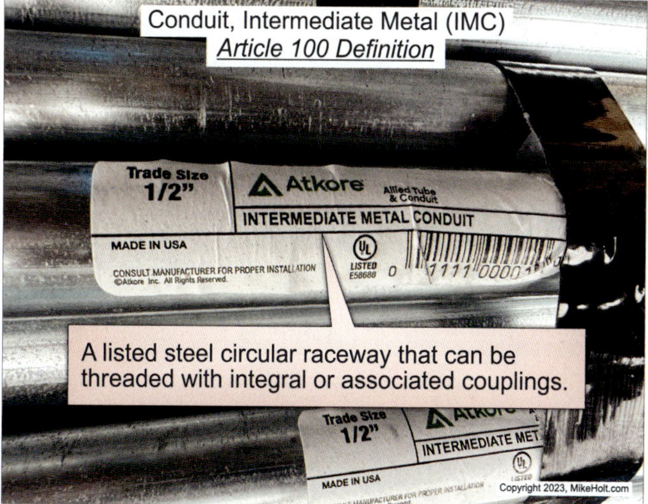
Conduit, Intermediate Metal (IMC)
Article 100 Definition
Trade Size 1/2"
Atkore
INTERMEDIATE METAL CONDUIT
MADE IN USA
A listed steel circular raceway that can be threaded with integral or associated couplings.
Copyright 2023, MikeHolt.com

▶Figure 100–28

Conduit, Liquidtight Flexible Metal (LFMC). A raceway of circular cross section (having an outer liquidtight, nonmetallic, sunlight-resistant jacket over an inner flexible metal core) with associated connectors and fittings listed for the installation of electrical conductors. ▶Figure 100–29

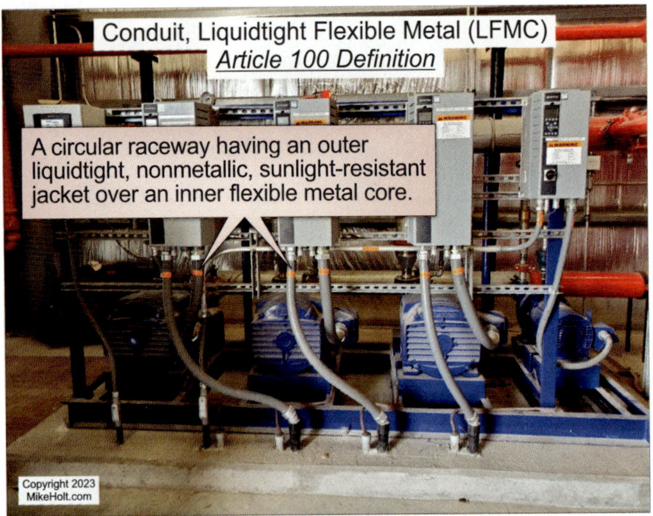
Conduit, Liquidtight Flexible Metal (LFMC)
Article 100 Definition
A circular raceway having an outer liquidtight, nonmetallic, sunlight-resistant jacket over an inner flexible metal core.
Copyright 2023 MikeHolt.com

▶Figure 100–29

Conduit, Liquidtight Flexible Nonmetallic (LFNC). A raceway of circular cross section (with an outer liquidtight, nonmetallic, sunlight-resistant jacket over a flexible inner core) with associated couplings, connectors, and fittings listed for the installation of electrical conductors. ▶Figure 100–30

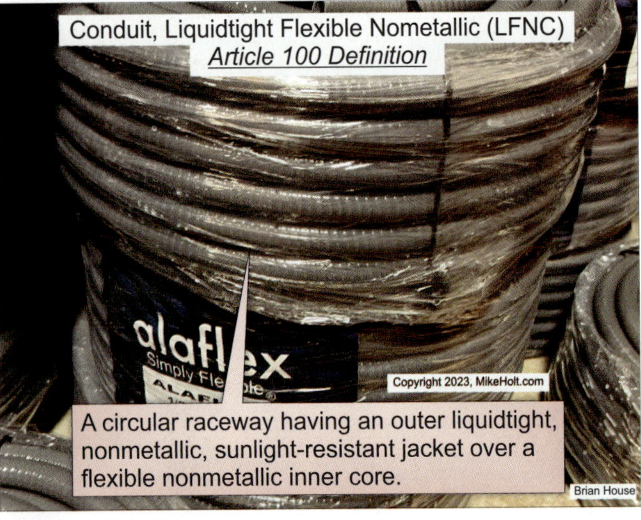
Conduit, Liquidtight Flexible Nometallic (LFNC)
Article 100 Definition
Copyright 2023, MikeHolt.com
A circular raceway having an outer liquidtight, nonmetallic, sunlight-resistant jacket over a flexible nonmetallic inner core.
Brian House

▶Figure 100–30

Conduit, Rigid Metal (RMC). A listed metal raceway of circular cross section with integral or associated couplings listed for the installation of electrical conductors. ▶Figure 100–31

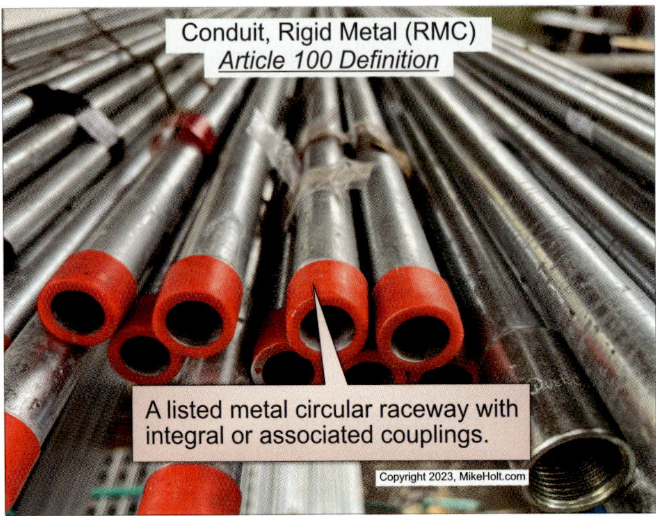
Conduit, Rigid Metal (RMC)
Article 100 Definition
A listed metal circular raceway with integral or associated couplings.
Copyright 2023, MikeHolt.com

▶Figure 100–31

Conduit, Rigid Polyvinyl Chloride (PVC). A rigid nonmetallic raceway of circular cross section with integral or associated couplings, connectors, and fittings listed for the installation of electrical conductors. ▶Figure 100–32

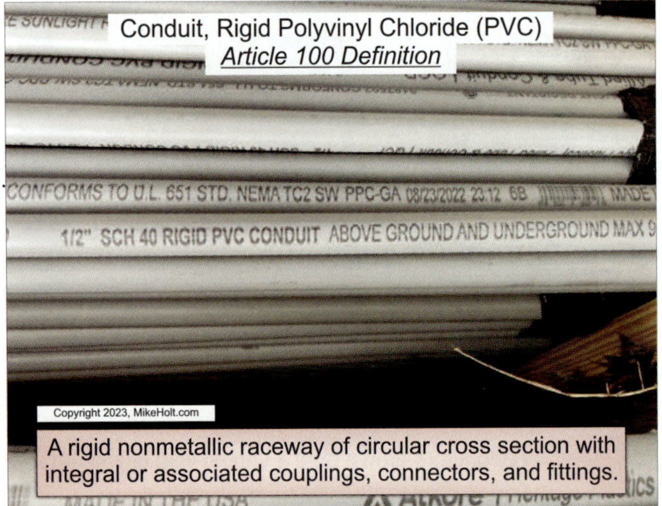
Conduit, Rigid Polyvinyl Chloride (PVC)
Article 100 Definition
CONFORMS TO U.L. 651 STD. NEMA TC2 SW PPC-GA
1/2" SCH 40 RIGID PVC CONDUIT ABOVE GROUND AND UNDERGROUND
Copyright 2023, MikeHolt.com
A rigid nonmetallic raceway of circular cross section with integral or associated couplings, connectors, and fittings.

▶Figure 100–32

Corrosive Environment. Areas or enclosures without adequate ventilation where electrical equipment is located, and pool sanitation chemicals are stored, handled, or dispensed (Article 680). ▶Figure 100–33

Note 1: Sanitation chemicals and pool water pose a risk of corrosion (gradually damaging or destroying materials) due to the presence of oxidizers (for example, calcium hypochlorite, sodium hypochlorite, bromine, and chlorinated isocyanurates) and chlorinating agents that release chlorine when dissolved in water.

Corrosive Environment
Article 100 Definition
Copyright 2023, MikeHolt.com
Areas or enclosures without adequate ventilation where electrical equipment is located and pool sanitation chemicals are stored, handled, or dispensed (680).

▸Figure 100–33

Dental Office. A building or portion of a building in which the following occur:

(1) Examinations and minor treatments or procedures performed under the continuous supervision of a dental professional

(2) Use of limited to minimal sedation and treatment or procedures that do not render the patient incapable of self-preservation under emergency conditions

(3) No overnight stays for patients or 24-hour operations

Disconnecting Means (Disconnect). A device that disconnects the circuit conductors from their power source. ▸Figure 100–34

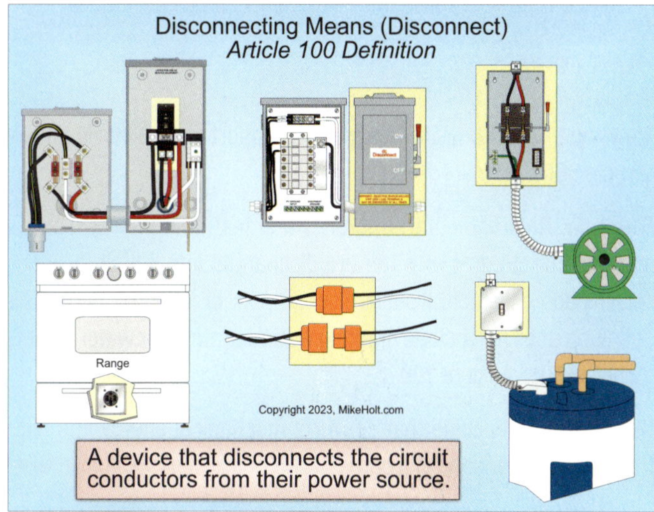
Disconnecting Means (Disconnect)
Article 100 Definition
Range
Copyright 2023, MikeHolt.com
A device that disconnects the circuit conductors from their power source.

▸Figure 100–34

Docking Facility. A fixed or floating structure that provides access to the water and to which boats are secured (Article 555). ▸Figure 100–35

Docking Facility
Article 100 Definition
Copyright 2023, MikeHolt.com
A fixed or floating structure that provides access to the water and to which boats are secured (555).

▸Figure 100–35

Electric Sign. A fixed, stationary, or portable self-contained, electrically operated and/or electrically illuminated piece of equipment with words or symbols designed to convey information or attract attention. ▸Figure 100–36

Electric Sign
Article 100 Definition
JVC
Copyright 2023, MikeHolt.com
Fixed, stationary, or portable equipment with illuminated words or symbols designed to convey information or attract attention.

▸Figure 100–36

Equipotential Plane. Conductive elements connected together to minimize voltage differences. ▸Figure 100–37

Exposed (as applied to wiring methods). On or attached to the surface of a building, or behind panels designed to allow access. ▸Figure 100–38

Feeder. The conductors between a service disconnect, transformer, generator, PV system output circuit, or other power-supply source and the branch-circuit overcurrent protective device. ▸Figure 100–39, ▸Figure 100–40, and ▸Figure 100–41

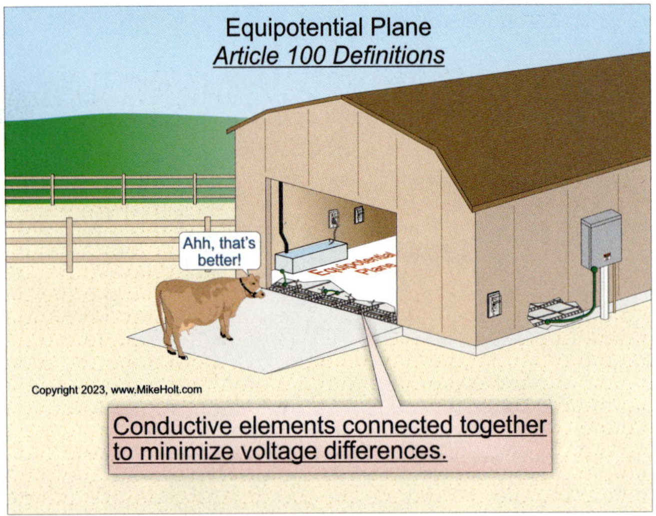
Equipotential Plane
Article 100 Definitions
Ahh, that's better!
Copyright 2023, www.MikeHolt.com
Conductive elements connected together to minimize voltage differences.

▸Figure 100–37

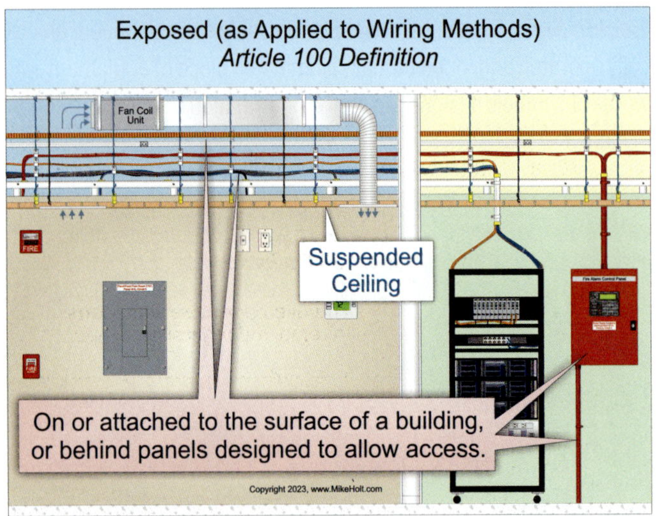
Exposed (as Applied to Wiring Methods)
Article 100 Definition
Fan Coil Unit
Suspended Ceiling
On or attached to the surface of a building, or behind panels designed to allow access.
Copyright 2023, www.MikeHolt.com

▸Figure 100–38

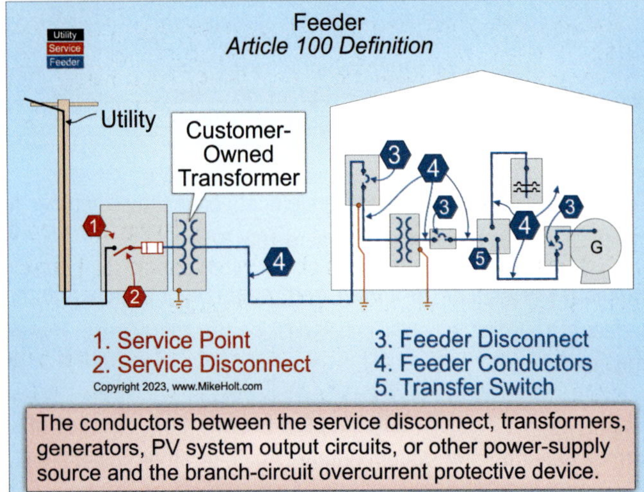
Feeder
Article 100 Definition
Utility
Service
Feeder
Utility
Customer-Owned Transformer
G
1. Service Point
2. Service Disconnect
3. Feeder Disconnect
4. Feeder Conductors
5. Transfer Switch
Copyright 2023, www.MikeHolt.com
The conductors between the service disconnect, transformers, generators, PV system output circuits, or other power-supply source and the branch-circuit overcurrent protective device.

▸Figure 100–39

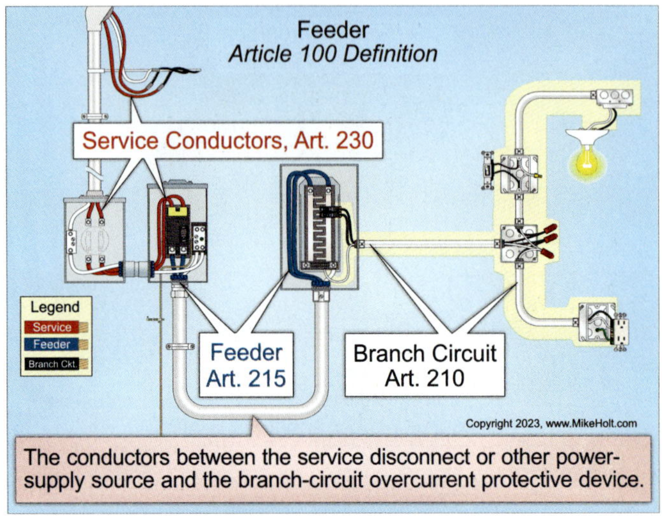
Feeder
Article 100 Definition
Service Conductors, Art. 230
Legend
Service
Feeder
Branch Ckt.
Feeder Art. 215
Branch Circuit Art. 210
Copyright 2023, www.MikeHolt.com
The conductors between the service disconnect or other power-supply source and the branch-circuit overcurrent protective device.

▸Figure 100–40

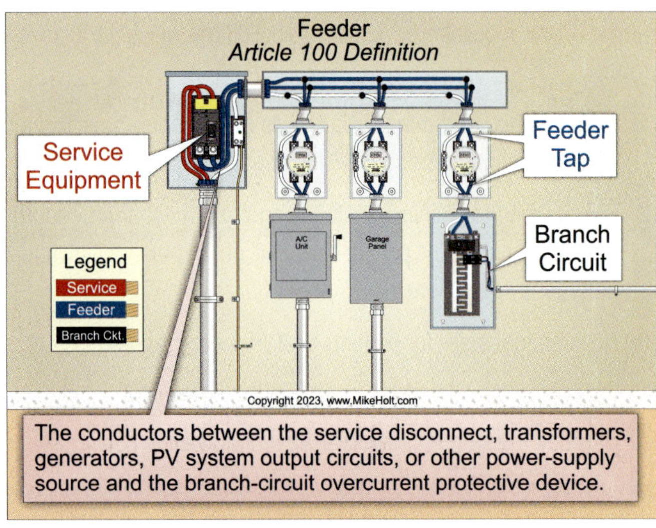
Feeder
Article 100 Definition
Service Equipment
Feeder Tap
Branch Circuit
Legend
Service
Feeder
Branch Ckt.
A/C Unit
Garage Panel
Copyright 2023, www.MikeHolt.com
The conductors between the service disconnect, transformers, generators, PV system output circuits, or other power-supply source and the branch-circuit overcurrent protective device.

▸Figure 100–41

Forming Shell. A housing designed to support a wet-niche luminaire (Article 680). ▸Figure 100–42

Fountain. An ornamental structure water feature from which one or more jets or streams of water are discharged into the air including splash pads, ornamental pools, display pools, or reflection pools. This definition does not include drinking water fountains or water coolers (Article 680). ▸Figure 100–43

Generator. A machine that converts mechanical energy into electrical energy by means of a prime mover or inverter. ▸Figure 100–44

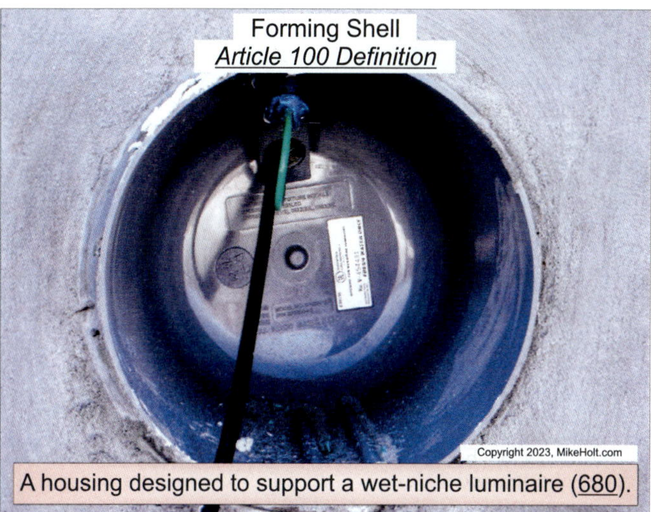
Forming Shell
Article 100 Definition
Copyright 2023, MikeHolt.com
A housing designed to support a wet-niche luminaire (680).

▸Figure 100–42

Fountain
Article 100 Definition
Copyright 2023, MikeHolt.com
An ornamental structure from which streams of water are discharged into splash pads, ornamental pools, display pools, or reflection pools.

▸Figure 100–43

Generator
Article 100 Definition
GENERAC
A machine that uses a prime mover to convert mechanical energy into electrical energy.

▸Figure 100–44

Ground. The Earth. ▸Figure 100–45

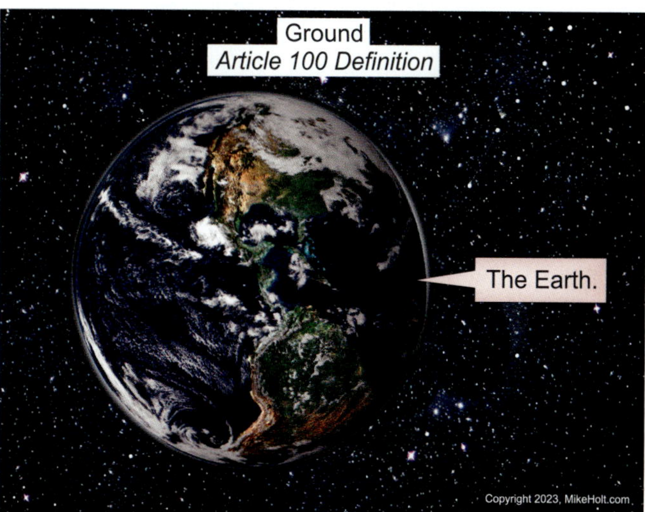
Ground
Article 100 Definition
The Earth.
Copyright 2023, MikeHolt.com

▸Figure 100–45

Ground Fault. An unintentional electrical connection between a phase conductor and equipment grounding conductors, metal parts of enclosures, metal raceways, or metal equipment. ▸Figure 100–46

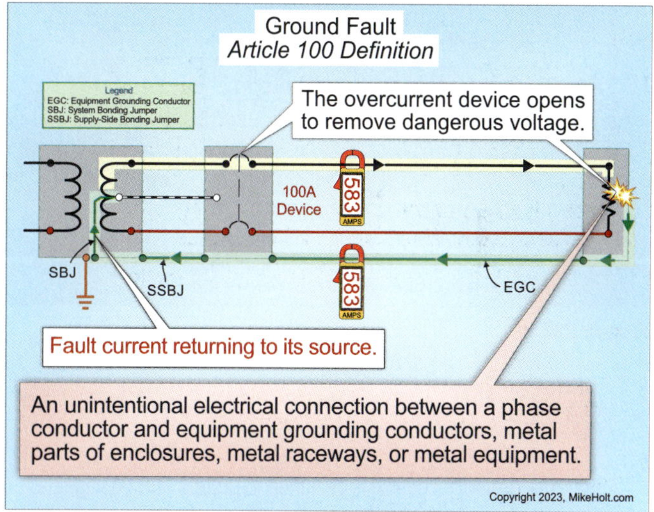
Ground Fault
Article 100 Definition
Legend
EGC: Equipment Grounding Conductor
SBJ: System Bonding Jumper
SSBJ: Supply-Side Bonding Jumper
The overcurrent device opens to remove dangerous voltage.
100A Device
SBJ
SSBJ
EGC
Fault current returning to its source.
An unintentional electrical connection between a phase conductor and equipment grounding conductors, metal parts of enclosures, metal raceways, or metal equipment.
Copyright 2023, MikeHolt.com

▸Figure 100–46

Ground-Fault Circuit Interrupter (GFCI). A device intended to protect people by de-energizing a circuit when ground-fault current exceeds the value established for a Class A device. ▸Figure 100–47

Note: A GFCI opens the circuit when the ground-fault current is 6 mA or higher, and it does not open when the ground-fault current is less than 4 mA. ▸Figure 100–48

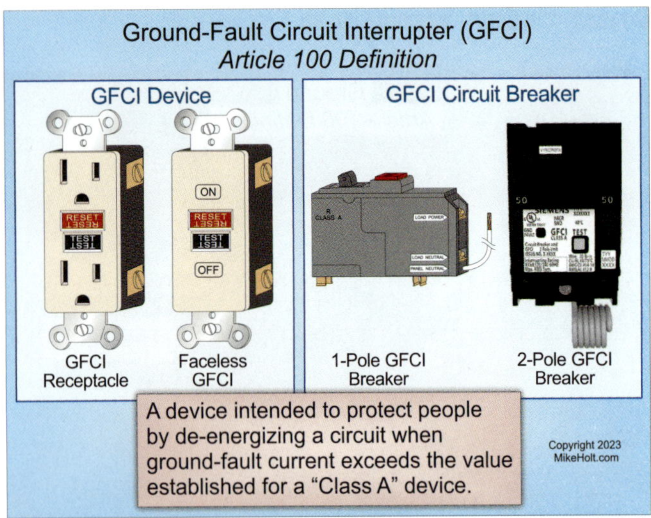
Ground-Fault Circuit Interrupter (GFCI)
Article 100 Definition
GFCI Device
GFCI Circuit Breaker
GFCI Receptacle
Faceless GFCI
1-Pole GFCI Breaker
2-Pole GFCI Breaker
A device intended to protect people by de-energizing a circuit when ground-fault current exceeds the value established for a "Class A" device.
Copyright 2023 MikeHolt.com

▸Figure 100–47

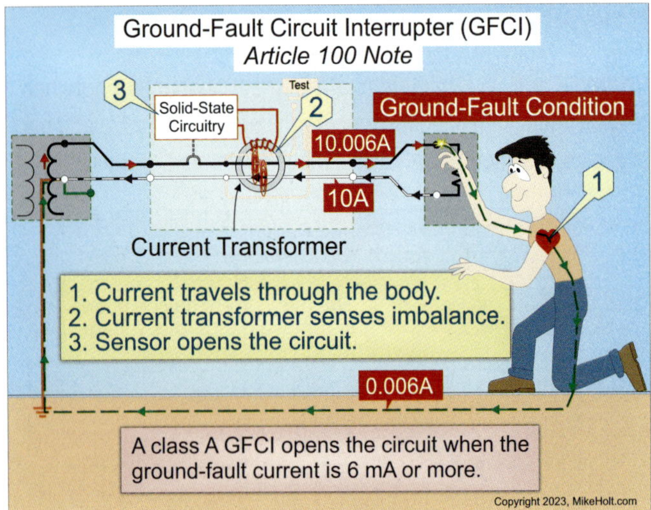
Ground-Fault Circuit Interrupter (GFCI)
Article 100 Note
Solid-State Circuitry
Test
Ground-Fault Condition
10.006A
10A
Current Transformer
1. Current travels through the body.
2. Current transformer senses imbalance.
3. Sensor opens the circuit.
0.006A
A class A GFCI opens the circuit when the ground-fault current is 6 mA or more.
Copyright 2023, MikeHolt.com

▸Figure 100–48

Author's Comment:

- A GFCI-protective device is designed to protect persons against electric shock and operates on the principle of monitoring the unbalanced current between the current-carrying circuit conductors. On a 120V circuit, the GFCI will monitor the unbalanced current between the phase and neutral conductors. On 240V circuits, monitoring is between circuit conductors. Receptacles, circuit breakers, cord sets, and other types of devices that incorporate GFCI protection are commercially available. ▸Figure 100–49
- GFCI devices should be tested monthly for functionality as recommended by the manufacturer's instructions.

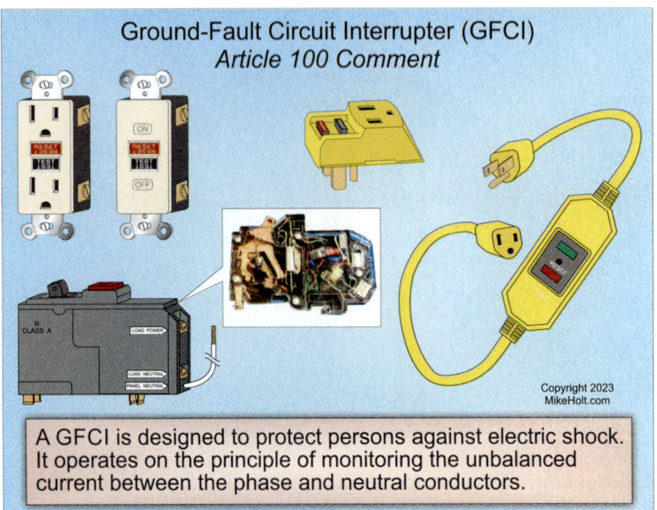
Ground-Fault Circuit Interrupter (GFCI)
Article 100 Comment
Copyright 2023 MikeHolt.com
A GFCI is designed to protect persons against electric shock. It operates on the principle of monitoring the unbalanced current between the phase and neutral conductors.

▸Figure 100–49

Ground-Fault Current Path, Effective (Effective Ground-Fault Current Path). An intentionally constructed low-impedance conductive path designed to carry ground-fault current during a ground-fault event to the power source. The purpose of the effective ground-fault current path is to assist in opening the circuit overcurrent protective device in the event of a ground fault. ▸Figure 100–50

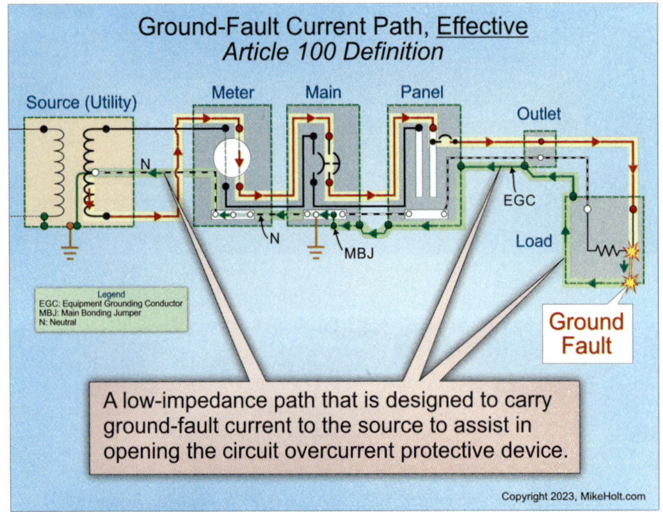
Ground-Fault Current Path, Effective
Article 100 Definition
Source (Utility)
Meter
Main
Panel
Outlet
N
EGC
Load
N
MBJ
Legend
EGC: Equipment Grounding Conductor
MBJ: Main Bonding Jumper
N: Neutral
Ground Fault
A low-impedance path that is designed to carry ground-fault current to the source to assist in opening the circuit overcurrent protective device.
Copyright 2023, MikeHolt.com

▸Figure 100–50

Author's Comment:

- The effective ground-fault current path is intended to help remove dangerous voltage from a ground fault by opening the circuit overcurrent protective device.

Grounded, Functionally (Functionally Grounded). A functionally grounded PV system that has an electrical ground reference for operational purposes that is not solidly grounded.

Note: A functionally grounded PV system is often connected to ground through an electronic means that is internal to an inverter or charge controller which provides ground-fault protection. Examples of operational purposes for functionally grounded systems include ground-fault detection and protection, as well as performance-related issues for some power sources.

Grounded (Grounding). Connected to the Earth (ground) or to a conductive body that extends the Earth connection. ▸Figure 100–51

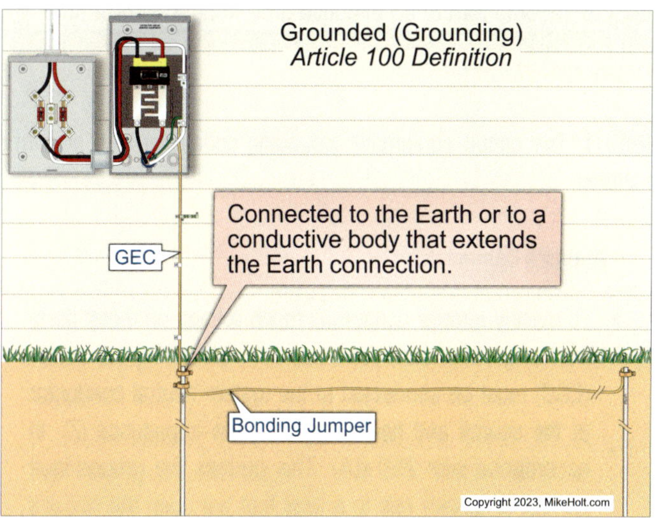
Grounded (Grounding)
Article 100 Definition
Connected to the Earth or to a conductive body that extends the Earth connection.
GEC
Bonding Jumper
Copyright 2023, MikeHolt.com

▸Figure 100–51

Author's Comment:

- An example of a "body that extends the ground (Earth) connection" is a termination to structural steel that is connected to the Earth either directly or by the termination to another grounding electrode in accordance with 250.52.

Grounded, Solidly (Solidly Grounded). Connected to ground (Earth) without inserting any resistor or impedance device. ▸Figure 100–52

Grounded Conductor. The system or circuit conductor intentionally connected to the ground (Earth). ▸Figure 100–53

Note: Although an equipment grounding conductor is grounded, it is not considered a grounded conductor.

<u>Grounded System, Impedance (Impedance Grounded System).</u> <u>An electrical system that is grounded by bonding the system neutral point to the metal parts of the enclosure through an impedance device.</u> ▸Figure 100–54

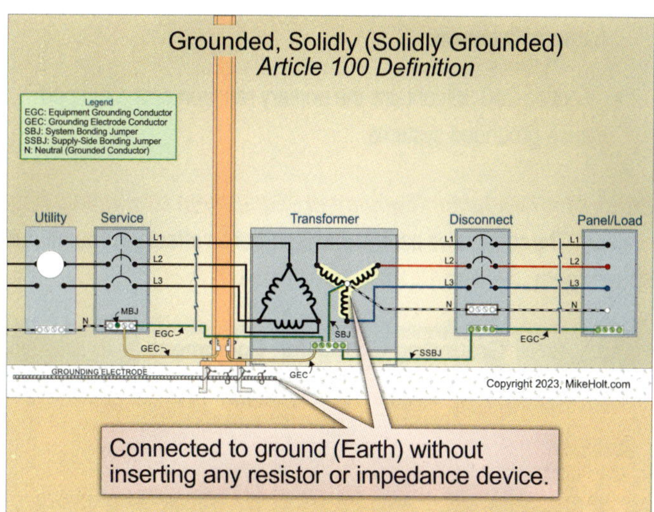
Grounded, Solidly (Solidly Grounded)
Article 100 Definition
Legend
EGC: Equipment Grounding Conductor
GEC: Grounding Electrode Conductor
SBJ: System Bonding Jumper
SSBJ: Supply-Side Bonding Jumper
N: Neutral (Grounded Conductor)
Utility
Service
Transformer
Disconnect
Panel/Load
L1
L2
L3
N
MBJ
EGC
GEC
SBJ
SSBJ
GROUNDING ELECTRODE
Copyright 2023, MikeHolt.com
Connected to ground (Earth) without inserting any resistor or impedance device.

▸Figure 100–52

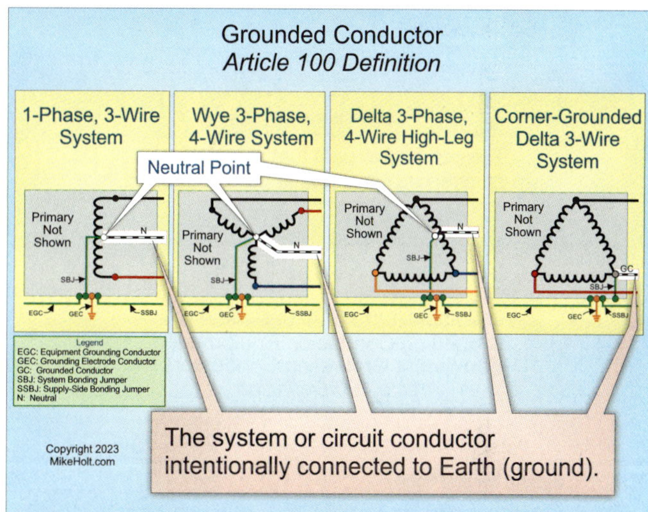
Grounded Conductor
Article 100 Definition
1-Phase, 3-Wire System
Wye 3-Phase, 4-Wire System
Delta 3-Phase, 4-Wire High-Leg System
Corner-Grounded Delta 3-Wire System
Neutral Point
Primary Not Shown
N
GC
SBJ
EGC
GEC
SSBJ
Legend
EGC: Equipment Grounding Conductor
GEC: Grounding Electrode Conductor
GC: Grounded Conductor
SBJ: System Bonding Jumper
SSBJ: Supply-Side Bonding Jumper
N: Neutral
Copyright 2023 MikeHolt.com
The system or circuit conductor intentionally connected to Earth (ground).

▸Figure 100–53

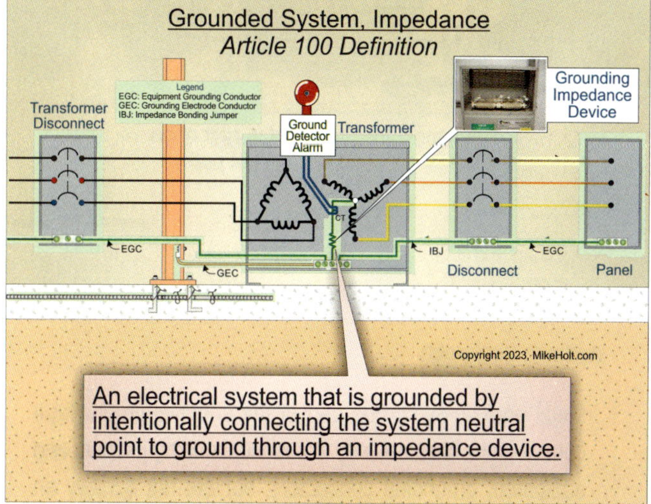
Grounded System, Impedance
Article 100 Definition
Legend
EGC: Equipment Grounding Conductor
GEC: Grounding Electrode Conductor
IBJ: Impedance Bonding Jumper
Transformer Disconnect
Ground Detector Alarm
Transformer
Grounding Impedance Device
CT
EGC
GEC
IBJ
Disconnect
Panel
Copyright 2023, MikeHolt.com
An electrical system that is grounded by intentionally connecting the system neutral point to ground through an impedance device.

▸Figure 100–54

Author's Comment:

- Section 250.36 contains the primary requirements for impedance grounded systems.

Grounding Conductor, Equipment (Equipment Grounding Conductor). The conductive path(s) that is part of an effective ground-fault current path. ▶**Figure 100–55** and ▶**Figure 100–56**

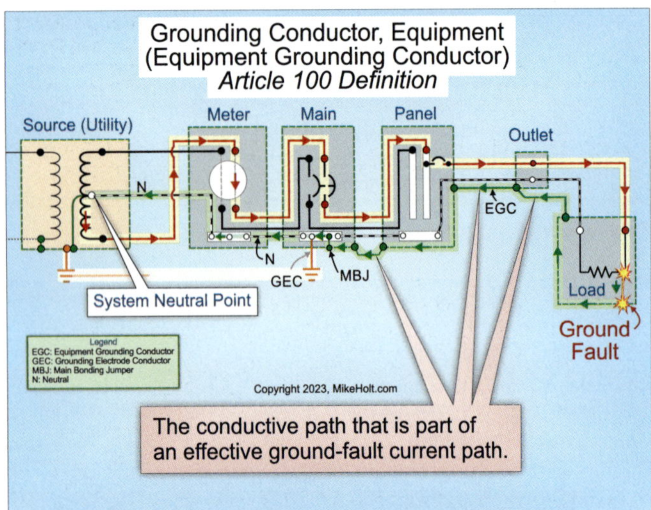

Grounding Conductor, Equipment
(Equipment Grounding Conductor)
Article 100 Definition
Source (Utility)
Meter
Main
Panel
Outlet
N
EGC
N
GEC
MBJ
System Neutral Point
Load
Ground Fault
Legend
EGC: Equipment Grounding Conductor
GEC: Grounding Electrode Conductor
MBJ: Main Bonding Jumper
N: Neutral
Copyright 2023, MikeHolt.com
The conductive path that is part of an effective ground-fault current path.

▶**Figure 100–55**

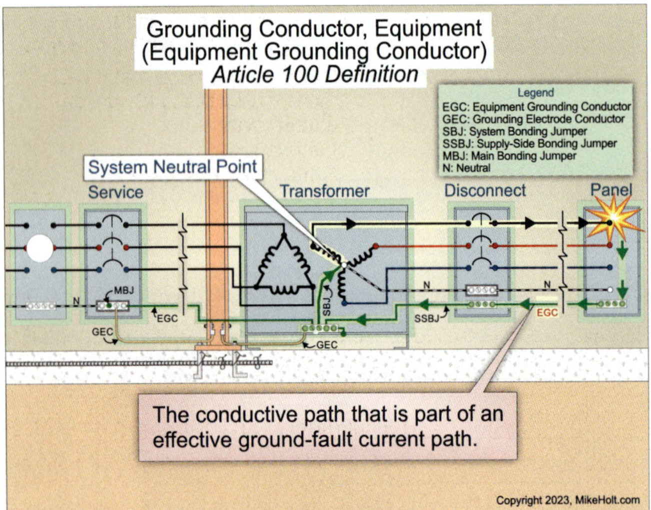

Grounding Conductor, Equipment
(Equipment Grounding Conductor)
Article 100 Definition
Legend
EGC: Equipment Grounding Conductor
GEC: Grounding Electrode Conductor
SBJ: System Bonding Jumper
SSBJ: Supply-Side Bonding Jumper
MBJ: Main Bonding Jumper
N: Neutral
System Neutral Point
Service
Transformer
Disconnect
Panel
MBJ
N
EGC
GEC
SBJ
SSBJ
GEC
N
N
EGC
The conductive path that is part of an effective ground-fault current path.
Copyright 2023, MikeHolt.com

▶**Figure 100–56**

Author's Comment:

- Metal enclosures can be part of the effective ground-fault current path. They are used to connect bonding jumpers and equipment grounding conductors, but are not actually an equipment grounding conductor [250.109]. ▶**Figure 100–57**

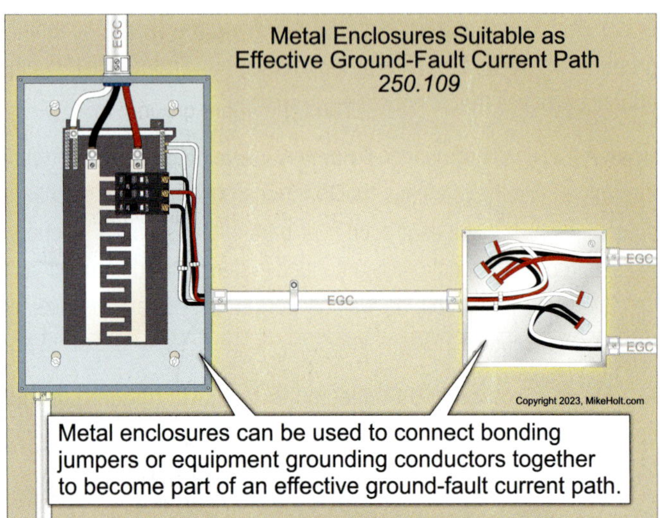

Metal Enclosures Suitable as
Effective Ground-Fault Current Path
250.109
EGC
EGC
EGC
EGC
Copyright 2023, MikeHolt.com
Metal enclosures can be used to connect bonding jumpers or equipment grounding conductors together to become part of an effective ground-fault current path.

▶**Figure 100–57**

Note 1: The circuit equipment grounding conductor also performs bonding.

Author's Comment:

- To quickly remove dangerous touch voltage on metal parts from a ground fault, the equipment grounding conductor (EGC) must be connected to the system neutral conductor at the source and have sufficiently low impedance (Z), in accordance with 250.4(A). This permits the ground-fault current to quickly rise to a level that will open the circuit's overcurrent protective device [250.4(A)(3)]. ▶**Figure 100–58**

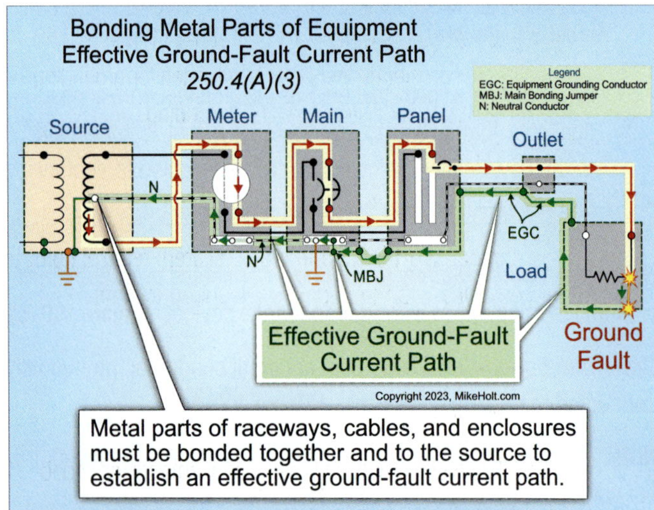

Bonding Metal Parts of Equipment
Effective Ground-Fault Current Path
250.4(A)(3)
Legend
EGC: Equipment Grounding Conductor
MBJ: Main Bonding Jumper
N: Neutral Conductor
Source
Meter
Main
Panel
Outlet
N
EGC
Load
N
MBJ
Effective Ground-Fault Current Path
Ground Fault
Copyright 2023, MikeHolt.com
Metal parts of raceways, cables, and enclosures must be bonded together and to the source to establish an effective ground-fault current path.

▶**Figure 100–58**

Note 2: An equipment grounding conductor can be any one or a combination of the types listed in 250.118(A). ▶**Figure 100–59**

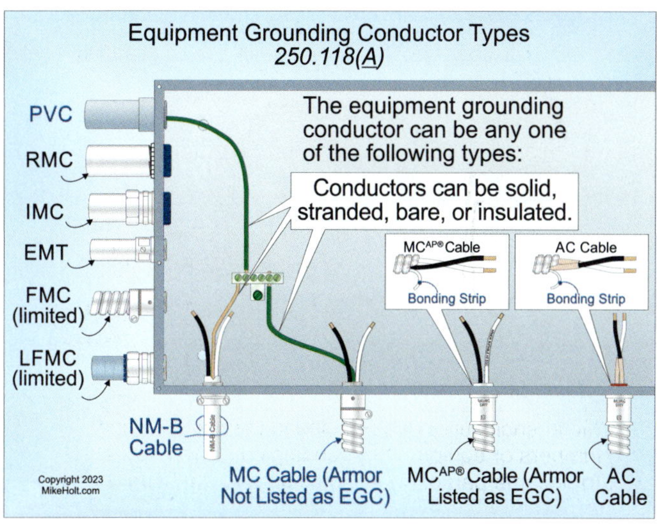
Equipment Grounding Conductor Types
250.118(A)
PVC
RMC
IMC
EMT
FMC (limited)
LFMC (limited)
The equipment grounding conductor can be any one of the following types:
Conductors can be solid, stranded, bare, or insulated.
MCAP® Cable
AC Cable
Bonding Strip
Bonding Strip
NM-B Cable
MC Cable (Armor Not Listed as EGC)
MCAP® Cable (Armor Listed as EGC)
AC Cable
Copyright 2023 MikeHolt.com

▶Figure 100–59

Author's Comment:

- Equipment grounding conductors include:
  - a bare or insulated conductor
  - rigid metal conduit
  - intermediate metal conduit
  - electrical metallic tubing
  - listed flexible metal conduit as limited by 250.118(A)(5)
  - listed liquidtight flexible metal conduit as limited by 250.118(A)(6)
  - armored cable
  - the copper metal sheath of mineral-insulated cable
  - metal-clad cable as limited by 250.118(A)(10)
  - metal cable trays as limited by 250.118(A)(11) and 392.60
  - electrically continuous metal raceways listed for grounding
  - surface metal raceways listed for grounding
  - metal enclosures

Grounding Conductor, Impedance (Impedance Grounding Conductor). A conductor that connects the system neutral point to the impedance device in an impedance grounded system. ▶Figure 100–60

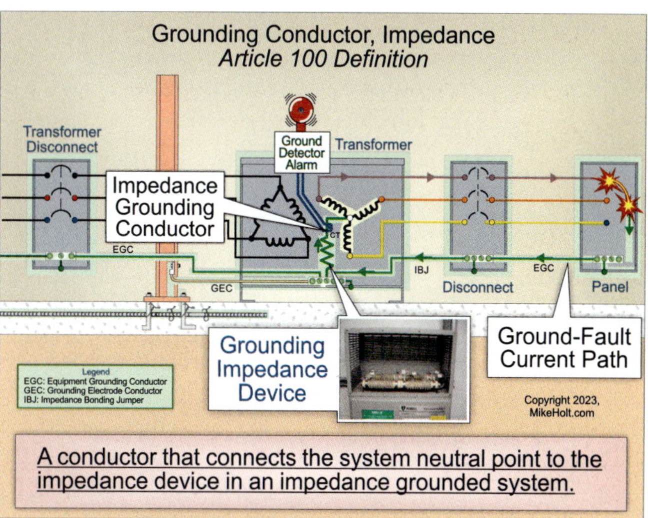
Grounding Conductor, Impedance
Article 100 Definition
Transformer Disconnect
Ground Detector Alarm
Transformer
Impedance Grounding Conductor
EGC
GEC
IBJ
Disconnect
EGC
Panel
Grounding Impedance Device
Ground-Fault Current Path
Legend
EGC: Equipment Grounding Conductor
GEC: Grounding Electrode Conductor
IBJ: Impedance Bonding Jumper
Copyright 2023, MikeHolt.com
A conductor that connects the system neutral point to the impedance device in an impedance grounded system.

▶Figure 100–60

Author's Comment:

- Section 250.36 contains the primary requirements for impedance grounding conductors.

Grounding Electrode. A conducting object used to make a direct electrical connection to the Earth [250.50 through 250.70]. ▶Figure 100–61

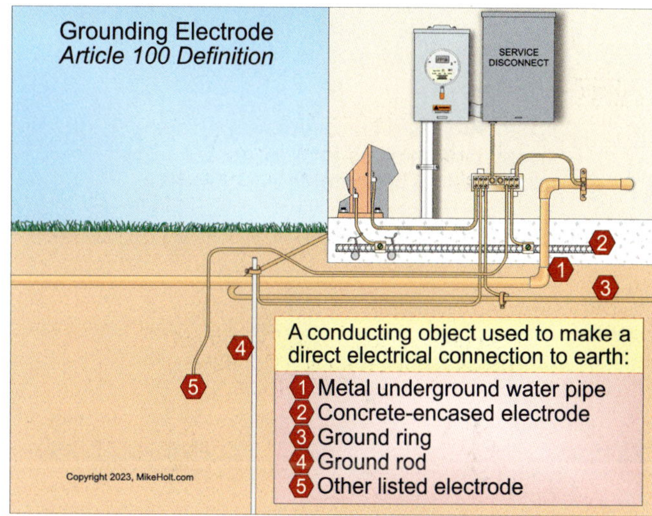
Grounding Electrode
Article 100 Definition
SERVICE DISCONNECT
A conducting object used to make a direct electrical connection to earth:
1 Metal underground water pipe
2 Concrete-encased electrode
3 Ground ring
4 Ground rod
5 Other listed electrode
Copyright 2023, MikeHolt.com

▶Figure 100–61

Grounding Electrode Conductor (GEC). The conductor used to connect the system neutral conductor, grounded-phase conductor, or the equipment to the grounding electrode system. ▶Figure 100–62

Handhole Enclosure. An underground enclosure with an open or closed bottom that is sized to allow personnel to reach into but not enter the enclosure. ▶Figure 100–63

Author's Comment:

- For the installation requirements for handhole enclosures, see 314.30.

Health Care Facilities. Buildings, portions of buildings, or mobile enclosures in which medical, dental, psychiatric, nursing, obstetrical, or surgical care is provided for humans.

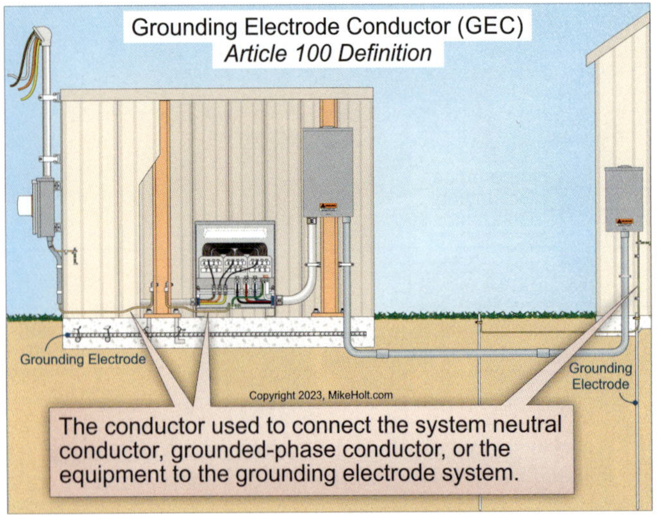
Grounding Electrode Conductor (GEC)
Article 100 Definition
Grounding Electrode
Grounding Electrode
Copyright 2023, MikeHolt.com
The conductor used to connect the system neutral conductor, grounded-phase conductor, or the equipment to the grounding electrode system.

▸Figure 100–62

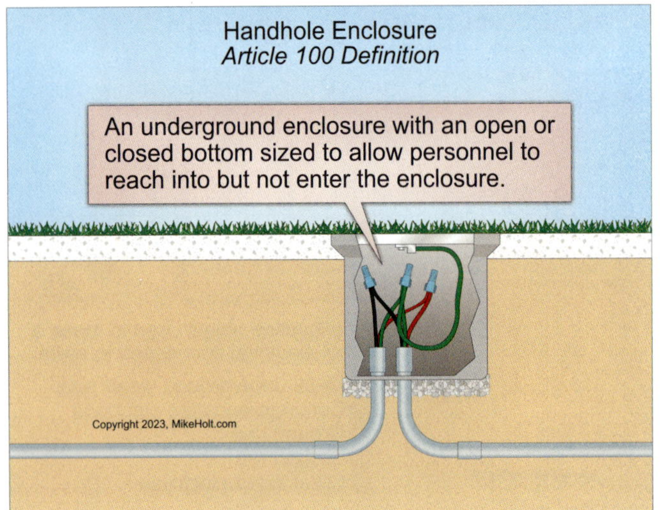
Handhole Enclosure
Article 100 Definition
An underground enclosure with an open or closed bottom sized to allow personnel to reach into but not enter the enclosure.
Copyright 2023, MikeHolt.com

▸Figure 100–63

Note: Examples of health care facilities include, but are not limited to, hospitals, nursing homes, limited-care facilities, supervisory-care facilities, clinics, medical/dental offices, and ambulatory care facilities.

Hermetic Refrigerant Motor-Compressor. A compressor and motor enclosed in the same housing and operating in refrigerant. ▸Figure 100–64

Hydromassage Bathtub. A permanently installed bathtub with a recirculating piping system designed to accept, circulate, and discharge water after each use (Article 680). ▸Figure 100–65

Identified (as applied to equipment). Recognized as suitable for a specific purpose, function, use, environment, or application. ▸Figure 100–66

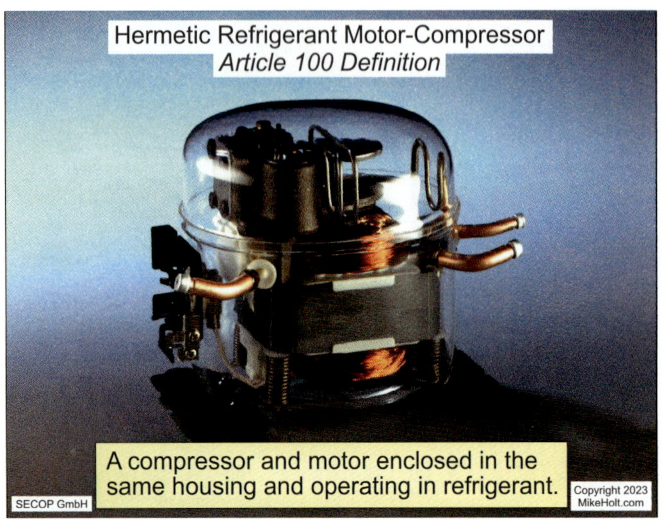
Hermetic Refrigerant Motor-Compressor
Article 100 Definition
A compressor and motor enclosed in the same housing and operating in refrigerant.
SECOP GmbH
Copyright 2023 MikeHolt.com

▸Figure 100–64

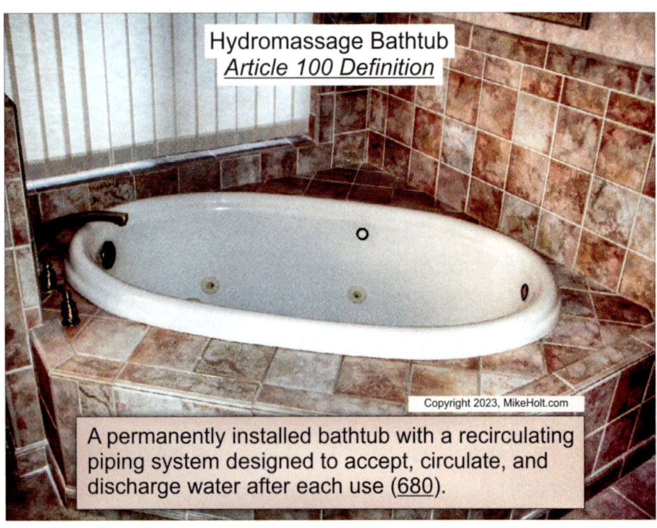
Hydromassage Bathtub
Article 100 Definition
Copyright 2023, MikeHolt.com
A permanently installed bathtub with a recirculating piping system designed to accept, circulate, and discharge water after each use (680).

▸Figure 100–65

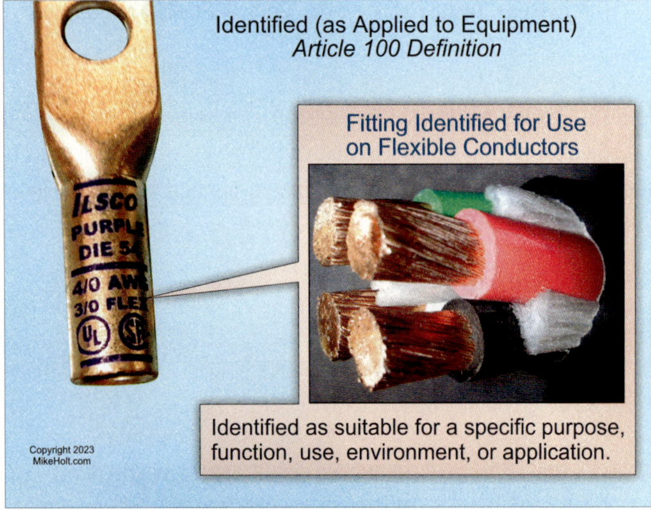
Identified (as Applied to Equipment)
Article 100 Definition
Fitting Identified for Use on Flexible Conductors
Identified as suitable for a specific purpose, function, use, environment, or application.
Copyright 2023 MikeHolt.com

▸Figure 100–66

Author's Comment:

- According to 110.3(A)(1) Note 2, "Suitability of equipment use may be identified by a description marked on, or provided with, a product to identify the suitability of the product for a specific purpose, environment, or application. Special conditions of use or other limitations may be marked on the equipment, in the product instructions, or included in the appropriate listing and labeling information. Suitability of equipment may be evidenced by listing or labeling."

Information Technology Equipment (ITE). Equipment used for the creation and manipulation of data, voice, and video. ▸Figure 100–67

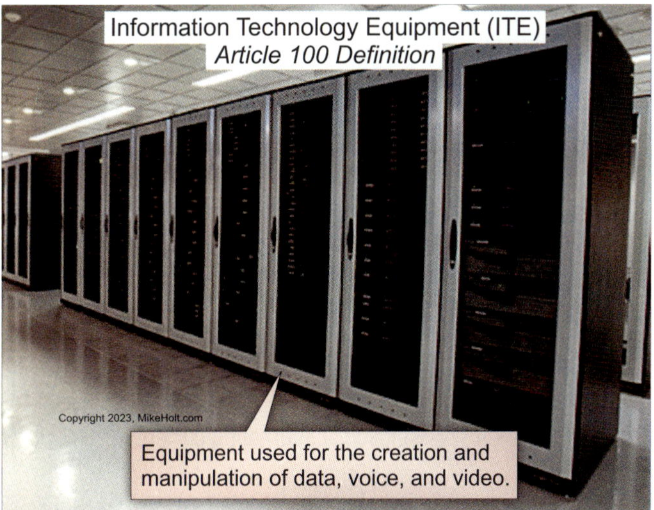
Information Technology Equipment (ITE)
Article 100 Definition
Copyright 2023, MikeHolt.com
Equipment used for the creation and manipulation of data, voice, and video.

▸Figure 100–67

Intersystem Bonding Termination. A device that provides a means to connect intersystem bonding conductors for communications systems to the grounding electrode system in accordance with 250.94. ▸Figure 100–68

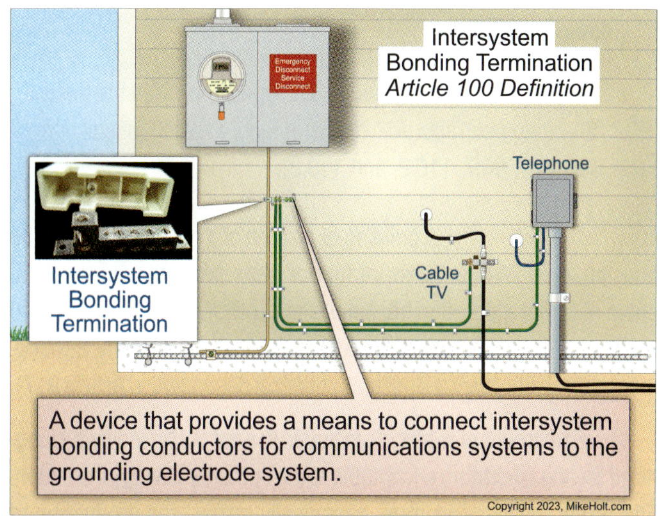
Intersystem Bonding Termination
Article 100 Definition
Telephone
Cable TV
Intersystem Bonding Termination
A device that provides a means to connect intersystem bonding conductors for communications systems to the grounding electrode system.
Copyright 2023, MikeHolt.com

▸Figure 100–68

Inverter. Equipment that changes direct current to alternating current. ▸Figure 100–69

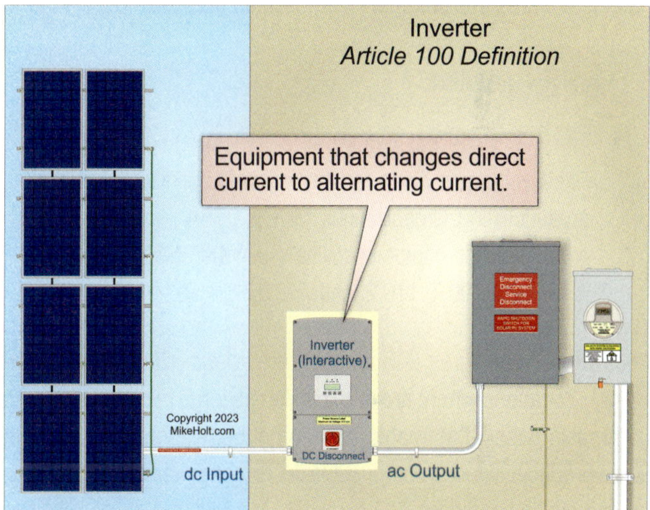
Inverter
Article 100 Definition
Equipment that changes direct current to alternating current.
Inverter (Interactive)
DC Disconnect
Copyright 2023 MikeHolt.com
dc Input
ac Output

▸Figure 100–69

Labeled. Equipment or materials that have a label, symbol, or other identifying mark in the form of a sticker, decal, printed label, or with the identifying mark molded or stamped into the product by a recognized testing laboratory acceptable to the authority having jurisdiction. ▸Figure 100–70

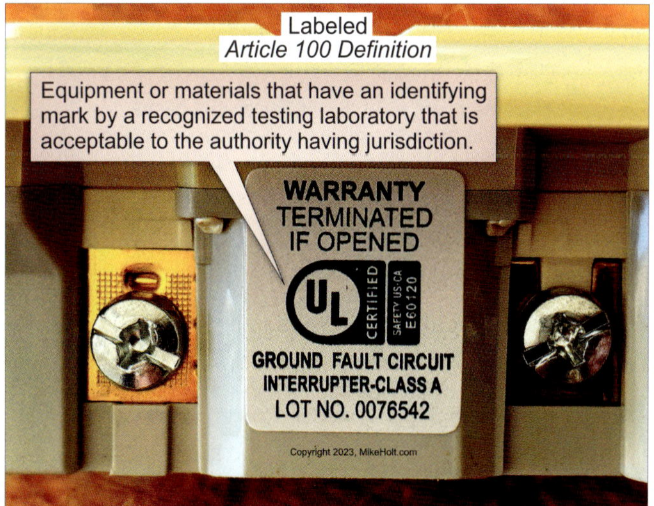
Labeled
Article 100 Definition
Equipment or materials that have an identifying mark by a recognized testing laboratory that is acceptable to the authority having jurisdiction.
WARRANTY TERMINATED IF OPENED
UL CERTIFIED
SAFETY US-CA E60120
GROUND FAULT CIRCUIT INTERRUPTER-CLASS A
LOT NO. 0076542
Copyright 2023, MikeHolt.com

▸Figure 100–70

Note: When a listed product is of such a size, shape, material, or surface texture that it is not possible to legibly apply the complete label to the product, it may appear on the smallest unit container in which the product is packaged.

Author's Comment:

- Labeling and listing of equipment typically provide the basis for equipment approval by the authority having jurisdiction [90.4(B), 90.7, 110.2, and 110.3].

Limited-Care Facility. A building or an area of a building used for the housing, on a 24-hour basis, of four or more persons who are incapable of self-preservation because of age, physical limitations due to accident or illness, or limitations such as intellectual disability, developmental disability, mental illness, or chemical dependency (Article 517).

Listed. Equipment or materials included in a list published by a recognized testing laboratory acceptable to the authority having jurisdiction. The listing organization must periodically inspect the production of listed equipment or material to ensure they meet appropriate designated standards and suitable for a specified purpose.

Author's Comment:

- The *NEC* does not require all electrical equipment to be listed, but some *Code* requirements do specifically call for product listing. Organizations such as OSHA are increasingly requiring listed equipment to be used when such equipment is available [90.7, 110.2, and 110.3].

Locations, Hazardous (Classified) Hazardous (Classified) Locations). Locations where fire or explosion hazards might exist due to flammable gases, flammable liquid-produced vapors, combustible liquid-produced vapors, combustible dusts, combustible fiber/flyings, or ignitible fibers/flyings. ▸Figure 100–71

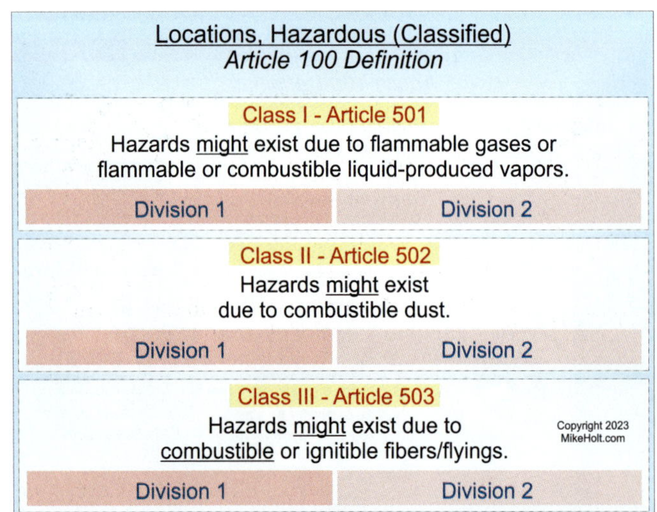
Locations, Hazardous (Classified)
Article 100 Definition
Class I - Article 501
Hazards might exist due to flammable gases or flammable or combustible liquid-produced vapors.
Division 1
Division 2
Class II - Article 502
Hazards might exist due to combustible dust.
Division 1
Division 2
Class III - Article 503
Hazards might exist due to combustible or ignitible fibers/flyings.
Copyright 2023 MikeHolt.com
Division 1
Division 2

▸Figure 100–71

Author's Comment:

- Article 500 contains important information about hazardous (classified) locations.

Low-Voltage Contact Limit. A voltage not exceeding the following values (Article 680): ▸Figure 100–72

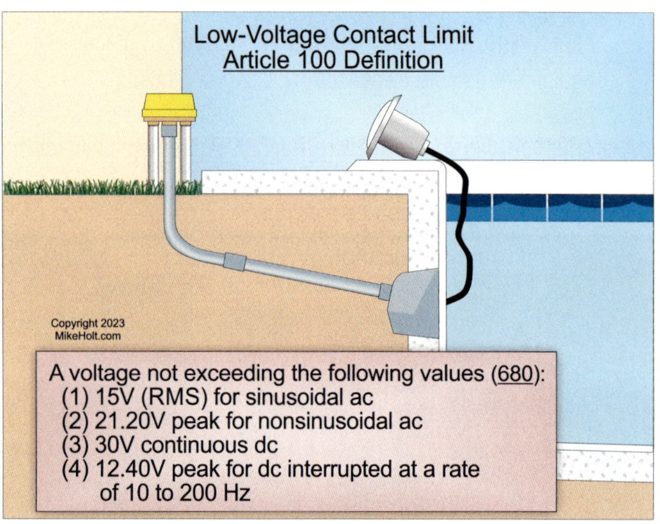
Low-Voltage Contact Limit
Article 100 Definition
Copyright 2023 MikeHolt.com
A voltage not exceeding the following values (680):
(1) 15V (RMS) for sinusoidal ac
(2) 21.20V peak for nonsinusoidal ac
(3) 30V continuous dc
(4) 12.40V peak for dc interrupted at a rate of 10 to 200 Hz

▸Figure 100–72

(1) 15V (RMS) for sinusoidal alternating current

(2) 21.20V peak for nonsinusoidal alternating current

(3) 30V for continuous direct current

(4) 12.40V peak for direct current that is interrupted at a rate of 10 to 200 Hz

Luminaire. A complete lighting unit consisting of a light source with parts designed to position the light source and connect it to the power supply. It may also include parts to protect and distribute the light. ▸Figure 100–73

Luminaire, Wet-Niche (Wet-Niche Luminaire). A luminaire intended to be installed in a forming shell where it will be completely surrounded by water (Article 680). ▸Figure 100–74

Marina. A facility, generally on the waterfront, which stores and services boats in berths, on moorings, and in dry storage or dry stack storage (Article 555).

Multioutlet Assembly. A surface, flush, or freestanding assembly containing receptacles. ▸Figure 100–75

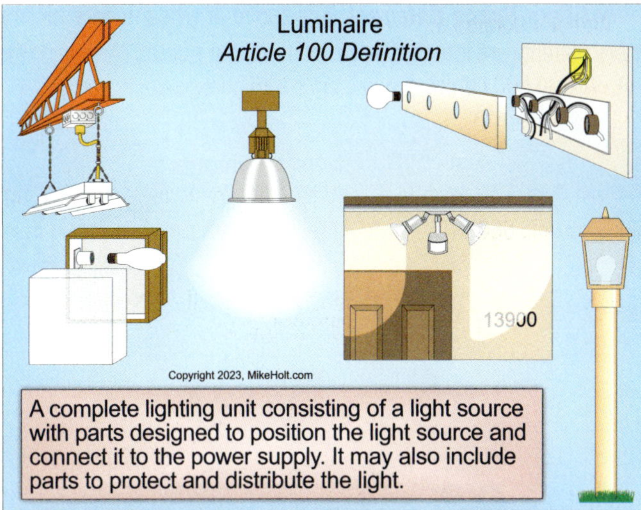
Luminaire
Article 100 Definition
13900
Copyright 2023, MikeHolt.com
A complete lighting unit consisting of a light source with parts designed to position the light source and connect it to the power supply. It may also include parts to protect and distribute the light.

▸Figure 100–73

Luminaire, Wet-Niche
Article 100 Definition
WARNING
RISK OF ELECTRICAL SHOCK OR ELECTROCUTION
Copyright 2023, MikeHolt.com
A luminaire intended to be installed in a forming shell where it will be completely surrounded by water (680).

▸Figure 100–74

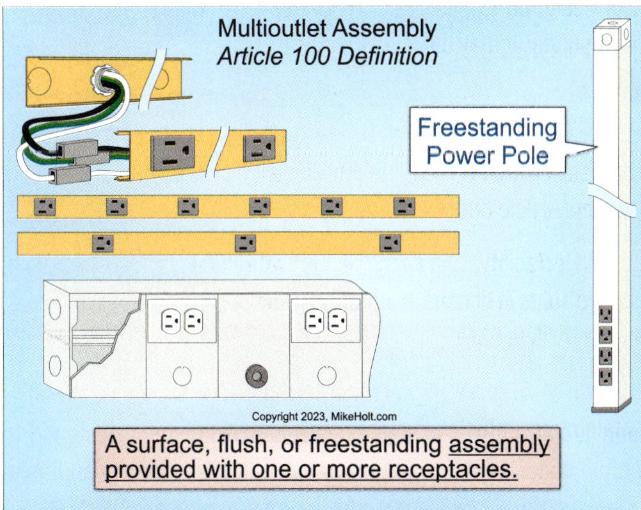
Multioutlet Assembly
Article 100 Definition
Freestanding Power Pole
Copyright 2023, MikeHolt.com
A surface, flush, or freestanding assembly provided with one or more receptacles.

▸Figure 100–75

Author's Comment:

- Portable assemblies such as power strips are relocatable power taps, not multioutlet assemblies. ▸Figure 100–76

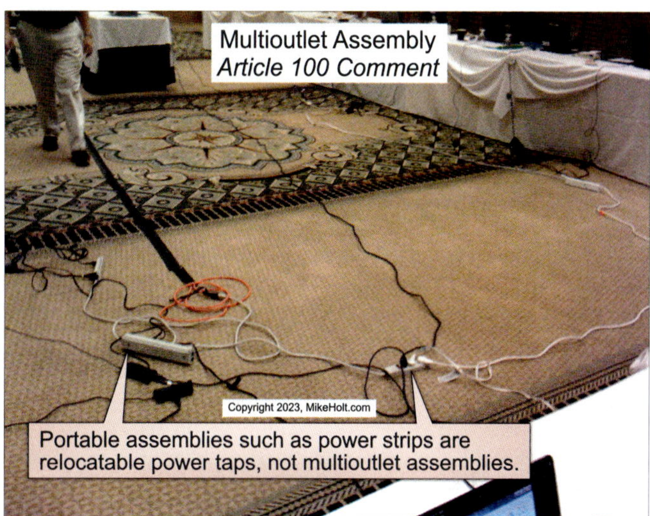
Multioutlet Assembly
Article 100 Comment
Copyright 2023, MikeHolt.com
Portable assemblies such as power strips are relocatable power taps, not multioutlet assemblies.

▸Figure 100–76

- Article 380 contains the primary requirements for multioutlet assemblies.

Neutral Conductor. The conductor connected to the neutral point of a system that is intended to carry current under normal conditions. ▸Figure 100–77

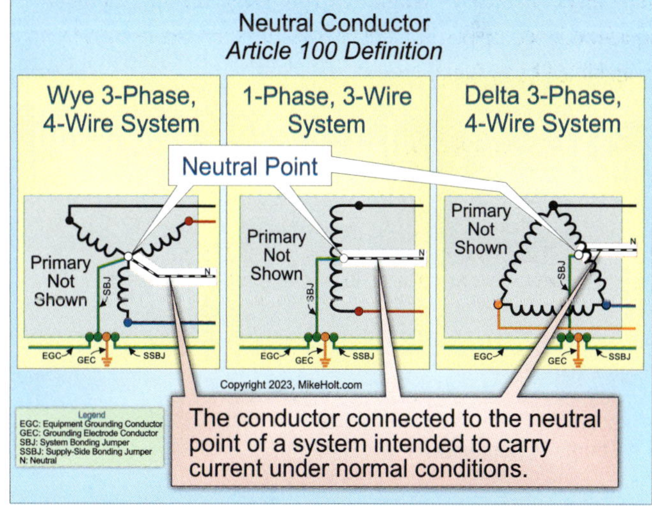
Neutral Conductor
Article 100 Definition
Wye 3-Phase, 4-Wire System
1-Phase, 3-Wire System
Delta 3-Phase, 4-Wire System
Neutral Point
Primary Not Shown
Primary Not Shown
Primary Not Shown
SBJ
N
EGC
GEC
SSBJ
Copyright 2023, MikeHolt.com
Legend
EGC: Equipment Grounding Conductor
GEC: Grounding Electrode Conductor
SBJ: System Bonding Jumper
SSBJ: Supply-Side Bonding Jumper
N: Neutral
The conductor connected to the neutral point of a system intended to carry current under normal conditions.

▸Figure 100–77

Neutral Point. The common point of a 4-wire, three-phase, wye-connected system; the midpoint of a 3-wire, single-phase system; or the midpoint of the single-phase portion of a three-phase, delta-connected system. ▸Figure 100–78

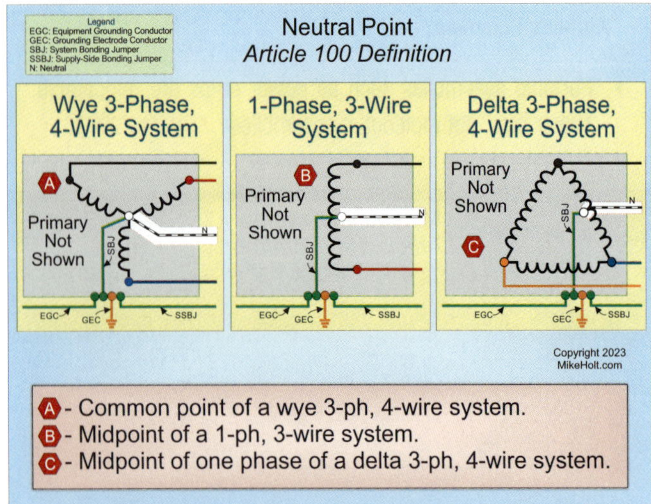
Neutral Point
Article 100 Definition
Legend
EGC: Equipment Grounding Conductor
GEC: Grounding Electrode Conductor
SBJ: System Bonding Jumper
SSBJ: Supply-Side Bonding Jumper
N: Neutral
Wye 3-Phase, 4-Wire System
Primary Not Shown
1-Phase, 3-Wire System
Primary Not Shown
Delta 3-Phase, 4-Wire System
Primary Not Shown
Copyright 2023 MikeHolt.com
A - Common point of a wye 3-ph, 4-wire system.
B - Midpoint of a 1-ph, 3-wire system.
C - Midpoint of one phase of a delta 3-ph, 4-wire system.

▶Figure 100–78

Overcurrent Protective Device, Branch-Circuit (Branch-Circuit Overcurrent Protective Device). A device capable of providing protection from an overload, short circuit, or ground fault for service, feeder, and branch circuits.

Panelboard. An assembly with buses and overcurrent protective devices designed to be placed in a cabinet or enclosure. ▶Figure 100–79

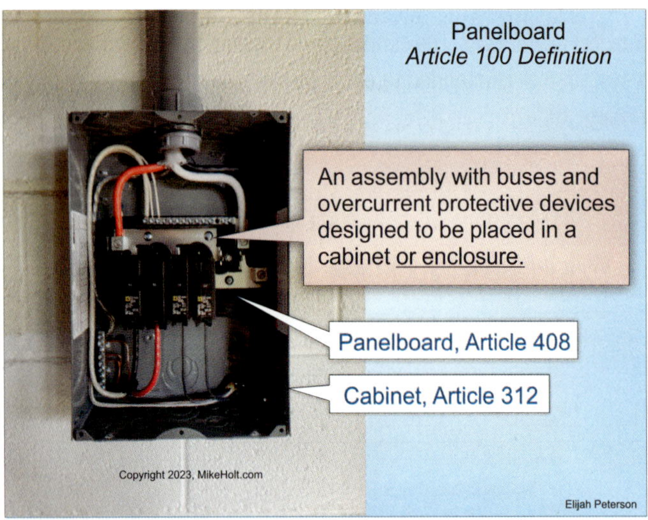
Panelboard
Article 100 Definition
An assembly with buses and overcurrent protective devices designed to be placed in a cabinet or enclosure.
Panelboard, Article 408
Cabinet, Article 312
Copyright 2023, MikeHolt.com
Elijah Peterson

▶Figure 100–79

Author's Comment:

- The slang term in the electrical field for a panelboard is "the guts." The requirements for panelboards are contained in Article 408.

Patient Bed Location. The location of an inpatient sleeping bed of a Category 1 space (Article 517).

Patient Care Space Category. Any space of a health care facility where patients are intended to be examined or treated (Article 517). ▶Figure 100–80

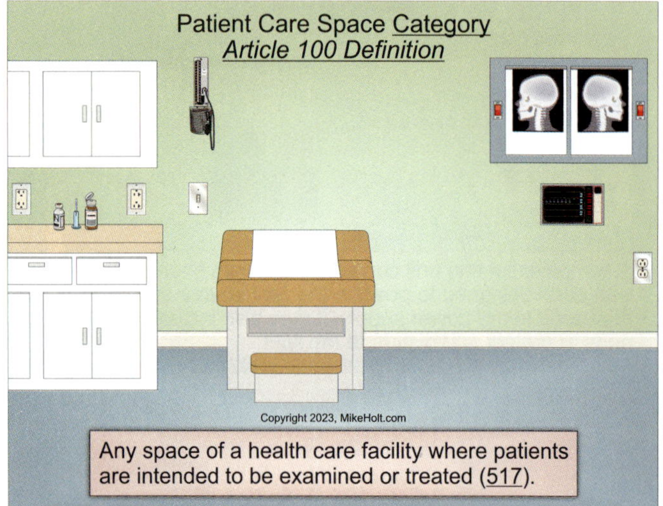
Patient Care Space Category
Article 100 Definition
Copyright 2023, MikeHolt.com
Any space of a health care facility where patients are intended to be examined or treated (517).

▶Figure 100–80

Note 2: Business offices, corridors, lounges, day rooms, dining rooms, or similar areas are not classified as patient care spaces.

Patient Care Vicinity. A space extending 6 ft beyond the patient bed, chair, table, treadmill (or other device that supports the patient during examination and treatment), and extending vertically to 7 ft 6 in. above the floor (Article 517). ▶Figure 100–81

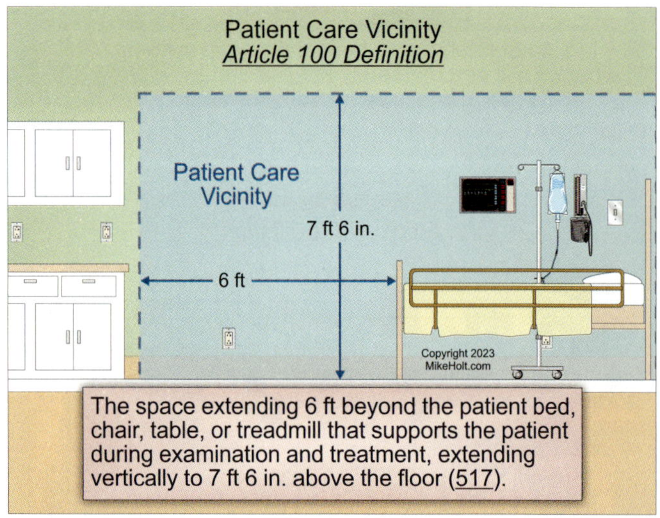
Patient Care Vicinity
Article 100 Definition
Patient Care Vicinity
7 ft 6 in.
6 ft
Copyright 2023 MikeHolt.com
The space extending 6 ft beyond the patient bed, chair, table, or treadmill that supports the patient during examination and treatment, extending vertically to 7 ft 6 in. above the floor (517).

▶Figure 100–81

Pool. Manufactured or field-constructed equipment designed to contain water on a permanent or semipermanent basis and used for swimming, wading, immersion, or other purposes (Article 680).

Author's Comment:

- The definition of a pool includes baptisteries (immersion pools) which must comply with the requirements of Article 680.
- An aboveground pool having a maximum water depth greater than 42 in. is considered a permanent pool. See the definition of "storable pool."

Pool, Permanently Installed (Permanently Installed Pool). Pools constructed or installed in the ground or partially in the ground, and pools installed inside of a building (Article 680). ▸Figure 100–82

Pool, Permanently Installed
Article 100 Definition
Copyright 2023
MikeHolt.com
A pool constructed or installed in the ground or partially in the ground, and all pools installed inside of a building (680).

▸Figure 100–82

Pool, Storable (Storable Pool). A pool installed entirely on or above the ground designed for ease of relocation regardless of water depth (Article 680). ▸Figure 100–83

Pool, Storable
Article 100 Definition
Copyright 2023, www.MikeHolt.com
A pool installed entirely on or above the ground designed for ease of relocation regardless of water depth (680).

▸Figure 100–83

PV Module. A PV module is a unit of environmentally protected solar cells and components designed to produce dc power. ▸Figure 100–84

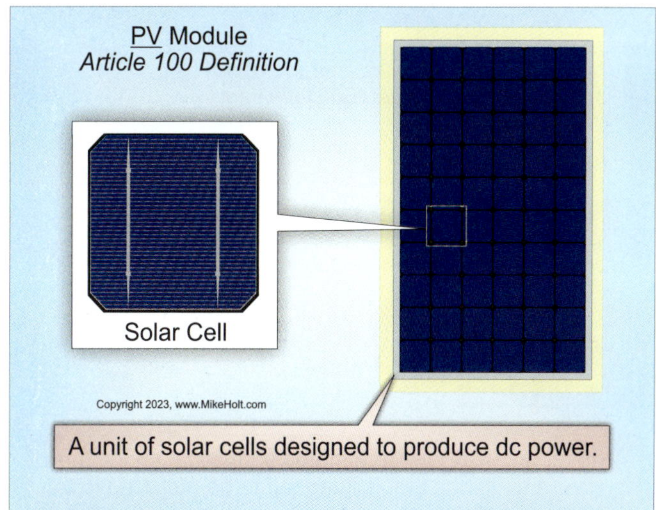
PV Module
Article 100 Definition
Solar Cell
Copyright 2023, www.MikeHolt.com
A unit of solar cells designed to produce dc power.

▸Figure 100–84

Author's Comment:

- PV modules use sunlight to generate dc electricity by using light (photons) to move electrons in a semiconductor. This is known as the "photovoltaic effect."

PV System. The components, circuits, and equipment up to and including the PV system disconnect, that in combination convert solar energy into electrical energy. ▸Figure 100–85

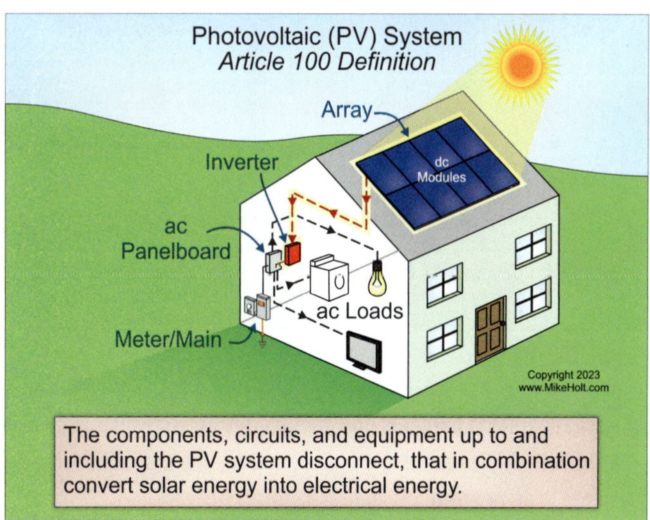
Photovoltaic (PV) System
Article 100 Definition
Array
Inverter
dc Modules
ac Panelboard
ac Loads
Meter/Main
Copyright 2023
www.MikeHolt.com
The components, circuits, and equipment up to and including the PV system disconnect, that in combination convert solar energy into electrical energy.

▸Figure 100–85

Raceway, Surface Metal (Surface Metal Raceway). A metal raceway with associated fittings in which conductors are placed after the raceway has been installed as a complete system. ▸Figure 100–86

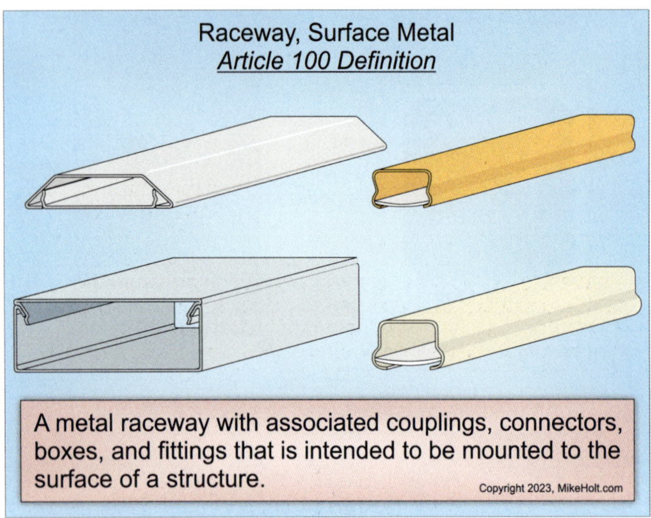
Raceway, Surface Metal
Article 100 Definition
A metal raceway with associated couplings, connectors, boxes, and fittings that is intended to be mounted to the surface of a structure.
Copyright 2023, MikeHolt.com

▸Figure 100–86

Receptacle. A contact device installed at an outlet for the connection of an attachment plug, or for the connection of equipment designed to mate with the contact device. ▸Figure 100–87

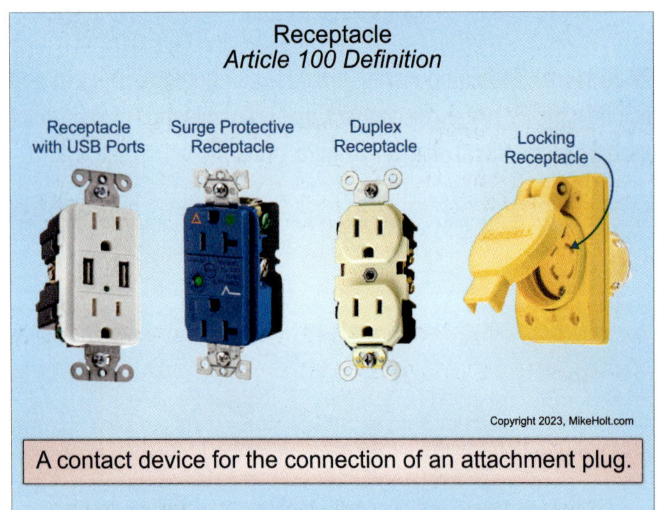
Receptacle
Article 100 Definition
Receptacle with USB Ports
Surge Protective Receptacle
Duplex Receptacle
Locking Receptacle
Copyright 2023, MikeHolt.com
A contact device for the connection of an attachment plug.

▸Figure 100–87

A single receptacle contains one contact device on the same a yoke or strap. A multiple receptacle has more than one contact device on the same yoke or strap. ▸Figure 100–88

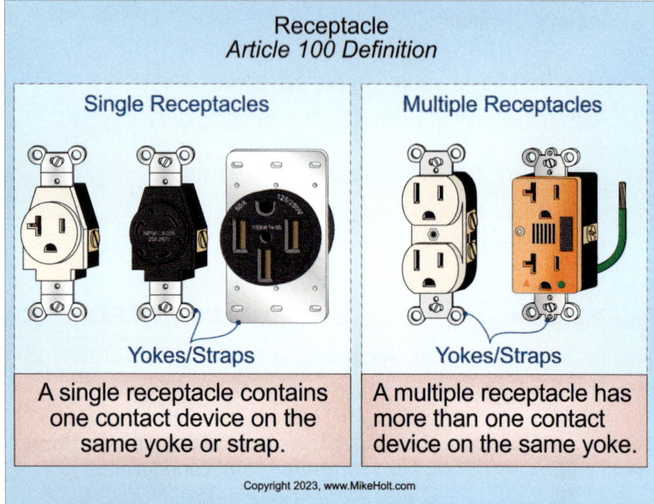
Receptacle
Article 100 Definition
Single Receptacles
Multiple Receptacles
Yokes/Straps
Yokes/Straps
A single receptacle contains one contact device on the same yoke or strap.
A multiple receptacle has more than one contact device on the same yoke.
Copyright 2023, www.MikeHolt.com

▸Figure 100–88

Author's Comment:

- A yoke (also called a "strap") is the metal mounting structure for such items as receptacles, switches, switches with pilot lights, and switch/receptacles to name a few.

Note: A duplex receptacle is an example of a multiple receptacle with two receptacles on the same yoke or strap.

Separately Derived System. An electrical power supply output having no direct connection(s) to the circuit conductors of any other electrical source other than those established by grounding and bonding connections. ▸Figure 100–89 and ▸Figure 100–90

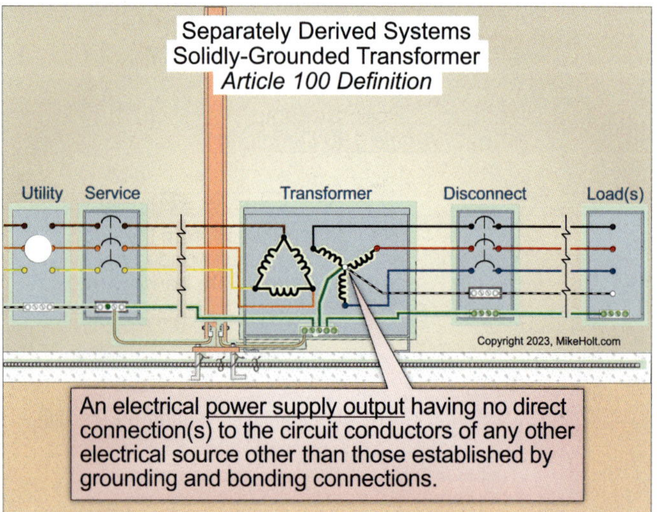
Separately Derived Systems
Solidly-Grounded Transformer
Article 100 Definition
Utility
Service
Transformer
Disconnect
Load(s)
Copyright 2023, MikeHolt.com
An electrical power supply output having no direct connection(s) to the circuit conductors of any other electrical source other than those established by grounding and bonding connections.

▸Figure 100–89

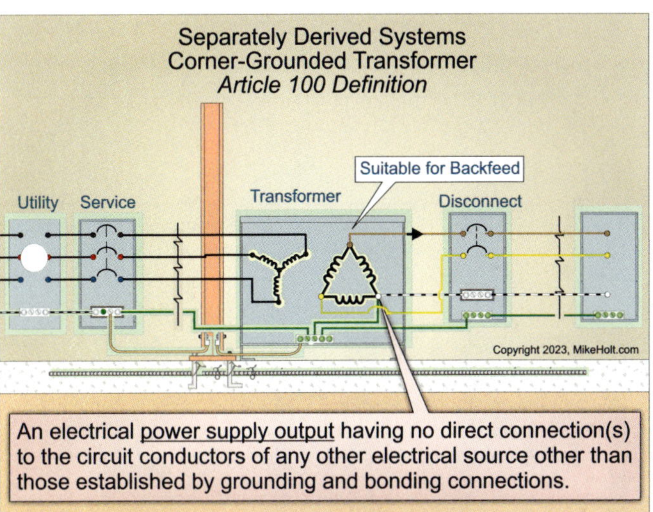
Separately Derived Systems
Corner-Grounded Transformer
Article 100 Definition
Suitable for Backfeed
Utility
Service
Transformer
Disconnect
Copyright 2023, MikeHolt.com
An electrical power supply output having no direct connection(s) to the circuit conductors of any other electrical source other than those established by grounding and bonding connections.

▸Figure 100–90

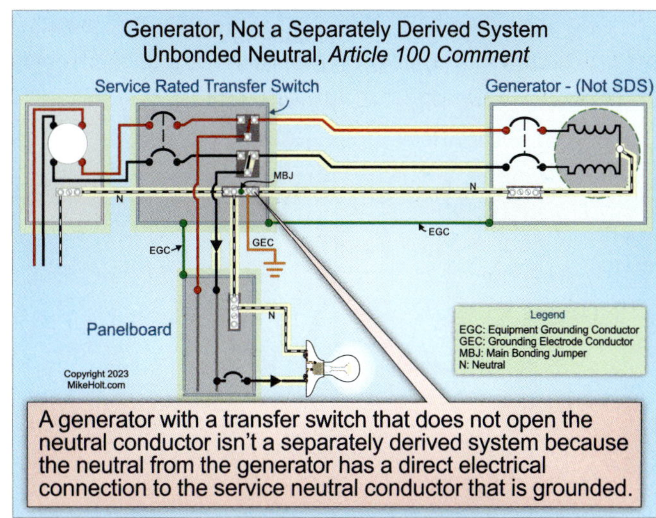
Generator, Not a Separately Derived System
Unbonded Neutral, Article 100 Comment
Service Rated Transfer Switch
Generator - (Not SDS)
MBJ
N
EGC
GEC
Panelboard
Legend
EGC: Equipment Grounding Conductor
GEC: Grounding Electrode Conductor
MBJ: Main Bonding Jumper
N: Neutral
Copyright 2023 MikeHolt.com
A generator with a transfer switch that does not open the neutral conductor isn't a separately derived system because the neutral from the generator has a direct electrical connection to the service neutral conductor that is grounded.

▸Figure 100–92

Author's Comment:

- A generator with a transfer switch that does not open the neutral conductor is not a separately derived system because the neutral from the generator has a direct electrical connection to the service neutral conductor that is grounded. ▸Figure 100-91 and ▸Figure 100-92

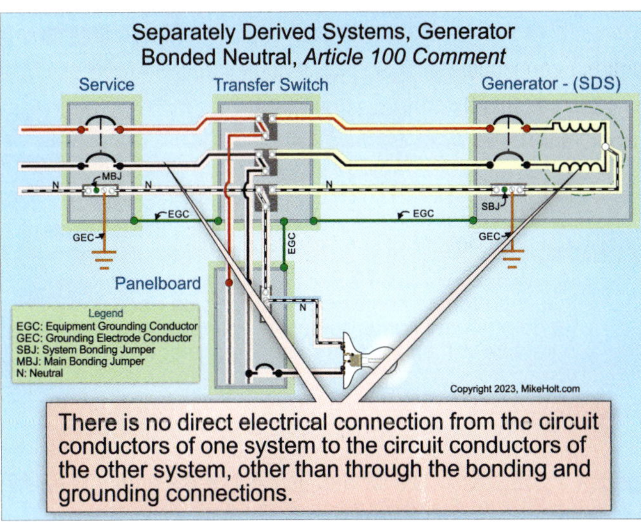
Separately Derived Systems, Generator
Bonded Neutral, Article 100 Comment
Service
Transfer Switch
Generator - (SDS)
MBJ
N
EGC
SBJ
GEC
Panelboard
Legend
EGC: Equipment Grounding Conductor
GEC: Grounding Electrode Conductor
SBJ: System Bonding Jumper
MBJ: Main Bonding Jumper
N: Neutral
Copyright 2023, MikeHolt.com
There is no direct electrical connection from the circuit conductors of one system to the circuit conductors of the other system, other than through the bonding and grounding connections.

▸Figure 100–91

- Section 250.30 contains important information on the use of the term "Separately Derived System."

Service. The conductors and equipment connecting the serving electric utility to the premises wiring system. ▸Figure 100-93

Service
Article 100 Definition
The conductors and equipment connecting the serving electric utility to the wiring system of the premises served.
Copyright 2023, www.MikeHolt.com

▸Figure 100–93

Service Conductors. The conductors from the serving electric utility service point to the service disconnect. ▸Figure 100–94

Author's Comment:

- Service conductors can include overhead service conductors, overhead service-entrance conductors, and underground service conductors. These conductors are not under the exclusive control of the serving electric utility, which means they are owned by the customer and are covered by the requirements in Article 230.

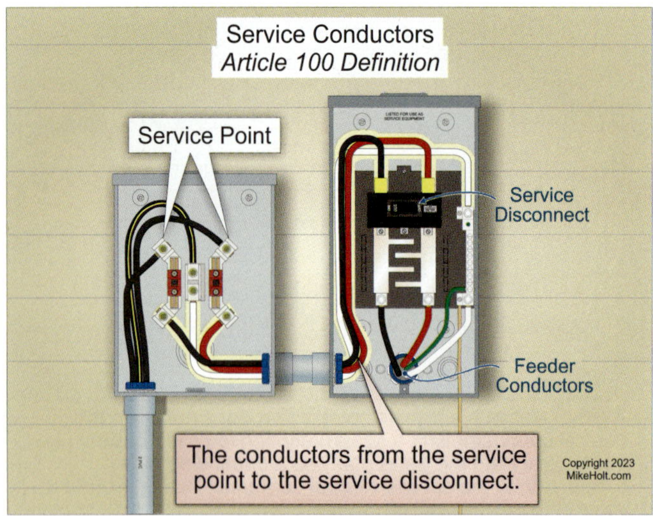
Service Conductors
Article 100 Definition
Service Point
Service Disconnect
Feeder Conductors
The conductors from the service point to the service disconnect.
Copyright 2023 MikeHolt.com

▸Figure 100–94

Service Equipment (Service Disconnect). Equipment such as circuit breakers or switches connected to the serving electric utility and intended to disconnect the power from the serving electric utility. ▸Figure 100–95 and ▸Figure 100–96

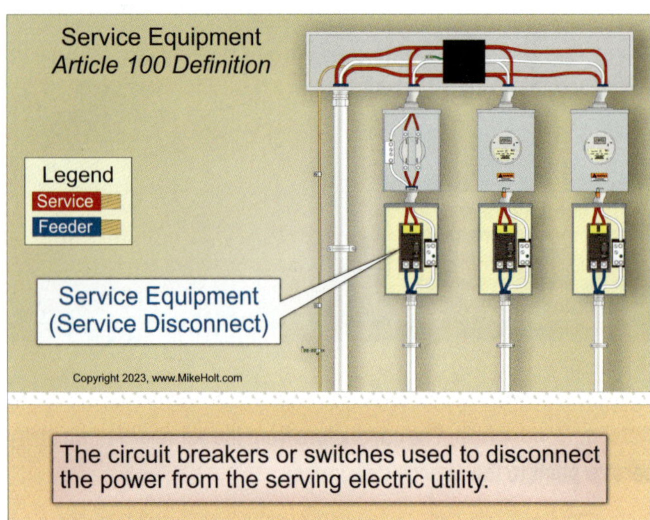
Service Equipment
Article 100 Definition
Legend
Service
Feeder
Service Equipment
(Service Disconnect)
Copyright 2023, www.MikeHolt.com
The circuit breakers or switches used to disconnect the power from the serving electric utility.

▸Figure 100–95

Author's Comment:

- Service equipment is often referred to as the "service disconnect" or "service main."
- Meter socket enclosures are not considered service equipment [230.66(B)].
- It is important to know where a service begins and where it ends to properly apply the *Code* requirements. The service can begin either before or after the metering equipment. ▸Figure 100–97

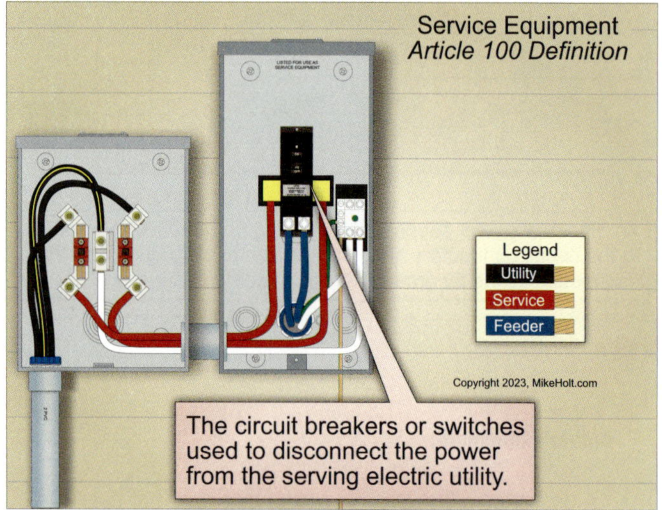
Service Equipment
Article 100 Definition
Legend
Utility
Service
Feeder
Copyright 2023, MikeHolt.com
The circuit breakers or switches used to disconnect the power from the serving electric utility.

▸Figure 100–96

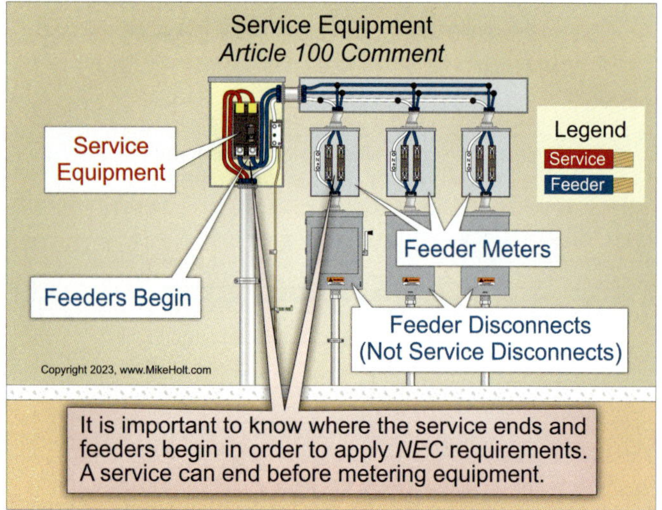
Service Equipment
Article 100 Comment
Service Equipment
Legend
Service
Feeder
Feeder Meters
Feeders Begin
Feeder Disconnects
(Not Service Disconnects)
Copyright 2023, www.MikeHolt.com
It is important to know where the service ends and feeders begin in order to apply NEC requirements. A service can end before metering equipment.

▸Figure 100–97

Special Permission. The written consent of the authority having jurisdiction.

Structure. That which is built or constructed, other than equipment. ▸Figure 100–98

Switch, General-Use Snap (General-Use Snap Switch). A switch constructed to be installed in a device box or a box cover.

Transformer. Equipment, either single-phase or three-phase, that uses electromagnetic induction to convert current and voltage in a primary circuit into current and voltage in a secondary circuit. ▸Figure 100–99

Author's Comment:

- Article 450 contains the primary requirements for transformers.

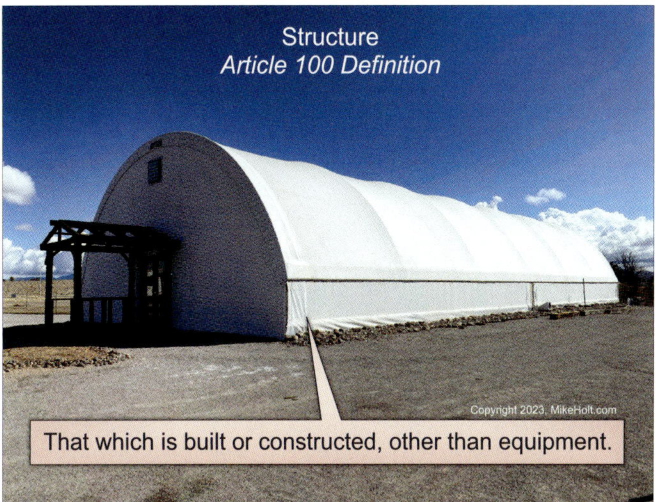
Structure
Article 100 Definition
Copyright 2023, MikeHolt.com
That which is built or constructed, other than equipment.

▶Figure 100–98

Transformer
Article 100 Definition
Copyright 2023, www.MikeHolt.com
Equipment that uses electromagnetic induction to convert current and voltage in a primary circuit into current and voltage in a secondary circuit.
Mario Valdes

▶Figure 100–99

Tubing, Electrical Metallic (EMT). An unthreaded thinwall circular metallic raceway used for the installation of electrical conductors. When joined together with listed fittings and enclosures as a complete system, it is a reliable wiring method providing both physical protection for conductors as well an effective ground-fault current path. ▶Figure 100–100

Tubing, Electrical Nonmetallic (ENT). A pliable corrugated circular raceway of circular cross section with integral or associated couplings, connectors, and fittings that are listed for the installation of electrical conductors. It is composed of a material that is resistant to moisture and chemical atmospheres and is flame retardant. ▶Figure 100–101

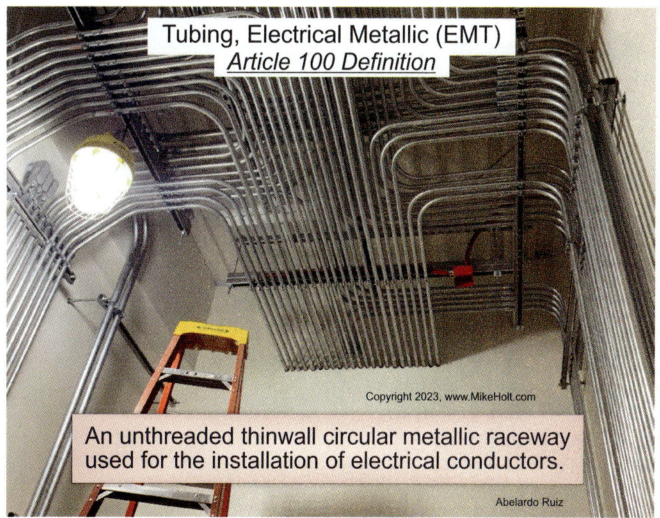
Tubing, Electrical Metallic (EMT)
Article 100 Definition
Copyright 2023, www.MikeHolt.com
An unthreaded thinwall circular metallic raceway used for the installation of electrical conductors.
Abelardo Ruiz

▶Figure 100–100

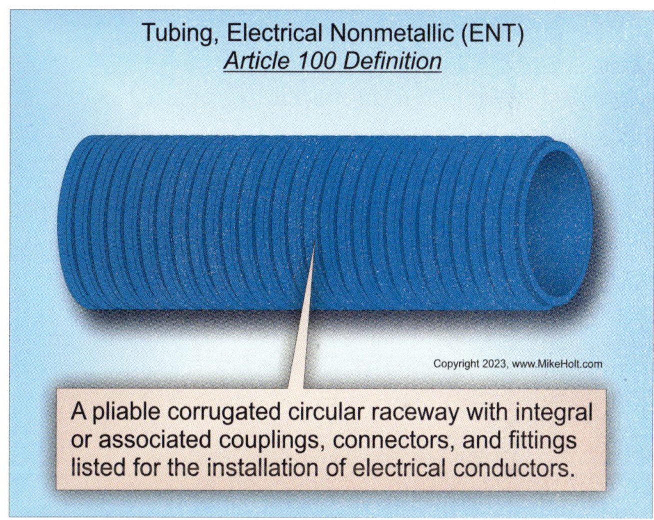
Tubing, Electrical Nonmetallic (ENT)
Article 100 Definition
Copyright 2023, www.MikeHolt.com
A pliable corrugated circular raceway with integral or associated couplings, connectors, and fittings listed for the installation of electrical conductors.

▶Figure 100–101

Author's Comment:

- Electrical nonmetallic tubing can be bent by hand with reasonable force and without other assistance.

Wireway, Metal (Metal Wireway). A sheet metal trough with hinged or removable covers for housing and protecting electrical conductors and cable, and in which conductors are placed after the raceway has been installed. ▶Figure 100–102

Wireway, Metal
Article 100 Definition
Copyright 2023, MikeHolt.com
A sheet metal trough with hinged or removable covers for housing and protecting electric wires and cable, and in which conductors are placed after the raceway has been installed.

▸Figure 100–102

GENERAL REQUIREMENTS FOR ELECTRICAL INSTALLATIONS

Introduction to Article 110—General Requirements for Electrical Installations

Article 110 is the first article in the *NEC* that contains requirements as opposed to overall scope information or definitions. It contains the general rules that apply to all installations and, as such, is the foundation of the *Code*. Topics covered in our material for Article 110 include:

- How equipment is approved
- How to determine when or where equipment can be used
- How to arrange equipment so it is safe to operate and maintain for the end user
- How to identify the characteristics of the systems being installed so future alterations, service, or maintenance can be completed safely

This article is divided into five parts. The first two cover systems under 1000V, nominal and are the only parts of this article covered in this material. As you begin your journey to understanding the *NEC*, remember that many other *Code* rules were written with the understanding that you will come to Article 100 to determine the general requirements. Set yourself up for success by taking the time to read and understand each of these rules.

Part I. General Requirements

110.1 Scope

Article 110 covers the general requirements for the examination, approval, installation, use, and access to spaces around electrical equipment. ▸Figure 110–1

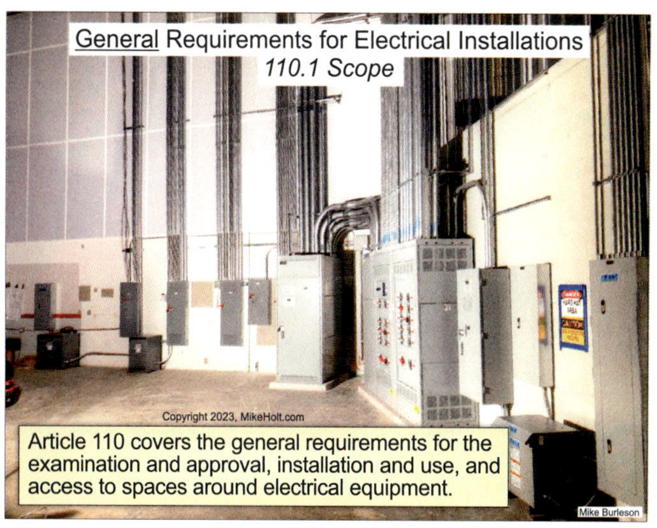
General Requirements for Electrical Installations
110.1 Scope
Copyright 2023, MikeHolt.com
Article 110 covers the general requirements for the examination and approval, installation and use, and access to spaces around electrical equipment.
Mike Burleson

▸Figure 110–1

Note: For information regarding ADA accessibility design, see Annex J.

Author's Comment:

- Requirements for people with disabilities include things like mounting heights for switches, receptacles and the requirements for the distance that objects (such as wall sconces) protrude from a wall.

110.2 Approval of Conductors and Equipment

The authority having jurisdiction must approve all electrical conductors and equipment. ▶Figure 110–2

Approval of Conductors and Equipment
110.2
Okay
Can I use this unlisted equipment?
Copyright 2023, MikeHolt.com
The authority having jurisdiction must approve all electrical conductors and equipment.

▶Figure 110–2

According to Article 100, "Approved" means acceptable to the authority having jurisdiction (AHJ), usually the electrical inspector. Product listing does not mean the product is approved, but it can be a basis for approval. ▶Figure 110–3

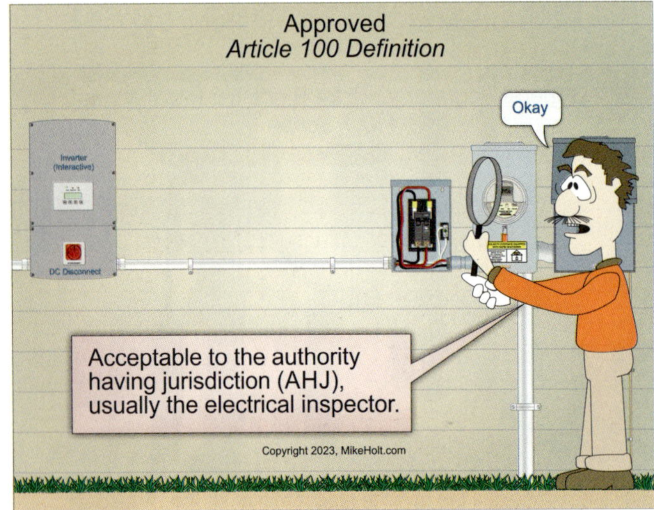
Approved
Article 100 Definition
Okay
DC Disconnect
Acceptable to the authority having jurisdiction (AHJ), usually the electrical inspector.
Copyright 2023, MikeHolt.com

▶Figure 110–3

According to Article 100, "Authority Having Jurisdiction (AHJ)" refers the organization, office, or individual responsible for approving equipment, materials, or an installation. See 90.4 and 90.7 for more information. ▶Figure 110–4

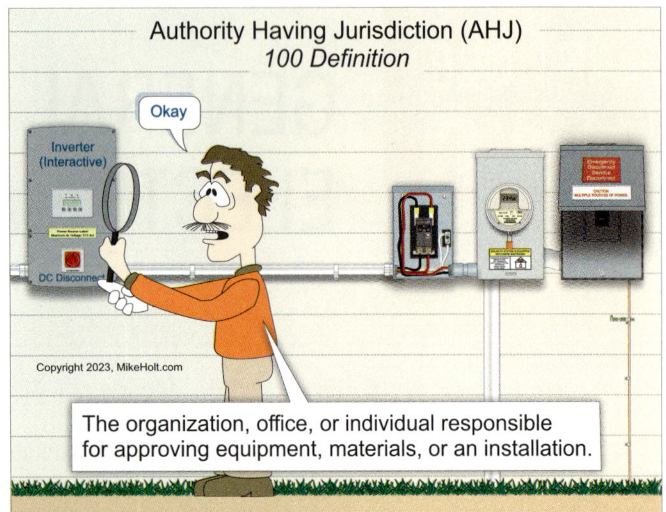
Authority Having Jurisdiction (AHJ)
100 Definition
Okay
Inverter (Interactive)
DC Disconnect
Copyright 2023, MikeHolt.com
The organization, office, or individual responsible for approving equipment, materials, or an installation.

▶Figure 110–4

110.3 Use of Equipment

(A) Guidelines for Approval. The authority having jurisdiction must approve equipment. In doing so, consideration must be given to the following:

(1) Suitability for installation and use in accordance with the *NEC*

Note 1: Equipment may be new, reconditioned, refurbished, or remanufactured.

Note 2: Suitability of equipment use may be identified by a description marked on (or provided with) a product to identify the suitability of the product for a specific purpose, environment, or application. Special conditions of use or other limitations may be marked on the equipment, in the product instructions, or included in the appropriate listing and labeling information. Suitability of equipment may be evidenced by listing or labeling.

According to Article 100, "Identified (as Applied to Equipment)" means that it is recognized as suitable for a specific purpose, function, use, environment, or application. ▶Figure 110–5

(2) Mechanical strength and durability

(3) Wire-bending and connection space

(4) Electrical insulation

(5) Heating effects under all conditions of use

(6) Arcing effects

(7) Classification by type, size, voltage, current capacity, and specific use

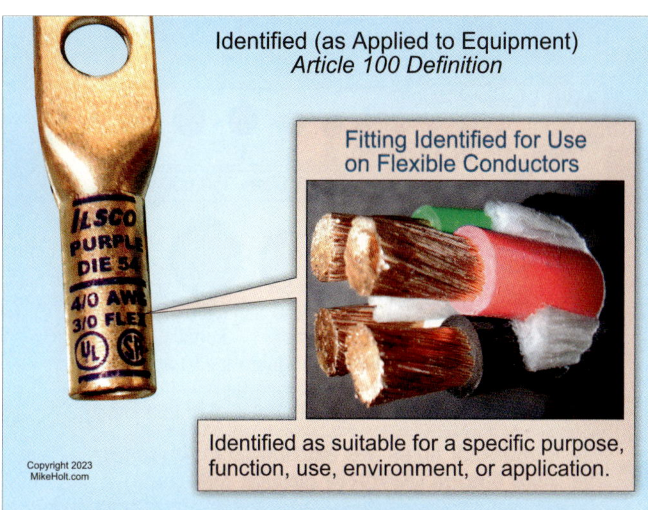
Identified (as Applied to Equipment)
Article 100 Definition
Fitting Identified for Use on Flexible Conductors
ILSCO PURPLE DIE 54
4/0 AWG 3/0 FLEX
Identified as suitable for a specific purpose, function, use, environment, or application.
Copyright 2023 MikeHolt.com

▸Figure 110–5

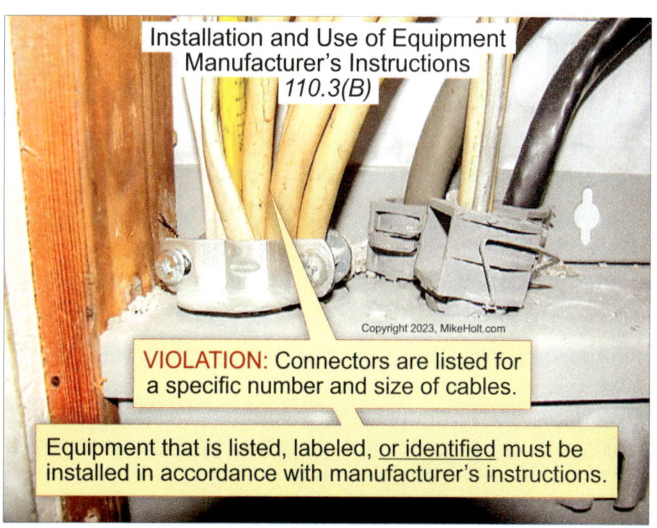
Installation and Use of Equipment
Manufacturer's Instructions
110.3(B)
Copyright 2023, MikeHolt.com
VIOLATION: Connectors are listed for a specific number and size of cables.
Equipment that is listed, labeled, or identified must be installed in accordance with manufacturer's instructions.

▸Figure 110–6

(8) Cybersecurity for network-connected life safety equipment to address its ability to withstand unauthorized updates and malicious attacks while continuing to perform its intended life safety functionality

Note 3: See the IEC 62443 series of standards for industrial automation and control systems, the UL 2900 series of standards for software cybersecurity for network connectible products, and UL 5500, *Standard for Remote Software Updates*, which are standards that provide frameworks to mitigate current and future security cybersecurity vulnerabilities and address software integrity in systems of electrical equipment.

(9) Other factors contributing to the practical safeguarding of persons using or in contact with the equipment

(B) Installation and Use. Equipment that is listed, labeled, or identified must be installed in accordance with manufacturer's instructions. ▸Figure 110–6

According to Article 100, "Labeled" mean equipment or materials that have a label, symbol, or other identifying mark in the form of a sticker, decal, printed label, or with the identifying mark molded or stamped into the product by a recognized testing laboratory acceptable to the authority having jurisdiction. ▸Figure 110–7

Note: The installation instructions can be provided in the form of printed material, quick response (QR) code, or the address on the Internet where users can download the required instructions. ▸Figure 110–8

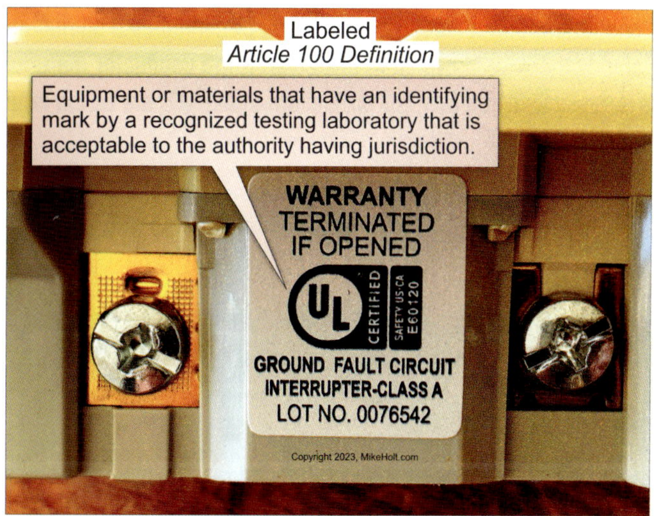
Labeled
Article 100 Definition
Equipment or materials that have an identifying mark by a recognized testing laboratory that is acceptable to the authority having jurisdiction.
WARRANTY TERMINATED IF OPENED
UL CERTIFIED SAFETY US-CA E60120
GROUND FAULT CIRCUIT INTERRUPTER-CLASS A
LOT NO. 0076542
Copyright 2023, MikeHolt.com

▸Figure 110–7

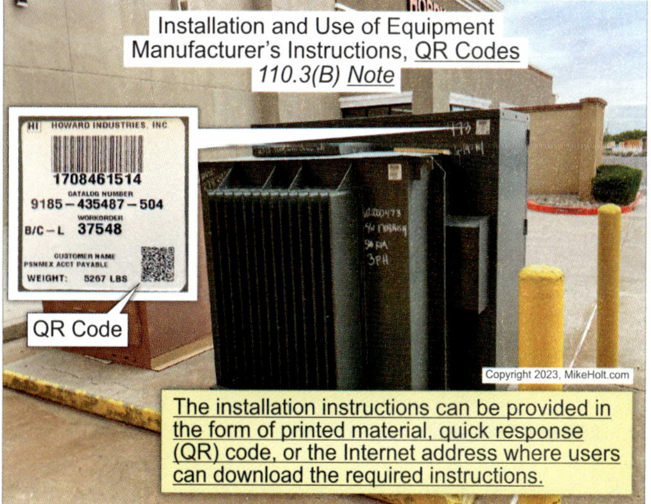
Installation and Use of Equipment
Manufacturer's Instructions, QR Codes
110.3(B) Note
HOWARD INDUSTRIES, INC.
1708461514
CATALOG NUMBER
9185 – 435487 – 504
WORKORDER
B/C – L 37548
WEIGHT: 5267 LBS
QR Code
Copyright 2023, MikeHolt.com
The installation instructions can be provided in the form of printed material, quick response (QR) code, or the Internet address where users can download the required instructions.

▸Figure 110–8

Author's Comment:

- Many electricians simply throw away installation instructions, but that excuse is now becoming less valid since manufacturers are starting to use QR codes on electrical equipment, so the instructions are always readily available.

(C) Product Listing. Product testing, evaluation, and listing must be performed by a recognized qualified testing laboratory in accordance with standards that achieve effective safety to comply with the *NEC*.

Note: OSHA recognizes qualified electrical testing laboratories that provide product certification that meets their electrical standards.

110.5 Conductor Material

Conductors must be copper, aluminum, or copper-clad aluminum unless otherwise provided in this *Code*. If the conductor material is not specified in a rule, the sizes given in the *NEC* are based on a copper conductor. ▸Figure 110–9

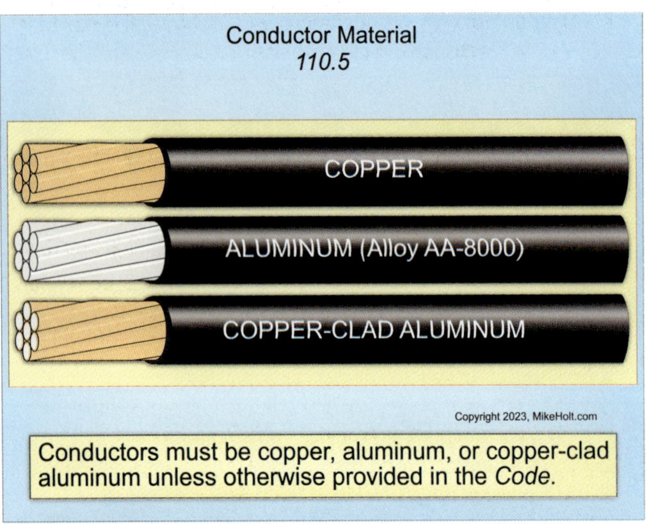
Conductor Material
110.5
COPPER
ALUMINUM (Alloy AA-8000)
COPPER-CLAD ALUMINUM
Copyright 2023, MikeHolt.com
Conductors must be copper, aluminum, or copper-clad aluminum unless otherwise provided in the Code.

▸Figure 110–9

110.6 Conductor Sizes

Conductor sizes are expressed in American Wire Gauge (AWG) or circular mils (cmil). ▸Figure 110–10

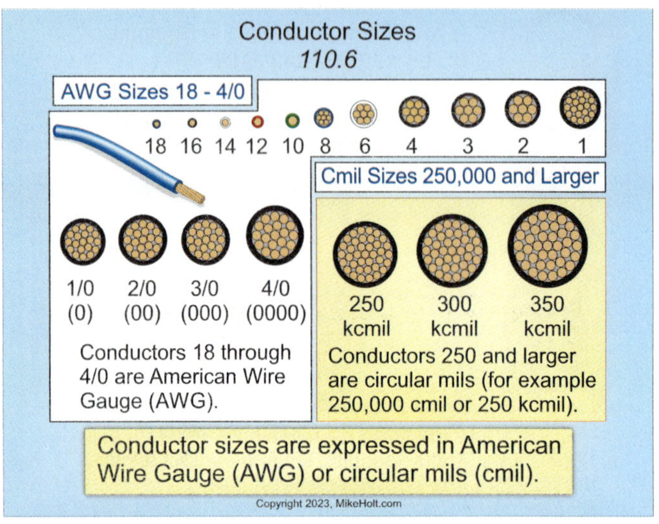
Conductor Sizes
110.6
AWG Sizes 18 - 4/0
18 16 14 12 10 8 6 4 3 2 1
Cmil Sizes 250,000 and Larger
1/0 (0) 2/0 (00) 3/0 (000) 4/0 (0000)
250 kcmil 300 kcmil 350 kcmil
Conductors 18 through 4/0 are American Wire Gauge (AWG).
Conductors 250 and larger are circular mils (for example 250,000 cmil or 250 kcmil).
Conductor sizes are expressed in American Wire Gauge (AWG) or circular mils (cmil).
Copyright 2023, MikeHolt.com

▸Figure 110–10

Author's Comment:

- Chapter 9, Table 8 gives the circular mil area of AWG conductors.

110.7 Wiring Integrity

Electrical installations must be free from short circuits, ground faults, or neutral to ground connections unless required or permitted by the *Code*. ▸Figure 110–11, ▸Figure 110–12, and ▸Figure 110–13

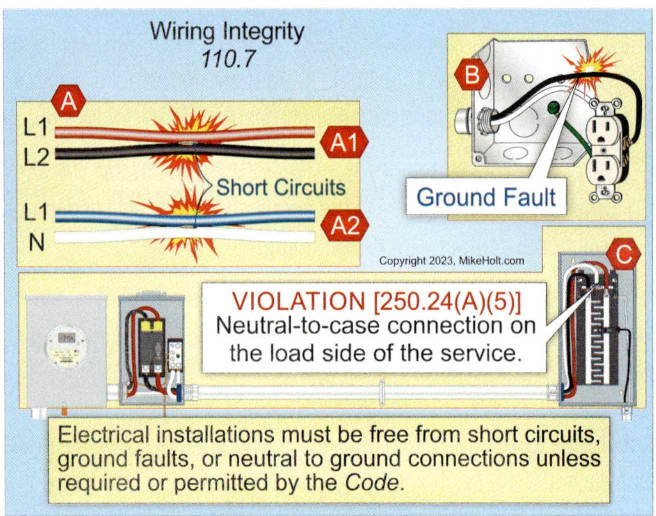
Wiring Integrity
110.7
A
L1
L2
A1
Short Circuits
L1
N
A2
B
Ground Fault
C
Copyright 2023, MikeHolt.com
VIOLATION [250.24(A)(5)]
Neutral-to-case connection on the load side of the service.
Electrical installations must be free from short circuits, ground faults, or neutral to ground connections unless required or permitted by the Code.

▸Figure 110–11

110.8 Suitable Wiring Methods

The only wiring methods permitted to be installed in buildings, occupancies, or premises are those recognized by the *NEC*. ▸Figure 110–14

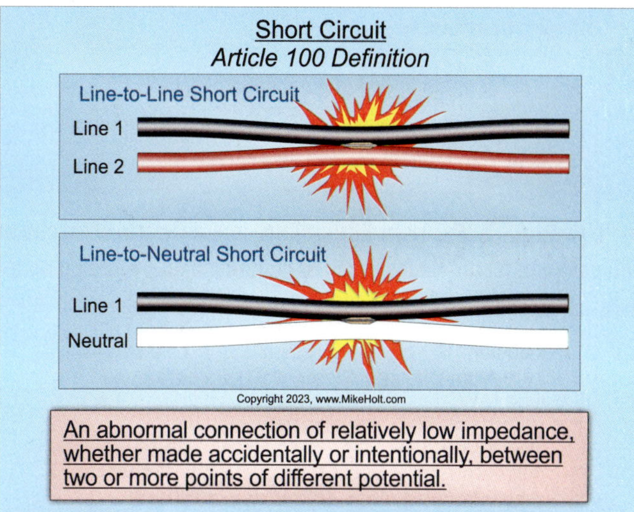
Short Circuit
Article 100 Definition
Line-to-Line Short Circuit
Line 1
Line 2
Line-to-Neutral Short Circuit
Line 1
Neutral
Copyright 2023, www.MikeHolt.com
An abnormal connection of relatively low impedance, whether made accidentally or intentionally, between two or more points of different potential.

▸Figure 110–12

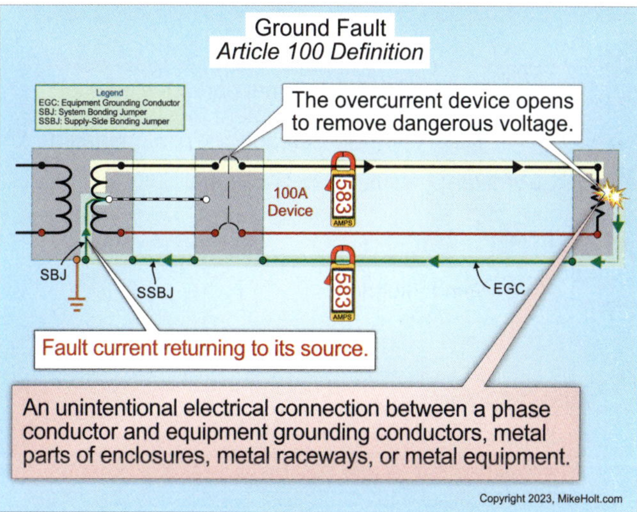
Ground Fault
Article 100 Definition
Legend
EGC: Equipment Grounding Conductor
SBJ: System Bonding Jumper
SSBJ: Supply-Side Bonding Jumper
The overcurrent device opens to remove dangerous voltage.
100A Device
583
583
SBJ
SSBJ
EGC
Fault current returning to its source.
An unintentional electrical connection between a phase conductor and equipment grounding conductors, metal parts of enclosures, metal raceways, or metal equipment.
Copyright 2023, MikeHolt.com

▸Figure 110–13

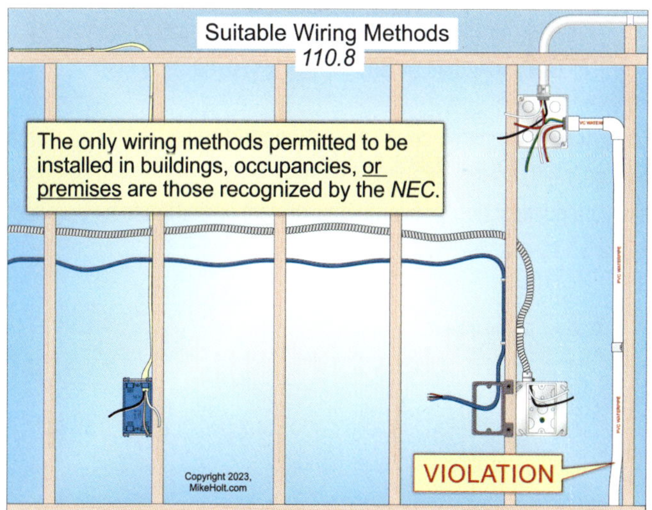
Suitable Wiring Methods
110.8
The only wiring methods permitted to be installed in buildings, occupancies, or premises are those recognized by the NEC.
Copyright 2023, MikeHolt.com
VIOLATION

▸Figure 110–14

110.11 Deteriorating Agents

Electrical equipment and conductors must be suitable for the environment and the conditions for which they will be used. Consideration must also be given to the presence of corrosive gases, fumes, vapors, liquids, or other substances that can have a deteriorating effect on conductors and equipment. ▸Figure 110–15

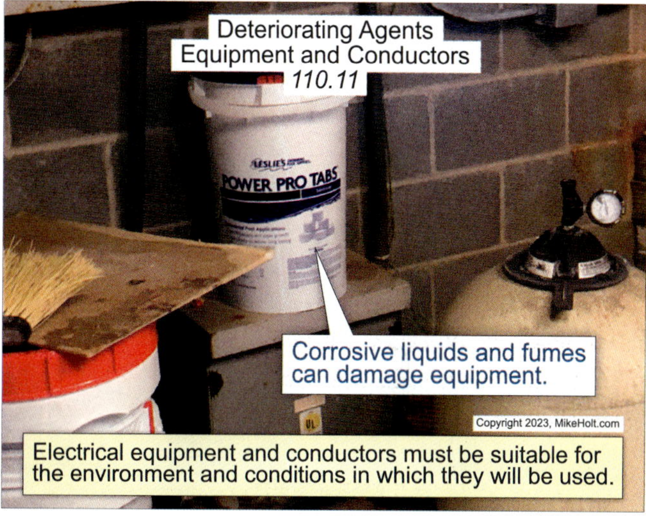
Deteriorating Agents
Equipment and Conductors
110.11
POWER PRO TABS
Corrosive liquids and fumes can damage equipment.
Copyright 2023, MikeHolt.com
Electrical equipment and conductors must be suitable for the environment and conditions in which they will be used.

▸Figure 110–15

Equipment identified for indoor use must be protected against damage from the weather during construction.

Note 1: Raceways, cable trays, cable armor, boxes, cable sheathing, cabinets, enclosures, elbows, couplings, fittings, supports, and support hardware must be suitable for the environment. See 300.6. ▸Figure 110–16

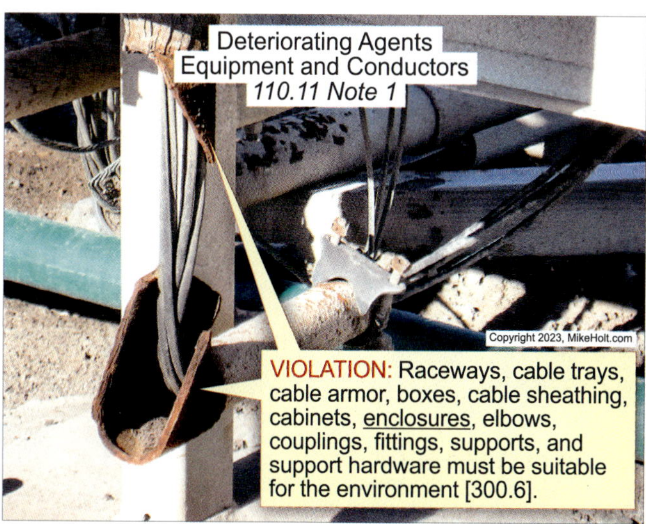
Deteriorating Agents
Equipment and Conductors
110.11 Note 1
Copyright 2023, MikeHolt.com
VIOLATION: Raceways, cable trays, cable armor, boxes, cable sheathing, cabinets, enclosures, elbows, couplings, fittings, supports, and support hardware must be suitable for the environment [300.6].

▸Figure 110–16

Note 2: Some cleaning and lubricating compounds contain chemicals that can cause plastic to deteriorate.

Note 3: For NEMA enclosure-type designations, see Table 110.28.

Note 4: For minimum flood provisions, see the *International Building Code* (IBC) and the *International Residential Code* (IRC).

110.12 Mechanical Execution of Work

Electrical equipment must be installed in a professional and skillful manner. ▶Figure 110–17

Mechanical Execution of Work
110.12
Electrical equipment must be installed in a professional and skillful manner.
Copyright 2023, MikeHolt.com

▶Figure 110–17

Note: For information on accepted industry practices, see ANSI/NECA 1, *Standard for Good Workmanship in Electrical Construction*, and other ANSI-approved installation standards. ▶Figure 110–18

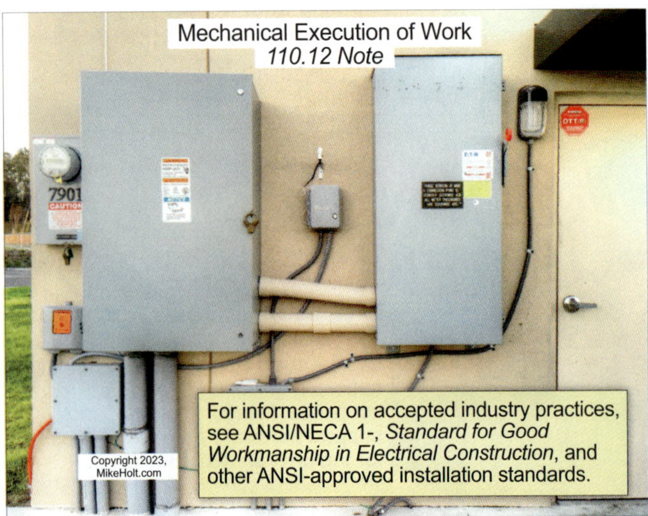
Mechanical Execution of Work
110.12 Note
For information on accepted industry practices, see ANSI/NECA 1-, Standard for Good Workmanship in Electrical Construction, and other ANSI-approved installation standards.
Copyright 2023, MikeHolt.com

▶Figure 110–18

Author's Comment:

- This rule is perhaps one of the most subjective of the entire *Code,* and its application is still ultimately a judgment call made by the authority having jurisdiction.

(B) Integrity of Electrical Equipment. Internal parts of electrical equipment must not be damaged or contaminated by foreign material such as paint, plaster, cleaners, and so forth. ▶Figure 110–19

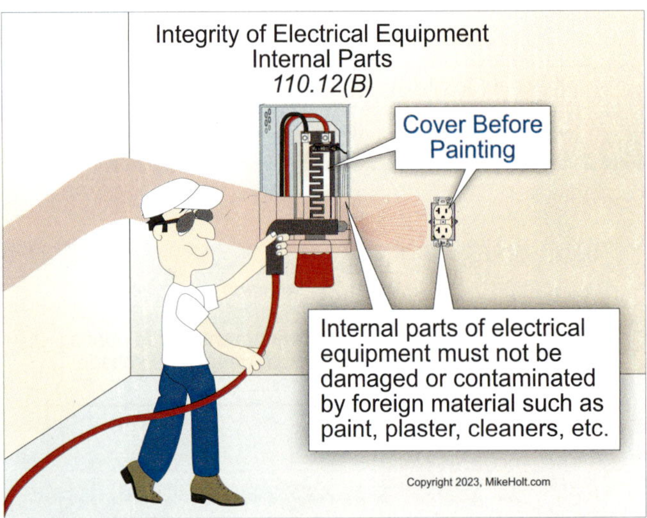
Integrity of Electrical Equipment
Internal Parts
110.12(B)
Cover Before Painting
Internal parts of electrical equipment must not be damaged or contaminated by foreign material such as paint, plaster, cleaners, etc.
Copyright 2023, MikeHolt.com

▶Figure 110–19

Author's Comment:

- Precautions must be taken to provide protection from the contamination of internal parts of panelboards and receptacles during building construction. Be sure the electrical equipment is properly masked and protected before drywall, painting, or other phases of the project that can contaminate or cause damage begins. ▶Figure 110–20

Electrical equipment containing damaged parts (such as items broken, bent, or cut), or those that have been deteriorated by corrosion, chemical action, or overheating are not permitted to be installed. ▶Figure 110–21

Author's Comment:

- Damaged parts include cracked insulators, arc shields not in place, overheated fuse clips, and damaged or missing switch handles or circuit-breaker handles.

1st Printing

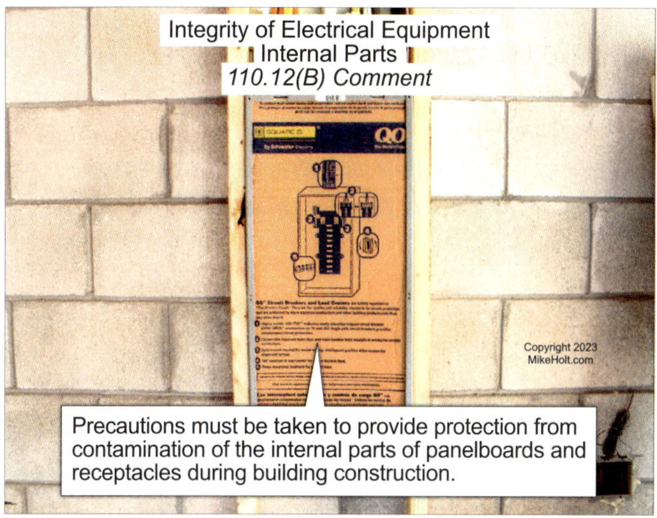
Integrity of Electrical Equipment
Internal Parts
110.12(B) Comment
Copyright 2023
MikeHolt.com
Precautions must be taken to provide protection from contamination of the internal parts of panelboards and receptacles during building construction.

▸Figure 110–20

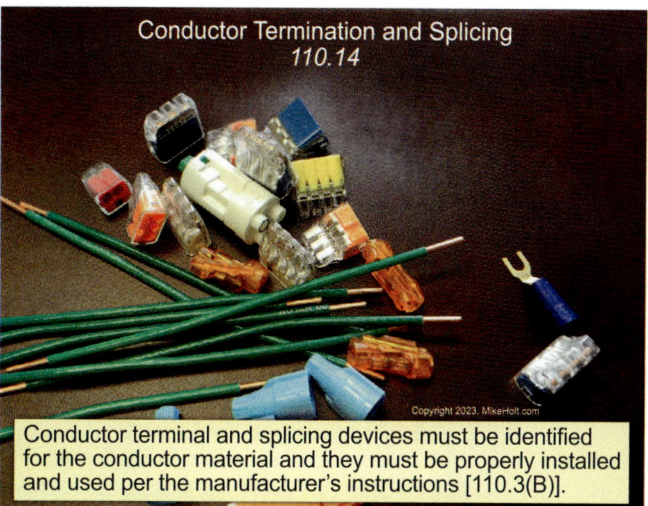
Conductor Termination and Splicing
110.14
Copyright 2023, MikeHolt.com
Conductor terminal and splicing devices must be identified for the conductor material and they must be properly installed and used per the manufacturer's instructions [110.3(B)].

▸Figure 110–22

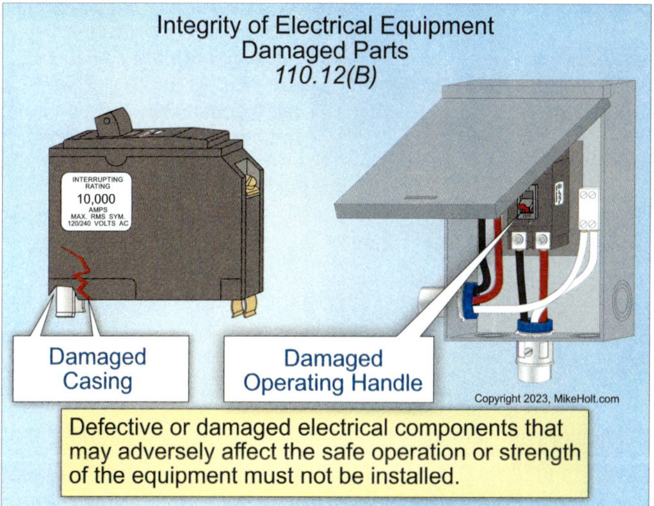
Integrity of Electrical Equipment
Damaged Parts
110.12(B)
INTERRUPTING RATING
10,000
AMPS
MAX. RMS SYM.
120/240 VOLTS AC
Damaged
Casing
Damaged
Operating Handle
Copyright 2023, MikeHolt.com
Defective or damaged electrical components that may adversely affect the safe operation or strength of the equipment must not be installed.

▸Figure 110–21

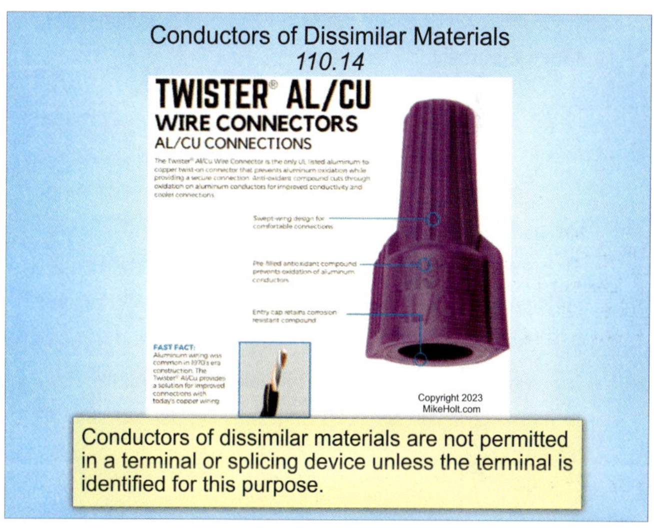
Conductors of Dissimilar Materials
110.14
TWISTER® AL/CU
WIRE CONNECTORS
AL/CU CONNECTIONS
FAST FACT:
Copyright 2023
MikeHolt.com
Conductors of dissimilar materials are not permitted in a terminal or splicing device unless the terminal is identified for this purpose.

▸Figure 110–23

110.14 Conductor Termination and Splicing

Conductor terminal and splicing devices must be identified for the conductor material and must be properly installed and used in accordance with the manufacturer's instructions [110.3(B)]. ▸Figure 110–22

Conductors of dissimilar materials are not permitted in a terminal or splicing device where contact occurs between dissimilar conductors—unless identified for the purpose and conditions of use. ▸Figure 110–23

According to Article 100, "Identified "Identified (as Applied to Equipment)" means recognized as suitable for a specific purpose, function, use, environment, or application. ▸Figure 110–24

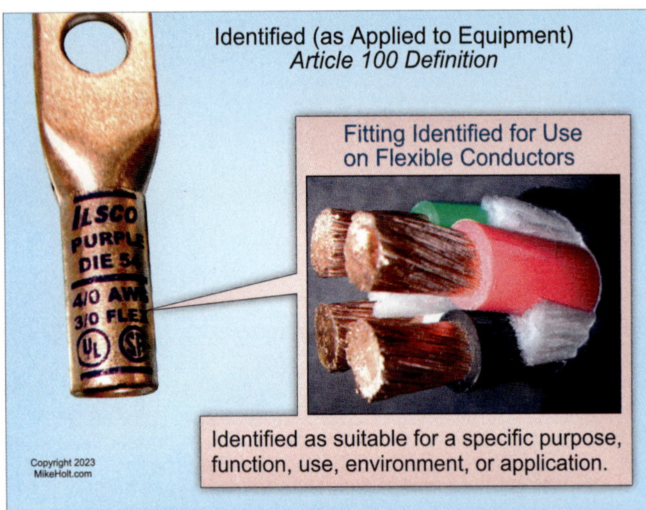
Identified (as Applied to Equipment)
Article 100 Definition
Fitting Identified for Use on Flexible Conductors
Identified as suitable for a specific purpose, function, use, environment, or application.
Copyright 2023 MikeHolt.com

▸Figure 110–24

Author's Comment:

- Conductor terminals suitable for aluminum wire only will be marked "AL." Those acceptable for copper wire will be marked "CU." Terminals suitable for copper, copper-clad-aluminum, and aluminum conductors will be marked "CU-AL" or "AL-CU." For 6 AWG and smaller, the markings can be printed on the container or on an information sheet inside the container. A "7" or "75" indicates a 75°C rated terminal, and a "9" or "90" indicates a 90°C rated terminal. If a terminal bears no marking, it can be used only with copper conductors. ▸Figure 110–25

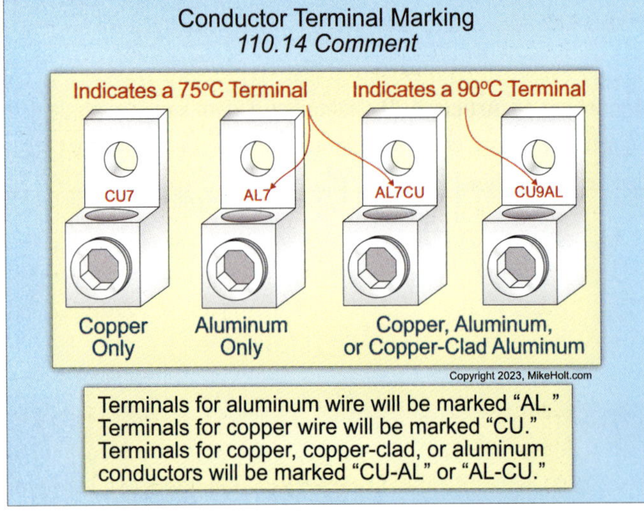
Conductor Terminal Marking
110.14 Comment
Indicates a 75°C Terminal
Indicates a 90°C Terminal
CU7
AL7
AL7CU
CU9AL
Copper Only
Aluminum Only
Copper, Aluminum, or Copper-Clad Aluminum
Copyright 2023, MikeHolt.com
Terminals for aluminum wire will be marked "AL." Terminals for copper wire will be marked "CU." Terminals for copper, copper-clad, or aluminum conductors will be marked "CU-AL" or "AL-CU."

▸Figure 110–25

- Aluminum wire that was installed prior to the 1972 was the same wire used for utility power transmission lines. This aluminum wire had a major problem with oxidation at terminations and it required an antioxidant at terminations. When the antioxidant was not properly applied to the wire termination, fires were common at the termination. Since 1983, the *National Electrical Code* [310.3(B)] has required aluminum wire to be made from an aluminum alloy (AA-8000). This conductor does not require an antioxidant at terminations. ▸Figure 110–26

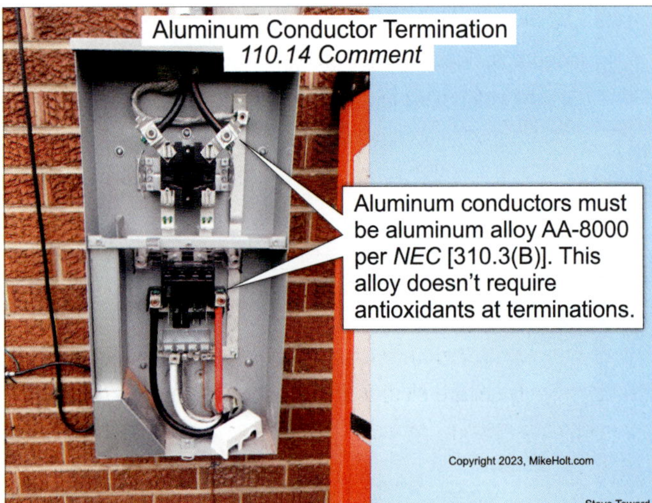
Aluminum Conductor Termination
110.14 Comment
Aluminum conductors must be aluminum alloy AA-8000 per NEC [310.3(B)]. This alloy doesn't require antioxidants at terminations.
Copyright 2023, MikeHolt.com
Steve Toward

▸Figure 110–26

Connectors and terminals for conductors more finely stranded than Class B and Class C must be identified for the use of finely stranded conductors. ▸Figure 110–27

Finely Stranded Conductors Connection and Termination
110.14
VIOLATION: Terminal not Identified for finely stranded conductors
Logan M. Millington
Copyright 2023, MikeHolt.com
Connectors and terminals for conductors more finely stranded than Class B and Class C must be identified for the use of finely stranded conductors.

▸Figure 110–27

Author's Comment:

- Conductor terminations must comply with the manufacturer's instructions as required by 110.3(B). For example, if the instructions for the device are written, "Suitable for 18-12 AWG Stranded," then only stranded conductors can be used with the terminating device. If they are written, "Suitable for 18-12 AWG Solid," then only solid conductors are permitted, and if the instructions are written, "Suitable for 18-12 AWG," then either solid or stranded conductors can be used with the terminating device.
- Few terminations are listed for mixing aluminum and copper conductors, but if they are, that will be marked on the product package or terminal device. The reason copper and aluminum should not be in contact with each other is because corrosion develops between the two different metals due to galvanic action. This results in increased contact resistance at the splicing device, and increased resistance can cause the splice to overheat and result in a fire.

(A) Conductor Terminations. Conductor terminals must ensure a mechanically secure electrical connection by the use of pressure connectors or splicing devices. ▸Figure 110–28

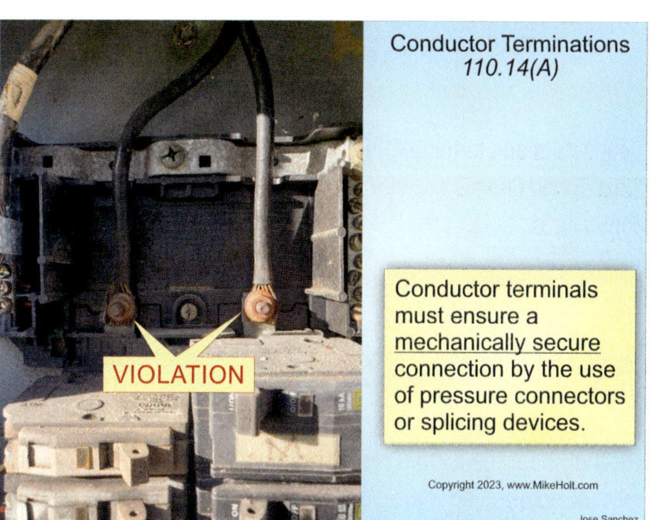
Conductor Terminations
110.14(A)
VIOLATION
Conductor terminals must ensure a mechanically secure connection by the use of pressure connectors or splicing devices.
Copyright 2023, www.MikeHolt.com
Jose Sanchez

▸Figure 110–28

Terminals are only listed for one conductor, unless marked otherwise. Terminals for more than one conductor must be identified for this purpose, either within the equipment instructions or on the terminal itself. ▸Figure 110–29

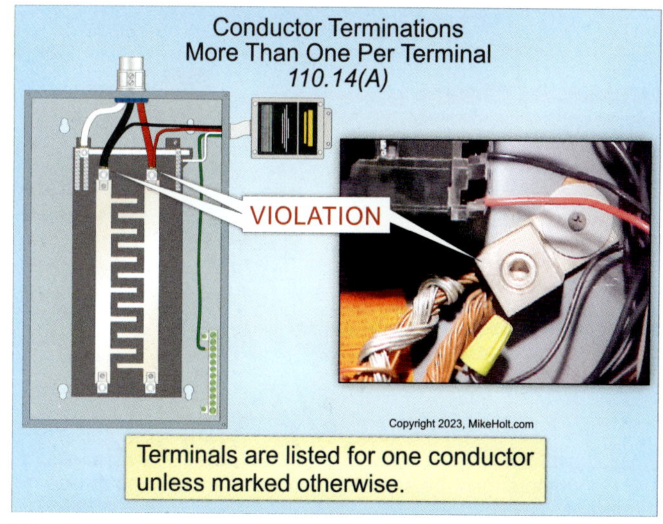
Conductor Terminations
More Than One Per Terminal
110.14(A)
VIOLATION
Copyright 2023, MikeHolt.com
Terminals are listed for one conductor unless marked otherwise.

▸Figure 110–29

Author's Comment:

- Split-bolt connectors are commonly listed for only two conductors, although some are listed for three. However, it is a common industry practice to terminate as many conductors as possible within a split-bolt connector, even though this violates the *NEC*. ▸Figure 110–30

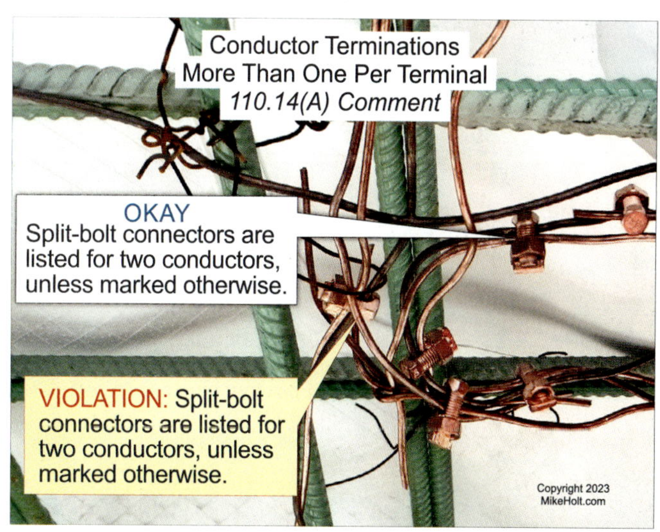
Conductor Terminations
More Than One Per Terminal
110.14(A) Comment
OKAY
Split-bolt connectors are listed for two conductors, unless marked otherwise.
VIOLATION: Split-bolt connectors are listed for two conductors, unless marked otherwise.
Copyright 2023
MikeHolt.com

▸Figure 110–30

(B) Conductor Splices. Conductors must be spliced by a splicing device that is identified for the purpose. All splices, joints, and free ends of conductors must be covered with an identified insulating device. ▸Figure 110–31

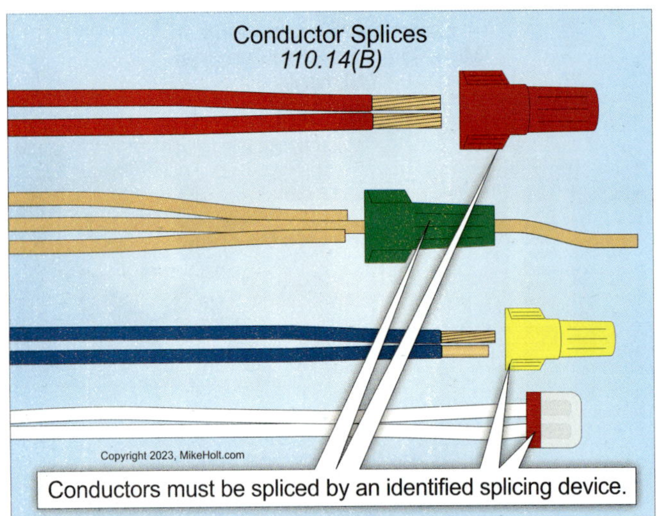
Conductor Splices
110.14(B)
Copyright 2023, MikeHolt.com
Conductors must be spliced by an identified splicing device.

▸Figure 110–31

Author's Comment:

- To prevent an electrical hazard, the free ends of conductors must be insulated to prevent the exposed end(s) from touching energized parts. This requirement can be met by using an insulated twist-on or push-on wire connector. ▸Figure 110–32

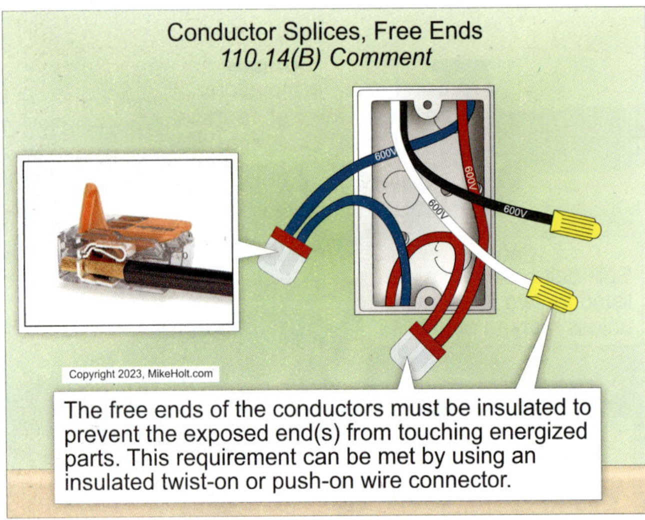
Conductor Splices, Free Ends
110.14(B) Comment
600V
Copyright 2023, MikeHolt.com
The free ends of the conductors must be insulated to prevent the exposed end(s) from touching energized parts. This requirement can be met by using an insulated twist-on or push-on wire connector.

▸Figure 110–32

- Pre-twisting conductors before applying twist-on wire connectors has been a very common practice in the field for years. The question (and subsequent debate) has always been, "Is pre-twisting required?" The *NEC* does not require that practice and, in fact, Ideal® made a statement about their Wing-Nut® twist-on connectors which said, "Pre-twisting is acceptable, but not required." Always follow the manufacturer's instructions and there will be no question [110.3(B)]. ▸Figure 110–33

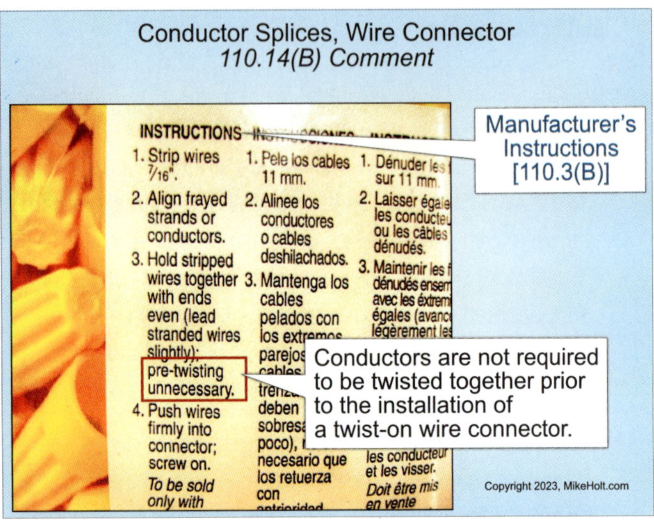
Conductor Splices, Wire Connector
110.14(B) Comment
INSTRUCTIONS
1. Strip wires 7/16".
2. Align frayed strands or conductors.
3. Hold stripped wires together with ends even (lead stranded wires slightly); pre-twisting unnecessary.
4. Push wires firmly into connector; screw on.
To be sold only with
Manufacturer's Instructions [110.3(B)]
Conductors are not required to be twisted together prior to the installation of a twist-on wire connector.
Copyright 2023, MikeHolt.com

▸Figure 110–33

Single direct burial types UF or USE conductors can be spliced underground with a device listed for direct burial [300.5(E) and 300.15(G)]. ▸Figure 110–34

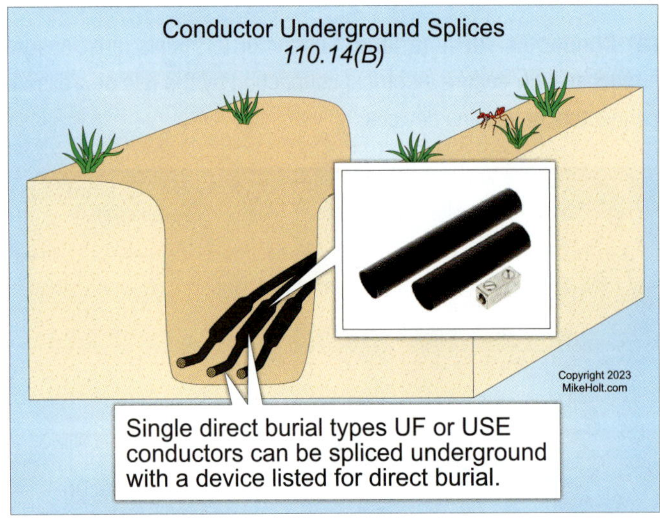
Conductor Underground Splices
110.14(B)
Copyright 2023 MikeHolt.com
Single direct burial types UF or USE conductors can be spliced underground with a device listed for direct burial.

▸Figure 110–34

The individual conductors of multiconductor UF or USE cable can be spliced underground with an underground listed splice kit that encapsulates the conductors and cable jacket.

Author's Comment:

- Electrical connection failures are the cause of many equipment and building fires. Improper terminations, poor workmanship, not following the manufacturer's instructions, and improper torquing can cause poor electrical connections. Improper electrical terminations can damage and melt conductor insulation resulting in short circuits and ground faults.

(D) Torquing of Terminal Connections. Tightening torque values for terminal connections must be as indicated on equipment or instructions. The tool or device used to achieve torque values must be approved by the authority having jurisdiction. ▶Figure 110–35

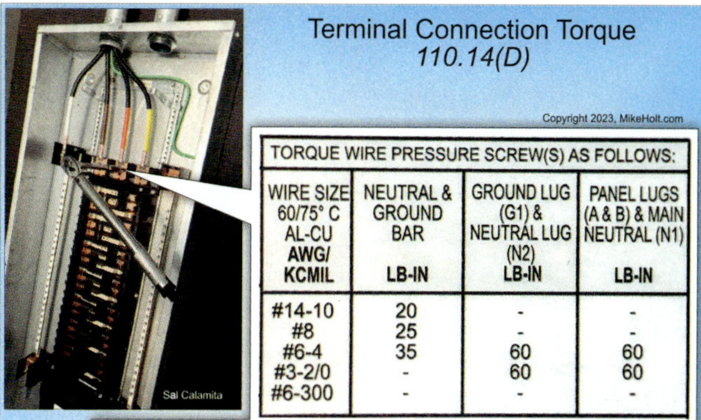
Terminal Connection Torque
110.14(D)
Copyright 2023, MikeHolt.com
Sal Calamita
Tightening torque values for terminal connections must be as indicated on equipment or installation instructions. An approved means must be used to achieve the indicated torque value.

TORQUE WIRE PRESSURE SCREW(S) AS FOLLOWS:

WIRE SIZE 60/75° C AL-CU AWG/ KCMIL	NEUTRAL & GROUND BAR LB-IN	GROUND LUG (G1) & NEUTRAL LUG (N2) LB-IN	PANEL LUGS (A & B) & MAIN NEUTRAL (N1) LB-IN
#14-10	20	-	-
#8	25	-	-
#6-4	35	60	60
#3-2/0	-	60	60
#6-300	-	-	-

▶Figure 110–35

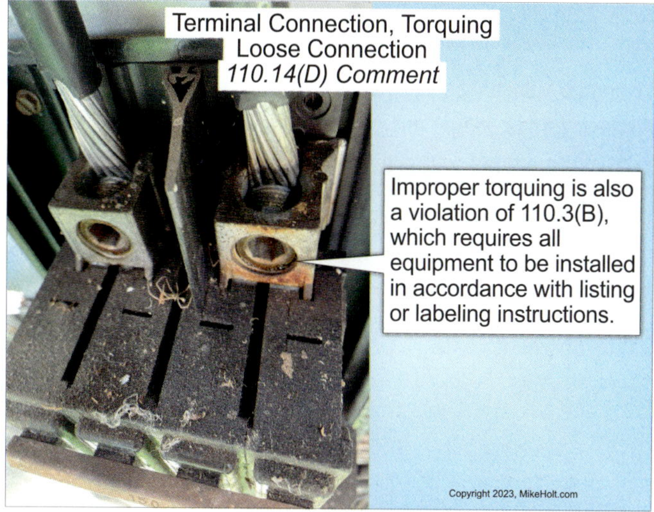
Terminal Connection, Torquing
Loose Connection
110.14(D) Comment
Improper torquing is also a violation of 110.3(B), which requires all equipment to be installed in accordance with listing or labeling instructions.
Copyright 2023, MikeHolt.com

▶Figure 110–36

Author's Comment:

- Conductors must terminate on device and equipment terminals that have been properly tightened in accordance with the manufacturer's torque specifications included with equipment instructions. Failure to torque terminals properly can result in excessive heating of terminals or splicing devices due to a loose connection. A loose connection can also lead to a glowing arc which increases the heating of the terminal and may ultimately cause a short circuit or ground fault. Any of these can result in a fire or other failure, including an arc flash event. ▶Figure 110–36 and ▶Figure 110–37

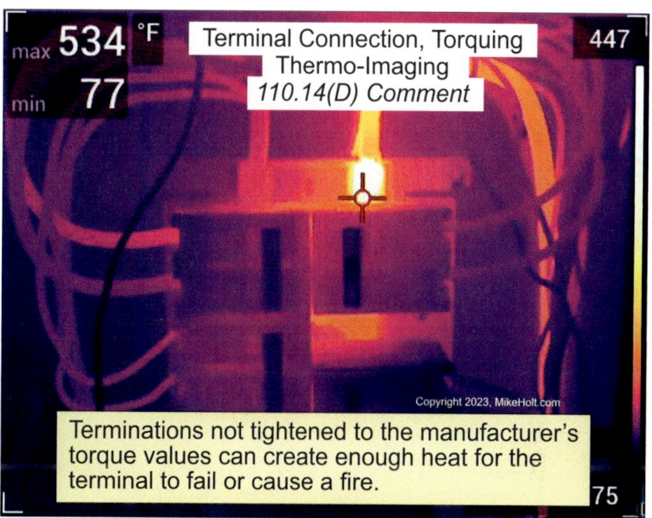
max 534 °F
min 77
447
Terminal Connection, Torquing
Thermo-Imaging
110.14(D) Comment
Copyright 2023, MikeHolt.com
Terminations not tightened to the manufacturer's torque values can create enough heat for the terminal to fail or cause a fire.
75

▶Figure 110–37

Note 1: Examples of approved means of achieving the indicated torque values include the use of torque tools or devices (such as shear bolts or breakaway-style devices) with visual indicators that demonstrate the proper torque has been applied. ▶Figure 110–38

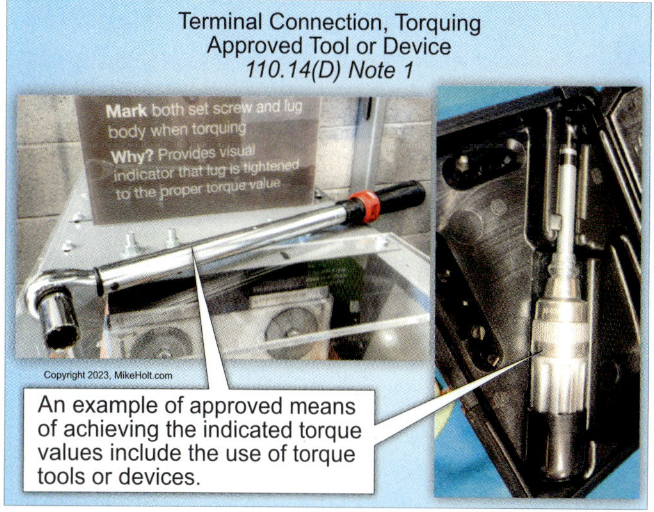
Terminal Connection, Torquing
Approved Tool or Device
110.14(D) Note 1
Mark both set screw and lug body when torquing
Why? Provides visual indicator that lug is tightened to the proper torque value
Copyright 2023, MikeHolt.com
An example of approved means of achieving the indicated torque values include the use of torque tools or devices.

▶Figure 110–38

Note 2: In the absence of manufacturer's torque requirements, see Annex I or UL Standard 486A-486B, *Standard for Safety-Wire Connectors,* for torque values. The equipment manufacturer can be contacted if numeric torque values are not indicated on the equipment or the instructions are not available.

Note 3: For information for torquing threaded connections and terminations, see NFPA 70B, *Recommended Practice for Electrical Equipment Maintenance*, Section 8.11. ▸**Figure 110–39**

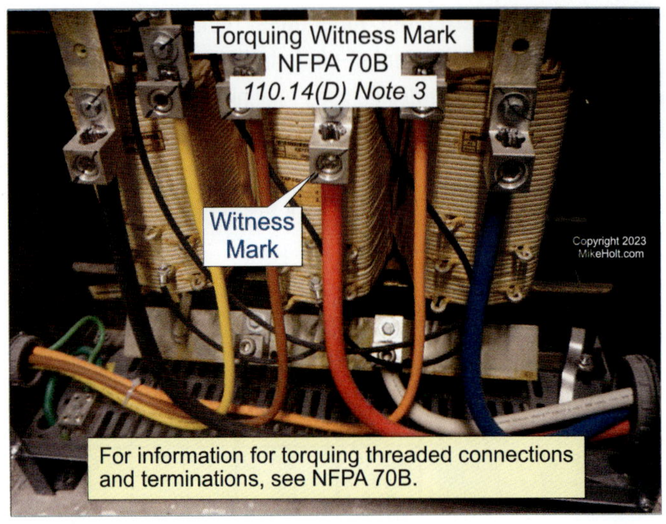
Torquing Witness Mark
NFPA 70B
110.14(D) Note 3
Witness Mark
Copyright 2023 MikeHolt.com
For information for torquing threaded connections and terminations, see NFPA 70B.

▸**Figure 110–39**

CHAPTER
1

REVIEW QUESTIONS

NFPA
70
nec

Please use the 2023 *Code* book to answer the following questions.

Article 100—Definitions

1. Capable of being removed or exposed without damaging the building structure or finish or not permanently closed in or blocked by the structure, other electrical equipment, other building systems, or finish of the building refers to _____.

   (a) wiring methods that are accessible
   (b) equipment that is accessible
   (c) being readily accessible
   (d) being serviceable

2. "_____" means acceptable to the authority having jurisdiction.

   (a) Identified
   (b) Listed
   (c) Approved
   (d) Labeled

3. A device that, when inserted in a receptacle, establishes a connection between the conductors of the attached flexible cord and the conductors connected permanently to the receptacle is known as a(an) "_____."

   (a) attachment plug
   (b) plug cap
   (c) plug
   (d) any of these

4. In many circumstances, the _____ or his or her designated agent assumes the role of the authority having jurisdiction.

   (a) property owner
   (b) developer
   (c) general contractor
   (d) insurance underwriter

5. "Bonded" is defined as _____ to establish electrical continuity and conductivity.

   (a) isolated
   (b) guarded
   (c) connected
   (d) separated

6. The connection between two or more portions of the equipment grounding conductor is the definition of a(an) "_____."

   (a) system bonding jumper
   (b) main bonding jumper
   (c) equipment ground-fault jumper
   (d) equipment bonding jumper

7. The connection between the grounded circuit conductor and the equipment grounding conductor, or the supply-side bonding jumper, or both, at the service is the "_____ bonding jumper."

   (a) main
   (b) system
   (c) equipment
   (d) circuit

8. A conductor installed on the supply side of a service or within a service equipment enclosure, or for a separately derived system, to ensure the required electrical conductivity between metal parts required to be electrically connected is known as the "_____."

   (a) supply-side bonding jumper
   (b) ungrounded conductor
   (c) electrical supply source
   (d) grounding electrode conductor

9. The connection between the grounded circuit conductor and the supply-side bonding jumper or equipment grounding conductor, or both, at a _____ is called a "system bonding jumper."

   (a) service disconnect
   (b) separately derived system
   (c) motor control center
   (d) separate building or structure disconnect

10. The circuit conductors between the final overcurrent device protecting the circuit and the outlet(s) are known as "_____ conductors."

   (a) feeder
   (b) branch-circuit
   (c) home run
   (d) main circuit

11. The *NEC* defines a(an) "_____" as a structure that stands alone or that is separated from adjoining structures by fire walls.

   (a) unit
   (b) apartment
   (c) building
   (d) utility

12. A cable tray system is a unit or assembly of units or sections and associated fittings forming a _____ system used to securely fasten or support cables and raceways.

   (a) structural
   (b) flexible
   (c) movable
   (d) secure

13. Type _____ cable is a fabricated assembly of insulated conductors in a flexible interlocked metallic armor.

   (a) AC
   (b) TC
   (c) NM
   (d) MA

14. Coaxial cable is a cylindrical assembly composed of a conductor centered inside a metallic tube or shield, separated by a(an) _____ material and usually covered by an insulating jacket.

   (a) insulating
   (b) conductive
   (c) isolating
   (d) dielectric

15. Type _____ cable is a factory assembly of insulated circuit conductors in an armor of interlocking metal tape, or a smooth or corrugated metallic sheath.

   (a) AC
   (b) MC
   (c) NM
   (d) CMS

16. Type _____ cable is a cable with insulated conductors within an overall nonmetallic jacket.

   (a) AC
   (b) MC
   (c) NM
   (d) TC

17. Type _____ cable is a factory assembly of two or more insulated conductors, with or without associated bare or covered grounding conductors, under a nonmetallic jacket.

   (a) NM
   (b) TC
   (c) SE
   (d) UF

18. Type _____ cable is a factory assembly of one or more insulated conductors with an integral or an overall covering of nonmetallic material suitable for direct burial in the earth.

   (a) NM
   (b) UF
   (c) SE
   (d) TC

19. _____ is a raceway of circular cross section made of a helically wound, formed, interlocked metal strip.

   (a) Type MC cable
   (b) Type AC cable
   (c) LFMC
   (d) FMC

20. _____ is a raceway of circular cross section having an outer liquidtight, nonmetallic, sunlight-resistant jacket over an inner flexible metal core.

   (a) FMC
   (b) LFNMC
   (c) LFMC
   (d) Vinyl-Clad Type MC

1st Printing

21. A rigid nonmetallic raceway of circular cross section, with integral or associated couplings, connectors, and fittings for the installation of electrical conductors and cables describes _____.

    (a) ENT
    (b) RMC
    (c) IMC
    (d) PVC

22. Areas or enclosures without adequate ventilation, where electrical equipment is located and pool sanitation chemicals are stored, handled, or dispensed is the definition of a _____.

    (a) hazardous area
    (b) restricted area
    (c) corrosive environment
    (d) wet location

23. A(An) _____ is a device, or group of devices, by which the conductors of a circuit can be disconnected from their source of supply.

    (a) feeder
    (b) enclosure
    (c) disconnecting means
    (d) conductor interrupter

24. A fixed, stationary, or portable self-contained, electrically operated and/or electrically illuminated utilization equipment with words or symbols designed to convey information or attract attention is the definition of _____.

    (a) an electric sign
    (b) equipment
    (c) appliances
    (d) exit lighting

25. "Likely to become energized" is defined as conductive material that could become energized because of _____ or electrical spacing.

    (a) improper installation
    (b) poor maintenance
    (c) the failure of electrical insulation
    (d) power surges

26. A(An) _____ at agricultural buildings is where conductive elements are connected together to minimize voltage differences.

    (a) voltage gradient
    (b) equipotential plane
    (c) supplementary grounding system
    (d) current dissipation system

27. "Exposed (as applied to _____)," is defined as on or attached to the surface, or behind access panels designed to allow access.

    (a) equipment
    (b) luminaires
    (c) wiring methods
    (d) motors

28. The *NEC* defines a "_____" as all circuit conductors between the service equipment, the source of a separately derived system, or other power supply source, and the final branch-circuit overcurrent device.

    (a) service
    (b) feeder
    (c) branch circuit
    (d) all of these

29. A fountain is defined as an ornamental structure or recreational water feature from which one or more jets or streams of water are discharged into the air, including splash pads, and _____ pools.

    (a) ornamental
    (b) wading
    (c) seasonal
    (d) permanently installed

30. A generator is a machine that converts mechanical energy into electrical energy by means of a _____ and alternator and/or inverter.

    (a) converter
    (b) rectifier
    (c) prime mover
    (d) turbine

31. Earth, as used in the *NEC* best describes the term _____.

    (a) bonded
    (b) ground
    (c) effective ground-fault current path
    (d) guarded

32. A(An) _____ is an unintentional, electrically conductive connection between an ungrounded conductor of an electrical circuit, and the normally noncurrent-carrying conductors, metal enclosures, metal raceways, metal equipment, or earth.

    (a) grounded conductor
    (b) ground fault
    (c) equipment ground
    (d) bonding jumper

33. Connected (connecting) to ground or to a conductive body that extends the ground connection is called "_____."

    (a) equipment grounding
    (b) bonded
    (c) grounded
    (d) all of these

34. A system or circuit conductor that is intentionally grounded is called a(an) "_____."

    (a) grounding conductor
    (b) unidentified conductor
    (c) grounded conductor
    (d) grounding electrode conductor

35. A(An) _____ grounded system is an electrical system that is grounded by intentionally connecting the system neutral point to ground through an impedance device.

    (a) impedance
    (b) solidly
    (c) isolated
    (d) separately

36. A functionally grounded system has an electrical ground reference for operational purposes that is not _____ grounded.

    (a) effectively
    (b) sufficiently
    (c) solidly
    (d) any of these

37. A functionally grounded system is often connected to ground through an electronic means internal to an inverter or charge controller that provides _____.

    (a) overcurrent protection
    (b) ground-fault protection
    (c) arc-fault protection
    (d) current-limiting properties

38. Connected to ground without the insertion of any resistor or impedance device is referred to as "_____."

    (a) grounded
    (b) solidly grounded
    (c) effectively grounded
    (d) a grounding conductor

39. A(An) "_____" is a device intended for the protection of personnel that functions to de-energize a circuit or portion thereof within an established period of time when a ground-fault current exceeds the values established for a Class A device.

    (a) dual-element fuse
    (b) inverse time breaker
    (c) ground-fault circuit interrupter
    (d) safety switch

40. A Class A GFCI trips when the ground-fault current is _____ or higher.

    (a) 4 mA
    (b) 5 mA
    (c) 6 mA
    (d) 7 mA

41. An effective ground-fault current path is an intentionally constructed, low-impedance electrically conductive path designed and intended to carry current during a ground-fault event from the point of a ground fault on a wiring system to _____.

    (a) ground
    (b) earth
    (c) the electrical supply source
    (d) the grounding electrode

42. A(An) _____ is a conductive path(s) that is part of an effective ground-fault current path and connects normally noncurrent-carrying metal parts of equipment together and to the system grounded conductor or to the grounding electrode conductor, or both.

    (a) grounding electrode conductor
    (b) main bonding jumper
    (c) system bonding jumper
    (d) equipment grounding conductor

43. An impedance grounding conductor is a conductor that connects the system _____ to the impedance device in an impedance grounded system.

    (a) main bonding jumper
    (b) neutral point
    (c) supply-side bonding jumper
    (d) load-side bonding jumper

1st Printing

44. A conducting object through which a direct connection to earth is established is a "_____."

(a) bonding conductor
(b) grounding conductor
(c) grounding electrode
(d) grounded conductor

45. A conductor used to connect the system grounded conductor, or the equipment to a grounding electrode or to a point on the grounding electrode system, is called the "_____ conductor."

(a) main grounding
(b) common main
(c) equipment grounding
(d) grounding electrode

46. A handhole enclosure is an enclosure for use in underground systems, provided with an open or closed bottom, and sized to allow personnel to _____.

(a) enter and exit freely
(b) reach into but not enter
(c) have full working space
(d) visually examine the interior

47. Health care facilities are defined as buildings or portions of buildings, or mobile enclosures in which human medical, dental, _____, or surgical care are provided.

(a) psychiatric
(b) nursing
(c) obstetrical
(d) any of these

48. Recognized as suitable for the specific purpose, function, use, environment, and application is the definition of "_____."

(a) labeled
(b) identified (as applied to equipment)
(c) listed
(d) approved

49. Information and technology equipment and systems are used for creation and manipulation of _____.

(a) data
(b) voice
(c) video
(d) all of these

50. A device that provides a means to connect intersystem bonding conductors for _____ systems to the grounding electrode system defines the term "intersystem bonding termination."

(a) limited-energy
(b) low-voltage
(c) communications
(d) power and lighting

51. A(An) _____ is equipment that changes dc to ac.

(a) diode
(b) rectifier
(c) transistor
(d) inverter

52. Equipment or materials to which a label, symbol, or other identifying mark of a product evaluation organization that is acceptable to the authority having jurisdiction has been attached is known as "_____."

(a) listed
(b) labeled
(c) approved
(d) identified

53. A "limited care facility" is defined as a building or portion thereof used on a(an) _____ basis for the housing of four or more persons who are incapable of self-preservation because of age; physical limitation due to accident or illness; or limitations such as intellectual disability/developmental disability, mental illness, or chemical dependency.

(a) occasional
(b) 10-hour or less per day
(c) 24-hour
(d) temporary

54. Equipment, materials, or services included in a list published by an organization that is acceptable to the authority having jurisdiction defines the term "_____."

(a) booked
(b) a digest
(c) a manifest
(d) listed

55. Hazardous (classified) locations are defined as those spaces or areas where fire or explosion hazards might exist due to _____.

(a) flammable gases or vapors
(b) combustible dusts
(c) ignitible fibers/flyings
(d) any of these

56. For pools, fountains, and similar installations, the "low-voltage contact limit" is a voltage not exceeding _____.

(a) 15V (RMS) for sinusoidal ac or 21.20V peak for nonsinusoidal ac
(b) 30V for continuous dc
(c) 12.40V peak for dc that is interrupted at a rate of 10 to 200 Hz
(d) all of these

57. A "luminaire" is a complete lighting unit consisting of a light source such as a lamp or lamps, together with the parts designed to position the _____ and connect it to the power supply.

(a) lampholder
(b) light source
(c) fixture
(d) bulb

58. A "wet-niche luminaire" is intended to be installed in a _____ surrounded by water.

(a) transformer
(b) forming shell
(c) hydromassage bathtub
(d) all of these

59. A "neutral conductor" is the conductor connected to the _____ of a system, which is intended to carry current under normal conditions.

(a) grounding electrode
(b) neutral point
(c) intersystem bonding termination
(d) electrical grid

60. The _____ is the "neutral point."

(a) common point on a wye-connection in a polyphase system
(b) midpoint on a single-phase, 3-wire system
(c) midpoint of a single-phase portion of a 3-phase delta system
(d) any of these

61. A panel, including buses and automatic overcurrent devices, designed to be placed in a cabinet, enclosure, or cutout box and accessible only from the front is known as a "_____."

(a) switchboard
(b) disconnect
(c) panelboard
(d) switchgear

62. A patient "_____" is the location of a patient sleeping bed, or the bed or procedure table of a Category 1 space.

(a) bed location
(b) care area
(c) observation area
(d) sterile area

63. The "patient care space category" is any space of a health care facility where patients are intended to be _____.

(a) admitted
(b) evaluated
(c) registered
(d) examined or treated

64. Permanently installed pools are those that are constructed or installed in the ground or partially in the ground, and all pools installed inside of a building, whether or not served by electrical circuits of any nature.

(a) in the ground
(b) partially in the ground
(c) inside of a building
(d) any of these

65. A "PV dc circuit" is any dc conductor in PV source circuits, PV string circuits, and PV _____ converter circuits.

(a) ac-to-dc
(b) dc-to-ac
(c) dc-to-dc
(d) any of these

66. A "PV _____" is a complete, environmentally protected unit consisting of solar cells and other components, designed to produce dc power.

(a) interface
(b) battery
(c) module
(d) cell bank

67. The *NEC* defines a(an) "_____" as one who has skills and knowledge related to the construction and operation of the electrical equipment and installations and has received safety training to recognize and avoid the hazards involved.

(a) inspector
(b) master electrician
(c) journeyman electrician
(d) qualified person

68. A "surface metal raceway" is a metal raceway that is intended to be mounted to the surface of a structure, with associated couplings, connectors, boxes, and fittings for the _____ of electrical conductors.

(a) installation
(b) protection
(c) routing
(d) enclosure

69. A contact device installed at an outlet for the connection of an attachment plug is known as a(an) "_____."

(a) attachment point
(b) tap
(c) receptacle
(d) wall plug

70. A single "receptacle" is a single contact device with no other contact device on the same _____.

(a) circuit
(b) yoke or strap
(c) run
(d) equipment

71. A duplex "receptacle" is an example of a multiple receptacle that has two receptacles on the same _____.

(a) yoke or strap
(b) strap
(c) device
(d) cover plate

72. Article 100 contains only those definitions essential to the application of this *Code*. An article number in parentheses following the definition indicates that the definition only applies to that article.

(a) True
(b) False

73. A "_____ system" is an electrical power supply output, other than a service, having no direct connection(s) to circuit conductors of any other electrical source other than those established by grounding and bonding connections.

(a) separately derived
(b) classified
(c) direct
(d) emergency

74. The conductors and equipment connecting the serving utility to the wiring system of the premises served is called a "_____."

(a) branch circuit
(b) feeder
(c) service
(d) service attachment

75. "Service conductors" are the conductors from the service point to the _____.

(a) service disconnecting means
(b) panelboard
(c) switchgear
(d) fire switch

76. The "_____" is the necessary equipment, consisting of a circuit breaker(s) or switch(es) and fuse(s) and their accessories, connected to the serving utility and intended to constitute the main control and disconnect of the serving utility.

(a) service equipment
(b) feeder equipment
(c) feeder disconnect
(d) none of these

77. A "structure" is that which is _____, other than equipment.

(a) built
(b) constructed
(c) built or constructed
(d) none of these

78. A switch constructed so that it can be installed in device boxes or on box covers, or otherwise used in conjunction with wiring systems recognized by this *Code* is called a "_____ switch."

(a) transfer
(b) motor-circuit
(c) general-use snap
(d) bypass isolation

79. "_____" is an unthreaded thinwall raceway of circular cross section designed for the physical protection and routing of conductors and cables and for use as an equipment grounding conductor when installed utilizing appropriate fittings.

(a) LFNC
(b) EMT
(c) NUCC
(d) RTRC

80. "_____" is a pliable corrugated raceway of circular cross section, with integral or associated couplings, connectors, and fittings that are listed for the installation of electrical conductors.

(a) PVC
(b) ENT
(c) RMC
(d) IMC

Article 110—General Requirements For Electrical Installations

1. General requirements for the examination and approval, installation and use, access to and spaces about electrical conductors and equipment; enclosures intended for personnel entry; and tunnel installations are within the scope of _____.

(a) Article 800
(b) Article 300
(c) Article 110
(d) Annex J

2. The conductors and equipment required or permitted by this *Code* shall be acceptable only if _____.

(a) labeled
(b) listed
(c) approved
(d) identified

3. In judging equipment, considerations such as _____ shall be evaluated.

(a) mechanical strength
(b) wire-bending and connection space
(c) arcing effects
(d) all of these

4. In judging equipment, considerations such as cybersecurity for network-connected _____ to address its ability to withstand unauthorized updates and malicious attacks while continuing to perform its intended safety functionality shall be evaluated.

(a) normal equipment
(b) emergency equipment
(c) standby power equipment
(d) life safety equipment

5. Equipment that is _____ or identified for a use shall be installed and used in accordance with any instructions included in the listing, labeling, or identification.

(a) listed, labeled, or both
(b) listed
(c) marked
(d) suitable

6. The installation and use instructions for listed, labeled, or identified electrical equipment may be provided in the form of _____.

(a) printed material
(b) a quick response (QR) code
(c) an internet address to download instructions
(d) any of these

7. Product testing, evaluation, and listing (product certification) shall be performed by _____.

(a) recognized qualified electrical testing laboratories
(b) the manufacturer
(c) a qualified person
(d) an electrical engineer

8. If the conductor material is not specified, the sizes given in the *Code* shall apply to _____ conductors.

(a) aluminum
(b) copper-clad aluminum
(c) copper
(d) all of these

9. Conductor sizes are expressed in American Wire Gauge (AWG) or in _____.

(a) inches
(b) circular mils
(c) square inches
(d) cubic inches

10. Completed wiring installations shall be free from _____ other than as required or permitted elsewhere in this *Code*.

    (a) short circuits
    (b) ground faults
    (c) any connections to ground
    (d) all of these

11. Only wiring methods recognized as _____ are included in this *Code*.

    (a) expensive
    (b) efficient
    (c) suitable
    (d) cost effective

12. Unless identified for use in the operating environment, no conductors or equipment shall be _____ having a deteriorating effect on the conductors or equipment.

    (a) located in damp or wet locations
    (b) exposed to fumes, vapors, liquids, or gases
    (c) exposed to excessive temperatures
    (d) all of these

13. Equipment not _____ for outdoor use and equipment identified only for indoor use such as "dry locations" or "indoor use only," shall be protected against damage from the weather during construction.

    (a) listed
    (b) identified
    (c) suitable
    (d) marked

14. Some _____ can cause severe deterioration of many plastic materials used for insulating and structural applications in equipment.

    (a) cleaning and lubricating compounds
    (b) protective coatings
    (c) paints and enamels
    (d) detergents

15. Electrical equipment shall be installed _____.

    (a) in a professional and skillful manner
    (b) under the supervision of a licensed person
    (c) completely before being inspected
    (d) all of these

16. Internal parts of electrical equipment, including busbars, wiring terminals, insulators, and other surfaces, shall not be damaged or contaminated by foreign materials such as _____, or corrosive residues.

    (a) paint, plaster
    (b) cleaners
    (c) abrasives
    (d) any of these

17. Pressure terminal or pressure splicing connectors and soldering lugs shall be _____ for the material of the conductor and shall be properly installed and used.

    (a) listed
    (b) approved
    (c) identified
    (d) all of these

18. Connectors and terminals for conductors more finely stranded than Class B and Class C, as shown in Chapter 9, Table 10, shall be _____ for the specific conductor class or classes.

    (a) listed
    (b) approved
    (c) identified
    (d) all of these

19. Conductors of dissimilar metals shall not be intermixed in a terminal or splicing connector where physical contact occurs between dissimilar conductors unless the device is _____ for the purpose and conditions of use.

    (a) identified
    (b) listed
    (c) approved
    (d) designed

20. Connection of conductors to terminal parts shall ensure a mechanically secure electrical connection without damaging the conductors and shall be made by means of _____.

    (a) solder lugs
    (b) pressure connectors
    (c) splices to flexible leads
    (d) any of these

21. All _____ shall be covered with an insulation equivalent to that of the conductors or with an identified insulating device.

    (a) splices
    (b) joints
    (c) free ends of conductors
    (d) all of these

22. Tightening torque values for terminal connections shall be as indicated on equipment or in installation instructions provided by the manufacturer. An approved means shall be used to achieve the _____ torque value.

    (a) indicated
    (b) identified
    (c) maximum
    (d) minimum

23. Examples of approved means of achieving the indicated _____ values include torque tools or devices such as shear bolts or breakaway-style devices with visual indicators that demonstrate that the proper torque has been applied.

    (a) pressure
    (b) torque
    (c) tightening
    (d) tension

CHAPTER

2 WIRING AND PROTECTION

Introduction to Chapter 2—Wiring and Protection

Chapter 2 of the *Code* is divided into eleven articles containing the general rules for wiring and sizing circuits, overcurrent protection of conductors, overvoltage protection of equipment, and bonding and grounding. The rules in this chapter apply to all electrical installations covered by the *NEC*—except as modified in Chapters 5, 6, 7, or specifically referenced in Chapter 8 [90.3].

This chapter can be thought of as the preconstruction phase of a job because it is primarily focused on layout, sizing, and the protection of circuits. Every article in this chapter deals with a different aspect of designing safe wiring for an electrical system. The Chapter 2 articles covered by this material are:

- **Article 215—Feeders.** This article covers the requirements for the installation, sizing, and protection of feeders.
- **Article 250—Bonding and Grounding.** Article 250 covers the grounding requirements for providing a path to the Earth to reduce overvoltage from lightning, and the bonding requirements for the low-impedance fault current path necessary to facilitate the operation of overcurrent protective devices in the event of a ground fault.

ARTICLE
215

FEEDERS

Introduction to Article 215—Feeders

Article 215 contains the general requirements for feeder conductors which extend between a service disconnect, transformer, generator, PV system output circuit, or other power-supply source and the branch-circuit overcurrent protective device. Feeders have specific requirement permissions that differ from branch circuits making the proper identification of feeders critical. Topics covered in this material for Article 215 include:

- Scope
- Feeder Equipment Grounding Conductor

215.1 Scope

Article 215 covers the installation, conductor sizing, and overcurrent protection requirements for feeder conductors not over 1000V ac or 1500V dc. ▶Figure 215-1

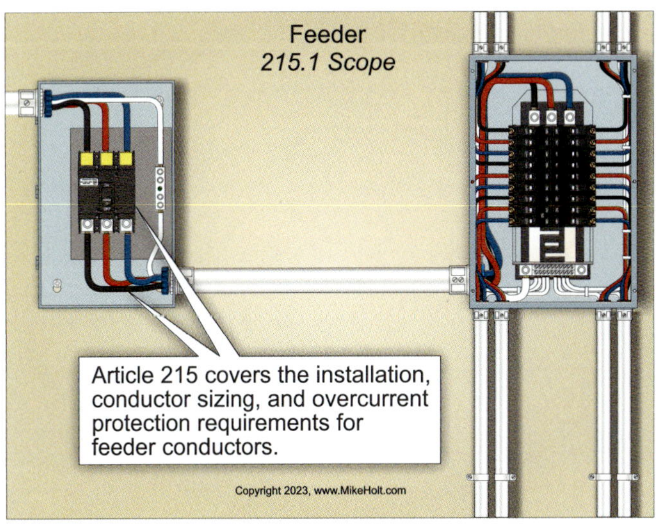
Feeder
215.1 Scope
Article 215 covers the installation, conductor sizing, and overcurrent protection requirements for feeder conductors.
Copyright 2023, www.MikeHolt.com

▶Figure 215-1

According to Article 100, "Feeders" are the conductors between the service disconnect, a separately derived system, or other power supply, and the final branch-circuit overcurrent protective device. ▶Figure 215-2 and ▶Figure 215-3

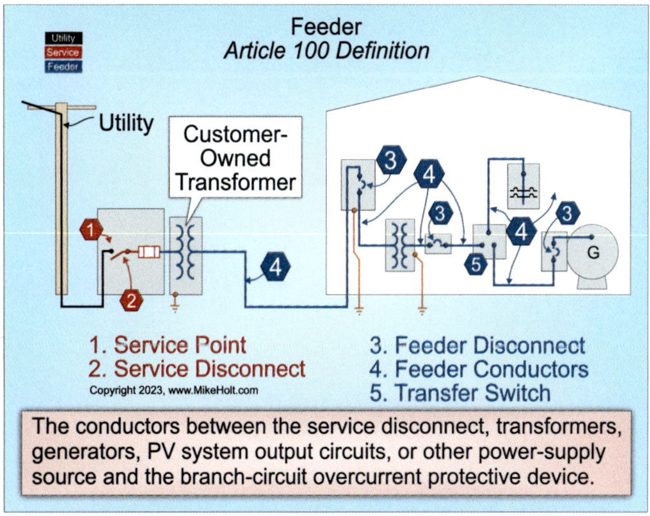
Feeder
Article 100 Definition
Utility
Service
Feeder
Utility
Customer-Owned Transformer
G
1. Service Point
2. Service Disconnect
3. Feeder Disconnect
4. Feeder Conductors
5. Transfer Switch
Copyright 2023, www.MikeHolt.com
The conductors between the service disconnect, transformers, generators, PV system output circuits, or other power-supply source and the branch-circuit overcurrent protective device.

▶Figure 215-2

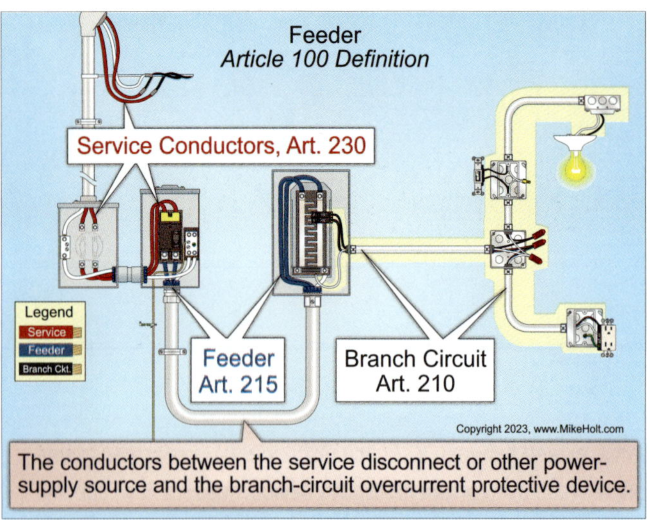
Feeder
Article 100 Definition
Service Conductors, Art. 230
Legend
Service
Feeder
Branch Ckt.
Feeder
Art. 215
Branch Circuit
Art. 210
Copyright 2023, www.MikeHolt.com
The conductors between the service disconnect or other power-supply source and the branch-circuit overcurrent protective device.

▸Figure 215-3

215.6 Feeder Equipment Grounding Conductor

A feeder must have an equipment grounding conductor. ▸Figure 215-4

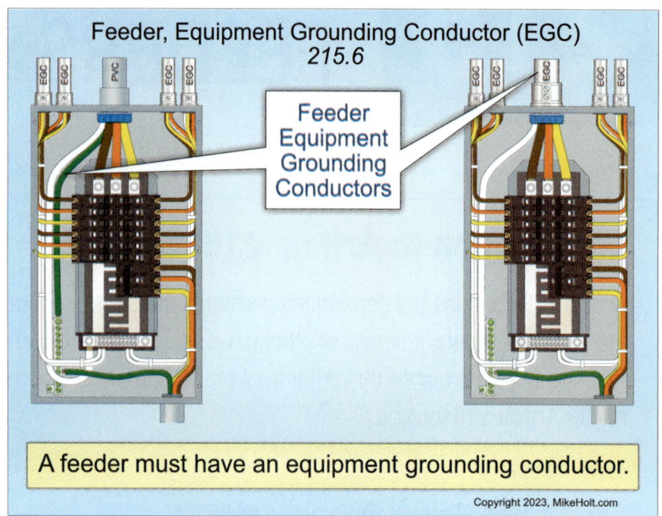
Feeder, Equipment Grounding Conductor (EGC)
215.6
EGC
PVC
Feeder
Equipment
Grounding
Conductors
A feeder must have an equipment grounding conductor.
Copyright 2023, MikeHolt.com

▸Figure 215-4

ARTICLE 250 GROUNDING AND BONDING

Introduction to Article 250—Grounding and Bonding

Article 250 covers the general requirements for bonding and grounding electrical installations. The terminology used in this article has been a source of much confusion over the years so pay careful attention to the definitions pertaining to Article 250. Understanding the difference between bonding and grounding will help you correctly apply the provisions of this article. Because of the massive size and scope of Article 250, Figure 250.1 in the *NEC* is provided as a reference for the locations of the different types of rules. Of the ten parts contained in this article only parts one through seven are covered in this material. Topics covered in this material for Article 250 include:

- General Requirements for Grounding and Bonding
- Objectionable Current
- Protection of Clamps and Fittings
- System Grounding Requirements
- Bonding Jumpers
- Generator Bonding
- Grounding Electrode System
- Service Equipment Bonding
- Piping System and Structural Steel Bonding
- Equipment Grounding conductors (EGCs)

Article 250 consists of ten parts:

- Part I. General
- Part II. System Grounding
- Part III. Grounding Electrode System and Grounding Electrode Conductor (GEC)
- Part IV. Enclosure, Raceway, and Service Cable Connections
- Part V. Bonding
- Part VI. Equipment Grounding Conductors (EGC)
- Part VII. Methods of EGC Connections
- Part VIII. Direct-Current Systems
- Part IX. Instruments, Meters, and Relays
- Part X. Grounding of Systems and Circuits of over 1000 Volts

Part I. General

250.1 Scope

Article 250 covers the general requirements for grounding and bonding electrical installations. ▶Figure 250–1

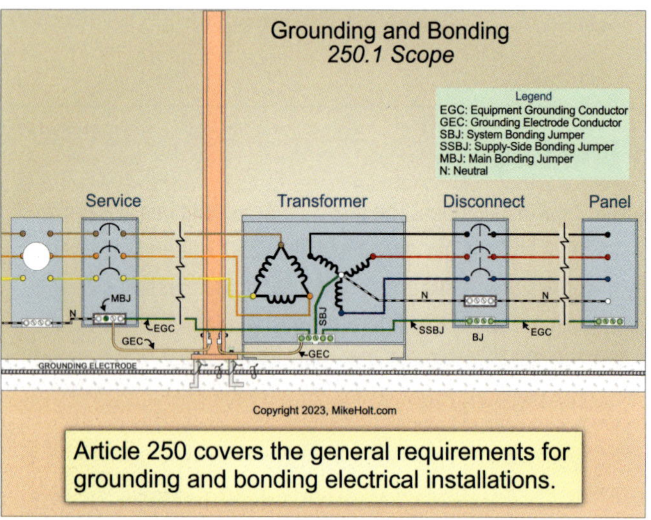
Grounding and Bonding
250.1 Scope
Legend
EGC: Equipment Grounding Conductor
GEC: Grounding Electrode Conductor
SBJ: System Bonding Jumper
SSBJ: Supply-Side Bonding Jumper
MBJ: Main Bonding Jumper
N: Neutral
Service
Transformer
Disconnect
Panel
MBJ
EGC
GEC
SBJ
GEC
SSBJ
BJ
EGC
N
N
GROUNDING ELECTRODE
Copyright 2023, MikeHolt.com
Article 250 covers the general requirements for grounding and bonding electrical installations.
▶Figure 250–1

Author's Comment:

- There are two completely different concepts being covered in this article: "grounding" which is the connection to the Earth, and "bonding" which is connecting conductive metal parts together to ensure electrical conductivity between metal parts. ▶Figure 250–2

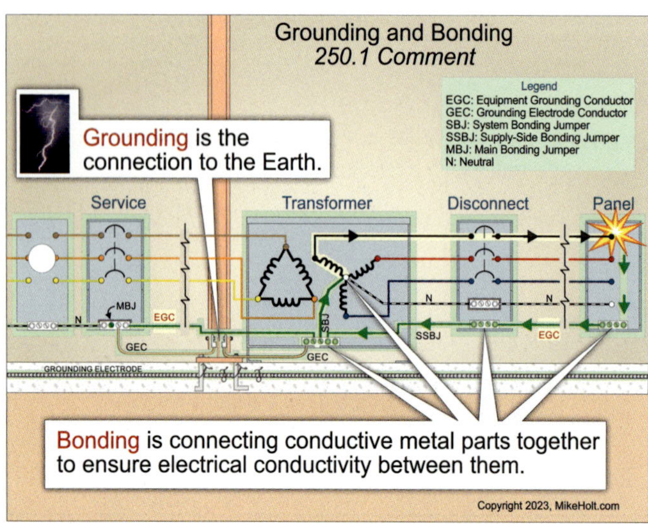
Grounding and Bonding
250.1 Comment
Legend
EGC: Equipment Grounding Conductor
GEC: Grounding Electrode Conductor
SBJ: System Bonding Jumper
SSBJ: Supply-Side Bonding Jumper
MBJ: Main Bonding Jumper
N: Neutral
Grounding is the connection to the Earth.
Service
Transformer
Disconnect
Panel
MBJ
EGC
GEC
SBJ
GEC
SSBJ
EGC
N
N
GROUNDING ELECTRODE
Bonding is connecting conductive metal parts together to ensure electrical conductivity between them.
Copyright 2023, MikeHolt.com
▶Figure 250–2

According to Article 100, "Bonding" means connected to establish electrical continuity and conductivity. ▶Figure 250–3

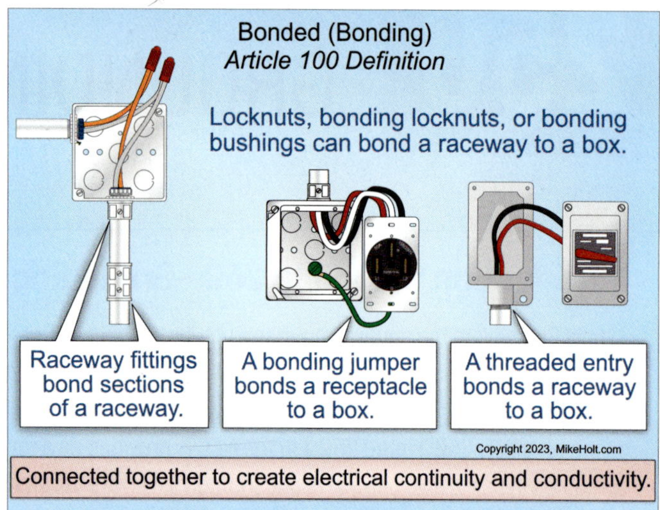
Bonded (Bonding)
Article 100 Definition
Locknuts, bonding locknuts, or bonding bushings can bond a raceway to a box.
Raceway fittings bond sections of a raceway.
A bonding jumper bonds a receptacle to a box.
A threaded entry bonds a raceway to a box.
Copyright 2023, MikeHolt.com
Connected together to create electrical continuity and conductivity.
▶Figure 250–3

According to Article 100, "Grounding" means the connection to the Earth (ground) or to a conductive body that extends the ground connection. ▶Figure 250–4

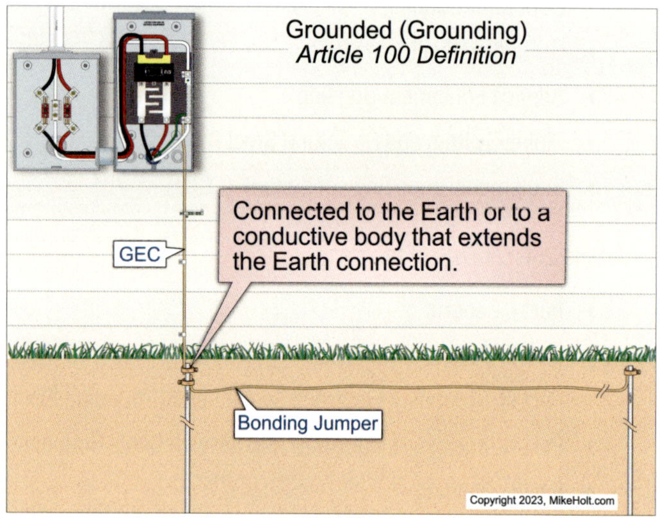
Grounded (Grounding)
Article 100 Definition
Connected to the Earth or to a conductive body that extends the Earth connection.
GEC
Bonding Jumper
Copyright 2023, MikeHolt.com
▶Figure 250–4

According to Article 100, "Ground" means the Earth. ▶Figure 250–5

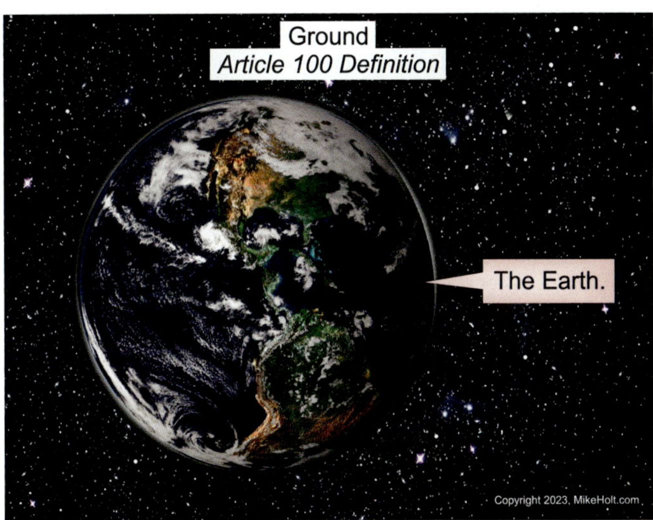

Ground
Article 100 Definition
The Earth.
Copyright 2023, MikeHolt.com

▸Figure 250–5

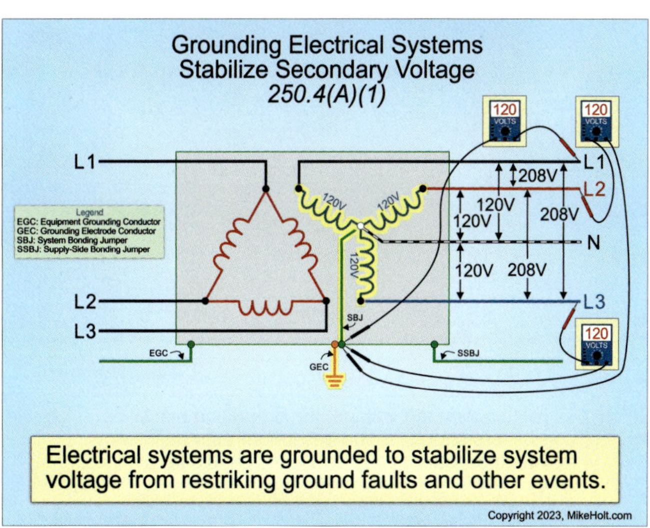

Grounding Electrical Systems
Stabilize Secondary Voltage
250.4(A)(1)
L1
L2
L3
N
120V
208V
EGC
GEC
SBJ
SSBJ
Electrical systems are grounded to stabilize system voltage from restriking ground faults and other events.
Copyright 2023, MikeHolt.com

▸Figure 250–7

250.4 Performance Requirements for Grounding and Bonding

(A) Grounded Systems.

(1) Grounding of Electrical Systems.

Reduce Inducted Voltage. Electrical systems are grounded to the Earth to reduce induced voltage on the system conductors from indirect lightning strikes. ▸Figure 250–6

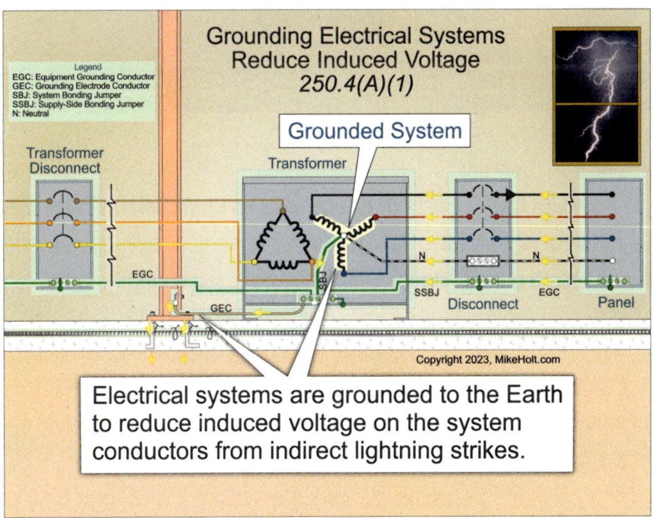

Grounding Electrical Systems
Reduce Induced Voltage
250.4(A)(1)
Grounded System
Transformer Disconnect
Transformer
Disconnect
Panel
EGC
GEC
SSBJ
Electrical systems are grounded to the Earth to reduce induced voltage on the system conductors from indirect lightning strikes.
Copyright 2023, MikeHolt.com

▸Figure 250–6

Stabilize System Voltage. Electrical systems are grounded to stabilize system voltage from restricting ground faults and other events. ▸Figure 250–7

Author's Comment:

- System grounding reduces induced voltage from indirect lightning. It stabilizes system voltage from restriking ground faults, thereby ensuring longer insulation life for motors, transformers, and other electrical equipment. ▸Figure 250–8

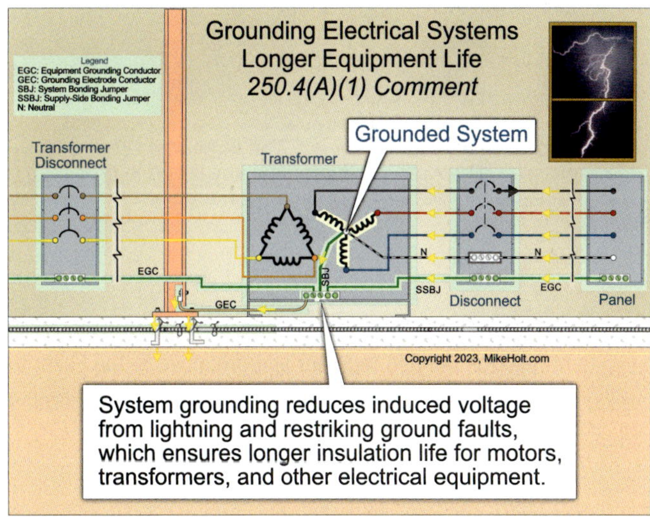

Grounding Electrical Systems
Longer Equipment Life
250.4(A)(1) Comment
Grounded System
Transformer Disconnect
Transformer
Disconnect
Panel
EGC
GEC
SSBJ
System grounding reduces induced voltage from lightning and restriking ground faults, which ensures longer insulation life for motors, transformers, and other electrical equipment.
Copyright 2023, MikeHolt.com

▸Figure 250–8

Note 1: To reduce induced voltage, the grounding electrode conductors should not be any longer than necessary, and unnecessary bends and loops should be avoided. ▸Figure 250–9 and ▸Figure 250–10

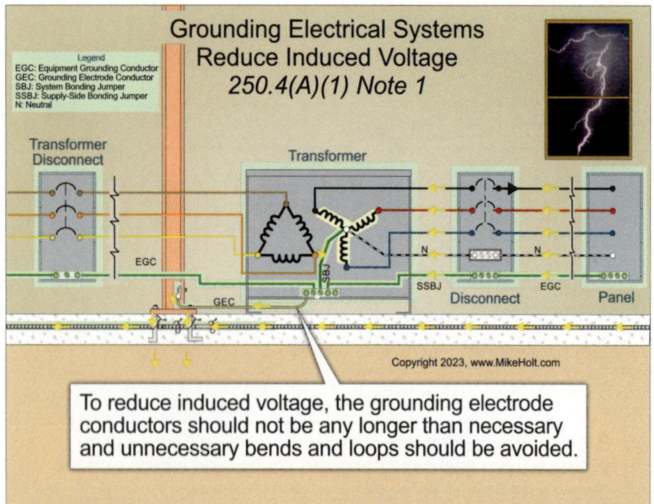

Grounding Electrical Systems
Reduce Induced Voltage
250.4(A)(1) Note 1
Legend
EGC: Equipment Grounding Conductor
GEC: Grounding Electrode Conductor
SBJ: System Bonding Jumper
SSBJ: Supply-Side Bonding Jumper
N: Neutral
Transformer Disconnect
Transformer
EGC
GEC
SBJ
N
N
SSBJ
Disconnect
EGC
Panel
Copyright 2023, www.MikeHolt.com
To reduce induced voltage, the grounding electrode conductors should not be any longer than necessary and unnecessary bends and loops should be avoided.

▸Figure 250–9

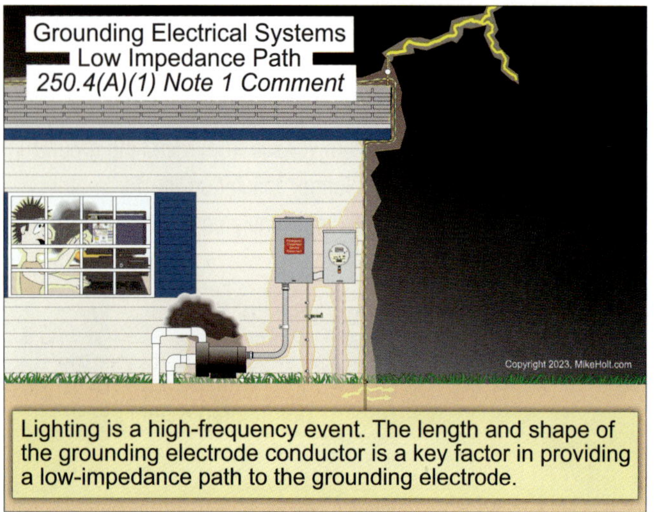

Grounding Electrical Systems
Low Impedance Path
250.4(A)(1) Note 1 Comment
Copyright 2023, MikeHolt.com
Lighting is a high-frequency event. The length and shape of the grounding electrode conductor is a key factor in providing a low-impedance path to the grounding electrode.

▸Figure 250–10

(2) Grounding Metal Parts of Equipment. Metal parts of electrical equipment must be bonded together and grounded to the Earth to reduce induced voltage on the metal parts from indirect lightning strikes. ▸Figure 250–11

Danger

DANGER: Failure to ground metal parts to the Earth can result in millions of volts of induced voltage on the metal parts generated by an indirect lightning strike. This energy seeks a path to the Earth within the building—possibly resulting in a fire and/or electric shock from a side flash. ▸Figure 250–12

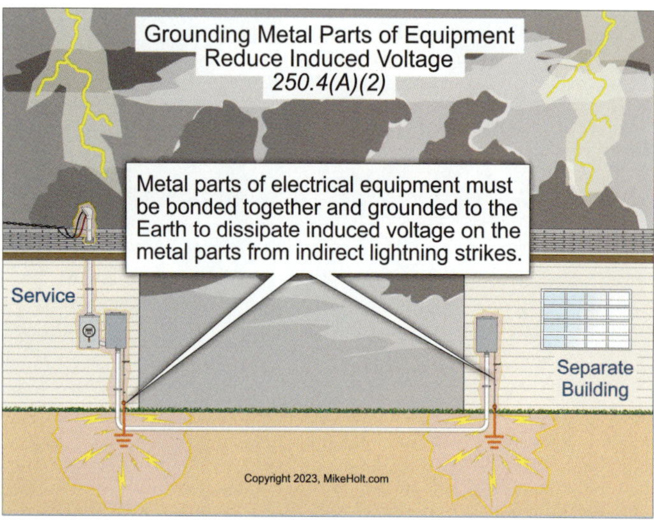

Grounding Metal Parts of Equipment
Reduce Induced Voltage
250.4(A)(2)
Metal parts of electrical equipment must be bonded together and grounded to the Earth to dissipate induced voltage on the metal parts from indirect lightning strikes.
Service
Separate Building
Copyright 2023, MikeHolt.com

▸Figure 250–11

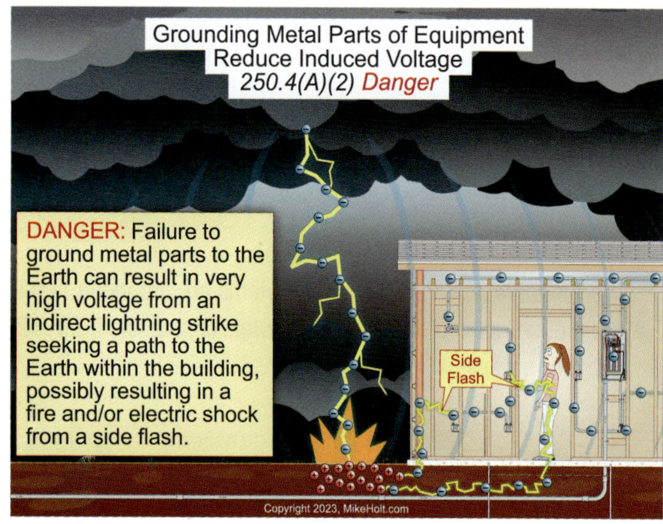

Grounding Metal Parts of Equipment
Reduce Induced Voltage
250.4(A)(2) Danger
DANGER: Failure to ground metal parts to the Earth can result in very high voltage from an indirect lightning strike seeking a path to the Earth within the building, possibly resulting in a fire and/or electric shock from a side flash.
Side Flash
Copyright 2023, MikeHolt.com

▸Figure 250–12

(3) Bonding Metal Parts of Equipment to Establish an Effective Ground-Fault Current Path. Metal parts of raceways, cables, and enclosures must be bonded together and to the source to establish an effective ground-fault current path. ▸Figure 250–13

According to Article 100, "Effective Ground-Fault Current Path" is an intentionally constructed low-impedance conductive path designed to carry fault current from the point of a ground fault to the source for the purpose of opening the circuit overcurrent protective device. ▸Figure 250–14

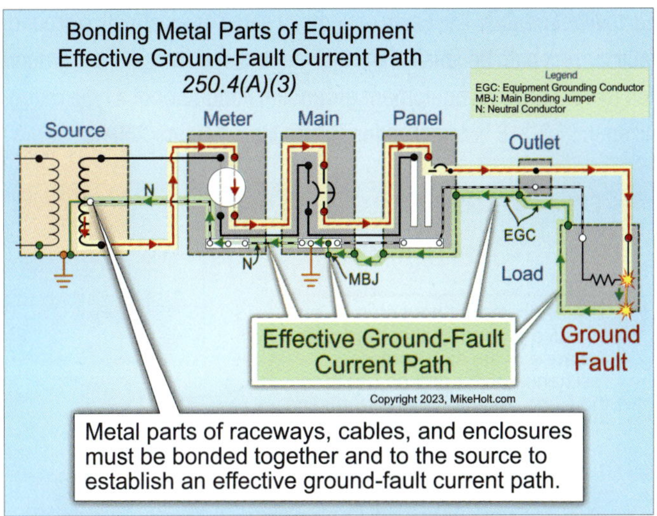
Bonding Metal Parts of Equipment
Effective Ground-Fault Current Path
250.4(A)(3)
Legend
EGC: Equipment Grounding Conductor
MBJ: Main Bonding Jumper
N: Neutral Conductor
Source
Meter
Main
Panel
Outlet
N
EGC
MBJ
Load
Effective Ground-Fault Current Path
Ground Fault
Copyright 2023, MikeHolt.com
Metal parts of raceways, cables, and enclosures must be bonded together and to the source to establish an effective ground-fault current path.

▸Figure 250–13

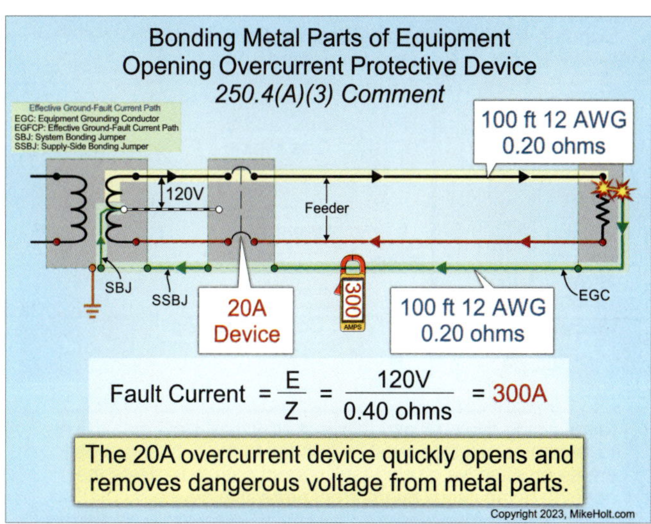
Bonding Metal Parts of Equipment
Opening Overcurrent Protective Device
250.4(A)(3) Comment
100 ft 12 AWG
0.20 ohms
120V
Feeder
SBJ
SSBJ
20A Device
300
100 ft 12 AWG
0.20 ohms
EGC
Fault Current = E/Z = 120V/0.40 ohms = 300A
The 20A overcurrent device quickly opens and removes dangerous voltage from metal parts.
Copyright 2023, MikeHolt.com

▸Figure 250–15

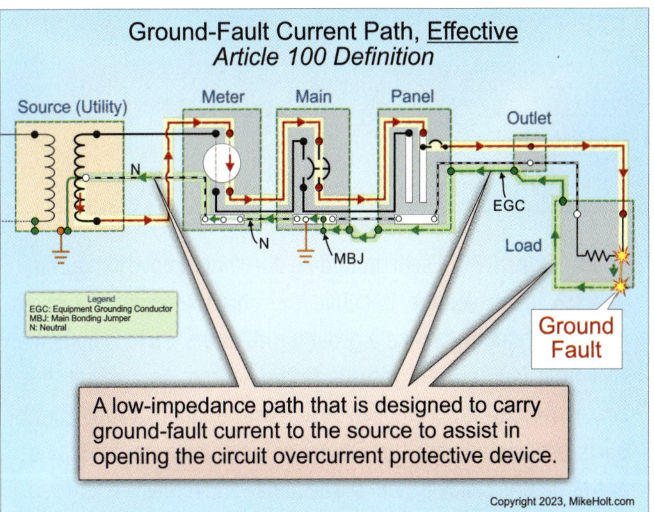
Ground-Fault Current Path, Effective
Article 100 Definition
Source (Utility)
Meter
Main
Panel
Outlet
N
EGC
MBJ
Load
Legend
EGC: Equipment Grounding Conductor
MBJ: Main Bonding Jumper
N: Neutral
Ground Fault
A low-impedance path that is designed to carry ground-fault current to the source to assist in opening the circuit overcurrent protective device.
Copyright 2023, MikeHolt.com

▸Figure 250–14

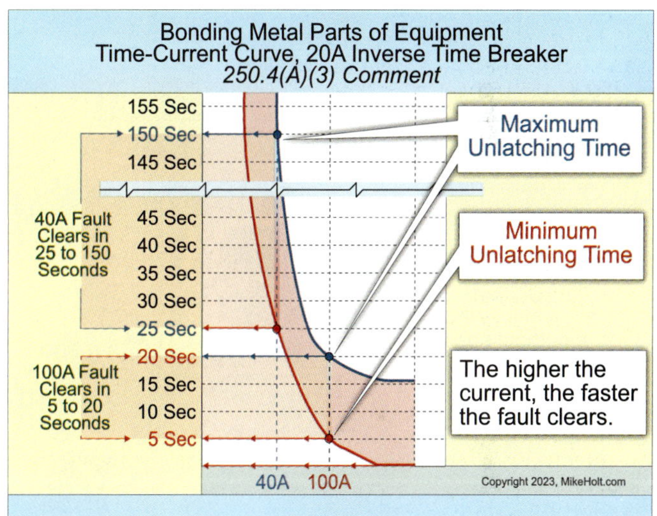
Bonding Metal Parts of Equipment
Time-Current Curve, 20A Inverse Time Breaker
250.4(A)(3) Comment
155 Sec
150 Sec
145 Sec
45 Sec
40 Sec
35 Sec
30 Sec
25 Sec
20 Sec
15 Sec
10 Sec
5 Sec
40A Fault Clears in 25 to 150 Seconds
100A Fault Clears in 5 to 20 Seconds
Maximum Unlatching Time
Minimum Unlatching Time
The higher the current, the faster the fault clears.
40A
100A
Copyright 2023, MikeHolt.com

▸Figure 250–16

Author's Comment:

- The purpose of the effective ground-fault current path is to quickly remove dangerous voltage on metal parts from a ground fault. The effective ground-fault current path must have sufficiently low impedance to the source so fault current will quickly rise to a level that will open the circuit overcurrent protective device. ▸Figure 250–15
- The time it takes for an overcurrent protective device to open is dependent on the magnitude of the fault current. A higher fault current value will result in a shorter clearing time for the overcurrent protective device. For example, a 20A overcurrent protective device with an overload of 40A (two times the 20A rating) takes 25 to 150 seconds to open. The same device at 100A (five times the 20A rating) trips in 5 to 20 seconds. ▸Figure 250–16

(4) Bonding Metal Piping and Structural Steel. Metal piping systems and exposed structural steel that is likely to become energized must be bonded to the source to facilitate opening of the circuit overcurrent protective device during a ground fault. ▸Figure 250–17

According to Article 100, "Energized, Likely to Become (Likely to Become Energized)" is conductive material that could become energized because of the failure of electrical insulation or electrical spacing. ▸Figure 250–18

(5) Effective Ground-Fault Current Path.

Opening Overcurrent Protective Device. Metal raceways, cables, and enclosures must be bonded together and to the source to create an effective ground-fault current path to facilitate the opening of the circuit overcurrent protective device. ▸Figure 250–19

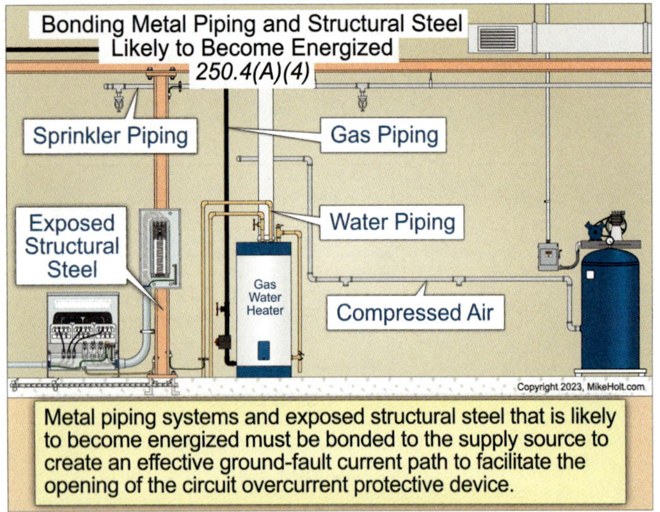

Bonding Metal Piping and Structural Steel
Likely to Become Energized
250.4(A)(4)
Sprinkler Piping
Gas Piping
Exposed Structural Steel
Water Piping
Gas Water Heater
Compressed Air
Copyright 2023, MikeHolt.com
Metal piping systems and exposed structural steel that is likely to become energized must be bonded to the supply source to create an effective ground-fault current path to facilitate the opening of the circuit overcurrent protective device.

▸Figure 250–17

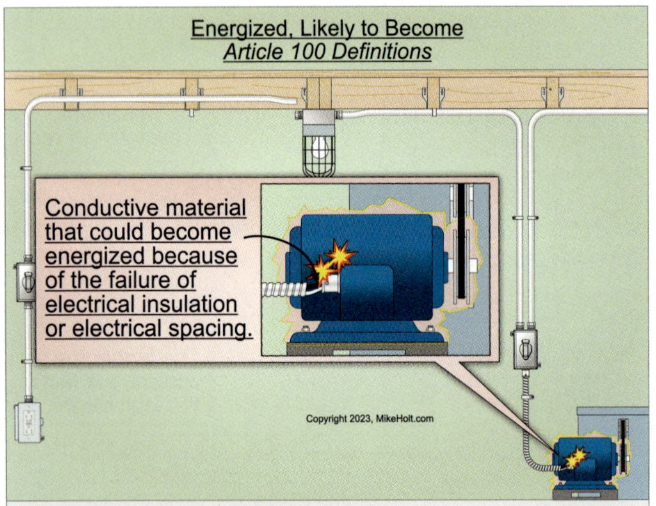

Energized, Likely to Become
Article 100 Definitions
Conductive material that could become energized because of the failure of electrical insulation or electrical spacing.
Copyright 2023, MikeHolt.com

▸Figure 250–18

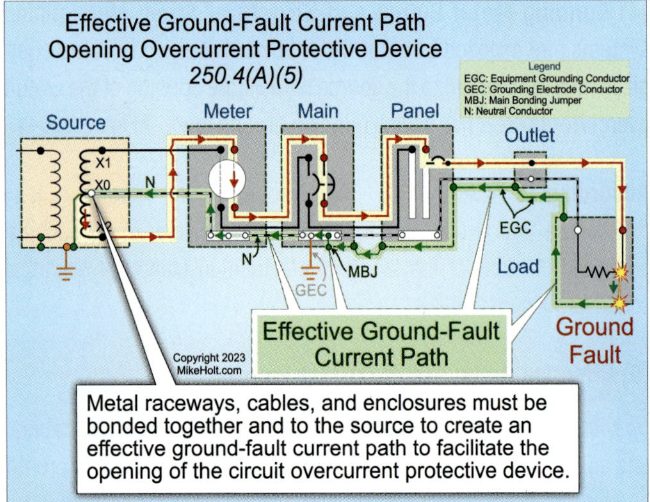

Effective Ground-Fault Current Path
Opening Overcurrent Protective Device
250.4(A)(5)
Legend
EGC: Equipment Grounding Conductor
GEC: Grounding Electrode Conductor
MBJ: Main Bonding Jumper
N: Neutral Conductor
Source
Meter
Main
Panel
Outlet
X1
X0
N
EGC
Load
MBJ
GEC
Effective Ground-Fault Current Path
Ground Fault
Copyright 2023 MikeHolt.com
Metal raceways, cables, and enclosures must be bonded together and to the source to create an effective ground-fault current path to facilitate the opening of the circuit overcurrent protective device.

▸Figure 250–19

Earth Not Suitable. The Earth cannot not serve as an effective ground-fault current path because of the high contact resistance of the ground rod to the Earth. An equipment grounding conductor of a type recognized in 250.118 is required for all circuits. ▸Figure 250–20

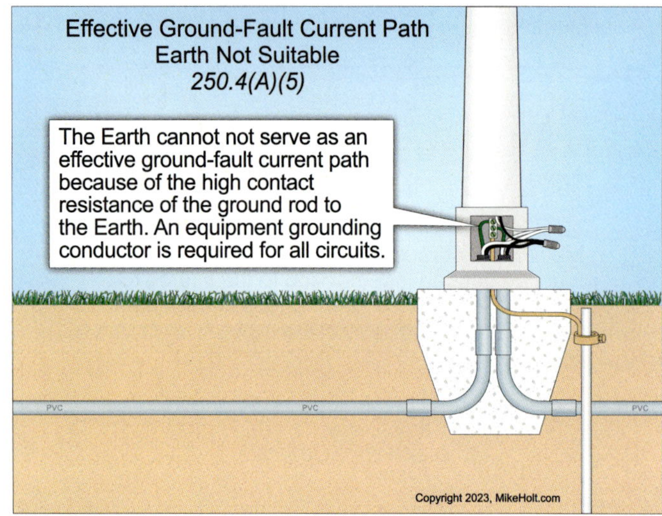

Effective Ground-Fault Current Path
Earth Not Suitable
250.4(A)(5)
The Earth cannot not serve as an effective ground-fault current path because of the high contact resistance of the ground rod to the Earth. An equipment grounding conductor is required for all circuits.
PVC
Copyright 2023, MikeHolt.com

▸Figure 250–20

Danger

DANGER: Earth grounding does not remove dangerous touch voltage because the contact resistance of a grounding electrode (like a ground rod) to the Earth is so high, very little fault current returns to the source. As a result, the circuit overcurrent protective device will not open, and all metal parts associated with the electrical installation, metal piping, and structural building steel will become—and remain—energized. ▸Figure 250–21

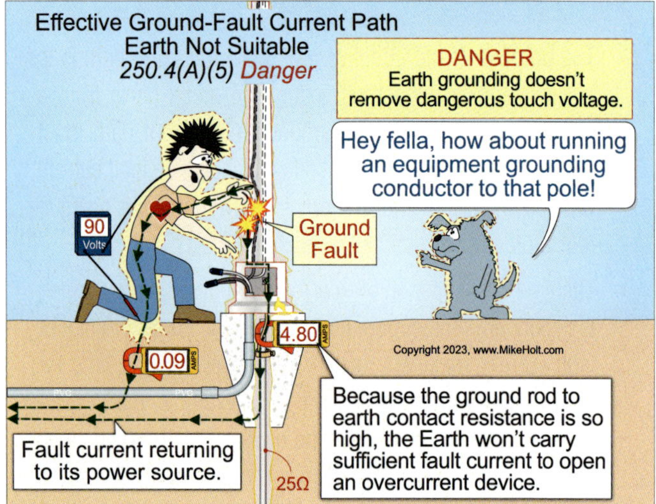

Effective Ground-Fault Current Path
Earth Not Suitable
250.4(A)(5) Danger
DANGER
Earth grounding doesn't remove dangerous touch voltage.
Hey fella, how about running an equipment grounding conductor to that pole!
90 Volts
Ground Fault
0.09
4.80
Copyright 2023, www.MikeHolt.com
Fault current returning to its power source.
25Ω
Because the ground rod to earth contact resistance is so high, the Earth won't carry sufficient fault current to open an overcurrent device.

▸Figure 250–21

▶ Example

Question: *What will the maximum fault current be when there is a 120V ground fault to the metal parts of a light pole that is grounded to a 25Ω ground rod, but not bonded to an effective ground-fault current path?* ▶Figure 250–22

(a) 3.70A (b) 4.80A (c) 5.20A (d) 6.40A

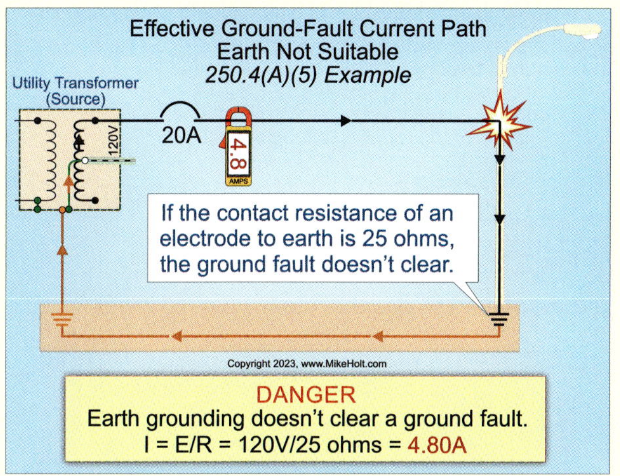
Effective Ground-Fault Current Path
Earth Not Suitable
250.4(A)(5) Example
Utility Transformer (Source)
120V
20A
4.8
AMPS
If the contact resistance of an electrode to earth is 25 ohms, the ground fault doesn't clear.
Copyright 2023, www.MikeHolt.com
DANGER
Earth grounding doesn't clear a ground fault.
I = E/R = 120V/25 ohms = 4.80A

▶Figure 250–22

Solution:

I = Volts/Resistance

I = 120V/25Ω

I = 4.80A

Answer: *(b) 4.80A*

Earth Shells

According to ANSI/IEEE 142, *Recommended Practice for Grounding of Industrial and Commercial Power Systems* (Green Book) [4.1.1], the resistance of the soil outward from a 10-ft ground rod is equal to the sum of the series resistances of the Earth shells. The shell nearest the ground rod has the highest resistance, and each shell further out has progressively larger areas and lower resistances. Do not be concerned if you do not understand this statement, just review the table below.

Distance from Rod	Soil Contact Resistance
1 ft (Shell 1)	68% of total contact resistance
3 ft (Shells 1 and 2)	75% of total contact resistance
5 ft (Shells 1, 2, and 3)	86% of total contact resistance

Contact Resistance. The Earth is an excellent conductor due to an almost limitless number of parallel paths over which electrons can flow. However, the problem lies in the contact resistance between the grounding electrode and the Earth. The surface area of the electrode contacting the Earth is minimal compared to the Earth itself.

Since voltage is directly proportional to resistance (Ohm's Law), the voltage gradient of the Earth around an energized rod (assuming a 120V ground fault) will be as follows: ▶Figure 250–23 and ▶Figure 250–24

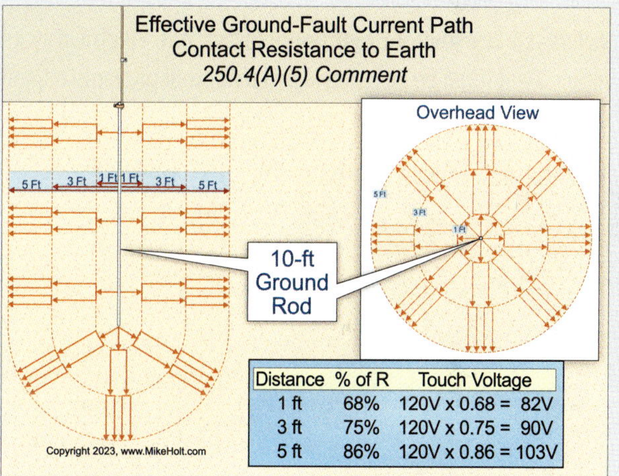
Effective Ground-Fault Current Path
Contact Resistance to Earth
250.4(A)(5) Comment
Overhead View
5 Ft
3 Ft
1 Ft
1 Ft
3 Ft
5 Ft
10-ft Ground Rod
Distance % of R Touch Voltage
1 ft 68% 120V x 0.68 = 82V
3 ft 75% 120V x 0.75 = 90V
5 ft 86% 120V x 0.86 = 103V
Copyright 2023, www.MikeHolt.com

▶Figure 250–23

Distance from Rod	Soil Contact Resistance	Voltage Gradient
1 ft (Shell 1)	68%	82V
3 ft (Shells 1 and 2)	75%	90V
5 ft (Shells 1, 2, and 3)	86%	103V

• • •

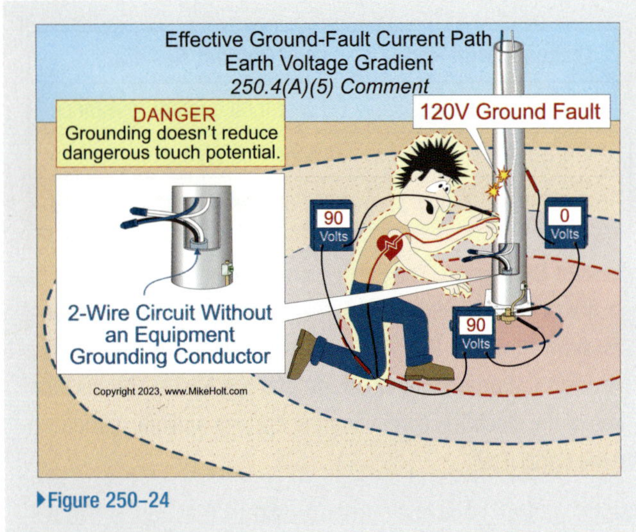

Effective Ground-Fault Current Path
Earth Voltage Gradient
250.4(A)(5) Comment
DANGER
Grounding doesn't reduce dangerous touch potential.
120V Ground Fault
90 Volts
0 Volts
90 Volts
2-Wire Circuit Without an Equipment Grounding Conductor
Copyright 2023, www.MikeHolt.com

▸Figure 250–24

250.6 Objectionable Current

(A) Arranged to Prevent Objectionable Current. Electrical systems and equipment must be installed in a manner that prevents objectionable current flowing on metal parts. ▸Figure 250–25

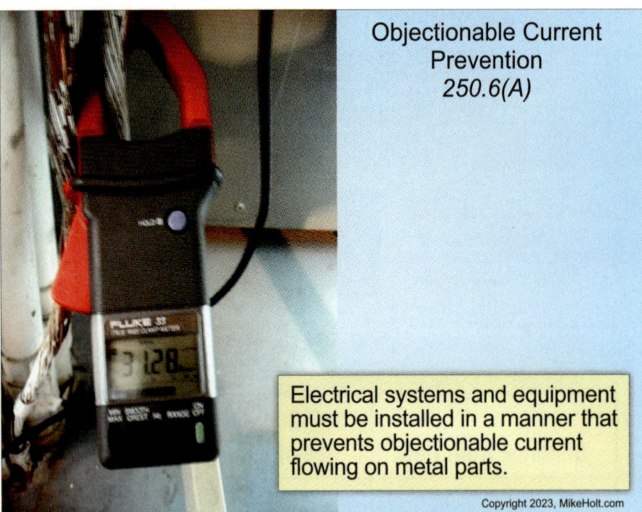

Objectionable Current
Prevention
250.6(A)
Electrical systems and equipment must be installed in a manner that prevents objectionable current flowing on metal parts.
Copyright 2023, MikeHolt.com

▸Figure 250–25

Objectionable Current

Objectionable neutral current occurs because of improper neutral-to-case connections or wiring errors that violate 250.24(B).

Panelboards. Objectionable neutral current will flow on metal parts and equipment grounding conductor when the neutral conductor is connected to the metal case of a panelboard on the load-side of the service equipment in violation of 250.24(B). ▸Figure 250–26

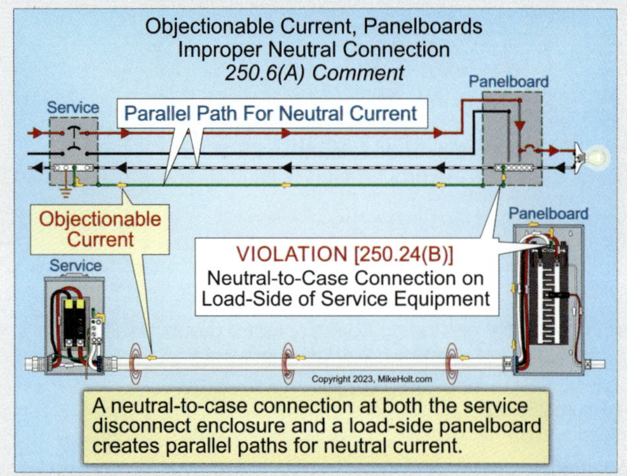

Objectionable Current, Panelboards
Improper Neutral Connection
250.6(A) Comment
Panelboard
Service
Parallel Path For Neutral Current
Objectionable Current
Panelboard
Service
VIOLATION [250.24(B)]
Neutral-to-Case Connection on Load-Side of Service Equipment
Copyright 2023, MikeHolt.com
A neutral-to-case connection at both the service disconnect enclosure and a load-side panelboard creates parallel paths for neutral current.

▸Figure 250–26

Transformers. Objectionable neutral current will flow on metal parts if the neutral conductor is connected to the circuit equipment grounding conductor at both the transformer and any other location on the load side of the system bonding jumper in violation of 250.30(A)(1). ▸Figure 250–27

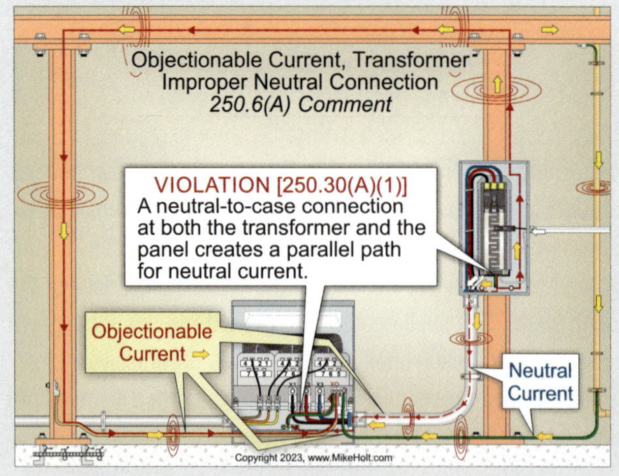

Objectionable Current, Transformer
Improper Neutral Connection
250.6(A) Comment
VIOLATION [250.30(A)(1)]
A neutral-to-case connection at both the transformer and the panel creates a parallel path for neutral current.
Objectionable Current
Neutral Current
Copyright 2023, www.MikeHolt.com

▸Figure 250–27

Generators. Objectionable neutral current will flow on metal parts and the equipment grounding conductor if a generator is connected to a transfer switch with a solidly connected neutral, and a neutral-to-case connection is made at the generator in violation of 250.20(A). ▶Figure 250–28

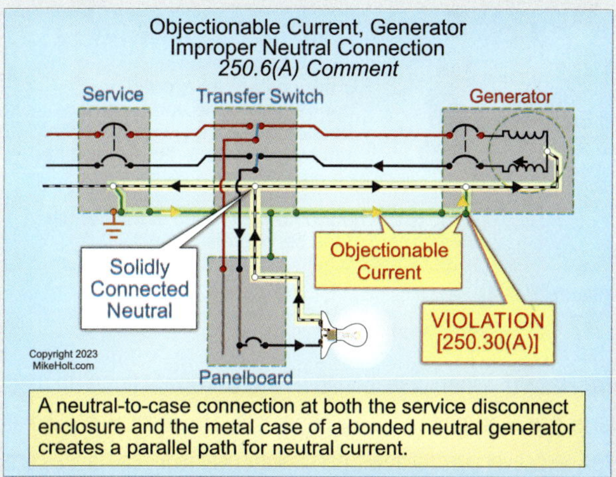
Objectionable Current, Generator
Improper Neutral Connection
250.6(A) Comment
Service
Transfer Switch
Generator
Solidly Connected Neutral
Objectionable Current
VIOLATION [250.30(A)]
Panelboard
Copyright 2023 MikeHolt.com
A neutral-to-case connection at both the service disconnect enclosure and the metal case of a bonded neutral generator creates a parallel path for neutral current.

▶Figure 250–28

Disconnects. Objectionable neutral current will flow on metal parts and the equipment grounding conductor if the neutral conductor is connected to the metal case of a remote building disconnect that is not part of the service disconnect in violation of 250.22(B)(1). ▶Figure 250–29

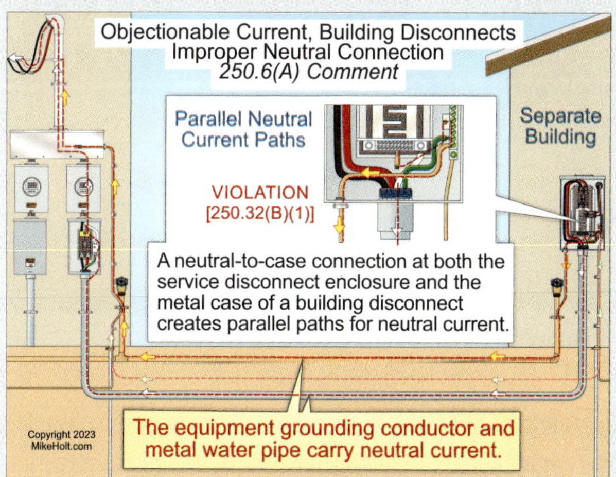
Objectionable Current, Building Disconnects
Improper Neutral Connection
250.6(A) Comment
Parallel Neutral Current Paths
VIOLATION [250.32(B)(1)]
Separate Building
A neutral-to-case connection at both the service disconnect enclosure and the metal case of a building disconnect creates parallel paths for neutral current.
Copyright 2023 MikeHolt.com
The equipment grounding conductor and metal water pipe carry neutral current.

▶Figure 250–29

Wiring Errors. Objectionable neutral current will flow on metal parts and equipment grounding conductors if the neutral conductor from one system is used as the neutral conductor for a different system. ▶Figure 250–30

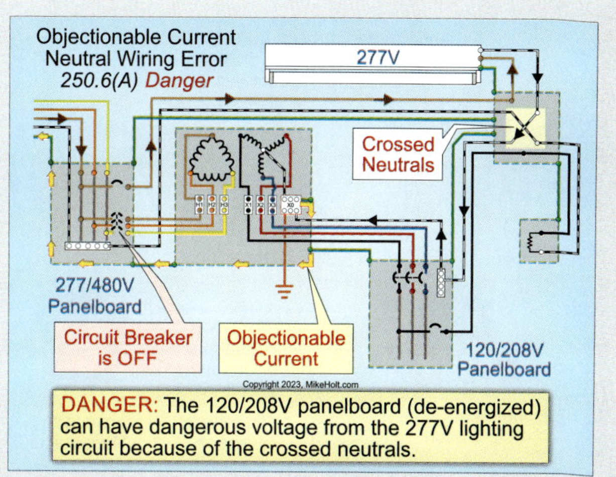
Objectionable Current
Neutral Wiring Error
250.6(A) Danger
277V
Crossed Neutrals
277/480V Panelboard
Circuit Breaker is OFF
Objectionable Current
120/208V Panelboard
Copyright 2023, MikeHolt.com
DANGER: The 120/208V panelboard (de-energized) can have dangerous voltage from the 277V lighting circuit because of the crossed neutrals.

▶Figure 250–30

Improper Wiring. Objectionable neutral current will flow on the equipment grounding conductor if the circuit equipment grounding conductor is used as a neutral conductor such as where:

- A 230V time-clock motor is replaced with a 115V time-clock motor, and the circuit equipment grounding conductor is used for neutral return current.
- A 115V water filter is wired to a 240V well-pump motor circuit, and the circuit equipment grounding conductor is used for neutral return current. ▶Figure 250–31

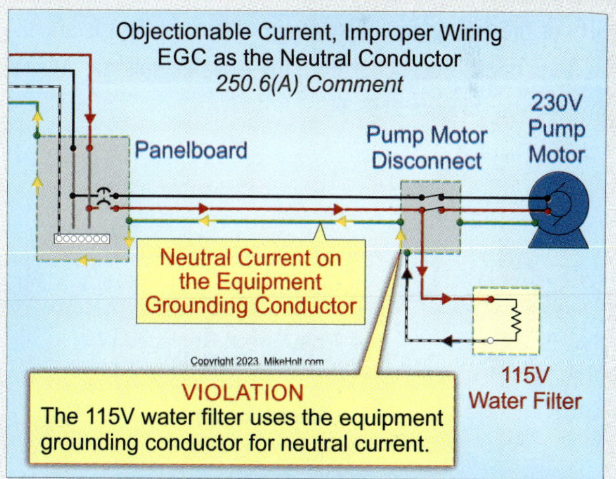
Objectionable Current, Improper Wiring
EGC as the Neutral Conductor
250.6(A) Comment
230V Pump Motor
Panelboard
Pump Motor Disconnect
Neutral Current on the Equipment Grounding Conductor
Copyright 2023, MikeHolt.com
VIOLATION
The 115V water filter uses the equipment grounding conductor for neutral current.
115V Water Filter

▶Figure 250–31

- The circuit equipment grounding conductor is used for neutral return current. ▶Figure 250–32

• • •

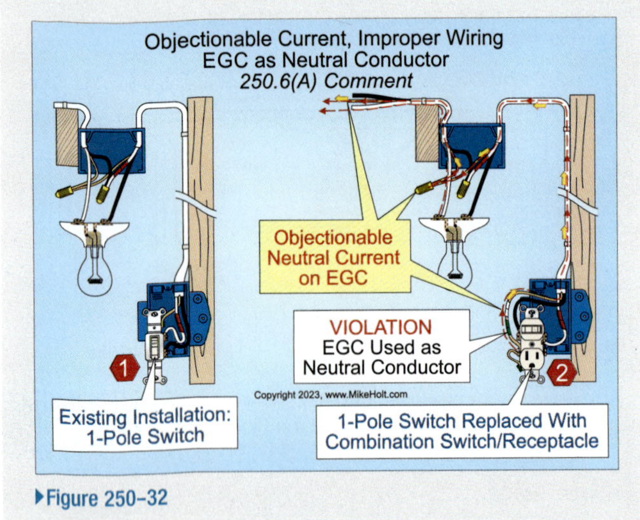
Objectionable Current, Improper Wiring
EGC as Neutral Conductor
250.6(A) Comment
Objectionable Neutral Current on EGC
VIOLATION
EGC Used as Neutral Conductor
1
2
Existing Installation: 1-Pole Switch
1-Pole Switch Replaced With Combination Switch/Receptacle
Copyright 2023, www.MikeHolt.com

▸Figure 250–32

Dangers of Objectionable Current

Objectionable neutral current on metal parts can cause electric shock, fires, and the improper operation of electronic equipment and overcurrent protective devices such as GFPEs, GFCIs, SPGFCIs, and AFCIs.

Shock Hazard. When objectionable neutral current flows on metal parts or the equipment grounding conductor, electric shock—and even death—can occur from the elevated voltage. ▸Figure 250–33 and ▸Figure 250–34

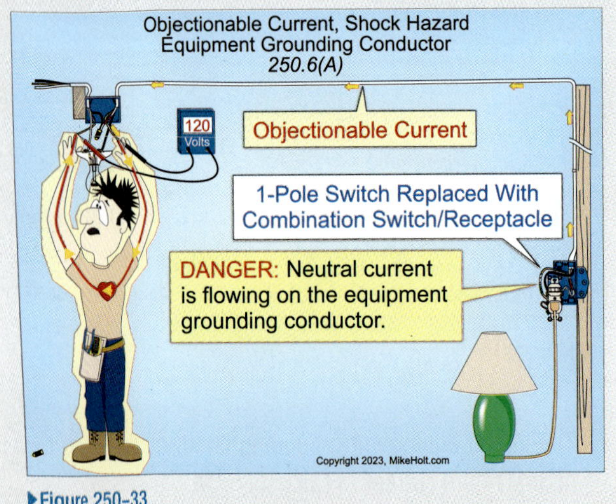
Objectionable Current, Shock Hazard
Equipment Grounding Conductor
250.6(A)
120 Volts
Objectionable Current
1-Pole Switch Replaced With Combination Switch/Receptacle
DANGER: Neutral current is flowing on the equipment grounding conductor.
Copyright 2023, MikeHolt.com

▸Figure 250–33

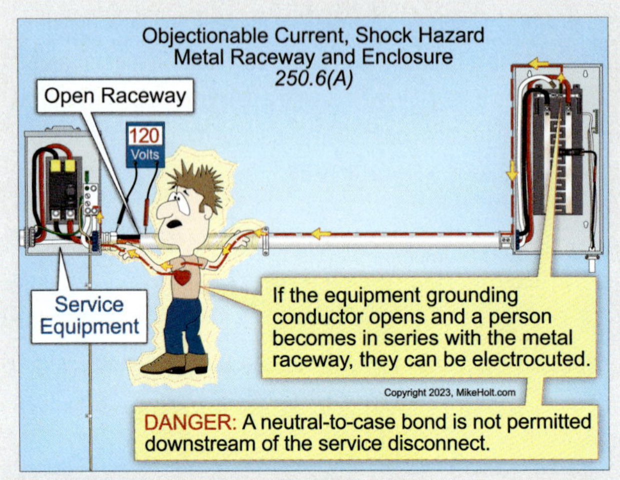
Objectionable Current, Shock Hazard
Metal Raceway and Enclosure
250.6(A)
Open Raceway
120 Volts
Service Equipment
If the equipment grounding conductor opens and a person becomes in series with the metal raceway, they can be electrocuted.
DANGER: A neutral-to-case bond is not permitted downstream of the service disconnect.
Copyright 2023, MikeHolt.com

▸Figure 250–34

Fire Hazard. When objectionable neutral current flows on metal parts, a fire can ignite adjacent combustible material. Heat is generated whenever current flows, particularly over high-resistance parts. In addition, arcing at loose connections is especially dangerous in areas containing easily ignitible and explosive gases, vapors, or dust. ▸Figure 250–35

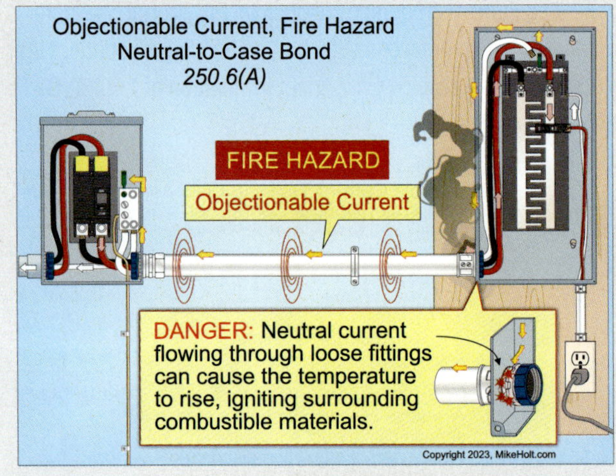
Objectionable Current, Fire Hazard
Neutral-to-Case Bond
250.6(A)
FIRE HAZARD
Objectionable Current
DANGER: Neutral current flowing through loose fittings can cause the temperature to rise, igniting surrounding combustible materials.
Copyright 2023, MikeHolt.com

▸Figure 250–35

Operation of Overcurrent Protective Devices. When objectionable neutral current travels on metal parts, electronic overcurrent protective devices equipped with ground-fault protection can trip because some neutral current flows on the circuit equipment grounding conductor—instead of on the neutral conductor.

(C) Currents Not Classified as Objectionable Currents. Currents resulting from abnormal conditions such as ground faults and currents resulting from required grounding and bonding connections, are not classified as objectionable current for the purposes specified in 250.6(A) and (B).

250.8 Connection of Grounding and Bonding Conductors

(A) Permitted Methods. Equipment grounding conductors, grounding electrode conductors, and bonding jumpers must be connected by one or more of the following methods:

(1) Listed pressure connectors ▸Figure 250–36

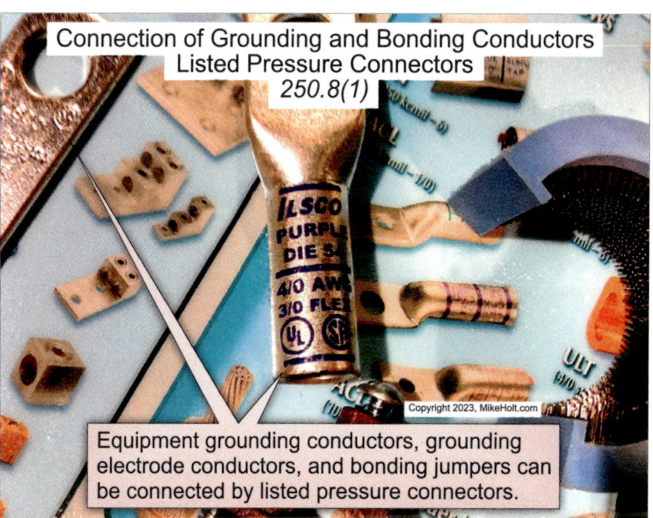
Connection of Grounding and Bonding Conductors
Listed Pressure Connectors
250.8(1)
ILSCO
PURPLE
DIE 54
4/0 AWG
3/0 FLEX
Copyright 2023, MikeHolt.com
Equipment grounding conductors, grounding electrode conductors, and bonding jumpers can be connected by listed pressure connectors.

▸Figure 250–36

(2) Terminal bars

(3) Pressure connectors listed for grounding and bonding

(4) Exothermic welding

(5) Machine screws that engage at least two threads or are secured with a nut

(6) Thread-forming machine screws that engage at least two threads in the enclosure

(7) Connections that are part of a listed assembly

(8) Other listed means

Author's Comment:

- The requirements contained in 250.8 only apply to the termination of conductors–not the termination of grounding and bonding terminals.

According to Article 100, "Listed" means equipment or materials included in a list published by a recognized testing laboratory acceptable to the authority having jurisdiction.

250.10 Protection of Ground Clamps and Fittings

Ground clamps and fittings subject to physical damage must be protected. ▸Figure 250–37

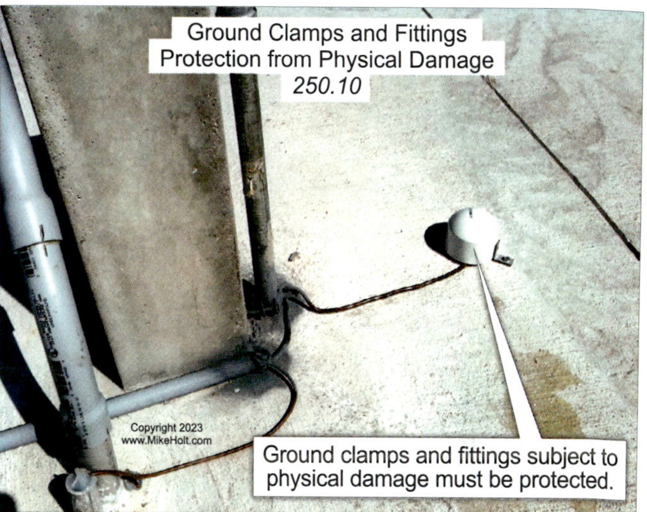
Ground Clamps and Fittings
Protection from Physical Damage
250.10
Copyright 2023
www.MikeHolt.com
Ground clamps and fittings subject to physical damage must be protected.

▸Figure 250–37

250.12 Clean Surfaces

Nonconductive coatings (such as paint) on equipment to be bonded or grounded must be removed to ensure electrical continuity, or the termination fittings must be designed to make such removal unnecessary.

Author's Comment:

- Fittings such as locknuts are designed to cut through nonconductive coatings and establish the intended electrical continuity when they are properly tightened.
- The tarnish on copper water pipe need not be removed before making a termination because copper-oxide does not interfere with the copper conductor conductivity.

Part II. System Grounding and Bonding

250.20 Systems Required to be Grounded

(A) Systems Below 50V. The secondary of a transformer operating below 50V is not required to be bonded or grounded unless the transformer's primary supply is from a(an): ▶Figure 250-38

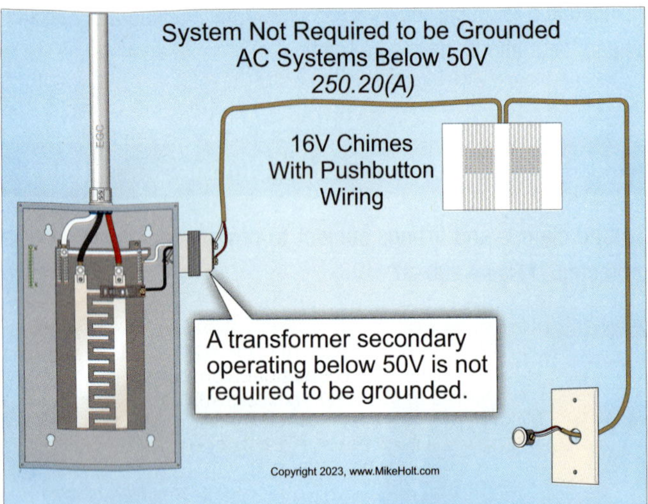
System Not Required to be Grounded
AC Systems Below 50V
250.20(A)
16V Chimes
With Pushbutton
Wiring
A transformer secondary operating below 50V is not required to be grounded.
Copyright 2023, www.MikeHolt.com

▶Figure 250-38

(1) 277V or 480V system

(2) Ungrounded system

(B) Systems 50V to 1000V. The following systems must be grounded if the neutral conductor is used as a circuit conductor:

(1) Single-phase systems ▶Figure 250-39

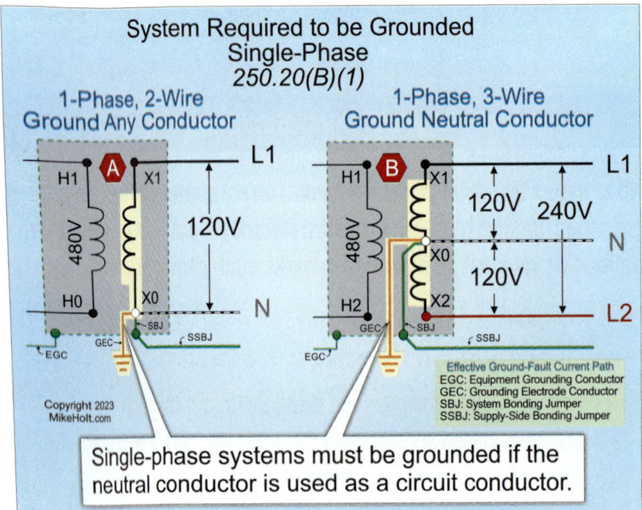
System Required to be Grounded
Single-Phase
250.20(B)(1)
1-Phase, 2-Wire
Ground Any Conductor
1-Phase, 3-Wire
Ground Neutral Conductor
H1
X1
480V
120V
H0
X0
L1
N
SBJ
SSBJ
GEC
EGC
H2
X2
120V
240V
L2
Effective Ground-Fault Current Path
EGC: Equipment Grounding Conductor
GEC: Grounding Electrode Conductor
SBJ: System Bonding Jumper
SSBJ: Supply-Side Bonding Jumper
Copyright 2023 MikeHolt.com
Single-phase systems must be grounded if the neutral conductor is used as a circuit conductor.

▶Figure 250-39

(2) Three-phase, wye-connected systems ▶Figure 250-40

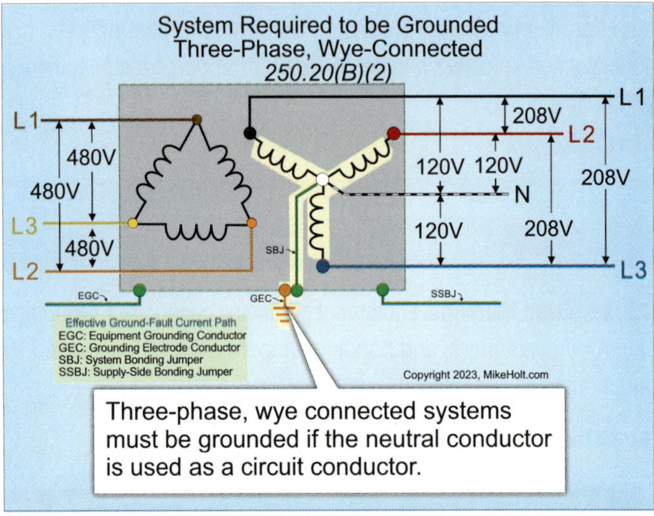
System Required to be Grounded
Three-Phase, Wye-Connected
250.20(B)(2)
L1
L2
L3
480V
208V
120V
N
SBJ
EGC
GEC
SSBJ
Effective Ground-Fault Current Path
EGC: Equipment Grounding Conductor
GEC: Grounding Electrode Conductor
SBJ: System Bonding Jumper
SSBJ: Supply-Side Bonding Jumper
Copyright 2023, MikeHolt.com
Three-phase, wye connected systems must be grounded if the neutral conductor is used as a circuit conductor.

▶Figure 250-40

(3) Three-phase, high-leg delta-connected systems ▶Figure 250-41

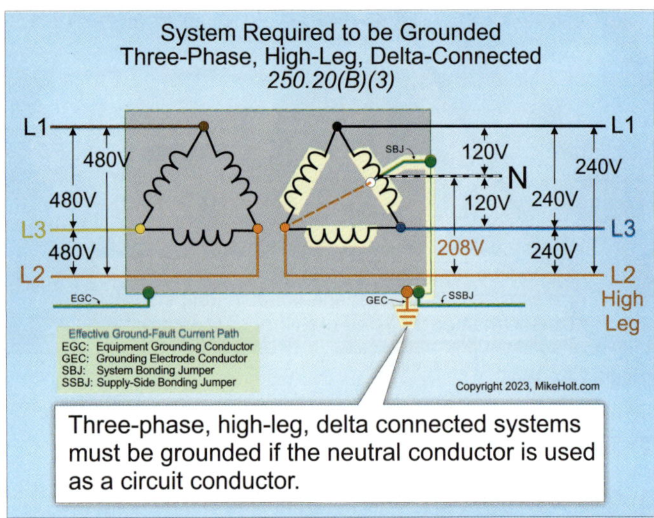
System Required to be Grounded
Three-Phase, High-Leg, Delta-Connected
250.20(B)(3)
L1
L3
L2
480V
120V
240V
208V
N
SBJ
EGC
GEC
SSBJ
L2
High
Leg
Effective Ground-Fault Current Path
EGC: Equipment Grounding Conductor
GEC: Grounding Electrode Conductor
SBJ: System Bonding Jumper
SSBJ: Supply-Side Bonding Jumper
Copyright 2023, MikeHolt.com
Three-phase, high-leg, delta connected systems must be grounded if the neutral conductor is used as a circuit conductor.

▶Figure 250-41

250.21 Ungrounded Systems

(B) Ground Detectors. Ungrounded systems from 50V to 1000V or less are not required to be grounded if:

(1) The ungrounded systems operating between 120V and 1000V as permitted in 250.21(A) must have a secondary ground detector sensing equipment.

(2) The secondary ground detection sensing equipment must be connected as close as practicable to where the system receives its supply. ▶Figure 250-42

1st Printing

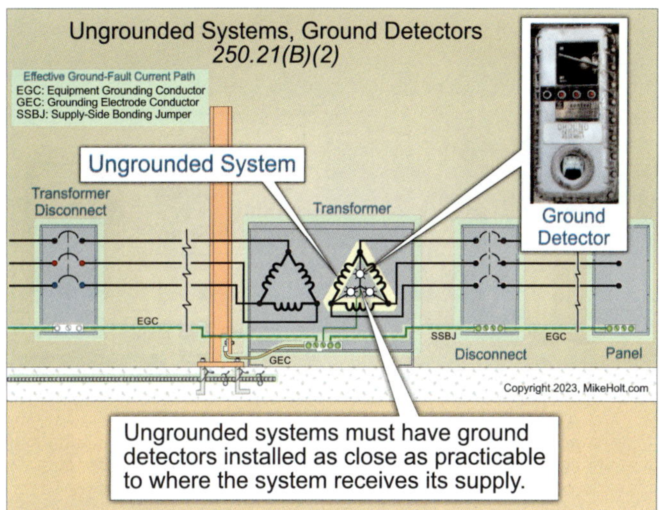
Ungrounded Systems, Ground Detectors
250.21(B)(2)
Effective Ground-Fault Current Path
EGC: Equipment Grounding Conductor
GEC: Grounding Electrode Conductor
SSBJ: Supply-Side Bonding Jumper
Ungrounded System
Transformer Disconnect
Transformer
Ground Detector
EGC
SSBJ
EGC
GEC
Disconnect
Panel
Copyright 2023, MikeHolt.com
Ungrounded systems must have ground detectors installed as close as practicable to where the system receives its supply.

▸Figure 250–42

(C) Marking. Ungrounded systems must be legibly marked "CAUTION UNGROUNDED SYSTEM OPERATING — _____ VOLTS BETWEEN CONDUCTORS" with sufficient durability to withstand the environment involved at the source or first disconnect of the system. ▸Figure 250–43

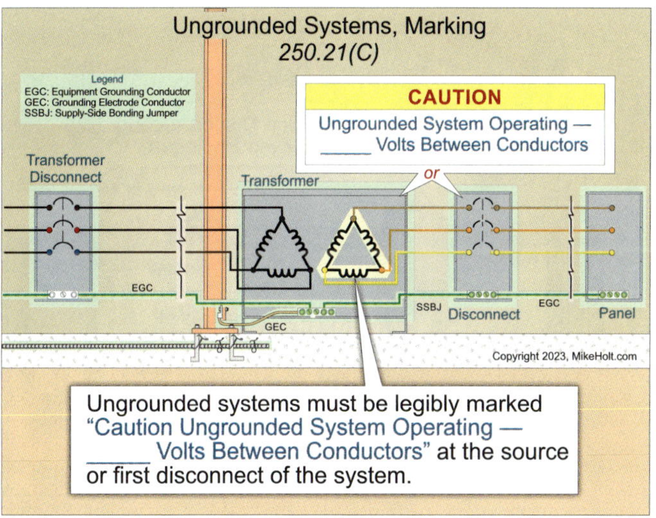
Ungrounded Systems, Marking
250.21(C)
Legend
EGC: Equipment Grounding Conductor
GEC: Grounding Electrode Conductor
SSBJ: Supply-Side Bonding Jumper
CAUTION
Ungrounded System Operating —
_____ Volts Between Conductors
or
Transformer Disconnect
Transformer
EGC
SSBJ
Disconnect
EGC
Panel
GEC
Copyright 2023, MikeHolt.com
Ungrounded systems must be legibly marked "Caution Ungrounded System Operating — _____ Volts Between Conductors" at the source or first disconnect of the system.

▸Figure 250–43

250.24 Service Grounding

(A) Service Equipment, Grounding. A premises wiring system supplied by a grounded service must have a grounding electrode conductor connected to the service neutral conductor in accordance with the following:

(1) General. The grounding electrode conductor connection to the neutral conductor at service equipment must be made at any accessible point from the load end of the overhead service conductors, service drop, underground service conductors, or service lateral to the terminal or bus to which the service neutral conductor is connected at the service disconnect. ▸Figure 250–44

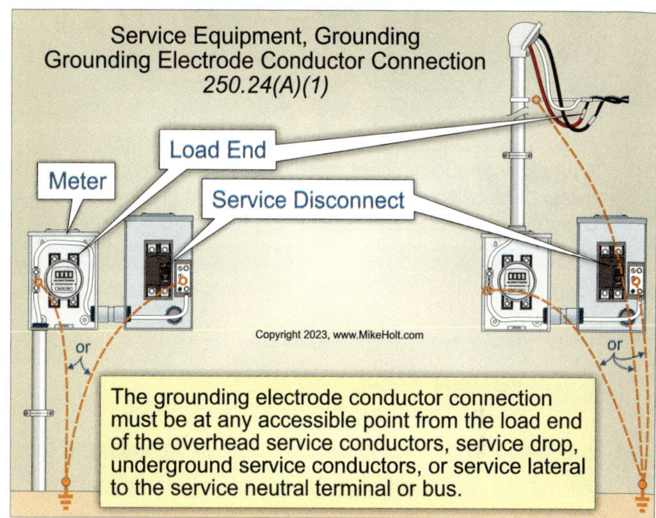
Service Equipment, Grounding
Grounding Electrode Conductor Connection
250.24(A)(1)
Load End
Meter
Service Disconnect
Copyright 2023, www.MikeHolt.com
or
or
The grounding electrode conductor connection must be at any accessible point from the load end of the overhead service conductors, service drop, underground service conductors, or service lateral to the service neutral terminal or bus.

▸Figure 250–44

Author's Comment:

- Some inspectors require the grounding electrode conductor connection to the service neutral conductor to be made at the meter socket enclosure, while others insist the connection be made only within the service disconnect. Grounding at either location complies with this rule, but be sure you know the local utility company's policy on connections inside the meter socket.

(4) Service Equipment, Main Bonding Jumper. If the main bonding jumper specified in 250.28 is a wire or busbar, the grounding electrode conductor is permitted to terminate to the equipment grounding terminal, bar, or bus to which the main bonding jumper is connected, instead of the neutral terminal.

(B) Load-Side Bonding Connections. A neutral conductor cannot be connected to metal parts of equipment or the equipment grounding conductor(s) on the load side of the service disconnect. ▸Figure 250–45

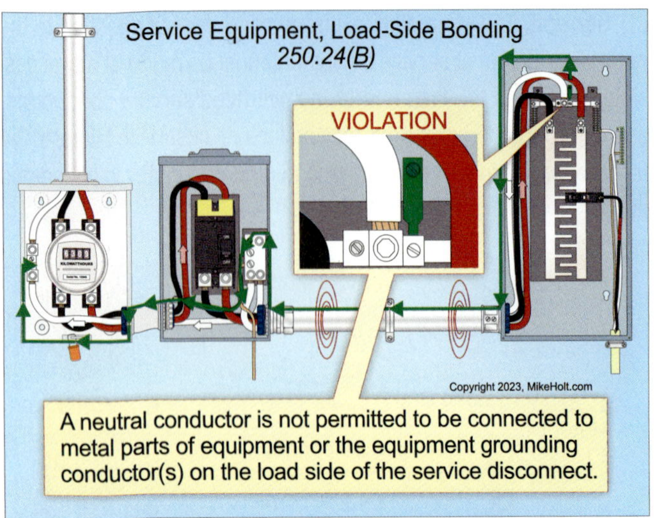
Service Equipment, Load-Side Bonding
250.24(B)
VIOLATION
Copyright 2023, MikeHolt.com
A neutral conductor is not permitted to be connected to metal parts of equipment or the equipment grounding conductor(s) on the load side of the service disconnect.

▸Figure 250–45

Author's Comment:

- If a neutral-to-case connection is made on the load side of the service disconnect, objectionable neutral current will flow on conductive metal parts of electrical equipment [250.6(A)]. Objectionable neutral current on metal parts of electrical equipment can be extremely dangerous. It does not take much current to cause electric shock or death (from ventricular fibrillation), as well as a fire. ▸Figure 250–46

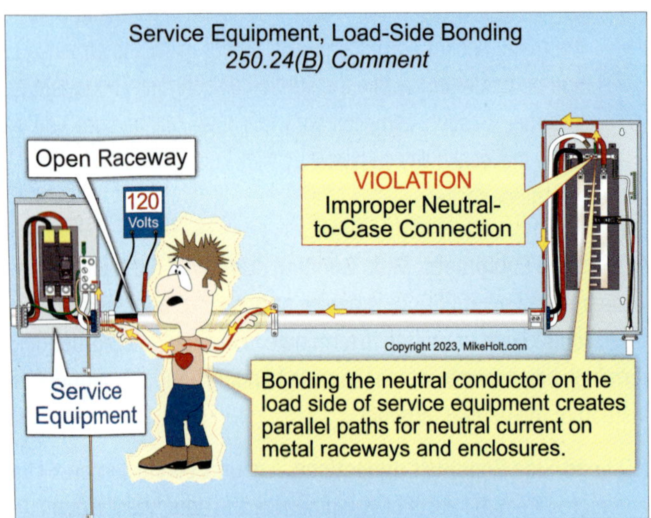
Service Equipment, Load-Side Bonding
250.24(B) Comment
Open Raceway
120
Volts
VIOLATION
Improper Neutral-to-Case Connection
Copyright 2023, MikeHolt.com
Service Equipment
Bonding the neutral conductor on the load side of service equipment creates parallel paths for neutral current on metal raceways and enclosures.

▸Figure 250–46

(C) Main Bonding Jumper. A main bonding jumper is required to bond the equipment grounding conductor to the neutral conductor in each service disconnect enclosure in accordance with 250.28. ▸Figure 250–47

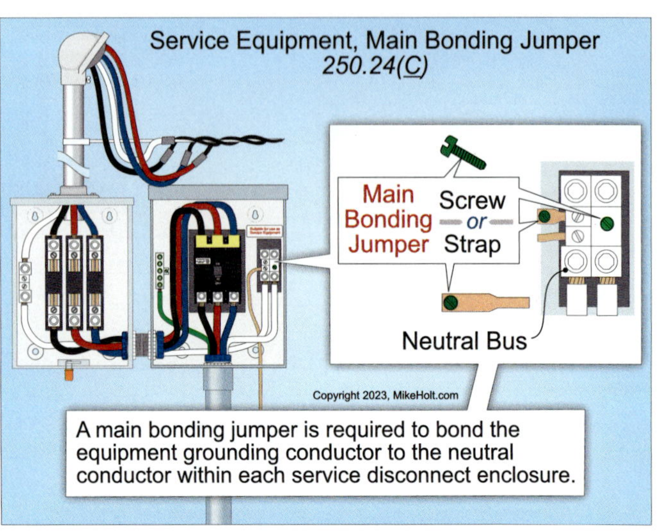
Service Equipment, Main Bonding Jumper
250.24(C)
Main Bonding Jumper
Screw or Strap
Neutral Bus
Copyright 2023, MikeHolt.com
A main bonding jumper is required to bond the equipment grounding conductor to the neutral conductor within each service disconnect enclosure.

▸Figure 250–47

According to Article 100, "Main Bonding Jumper" is a wire, screw, or busbar used to connect the service neutral conductor to the equipment grounding conductor, supply-side bonding jumper (or both) at the service disconnect enclosure. ▸Figure 250–48 and ▸Figure 250–49

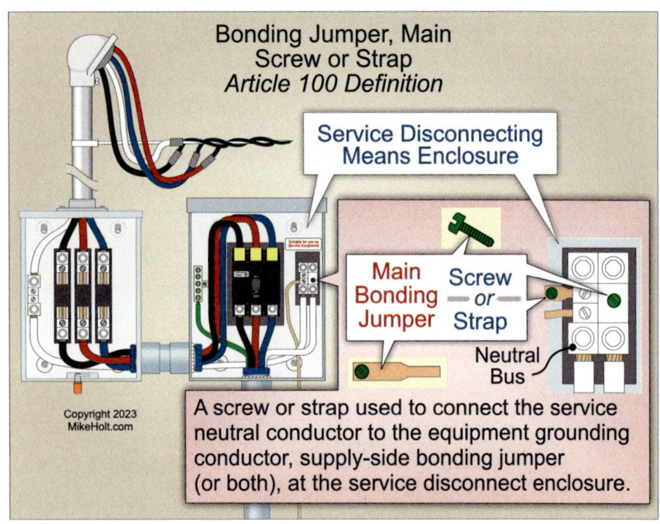
Bonding Jumper, Main
Screw or Strap
Article 100 Definition
Service Disconnecting Means Enclosure
Main Bonding Jumper
Screw or Strap
Neutral Bus
Copyright 2023
MikeHolt.com
A screw or strap used to connect the service neutral conductor to the equipment grounding conductor, supply-side bonding jumper (or both), at the service disconnect enclosure.

▸Figure 250–48

(D) Neutral Conductor Brought to Service Equipment. A neutral conductor must be installed and routed with the phase conductors and be connected to the neutral terminal or bus at each service disconnect enclosure. ▸Figure 250–50 and ▸Figure 250–51

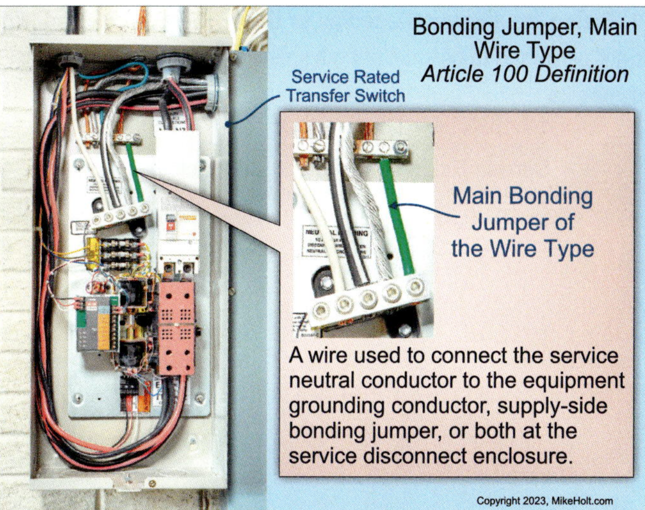
Bonding Jumper, Main
Wire Type
Article 100 Definition
Service Rated
Transfer Switch
Main Bonding
Jumper of
the Wire Type
A wire used to connect the service neutral conductor to the equipment grounding conductor, supply-side bonding jumper, or both at the service disconnect enclosure.
Copyright 2023, MikeHolt.com

▶Figure 250–49

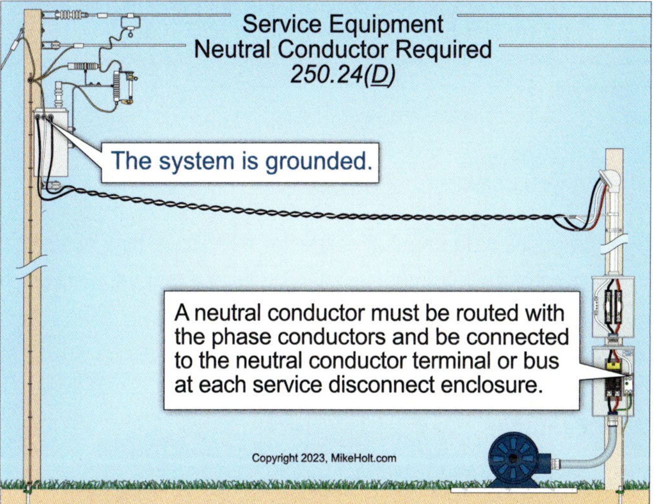
Service Equipment
Neutral Conductor Required
250.24(D)
The system is grounded.
A neutral conductor must be routed with the phase conductors and be connected to the neutral conductor terminal or bus at each service disconnect enclosure.
Copyright 2023, MikeHolt.com

▶Figure 250–50

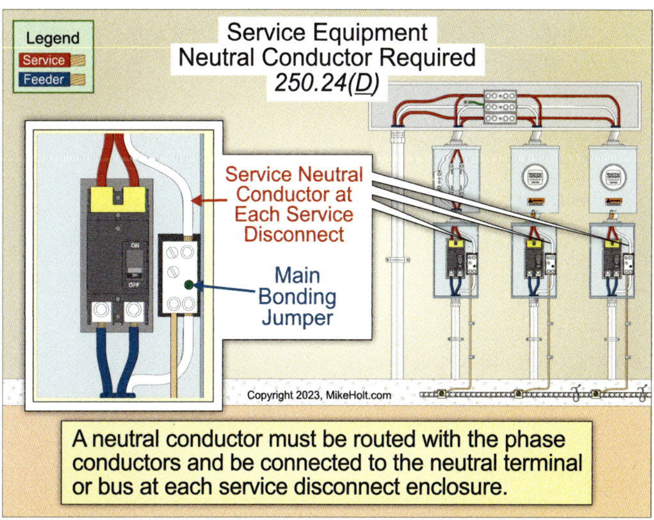
Legend
Service
Feeder
Service Equipment
Neutral Conductor Required
250.24(D)
Service Neutral
Conductor at
Each Service
Disconnect
Main
Bonding
Jumper
Copyright 2023, MikeHolt.com
A neutral conductor must be routed with the phase conductors and be connected to the neutral terminal or bus at each service disconnect enclosure.

▶Figure 250–51

Author's Comment:

- A neutral conductor must be routed with the phase conductors and connected to the neutral conductor terminal or bus at each service disconnect enclosure, regardless of whether line-to-neutral loads are supplied.
- The service neutral conductor provides the effective ground-fault current path to the source to remove dangerous voltage from a ground fault by opening the circuit overcurrent protective device [250.4(A)(3) and 250.4(A)(5)]. ▶Figure 250–52

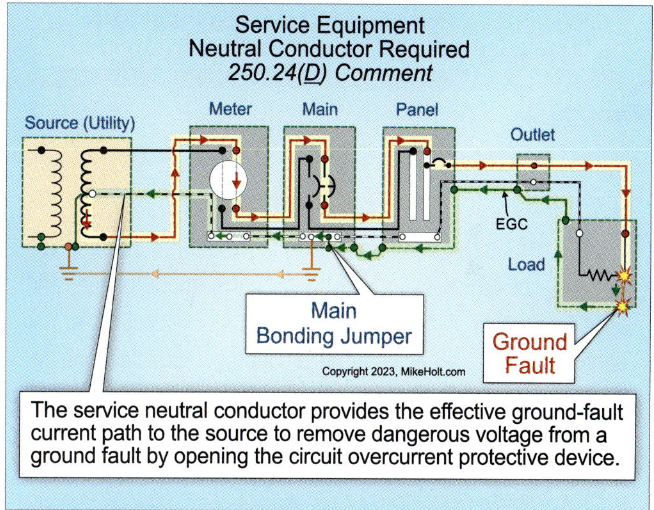
Service Equipment
Neutral Conductor Required
250.24(D) Comment
Source (Utility)
Meter
Main
Panel
Outlet
EGC
Load
Main
Bonding Jumper
Ground
Fault
Copyright 2023, MikeHolt.com
The service neutral conductor provides the effective ground-fault current path to the source to remove dangerous voltage from a ground fault by opening the circuit overcurrent protective device.

▶Figure 250–52

Author's Comment:

- The main bonding jumper is a vital component of bonding. It facilitates the operation of overcurrent protective devices and is a critical part of the grounding system since it bonds the neutral conductor, service enclosure, and the equipment grounding conductor to the grounding electrode system via the grounding electrode conductor.

Danger

DANGER: If the neutral conductor is opened, dangerous voltage may be present on metal parts under normal conditions, providing the potential for electric shock. If the Earth's ground resistance is 25Ω and the load's resistance is 25Ω, the voltage drop across each of these resistances will be half of the voltage source. Since the neutral is connected to the service disconnect, all metal parts will be elevated 60V above the Earth's voltage for a 120/240V system. ▶Figure 250–53

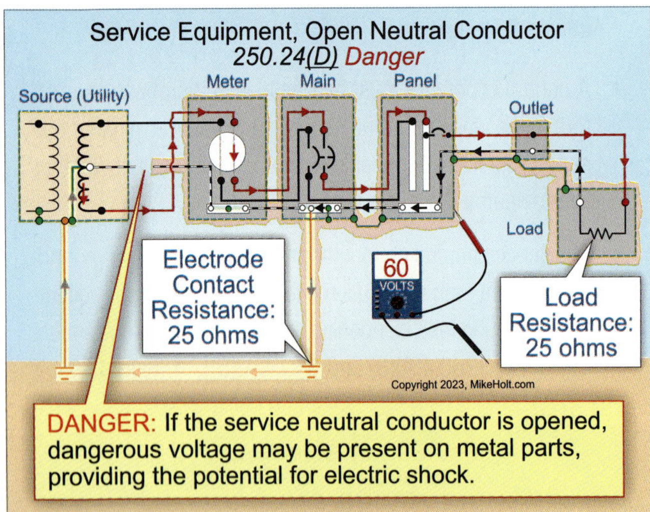
Service Equipment, Open Neutral Conductor
250.24(D) Danger
Source (Utility)
Meter
Main
Panel
Outlet
Load
Electrode Contact Resistance: 25 ohms
60 VOLTS
Load Resistance: 25 ohms
Copyright 2023, MikeHolt.com
DANGER: If the service neutral conductor is opened, dangerous voltage may be present on metal parts, providing the potential for electric shock.

▸Figure 250-53

Danger

DANGER: Dangerous voltage from a ground fault will not be removed from metal parts, metal piping, and structural steel if the service-disconnect enclosure is not connected to the service neutral conductor. This is because the contact resistance of a grounding electrode to the Earth is so great that insufficient ground-fault current returns to the source if that is the only ground-fault current return path available to open the circuit overcurrent protective device. ▸Figure 250-54

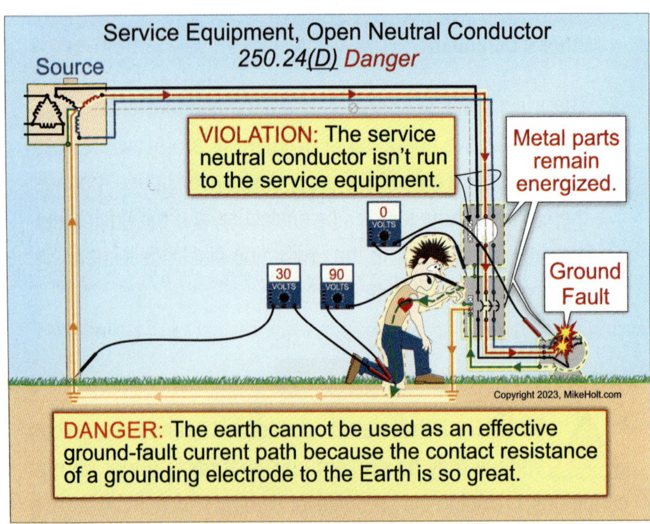
Service Equipment, Open Neutral Conductor
250.24(D) Danger
Source
VIOLATION: The service neutral conductor isn't run to the service equipment.
Metal parts remain energized.
0 VOLTS
30 VOLTS
90 VOLTS
Ground Fault
Copyright 2023, MikeHolt.com
DANGER: The earth cannot be used as an effective ground-fault current path because the contact resistance of a grounding electrode to the Earth is so great.

▸Figure 250-54

The neutral conductor(s) must be sized in accordance with 250.24(D)(1) and (2) as follows:

(1) Sizing for a Single Raceway or Cable. The neutral conductor is not permitted to be smaller than specified in Table 250.102(C)(1). ▸Figure 250-55

Service Equipment, Neutral Conductor Sizing
Single Raceway
250.24(D)(1)
Copyright 2023,MikeHolt.com
The service neutral conductor is not permitted to be smaller than specified in Table 250.102(C)(1).

▸Figure 250-55

Author's Comment:

- In addition, the neutral conductor must have the capacity to carry the maximum unbalanced neutral current in accordance with 220.61.

▸ Example

Question: *What is the minimum size copper service neutral conductor required when the service phase conductors are 4/0 AWG?* ▸Figure 250-56

(a) 3 AWG *(b) 2 AWG* *(c) 1 AWG* *(d) 1/0 AWG*

Solution:

2 AWG [Table 250.102(C)(1)].

Answer: *(b) 2 AWG*

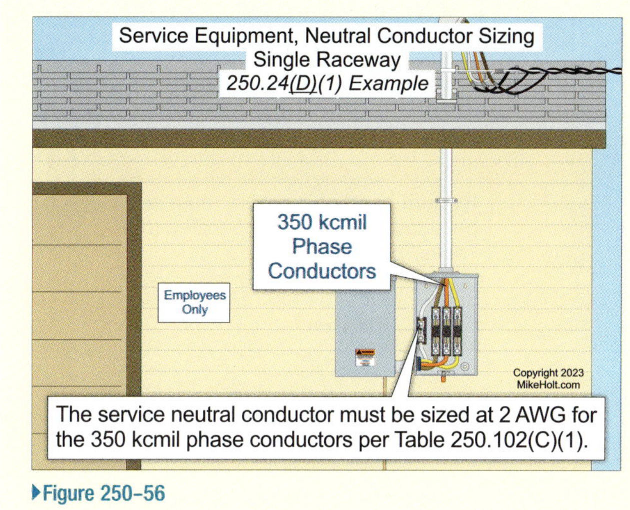
Service Equipment, Neutral Conductor Sizing
Single Raceway
250.24(D)(1) Example
350 kcmil Phase Conductors
Employees Only
Copyright 2023 MikeHolt.com
The service neutral conductor must be sized at 2 AWG for the 350 kcmil phase conductors per Table 250.102(C)(1).

▸Figure 250–56

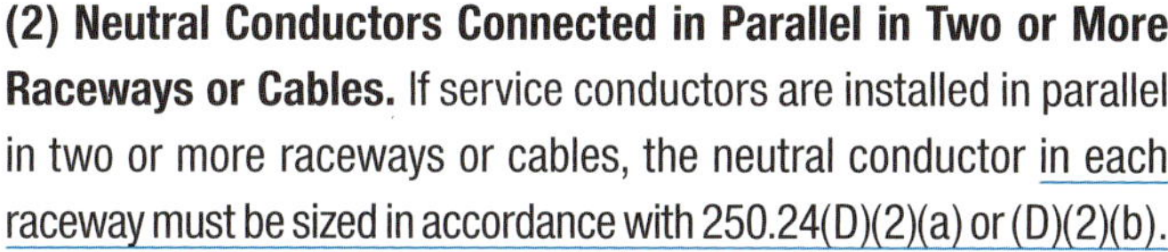

(2) Neutral Conductors Connected in Parallel in Two or More Raceways or Cables. If service conductors are installed in parallel in two or more raceways or cables, the neutral conductor in each raceway must be sized in accordance with 250.24(D)(2)(a) or (D)(2)(b).

(a) The neutral conductor in each raceway must be sized in accordance with Table 250.102(C)(1), based on the circular mil area of the largest phase conductor in each raceway, but not smaller than 1/0 AWG.

(b) The neutral conductors must be sized based on the sum of the circular mil areas of the largest phase conductors from each set connected in parallel in each raceway in accordance with Table 250.102(C)(2)(2).

Note: See 310.10(G) for neutral conductors connected in parallel.

(3) Delta-Connected Service. The grounded conductor of a three-phase, 3-wire delta service must have an ampacity of not less than that of the phase conductors.

(E) Grounding Electrode Conductor. The grounding electrode conductor at service equipment must be sized in accordance with 250.66. ▸Figure 250–57 and ▸Figure 250–58

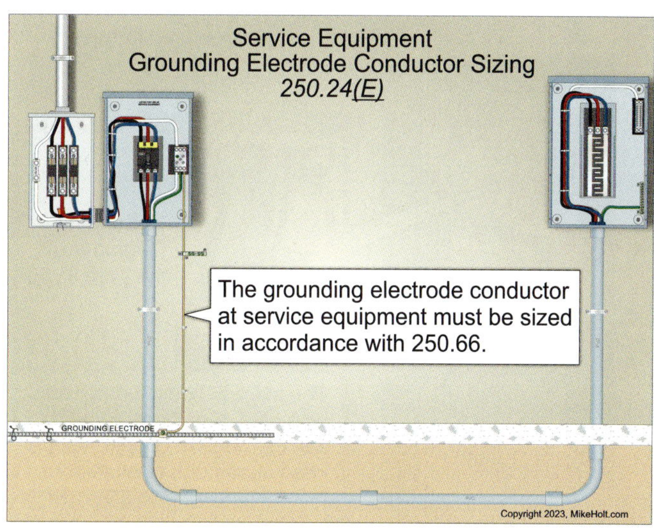
Service Equipment
Grounding Electrode Conductor Sizing
250.24(E)
The grounding electrode conductor at service equipment must be sized in accordance with 250.66.
GROUNDING ELECTRODE
Copyright 2023, MikeHolt.com

▸Figure 250–57

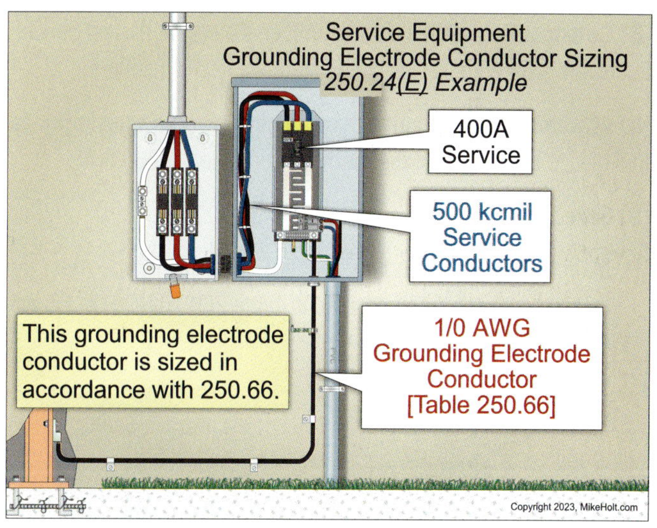
Service Equipment
Grounding Electrode Conductor Sizing
250.24(E) Example
400A Service
500 kcmil Service Conductors
This grounding electrode conductor is sized in accordance with 250.66.
1/0 AWG Grounding Electrode Conductor [Table 250.66]
Copyright 2023, MikeHolt.com

▸Figure 250–58

250.28 Main Bonding Jumper and System Bonding Jumper

Main and system bonding jumpers must be installed as follows:

(A) Material. The bonding jumper can be a wire, bus, or screw. ▸Figure 250–59

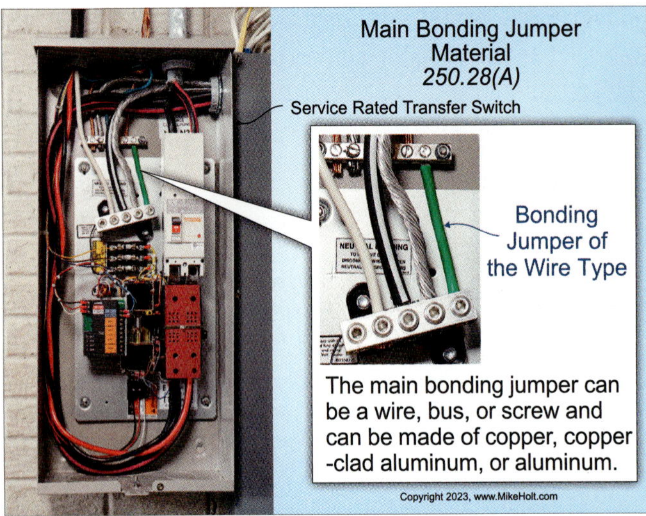
Main Bonding Jumper
Material
250.28(A)
Service Rated Transfer Switch
Bonding
Jumper of
the Wire Type
The main bonding jumper can be a wire, bus, or screw and can be made of copper, copper -clad aluminum, or aluminum.
Copyright 2023, www.MikeHolt.com

▸Figure 250–59

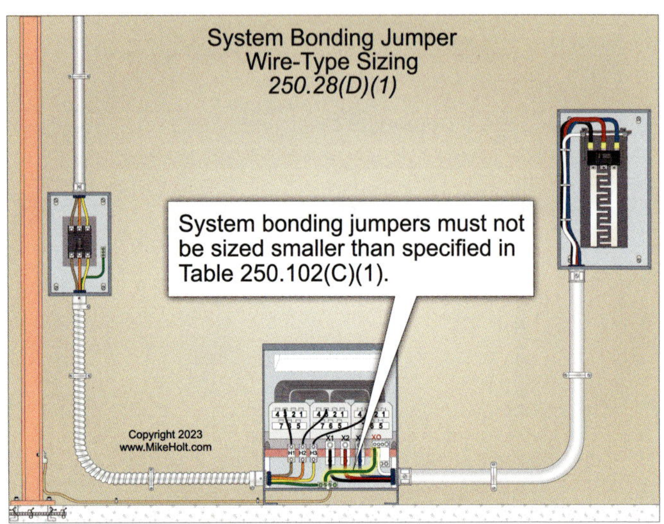
System Bonding Jumper
Wire-Type Sizing
250.28(D)(1)
System bonding jumpers must not be sized smaller than specified in Table 250.102(C)(1).
Copyright 2023
www.MikeHolt.com

▸Figure 250–61

(B) Construction. If the bonding jumper is a screw, it must be identified with a green finish visible when the screw is installed.

(C) Attachment. Main and system bonding jumpers must terminate to a device by any one of the methods contained in 250.8(A).

(D) Size.

(1) Main and system bonding jumpers of the wire type must not be sized smaller than specified in Table 250.102(C)(1). ▸Figure 250–60 and ▸Figure 250–61

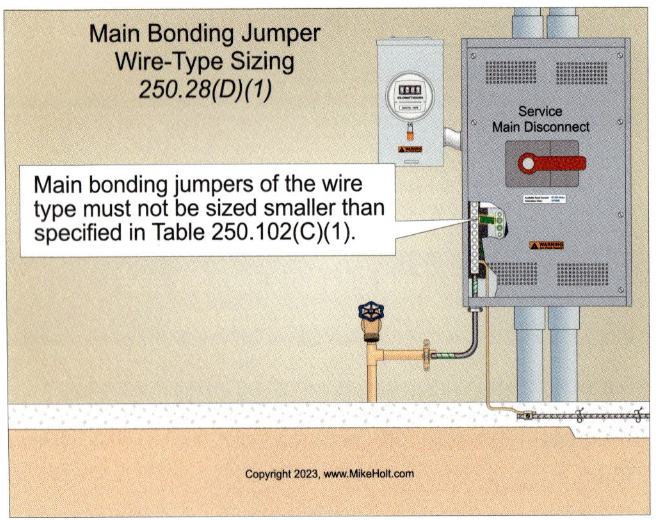
Main Bonding Jumper
Wire-Type Sizing
250.28(D)(1)
Service
Main Disconnect
Main bonding jumpers of the wire type must not be sized smaller than specified in Table 250.102(C)(1).
Copyright 2023, www.MikeHolt.com

▸Figure 250–60

Author's Comment:

- The primary purpose of the main and system bonding jumpers is to create a path for fault current to flow from a fault to the source to open the circuit overcurrent protective device.

Danger

DANGER: Metal parts of electrical equipment, as well as metal piping and structural steel, will become and remain energized with dangerous voltage from a ground fault if a main bonding jumper or system bonding jumper is not installed. A missing main or system bonding jumper causes an opening in the effective ground-fault current path back to the source and creates a condition where overcurrent protective devices will not open during a ground-fault condition. ▸Figure 250–62 and ▸Figure 250–63

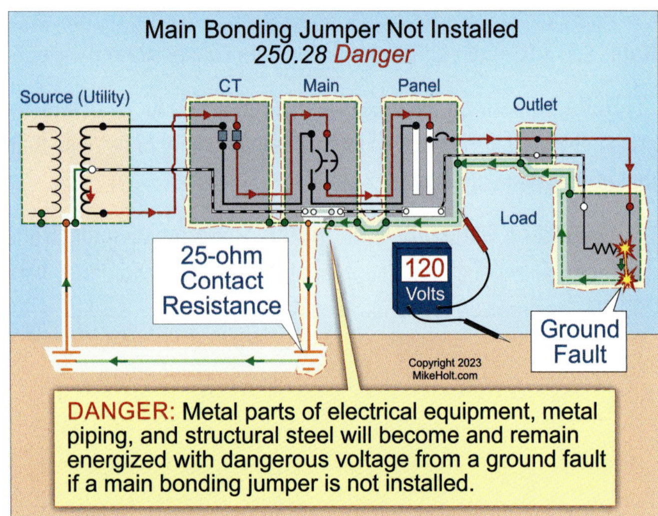
Main Bonding Jumper Not Installed
250.28 Danger
Source (Utility)
CT
Main
Panel
Outlet
Load
25-ohm
Contact
Resistance
120
Volts
Ground
Fault
Copyright 2023
MikeHolt.com
DANGER: Metal parts of electrical equipment, metal piping, and structural steel will become and remain energized with dangerous voltage from a ground fault if a main bonding jumper is not installed.

▸Figure 250–62

1st Printing

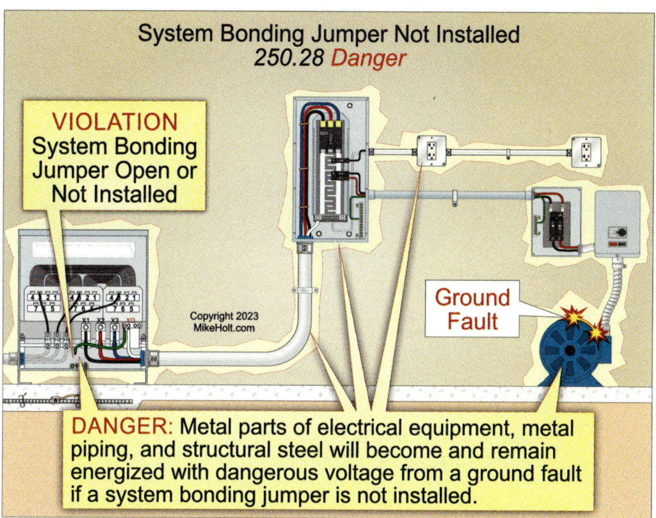
System Bonding Jumper Not Installed
250.28 Danger
VIOLATION
System Bonding Jumper Open or Not Installed
Ground Fault
Copyright 2023 MikeHolt.com
DANGER: Metal parts of electrical equipment, metal piping, and structural steel will become and remain energized with dangerous voltage from a ground fault if a system bonding jumper is not installed.

▸Figure 250–63

250.30 Transformer Separately Derived Systems

According to Article 100, "Separately Derived System" is an electrical power supply output having no direct connection(s) to the circuit conductors of any other electrical source other than those established by grounding and bonding connections. ▸Figure 250–64

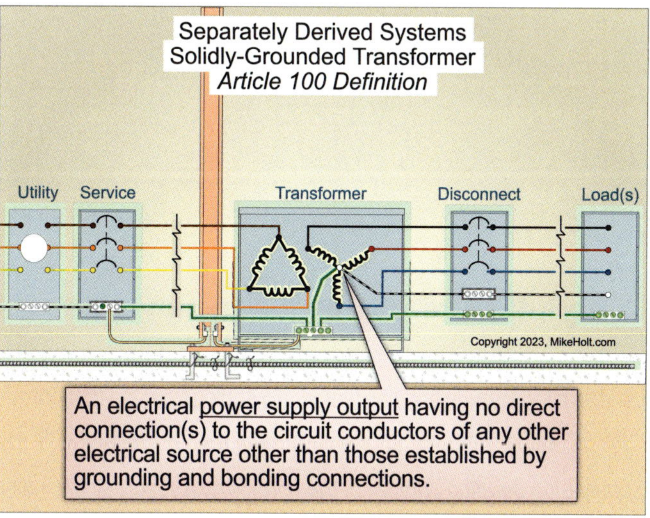
Separately Derived Systems
Solidly-Grounded Transformer
Article 100 Definition
Utility
Service
Transformer
Disconnect
Load(s)
Copyright 2023, MikeHolt.com
An electrical power supply output having no direct connection(s) to the circuit conductors of any other electrical source other than those established by grounding and bonding connections.

▸Figure 250–64

- Transformers, other than autotransformers, are separately derived because the primary conductors have no direct electrical connection from the circuit conductors of one system to the circuit conductors of another.

(A) Grounded Systems. Separately derived transformer systems must be bonded and grounded in accordance with 250.30(A)(1) through (A)(8). A neutral-to-case connection is not permitted to be made on the load side of the system bonding jumper.

A neutral conductor is not permitted to be connected to metal parts of equipment or equipment grounding conductors on the load side of the system bonding jumper.

(1) System Bonding Jumper. A system bonding jumper must be installed at the secondary neutral point or the secondary disconnect neutral terminal, but not both. The system bonding jumper must comply with 250.28 and sized in accordance with 250.102(C). ▸Figure 250–65

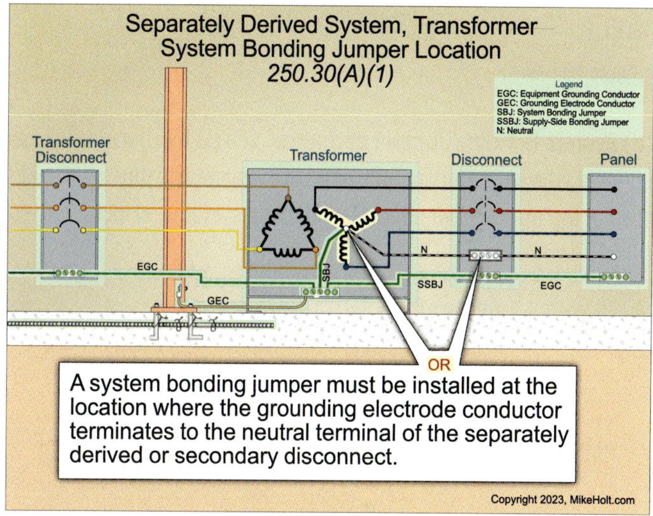
Separately Derived System, Transformer
System Bonding Jumper Location
250.30(A)(1)
Legend
EGC: Equipment Grounding Conductor
GEC: Grounding Electrode Conductor
SBJ: System Bonding Jumper
SSBJ: Supply-Side Bonding Jumper
N: Neutral
Transformer Disconnect
Transformer
Disconnect
Panel
EGC
GEC
SBJ
N
N
SSBJ
EGC
OR
A system bonding jumper must be installed at the location where the grounding electrode conductor terminates to the neutral terminal of the separately derived or secondary disconnect.
Copyright 2023, MikeHolt.com

▸Figure 250–65

Author's Comment:

- Section 250.30(A)(5) requires the termination of a grounding electrode conductor to the same point where the system bonding jumper has been installed.

According to Article 100, "System Bonding Jumper" is the connection between the neutral conductor or grounded-phase conductor and the equipment grounding conductor, supply-side bonding jumper, or both at a transformer separately derived system. ▸Figure 250–66

Ex 2: If a building or structure is supplied by a feeder from an outdoor transformer separately derived system, a system bonding jumper at both the source and the first disconnect is permitted if doing so does not establish a parallel path for the neutral current. The neutral conductor is not permitted to be smaller than the size specified for the system bonding jumper, and it is not required to be larger than the phase conductor(s).

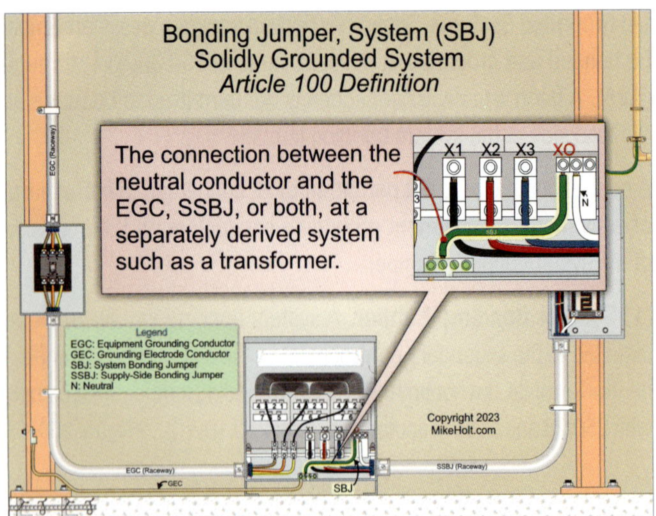
Bonding Jumper, System (SBJ)
Solidly Grounded System
Article 100 Definition
The connection between the neutral conductor and the EGC, SSBJ, or both, at a separately derived system such as a transformer.
X1 X2 X3 XO
Legend
EGC: Equipment Grounding Conductor
GEC: Grounding Electrode Conductor
SBJ: System Bonding Jumper
SSBJ: Supply-Side Bonding Jumper
N: Neutral
Copyright 2023 MikeHolt.com
SBJ

▸Figure 250–66

(a) System Bonding Jumper at Source. The system bonding jumper connects the secondary neutral point of the system to the metal enclosure of the transformer separately derived system. ▸Figure 250–67

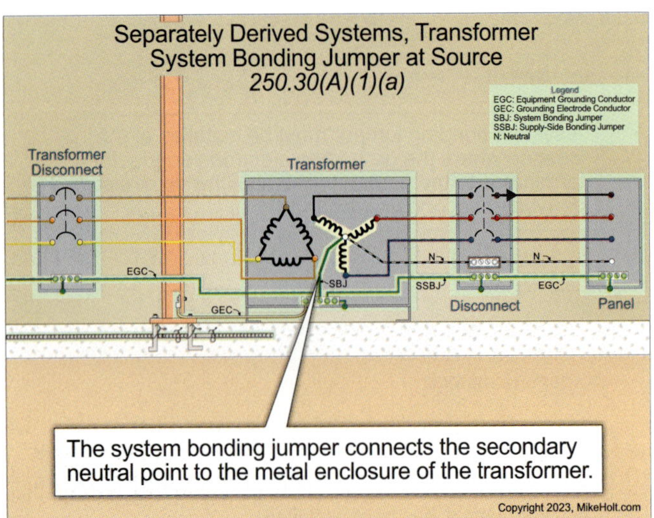
Separately Derived Systems, Transformer
System Bonding Jumper at Source
250.30(A)(1)(a)
Legend
EGC: Equipment Grounding Conductor
GEC: Grounding Electrode Conductor
SBJ: System Bonding Jumper
SSBJ: Supply-Side Bonding Jumper
N: Neutral
Transformer Disconnect
Transformer
EGC
SBJ
SSBJ
EGC
GEC
Disconnect
Panel
The system bonding jumper connects the secondary neutral point to the metal enclosure of the transformer.
Copyright 2023, MikeHolt.com

▸Figure 250–67

(b) System Bonding Jumper at First Disconnecting Means. The system bonding jumper connects the neutral conductor of the transformer secondary to the metal enclosure at the secondary disconnect. ▸Figure 250–68

Caution

CAUTION: Dangerous objectionable neutral current will flow on conductive metal parts of electrical equipment, metal piping, and structural steel in violation of 250.6(A). ▸Figure 250–69

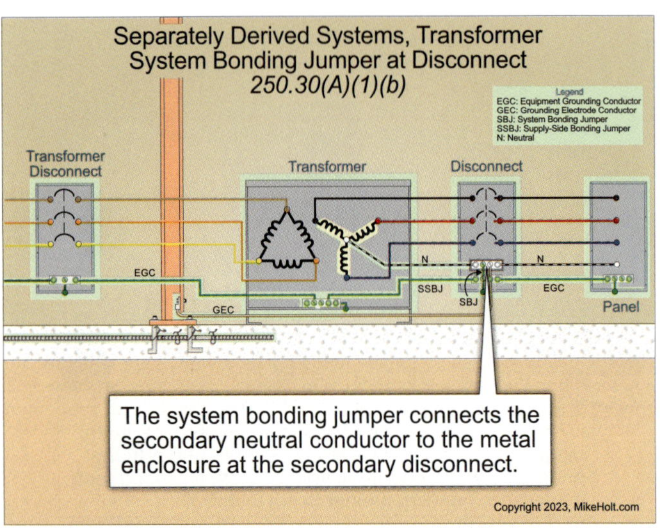
Separately Derived Systems, Transformer
System Bonding Jumper at Disconnect
250.30(A)(1)(b)
Legend
EGC: Equipment Grounding Conductor
GEC: Grounding Electrode Conductor
SBJ: System Bonding Jumper
SSBJ: Supply-Side Bonding Jumper
N: Neutral
Transformer Disconnect
Transformer
Disconnect
EGC
GEC
SSBJ
SBJ
EGC
Panel
The system bonding jumper connects the secondary neutral conductor to the metal enclosure at the secondary disconnect.
Copyright 2023, MikeHolt.com

▸Figure 250–68

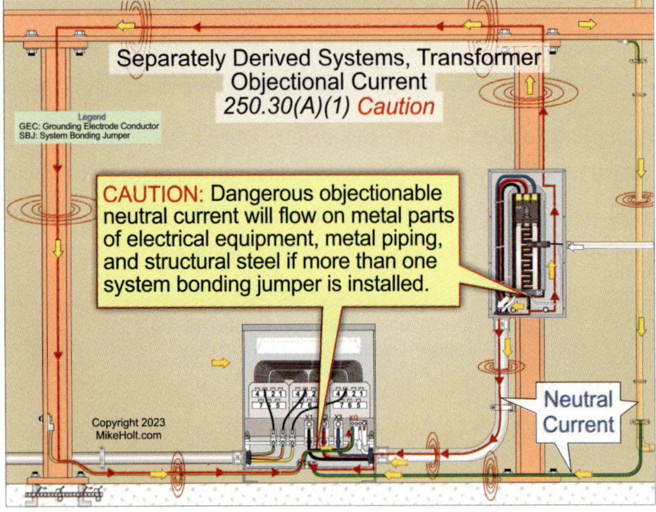
Separately Derived Systems, Transformer
Objectional Current
250.30(A)(1) Caution
Legend
GEC: Grounding Electrode Conductor
SBJ: System Bonding Jumper
CAUTION: Dangerous objectionable neutral current will flow on metal parts of electrical equipment, metal piping, and structural steel if more than one system bonding jumper is installed.
Neutral Current
Copyright 2023 MikeHolt.com

▸Figure 250–69

(2) Supply-Side Bonding Jumper to Disconnect.

Nonflexible Metal Raceway. A nonflexible metal raceway can be used as a supply-side bonding jumper if installed from the transformer enclosure to the secondary disconnect enclosure. ▸Figure 250–70

Supply-Side Bonding Jumper of the Wire-Type. A supply-side bonding jumper of the wire-type can be used if installed from the transformer enclosure grounding terminal to the secondary disconnect enclosure grounding terminal. ▸Figure 250–71

1st Printing

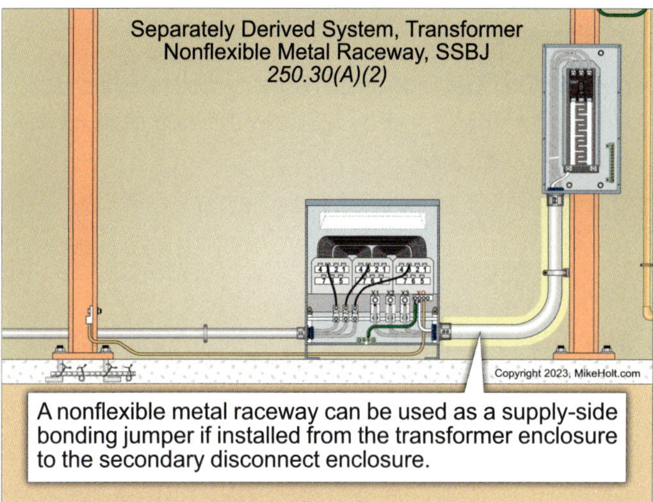
Separately Derived System, Transformer
Nonflexible Metal Raceway, SSBJ
250.30(A)(2)
Copyright 2023, MikeHolt.com
A nonflexible metal raceway can be used as a supply-side bonding jumper if installed from the transformer enclosure to the secondary disconnect enclosure.

▸Figure 250–70

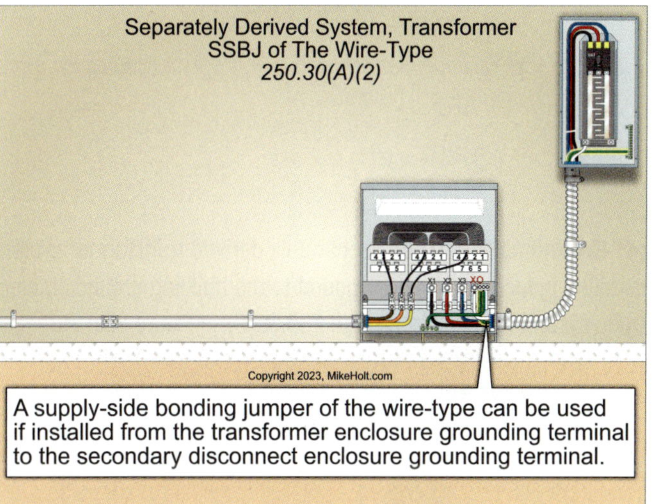
Separately Derived System, Transformer
SSBJ of The Wire-Type
250.30(A)(2)
Copyright 2023, MikeHolt.com
A supply-side bonding jumper of the wire-type can be used if installed from the transformer enclosure grounding terminal to the secondary disconnect enclosure grounding terminal.

▸Figure 250–71

Author's Comment:

- The supply-side bonding jumper can be RMC, IMC, or EMT run between the transformer separately derived system enclosure and the secondary system disconnect enclosure. A nonmetallic or flexible raceway must have a supply-side bonding jumper of the wire type.

(1) A supply-side bonding jumper of the wire type must be sized in accordance with 250.102(C) based on the size or area of the secondary phase conductors in the raceway or cable.

▸ **Example**

Question: *What size supply-side bonding jumper is required for flexible metal conduit containing 300 kcmil transformer secondary conductors?* ▸**Figure 250–72**

(a) 4 AWG *(b) 2 AWG* *(c) 1/0 AWG* *(d) 3/0 AWG*

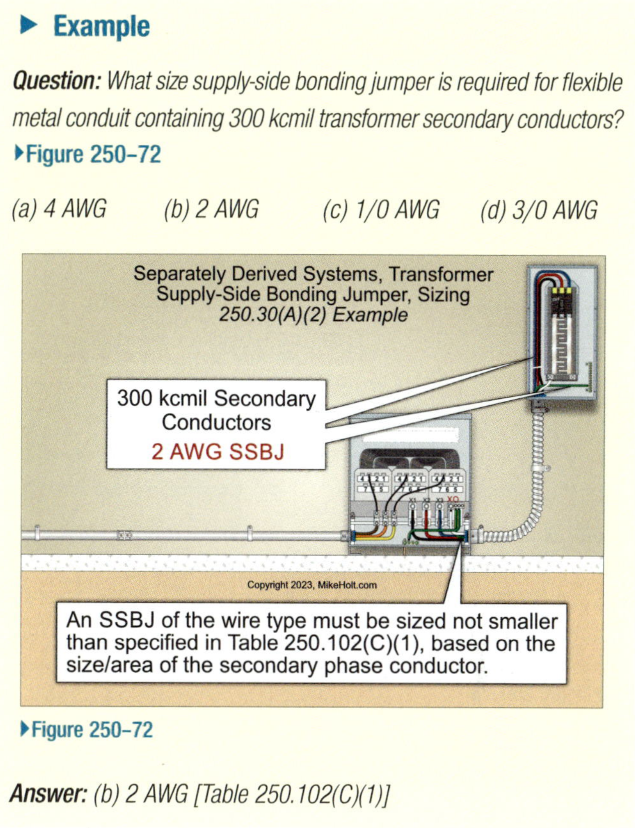
Separately Derived Systems, Transformer
Supply-Side Bonding Jumper, Sizing
250.30(A)(2) Example
300 kcmil Secondary Conductors
2 AWG SSBJ
Copyright 2023, MikeHolt.com
An SSBJ of the wire type must be sized not smaller than specified in Table 250.102(C)(1), based on the size/area of the secondary phase conductor.

▸Figure 250–72

Answer: *(b) 2 AWG [Table 250.102(C)(1)]*

(3) Neutral Conductor Size. The neutral conductor between the transformer separately derived system and the secondary system disconnect is not required to be larger than the phase conductors. If the system bonding jumper is installed at the secondary system disconnect, instead of at the transformer separately derived system, the following apply:

(a) Single Raceway. A secondary neutral conductor must be run from the transformer separately derived system to the secondary system disconnect, and the secondary neutral conductor must be sized in accordance with Table 250.102(C)(1) based on the size or area of the secondary phase conductor.

▶ Example

Question: *What size neutral conductor is required for a 75 kVA transformer with 250 kcmil secondary conductors?* ▸Figure 250–73

(a) 2 AWG (b) 1/0 AWG (c) 4/0 AWG (d) 250 kcmil

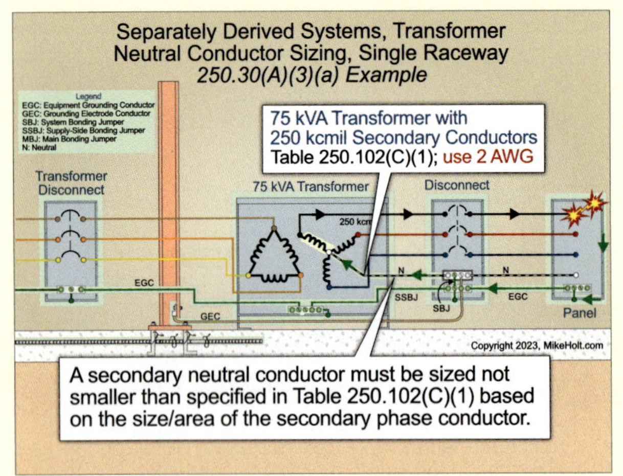
Separately Derived Systems, Transformer
Neutral Conductor Sizing, Single Raceway
250.30(A)(3)(a) Example
75 kVA Transformer with
250 kcmil Secondary Conductors
Table 250.102(C)(1); use 2 AWG
Transformer Disconnect
75 kVA Transformer
Disconnect
Panel
A secondary neutral conductor must be sized not smaller than specified in Table 250.102(C)(1) based on the size/area of the secondary phase conductor.
Copyright 2023, MikeHolt.com

▸Figure 250–73

Answer: *(a) 2 AWG [Table 250.102(C)(1)]*

▶ Example

Question: *The minimum secondary neutral conductor size for a 112.50 kVA transformer is ____ if the secondary paralleled phase conductors are 3/0 AWG kcmil.*

(a) 4 AWG in each raceway (b) 2 AWG in each raceway
(c) 1/0 AWG in each raceway (d) 3/0 AWG in each raceway

Solution:

Step 1: *Determine the equivalent area for two 3/0 AWG conductors from Chapter 9, Table 8:*

3/0 AWG = 167,800 circular mils
2 conductors × 167,800 cmil = 335,600 cmil [Table 250.102(C)(1)]

Step 2: *Size the neutral conductor in each raceway to Table 250.102(C)(1) based on 3/0 AWG phase conductors per raceway: 2 AWG.*

Step 3: *The minimum parallel conductor is 1/0 in accordance with 310.10(G): 1/0 AWG.*

Answer: *(c) 1/0 AWG in each raceway*

(b) Paralleled in Two or More Raceways or Cables. The neutral conductor(s) in each raceway or cable set connected in parallel is sized based on the largest phase conductor in each raceway or cable in accordance with Table 250.102(C)(1), but not smaller than 1/0 AWG. ▸Figure 250–74

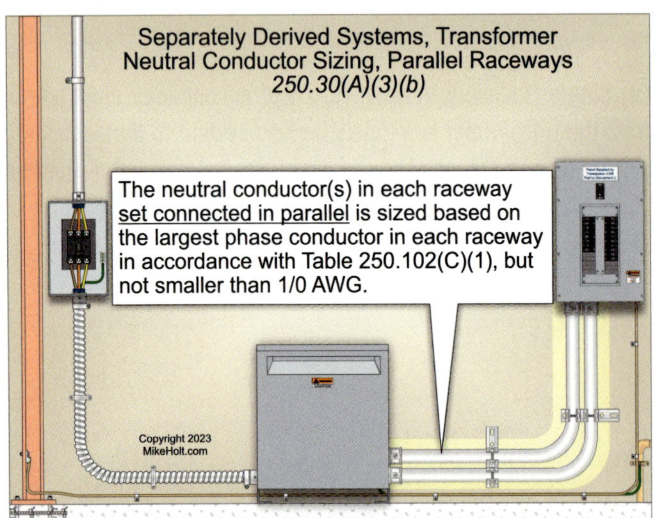
Separately Derived Systems, Transformer
Neutral Conductor Sizing, Parallel Raceways
250.30(A)(3)(b)
The neutral conductor(s) in each raceway set connected in parallel is sized based on the largest phase conductor in each raceway in accordance with Table 250.102(C)(1), but not smaller than 1/0 AWG.
Copyright 2023 MikeHolt.com

▸Figure 250–74

(4) Grounding Electrode. Separately derived transformer system installed indoors must be grounded to the building grounding electrode system in accordance with 250.30(C). ▸Figure 250–75

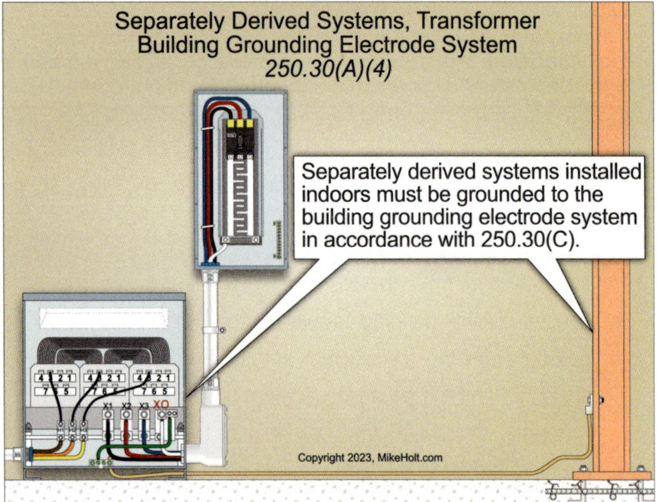
Separately Derived Systems, Transformer
Building Grounding Electrode System
250.30(A)(4)
Separately derived systems installed indoors must be grounded to the building grounding electrode system in accordance with 250.30(C).
Copyright 2023, MikeHolt.com

▸Figure 250–75

Separately derived transformer systems located outdoors must be grounded in accordance with 250.30(C).

(5) Grounding Electrode Conductor. The grounding electrode conductor for a transformer separately derived system must be sized in accordance with 250.66.

The grounding electrode conductor must terminate to the neutral conductor at the same point where the system bonding jumper is connected. ▶Figure 250–76

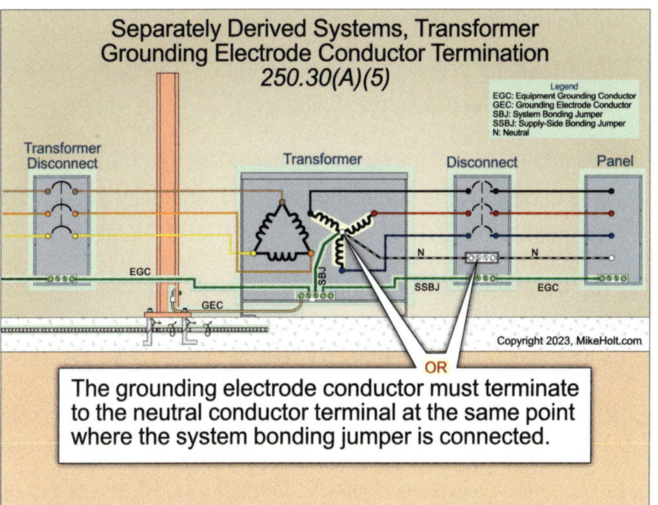
Separately Derived Systems, Transformer
Grounding Electrode Conductor Termination
250.30(A)(5)
Legend
EGC: Equipment Grounding Conductor
GEC: Grounding Electrode Conductor
SBJ: System Bonding Jumper
SSBJ: Supply-Side Bonding Jumper
N: Neutral
Transformer Disconnect
Transformer
Disconnect
Panel
EGC
GEC
SBJ
SSBJ
N
Copyright 2023, MikeHolt.com
OR
The grounding electrode conductor must terminate to the neutral conductor terminal at the same point where the system bonding jumper is connected.

▶Figure 250–76

Author's Comment:

- To prevent objectionable neutral current from flowing onto metal parts [250.6], the grounding electrode conductor must originate at the same point on the transformer separately derived system as where the system bonding jumper is connected [250.30(A)(1)].

Ex 1: If the system bonding jumper is a wire or busbar [250.30(A)(1)], the grounding electrode conductor can terminate at the grounding terminal, bar, or bus where the system bonding jumper terminates, instead of on the neutral terminal. ▶Figure 250–77

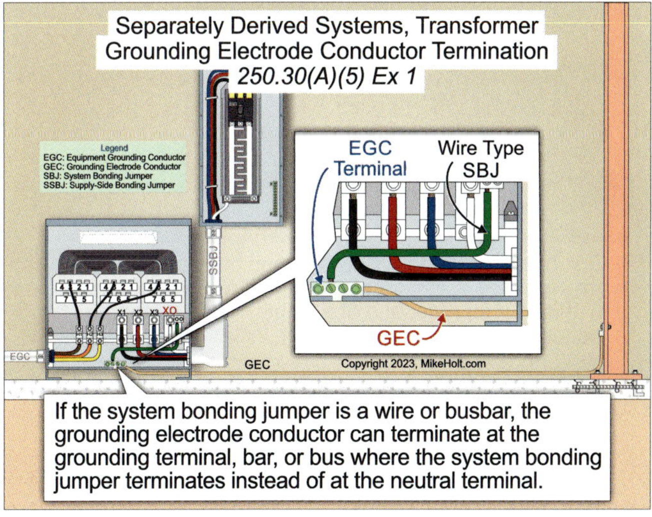
Separately Derived Systems, Transformer
Grounding Electrode Conductor Termination
250.30(A)(5) Ex 1
Legend
EGC: Equipment Grounding Conductor
GEC: Grounding Electrode Conductor
SBJ: System Bonding Jumper
SSBJ: Supply-Side Bonding Jumper
EGC Terminal
Wire Type SBJ
GEC
SSBJ
EGC
Copyright 2023, MikeHolt.com
If the system bonding jumper is a wire or busbar, the grounding electrode conductor can terminate at the grounding terminal, bar, or bus where the system bonding jumper terminates instead of at the neutral terminal.

▶Figure 250–77

▶ Grounding Electrode Conductor Example 1

Question: *What size grounding electrode conductor is required for a 45 kVA, three-phase, 480V to 120/208V transformer when the secondary conductors are sized at 1/0 AWG?* ▶Figure 250–78

(a) 6 AWG (b) 4 AWG (c) 3 AWG (d) 2 AWG

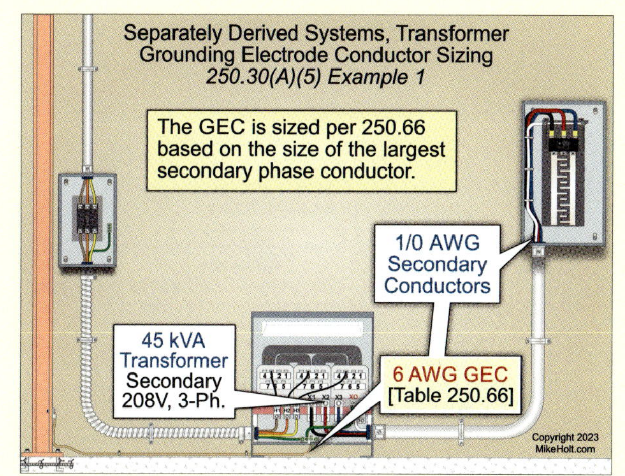
Separately Derived Systems, Transformer
Grounding Electrode Conductor Sizing
250.30(A)(5) Example 1
The GEC is sized per 250.66 based on the size of the largest secondary phase conductor.
1/0 AWG Secondary Conductors
45 kVA Transformer Secondary 208V, 3-Ph.
6 AWG GEC [Table 250.66]
Copyright 2023 MikeHolt.com

▶Figure 250–78

Answer: *(a) 6 AWG [Table 250.66]*

▶ Grounding Electrode Conductor Example 2

Question: *What size grounding electrode conductor is required for a 75 kVA, three-phase, 480V to 120/208V transformer when the secondary conductors are sized at 4/0 AWG?* ▶Figure 250–79

(a) 6 AWG (b) 4 AWG (c) 3 AWG (d) 2 AWG

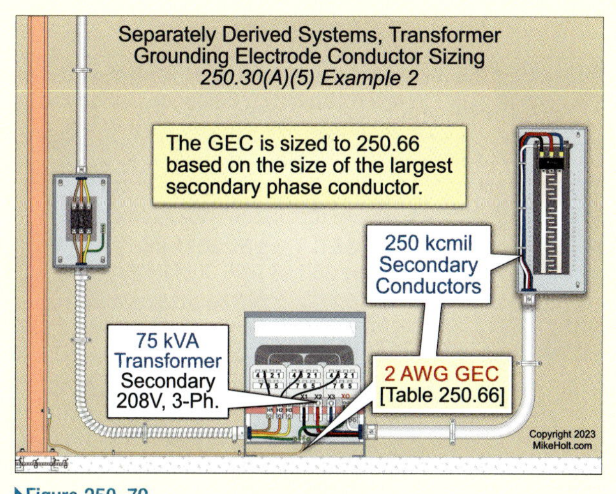
Separately Derived Systems, Transformer
Grounding Electrode Conductor Sizing
250.30(A)(5) Example 2
The GEC is sized to 250.66 based on the size of the largest secondary phase conductor.
250 kcmil Secondary Conductors
75 kVA Transformer Secondary 208V, 3-Ph.
2 AWG GEC [Table 250.66]
Copyright 2023 MikeHolt.com

▶Figure 250–79

Answer: *(d) 2 AWG [Table 250.66]*

▶ Grounding Electrode Conductor Example 3

Question: *What size grounding electrode conductor is required for a 112.50 kVA, three-phase, 480V to 120/208V transformer when the secondary conductors are sized at 600 kcmil?* ▸**Figure 250–80**

(a) 1/0 AWG (b) 2/0 AWG (c) 3/0 AWG (d) 4/0 AWG

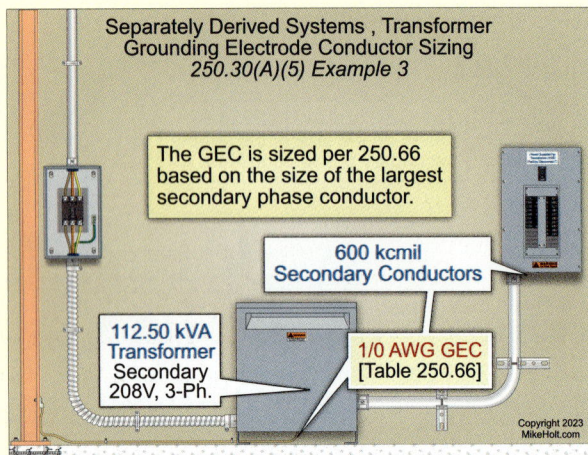

Separately Derived Systems , Transformer
Grounding Electrode Conductor Sizing
250.30(A)(5) Example 3
The GEC is sized per 250.66 based on the size of the largest secondary phase conductor.
600 kcmil Secondary Conductors
112.50 kVA Transformer Secondary 208V, 3-Ph.
1/0 AWG GEC [Table 250.66]
Copyright 2023 MikeHolt.com

▸Figure 250–80

Answer: *(b) 2/0 AWG*

(6) Common Grounding Electrode Conductor, Multiple Separately Derived Transformer Systems. Where there are multiple transformer separately derived systems, a grounding electrode conductor tap from each of them to a common grounding electrode conductor is permitted. This connection must be made at the same point on the transformer separately derived system secondary as where the system bonding jumper is connected [250.30(A)(1)]. ▸**Figure 250–81**

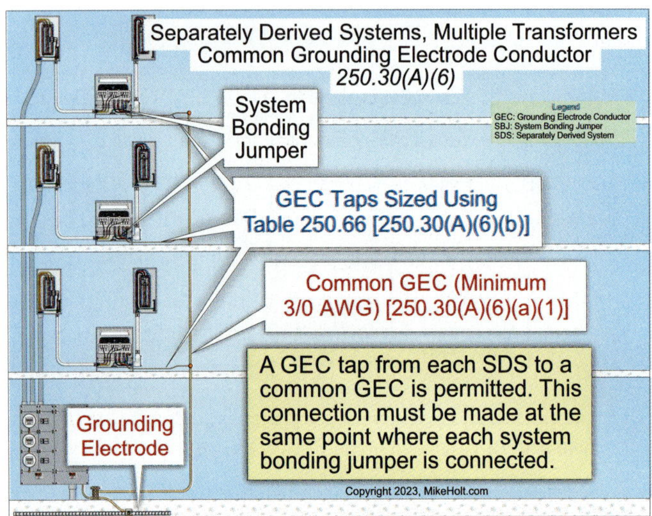

Separately Derived Systems, Multiple Transformers
Common Grounding Electrode Conductor
250.30(A)(6)
System Bonding Jumper
Legend
GEC: Grounding Electrode Conductor
SBJ: System Bonding Jumper
SDS: Separately Derived System
GEC Taps Sized Using Table 250.66 [250.30(A)(6)(b)]
Common GEC (Minimum 3/0 AWG) [250.30(A)(6)(a)(1)]
A GEC tap from each SDS to a common GEC is permitted. This connection must be made at the same point where each system bonding jumper is connected.
Grounding Electrode
Copyright 2023, MikeHolt.com

▸Figure 250–81

(a) Common Grounding Electrode Conductor. The common grounding electrode conductor can be any of the following:

(1) An unspliced conductor not smaller than 3/0 AWG copper or 250 kcmil aluminum

(2) Interior metal water pipe not more than 5 ft from the point of entrance to the building [250.68(C)(1)]

(3) The metal frame of the building in accordance with 250.68(C)(2) or connected to the grounding electrode system by a conductor not smaller than 3/0 AWG copper or 250 kcmil aluminum

(b) Tap Conductor Size. Grounding electrode conductor taps must be sized in accordance with Table 250.66, based on the area of the largest secondary phase conductor.

Ex: If the only electrodes present are ground rods [250.66(A)], concrete-encased electrodes [250.66(B)], or ground rings [250.66(C)], the size of the common grounding electrode conductor is not required to be larger than the largest conductor required by 250.66(A), (B), or (C) for the type of electrode that is present.

(c) Connections. Tap connections to the common grounding electrode conductor must be made at an accessible location by any of the following methods:

(1) A connector listed as "bonding and grounding equipment"

(2) Listed connections to aluminum or copper busbars not less than ¼ in. thick × 2 in. wide, and of a length to accommodate the terminations necessary for the installation ▸**Figure 250–82**

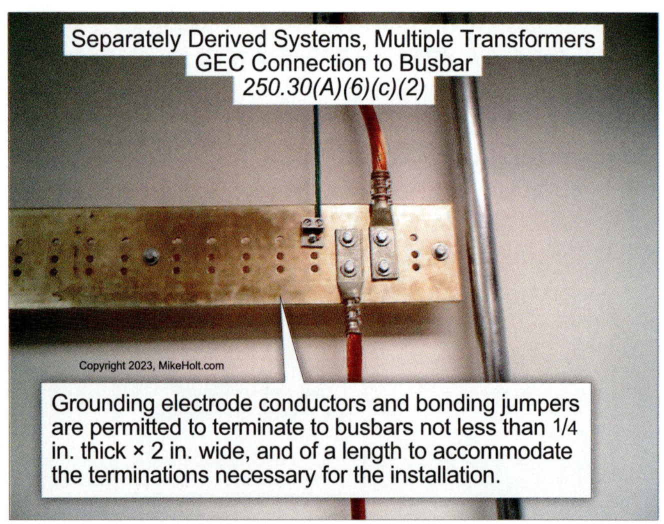

Separately Derived Systems, Multiple Transformers
GEC Connection to Busbar
250.30(A)(6)(c)(2)
Copyright 2023, MikeHolt.com
Grounding electrode conductors and bonding jumpers are permitted to terminate to busbars not less than 1/4 in. thick × 2 in. wide, and of a length to accommodate the terminations necessary for the installation.

▸Figure 250–82

(3) Exothermic Welding. Tap grounding electrode conductors must remain without a splice or joint.

(7) Installation. The grounding electrode conductor must comply with 250.64(A), (B), (C), and (E).

Author's Comment:

- According to 250.64, the grounding electrode conductor must be copper where within 18 in. of the surface of the Earth [250.64(A)], securely fastened to the surface on which it is carried [250.64(B)(1)], and adequately protected if exposed to physical damage [250.64(B)(2) and (3)]. In addition, ferrous metal enclosures enclosing a grounding electrode conductor must be made electrically continuous from the point of attachment to cabinets or equipment to the grounding electrode [250.64(E)].

(C) Outdoor Source. If located outdoors, the grounding electrode connection must be made at the transformer separately derived system. ▸Figure 250–83

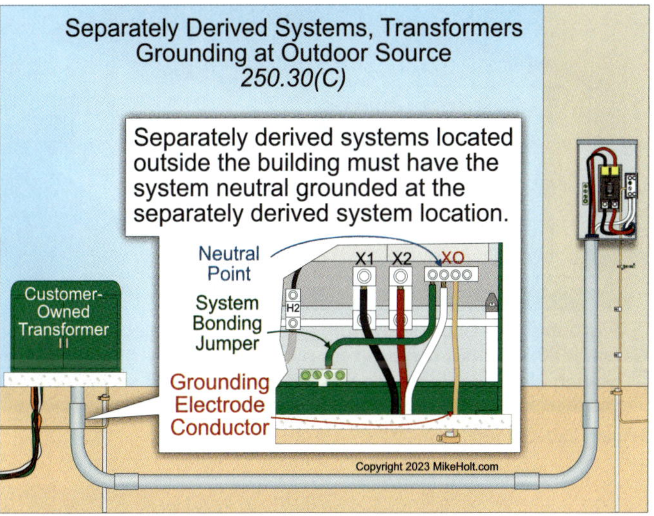
Separately Derived Systems, Transformers
Grounding at Outdoor Source
250.30(C)
Separately derived systems located outside the building must have the system neutral grounded at the separately derived system location.
Neutral Point
X1
X2
XO
H2
System Bonding Jumper
Grounding Electrode Conductor
Customer-Owned Transformer
Copyright 2023 MikeHolt.com

▸Figure 250–83

Generator Separately Derived Systems

According to Article 100, "Separately Derived System" is an electrical power supply output having no direct connection(s) to the circuit conductors of any other electrical source other than those established by grounding and bonding connections. ▸Figure 250–84

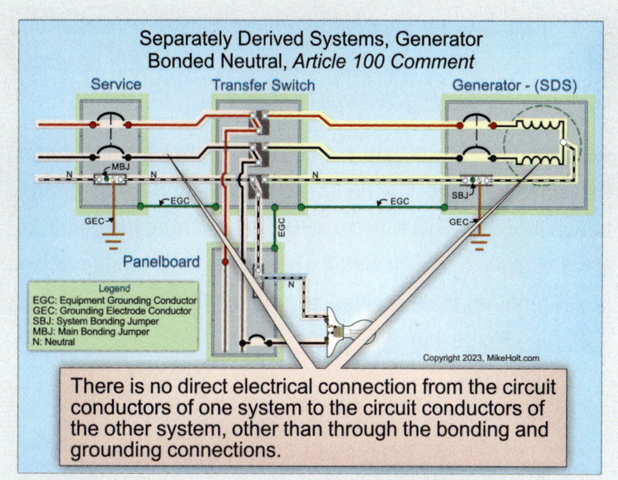
Separately Derived Systems, Generator
Bonded Neutral, *Article 100 Comment*
Service
Transfer Switch
Generator - (SDS)
MBJ
N
EGC
SBJ
GEC
Panelboard
Legend
EGC: Equipment Grounding Conductor
GEC: Grounding Electrode Conductor
SBJ: System Bonding Jumper
MBJ: Main Bonding Jumper
N: Neutral
Copyright 2023, MikeHolt.com
There is no direct electrical connection from the circuit conductors of one system to the circuit conductors of the other system, other than through the bonding and grounding connections.

▸Figure 250–84

(A) Grounded Systems. A generator with a disconnect supplying a switched-neutral transfer switch must be bonded and grounded in accordance with the following. ▸Figure 250–85

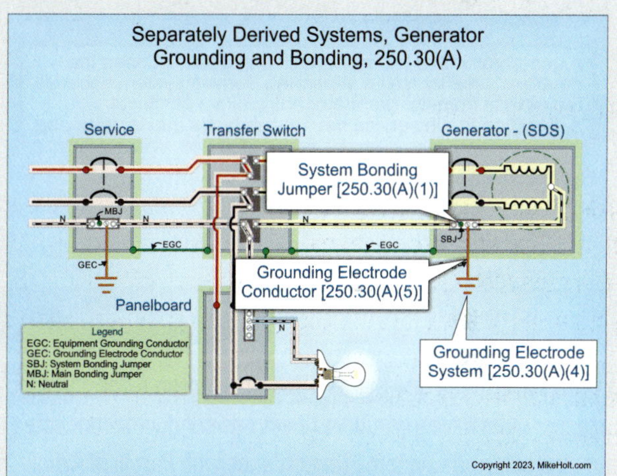
Separately Derived Systems, Generator
Grounding and Bonding, 250.30(A)
Service
Transfer Switch
Generator - (SDS)
System Bonding Jumper [250.30(A)(1)]
MBJ
N
EGC
SBJ
GEC
Grounding Electrode Conductor [250.30(A)(5)]
Panelboard
Grounding Electrode System [250.30(A)(4)]
Legend
EGC: Equipment Grounding Conductor
GEC: Grounding Electrode Conductor
SBJ: System Bonding Jumper
MBJ: Main Bonding Jumper
N: Neutral
Copyright 2023, MikeHolt.com

▸Figure 250–85

(1) System Bonding Jumper. A system bonding jumper must be installed at the secondary neutral point.

(4) Grounding Electrode. A separately derived generator system installed indoors must be grounded to the building grounding electrode system. Separately derived generator systems located outdoors must have the grounding electrode connection made at the generator separately derived system in accordance with 250.30(C).

(5) Grounding Electrode Conductor. The grounding electrode conductor must terminate to the neutral terminal where the system bonding jumper is connected.

• • •

Ex 1: If the system bonding jumper is a wire or busbar, the grounding electrode conductor can terminate at the generator equipment grounding terminal.

According to 250.30 Note 1, a generator with a transfer switch that does not open the neutral is not a generator separately derived system. This is because the neutral from the generator has a direct connection with the service neutral conductor, and is not required to be bonded or grounded in accordance with 250.30. ▸Figure 250–86

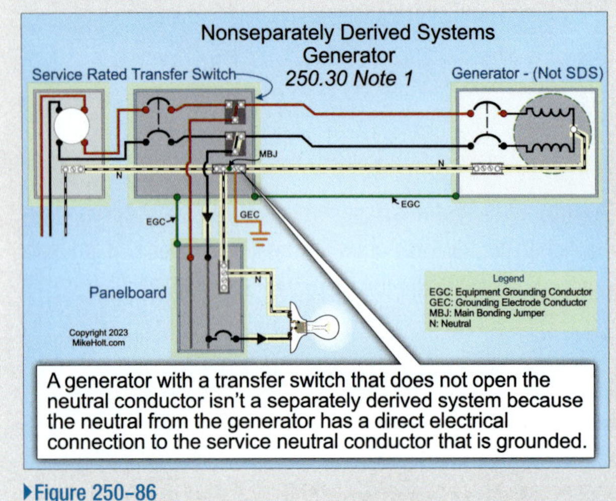
Nonseparately Derived Systems
Generator
250.30 Note 1
Service Rated Transfer Switch
Generator - (Not SDS)
MBJ
N
EGC
GEC
Panelboard
Legend
EGC: Equipment Grounding Conductor
GEC: Grounding Electrode Conductor
MBJ: Main Bonding Jumper
N: Neutral
Copyright 2023 MikeHolt.com
A generator with a transfer switch that does not open the neutral conductor isn't a separately derived system because the neutral from the generator has a direct electrical connection to the service neutral conductor that is grounded.

▸Figure 250–86

250.32 Buildings Supplied by a Feeder

(A) Grounding Electrode System and Conductor. A building supplied by a feeder must have a grounding electrode conductor connected to a grounding electrode system in accordance with Part III of Article 250. ▸Figure 250–87

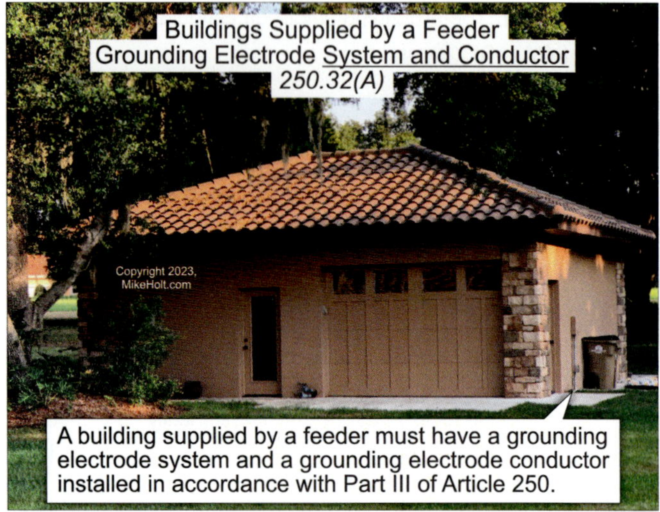
Buildings Supplied by a Feeder
Grounding Electrode System and Conductor
250.32(A)
Copyright 2023, MikeHolt.com
A building supplied by a feeder must have a grounding electrode system and a grounding electrode conductor installed in accordance with Part III of Article 250.

▸Figure 250–87

Ex: A grounding electrode system and grounding electrode conductor is not required for a building if it is supplied by a single branch circuit or multiwire branch circuit. ▸Figure 250–88

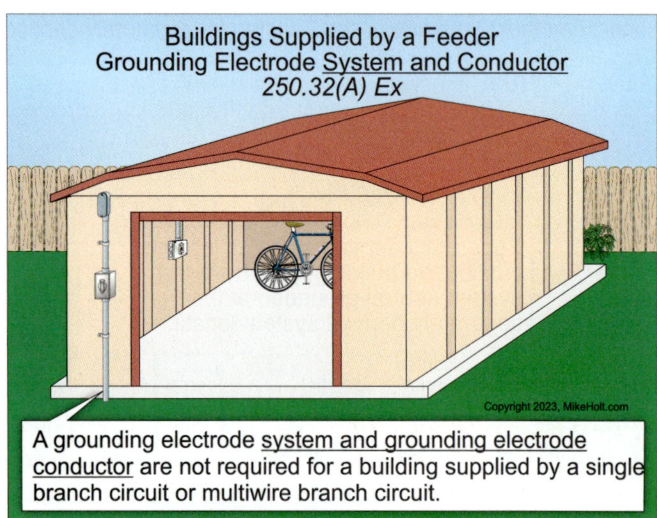
Buildings Supplied by a Feeder
Grounding Electrode System and Conductor
250.32(A) Ex
Copyright 2023, MikeHolt.com
A grounding electrode system and grounding electrode conductor are not required for a building supplied by a single branch circuit or multiwire branch circuit.

▸Figure 250–88

(B) Equipment Grounding Conductor.

(1) The metal parts of the building disconnect must be connected to the feeder equipment grounding conductor of a type described in 250.118(A). ▸Figure 250–89

Where the supply circuit equipment grounding conductor is of the wire type, it must be sized in accordance with 250.122.

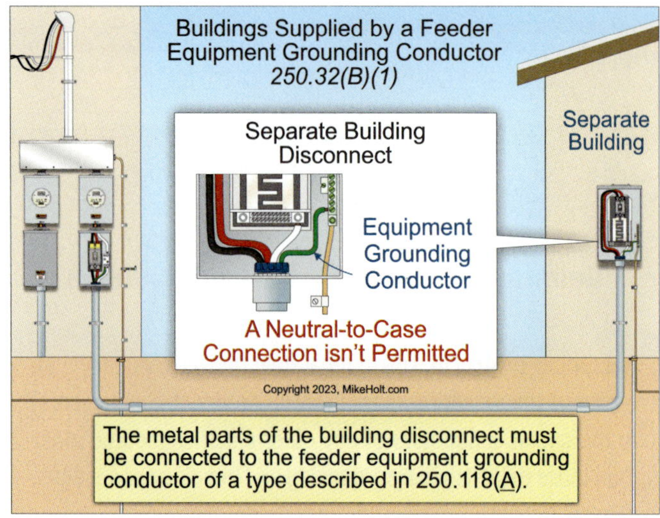
Buildings Supplied by a Feeder
Equipment Grounding Conductor
250.32(B)(1)
Separate Building Disconnect
Equipment Grounding Conductor
A Neutral-to-Case Connection isn't Permitted
Separate Building
Copyright 2023, MikeHolt.com
The metal parts of the building disconnect must be connected to the feeder equipment grounding conductor of a type described in 250.118(A).

▸Figure 250–89

1st Printing

Caution

CAUTION: To prevent dangerous objectionable neutral current from flowing on metal parts [250.6(A)], the supply circuit neutral conductor is not permitted to be connected to the remote building disconnect metal enclosure. [250.142(B)]. ▸Figure 250–90

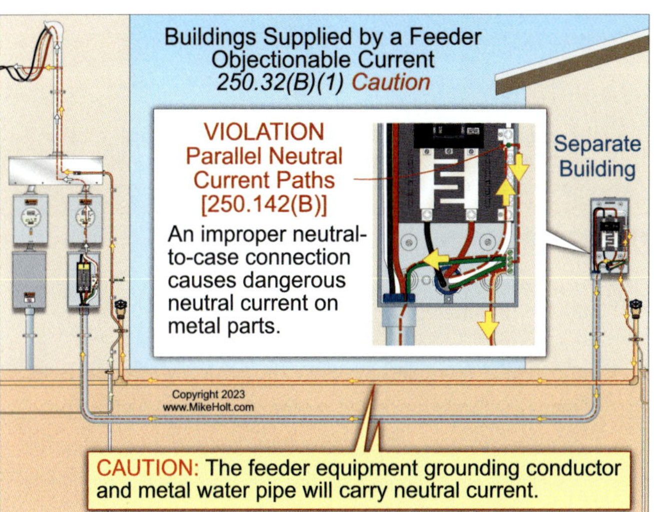
Buildings Supplied by a Feeder
Objectionable Current
250.32(B)(1) Caution
VIOLATION
Parallel Neutral
Current Paths
[250.142(B)]
An improper neutral-to-case connection causes dangerous neutral current on metal parts.
Separate Building
Copyright 2023
www.MikeHolt.com
CAUTION: The feeder equipment grounding conductor and metal water pipe will carry neutral current.

▸Figure 250–90

Ex 1: The neutral conductor can serve as the ground-fault return path for the building disconnect for existing installations where there are no continuous metallic paths between buildings and structures, ground-fault protection of equipment is not installed on the supply side of the circuit, and the neutral conductor is sized no smaller than the larger of:

(1) The maximum unbalanced calculated neutral load in accordance with 220.61

(2) The minimum equipment grounding conductor size in accordance with 250.122

(E) Grounding Electrode Conductor Size. The grounding electrode conductor must terminate to the equipment grounding terminal of the disconnect (not the neutral terminal) and must be sized in accordance with 250.66.

▶ Example

Question: *What size grounding electrode conductor is required for a building disconnect supplied with a 3/0 AWG feeder with a concrete-encased electrode?* ▸Figure 250–91

(a) 4 AWG (b) 2 AWG (c) 1 AWG (d) 1/0 AWG

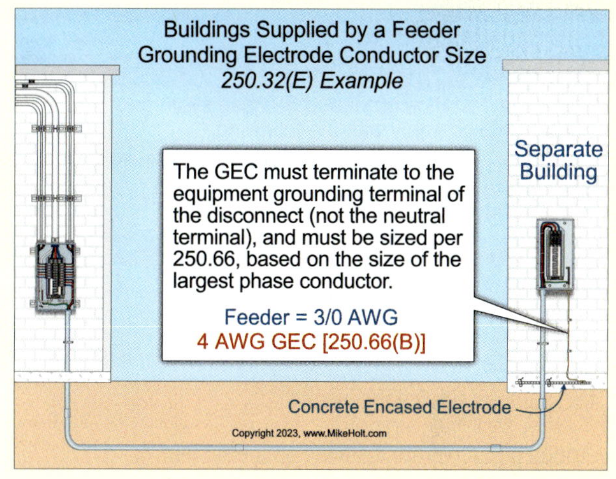
Buildings Supplied by a Feeder
Grounding Electrode Conductor Size
250.32(E) Example
Separate Building
The GEC must terminate to the equipment grounding terminal of the disconnect (not the neutral terminal), and must be sized per 250.66, based on the size of the largest phase conductor.
Feeder = 3/0 AWG
4 AWG GEC [250.66(B)]
Concrete Encased Electrode
Copyright 2023, www.MikeHolt.com

▸Figure 250–91

Answer: *(a) 4 AWG*

Note: *If the grounding electrode conductor is connected to a concrete-encased electrode(s), the portion of the conductor that connects only to the concrete-encased electrode(s) is not required to be larger than 4 AWG copper [250.66(B)].*

Author's Comment:

- If the grounding electrode conductor is connected to a rod(s), the portion of the conductor that connects only to the rod(s) is not required to be larger than 6 AWG copper [250.66(A)].

250.36 Impedance Grounded Systems—480V to 1000V

To limit ground-fault current to a low value, an impedance grounded system with a grounding impedance device, typically a resistor, is permitted to be installed on three-phase systems of 480V up to 1000V where all the following conditions are met: ▸Figure 250–92

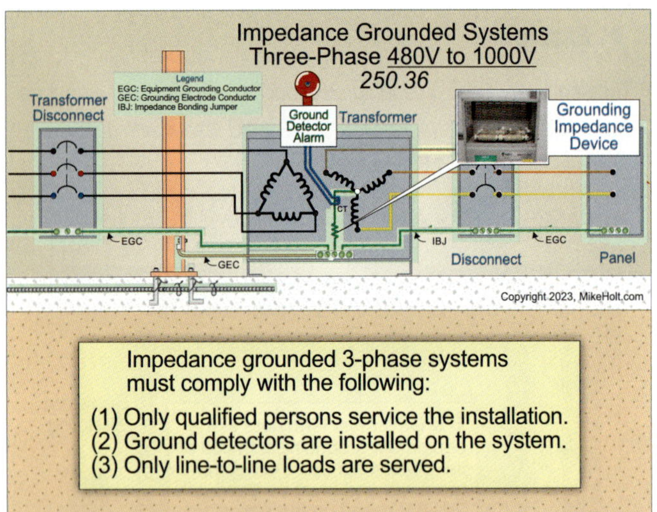

Impedance Grounded Systems
Three-Phase 480V to 1000V
250.36
Legend
EGC: Equipment Grounding Conductor
GEC: Grounding Electrode Conductor
IBJ: Impedance Bonding Jumper
Transformer Disconnect
Ground Detector Alarm
Transformer
Grounding Impedance Device
CT
EGC
GEC
IBJ
EGC
Disconnect
Panel
Copyright 2023, MikeHolt.com
Impedance grounded 3-phase systems must comply with the following:
(1) Only qualified persons service the installation.
(2) Ground detectors are installed on the system.
(3) Only line-to-line loads are served.

▸Figure 250–92

(1) Conditions of maintenance and supervision ensure that only qualified persons service the installation.

(2) Ground detectors are installed on the system.

(3) Only line-to-line loads are served.

Note: Impedance grounding is an effective tool for reducing arc-flash hazards, see Annex O of NFPA 70E, *Standard for Electrical Safety in the Workplace.* ▸**Figure 250–93**

Impedance Grounded Systems
Reduces Arc-Flash Hazards
250.36 Note
Copyright 2023, MikeHolt.com
In accordance with NFPA 70E Annex O, impedance grounding is an effective tool for reducing arc-flash hazards.

▸Figure 250–93

According to Article 100, "Impedance Grounded System" is an electrical system that is grounded by bonding the system neutral point to the metal parts of the enclosure through an impedance device. ▸**Figure 250–94**

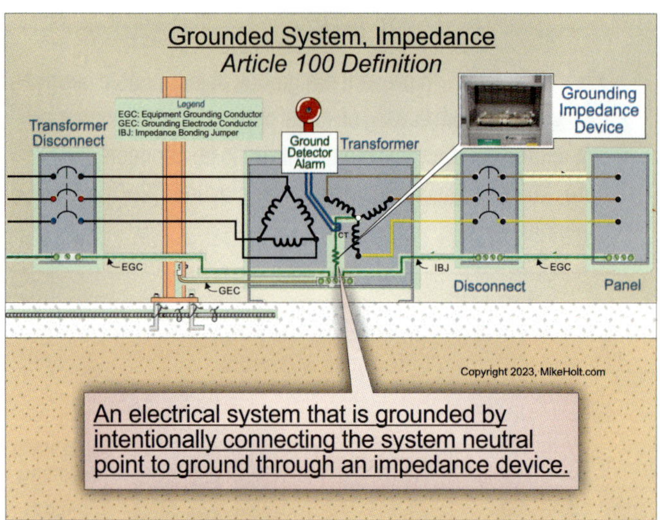

Grounded System, Impedance
Article 100 Definition
Legend
EGC: Equipment Grounding Conductor
GEC: Grounding Electrode Conductor
IBJ: Impedance Bonding Jumper
Transformer Disconnect
Ground Detector Alarm
Transformer
Grounding Impedance Device
CT
EGC
GEC
IBJ
EGC
Disconnect
Panel
Copyright 2023, MikeHolt.com
An electrical system that is grounded by intentionally connecting the system neutral point to ground through an impedance device.

▸Figure 250–94

Author's Comment:

- Impedance grounded systems are generally referred to as "high-resistance grounded systems" in the industry. These systems are generally used where sudden interruption of power will create increased hazards and when a reduction of incident energy is needed for worker safety.
- High-resistance grounding will insert an impedance in the ground return path and will typically limit the fault current to 10A or less, leaving insufficient fault energy and thereby reducing the arc-flash hazard level. High-resistance grounding will not affect arc-flash energy for line-to-line faults NFPA 70E, *Standard for Electrical Safety in the Workplace.*

(A) Grounding Impedance Device Location. A grounding impedance device must be installed between the impedance grounding conductor and the transformer secondary neutral point. ▸**Figure 250–95**

According to Article 100, "Impedance Grounding Conductor" is a conductor that connects the system neutral point to the impedance device in an impedance grounded system. ▸**Figure 250–96**

Part III. Grounding Electrode System and Grounding Electrode Conductor

250.50 Grounding Electrode System

According to Article 100, "Grounding Electrode" is a conducting object used to make a direct electrical connection to the Earth [250.50 through 250.70]. ▸**Figure 250–97**

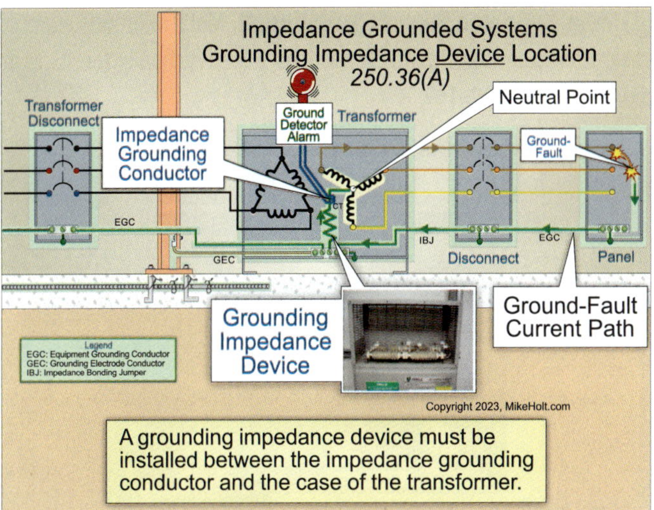
Impedance Grounded Systems
Grounding Impedance Device Location
250.36(A)
Neutral Point
Transformer Disconnect
Impedance Grounding Conductor
Ground Detector Alarm
Transformer
Ground-Fault
EGC
GEC
IBJ
Disconnect
EGC
Panel
Grounding Impedance Device
Ground-Fault Current Path
Legend
EGC: Equipment Grounding Conductor
GEC: Grounding Electrode Conductor
IBJ: Impedance Bonding Jumper
Copyright 2023, MikeHolt.com
A grounding impedance device must be installed between the impedance grounding conductor and the case of the transformer.

▸Figure 250–95

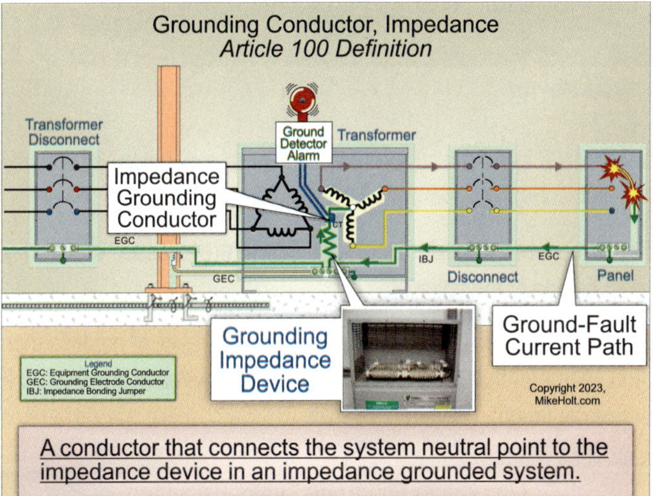
Grounding Conductor, Impedance
Article 100 Definition
Transformer Disconnect
Ground Detector Alarm
Transformer
Impedance Grounding Conductor
EGC
GEC
IBJ
Disconnect
EGC
Panel
Grounding Impedance Device
Ground-Fault Current Path
Legend
EGC: Equipment Grounding Conductor
GEC: Grounding Electrode Conductor
IBJ: Impedance Bonding Jumper
Copyright 2023, MikeHolt.com
A conductor that connects the system neutral point to the impedance device in an impedance grounded system.

▸Figure 250–96

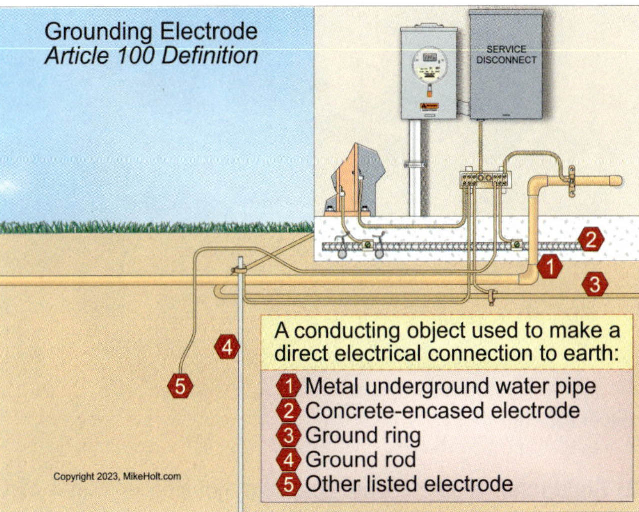
Grounding Electrode
Article 100 Definition
SERVICE DISCONNECT
A conducting object used to make a direct electrical connection to earth:
1 Metal underground water pipe
2 Concrete-encased electrode
3 Ground ring
4 Ground rod
5 Other listed electrode
Copyright 2023, MikeHolt.com

▸Figure 250–97

A grounding electrode system is comprised of bonding together the grounding electrodes described in 250.52(A)(1) through (A)(8) that are present at a building or structure. ▸Figure 250–98

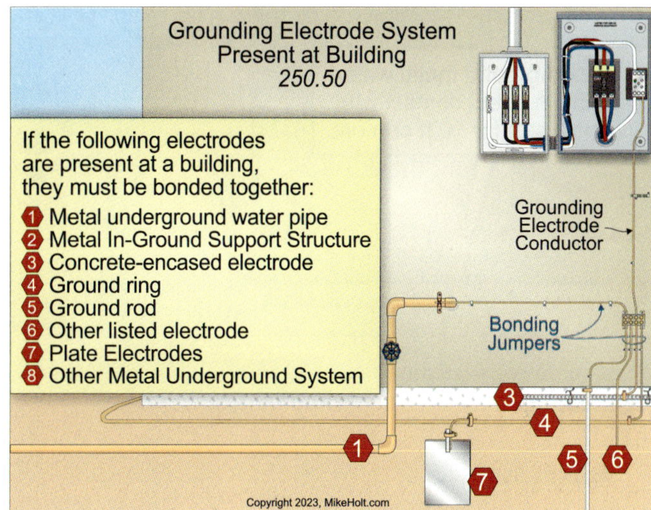
Grounding Electrode System
Present at Building
250.50
If the following electrodes are present at a building, they must be bonded together:
1 Metal underground water pipe
2 Metal In-Ground Support Structure
3 Concrete-encased electrode
4 Ground ring
5 Ground rod
6 Other listed electrode
7 Plate Electrodes
8 Other Metal Underground System
Grounding Electrode Conductor
Bonding Jumpers
Copyright 2023, MikeHolt.com

▸Figure 250–98

Ex: Concrete-encased electrodes are not required for existing buildings or structures if the rebar is not accessible without chipping up the concrete. ▸Figure 250–99

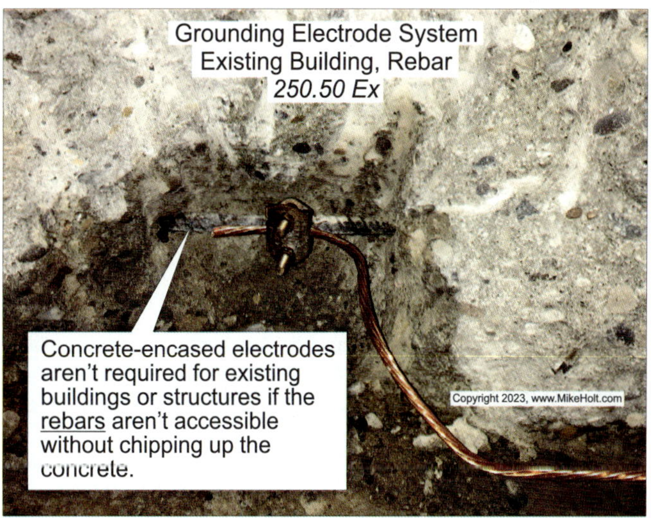
Grounding Electrode System
Existing Building, Rebar
250.50 Ex
Concrete-encased electrodes aren't required for existing buildings or structures if the rebars aren't accessible without chipping up the concrete.
Copyright 2023, www.MikeHolt.com

▸Figure 250–99

250.52 Grounding Electrode Types

(A) Electrodes Permitted.

(1) Underground Metal Water Pipe Electrode. Underground metal water pipe in direct contact with the Earth for 10 ft or more. ▸Figure 250–100

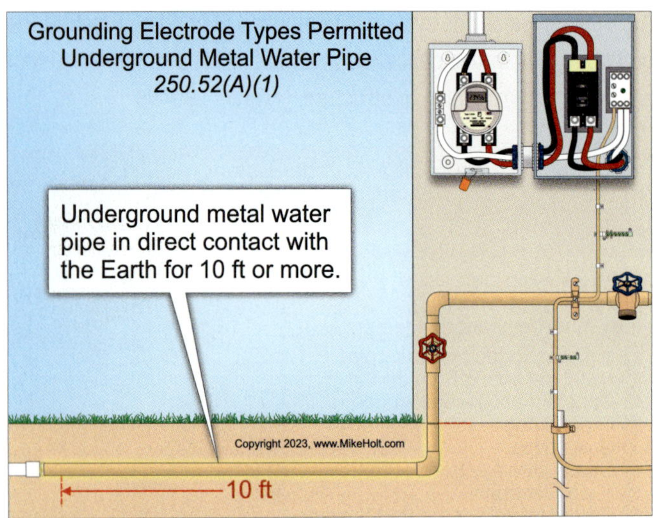

Grounding Electrode Types Permitted
Underground Metal Water Pipe
250.52(A)(1)
Underground metal water pipe in direct contact with the Earth for 10 ft or more.
Copyright 2023, www.MikeHolt.com
10 ft

▸Figure 250–100

Author's Comment:

- Controversy about using metal underground water piping as a grounding electrode has existed since the early 1900s. The water industry believes that neutral current flowing on water piping corrodes the metal. For more information, contact the American Water Works Association about their report, *Effects of Electrical Grounding on Pipe Integrity and Shock Hazard*, Catalog No. 90702, 1.800.926.7337. ▸Figure 250–101

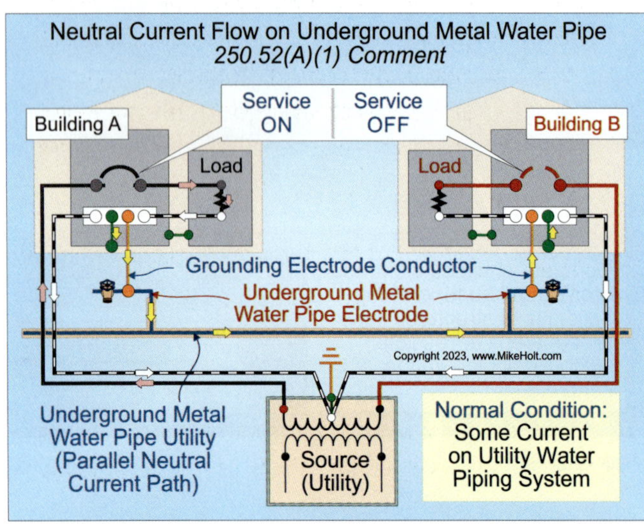

Neutral Current Flow on Underground Metal Water Pipe
250.52(A)(1) Comment
Service ON
Service OFF
Building A
Building B
Load
Load
Grounding Electrode Conductor
Underground Metal Water Pipe Electrode
Copyright 2023, www.MikeHolt.com
Underground Metal Water Pipe Utility (Parallel Neutral Current Path)
Source (Utility)
Normal Condition: Some Current on Utility Water Piping System

▸Figure 250–101

- Where there is a common metal underground water piping system, it is possible for the service neutral to be open and not show any symptoms that are typically associated with open service neutrals. This can create a dangerous condition for water workers who open the underground water pipe when it is acting as the service neutral.

(2) Metal In-Ground Support Structure(s). Metal in-ground support structure(s) in direct contact with the Earth vertically for 10 ft or more. ▸Figure 250–102

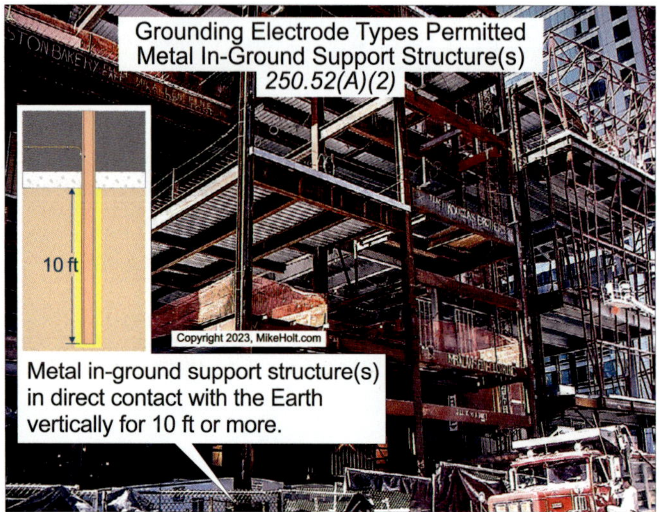

Grounding Electrode Types Permitted
Metal In-Ground Support Structure(s)
250.52(A)(2)
10 ft
Copyright 2023, MikeHolt.com
Metal in-ground support structure(s) in direct contact with the Earth vertically for 10 ft or more.

▸Figure 250–102

Note: Metal in-ground support structures include—but are not limited to—pilings, casings, and other structural metal.

(3) Concrete-Encased Electrode. Concrete-encased electrodes must be one of the following:

(1) Rebar. One or more pieces of conductive rebar of not less than ½ in. diameter that are connected by steel tie wires to create a 20 ft or greater length. ▸Figure 250–103

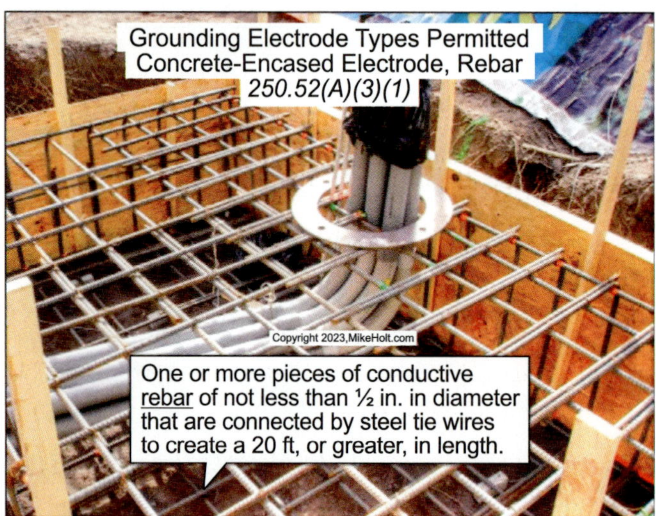

Grounding Electrode Types Permitted
Concrete-Encased Electrode, Rebar
250.52(A)(3)(1)
Copyright 2023, MikeHolt.com
One or more pieces of conductive rebar of not less than ½ in. in diameter that are connected by steel tie wires to create a 20 ft, or greater, in length.

▸Figure 250–103

(2) Conductor. A bare copper conductor not smaller than 4 AWG and 20 ft or greater in length. ▸Figure 250–104

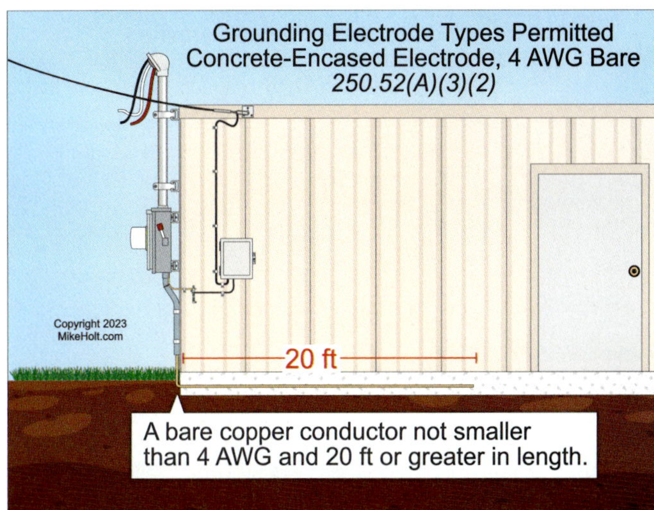
Grounding Electrode Types Permitted
Concrete-Encased Electrode, 4 AWG Bare
250.52(A)(3)(2)
Copyright 2023 MikeHolt.com
20 ft
A bare copper conductor not smaller than 4 AWG and 20 ft or greater in length.

▸Figure 250-104

Rebar or Conductor. The rebar or bare copper conductor used as part of the concrete-encased electrode must be encased by at least 2 in. of concrete that is in direct contact with the Earth. ▸Figure 250-105

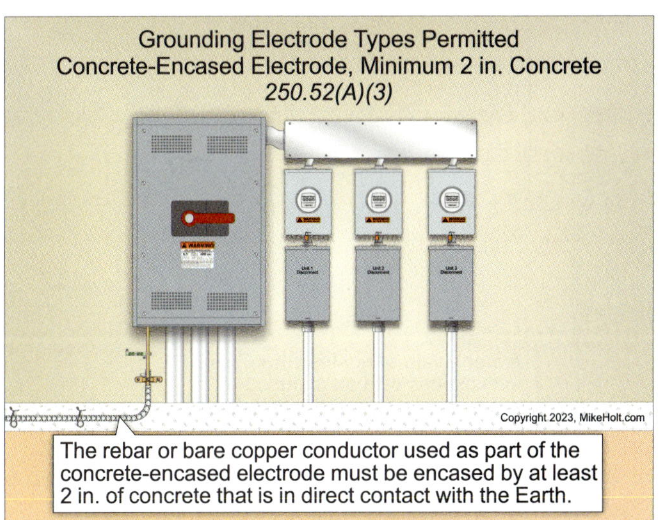
Grounding Electrode Types Permitted
Concrete-Encased Electrode, Minimum 2 in. Concrete
250.52(A)(3)
Copyright 2023, MikeHolt.com
The rebar or bare copper conductor used as part of the concrete-encased electrode must be encased by at least 2 in. of concrete that is in direct contact with the Earth.

▸Figure 250-105

The concrete-encased electrode can be horizontal or vertical within a foundation or footing that is in direct contact with the Earth. If multiple concrete-encased electrodes are present at a building, only one is required to serve as a grounding electrode.

Note: Rebar in concrete that is not in direct contact with the Earth because of insulation, vapor barriers, or similar items is not considered to be a concrete-encased electrode. ▸Figure 250-106

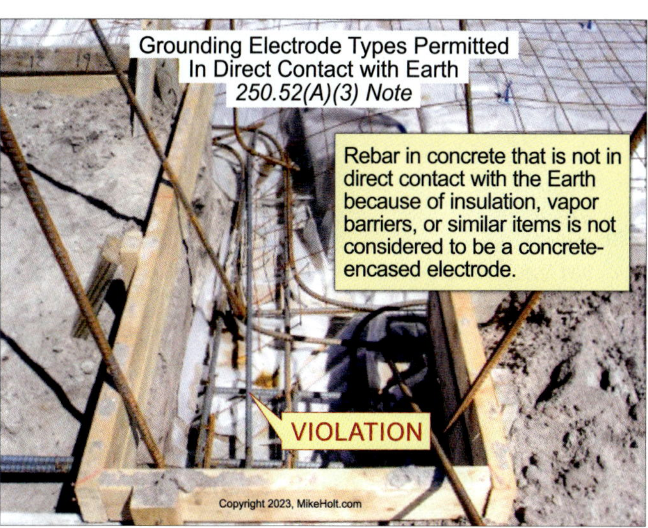
Grounding Electrode Types Permitted
In Direct Contact with Earth
250.52(A)(3) Note
Rebar in concrete that is not in direct contact with the Earth because of insulation, vapor barriers, or similar items is not considered to be a concrete-encased electrode.
VIOLATION
Copyright 2023, MikeHolt.com

▸Figure 250-106

Author's Comment:

- A grounding electrode conductor connected to a concrete-encased grounding electrode is not required to be larger than 4 AWG copper [250.66(B)].
- A concrete-encased grounding electrode is also called a "Ufer Ground," named after a consultant working for the U.S. Army during World War II. The technique Herbert G. Ufer created was necessary because the site needing grounding had no underground water table and little rainfall. The desert site was a series of bomb storage vaults near Flagstaff, Arizona. This type of grounding electrode generally offers the lowest ground resistance for the cost. In fact, Mr. Ufer's method is so effective that ground rods are not necessary!

(4) Ground Ring. A direct buried bare copper conductor not smaller than 2 AWG encircling a building. ▸Figure 250-107

Author's Comment:

- A ground ring encircling a building must not be installed less than 30 in. below the surface of the Earth [250.53(F)].

(5) Ground Rod.

(2) Ground Rod Length. Ground rods at least 8 ft in length in contact with the Earth. ▸Figure 250-108

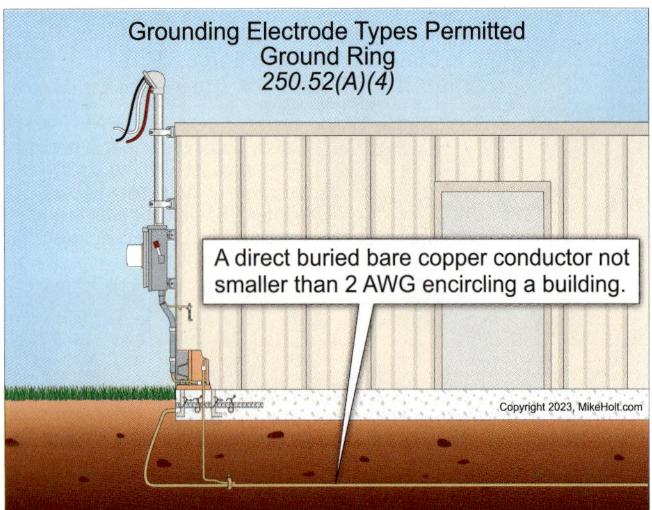
Grounding Electrode Types Permitted
Ground Ring
250.52(A)(4)
A direct buried bare copper conductor not smaller than 2 AWG encircling a building.
Copyright 2023, MikeHolt.com

▸Figure 250-107

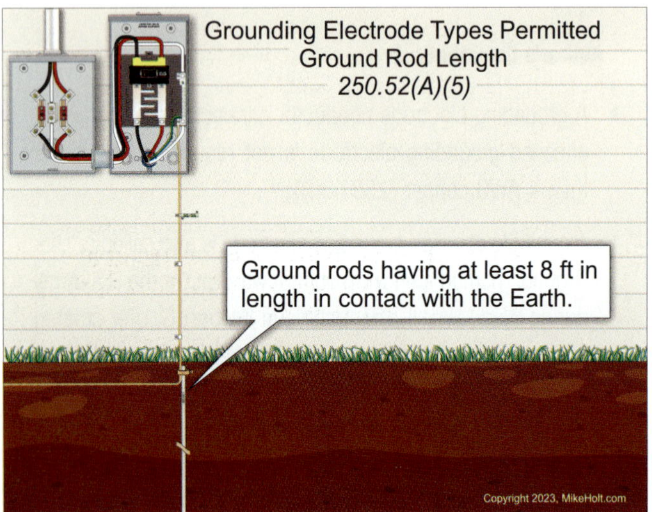
Grounding Electrode Types Permitted
Ground Rod Length
250.52(A)(5)
Ground rods having at least 8 ft in length in contact with the Earth.
Copyright 2023, MikeHolt.com

▸Figure 250-108

Author's Comment:

- The grounding electrode conductor, if it is the sole connection to the rod(s), is not required to be larger than 6 AWG copper [250.66(A)].
- The diameter of a ground rod has an insignificant effect on the contact resistance of a rod(s) to the Earth. However, larger diameter rods (¾ in. and 1 in.) are sometimes installed where mechanical strength is desired, or is needed to compensate for the loss of the electrode's metal due to corrosion.

(6) Listed Electrode. Other listed grounding electrodes. ▸Figure 250-109

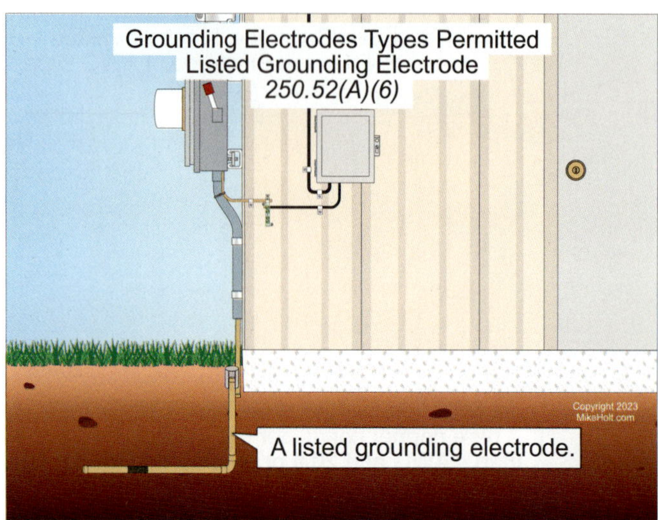
Grounding Electrodes Types Permitted
Listed Grounding Electrode
250.52(A)(6)
A listed grounding electrode.
Copyright 2023
MikeHolt.com

▸Figure 250-109

(7) Plate Electrode. A steel plate of not less than ¼ in. thick with an exposed surface area of not less than 288 sq in. (2 ft). ▸Figure 250-110

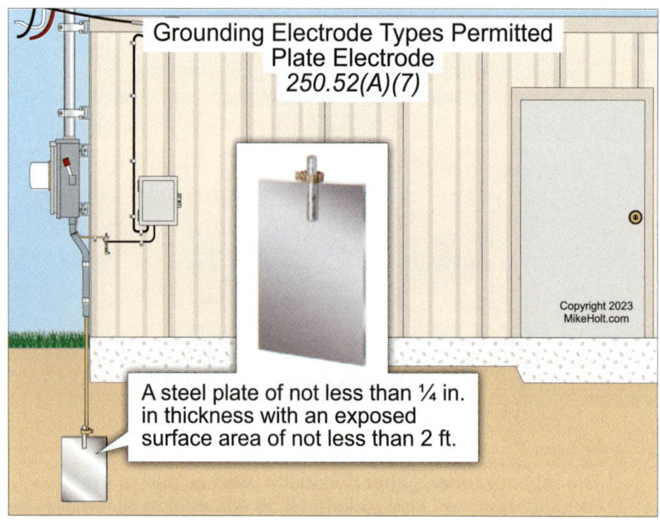
Grounding Electrode Types Permitted
Plate Electrode
250.52(A)(7)
A steel plate of not less than ¼ in. in thickness with an exposed surface area of not less than 2 ft.
Copyright 2023
MikeHolt.com

▸Figure 250-110

(8) Metal Underground Systems. Metal underground piping and metal well casings. ▸Figure 250-111

Author's Comment:

- The grounding electrode conductor to the metal underground system must be sized in accordance with Table 250.66.

(B) Not Permitted for Use as a Grounding Electrode.

(1) Underground metal gas piping systems are not permitted to be used as a grounding electrode. ▸Figure 250-112

Grounding Electrode Types Permitted
Metal Underground Systems
250.52(A)(8)
Copyright 2023, www.MikeHolt.com
Metal underground piping and metal well casings.

▸Figure 250–111

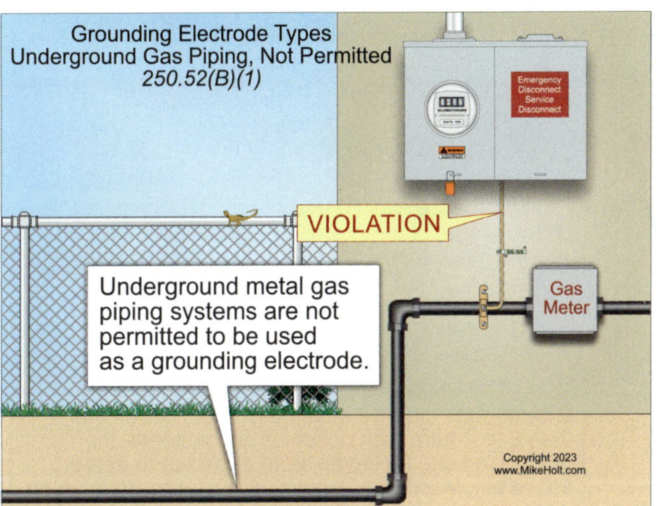
Grounding Electrode Types
Underground Gas Piping, Not Permitted
250.52(B)(1)
Emergency Disconnect Service Disconnect
VIOLATION
Gas Meter
Underground metal gas piping systems are not permitted to be used as a grounding electrode.
Copyright 2023 www.MikeHolt.com

▸Figure 250–112

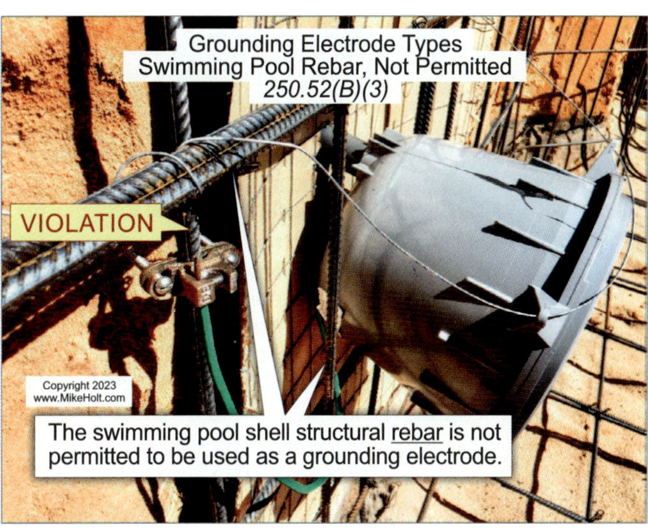
Grounding Electrode Types
Swimming Pool Rebar, Not Permitted
250.52(B)(3)
VIOLATION
Copyright 2023 www.MikeHolt.com
The swimming pool shell structural rebar is not permitted to be used as a grounding electrode.

▸Figure 250–113

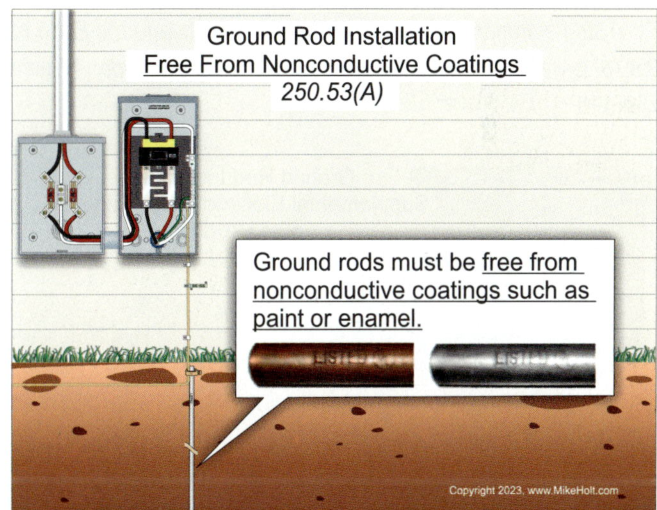
Ground Rod Installation
Free From Nonconductive Coatings
250.53(A)
Ground rods must be free from nonconductive coatings such as paint or enamel.
Copyright 2023, www.MikeHolt.com

▸Figure 250–114

(2) Aluminum is not permitted to be used as a grounding electrode.

(3) The swimming pool shell structural rebar described in 680.26(B)(1) and (B)(2) is not permitted to be used as a grounding electrode. ▸Figure 250–113

250.53 Grounding Electrode Installation

(A) Ground Rods. Ground rods must be free from nonconductive coatings such as paint or enamel. ▸Figure 250–114

(1) Below Permanent Moisture Level. If practicable, rod, pipe, and plate electrodes must be embedded below the permanent moisture level.

(2) Supplemental Electrode. A single ground rod must be supplemented by an additional electrode. The supplemental electrode must be bonded to: ▸Figure 250–115

(1) Another ground rod

(2) The grounding electrode conductor

(3) The service neutral conductor

(4) A nonflexible metal service raceway

(5) The service-disconnect enclosure

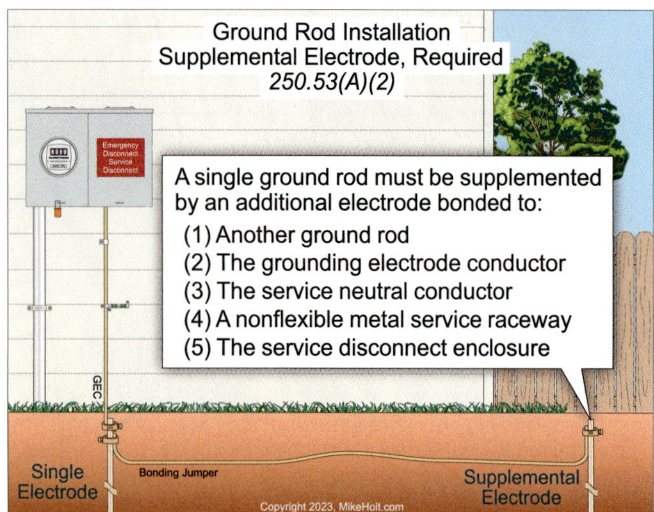
Ground Rod Installation
Supplemental Electrode, Required
250.53(A)(2)
A single ground rod must be supplemented by an additional electrode bonded to:
(1) Another ground rod
(2) The grounding electrode conductor
(3) The service neutral conductor
(4) A nonflexible metal service raceway
(5) The service disconnect enclosure
GEC
Single Electrode
Bonding Jumper
Supplemental Electrode
Copyright 2023, MikeHolt.com

▸Figure 250-115

Ex: A single ground rod having a contact resistance to the Earth of 25Ω or less is not required to have a supplemental electrode. ▸Figure 250-116

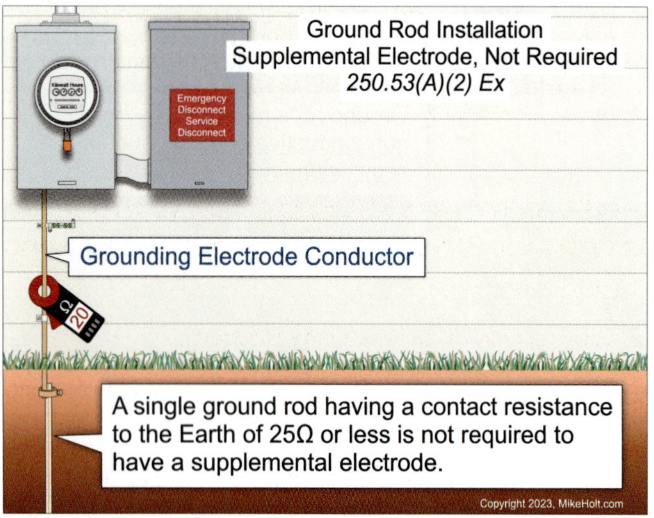
Ground Rod Installation
Supplemental Electrode, Not Required
250.53(A)(2) Ex
Emergency Disconnect Service Disconnect
Grounding Electrode Conductor
A single ground rod having a contact resistance to the Earth of 25Ω or less is not required to have a supplemental electrode.
Copyright 2023, MikeHolt.com

▸Figure 250-116

(3) Supplemental Ground Rod, Spacing. A ground rod serving as a supplemental electrode must be at least 6 ft apart from the other ground rod. ▸Figure 250-117

(4) Rod Electrodes. Ground rods must be driven to a depth of not less than 8 ft. Where rock bottom is encountered, the ground rod can be driven at an angle not to exceed 45 degrees or be placed in a trench that is at least 30 in. deep. ▸Figure 250-118

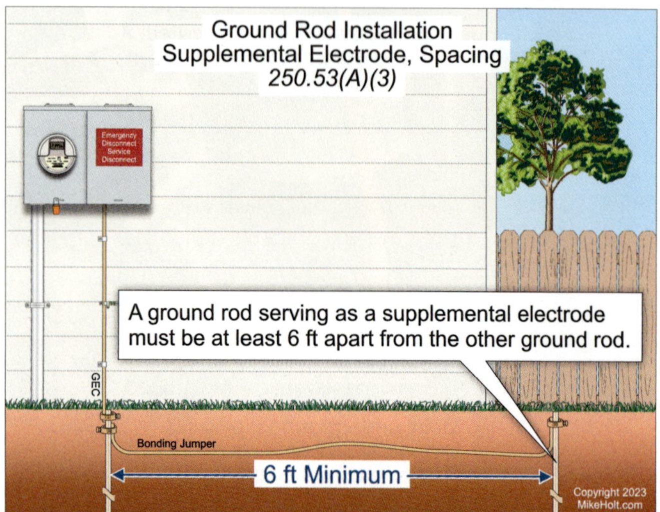
Ground Rod Installation
Supplemental Electrode, Spacing
250.53(A)(3)
A ground rod serving as a supplemental electrode must be at least 6 ft apart from the other ground rod.
GEC
Bonding Jumper
6 ft Minimum
Copyright 2023 MikeHolt.com

▸Figure 250-117

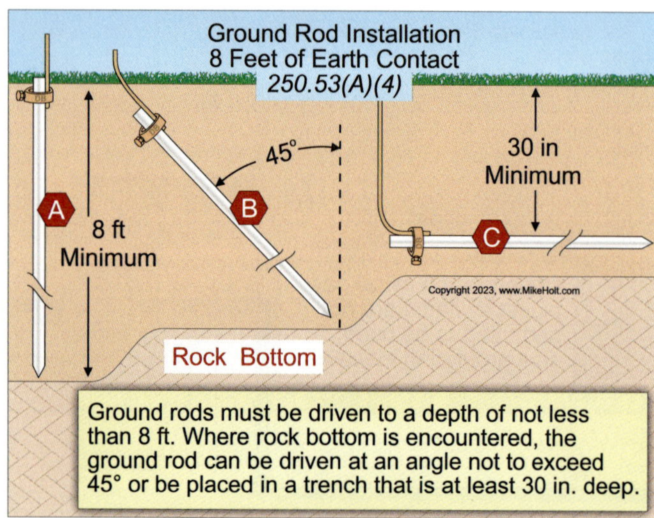
Ground Rod Installation
8 Feet of Earth Contact
250.53(A)(4)
45°
30 in Minimum
A
B
C
8 ft Minimum
Copyright 2023, www.MikeHolt.com
Rock Bottom
Ground rods must be driven to a depth of not less than 8 ft. Where rock bottom is encountered, the ground rod can be driven at an angle not to exceed 45° or be placed in a trench that is at least 30 in. deep.

▸Figure 250-118

The upper end of the ground rod must be flush with or below ground level, unless the grounding electrode conductor attachment is protected against physical damage as specified in 250.10. ▸Figure 250-119

Author's Comment:

- When the grounding electrode attachment fitting is underground (below ground level), it must be listed for direct soil burial [250.70(A)].

(5) Plate Electrode. Plate electrodes must be installed no less than 30 in. below the surface of the Earth. ▸Figure 250-120

(B) Electrode Spacing. The building grounding electrode(s) must be at least 6 ft from other grounding electrode systems, such as the lightning protection grounding electrode(s). ▸Figure 250-121

Ground Rod Installation
Protection from Physical Damage
250.53(A)(4)
Copyright 2023
MikeHolt.com
The upper end of the ground rod must be flush with or below ground level, unless the grounding electrode conductor attachment is protected against physical damage per 250.10.

▸Figure 250–119

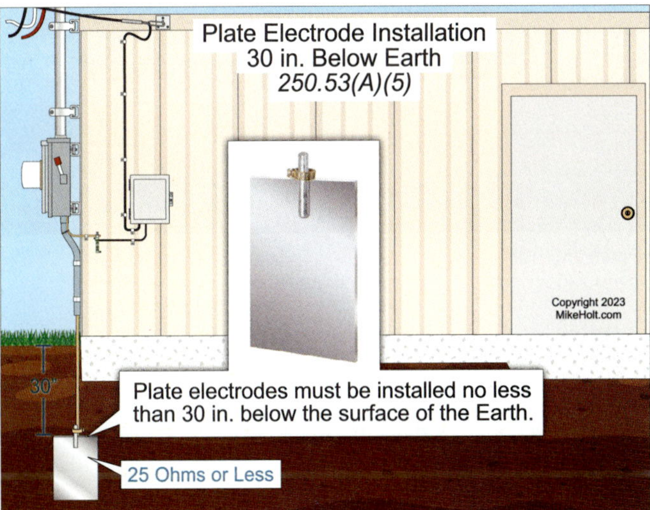

Plate Electrode Installation
30 in. Below Earth
250.53(A)(5)
Copyright 2023
MikeHolt.com
30"
Plate electrodes must be installed no less than 30 in. below the surface of the Earth.
25 Ohms or Less

▸Figure 250–120

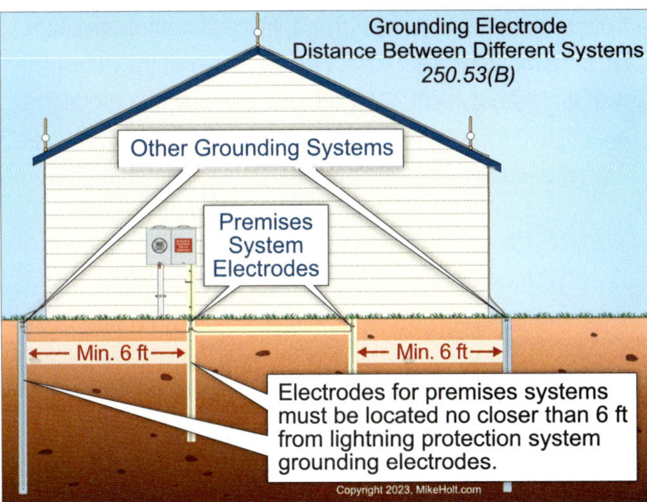

Grounding Electrode
Distance Between Different Systems
250.53(B)
Other Grounding Systems
Premises
System
Electrodes
Min. 6 ft
Min. 6 ft
Electrodes for premises systems must be located no closer than 6 ft from lightning protection system grounding electrodes.
Copyright 2023, MikeHolt.com

▸Figure 250–121

(C) Grounding Electrode Bonding Jumper. Grounding electrode bonding jumpers must be copper when within 18 in. of the Earth [250.64(A)]. Exposed grounding electrode bonding jumpers must be securely fastened to the surface and protected from physical damage [250.64(B)]. Grounding electrode bonding jumpers installed in metal raceways must be bonded at both ends [250.64(E)]. The bonding jumper to each electrode must be sized in accordance with 250.66. ▸Figure 250–122

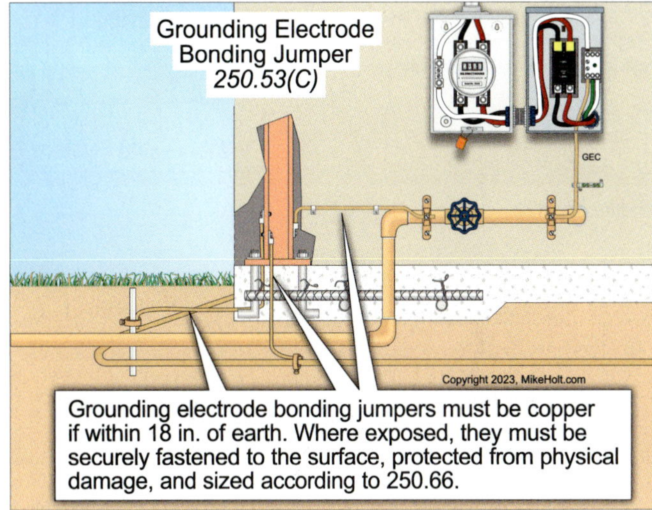

Grounding Electrode
Bonding Jumper
250.53(C)
GEC
Copyright 2023, MikeHolt.com
Grounding electrode bonding jumpers must be copper if within 18 in. of earth. Where exposed, they must be securely fastened to the surface, protected from physical damage, and sized according to 250.66.

▸Figure 250–122

When the grounding electrode conductor termination is encased in concrete or buried, the termination fittings must be listed for this purpose [250.70(A)].

(D) Underground Metal Water Pipe Electrode.

(1) Continuity. The continuity of interior metal water piping systems must not rely on water meters or filtering devices. ▸Figure 250–123

(2) Water Pipe Supplemental Electrode. When an underground metal water pipe grounding electrode is present, it must be supplemented by any of the following electrodes:

- Metal frame of the building electrode [250.52(A)(2)]
- Concrete-encased electrode [250.52(A)(3)]
- Rod electrode [250.52(A)(5)]
- Other type of listed electrode [250.52(A)(6)]
- Metal underground piping electrode [250.52(A)(8)]

The grounding electrode conductor for the supplemental electrode must be bonded to any of the following: ▸Figure 250–124

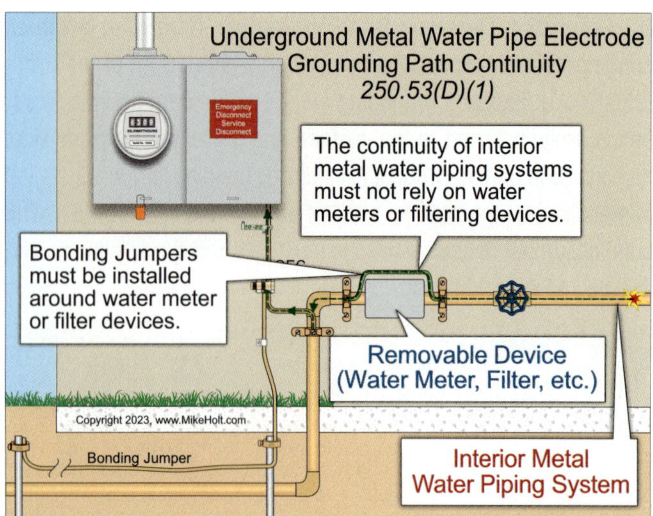
Underground Metal Water Pipe Electrode
Grounding Path Continuity
250.53(D)(1)
The continuity of interior metal water piping systems must not rely on water meters or filtering devices.
Bonding Jumpers must be installed around water meter or filter devices.
Removable Device (Water Meter, Filter, etc.)
Copyright 2023, www.MikeHolt.com
Bonding Jumper
Interior Metal Water Piping System

▸Figure 250–123

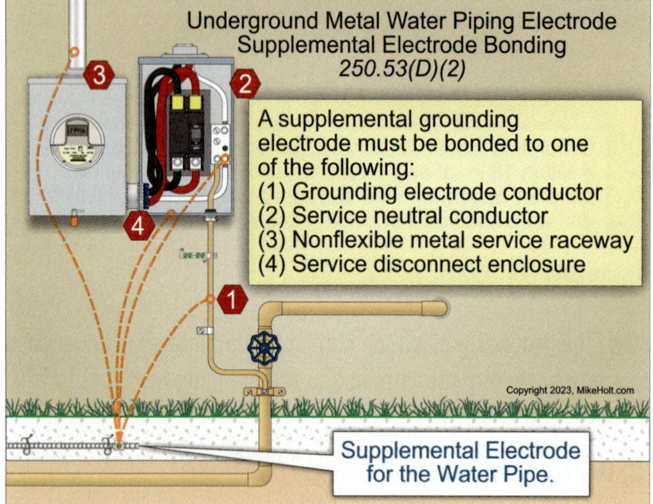
Underground Metal Water Piping Electrode
Supplemental Electrode Bonding
250.53(D)(2)
A supplemental grounding electrode must be bonded to one of the following:
(1) Grounding electrode conductor
(2) Service neutral conductor
(3) Nonflexible metal service raceway
(4) Service disconnect enclosure
Copyright 2023, MikeHolt.com
Supplemental Electrode for the Water Pipe.

▸Figure 250–124

(1) Grounding electrode conductor

(2) Service neutral conductor

(3) Nonflexible metal service raceway

(4) Service-disconnect enclosure

Author's Comment:

- Because a metal underground waterpipe electrode could be replaced by a plastic water pipe, the supplemental electrode must be installed as if it is the only electrode for the system.

Ex: The supplemental electrode can be bonded to interior metal water piping not more than 5 ft from the point of entrance to the building [250.68(C)(1)].

(E) Supplemental Rod Electrode Bonding Jumper Size. The grounding electrode bonding jumper to a ground rod that serves as a water pipe supplemental electrode is not required to be larger than 6 AWG copper.

(F) Ground Ring. The bare 2 AWG or larger copper conductor encircling a building [250.52(A)(4)] must be installed not less than 30 in. below the surface of the Earth. ▸Figure 250–125

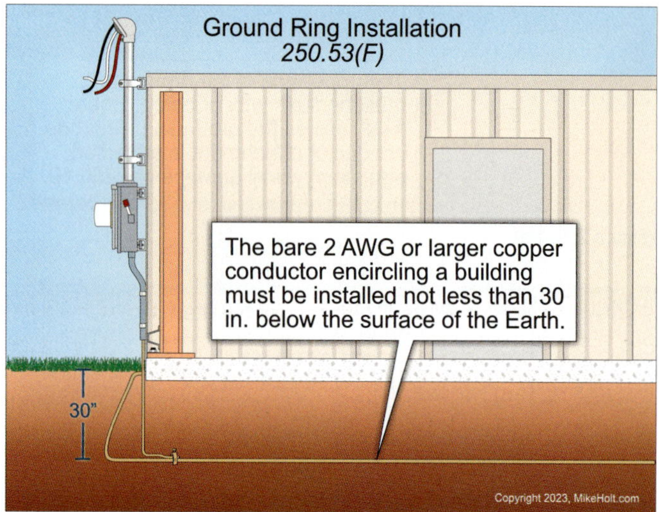
Ground Ring Installation
250.53(F)
The bare 2 AWG or larger copper conductor encircling a building must be installed not less than 30 in. below the surface of the Earth.
30"
Copyright 2023, MikeHolt.com

▸Figure 250–125

Soil Resistivity

The contact resistance of an electrode to the Earth is impacted by soil resistivity, which varies throughout the world. Soil resistivity is influenced by electrolytes, which consist of moisture, minerals, and dissolved salts. Because soil resistivity changes with moisture content, the contact resistance of a grounding system to the Earth varies with the seasons.

250.54 Auxiliary Grounding Electrodes

Grounding electrodes that are not required by the *NEC* are called "auxiliary electrodes" and connected to the equipment grounding conductors. Since they serve no purpose related to the electrical safety addressed by the *Code*, they have no *NEC* requirements. ▸Figure 250–126

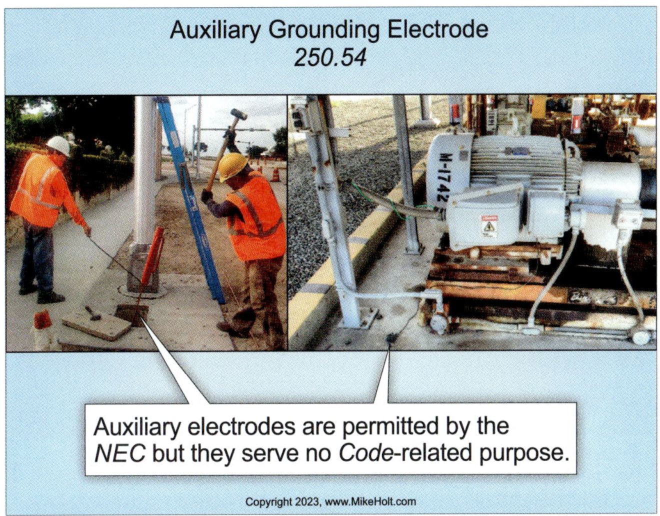
Auxiliary Grounding Electrode
250.54
Auxiliary electrodes are permitted by the NEC but they serve no Code-related purpose.
Copyright 2023, www.MikeHolt.com

▶Figure 250–126

If an auxiliary electrode is installed, it is not required to be bonded to the building grounding electrode system, to have the grounding conductor sized to 250.66, nor must it comply with the 25Ω single ground rod requirement of 250.53(A)(2) Ex. ▶Figure 250–127

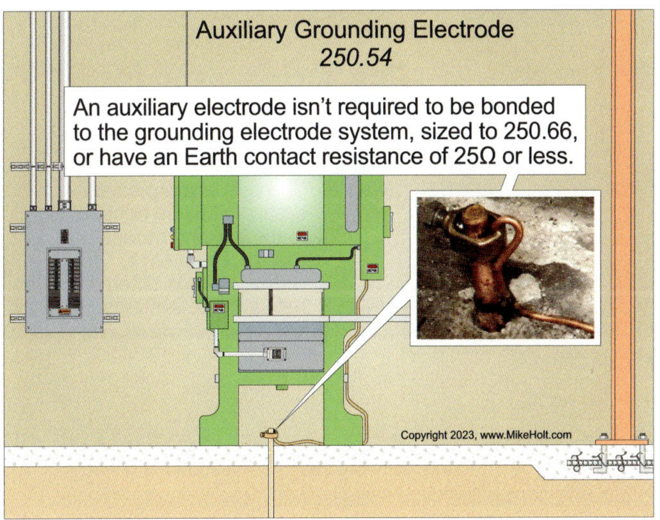
Auxiliary Grounding Electrode
250.54
An auxiliary electrode isn't required to be bonded to the grounding electrode system, sized to 250.66, or have an Earth contact resistance of 25Ω or less.
Copyright 2023, www.MikeHolt.com

▶Figure 250–127

Caution

CAUTION: An auxiliary electrode may cause damage to the generator electronics by providing a path for lightning to travel through the generating equipment. ▶Figure 250–128 and ▶Figure 250–129

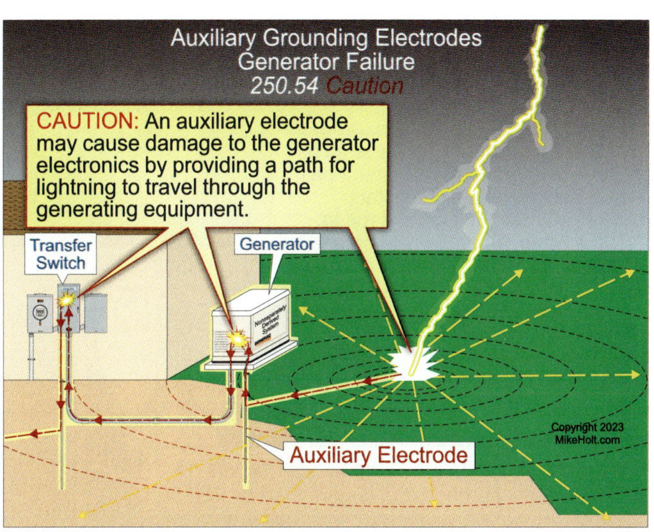
Auxiliary Grounding Electrodes
Generator Failure
250.54 Caution
CAUTION: An auxiliary electrode may cause damage to the generator electronics by providing a path for lightning to travel through the generating equipment.
Transfer Switch
Generator
Auxiliary Electrode
Copyright 2023 MikeHolt.com

▶Figure 250–128

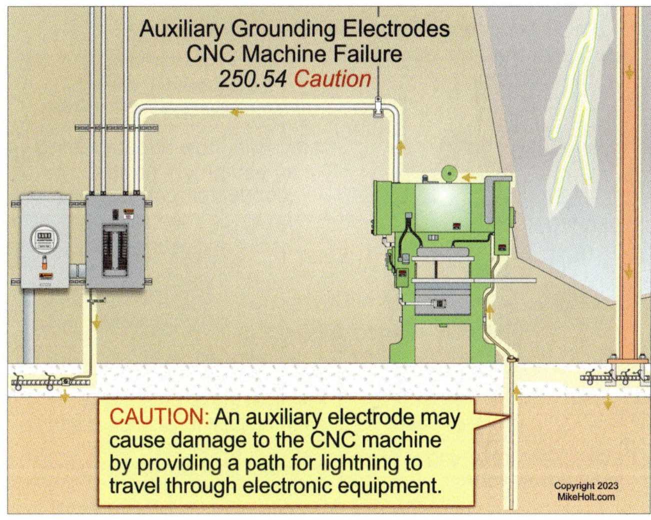
Auxiliary Grounding Electrodes
CNC Machine Failure
250.54 Caution
CAUTION: An auxiliary electrode may cause damage to the CNC machine by providing a path for lightning to travel through electronic equipment.
Copyright 2023 MikeHolt.com

▶Figure 250–129

The Earth is not to be considered the effective ground-fault current path specified in 250.4(A)(5). ▶Figure 250–130

Danger

DANGER: Because the contact resistance of an electrode to the Earth is so great, very little fault current returns to the source if the Earth is the only fault-current return path. As a result, the circuit overcurrent protective device will not open and clear the ground fault, and all metal parts associated with the electrical installation, metal piping, and structural building steel will become and remain energized. ▶Figure 250–131

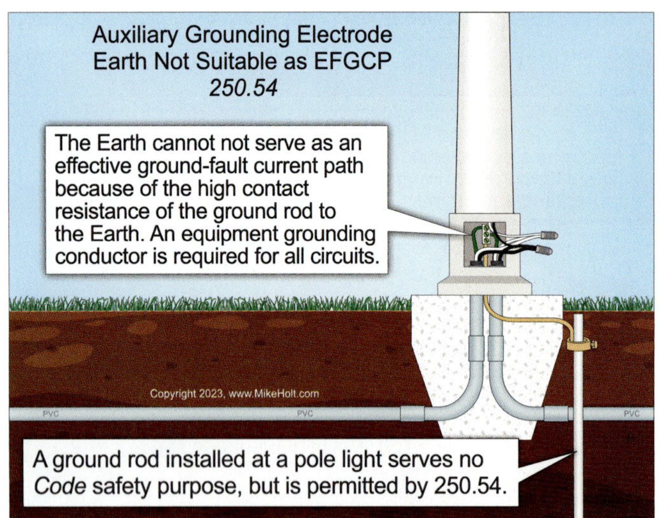
Auxiliary Grounding Electrode
Earth Not Suitable as EFGCP
250.54
The Earth cannot not serve as an effective ground-fault current path because of the high contact resistance of the ground rod to the Earth. An equipment grounding conductor is required for all circuits.
Copyright 2023, www.MikeHolt.com
A ground rod installed at a pole light serves no Code safety purpose, but is permitted by 250.54.

▸Figure 250–130

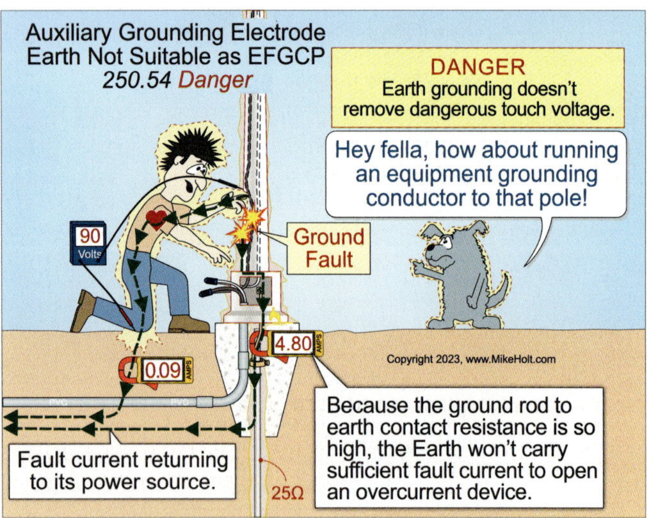
Auxiliary Grounding Electrode
Earth Not Suitable as EFGCP
250.54 Danger
DANGER
Earth grounding doesn't remove dangerous touch voltage.
Hey fella, how about running an equipment grounding conductor to that pole!
90 Volts
Ground Fault
4.80
0.09
Copyright 2023, www.MikeHolt.com
Fault current returning to its power source.
25Ω
Because the ground rod to earth contact resistance is so high, the Earth won't carry sufficient fault current to open an overcurrent device.

▸Figure 250–131

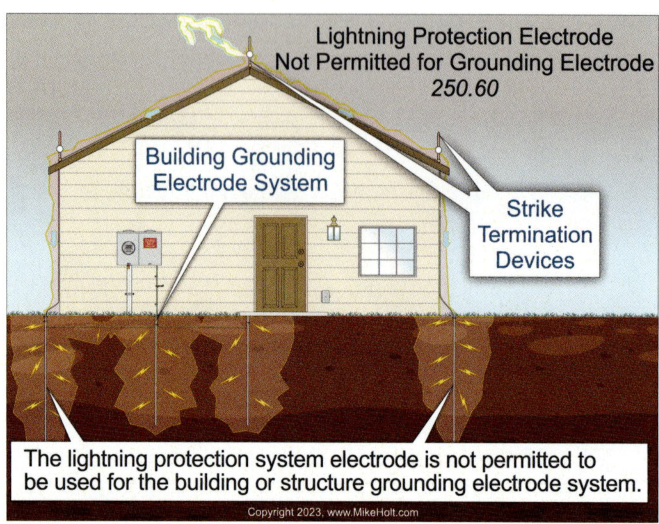
Lightning Protection Electrode
Not Permitted for Grounding Electrode
250.60
Building Grounding Electrode System
Strike Termination Devices
The lightning protection system electrode is not permitted to be used for the building or structure grounding electrode system.
Copyright 2023, www.MikeHolt.com

▸Figure 250–132

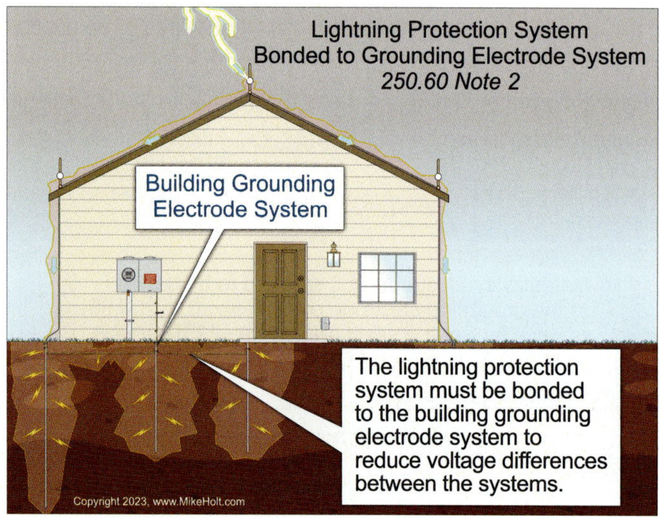
Lightning Protection System
Bonded to Grounding Electrode System
250.60 Note 2
Building Grounding Electrode System
The lightning protection system must be bonded to the building grounding electrode system to reduce voltage differences between the systems.
Copyright 2023, www.MikeHolt.com

▸Figure 250–133

250.60 Lightning Protection Electrode

The lightning protection system electrode is not permitted to be used for the building or structure grounding electrode system required for service equipment [250.24(A)(1)], separately derived systems [250.30], or remote building feeder disconnect [250.32(A)]. ▸Figure 250–132

Note 1: See 250.106 for the bonding requirements of the lightning protection system to the building or structure grounding electrode system.

Note 2: Bonding together of all separate grounding electrodes will limit voltage differences between them and their associated wiring systems. ▸Figure 250–133

250.62 Grounding Electrode Conductor

Grounding electrode conductors can be copper, aluminum or copper-clad aluminum.

250.64 Grounding Electrode Conductor Installation

(A) Aluminum Conductors or Copper-Clad.

(1) Aluminum or copper-clad aluminum grounding electrode conductors are not permitted to be installed in direct contact with concrete.

(3) Aluminum or copper-clad aluminum grounding electrode conductors are not permitted to terminate within 18 in. of the Earth.

(B) Conductor Protection. If exposed, a grounding electrode conductor must be securely fastened to the surface on which it is carried.

(1) Not Exposed to Physical Damage. Grounding electrode conductors sized 6 AWG and larger not subject to physical damage can be installed exposed along the surface if securely fastened. ▸Figure 250–134

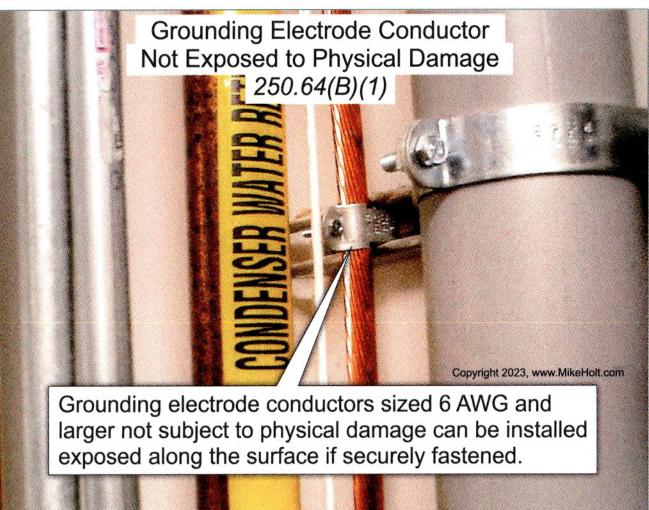
Grounding Electrode Conductor
Not Exposed to Physical Damage
250.64(B)(1)
CONDENSER WATER
Copyright 2023, www.MikeHolt.com
Grounding electrode conductors sized 6 AWG and larger not subject to physical damage can be installed exposed along the surface if securely fastened.

▸Figure 250–134

(2) Exposed to Physical Damage. Grounding electrode conductors sized 6 AWG and larger and exposed to physical damage must be protected in rigid metal conduit (RMC), intermediate metal conduit (IMC), electrical metallic tubing (EMT), Schedule 80 rigid polyvinyl chloride conduit (PVC), reinforced thermosetting resin conduit Type XW (RTRC-XW), or cable armor. ▸Figure 250–135

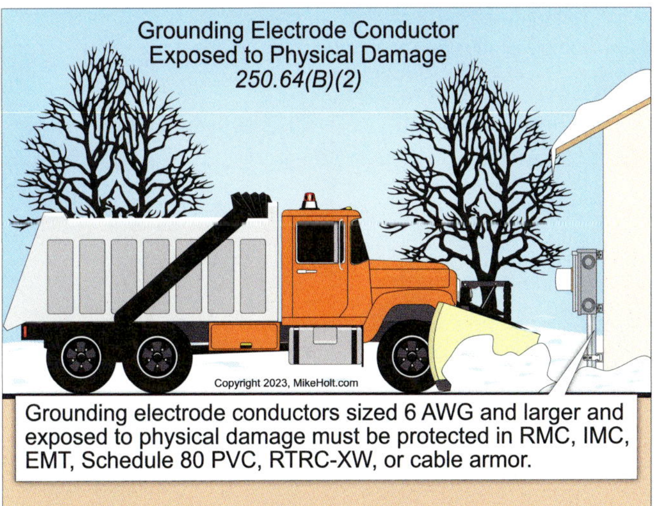
Grounding Electrode Conductor
Exposed to Physical Damage
250.64(B)(2)
Copyright 2023, MikeHolt.com
Grounding electrode conductors sized 6 AWG and larger and exposed to physical damage must be protected in RMC, IMC, EMT, Schedule 80 PVC, RTRC-XW, or cable armor.

▸Figure 250–135

(3) 8 AWG and Smaller. Grounding electrode conductors 8 AWG and smaller must be installed in RMC, IMC, Schedule 80 PVC, RTRC-XW, EMT, or cable armor.

Author's Comment:

- While Table 250.66 permits the use of 8 AWG copper as the grounding electrode conductor for the phase conductor typically used for a 100A service, using a GEC smaller than 6 AWG is not common.
- Where grounding electrode conductors are installed in RMC, IMC, or EMT, the metal raceways must be bonded at both ends per 250.64(E).

(4) Burial Depth Not Required. Grounding electrode conductors and bonding jumpers in contact with the Earth are not required to comply with the cover requirements of 300.5, but must be protected where subject to physical damage. ▸Figure 250–136

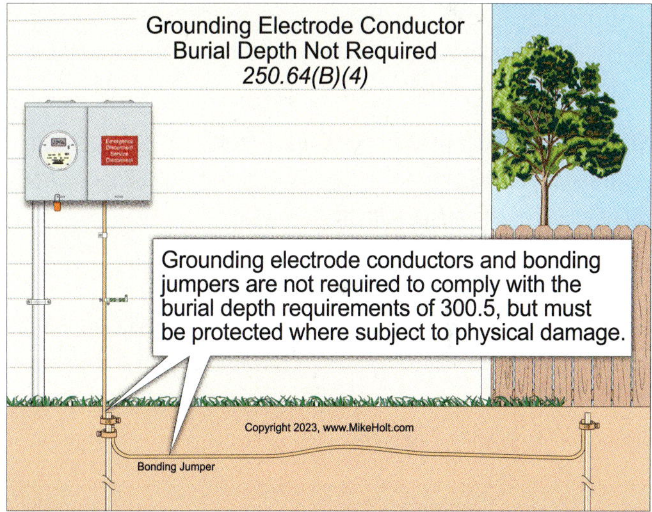
Grounding Electrode Conductor
Burial Depth Not Required
250.64(B)(4)
Grounding electrode conductors and bonding jumpers are not required to comply with the burial depth requirements of 300.5, but must be protected where subject to physical damage.
Copyright 2023, www.MikeHolt.com
Bonding Jumper

▸Figure 250–136

(C) Continuous. Grounding electrode conductor(s) must be installed without a splice or joint except by:

(1) Irreversible compression-type connectors or exothermic welding ▸Figure 250–137

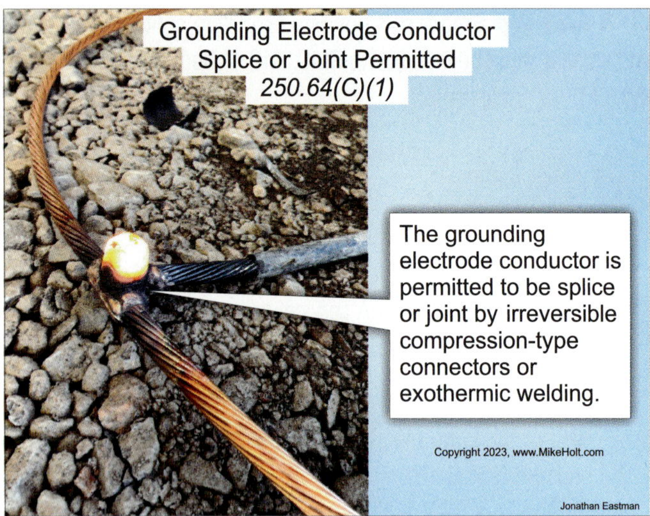
Grounding Electrode Conductor
Splice or Joint Permitted
250.64(C)(1)
The grounding electrode conductor is permitted to be splice or joint by irreversible compression-type connectors or exothermic welding.
Copyright 2023, www.MikeHolt.com
Jonathan Eastman

▸Figure 250-137

(2) Busbars connected together

(3) Bolted, riveted, or welded connections to the structural metal frames of buildings

(4) Threaded, welded, brazed, soldered, or bolted-flange connections to metal water piping

(D) Multiple Disconnect Enclosures. If a building contains two or more service or building feeder disconnects, the grounding electrode connections must comply with the following:

(1) Common Grounding Electrode Conductor and Taps.

Common Grounding Electrode Conductor. An unspliced common grounding electrode conductor sized in accordance with 250.66 based on the total area of the phase conductor(s) supplying the service disconnects. ▸Figure 250-138

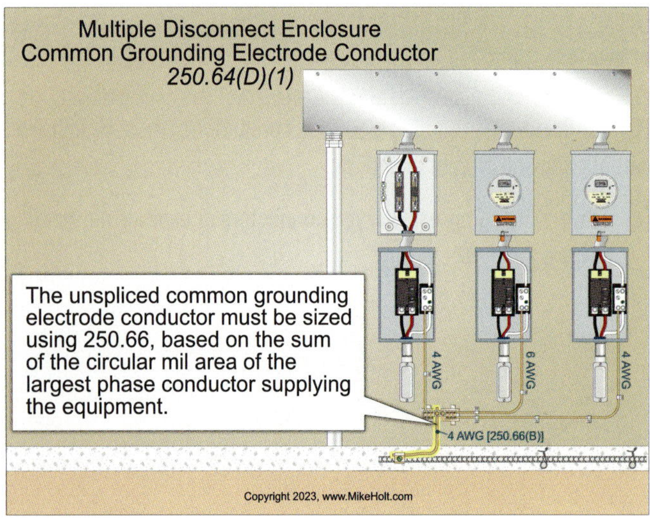
Multiple Disconnect Enclosure
Common Grounding Electrode Conductor
250.64(D)(1)
The unspliced common grounding electrode conductor must be sized using 250.66, based on the sum of the circular mil area of the largest phase conductor supplying the equipment.
4 AWG
6 AWG
4 AWG
4 AWG [250.66(B)]
Copyright 2023, www.MikeHolt.com

▸Figure 250-138

Grounding Electrode Taps. Grounding electrode conductor taps from each disconnect must be sized no smaller than specified in Table 250.66 and connected to the common grounding electrode conductor. ▸Figure 250-139

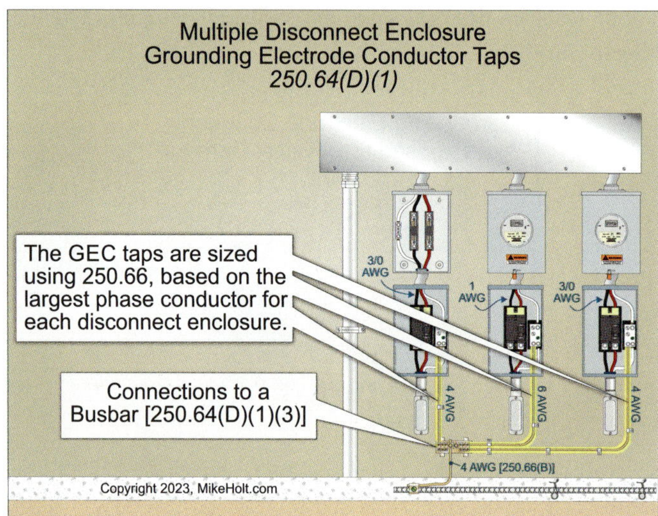
Multiple Disconnect Enclosure
Grounding Electrode Conductor Taps
250.64(D)(1)
The GEC taps are sized using 250.66, based on the largest phase conductor for each disconnect enclosure.
3/0 AWG
1 AWG
3/0 AWG
Connections to a Busbar [250.64(D)(1)(3)]
4 AWG
6 AWG
4 AWG
4 AWG [250.66(B)]
Copyright 2023, MikeHolt.com

▸Figure 250-139

The grounding electrode conductor taps must be connected to the common grounding electrode by any of the following methods:

(1) Exothermic welding

(2) Connectors listed as grounding and bonding equipment

(3) Connections to a busbar not less than ¼ in. thick × 2 in. wide that is securely fastened and installed in an accessible location ▸Figure 250-140

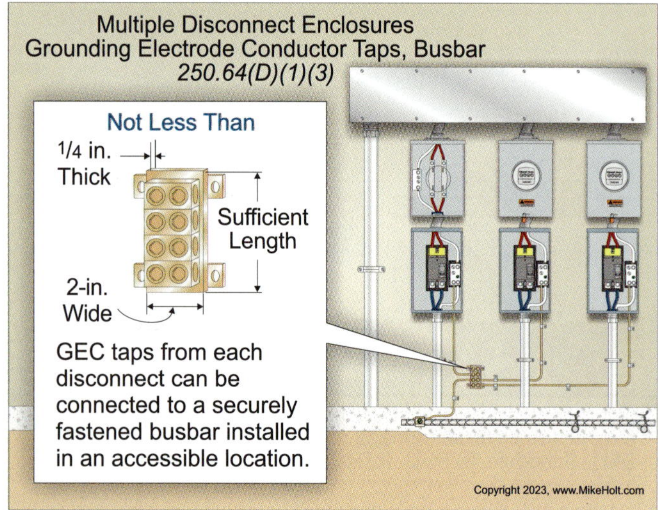
Multiple Disconnect Enclosures
Grounding Electrode Conductor Taps, Busbar
250.64(D)(1)(3)
Not Less Than
1/4 in. Thick
Sufficient Length
2-in. Wide
GEC taps from each disconnect can be connected to a securely fastened busbar installed in an accessible location.
Copyright 2023, www.MikeHolt.com

▸Figure 250-140

(2) Individual Grounding Electrode Conductors. A grounding electrode conductor from each service disconnect sized in accordance with 250.66 based on the phase conductor(s) supplying the service disconnect. ▸Figure 250–141

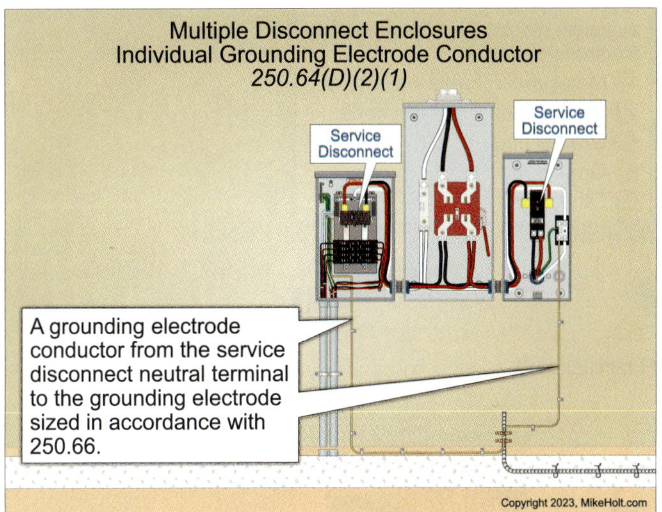
Multiple Disconnect Enclosures
Individual Grounding Electrode Conductor
250.64(D)(2)(1)
Service Disconnect
Service Disconnect
A grounding electrode conductor from the service disconnect neutral terminal to the grounding electrode sized in accordance with 250.66.
Copyright 2023, MikeHolt.com

▸Figure 250–141

(3) Supply Side of Disconnects. A grounding electrode conductor on the supply side of the service disconnects, sized in accordance with 250.66 based on the phase conductor(s) supplying the service connected to:

(1) The service neutral conductor ▸Figure 250–142

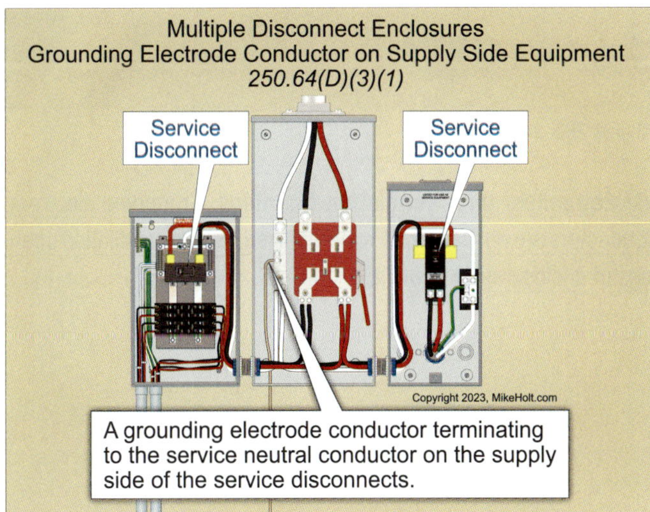
Multiple Disconnect Enclosures
Grounding Electrode Conductor on Supply Side Equipment
250.64(D)(3)(1)
Service Disconnect
Service Disconnect
Copyright 2023, MikeHolt.com
A grounding electrode conductor terminating to the service neutral conductor on the supply side of the service disconnects.

▸Figure 250–142

(2) The equipment grounding conductor of the feeder circuit

(3) The supply-side bonding jumper

(E) Ferrous Raceways, Cable Armor, and Enclosures Containing Grounding Electrode Conductors.

(1) General. Ferrous metal raceways containing the grounding electrode conductor must have each end of the raceway bonded to the grounding electrode conductor. ▸Figure 250–143

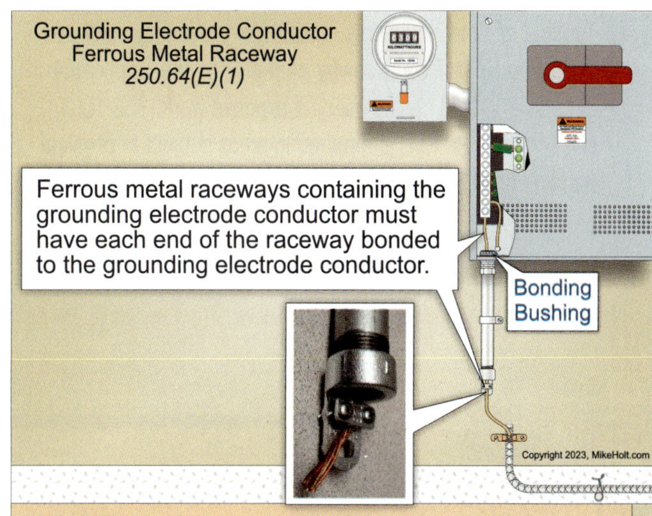
Grounding Electrode Conductor
Ferrous Metal Raceway
250.64(E)(1)
Ferrous metal raceways containing the grounding electrode conductor must have each end of the raceway bonded to the grounding electrode conductor.
Bonding Bushing
Copyright 2023, MikeHolt.com

▸Figure 250–143

(2) Methods. Ferrous metal raceways must be bonded in accordance with 250.92(B)(2) through (B)(4).

(3) Size. Bonding jumpers for ferrous metal raceways must be sized no smaller than the grounding electrode conductor in the raceway. ▸Figure 250–144

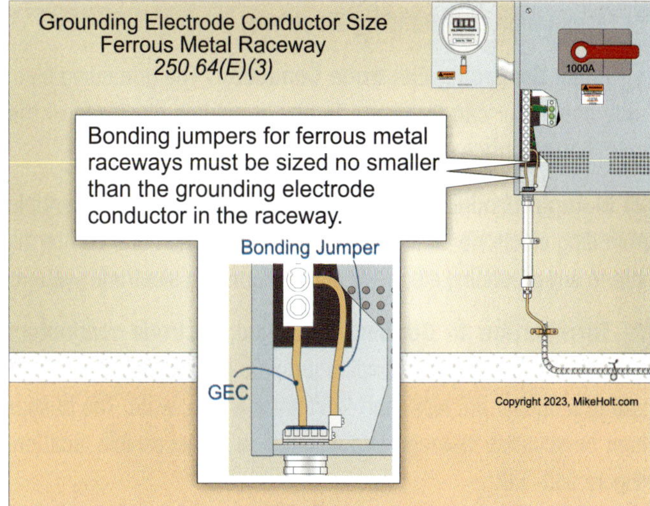
Grounding Electrode Conductor Size
Ferrous Metal Raceway
250.64(E)(3)
1000A
Bonding jumpers for ferrous metal raceways must be sized no smaller than the grounding electrode conductor in the raceway.
Bonding Jumper
GEC
Copyright 2023, MikeHolt.com

▸Figure 250–144

Author's Comment:

- Nonferrous metal raceways, such as aluminum rigid metal conduit, enclosing the grounding electrode conductor are not required to meet the "bonding each end of the raceway to the grounding electrode conductor" provisions of this section.
- To save of time and effort, install the grounding electrode conductor in a PVC raceway suitable for the application. Schedule 40 PVC can be used for exposed work [352.10(G)], but Schedule 80 PVC is required in areas subject to physical damage [250.64(B)(2)(3) and 352.10(K)]. ▶Figure 250–145

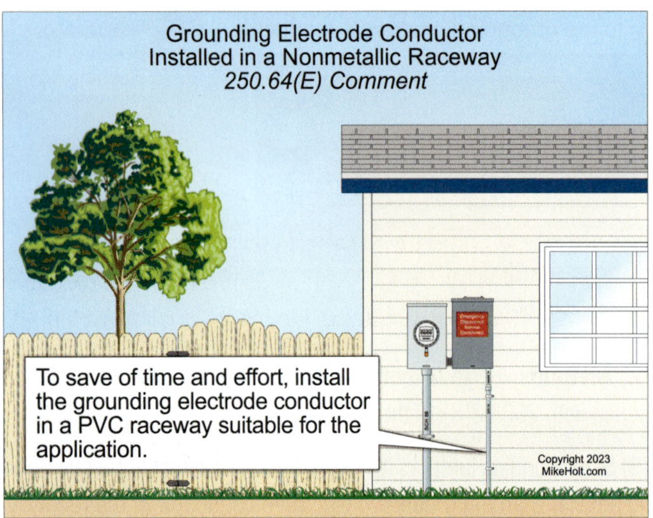
Grounding Electrode Conductor
Installed in a Nonmetallic Raceway
250.64(E) Comment
To save of time and effort, install the grounding electrode conductor in a PVC raceway suitable for the application.
Copyright 2023
MikeHolt.com

▶Figure 250–145

(F) Termination to Grounding Electrode.

(1) Single Grounding Electrode Conductor. The grounding electrode conductor can terminate to any grounding electrode of the grounding electrode system. ▶Figure 250–146

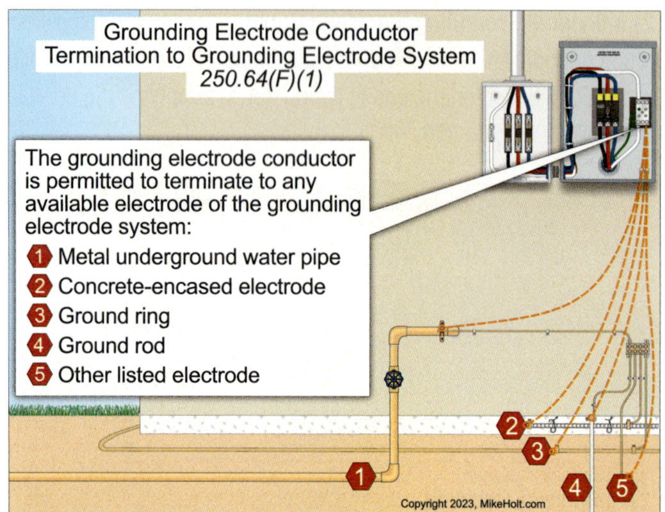
Grounding Electrode Conductor
Termination to Grounding Electrode System
250.64(F)(1)
The grounding electrode conductor is permitted to terminate to any available electrode of the grounding electrode system:
1 Metal underground water pipe
2 Concrete-encased electrode
3 Ground ring
4 Ground rod
5 Other listed electrode
Copyright 2023, MikeHolt.com

▶Figure 250–146

(2) Multiple Grounding Electrode Conductors. Where multiple grounding electrode conductors are installed, each one can terminate to any grounding electrode of the grounding electrode system.

(3) Termination to Busbar. Grounding electrode conductors and grounding electrode bonding jumpers are permitted to terminate to a busbar not less than ¼ in. thick × 2 in. wide. The busbar must be securely fastened and installed in an accessible location. ▶Figure 250–147

Grounding Electrode Conductor
Termination to Busbar
250.64(F)(3)
Grounding electrode conductors and grounding electrode bonding jumpers are permitted to terminate to a securely fastened busbar not less than ¼ in. thick × 2 in. wide, and of sufficient length.
Copyright 2023, www.MikeHolt.com

▶Figure 250–147

(G) Equipment with Ventilation Openings. Grounding electrode conductors are not permitted to be installed through ventilation openings of enclosures. ▶Figure 250–148

Grounding Electrode Conductor
Ventilation Openings
250.64(G)
EGC
EGC: Equipment Grounding Conductor
GEC: Grounding Electrode Conductor
SBJ: System Bonding Jumper
GEC
Grounding electrode conductors are not permitted to be installed through ventilation openings of enclosures.
SBJ
Mario Valdez
Copyright 2023, MikeHolt.com

▸Figure 250–148

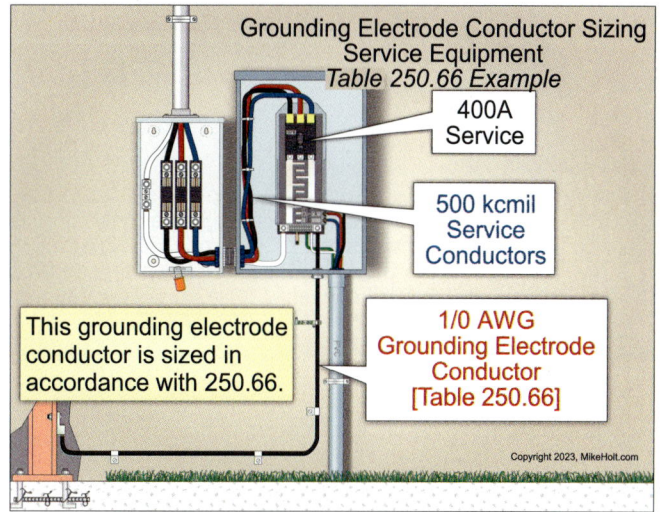

250.66 Sizing Grounding Electrode Conductors

According to Article 100, "Grounding Electrode Conductor" is the conductor used to connect the system neutral conductor, grounded-phase conductor, or equipment to the grounding electrode system. ▸Figure 250–149

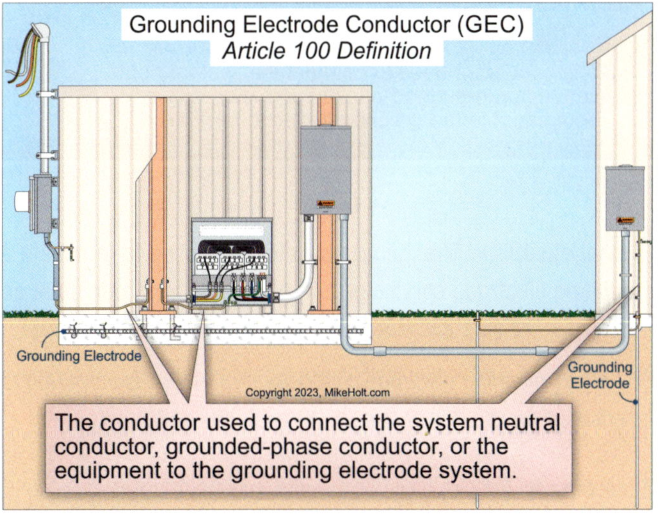
Grounding Electrode Conductor (GEC)
Article 100 Definition
Grounding Electrode
Grounding Electrode
Copyright 2023, MikeHolt.com
The conductor used to connect the system neutral conductor, grounded-phase conductor, or the equipment to the grounding electrode system.

▸Figure 250–149

Except as permitted in 250.66(A) through (C), grounding electrode conductors must be sized in accordance with Table 250.66. ▸Figure 250–150

Grounding Electrode Conductor Sizing
Service Equipment
Table 250.66 Example
400A Service
500 kcmil Service Conductors
This grounding electrode conductor is sized in accordance with 250.66.
1/0 AWG Grounding Electrode Conductor [Table 250.66]
Copyright 2023, MikeHolt.com

▸Figure 250–150

▸ Grounding Electrode Conductor, Transformer

Question: *What size grounding electrode conductor is required for a 112.50 kVA, three-phase, 480V to 120/208V transformer when the secondary conductors are sized at 600 kcmil?* ▸Figure 250–151

(a) 1/0 AWG *(b) 2/0 AWG* *(c) 3/0 AWG* *(d) 4/0 AWG*

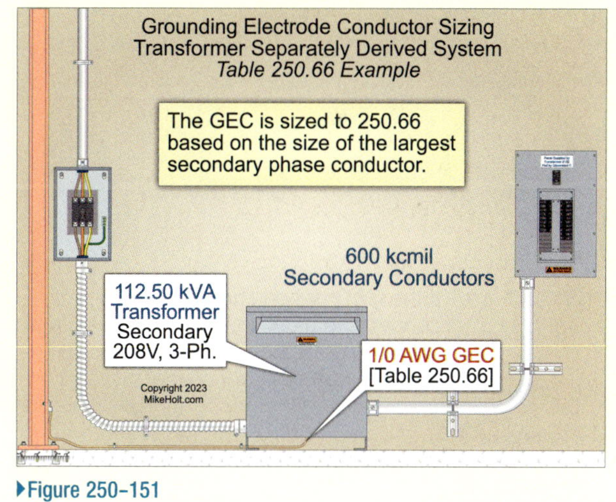
Grounding Electrode Conductor Sizing
Transformer Separately Derived System
Table 250.66 Example
The GEC is sized to 250.66 based on the size of the largest secondary phase conductor.
600 kcmil
Secondary Conductors
112.50 kVA
Transformer
Secondary
208V, 3-Ph.
1/0 AWG GEC
[Table 250.66]
Copyright 2023
MikeHolt.com

▸Figure 250–151

Answer: *(a) 1/0 AWG*

(A) Ground Rods. If a grounding electrode conductor or grounding electrode bonding jumper only connects to a ground rod [250.52(A)(5)], the grounding electrode conductor is not required to be larger than 6 AWG copper. ▸Figure 250–152

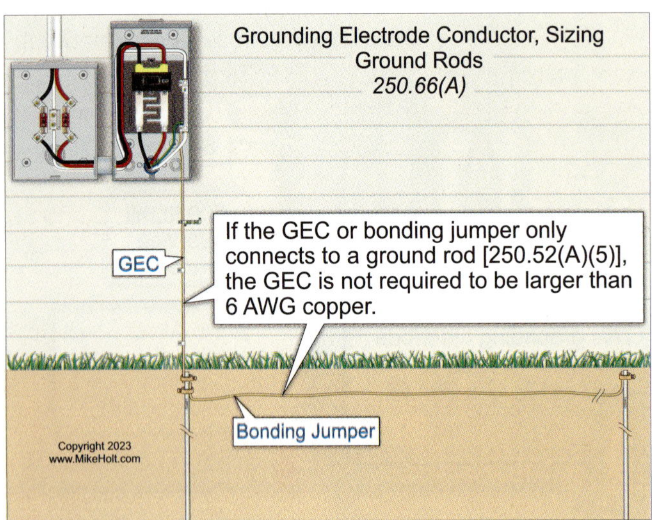
Grounding Electrode Conductor, Sizing
Ground Rods
250.66(A)
GEC
If the GEC or bonding jumper only connects to a ground rod [250.52(A)(5)], the GEC is not required to be larger than 6 AWG copper.
Bonding Jumper
Copyright 2023
www.MikeHolt.com

▸Figure 250–152

(B) Concrete-Encased Grounding Electrodes. If a grounding electrode conductor or bonding jumper only connects to a concrete-encased electrode [250.52(A)(3)], the grounding electrode conductor is not required to be larger than 4 AWG copper. ▸Figure 250–153

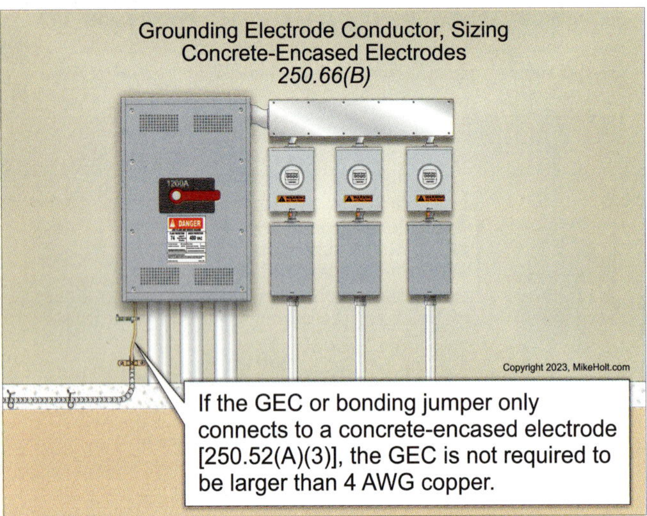
Grounding Electrode Conductor, Sizing
Concrete-Encased Electrodes
250.66(B)
Copyright 2023, MikeHolt.com
If the GEC or bonding jumper only connects to a concrete-encased electrode [250.52(A)(3)], the GEC is not required to be larger than 4 AWG copper.

▸Figure 250–153

250.68 Grounding Electrode Conductor Connection to Grounding Electrodes

According to Article 100, "Grounding Electrode Conductor (GEC)" is the conductor used to connect the system neutral conductor, grounded-phase conductor, or the equipment to the grounding electrode system. ▸Figure 250–154

Table 250.66 Grounding Electrode Conductor

AWG or Area of Parallel Copper Conductors	Copper Grounding Electrode Conductor
2 AWG or Smaller	8 AWG
1 or 1/0 AWG	6 AWG
2/0 or 3/0 AWG	4 AWG
Over 3/0 through 350 kcmil	2 AWG
Over 350 through 600 kcmil	1/0 AWG
Over 600 through 1100 kcmil	2/0 AWG
Over 1100 kcmil	3/0 AWG

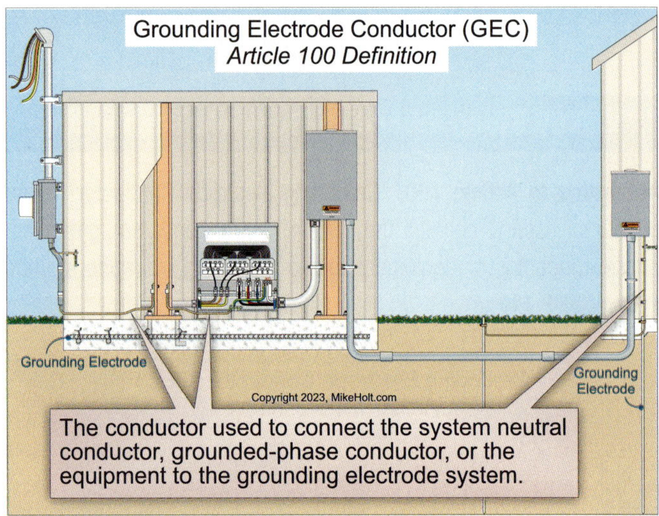
Grounding Electrode Conductor (GEC)
Article 100 Definition
Grounding Electrode
Grounding Electrode
Copyright 2023, MikeHolt.com
The conductor used to connect the system neutral conductor, grounded-phase conductor, or the equipment to the grounding electrode system.

▸Figure 250–154

(A) Accessibility. The mechanical elements used to terminate a grounding electrode conductor to a grounding electrode must be accessible. ▸Figure 250–155

Ex 1: The grounding electrode conductor termination is permitted to be encased in concrete or buried. ▸Figure 250–156

According to Article 100, "Accessible" means that it is capable of being removed or exposed without damaging the building structure or finish, or not permanently closed in or blocked by the building structure, other electrical equipment, other building systems, or the building finish.

Grounding Electrode Conductor Connection
Termination Must Be Accessible
250.68(A)
The grounding electrode conductor termination to a grounding electrode must be accessible.
Copyright 2023 MikeHolt.com

▶Figure 250-155

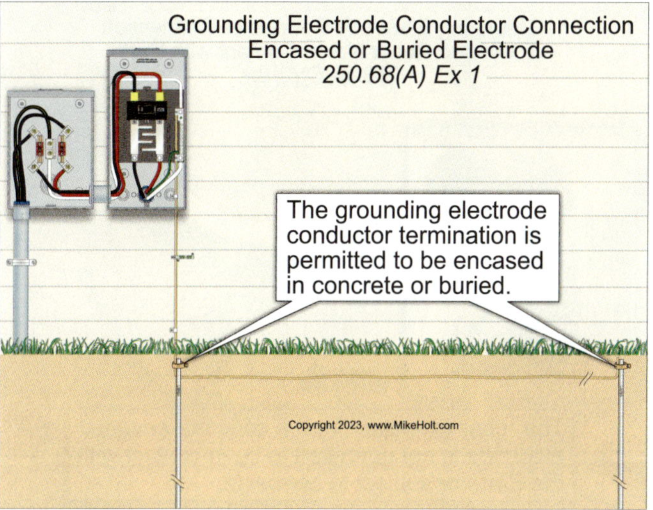
Grounding Electrode Conductor Connection
Encased or Buried Electrode
250.68(A) Ex 1
The grounding electrode conductor termination is permitted to be encased in concrete or buried.
Copyright 2023, www.MikeHolt.com

▶Figure 250-156

Author's Comment:

- If the grounding electrode attachment fitting is encased in concrete or buried in the Earth, it must be listed for direct soil burial [250.70(A)].
- In accordance with "*UL Guide Information KDER*," all grounding electrode connectors that are marked as suitable for direct burial use are also suitable for concrete encasement.

(B) Integrity of Underground Metal Water Pipe Electrode. A bonding jumper must be installed around insulated joints and equipment likely to be disconnected for repairs or replacement for an underground metal water piping system used as a grounding electrode. The bonding jumper must be of sufficient length to allow the removal of such equipment, while retaining the integrity of the grounding path. ▶Figure 250-157

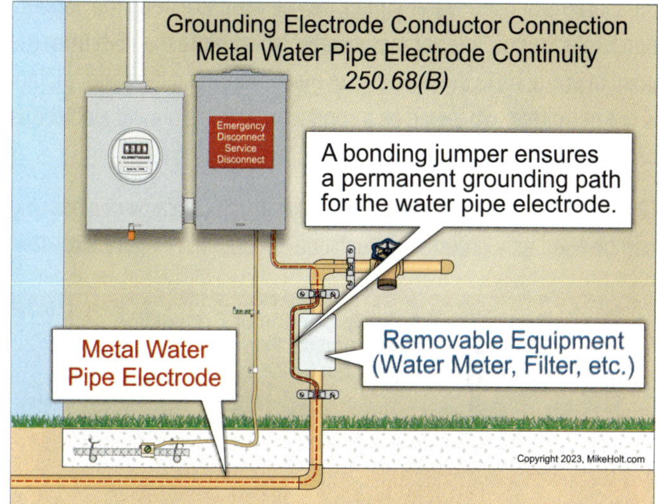
Grounding Electrode Conductor Connection
Metal Water Pipe Electrode Continuity
250.68(B)
Emergency Disconnect Service Disconnect
A bonding jumper ensures a permanent grounding path for the water pipe electrode.
Metal Water Pipe Electrode
Removable Equipment (Water Meter, Filter, etc.)
Copyright 2023, MikeHolt.com

▶Figure 250-157

According to Article 100, "Bonding Jumper" is a conductor that ensures electrical conductivity by connecting metal parts of equipment together. ▶Figure 250-158

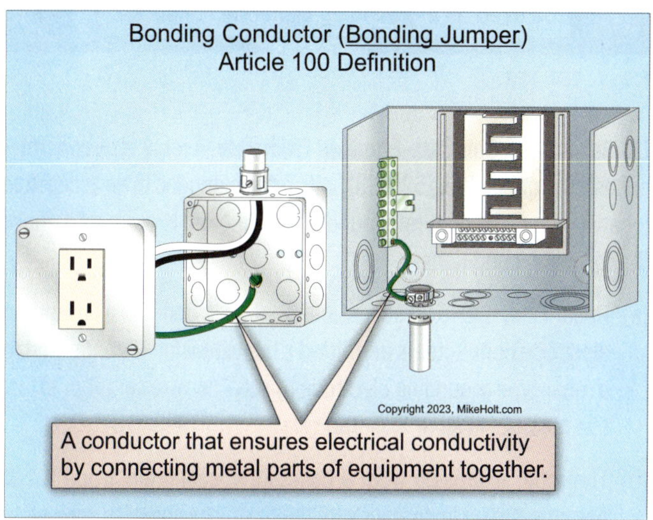
Bonding Conductor (Bonding Jumper)
Article 100 Definition
Copyright 2023, MikeHolt.com
A conductor that ensures electrical conductivity by connecting metal parts of equipment together.

▶Figure 250-158

(C) Grounding Electrode Conductor Connections. Grounding electrode conductors and bonding jumpers are permitted to terminate at the following locations and to be used to extend the connection to an electrode(s):

(1) Interior Metal Water Piping. Interior metal water piping that is electrically continuous with a metal underground water pipe electrode and is not more than 5 ft from the point of entrance to the building, as measured along the water piping, can be used to extend the connection to electrodes. Interior metal water piping more than 5 ft from the point of entrance to the building, as measured along the water piping, is not permitted to be used as a conductor to interconnect electrodes of the grounding electrode system.

(2) Metal Structural Frame. The metal structural frame of a building can be used as a grounding electrode conductor. ▸Figure 250–159

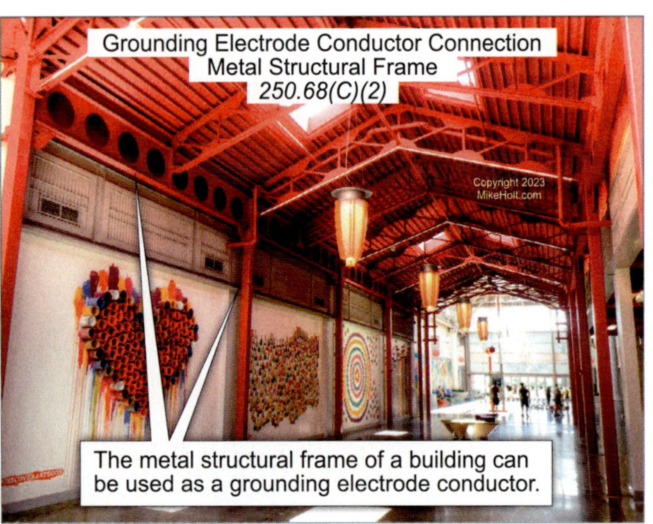
Grounding Electrode Conductor Connection
Metal Structural Frame
250.68(C)(2)
Copyright 2023
MikeHolt.com
The metal structural frame of a building can be used as a grounding electrode conductor.

▸Figure 250–159

(3) Rebar from Concrete-Encased Electrode. A rebar-type concrete-encased electrode [250.52(A)(3)] with rebar extended to an accessible location above the concrete foundation or footing is permitted under the following conditions:

(a) Rebar extended to an accessible location to connect a grounding electrode conductor is permitted if the extension is connected to a rebar-type grounding electrode by steel tie wires or other effective means. ▸Figure 250–160

(b) The rebar extension from a concrete-encased electrode is not permitted to be in contact with the Earth or subject to corrosion. ▸Figure 250–161

(c) The rebar extension is not permitted to be used as a conductor to interconnect the electrodes of grounding electrode systems.

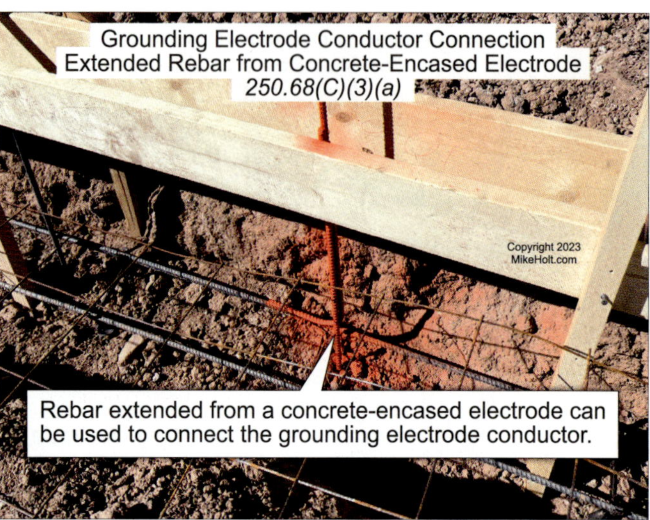
Grounding Electrode Conductor Connection
Extended Rebar from Concrete-Encased Electrode
250.68(C)(3)(a)
Copyright 2023
MikeHolt.com
Rebar extended from a concrete-encased electrode can be used to connect the grounding electrode conductor.

▸Figure 250–160

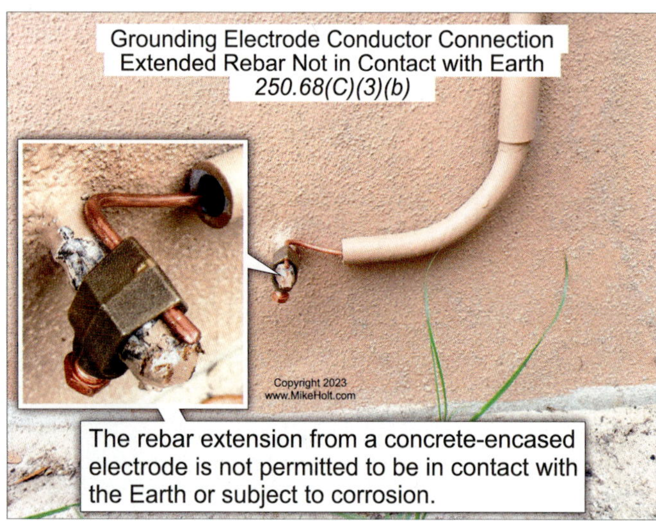
Grounding Electrode Conductor Connection
Extended Rebar Not in Contact with Earth
250.68(C)(3)(b)
Copyright 2023
www.MikeHolt.com
The rebar extension from a concrete-encased electrode is not permitted to be in contact with the Earth or subject to corrosion.

▸Figure 250–161

250.70 Grounding Electrode Conductor Termination Fittings

(A) General.

Termination. The grounding electrode conductor must terminate to the grounding electrode by exothermic welding, listed lugs, listed pressure connectors, listed clamps, or other means listed for the grounding electrode and the grounding electrode conductor. ▸Figure 250–162

Direct Burial or Concrete Encasement. When the termination to a grounding electrode encased in concrete or buried, the termination fitting must be listed for direct soil burial. ▸Figure 250–163

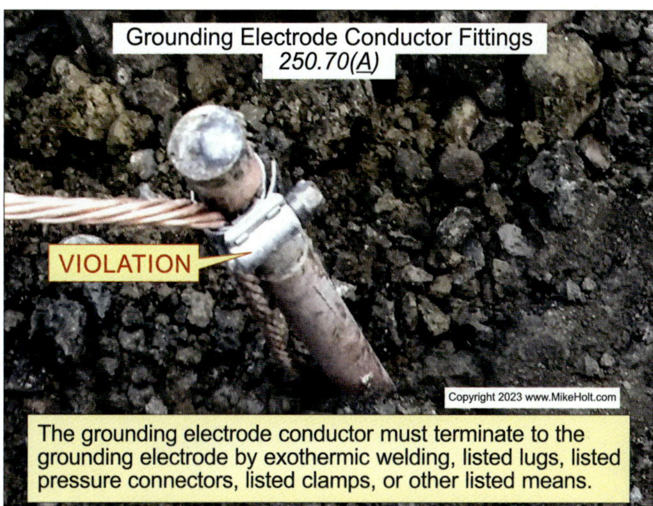
Grounding Electrode Conductor Fittings
250.70(A)
VIOLATION
Copyright 2023 www.MikeHolt.com
The grounding electrode conductor must terminate to the grounding electrode by exothermic welding, listed lugs, listed pressure connectors, listed clamps, or other listed means.

▸Figure 250–162

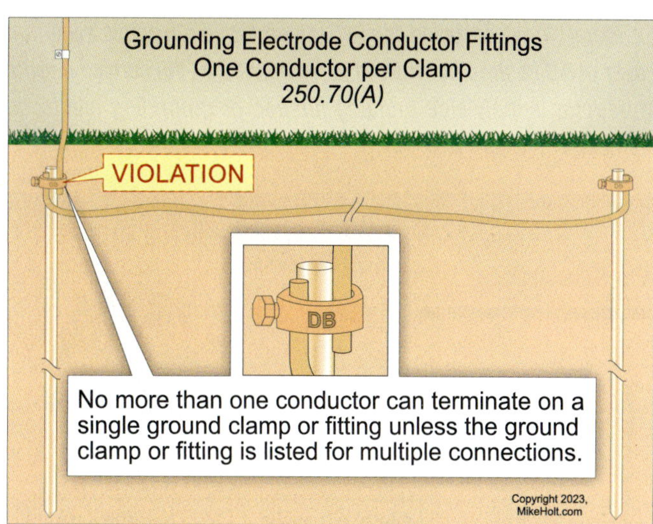
Grounding Electrode Conductor Fittings
One Conductor per Clamp
250.70(A)
VIOLATION
DB
No more than one conductor can terminate on a single ground clamp or fitting unless the ground clamp or fitting is listed for multiple connections.
Copyright 2023, MikeHolt.com

▸Figure 250–164

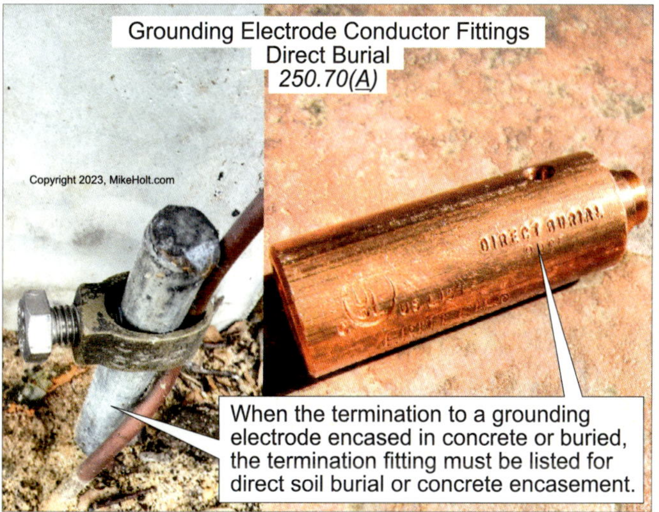
Grounding Electrode Conductor Fittings
Direct Burial
250.70(A)
Copyright 2023, MikeHolt.com
When the termination to a grounding electrode encased in concrete or buried, the termination fitting must be listed for direct soil burial or concrete encasement.

▸Figure 250–163

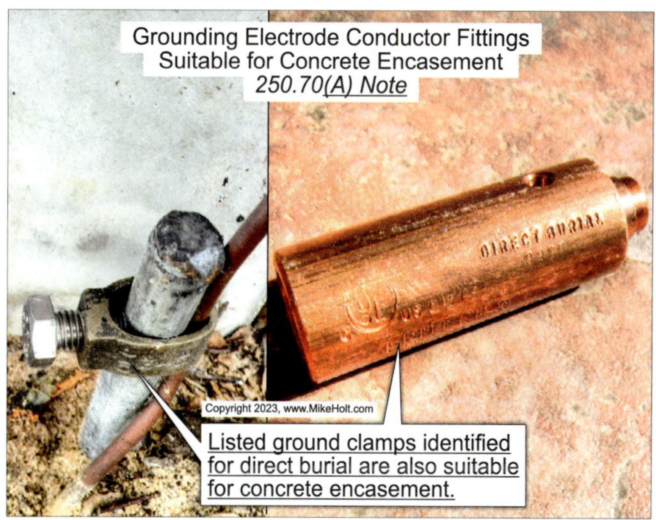
Grounding Electrode Conductor Fittings
Suitable for Concrete Encasement
250.70(A) Note
Copyright 2023, www.MikeHolt.com
Listed ground clamps identified for direct burial are also suitable for concrete encasement.

▸Figure 250–165

Only One Conductor. No more than one conductor can terminate on a single ground clamp or fitting, unless the ground clamp or fitting is listed for multiple connections. ▸Figure 250–164

Note: Listed ground clamps identified for direct burial are also suitable for concrete encasement. ▸Figure 250–165

Part IV. Enclosure and Raceway

250.80 Service Raceways and Enclosures

Metal raceways and enclosures containing service conductors must be connected to the service neutral conductor. ▸Figure 250–166

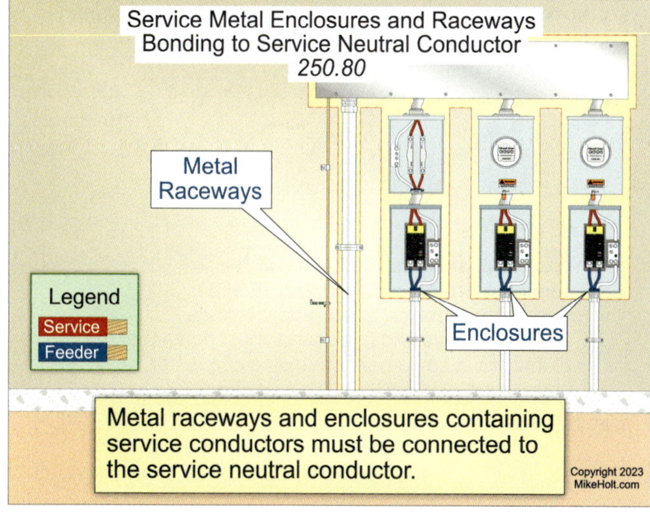
Service Metal Enclosures and Raceways
Bonding to Service Neutral Conductor
250.80
Metal Raceways
Legend
Service
Feeder
Enclosures
Metal raceways and enclosures containing service conductors must be connected to the service neutral conductor.
Copyright 2023 MikeHolt.com

▸Figure 250–166

Ex: Metal elbows installed in a PVC underground run with a minimum cover of 18 in. are not required to be bonded to the service neutral conductor, supply-side bonding jumper, or grounding electrode conductor. ▸Figure 250–167

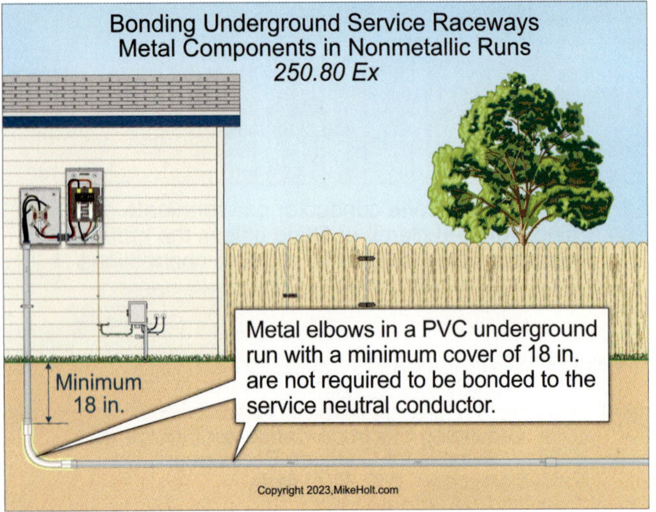
Bonding Underground Service Raceways
Metal Components in Nonmetallic Runs
250.80 Ex
Minimum 18 in.
Metal elbows in a PVC underground run with a minimum cover of 18 in. are not required to be bonded to the service neutral conductor.
Copyright 2023,MikeHolt.com

▸Figure 250–167

250.86 Other than Service Raceways and Enclosures

Metal raceways and enclosures containing feeder and branch circuit conductors must be connected to the circuit equipment grounding conductor. ▸Figure 250–168

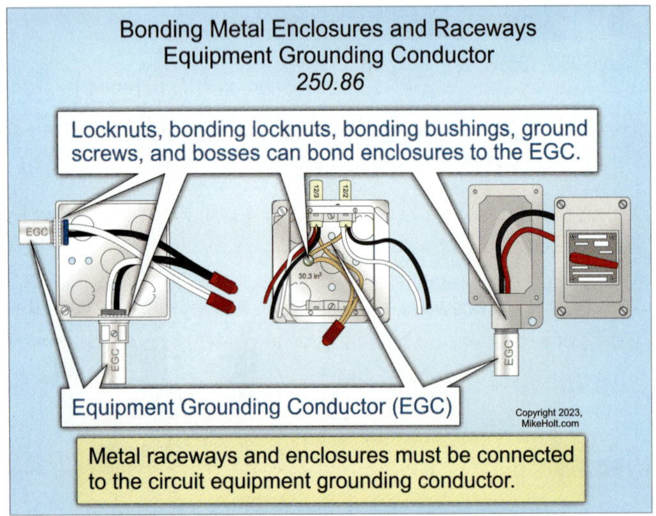
Bonding Metal Enclosures and Raceways
Equipment Grounding Conductor
250.86
Locknuts, bonding locknuts, bonding bushings, ground screws, and bosses can bond enclosures to the EGC.
EGC
EGC
EGC
Equipment Grounding Conductor (EGC)
Copyright 2023, MikeHolt.com
Metal raceways and enclosures must be connected to the circuit equipment grounding conductor.

▸Figure 250–168

Ex 2: Short sections of metal raceways used for the support or physical protection of cables are not required to be connected to the circuit equipment grounding conductor.

Ex 3: Metal elbows are not required to be bonded if the metal elbows have a minimum cover of 18 in. or are encased in not less than 2 in. of concrete. ▸Figure 250–169

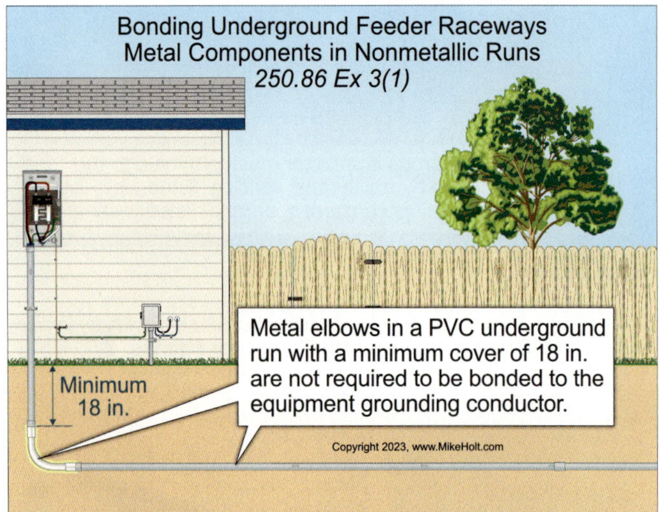
Bonding Underground Feeder Raceways
Metal Components in Nonmetallic Runs
250.86 Ex 3(1)
Minimum 18 in.
Metal elbows in a PVC underground run with a minimum cover of 18 in. are not required to be bonded to the equipment grounding conductor.
Copyright 2023, www.MikeHolt.com

▸Figure 250–169

Part V. Bonding

250.92 Bonding Metal Service Raceways and Enclosures

(A) Metal Raceways and Enclosures. Metal raceways and enclosures containing service conductors must be bonded in accordance with 250.92(B). ▸Figure 250–170

According to Article 100, "Service Conductors" are conductors from the serving electric utility service point to the service disconnect. ▸Figure 250–171

(B) Methods of Bonding Raceways. Metal raceways and enclosures containing service conductors must be bonded by one of the following methods:

(1) Service Neutral. Bonding metal raceways and enclosures to the service neutral conductor. ▸Figure 250–172

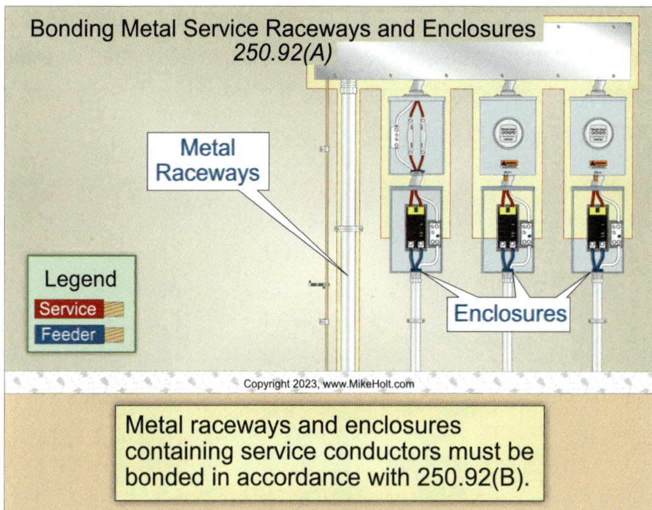
Bonding Metal Service Raceways and Enclosures
250.92(A)
Metal Raceways
Legend
Service
Feeder
Enclosures
Copyright 2023, www.MikeHolt.com
Metal raceways and enclosures containing service conductors must be bonded in accordance with 250.92(B).

▸Figure 250–170

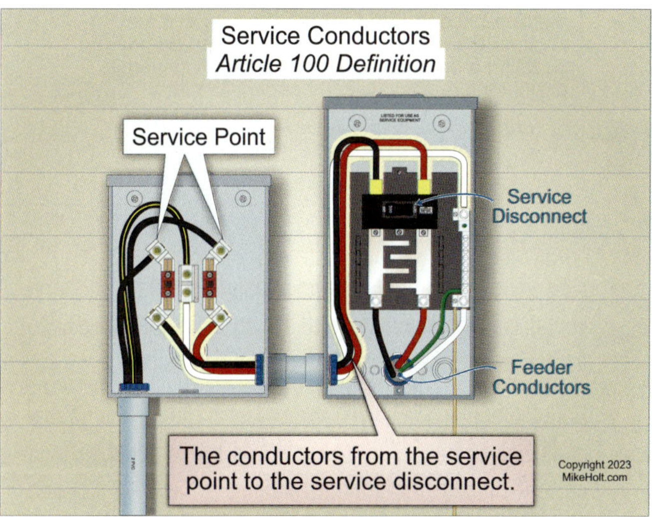
Service Conductors
Article 100 Definition
Service Point
Service Disconnect
Feeder Conductors
The conductors from the service point to the service disconnect.
Copyright 2023 MikeHolt.com

▸Figure 250–171

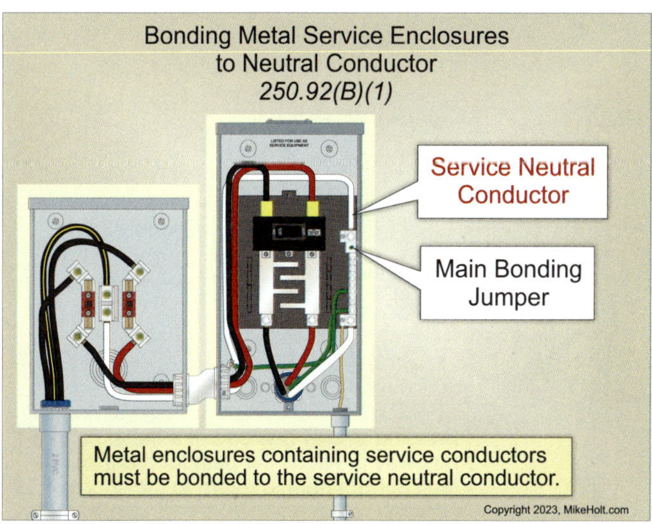
Bonding Metal Service Enclosures to Neutral Conductor
250.92(B)(1)
Service Neutral Conductor
Main Bonding Jumper
Metal enclosures containing service conductors must be bonded to the service neutral conductor.
Copyright 2023, MikeHolt.com

▸Figure 250–172

Author's Comment:

- A main bonding jumper is required to bond the service disconnect to the service neutral conductor [250.24(C) and 250.28].
- A supply-side bonding jumper can be used to bond metal service raceways to the neutral conductor.
- At the service disconnect, the service neutral conductor provides the effective ground-fault current path to the source [250.24(D)].
- A supply-side bonding jumper is not required to be installed in PVC conduit containing service-entrance conductors [250.142(A)(1) and 352.60 Ex 2]. ▸Figure 250–173

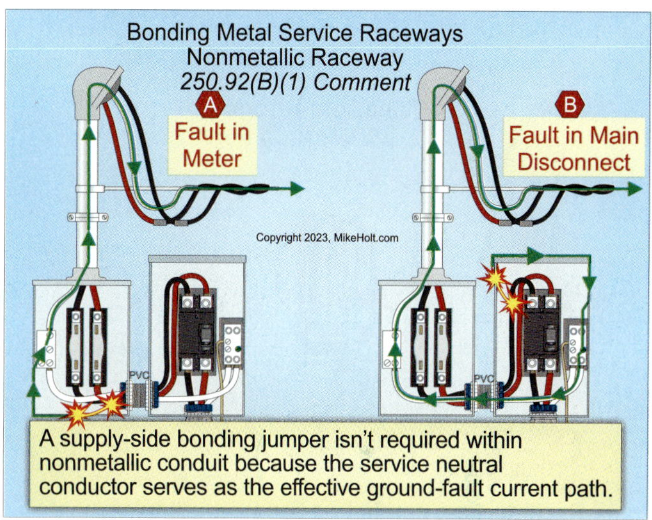
Bonding Metal Service Raceways
Nonmetallic Raceway
250.92(B)(1) Comment
A
Fault in Meter
B
Fault in Main Disconnect
Copyright 2023, MikeHolt.com
PVC
PVC
A supply-side bonding jumper isn't required within nonmetallic conduit because the service neutral conductor serves as the effective ground-fault current path.

▸Figure 250–173

(2) Threaded Entries. Bonding by tightening wrenchtight threaded couplings, threaded entries, or listed threaded hubs on enclosures. ▸Figure 250–174

(3) Threadless Fittings. Bonding by terminating metal raceways to threadless fittings. ▸Figure 250–175

(4) Other Listed Fittings. Bonding by the use of bonding-type locknuts, bonding wedges, or bonding bushings with bonding jumpers to the service neutral conductor as follows:

Ring Knockouts. Metal service raceways that terminates to a metal enclosure with ringed knockouts requires a bonding fitting with a bonding jumper to the service neutral conductor. ▸Figure 250–176

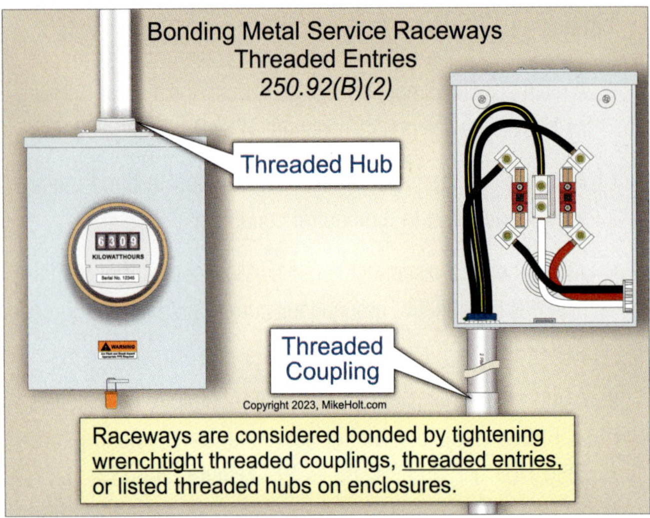
Bonding Metal Service Raceways
Threaded Entries
250.92(B)(2)
Threaded Hub
Threaded Coupling
Copyright 2023, MikeHolt.com
Raceways are considered bonded by tightening wrenchtight threaded couplings, threaded entries, or listed threaded hubs on enclosures.

▸Figure 250–174

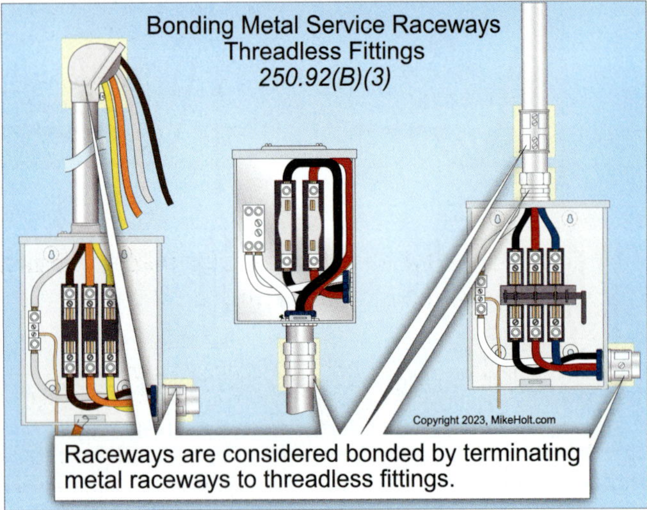
Bonding Metal Service Raceways
Threadless Fittings
250.92(B)(3)
Copyright 2023, MikeHolt.com
Raceways are considered bonded by terminating metal raceways to threadless fittings.

▸Figure 250–175

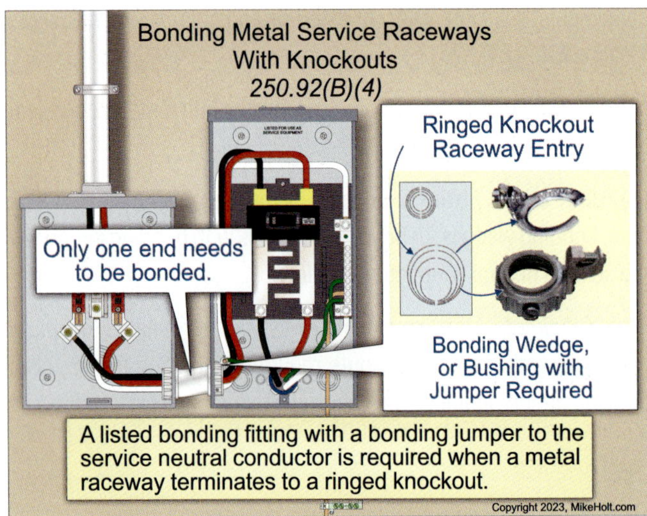
Bonding Metal Service Raceways
With Knockouts
250.92(B)(4)
Ringed Knockout
Raceway Entry
Only one end needs to be bonded.
Bonding Wedge, or Bushing with Jumper Required
A listed bonding fitting with a bonding jumper to the service neutral conductor is required when a metal raceway terminates to a ringed knockout.
Copyright 2023, MikeHolt.com

▸Figure 250–176

No Ringed Knockout. Metal service raceways that terminates to a metal enclosure without ringed knockouts can be bonded by using a bonding-type locknut, bonding wedge, or bonding bushing with a bonding jumper. ▸Figure 250–177

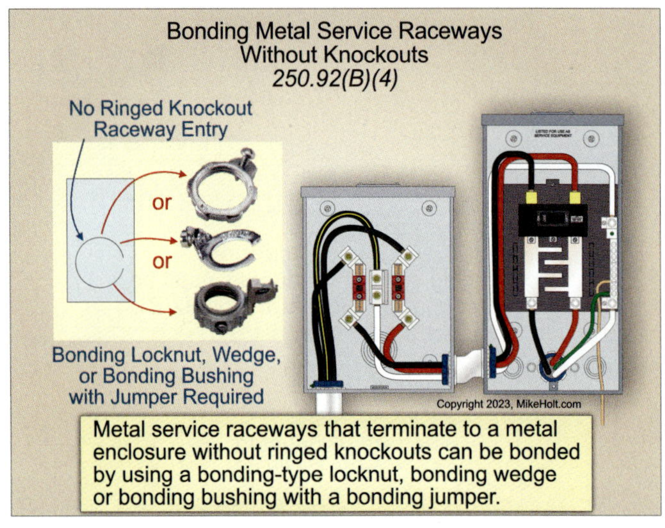
Bonding Metal Service Raceways
Without Knockouts
250.92(B)(4)
No Ringed Knockout
Raceway Entry
or
or
Bonding Locknut, Wedge, or Bonding Bushing with Jumper Required
Copyright 2023, MikeHolt.com
Metal service raceways that terminate to a metal enclosure without ringed knockouts can be bonded by using a bonding-type locknut, bonding wedge or bonding bushing with a bonding jumper.

▸Figure 250–177

Author's Comment:

- A bonding locknut differs from a standard locknut in that it contains a bonding screw with a sharp point that drives into the metal enclosure to ensure a solid connection.
- Bonding one end of a service raceway to the service neutral is all that is necessary to provide a low-impedance fault current path to the source required by 250.4(A)(3) and (A)(5). ▸Figure 250–178

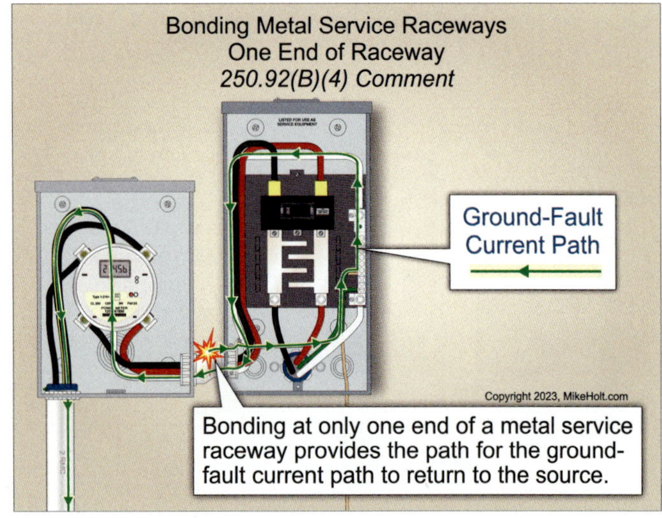
Bonding Metal Service Raceways
One End of Raceway
250.92(B)(4) Comment
Ground-Fault
Current Path
Copyright 2023, MikeHolt.com
Bonding at only one end of a metal service raceway provides the path for the ground-fault current path to return to the source.

▸Figure 250–178

250.94 Bonding for Communications Systems

According to Article 100, "Intersystem Bonding Termination" is a device that provides a means to connect intersystem bonding conductors for communications systems to the grounding electrode system in accordance with 250.94. ▸Figure 250–179

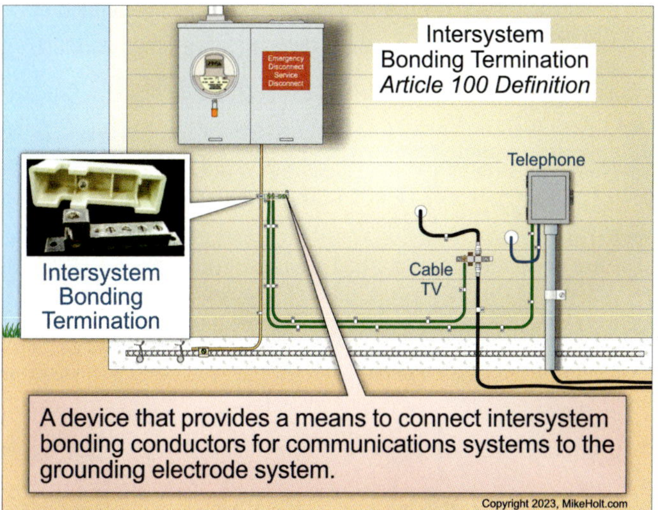
Intersystem
Bonding Termination
Article 100 Definition
Telephone
Cable TV
Intersystem Bonding Termination
A device that provides a means to connect intersystem bonding conductors for communications systems to the grounding electrode system.
Copyright 2023, MikeHolt.com

▸Figure 250–179

(A) Intersystem Bonding Termination Device. An intersystem bonding termination device must be installed at the service equipment, meter enclosures, or at the disconnect for a building supplied by a feeder and meet all the following requirements:

(1) Be accessible for connection and inspection ▸Figure 250–180

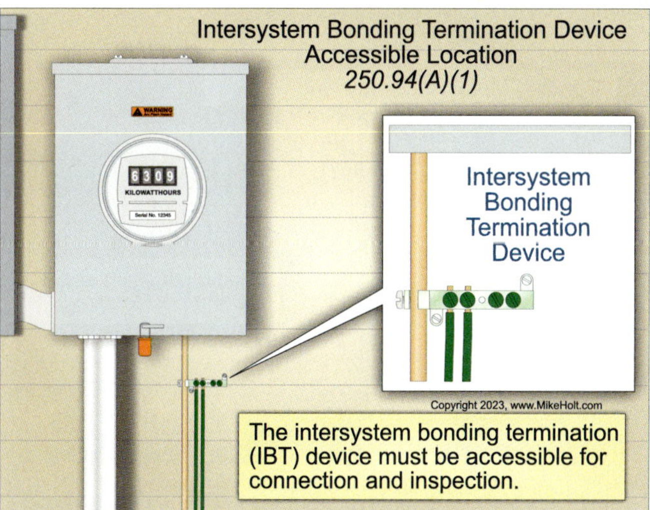
Intersystem Bonding Termination Device
Accessible Location
250.94(A)(1)
Intersystem Bonding Termination Device
Copyright 2023, www.MikeHolt.com
The intersystem bonding termination (IBT) device must be accessible for connection and inspection.

▸Figure 250–180

(2) Have a capacity for at least three intersystem bonding conductors

(3) Be installed not to interfere with the opening of any enclosure

(4) The intersystem bonding termination device (ITB) must be:

(a) Securely mounted to the metal service disconnect enclosure, metal meter enclosure, metal service raceway, or the grounding electrode conductor ▸Figure 250–181

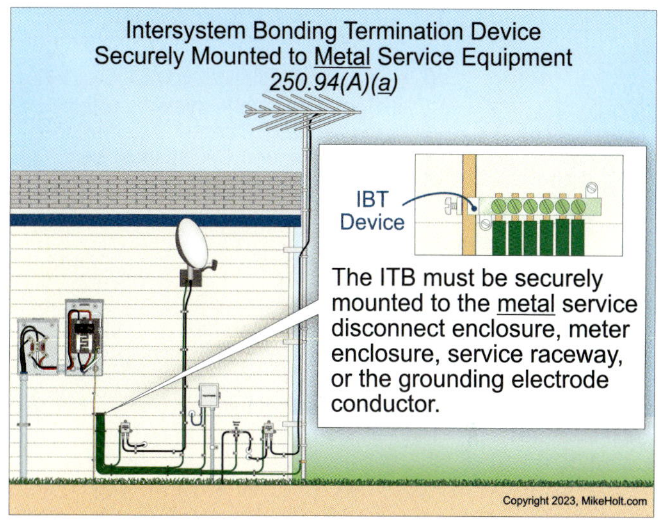
Intersystem Bonding Termination Device
Securely Mounted to Metal Service Equipment
250.94(A)(a)
IBT Device
The ITB must be securely mounted to the metal service disconnect enclosure, meter enclosure, service raceway, or the grounding electrode conductor.
Copyright 2023, MikeHolt.com

▸Figure 250–181

(b) Securely mounted to the metal remote building feeder disconnect enclosure or grounding electrode conductor ▸Figure 250–182

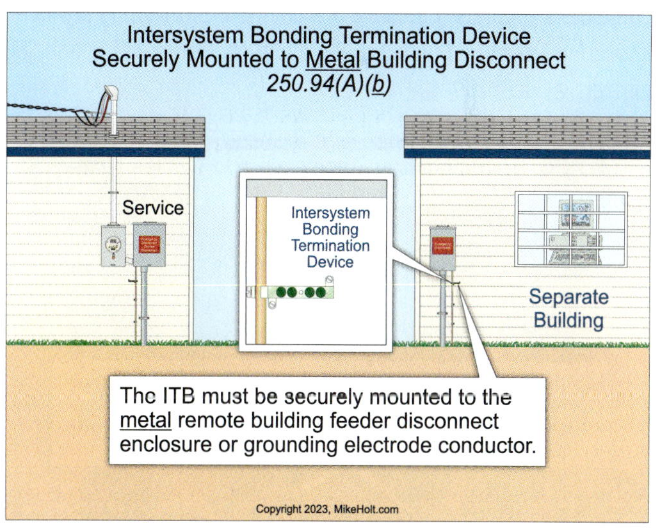
Intersystem Bonding Termination Device
Securely Mounted to Metal Building Disconnect
250.94(A)(b)
Service
Intersystem Bonding Termination Device
Separate Building
The ITB must be securely mounted to the metal remote building feeder disconnect enclosure or grounding electrode conductor.
Copyright 2023, MikeHolt.com

▸Figure 250–182

(5) Listed as grounding and bonding equipment

Ex: An intersystem bonding termination device is not required where communications systems are not likely to be used.

Note: Communications systems within the scope of Chapter 8 (telephone, antennas, and CATV) must be bonded to the intersystem bonding termination device. ▸Figure 250–183

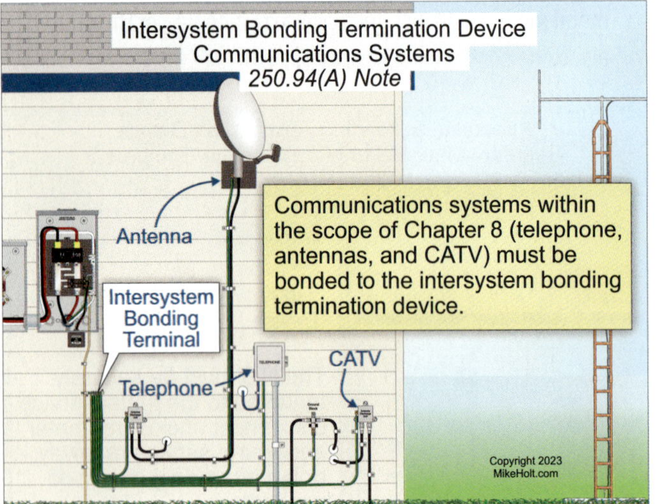
Intersystem Bonding Termination Device
Communications Systems
250.94(A) Note
Antenna
Intersystem Bonding Terminal
Communications systems within the scope of Chapter 8 (telephone, antennas, and CATV) must be bonded to the intersystem bonding termination device.
CATV
Telephone
Copyright 2023 MikeHolt.com

▸Figure 250–183

250.97 Bonding Metal Raceways and Metal Cables Containing 277V and 480V Circuits

Metal raceways and metal cables containing feeder or branch circuit conductors (operating at 277V or 480V) and terminating at ringed knockouts, must be bonded to the metal enclosure with a bonding jumper. ▸Figure 250–184

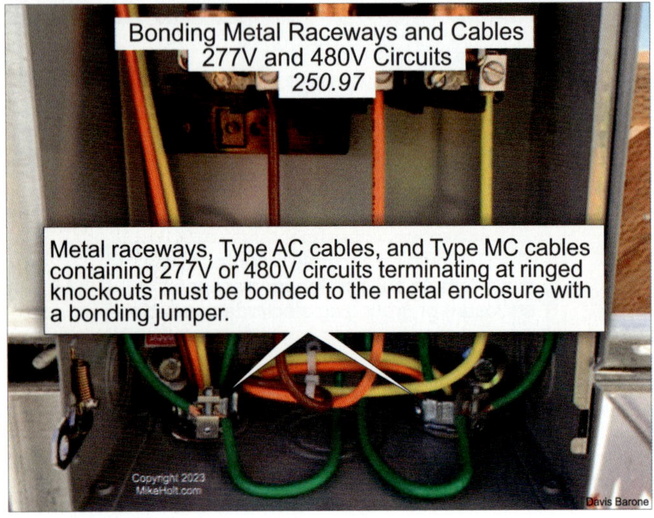
Bonding Metal Raceways and Cables
277V and 480V Circuits
250.97
Metal raceways, Type AC cables, and Type MC cables containing 277V or 480V circuits terminating at ringed knockouts must be bonded to the metal enclosure with a bonding jumper.
Copyright 2023 MikeHolt.com
Davis Barone

▸Figure 250–184

Author's Comment:

- Bonding jumpers for raceways and cables containing 277V or 480V circuits are required at ringed knockout terminations to ensure the ground-fault current path has the capacity to safely conduct the maximum ground-fault current likely to be imposed [110.10, 250.4(A)(5), and 250.96(A)]. Ringed knockouts are not listed to withstand the heat generated by a 277V ground fault, which generates five times as much heat as does a 120V ground fault. ▸Figure 250–185

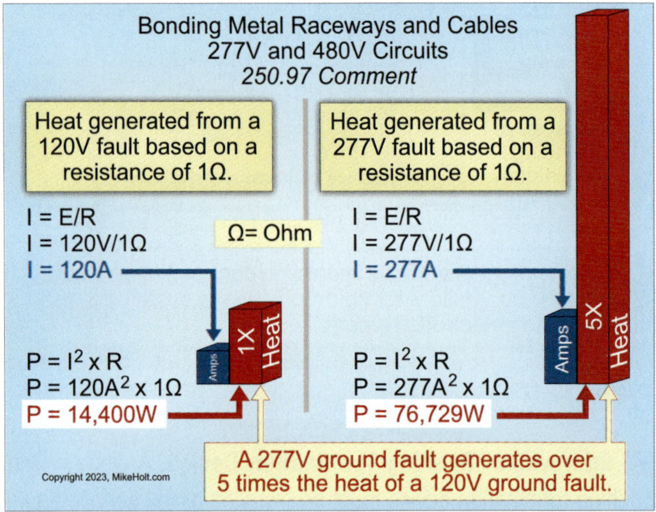
Bonding Metal Raceways and Cables
277V and 480V Circuits
250.97 Comment
Heat generated from a 120V fault based on a resistance of 1Ω.
Heat generated from a 277V fault based on a resistance of 1Ω.
I = E/R
I = 120V/1Ω
I = 120A
Ω= Ohm
I = E/R
I = 277V/1Ω
I = 277A
P = I² x R
P = 120A² x 1Ω
P = 14,400W
Amps
1X Heat
P = I² x R
P = 277A² x 1Ω
P = 76,729W
Amps
5X Heat
A 277V ground fault generates over 5 times the heat of a 120V ground fault.
Copyright 2023, MikeHolt.com

▸Figure 250–185

Ex: A bonding jumper is not required if reducing washers or ringed knockout are not encountered at metal raceway and metal cable terminations. ▸Figure 250–186

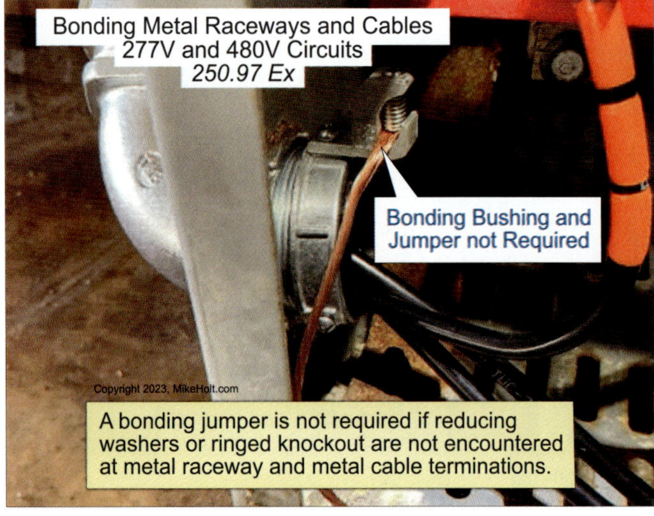
Bonding Metal Raceways and Cables
277V and 480V Circuits
250.97 Ex
Bonding Bushing and Jumper not Required
Copyright 2023, MikeHolt.com
A bonding jumper is not required if reducing washers or ringed knockout are not encountered at metal raceway and metal cable terminations.

▸Figure 250–186

250.98 Bonding Loosely Jointed Metal Raceways

Metal raceways with expansion fittings, expansion-deflection fittings, deflection fittings, or telescoping sections must be made electrically continuous using equipment bonding jumpers. ▶Figure 250–187

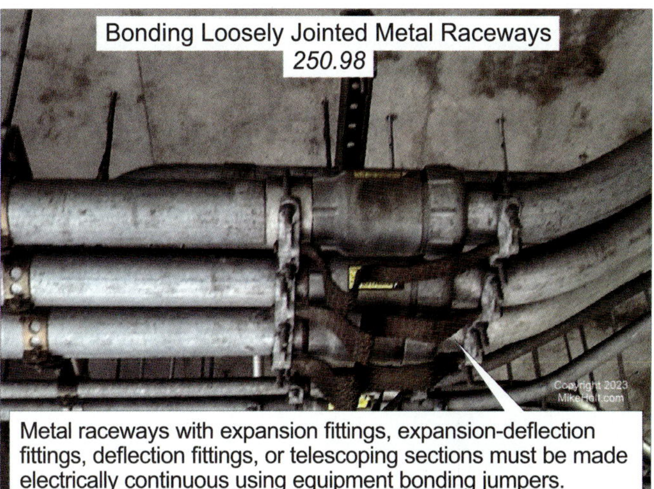
Bonding Loosely Jointed Metal Raceways
250.98
Copyright 2023
MikeHolt.com
Metal raceways with expansion fittings, expansion-deflection fittings, deflection fittings, or telescoping sections must be made electrically continuous using equipment bonding jumpers.

▶Figure 250–187

According to Article 100, "Equipment Bonding Jumper" is the conductor used to ensure electrical continuity between two or more portions of the equipment grounding conductor.

250.100 Bonding in Hazardous (Classified) Locations

Bonding in hazardous (classified) locations must be installed using one of the methods in 250.92(B)(2) through (4), whether or not an equipment grounding conductor of the wire type is installed.

250.102 Bonding Jumper Sizing

(C) Supply-Side Bonding Jumper Sizing.

According to Article 100, "Supply-Side Bonding Jumper" is the conductor installed on the supply side of a service, within the service equipment, or separately derived system that ensures conductivity between metal parts required to be electrically connected. ▶Figure 250–188, ▶Figure 250–189, and ▶Figure 250–190

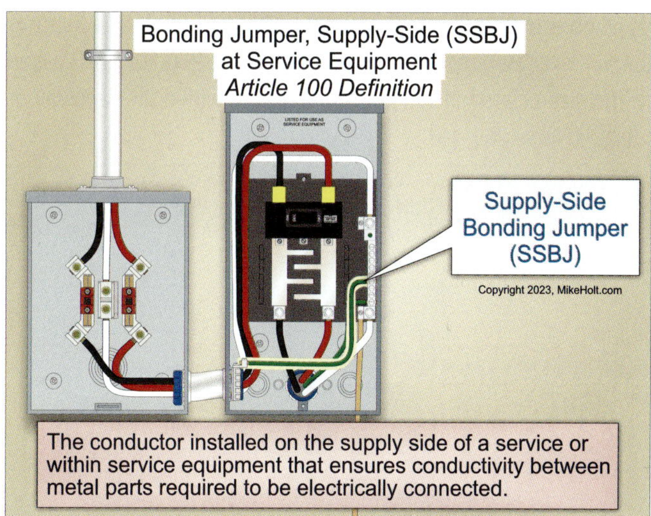
Bonding Jumper, Supply-Side (SSBJ)
at Service Equipment
Article 100 Definition
Supply-Side
Bonding Jumper
(SSBJ)
Copyright 2023, MikeHolt.com
The conductor installed on the supply side of a service or within service equipment that ensures conductivity between metal parts required to be electrically connected.

▶Figure 250–188

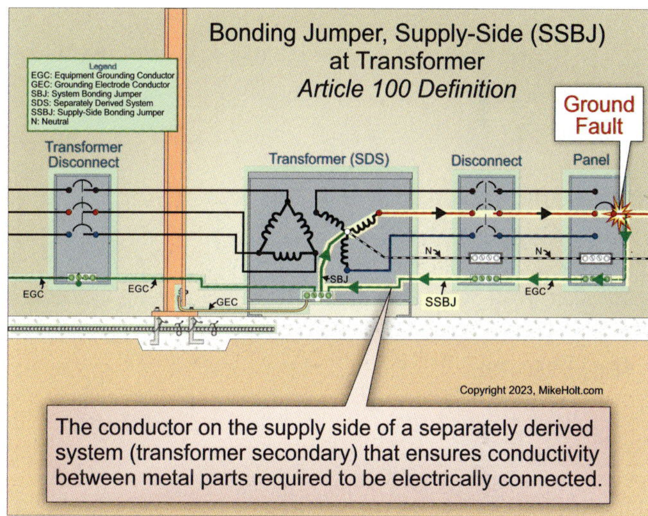
Bonding Jumper, Supply-Side (SSBJ)
at Transformer
Article 100 Definition
Legend
EGC: Equipment Grounding Conductor
GEC: Grounding Electrode Conductor
SBJ: System Bonding Jumper
SDS: Separately Derived System
SSBJ: Supply-Side Bonding Jumper
N: Neutral
Ground Fault
Transformer Disconnect
Transformer (SDS)
Disconnect
Panel
N
N
EGC
EGC
GEC
SBJ
SSBJ
EGC
Copyright 2023, MikeHolt.com
The conductor on the supply side of a separately derived system (transformer secondary) that ensures conductivity between metal parts required to be electrically connected.

▶Figure 250–189

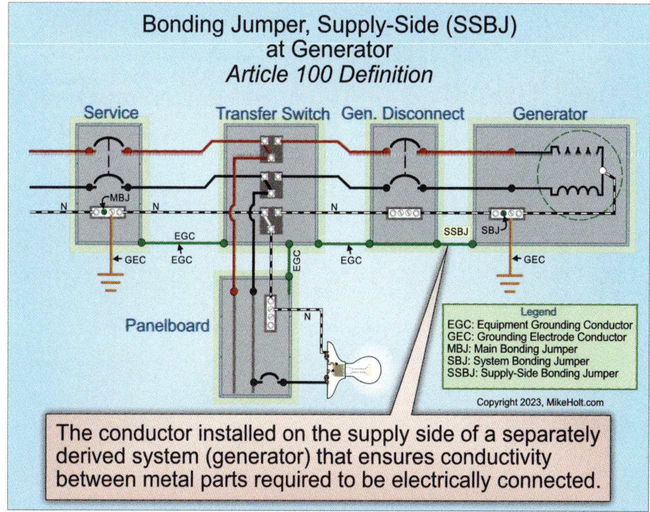
Bonding Jumper, Supply-Side (SSBJ)
at Generator
Article 100 Definition
Service
Transfer Switch
Gen. Disconnect
Generator
MBJ
N
N
N
EGC
GEC
EGC
EGC
EGC
SSBJ
SBJ
GEC
N
Panelboard
Legend
EGC: Equipment Grounding Conductor
GEC: Grounding Electrode Conductor
MBJ: Main Bonding Jumper
SBJ: System Bonding Jumper
SSBJ: Supply-Side Bonding Jumper
Copyright 2023, MikeHolt.com
The conductor installed on the supply side of a separately derived system (generator) that ensures conductivity between metal parts required to be electrically connected.

▶Figure 250–190

(1) Conductors in Single Raceway or Cable. Supply-side bonding jumpers must be sized in accordance with Table 250.102(C)(1) based on the size or area of the phase conductor within the raceway or cable. ▸Figure 250–191

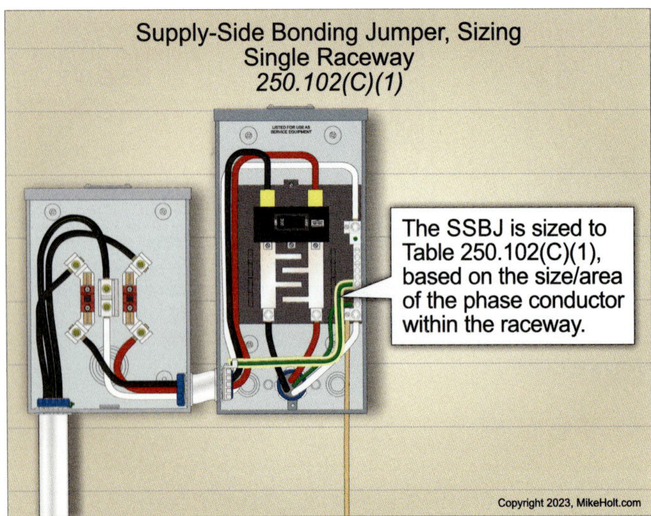
Supply-Side Bonding Jumper, Sizing
Single Raceway
250.102(C)(1)
The SSBJ is sized to Table 250.102(C)(1), based on the size/area of the phase conductor within the raceway.
Copyright 2023, MikeHolt.com

▸Figure 250–191

▸ Example

Question: *What size copper single supply-side bonding jumper is required for a raceways containing 3/0 AWG copper service conductors?* ▸Figure 250–192

(a) 1 AWG *(b) 2 AWG* *(c) 3 AWG* *(d) 4 AWG*

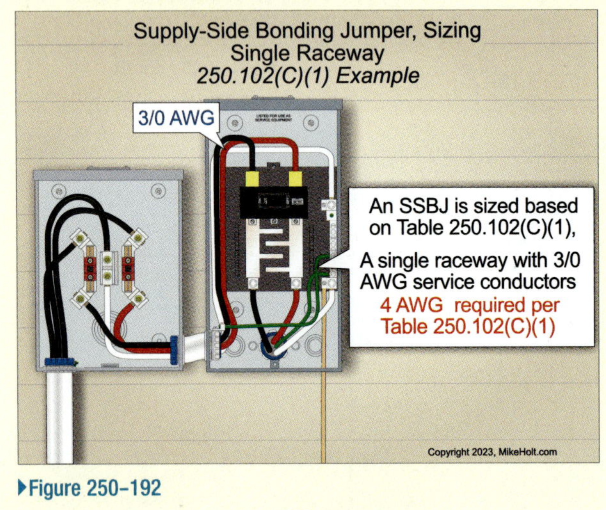
Supply-Side Bonding Jumper, Sizing
Single Raceway
250.102(C)(1) Example
3/0 AWG
An SSBJ is sized based on Table 250.102(C)(1),
A single raceway with 3/0 AWG service conductors
4 AWG required per Table 250.102(C)(1)
Copyright 2023, MikeHolt.com

▸Figure 250–192

Answer: *(d) 4 AWG*

(2) Parallel Conductors in Multiple Raceways or Cables. If the phase conductors are connected in parallel in multiple raceways or cables, the supply-side bonding jumper must be sized in accordance with either of the following:

(1) Individual Bonding Jumper for Each Raceway. An individual bonding jumper for each raceway or cable must be selected from Table 250.102(C)(1) based on the size or area of the largest phase conductors in each raceway or cable. ▸Figure 250–193

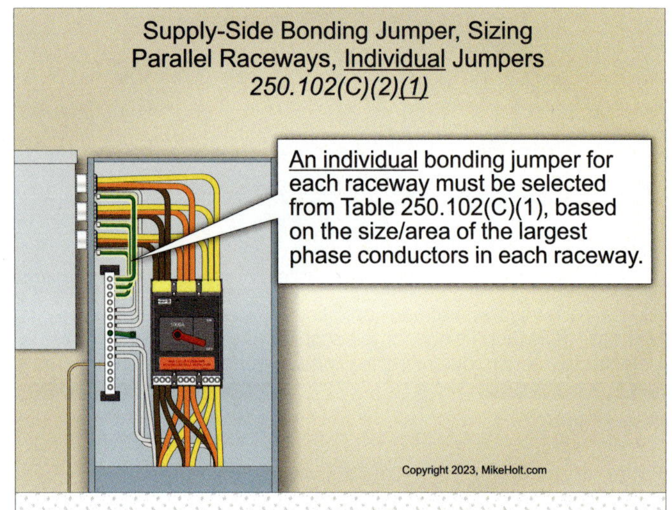
Supply-Side Bonding Jumper, Sizing
Parallel Raceways, Individual Jumpers
250.102(C)(2)(1)
An individual bonding jumper for each raceway must be selected from Table 250.102(C)(1), based on the size/area of the largest phase conductors in each raceway.
Copyright 2023, MikeHolt.com

▸Figure 250–193

▸ Example

Question: *What size individual copper supply-side bonding jumper is required for each of three metal raceways, if each raceway contains 600 kcmil copper service conductors in parallel?* ▸Figure 250–194

(a) 2 AWG *(b) 1 AWG* *(c) 1/0 AWG* *(d) 2/0 AWG*

Solution:

A single supply-side bonding jumper is permitted for multiple raceways based on the area of the supply-side 600 kcmil phase conductors.

Answer: *(c) 1/0 AWG*

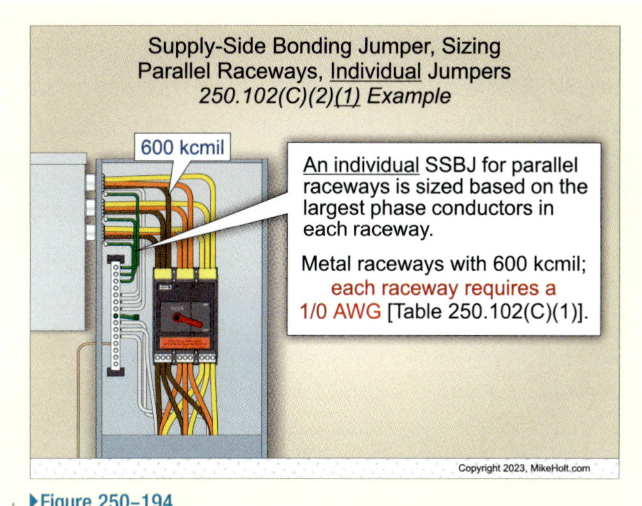
Supply-Side Bonding Jumper, Sizing
Parallel Raceways, Individual Jumpers
250.102(C)(2)(1) Example
600 kcmil
An individual SSBJ for parallel raceways is sized based on the largest phase conductors in each raceway.
Metal raceways with 600 kcmil; each raceway requires a 1/0 AWG [Table 250.102(C)(1)].
Copyright 2023, MikeHolt.com

▸Figure 250–194

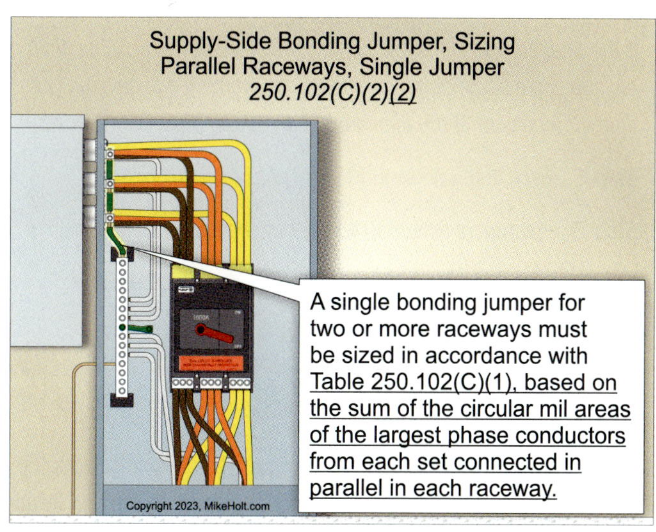
Supply-Side Bonding Jumper, Sizing
Parallel Raceways, Single Jumper
250.102(C)(2)(2)
A single bonding jumper for two or more raceways must be sized in accordance with Table 250.102(C)(1), based on the sum of the circular mil areas of the largest phase conductors from each set connected in parallel in each raceway.
Copyright 2023, MikeHolt.com

▸Figure 250–195

Table 250.102(C)(1) Neutral Conductor, Main Bonding Jumper, System Bonding Jumper, and Supply-Side Bonding Jumper

Size of Largest Phase Conductor Per Raceway or Equivalent Area for Parallel Conductors		Size of Bonding Jumper or Neutral Conductor
Copper	Aluminum or Copper-Clad Aluminum	Copper-Aluminum
2 or smaller	1/0 or smaller	8 CU–6 AL
1 or 1/0	2/0 or 3/0	6 CU–4 AL
2/0 or 3/0	Over 3/0 250 kcmil	4 CU–2 AL
Over 3/0–350 kcmil	Over 250–500 kcmil	2 CU–1/0 AL
Over 350–600 kcmil	Over 500–900 kcmil	1/0 CU–3/0 AL
Over 600–1100 kcmil	Over 900–1750 kcmil	2/0 CU–4/0 AL
Over 1100 kcmil	Over 1750 kcmil	See Note 1

If the total area of the parallel phase conductors exceeds 1100 kcmil, then the size of the single bonding jumper is not permitted to be sized less than 12.5 percent of the total are of the parallel phase conductors.

(2) Single Bonding Jumper for All Raceways. A single bonding jumper for two or more raceways or cables containing parallel conductors must be sized in accordance with Table 250.102(C)(1), based on the sum of the circular mil areas of all parallel phase conductors. ▸Figure 250–195

▸ Example

Question: *What size single copper supply-side bonding jumper is required for all three metal raceways, if each raceway contains 600 kcmil copper service conductors in parallel?* ▸Figure 250–196

(a) 4/0 AWG (b) 250 kcmil (c) 300 kcmil (d) 350 kcmil

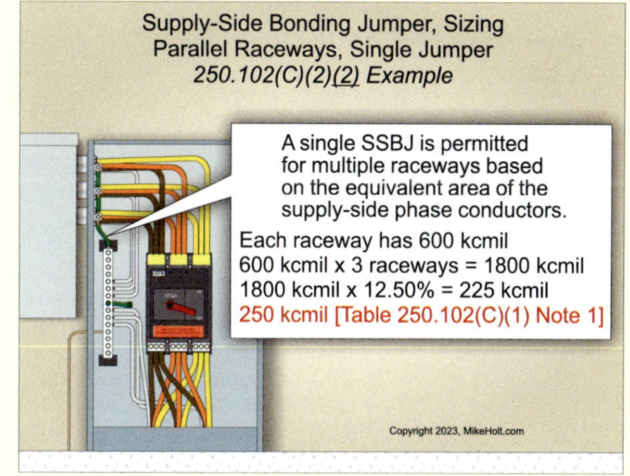
Supply-Side Bonding Jumper, Sizing
Parallel Raceways, Single Jumper
250.102(C)(2)(2) Example
A single SSBJ is permitted for multiple raceways based on the equivalent area of the supply-side phase conductors.
Each raceway has 600 kcmil
600 kcmil x 3 raceways = 1800 kcmil
1800 kcmil x 12.50% = 225 kcmil
250 kcmil [Table 250.102(C)(1) Note 1]
Copyright 2023, MikeHolt.com

▸Figure 250–196

Solution:

A single bonding jumper for two or more raceways or cables containing parallel conductors must be sized in accordance with Table 250.102(C)(1), based on the sum of the circular mil areas of all parallel phase conductors.

• • •

If the total area of the phase conductors exceeds 1,100 kcmil, then the size of the single bonding jumper is not permitted to be sized less than 12.5 percent of the total are of the parallel phase conductors.

Step 1: *Each raceway has 600 kcmil phase conductors.*

Step 2: *Total are of three 600 kcmil phase conductors = 1,800 kcmil*

Step.3: *SSBJ sized to 12.5 percent of 1,800 kcmil x 12.5% = 225 kcmil*

Answer: *(b) 250 kcmil*

Note 1: The term "supply conductors" includes phase conductors that do not have overcurrent protection on their supply side and terminate at the service disconnect or the first disconnect of a separately derived system.

Note 2: See Chapter 9, Table 8 for the circular mil area of conductors 18 AWG through 4/0 AWG.

(D) Load-Side Bonding Jumper Sizing. Bonding jumpers on the load side of feeder and branch-circuit overcurrent protective devices are sized in accordance with 250.122. ▶Figure 250–197

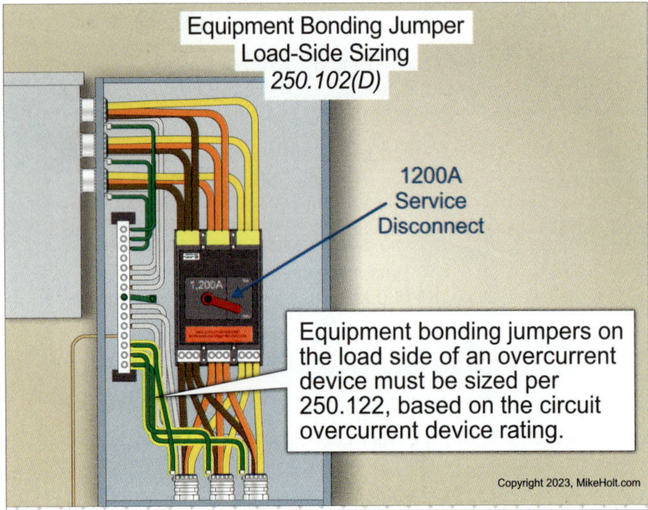
Equipment Bonding Jumper
Load-Side Sizing
250.102(D)
1200A
Service
Disconnect
Equipment bonding jumpers on the load side of an overcurrent device must be sized per 250.122, based on the circuit overcurrent device rating.
Copyright 2023, MikeHolt.com

▶Figure 250–197

▶ Example

Question: *What size equipment bonding jumper is required for each metal raceway where the circuit conductors are protected by a 1,200A overcurrent protective device?* ▶Figure 250–198

(a) 1/0 AWG (b) 2/0 AWG (c) 3/0 AWG (d) 4/0 AWG

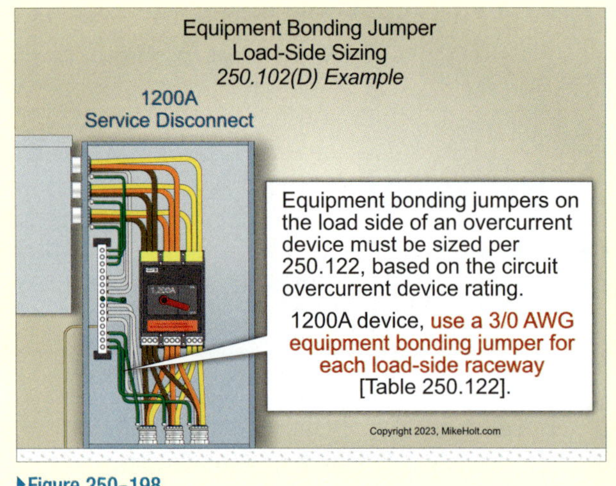
Equipment Bonding Jumper
Load-Side Sizing
250.102(D) Example
1200A
Service Disconnect
Equipment bonding jumpers on the load side of an overcurrent device must be sized per 250.122, based on the circuit overcurrent device rating.
1200A device, use a 3/0 AWG equipment bonding jumper for each load-side raceway [Table 250.122].
Copyright 2023, MikeHolt.com

▶Figure 250–198

Answer: *(c) 3/0 AWG [Table 250.122]*

If a single bonding jumper is used to bond two or more metal raceways, it must be sized in accordance with 250.122, based on the rating of the largest circuit overcurrent protective device.

(E) Installation of Bonding Jumpers.

(2) Outside a Raceway. Equipment bonding jumpers installed outside a raceway must be routed with the raceway, and the conductor cannot exceed 6 ft in length. ▶Figure 250–199

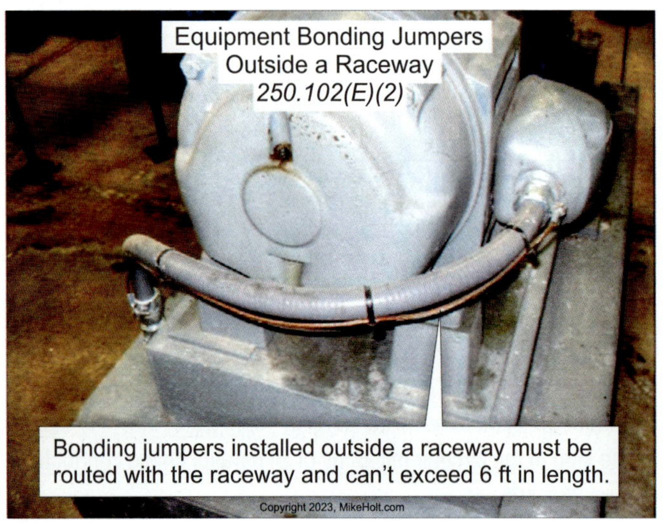
Equipment Bonding Jumpers
Outside a Raceway
250.102(E)(2)
Bonding jumpers installed outside a raceway must be routed with the raceway and can't exceed 6 ft in length.
Copyright 2023, MikeHolt.com

▶Figure 250–199

250.104 Bonding of Piping Systems and Exposed Structural Metal

(A) Metal Water Piping System. Electrically continuous metal water piping systems and metal sprinkler piping must be bonded in accordance with 250.104(A)(1), (A)(2), or (A)(3).

(1) Buildings Supplied by a Service. Electrically continuous metal water piping must be bonded to any one of the following: ▸Figure 250-200

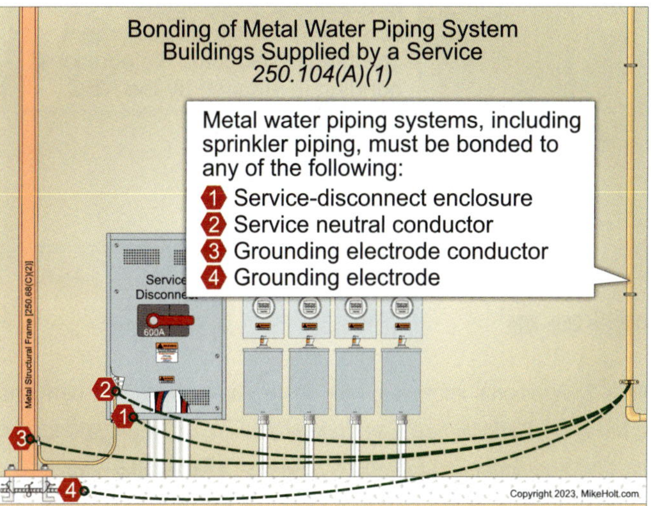
Bonding of Metal Water Piping System
Buildings Supplied by a Service
250.104(A)(1)
Metal water piping systems, including sprinkler piping, must be bonded to any of the following:
1 Service-disconnect enclosure
2 Service neutral conductor
3 Grounding electrode conductor
4 Grounding electrode
Service Disconnect
600A
Metal Structural Frame [250.68(C)(2)]
Copyright 2023, MikeHolt.com

▸Figure 250-200

(1) Service-disconnect enclosure

(2) Service neutral conductor

(3) Grounding electrode conductor if of sufficient size

(4) One of the grounding electrodes of the grounding electrode system if the grounding electrode conductor or bonding jumper to the electrode is of sufficient size

Author's Comment:

- The intent of this rule is to remove dangerous voltage on metal parts from a ground fault to electrically conductive metal water piping systems and metal sprinkler piping.

Metal water piping system bonding jumpers must be sized in accordance with Table 250.102(C)(1), based on the size or area of the service phase conductors. They are not required to be larger than 3/0 AWG copper or 250 kcmil aluminum or copper-clad aluminum, except as permitted in 250.104(A)(2) and (A)(3).

▸ Example

Question: *What size bonding jumper is required for a metal water piping system if the 300 kcmil service conductors are paralleled in two raceways?* ▸Figure 250-201

(a) 1/0 AWG (b) 2/0 AWG (c) 3/0 AWG (d) 4/0 AWG

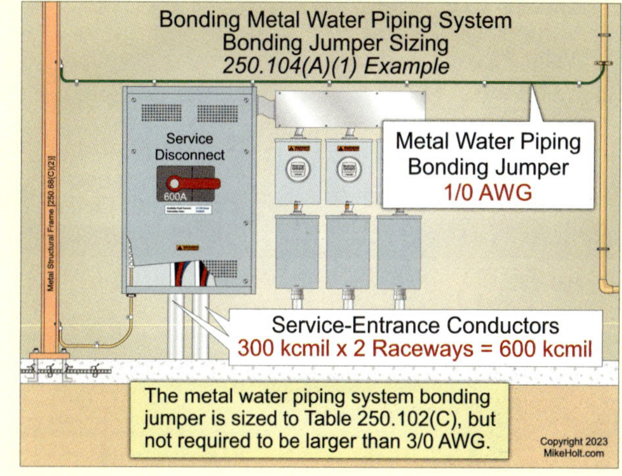
Bonding Metal Water Piping System
Bonding Jumper Sizing
250.104(A)(1) Example
Service Disconnect
600A
Metal Water Piping Bonding Jumper
1/0 AWG
Metal Structural Frame [250.68(C)(2)]
Service-Entrance Conductors
300 kcmil x 2 Raceways = 600 kcmil
The metal water piping system bonding jumper is sized to Table 250.102(C), but not required to be larger than 3/0 AWG.
Copyright 2023 MikeHolt.com

▸Figure 250-201

Solution:

A 1/0 AWG bonding jumper is required based on the 600 kcmil conductors (300 kcmil × 2 raceways) [250.102(C)(1)].

Answer: *(a) 1/0 AWG*

Author's Comment:

- Bonding is not required for isolated sections of metal water piping connected to a nonmetallic water piping system. In fact, these isolated sections of metal piping should not be bonded because they could become a shock hazard under certain conditions if they were bonded. ▸Figure 250-202

(2) Bonding Multiple-Occupancy Buildings. When an electrically continuous metal water piping system in an individual occupancy is metallically isolated from other occupancies in a building, the metal water piping system for that occupancy can be bonded to the equipment grounding terminal of the occupancy's switchgear, switchboard, or panelboard. The bonding jumper must be sized in accordance with 250.122 [250.102(D)]. ▸Figure 250-203

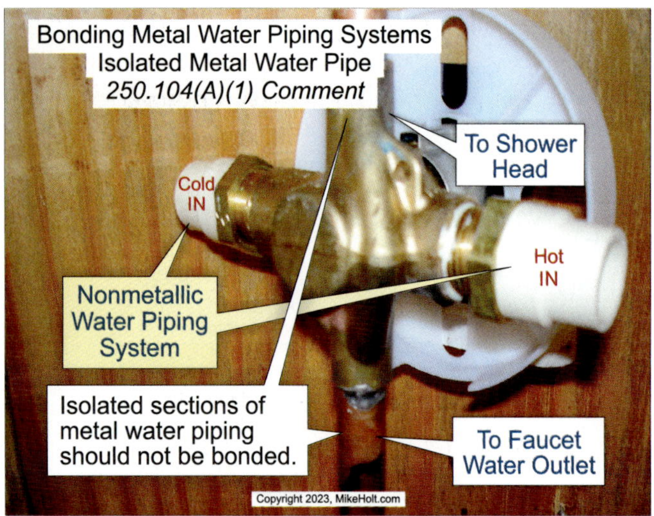
Bonding Metal Water Piping Systems
Isolated Metal Water Pipe
250.104(A)(1) Comment
To Shower Head
Cold IN
Hot IN
Nonmetallic Water Piping System
Isolated sections of metal water piping should not be bonded.
To Faucet Water Outlet
Copyright 2023, MikeHolt.com

▸Figure 250–202

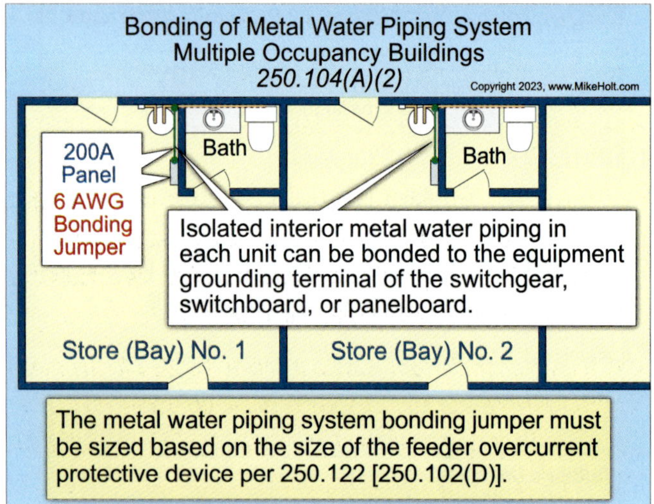
Bonding of Metal Water Piping System
Multiple Occupancy Buildings
250.104(A)(2)
Copyright 2023, www.MikeHolt.com
200A Panel
6 AWG Bonding Jumper
Bath
Bath
Isolated interior metal water piping in each unit can be bonded to the equipment grounding terminal of the switchgear, switchboard, or panelboard.
Store (Bay) No. 1
Store (Bay) No. 2
The metal water piping system bonding jumper must be sized based on the size of the feeder overcurrent protective device per 250.122 [250.102(D)].

▸Figure 250–203

(3) Buildings Supplied by a Feeder. The metal water piping system of a building supplied by a feeder must be bonded to one of the following:

(1) The equipment grounding terminal of the building's disconnect enclosure

(2) The feeder equipment grounding conductor

(3) One of the building's grounding electrodes of the grounding electrode system if the grounding electrode or bonding jumper to the electrode is of sufficient size

The bonding jumper is sized in accordance with 250.102(D) and is not required to be larger than the largest feeder phase or branch-circuit conductor supplying the building.

(B) Bonding Other Metal-Piping Systems. Metal-piping systems in or attached to a building must be bonded. The piping is considered bonded when it is connected to an appliance that is connected to the circuit equipment grounding conductor. ▸Figure 250–204

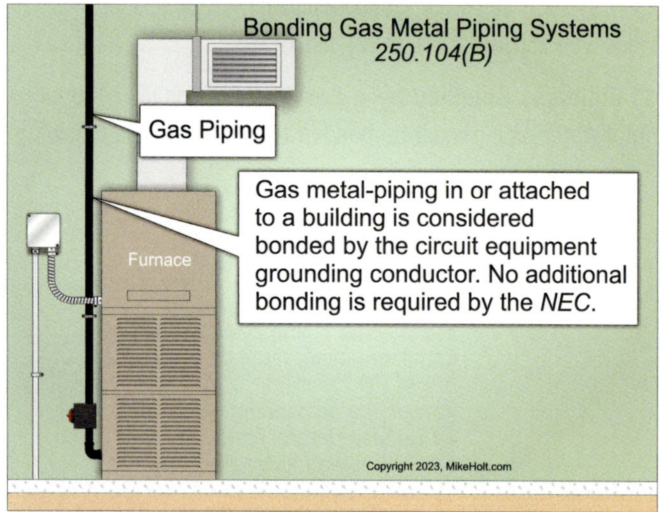
Bonding Gas Metal Piping Systems
250.104(B)
Gas Piping
Gas metal-piping in or attached to a building is considered bonded by the circuit equipment grounding conductor. No additional bonding is required by the NEC.
Furnace
Copyright 2023, MikeHolt.com

▸Figure 250–204

Note 2: Additional information for gas piping systems can be found in NFPA 54, *National Fuel Gas Code* and NFPA 780, *Standard for the Installation of Lightning Protection Systems.* ▸Figure 250–205

Bonding Gas Metal-Piping Systems
NFPA 54
250.104(B) Note 2
Copyright 2023, www.MikeHolt.com
The National Fuel Gas Code, NFPA 54 Section 7.13, contains further information about bonding gas piping.

▸Figure 250–205

Author's Comment:

- According to the *National Fuel Gas Code*, NFPA 54, section 7.12, you only need to bond CSST tubing if it is not of the "arc-resistant jacket type." See https://www.gastite.com/us/products/flashshield/flashshieldplus_csst/

(C) Bonding Exposed Structural Metal. Exposed structural metal that is interconnected to form a metal building frame must be bonded to any of the following: ▸Figure 250–206

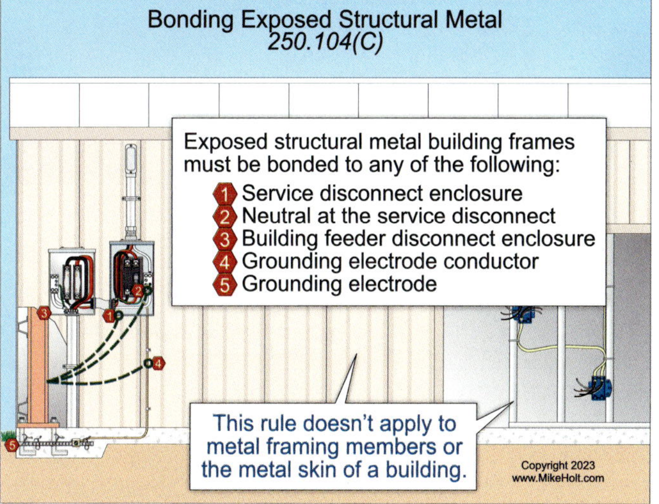
Bonding Exposed Structural Metal
250.104(C)
Exposed structural metal building frames must be bonded to any of the following:
1 Service disconnect enclosure
2 Neutral at the service disconnect
3 Building feeder disconnect enclosure
4 Grounding electrode conductor
5 Grounding electrode
This rule doesn't apply to metal framing members or the metal skin of a building.
Copyright 2023
www.MikeHolt.com

▸Figure 250–206

(1) The service-disconnect enclosure

(2) The neutral at the service disconnect

(3) The building's disconnect enclosure for those supplied by a feeder.

(4) The grounding electrode conductor sized in accordance with Table 250.102(C)(1)

(5) One of the grounding electrodes of the grounding electrode system if the grounding electrode conductor or bonding jumper to the electrode is sized in accordance with Table 250.102(C)(1)

The structural metal bonding conductor must be sized in accordance with Table 250.102(C)(1) based on the size or area of the supply phase conductors. It is not required to be larger than 3/0 AWG copper or 250 kcmil aluminum or copper-clad aluminum. The bonding jumper must be copper where within 18 in. of the surface of the Earth [250.64(A)], be securely fastened to the surface on which it is carried [250.64(B)], be adequately protected if exposed to physical damage [250.64(B)], and bonded at both ends if inside a metal raceway [250.64(E)]. In addition, all points of attachment must be accessible, except as permitted in 250.68(A) Ex 2.

(D) Transformers. Metal water piping systems and structural metal that is interconnected to form a building frame must be bonded to the transformer secondary winding in accordance with 250.104(D)(1) through (D)(3).

(1) Bonding Metal Water Pipe. Metal water piping systems in the area served by a transformer must be bonded to the secondary neutral conductor where the grounding electrode conductor is connected at the transformer. ▸Figure 250–207

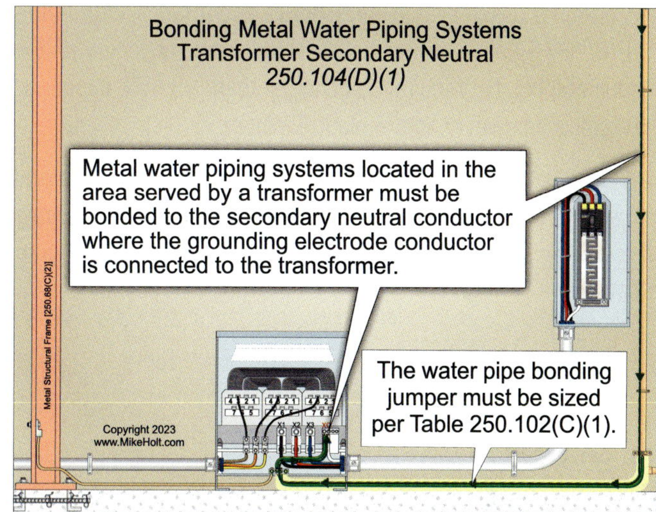
Bonding Metal Water Piping Systems
Transformer Secondary Neutral
250.104(D)(1)
Metal water piping systems located in the area served by a transformer must be bonded to the secondary neutral conductor where the grounding electrode conductor is connected to the transformer.
The water pipe bonding jumper must be sized per Table 250.102(C)(1).
Metal Structural Frame [250.68(C)(2)]
Copyright 2023
www.MikeHolt.com

▸Figure 250–207

The bonding jumper must be sized in accordance with Table 250.102(C)(1) based on the size or area of the secondary phase conductors. It is not required to be larger than 3/0 AWG copper or 250 kcmil aluminum or copper-clad aluminum.

Ex 2: The metal water piping system can be bonded to the metal structural building frame if it serves as the grounding electrode [250.52(A)(2)] or grounding electrode conductor [250.68(C)(2)] for the transformer. ▸Figure 250–208

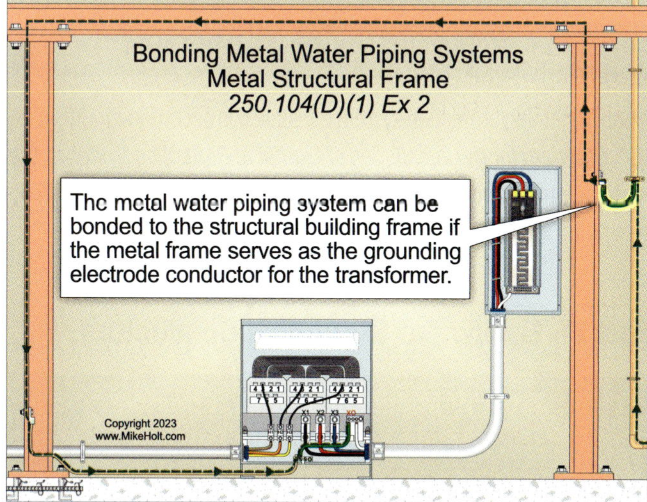
Bonding Metal Water Piping Systems
Metal Structural Frame
250.104(D)(1) Ex 2
The metal water piping system can be bonded to the structural building frame if the metal frame serves as the grounding electrode conductor for the transformer.
Copyright 2023
www.MikeHolt.com

▸Figure 250–208

(2) Bonding Exposed Structural Metal. Exposed structural metal that is interconnected to form the building frame in the area served by a transformer must be bonded to the secondary neutral conductor where the grounding electrode conductor is connected at the transformer.

The bonding jumper must be sized in accordance with Table 250.102(C)(1) based on the size or area of the secondary phase conductors. It is not required to be larger than 3/0 AWG copper or 250 kcmil aluminum or copper-clad aluminum.

Ex 1: Bonding to the transformer is not required if the metal structural frame serves as the grounding electrode [250.52(A)(2)] or grounding electrode conductor [250.68(C)(2)] for the transformer. ▸Figure 250–209

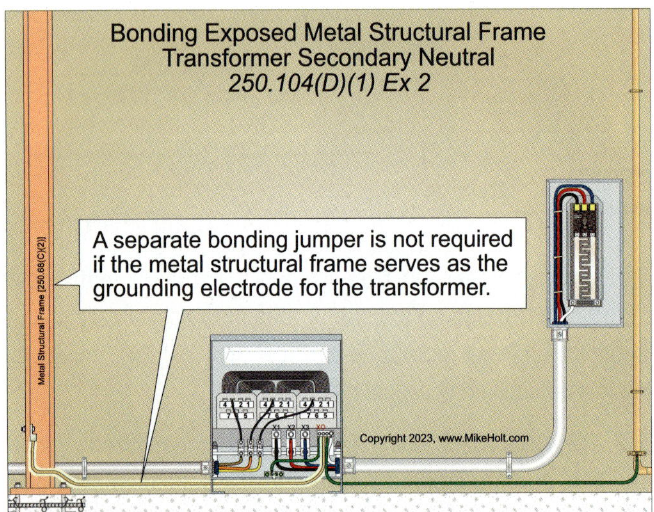
Bonding Exposed Metal Structural Frame
Transformer Secondary Neutral
250.104(D)(1) Ex 2
A separate bonding jumper is not required if the metal structural frame serves as the grounding electrode for the transformer.
Metal Structural Frame [250.68(C)(2)]
Copyright 2023, www.MikeHolt.com

▸Figure 250–209

250.106 Lightning Protection Systems

When a lightning protection system is installed in accordance with NFPA 780, *Standard for the Installation of Lightning Protection Systems*, the lightning protection electrode system must be bonded to the building grounding electrode system. ▸Figure 250–210

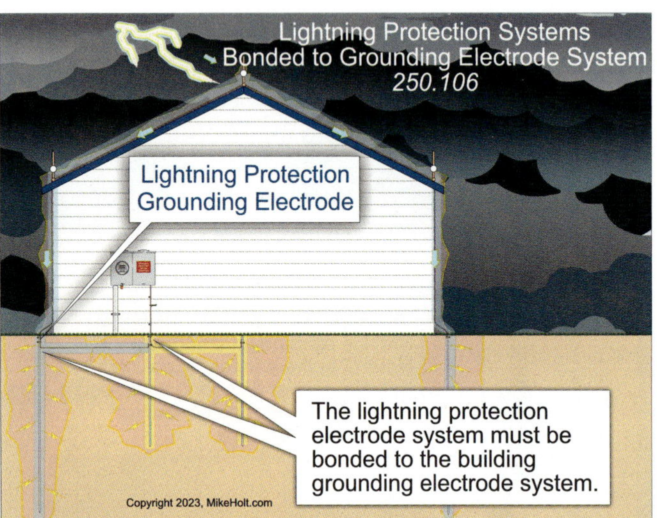
Lightning Protection Systems
Bonded to Grounding Electrode System
250.106
Lightning Protection Grounding Electrode
The lightning protection electrode system must be bonded to the building grounding electrode system.
Copyright 2023, MikeHolt.com

▸Figure 250–210

Part VI. Equipment Grounding Conductors

250.109 Metal Enclosures, Effective Ground-Fault Current Path

Metal enclosures can be used to connect bonding jumpers or equipment grounding conductors together to become a part of an effective ground-fault current path. ▸Figure 250–211

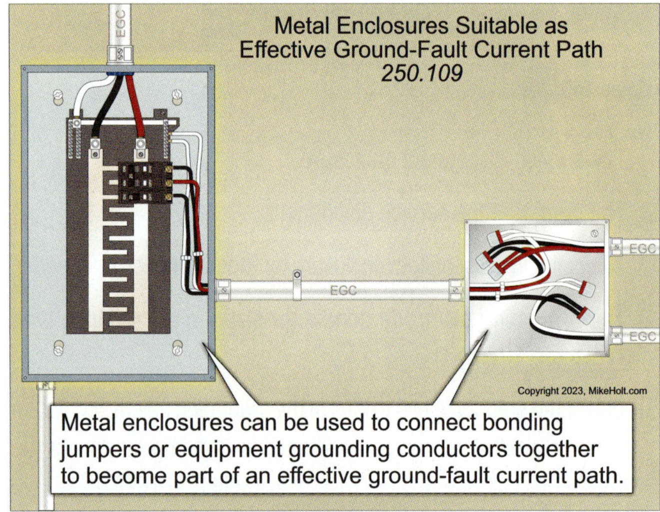
Metal Enclosures Suitable as
Effective Ground-Fault Current Path
250.109
EGC
EGC
EGC
EGC
Metal enclosures can be used to connect bonding jumpers or equipment grounding conductors together to become part of an effective ground-fault current path.
Copyright 2023, MikeHolt.com

▸Figure 250–211

Metal covers, metal plaster rings, and metal extension rings must be attached to metal enclosures to ensure an effective ground-fault current path. ▸Figure 250–212

250.114 Equipment Connected by Cord and Plug

Metal parts of cord-and-plug-connected equipment must be connected to the equipment grounding conductor of the circuit supplying the equipment under any of the following conditions:

Ex: Listed tools, appliances, and equipment covered in 250.114 list items (2) through (4) are not required to be connected to an equipment grounding conductor if protected by a system of double insulation or its equivalent. Double-insulated equipment must be distinctively marked.

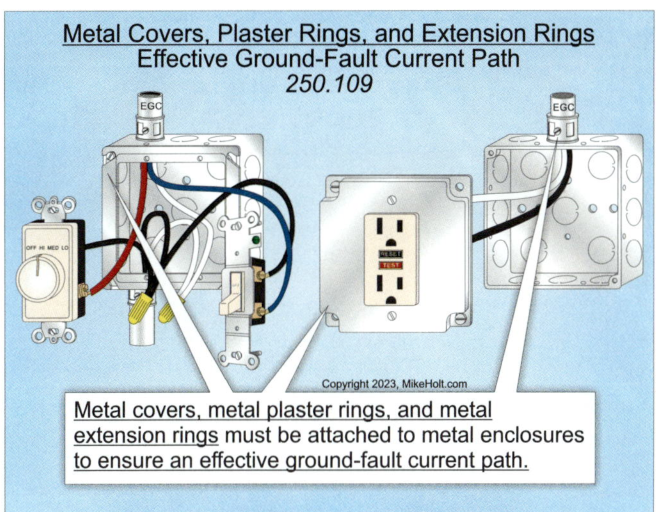
Metal Covers, Plaster Rings, and Extension Rings
Effective Ground-Fault Current Path
250.109
EGC
EGC
Copyright 2023, MikeHolt.com
Metal covers, metal plaster rings, and metal extension rings must be attached to metal enclosures to ensure an effective ground-fault current path.

▶Figure 250–212

(1) In hazardous (classified) locations [Articles 500 through 517]

(2) If operated at over 150V to ground.

Ex 1 to (2): Motors that are guarded.

Ex 2 to (2): Metal frames of exempted electrically heated appliances.

(3) In residential occupancies:

a. Refrigerators, freezers, ice makers, and air conditioners

b. Clothes-washing, clothes-drying, or dish-washing machines, ranges, kitchen waste disposals, sump pumps, and electrical aquarium equipment

c. Hand-held (stationary or fixed) and light industrial motor-operated tools

d. Motor-operated hedge clippers, lawn mowers, snow-blowers, and wet scrubbers

e. Portable handlamps and portable luminaires

(4) In other than residential occupancies:

a. Refrigerators, freezers, ice makers, and air conditioners

b. Clothes-washing, clothes-drying or dish-washing machines, IT equipment, sump pumps, and electrical aquarium equipment

c. Hand-held (stationary or fixed) and light industrial motor-operated tools

d. Motor-operated hedge clippers, lawn mowers, snow-blowers, and wet scrubbers

e. Portable handlamps and portable luminaires

f. Appliances used in damp or wet locations or by persons standing on the ground, standing on metal floors, or working inside metal tanks or boilers.

g. Tools likely to be used in wet or conductive locations.

Ex: Tools and portable handlamps or portable luminaires likely to be used in wet or conductive locations are not required to be connected to an equipment grounding conductor if supplied through an isolating transformer with an ungrounded secondary of not over 50V.

250.118 Types of Equipment Grounding Conductors

According to Article 100, "Equipment Grounding Conductor" a conductive path(s) that is part of an effective ground-fault current path. ▶Figure 250–213 and ▶Figure 250–214

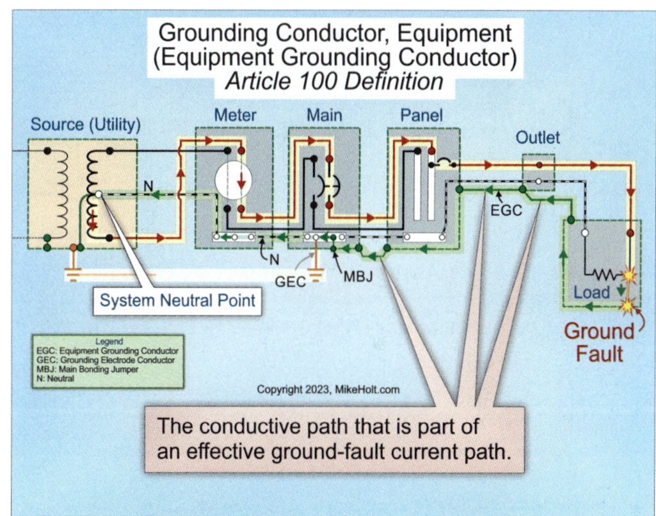
Grounding Conductor, Equipment
(Equipment Grounding Conductor)
Article 100 Definition
Source (Utility)
Meter
Main
Panel
Outlet
N
EGC
N
GEC
MBJ
System Neutral Point
Load
Ground Fault
Legend
EGC: Equipment Grounding Conductor
GEC: Grounding Electrode Conductor
MBJ: Main Bonding Jumper
N: Neutral
Copyright 2023, MikeHolt.com
The conductive path that is part of an effective ground-fault current path.

▶Figure 250–213

(A) Permitted. The equipment grounding conductor can be any one of the following types: ▶Figure 250–215

(1) Conductor sized in accordance with 250.122 ▶Figure 250–216

(2) Rigid metal conduit (RMC) ▶Figure 250–217

(3) Intermediate metal conduit (IMC) ▶Figure 250–218

(4) Electrical metallic tubing (EMT) ▶Figure 250–219

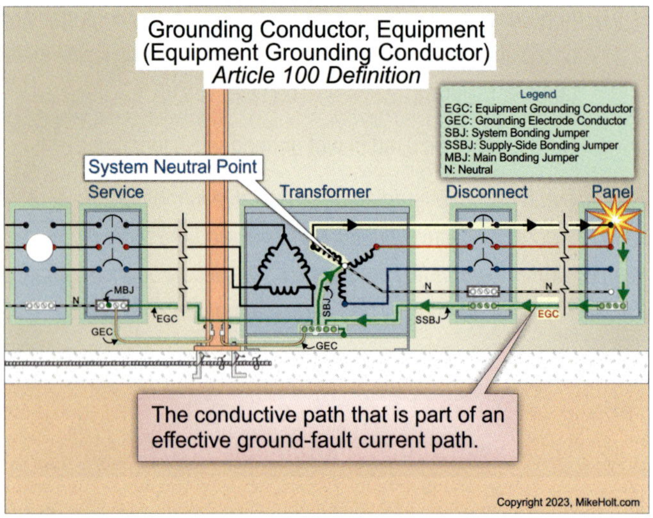
Grounding Conductor, Equipment
(Equipment Grounding Conductor)
Article 100 Definition
Legend
EGC: Equipment Grounding Conductor
GEC: Grounding Electrode Conductor
SBJ: System Bonding Jumper
SSBJ: Supply-Side Bonding Jumper
MBJ: Main Bonding Jumper
N: Neutral
System Neutral Point
Service
Transformer
Disconnect
Panel
The conductive path that is part of an effective ground-fault current path.
Copyright 2023, MikeHolt.com

▶Figure 250–214

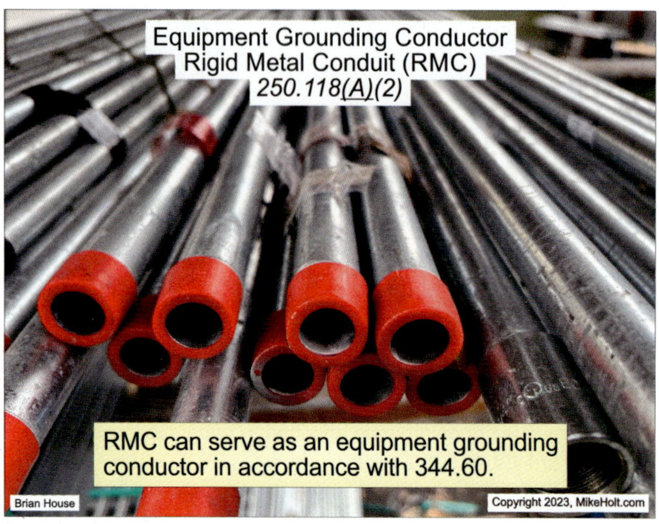
Equipment Grounding Conductor
Rigid Metal Conduit (RMC)
250.118(A)(2)
RMC can serve as an equipment grounding conductor in accordance with 344.60.
Brian House
Copyright 2023, MikeHolt.com

▶Figure 250–217

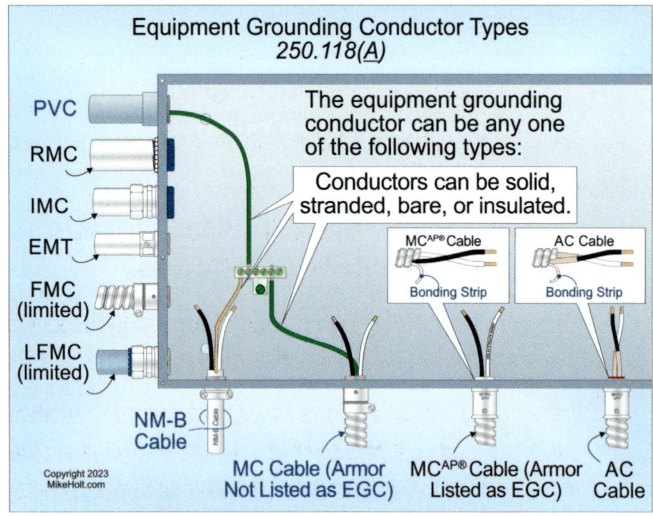
Equipment Grounding Conductor Types
250.118(A)
PVC
RMC
IMC
EMT
FMC (limited)
LFMC (limited)
The equipment grounding conductor can be any one of the following types:
Conductors can be solid, stranded, bare, or insulated.
MCAP® Cable
AC Cable
Bonding Strip
Bonding Strip
NM-B Cable
MC Cable (Armor Not Listed as EGC)
MCAP® Cable (Armor Listed as EGC)
AC Cable
Copyright 2023 MikeHolt.com

▶Figure 250–215

Equipment Grounding Conductor
Intermediate Metal Conduit (IMC)
250.118(A)(3)
IMC can serve as an equipment grounding conductor in accordance with 342.60.
Brian House
Copyright 2023, MikeHolt.com

▶Figure 250–218

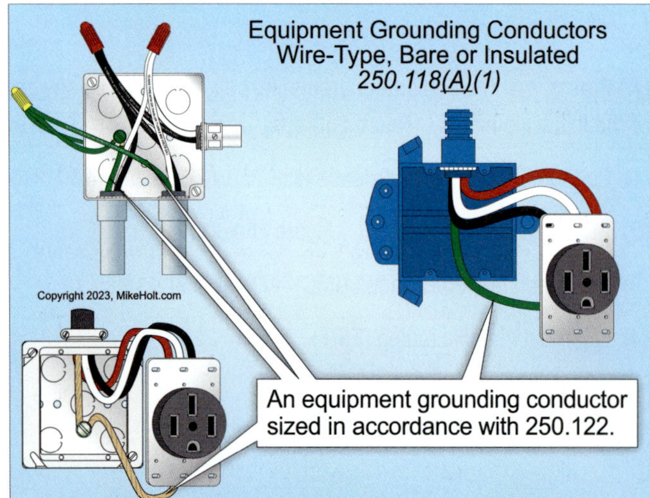
Equipment Grounding Conductors
Wire-Type, Bare or Insulated
250.118(A)(1)
Copyright 2023, MikeHolt.com
An equipment grounding conductor sized in accordance with 250.122.

▶Figure 250–216

Equipment Grounding Conductor
Electrical Metallic Tubing (EMT)
250.118(A)(4)
EMT can serve as an equipment grounding conductor in accordance with 358.60.
Brian House
Copyright 2023, MikeHolt.com

▶Figure 250–219

(5) Flexible metal conduit (FMC), where: ▸Figure 250–220

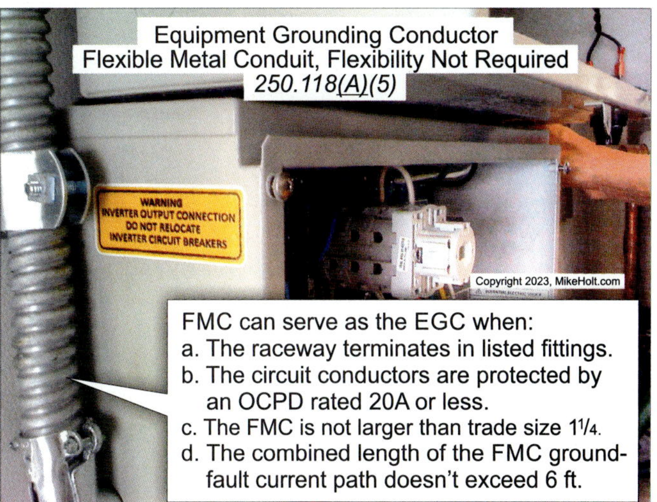
Equipment Grounding Conductor
Flexible Metal Conduit, Flexibility Not Required
250.118(A)(5)
WARNING
INVERTER OUTPUT CONNECTION
DO NOT RELOCATE
INVERTER CIRCUIT BREAKERS
Copyright 2023, MikeHolt.com
FMC can serve as the EGC when:
a. The raceway terminates in listed fittings.
b. The circuit conductors are protected by an OCPD rated 20A or less.
c. The FMC is not larger than trade size 1¼.
d. The combined length of the FMC ground-fault current path doesn't exceed 6 ft.

▸Figure 250–220

a. The raceway terminates in listed fittings.

b. The circuit conductors are protected by an overcurrent protective device rated 20A or less.

c. The size of the flexible metal conduit does not exceed 1¼ in.

d. The combined length of the flexible metal conduit in the same effective ground-fault current path does not exceed 6 ft.

e. If flexibility is required to minimize the transmission of vibration from equipment or to provide flexibility for equipment that requires movement after installation, an equipment grounding conductor or a bonding jumper of the wire type must be installed with the circuit conductors in accordance with 250.102(E). ▸Figure 250–221

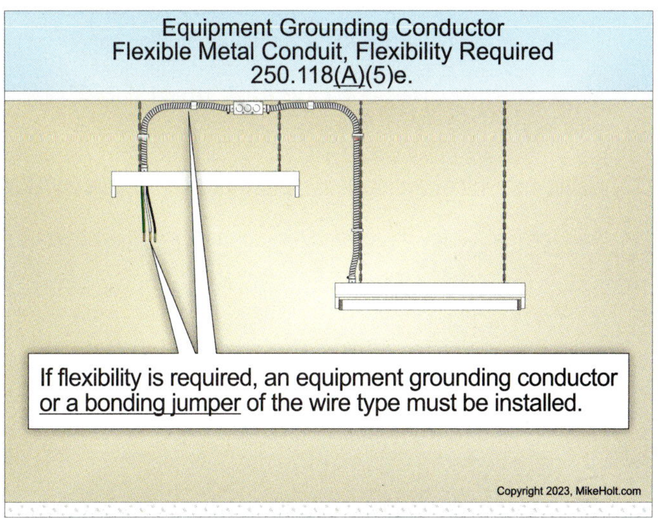
Equipment Grounding Conductor
Flexible Metal Conduit, Flexibility Required
250.118(A)(5)e.
If flexibility is required, an equipment grounding conductor or a bonding jumper of the wire type must be installed.
Copyright 2023, MikeHolt.com

▸Figure 250–221

(6) Liquidtight flexible metal conduit (LFMC), where: ▸Figure 250–222

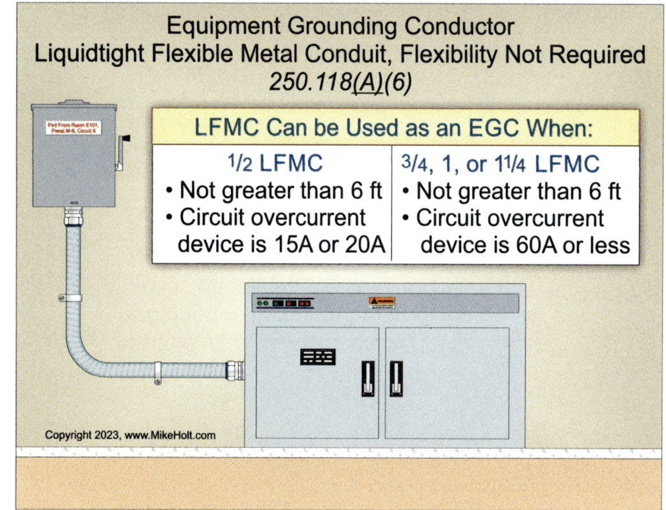
Equipment Grounding Conductor
Liquidtight Flexible Metal Conduit, Flexibility Not Required
250.118(A)(6)
LFMC Can be Used as an EGC When:
1/2 LFMC
• Not greater than 6 ft
• Circuit overcurrent device is 15A or 20A
3/4, 1, or 1 1/4 LFMC
• Not greater than 6 ft
• Circuit overcurrent device is 60A or less
Copyright 2023, www.MikeHolt.com

▸Figure 250–222

a. The raceway terminates in listed fittings.

b. For ½ in., the circuit conductors are protected by overcurrent protective devices rated 20A or less.

c. For ¾ through 1¼ in., the circuit conductors are protected by overcurrent protective devices rated 60A or less.

d. The combined length of the liquidtight flexible metal conduit in the same effective ground-fault current path does not exceed 6 ft.

e. If flexibility is required to minimize the transmission of vibration from equipment or to provide flexibility for equipment that requires movement after installation, an equipment grounding conductor of the wire type or a bonding jumper must be installed with the circuit conductors in accordance with 250.102(E).

(8) Type AC cable ▸Figure 250–223

Author's Comment:

- The internal aluminum bonding strip of Type AC cable is not an equipment grounding conductor, but it allows the interlocked armor of the cable to serve as an equipment grounding conductor because it reduces the impedance of the armored spirals to ensure a ground fault will be cleared. It is the aluminum bonding strip in combination with the cable armor that creates the circuit equipment grounding conductor. Once the bonding strip exits the cable it can be cut off because it no longer serves any purpose.

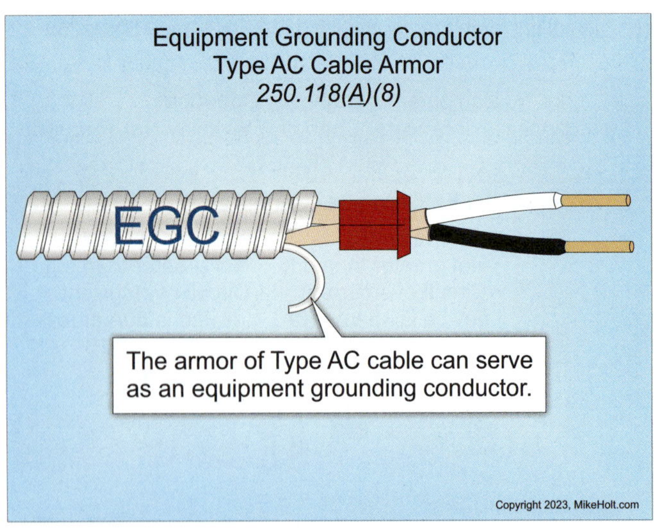
Equipment Grounding Conductor
Type AC Cable Armor
250.118(A)(8)
EGC
The armor of Type AC cable can serve as an equipment grounding conductor.
Copyright 2023, MikeHolt.com

▸Figure 250-223

(10) Type MC cable as follows:

a. An equipment grounding conductor of the wire-type is contained in traditional Type MC cable. ▸Figure 250-224

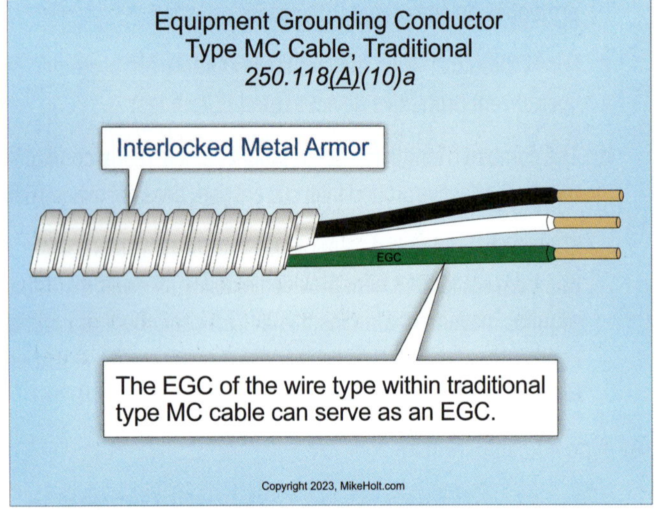
Equipment Grounding Conductor
Type MC Cable, Traditional
250.118(A)(10)a
Interlocked Metal Armor
EGC
The EGC of the wire type within traditional type MC cable can serve as an EGC.
Copyright 2023, MikeHolt.com

▸Figure 250-224

b. The combination of the metallic sheath and bare 10 AWG aluminum bonding/grounding conductor in MCAP. ▸Figure 250-225

Author's Comment:

▸ Once the bare aluminum grounding/bonding conductor of Type MC cable exits the cable, it can be cut off because it no longer serves any purpose. The effective ground-fault current path must be maintained using fittings specifically listed for Type MC$^{AP®}$ cable [330.6]. See 300.12, 300.15, and 330.108. ▸Figure 250-226

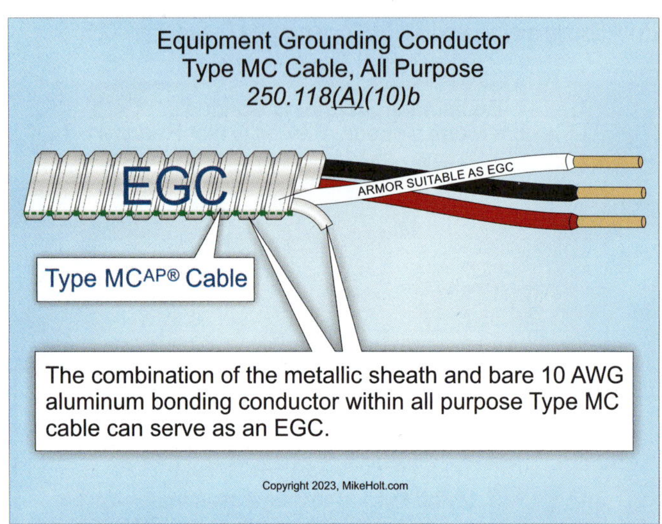
Equipment Grounding Conductor
Type MC Cable, All Purpose
250.118(A)(10)b
EGC
ARMOR SUITABLE AS EGC
Type MCAP® Cable
The combination of the metallic sheath and bare 10 AWG aluminum bonding conductor within all purpose Type MC cable can serve as an EGC.
Copyright 2023, MikeHolt.com

▸Figure 250-225

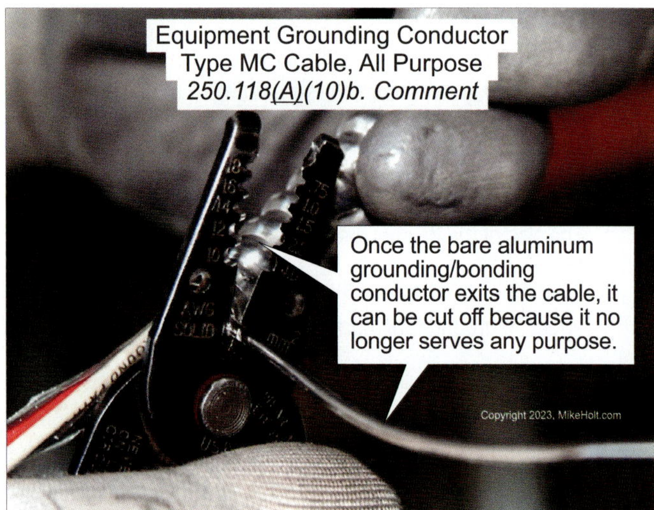
Equipment Grounding Conductor
Type MC Cable, All Purpose
250.118(A)(10)b. Comment
Once the bare aluminum grounding/bonding conductor exits the cable, it can be cut off because it no longer serves any purpose.
Copyright 2023, MikeHolt.com

▸Figure 250-226

c. The metallic sheath of smooth or corrugated tube-type MC cable listed and identified as an equipment grounding conductor.

(11) Metal cable trays in accordance with 392.10 and 392.60 ▸Figure 250-227

(13) Listed metal raceways, such as metal wireways ▸Figure 250-228

(14) Surface metal raceways listed for grounding ▸Figure 250-229

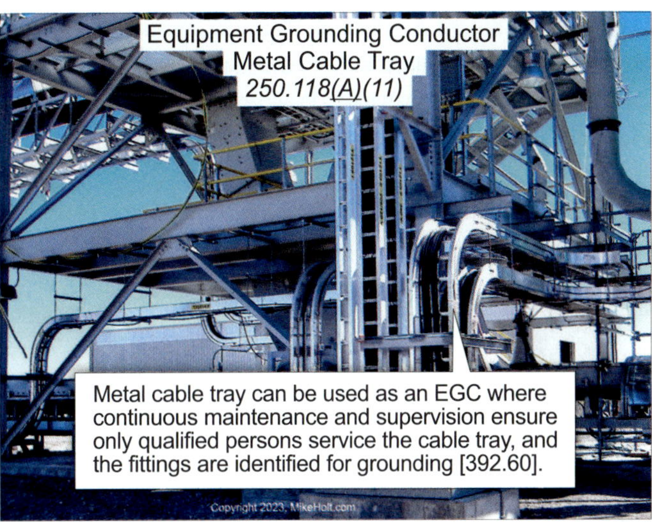
Equipment Grounding Conductor
Metal Cable Tray
250.118(A)(11)
Metal cable tray can be used as an EGC where continuous maintenance and supervision ensure only qualified persons service the cable tray, and the fittings are identified for grounding [392.60].
Copyright 2023, MikeHolt.com

▸Figure 250–227

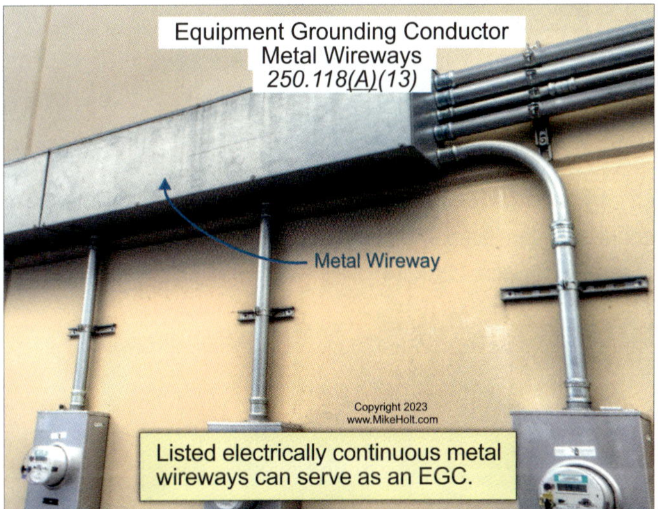
Equipment Grounding Conductor
Metal Wireways
250.118(A)(13)
Metal Wireway
Copyright 2023
www.MikeHolt.com
Listed electrically continuous metal wireways can serve as an EGC.

▸Figure 250–228

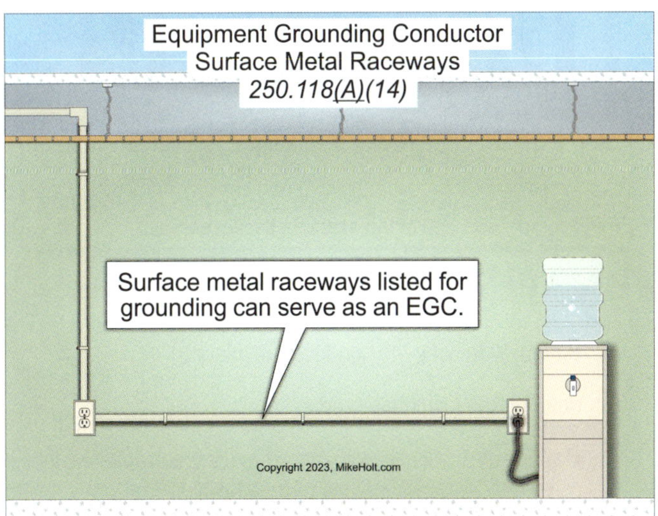
Equipment Grounding Conductor
Surface Metal Raceways
250.118(A)(14)
Surface metal raceways listed for grounding can serve as an EGC.
Copyright 2023, MikeHolt.com

▸Figure 250–229

According to Article 100, "Effective Ground-Fault Current Path" is an intentionally constructed low-impedance conductive path designed to carry ground-fault current during a ground-fault event to the power source. The purpose of the effective ground-fault current path is to assist in opening the circuit overcurrent protective device in the event of a ground fault. ▸Figure 250–230

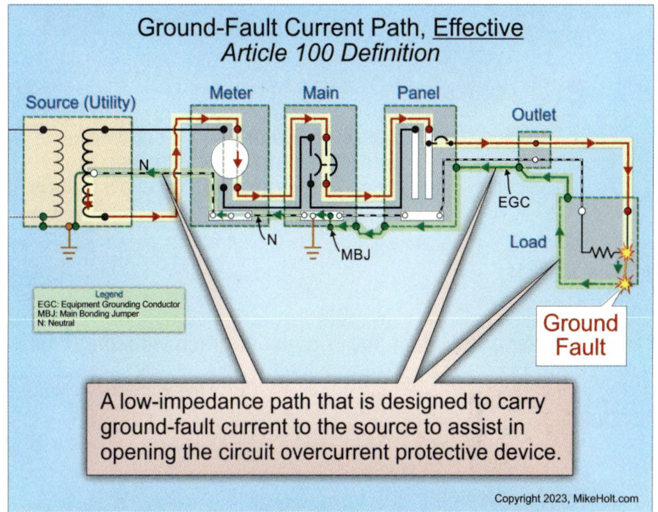
Ground-Fault Current Path, Effective
Article 100 Definition
Source (Utility)
Meter
Main
Panel
Outlet
N
EGC
Load
N
MBJ
Legend
EGC: Equipment Grounding Conductor
MBJ: Main Bonding Jumper
N: Neutral
Ground Fault
A low-impedance path that is designed to carry ground-fault current to the source to assist in opening the circuit overcurrent protective device.
Copyright 2023, MikeHolt.com

▸Figure 250–230

Author's Comment:

- In accordance with "*UL Guide Information DWTT*," listed offset nipples and metal fittings for metal cable, conduit, and tubing are considered suitable for grounding circuits where installed in accordance with the *NEC*, except as noted for flexible metal conduit fittings and liquid-tight flexible metal conduit fittings.

250.119 Identification of Wire-Type Equipment Grounding Conductors

(A) General. Unless required to be insulated in this *Code*, equipment grounding conductors can be bare or covered.

Conductors 6 AWG and Smaller. Insulated equipment grounding conductors 6 AWG and smaller, must have a continuous outer finish that is either green or green with one or more yellow stripes. ▸Figure 250–231

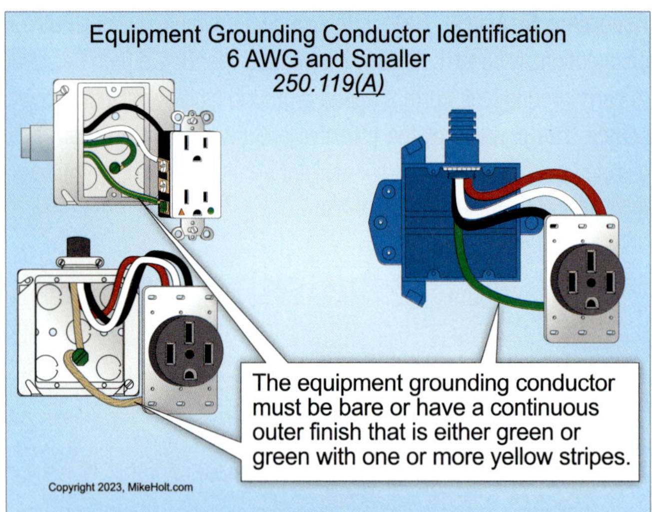
Equipment Grounding Conductor Identification
6 AWG and Smaller
250.119(A)
The equipment grounding conductor must be bare or have a continuous outer finish that is either green or green with one or more yellow stripes.
Copyright 2023, MikeHolt.com

▸Figure 250–231

Conductors with insulation that is green or green with one or more yellow stripes are not permitted to be used as phase or neutral conductors.

Author's Comment:

- The *NEC* does not require the color green to identify the grounding electrode conductor. ▸Figure 250–232

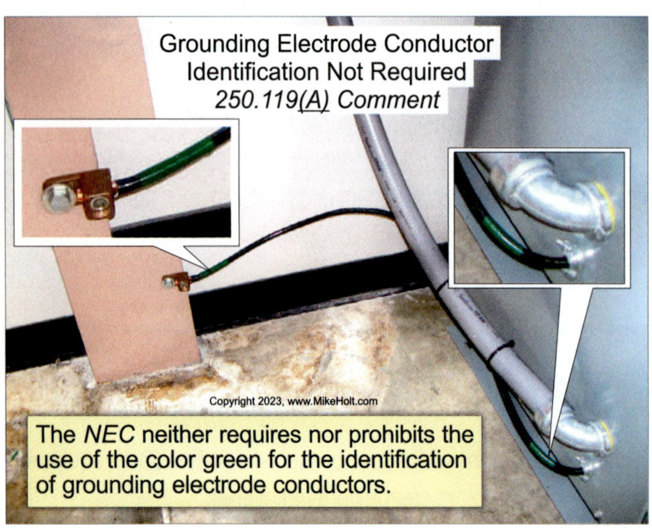
Grounding Electrode Conductor
Identification Not Required
250.119(A) Comment
Copyright 2023, www.MikeHolt.com
The NEC neither requires nor prohibits the use of the color green for the identification of grounding electrode conductors.

▸Figure 250–232

(B) Conductors 4 AWG and Larger. Insulated equipment grounding conductors 4 AWG and larger, must comply with 250.119(B)(1) and (B)(2).

(1) Identified Where Accessible. Insulated equipment grounding conductors 4 AWG and larger that do not comply with 250.119(A) must be reidentified with green marking in accordance with 250.119(B)(2) where the conductor is accessible. ▸Figure 250–233

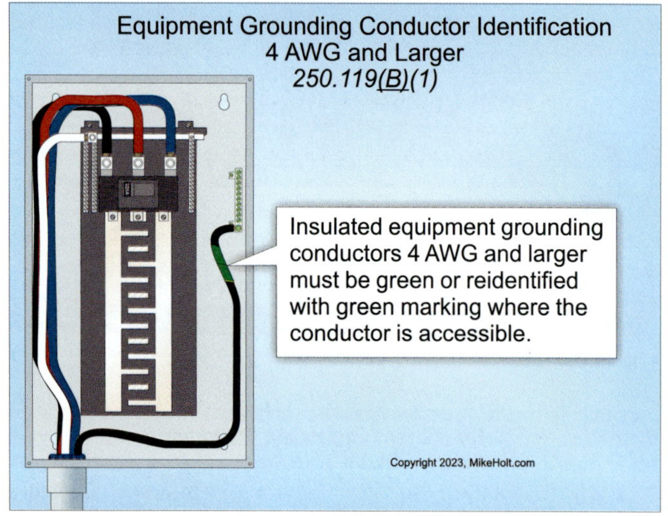
Equipment Grounding Conductor Identification
4 AWG and Larger
250.119(B)(1)
Insulated equipment grounding conductors 4 AWG and larger must be green or reidentified with green marking where the conductor is accessible.
Copyright 2023, MikeHolt.com

▸Figure 250–233

(2) Identification at Terminals. The equipment grounding conductor identification at terminations must comply with one of the following: ▸Figure 250–234

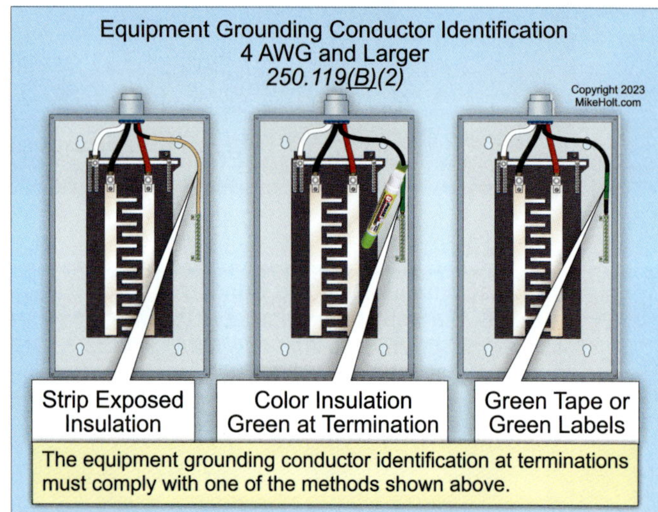
Equipment Grounding Conductor Identification
4 AWG and Larger
250.119(B)(2)
Copyright 2023 MikeHolt.com
Strip Exposed Insulation
Color Insulation Green at Termination
Green Tape or Green Labels
The equipment grounding conductor identification at terminations must comply with one of the methods shown above.

▸Figure 250–234

a. Bare by removing the conductor insulation.

b. Coloring the insulation green.

c. Marking the insulation with green tape or green adhesive labels.

(C) Multiconductor Cable. One or more insulated conductors, regardless of size in a multiconductor cable, at the time of installation are permitted to be permanently identified as equipment grounding conductors at every point where the conductors are accessible by one of the following means:

(1) Stripping the insulation from the entire exposed length.

(2) Coloring the exposed insulation green.

(3) Marking the exposed insulation with green tape or green adhesive labels and must encircle the conductor.

250.120 Equipment Grounding Conductor Installation

(A) Fittings Made Tight. The termination fitting for raceways, cable trays, or cable armor must be made tight using suitable tools.

(B) Aluminum and Copper-Clad Aluminum Conductors. Aluminum and copper-clad aluminum equipment grounding conductors must comply with the following:

(1) Aluminum and copper-clad aluminum equipment grounding conductors are not permitted to be installed where subject to corrosive conditions or in direct contact with concrete, masonry, or the Earth.

(2) Aluminum and copper-clad aluminum equipment grounding conductors are permitted within 18 in. of the bottom of any enclosure.

(3) Aluminum and copper-clad aluminum equipment grounding conductors are not permitted to terminate within 18 in. of the Earth.

250.122 Sizing Wire-Type Equipment Grounding Conductors

(A) General. Equipment grounding conductors must be sized in accordance with Table 250.122 and are not required to be larger than the largest circuit phase conductors. ▸Figure 250-235

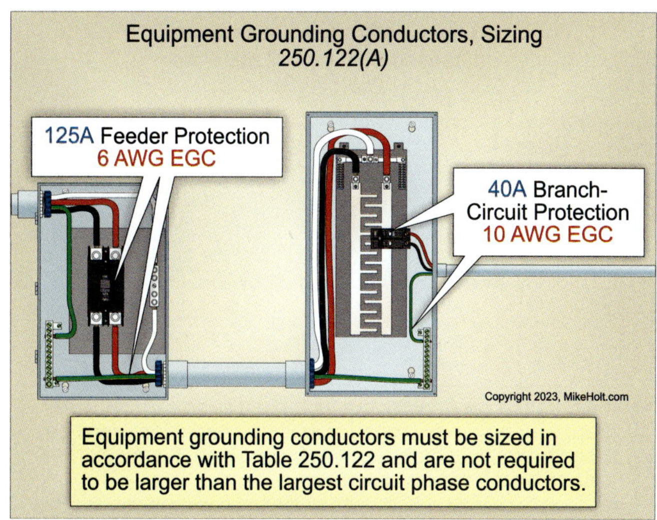
Equipment Grounding Conductors, Sizing
250.122(A)
125A Feeder Protection
6 AWG EGC
40A Branch-Circuit Protection
10 AWG EGC
Copyright 2023, MikeHolt.com
Equipment grounding conductors must be sized in accordance with Table 250.122 and are not required to be larger than the largest circuit phase conductors.

▸Figure 250-235

Table 250.122 Sizing Equipment Grounding Conductor

Overcurrent Protective Device Rating	Copper Conductor
15A	14 AWG
20A	12 AWG
25A–60A	10 AWG
70A–100A	8 AWG
110A–200A	6 AWG
225A–300A	4 AWG
350A–400A	3 AWG
450A–500A	2 AWG
600A	1 AWG
700A–800A	1/0 AWG
1000A	2/0 AWG
1200A	3/0 AWG

Note: Where necessary to comply with 250.4(A)(5) or (B)(4), the equipment grounding conductor might be required to be sized larger than given in this table.

(B) Increased in Size. If the phase conductors are larger than required by the *NEC*, such as for voltage drop consideration, the wire-type equipment grounding conductors must be proportionately increased in size based on the circular mil area of the phase conductors. ▸Figure 250-236

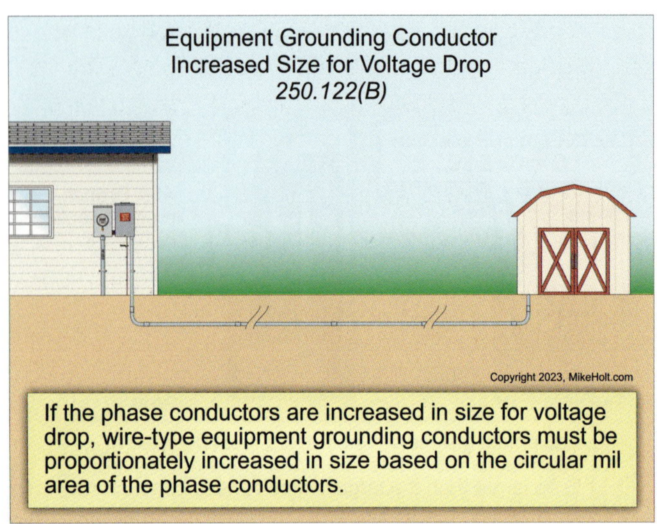
Equipment Grounding Conductor
Increased Size for Voltage Drop
250.122(B)
Copyright 2023, MikeHolt.com
If the phase conductors are increased in size for voltage drop, wire-type equipment grounding conductors must be proportionately increased in size based on the circular mil area of the phase conductors.

▸Figure 250–236

Ex: Equipment grounding conductors can be sized by a qualified person.

▸ Example

Question: *If the phase conductors for a 40A circuit are increased in size from 8 AWG to 6 AWG due to voltage drop, the circuit equipment grounding conductor must be increased in size from 10 AWG to ______.* ▸Figure 250–237

(a) 8 AWG *(b) 6 AWG* *(c) 4 AWG* *(d) 3 AWG*

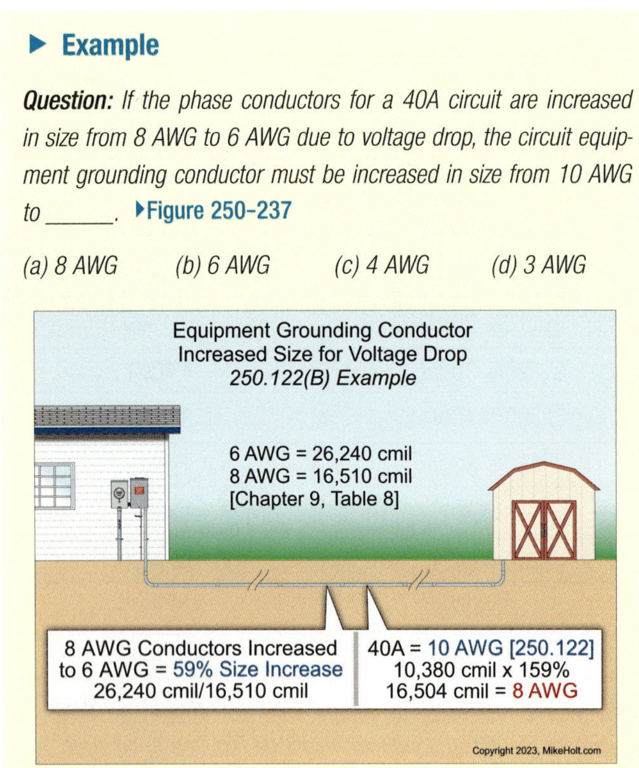
Equipment Grounding Conductor
Increased Size for Voltage Drop
250.122(B) Example
6 AWG = 26,240 cmil
8 AWG = 16,510 cmil
[Chapter 9, Table 8]
8 AWG Conductors Increased to 6 AWG = 59% Size Increase
26,240 cmil/16,510 cmil
40A = 10 AWG [250.122]
10,380 cmil x 159%
16,504 cmil = 8 AWG
Copyright 2023, MikeHolt.com

▸Figure 250–237

Solution:

The circular mil area of 6 AWG is 59 percent more than 8 AWG (26,240 cmil/16,510 cmil) [Chapter 9, Table 8].

According to Table 250.122, the circuit equipment grounding conductor for a 40A overcurrent protective device will be 10 AWG (10,380 cmil), but the circuit equipment grounding conductor for this circuit must be increased in size by a multiplier of 159 percent.

Conductor Size = 10,380 cmil × 159%
Conductor Size = 16,504 cmil

The circuit equipment grounding conductor must be increased to 8 AWG [Chapter 9, Table 8].

Answer: *(a) 8 AWG*

(C) Multiple Circuits. When multiple circuits are installed in the same raceway or cable tray, only one equipment grounding conductor, sized in accordance with Table 250.122, based on the largest overcurrent protective device is required. ▸Figure 250–238

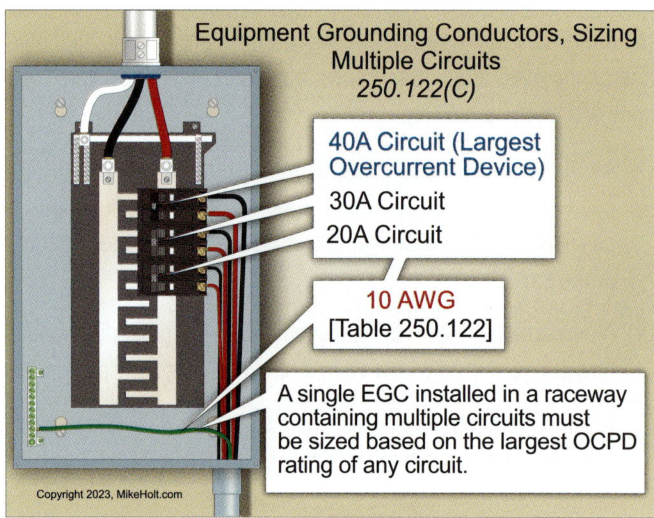
Equipment Grounding Conductors, Sizing
Multiple Circuits
250.122(C)
40A Circuit (Largest Overcurrent Device)
30A Circuit
20A Circuit
10 AWG
[Table 250.122]
A single EGC installed in a raceway containing multiple circuits must be sized based on the largest OCPD rating of any circuit.
Copyright 2023, MikeHolt.com

▸Figure 250–238

(D) Motor Branch Circuits. Equipment grounding conductors for motor circuits must be sized in accordance with 250.122(D)(1) or (D)(2).

(1) General. The equipment grounding conductor for a motor is sized in accordance with 250.122(A), based on the rating of the motor circuit branch-circuit short-circuit and ground-fault protective device. ▸Figure 250–239

Author's Comment:

- The equipment grounding conductor is not required to be larger than the motor circuit conductors. See 250.122(A).

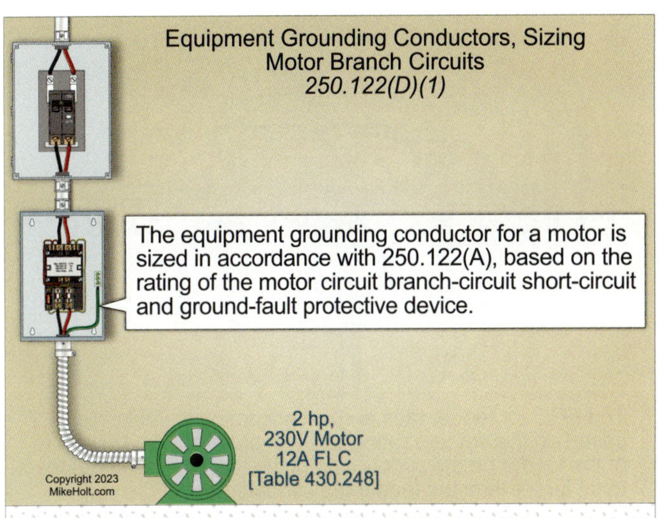
Equipment Grounding Conductors, Sizing
Motor Branch Circuits
250.122(D)(1)
The equipment grounding conductor for a motor is sized in accordance with 250.122(A), based on the rating of the motor circuit branch-circuit short-circuit and ground-fault protective device.
2 hp,
230V Motor
12A FLC
[Table 430.248]
Copyright 2023
MikeHolt.com

▸Figure 250-239

▸ Example

Question: *What size equipment grounding conductor of the wire type is required for a 14 AWG motor branch circuit [430.22], protected with a 2-pole, 40A circuit breaker in accordance with 430.22 and 430.52(C)(1)?* ▸**Figure 250-240**

(a) 14 AWG (b) 12 AWG (c) 10 AWG (d) 8 AWG

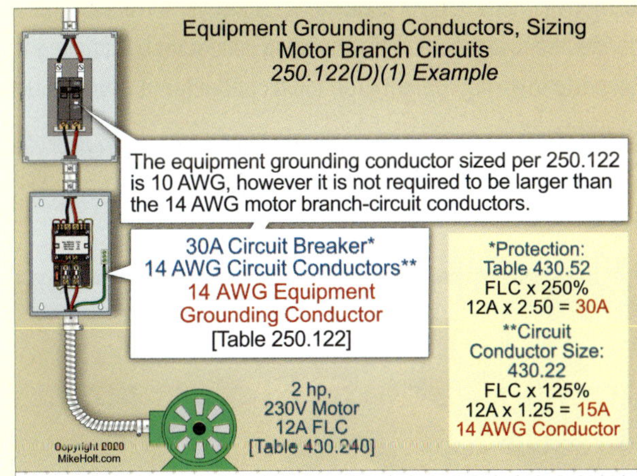
Equipment Grounding Conductors, Sizing
Motor Branch Circuits
250.122(D)(1) Example
The equipment grounding conductor sized per 250.122 is 10 AWG, however it is not required to be larger than the 14 AWG motor branch-circuit conductors.
30A Circuit Breaker*
14 AWG Circuit Conductors**
14 AWG Equipment
Grounding Conductor
[Table 250.122]
*Protection:
Table 430.52
FLC x 250%
12A x 2.50 = 30A
**Circuit
Conductor Size:
430.22
FLC x 125%
12A x 1.25 = 15A
14 AWG Conductor
2 hp,
230V Motor
12A FLC
[Table 430.248]

▸Figure 250-240

Solution:

The equipment grounding conductor sized to 250.122 is 10 AWG [250.122(D)(1)], however it is not required to be larger than the 14 AWG motor branch-circuit conductors [250.122(A)].

Answer: *(a) 14 AWG*

(F) Parallel Conductors. Where circuit conductors are installed in parallel in accordance with 310.10(G), an equipment grounding conductor of the wire type must be installed in accordance with the following:

(1) Raceways or Cable Trays.

(a) Parallel Conductors in a Single Raceway. Parallel conductors installed in a raceway require a wire-type equipment grounding conductor sized in accordance with Table 250.122.

(b) Parallel Conductors in Multiple Raceways. Parallel conductors installed in multiple raceways require a wire-type equipment grounding conductor in each raceway sized in accordance with Table 250.122. ▸**Figure 250-241** and ▸**Figure 250-242**

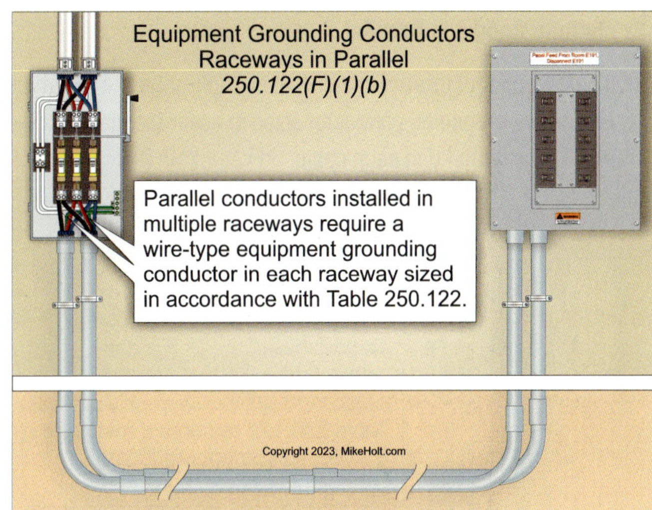
Equipment Grounding Conductors
Raceways in Parallel
250.122(F)(1)(b)
Parallel conductors installed in multiple raceways require a wire-type equipment grounding conductor in each raceway sized in accordance with Table 250.122.
Copyright 2023, MikeHolt.com

▸Figure 250-241

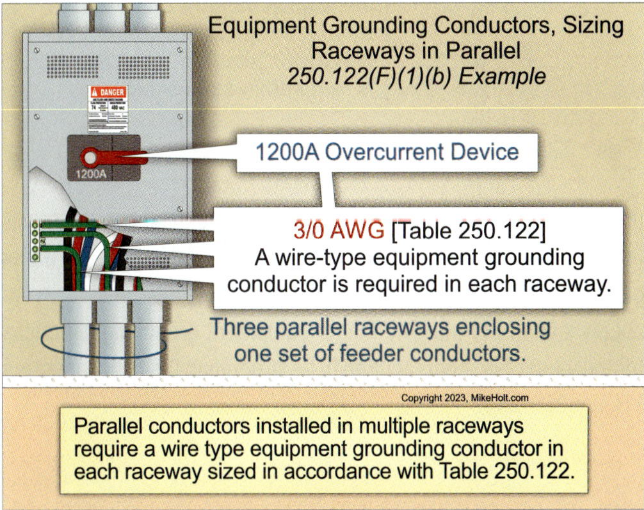
Equipment Grounding Conductors, Sizing
Raceways in Parallel
250.122(F)(1)(b) Example
1200A Overcurrent Device
1200A
3/0 AWG [Table 250.122]
A wire-type equipment grounding conductor is required in each raceway.
Three parallel raceways enclosing one set of feeder conductors.
Copyright 2023, MikeHolt.com
Parallel conductors installed in multiple raceways require a wire type equipment grounding conductor in each raceway sized in accordance with Table 250.122.

▸Figure 250-242

▶ **Example**

Question: *What size aluminum equipment grounding conductor of the wire type is required for a 4,000A feeder containing twelve parallel sets of 600 kcmil aluminum conductors per phase in PVC conduit?*

(a) 750 kcmil (b) 800 kcmil (c)1,000 kcmil (d) 1,250 kcmil

Solution:

According to Table 250.122, the equipment grounding conductor in each raceway must not be smaller than 750 kcmil, which is larger than the individual phase conductors!

Answer: *(a) 750 kcmil*

(2) Multiple Cables in Parallel.

(a) If parallel conductors are installed in multiple cables, a wire-type equipment grounding conductor sized in accordance with Table 250.122 is required in each cable. ▶Figure 250–243

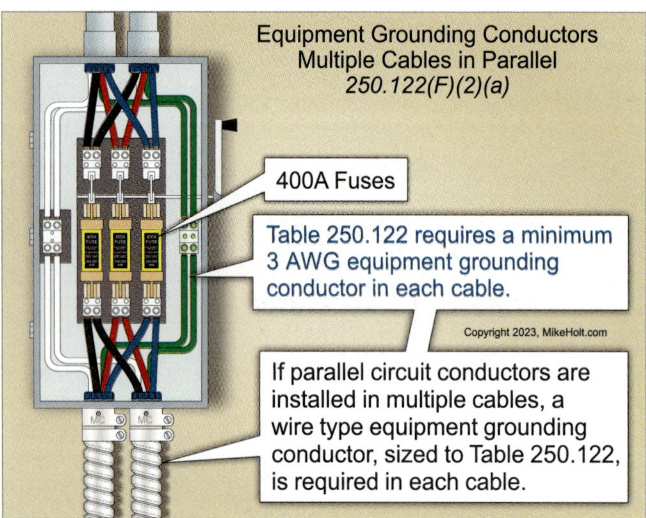
Equipment Grounding Conductors
Multiple Cables in Parallel
250.122(F)(2)(a)
400A Fuses
Table 250.122 requires a minimum 3 AWG equipment grounding conductor in each cable.
Copyright 2023, MikeHolt.com
If parallel circuit conductors are installed in multiple cables, a wire type equipment grounding conductor, sized to Table 250.122, is required in each cable.

▶Figure 250–243

(G) Feeder Tap Conductors. Equipment grounding conductors for feeder taps must be sized in accordance with Table 250.122 based on the ampere rating of the overcurrent protective device on the supply side of the tap. The feeder equipment grounding conductor for the feeder tap is not required to be larger than the tap conductors. ▶Figure 250–244

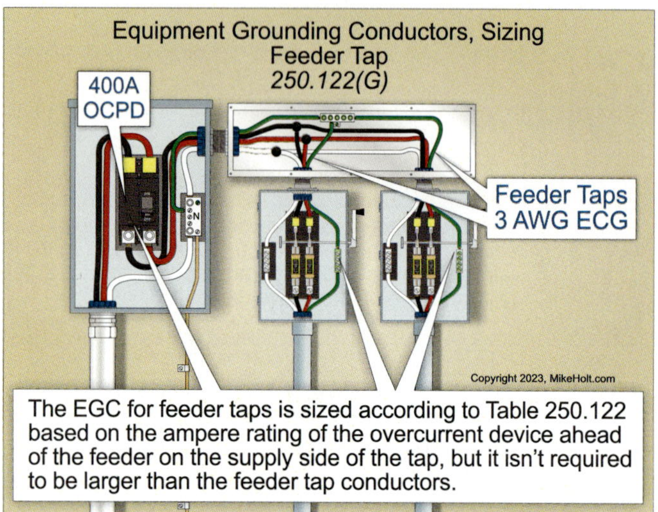
Equipment Grounding Conductors, Sizing
Feeder Tap
250.122(G)
400A OCPD
Feeder Taps 3 AWG ECG
Copyright 2023, MikeHolt.com
The EGC for feeder taps is sized according to Table 250.122 based on the ampere rating of the overcurrent device ahead of the feeder on the supply side of the tap, but it isn't required to be larger than the feeder tap conductors.

▶Figure 250–244

Part VII. Equipment Grounding Conductor Connections

250.134 Equipment Connected by Permanent Wiring Methods

Except as permitted for services or separately derived systems [250.142(A)], metal parts of equipment, raceways, and enclosures must be connected to an equipment grounding conductor by connecting the metal parts to an equipment grounding conductor of a type 250.118.

Ex 2: For direct-current circuits, the equipment grounding conductor is permitted to be run separately from the circuit conductors. ▶Figure 250–245

Equipment Grounding Conductor
Direct-Current Circuits
250.134(2) Ex 2
Copyright 2023, www.MikeHolt.com
For dc circuits, the equipment grounding conductor is permitted to be run separately from the circuit conductors.

▶Figure 250–245

250.138 Cord-and-Plug-Connected

(A) Equipment Grounding Conductor. Metal parts of cord-and-plug-connected equipment must be connected to an equipment grounding conductor that terminates to a grounding-type attachment plug. ▸Figure 250–246

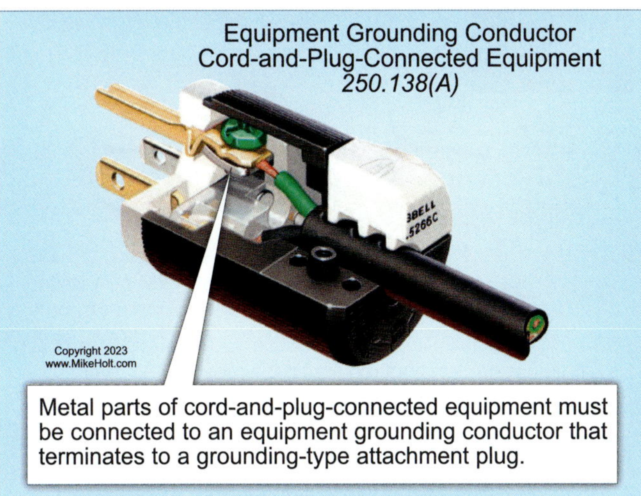
Equipment Grounding Conductor
Cord-and-Plug-Connected Equipment
250.138(A)
Copyright 2023
www.MikeHolt.com
Metal parts of cord-and-plug-connected equipment must be connected to an equipment grounding conductor that terminates to a grounding-type attachment plug.

▸Figure 250–246

250.140 Frames of Ranges, Ovens, and Clothes Dryers

The frames of electric ranges, wall-mounted ovens, counter-mounted cooking units, and clothes dryers must be connected to the circuit equipment grounding conductor in accordance with 250.140(A) or (B).

(A) Equipment Grounding Conductor. The circuit supplying electric ranges, ovens, cooktops, and clothes dryers must include an equipment grounding conductor connected to the frame of the appliance. ▸Figure 250–247

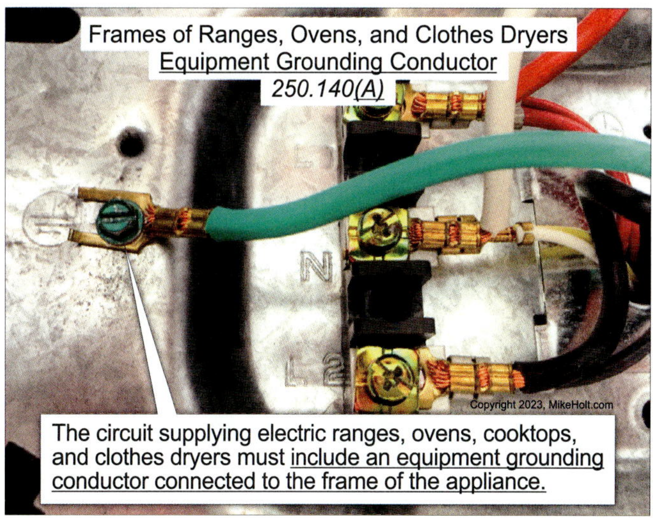
Frames of Ranges, Ovens, and Clothes Dryers
Equipment Grounding Conductor
250.140(A)
Copyright 2023, MikeHolt.com
The circuit supplying electric ranges, ovens, cooktops, and clothes dryers must include an equipment grounding conductor connected to the frame of the appliance.

▸Figure 250–247

(B) Neutral Conductor. For existing installations, if an equipment grounding conductor is not present in the outlet box, the frames of electric ranges, ovens, cooktops, and clothes dryers must be connected to the neutral conductor. ▸Figure 250–248

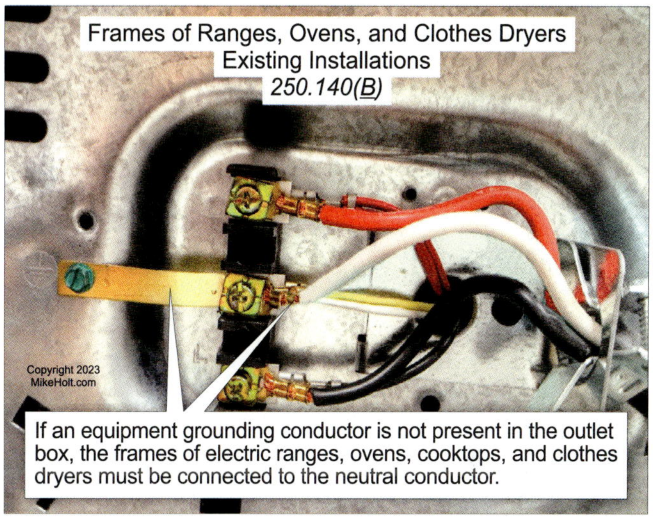
Frames of Ranges, Ovens, and Clothes Dryers
Existing Installations
250.140(B)
Copyright 2023
MikeHolt.com
If an equipment grounding conductor is not present in the outlet box, the frames of electric ranges, ovens, cooktops, and clothes dryers must be connected to the neutral conductor.

▸Figure 250–248

250.146 Connecting Receptacle Grounding Terminal to an Equipment Grounding Conductor

An equipment bonding conductor is required to connect the grounding terminals of a receptacle to a metal box, except as permitted in 250.146(A) through (D). ▸Figure 250–249

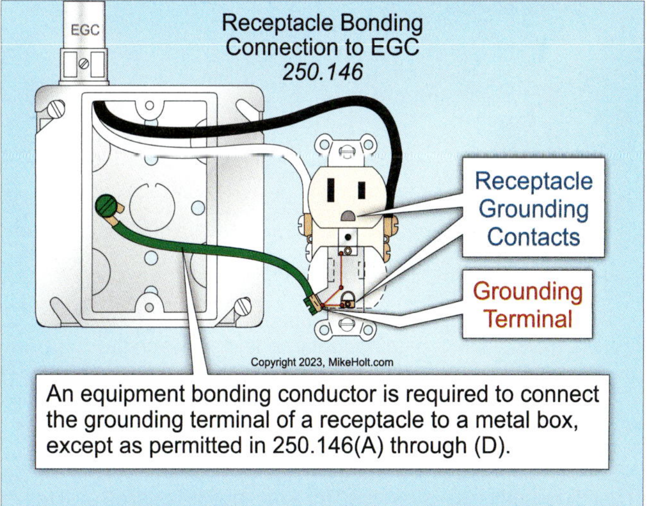
EGC
Receptacle Bonding
Connection to EGC
250.146
Receptacle Grounding Contacts
Grounding Terminal
Copyright 2023, MikeHolt.com
An equipment bonding conductor is required to connect the grounding terminal of a receptacle to a metal box, except as permitted in 250.146(A) through (D).

▸Figure 250–249

Author's Comment:

- The *NEC* does not restrict the position of the receptacle grounding terminal—it can be up, down, or sideways. *Code* proposals to specify the mounting position of receptacles have always been rejected. ▸Figure 250–250

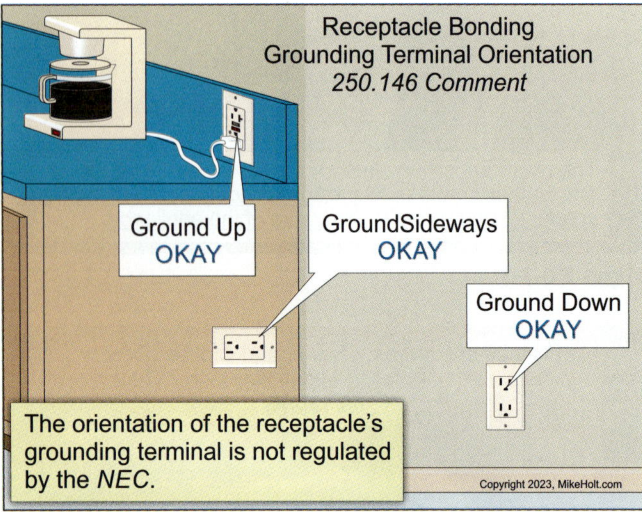
Receptacle Bonding
Grounding Terminal Orientation
250.146 Comment
Ground Up
OKAY
GroundSideways
OKAY
Ground Down
OKAY
The orientation of the receptacle's grounding terminal is not regulated by the *NEC*.
Copyright 2023, MikeHolt.com

▸Figure 250–250

(A) Surface-Mounted Box. A bonding jumper is not required for a receptacle having direct metal-to-metal contact between the receptacle mounting strap and a surface metal box. To ensure sufficient metal-to-metal contact, at least one of the insulating retaining washers on the yoke screw must be removed. ▸Figure 250–251

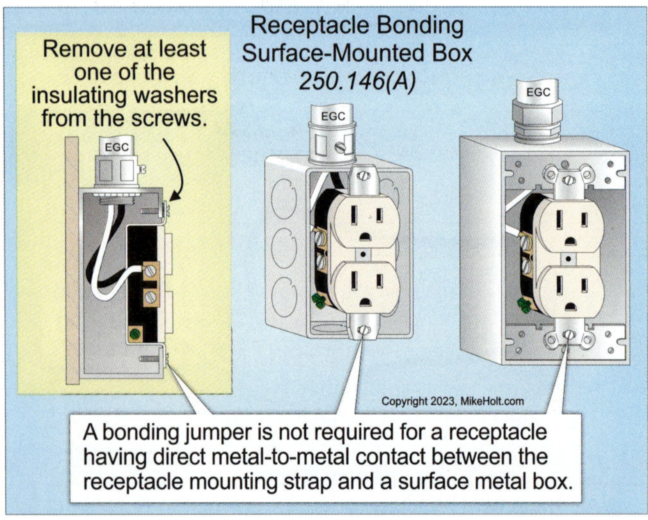
Receptacle Bonding
Surface-Mounted Box
250.146(A)
Remove at least one of the insulating washers from the screws.
EGC
EGC
EGC
A bonding jumper is not required for a receptacle having direct metal-to-metal contact between the receptacle mounting strap and a surface metal box.
Copyright 2023, MikeHolt.com

▸Figure 250–251

A bonding jumper is not required for a receptacle installed on a raised cover under both of the following conditions:

(1) The receptacle is attached to the metal cover with at least two fasteners that have a thread locking, or screw or nut locking means.

(2) The cover mounting holes are on a flat non-raised portion of the cover. ▸Figure 250–252

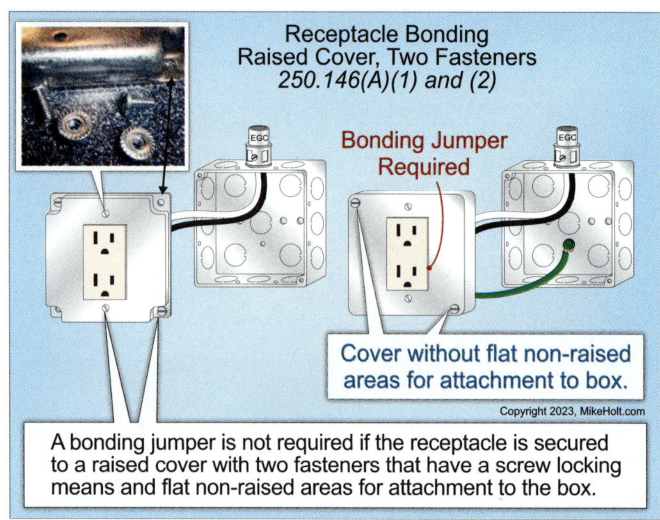
Receptacle Bonding
Raised Cover, Two Fasteners
250.146(A)(1) and (2)
EGC
Bonding Jumper Required
EGC
Cover without flat non-raised areas for attachment to box.
A bonding jumper is not required if the receptacle is secured to a raised cover with two fasteners that have a screw locking means and flat non-raised areas for attachment to the box.
Copyright 2023, MikeHolt.com

▸Figure 250–252

(B) Self-Grounding Receptacles. A bonding jumper is not required for a self-grounding receptacle mounted to a metal box. ▸Figure 250–253

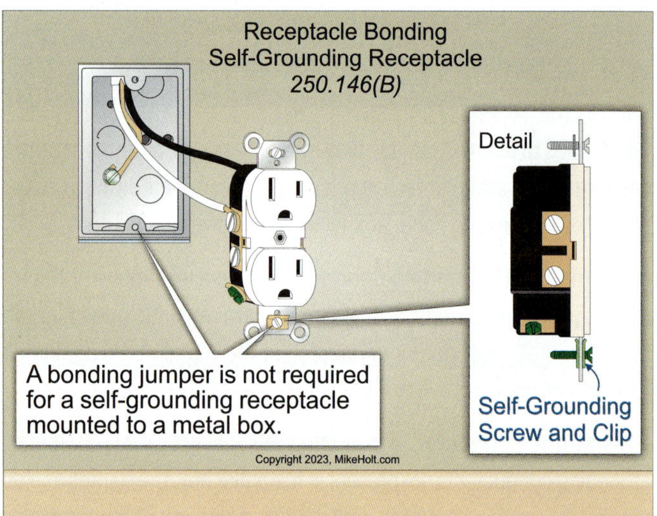
Receptacle Bonding
Self-Grounding Receptacle
250.146(B)
Detail
A bonding jumper is not required for a self-grounding receptacle mounted to a metal box.
Self-Grounding Screw and Clip
Copyright 2023, MikeHolt.com

▸Figure 250–253

Author's Comment:

- Receptacle yokes listed as self-grounding are considered bonded through the supporting screws connected to the metal box. ▸Figure 250–254

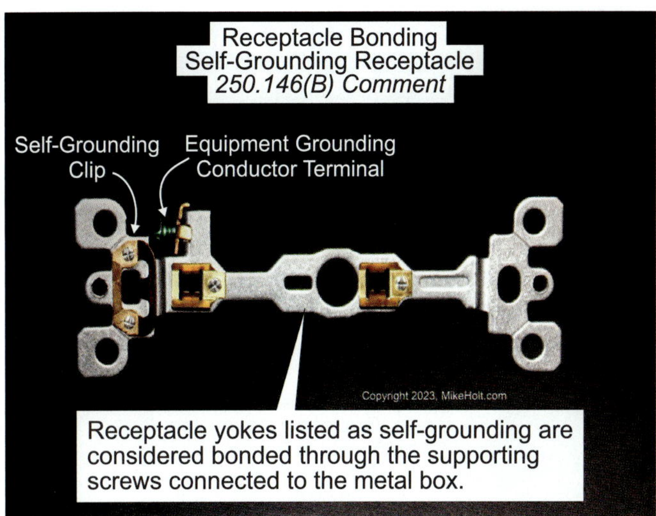
Receptacle Bonding
Self-Grounding Receptacle
250.146(B) Comment
Self-Grounding Clip
Equipment Grounding Conductor Terminal
Copyright 2023, MikeHolt.com
Receptacle yokes listed as self-grounding are considered bonded through the supporting screws connected to the metal box.

▸Figure 250-254

(C) Floor Boxes. Metal floor boxes must establish the bonding path between the receptacle yoke and a metal box.

(D) Isolated Ground Receptacles. The grounding terminal of an isolated ground receptacle must be connected to an insulated equipment grounding conductor. ▸Figure 250-255

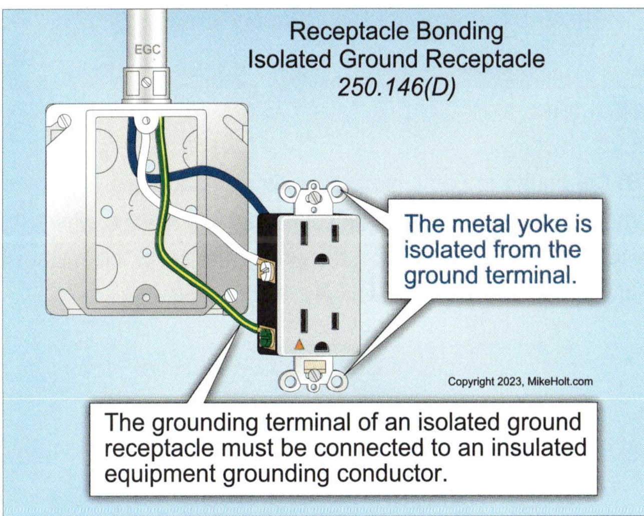
Receptacle Bonding
Isolated Ground Receptacle
250.146(D)
EGC
The metal yoke is isolated from the ground terminal.
Copyright 2023, MikeHolt.com
The grounding terminal of an isolated ground receptacle must be connected to an insulated equipment grounding conductor.

▸Figure 250-255

Author's Comment:

- Type AC cable containing an insulated equipment grounding conductor can be used to supply isolated ground receptacles because the metal armor of the cable is listed as an equipment grounding conductor [250.118(A)(8)]. ▸Figure 250-256

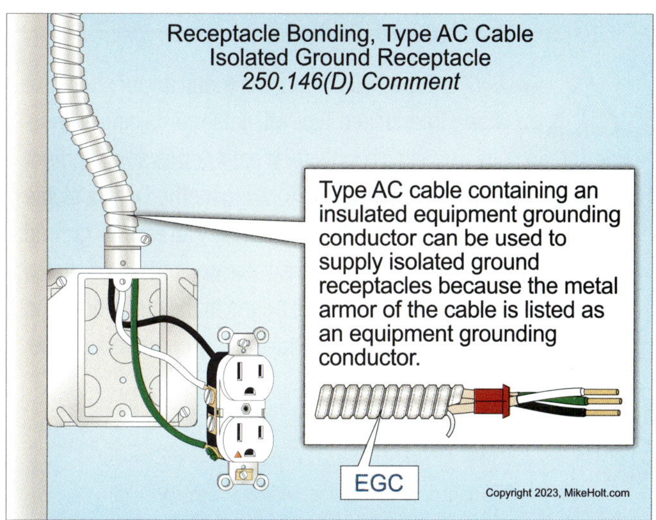
Receptacle Bonding, Type AC Cable
Isolated Ground Receptacle
250.146(D) Comment
Type AC cable containing an insulated equipment grounding conductor can be used to supply isolated ground receptacles because the metal armor of the cable is listed as an equipment grounding conductor.
EGC
Copyright 2023, MikeHolt.com

▸Figure 250-256

- Type MC[AP®] cable with a 10 AWG bare aluminum grounding/bonding conductor can be used to supply isolated ground receptacles because it is listed as an equipment grounding conductor [250.118(A)(10)(b)].
- An interlocked Type MC[AP®] cable is an acceptable wiring method to use for an isolated ground receptacle. ▸Figure 250-257

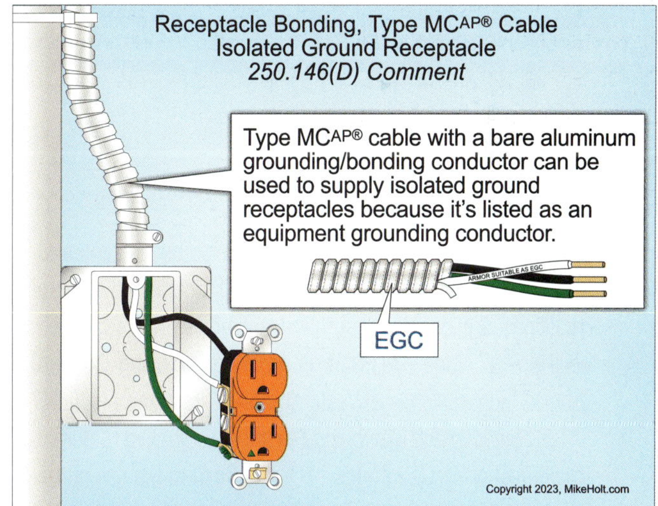
Receptacle Bonding, Type MCAP® Cable
Isolated Ground Receptacle
250.146(D) Comment
Type MCAP® cable with a bare aluminum grounding/bonding conductor can be used to supply isolated ground receptacles because it's listed as an equipment grounding conductor.
EGC
Copyright 2023, MikeHolt.com

▸Figure 250-257

Caution

CAUTION: Type MC Cable. The metal armor sheath of traditional interlocked Type MC cable containing an insulated equipment grounding conductor is not listed as an equipment grounding conductor. Therefore, this wiring method with a single equipment grounding conductor cannot supply an isolated ground receptacle. Type MC cable with two insulated equipment grounding conductors is acceptable since one bonds to the metal box, and the other one connects to the isolated ground receptacle. ▸Figure 250–258

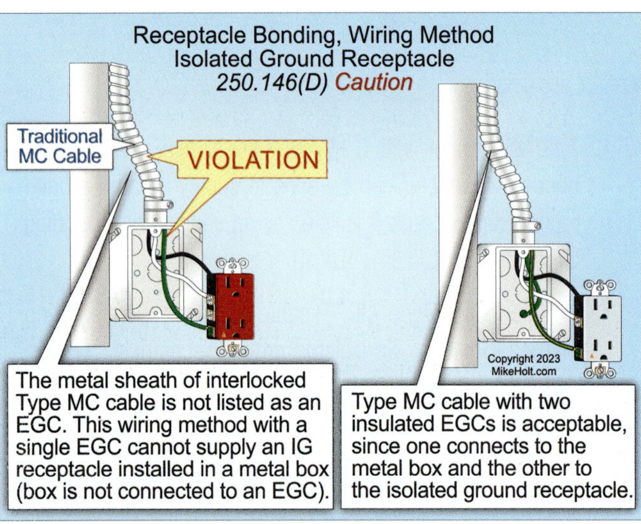
Receptacle Bonding, Wiring Method
Isolated Ground Receptacle
250.146(D) Caution
Traditional MC Cable
VIOLATION
The metal sheath of interlocked Type MC cable is not listed as an EGC. This wiring method with a single EGC cannot supply an IG receptacle installed in a metal box (box is not connected to an EGC).
Type MC cable with two insulated EGCs is acceptable, since one connects to the metal box and the other to the isolated ground receptacle.
Copyright 2023 MikeHolt.com

▸Figure 250–258

Author's Comment:

- When should an isolated ground receptacle be installed and how should the isolated ground system be designed? These questions are design issues and are not answered based on the *NEC* alone [90.2(C)]. In most cases, using isolated ground receptacles is a waste of money. For example, IEEE 1100, *Powering and Grounding Electronic Equipment* (Emerald Book) section 8.5.3.2 states, "The results from the use of the isolated ground method range from no observable effects, the desired effects, or worse noise conditions than when standard equipment bonding configurations are used to serve electronic load equipment."
- Few electrical installations truly require an isolated ground system. For those systems that can benefit from one, engineering opinions differ as to what is a proper design. Making matters worse—of those properly designed, few are correctly installed, and even fewer are properly maintained.

250.148 Continuity and Attachment of Equipment Grounding Conductors in Boxes

If circuit conductors are spliced or terminate to equipment in a box, the equipment grounding conductor must comply with 250.148(A) through (D).

(A) Connections and Splices. Equipment grounding conductors must be connected together in accordance with 110.14(B) and 250.8. ▸Figure 250–259

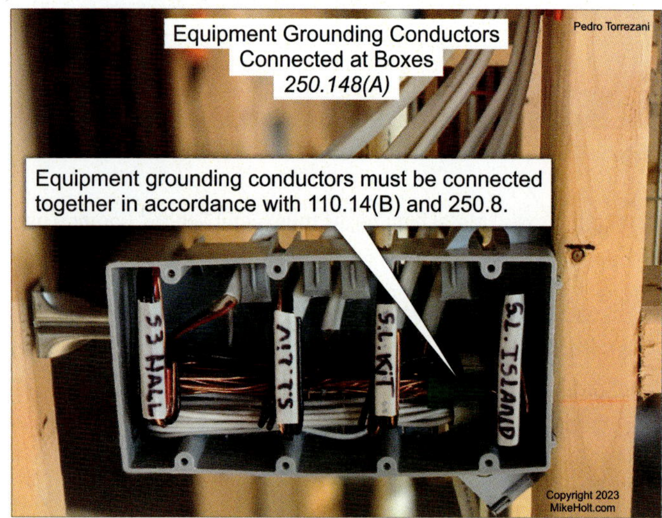
Equipment Grounding Conductors
Connected at Boxes
250.148(A)
Pedro Torrezani
Equipment grounding conductors must be connected together in accordance with 110.14(B) and 250.8.
S3 HALL
S.L.KIT
SL ISLAND
Copyright 2023 MikeHolt.com

▸Figure 250–259

(B) Continuity of Equipment Grounding Conductors. Equipment grounding conductors must be connected in a manner where the disconnection or removal of a receptacle, device, or luminaire will not interrupt its electrical continuity. ▸Figure 250–260

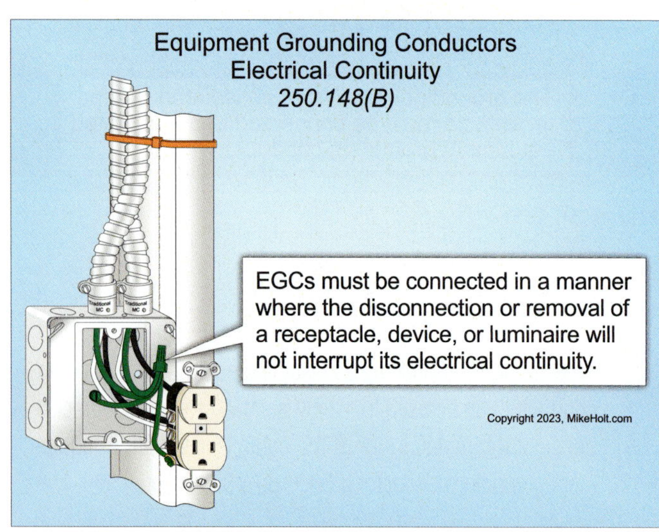
Equipment Grounding Conductors
Electrical Continuity
250.148(B)
EGCs must be connected in a manner where the disconnection or removal of a receptacle, device, or luminaire will not interrupt its electrical continuity.
Copyright 2023, MikeHolt.com

▸Figure 250–260

(C) Metal Boxes. Bonding jumpers and equipment grounding conductors must be connected to the metal box by a device that serves no other purpose. ▶Figure 250–261 and ▶Figure 250–262

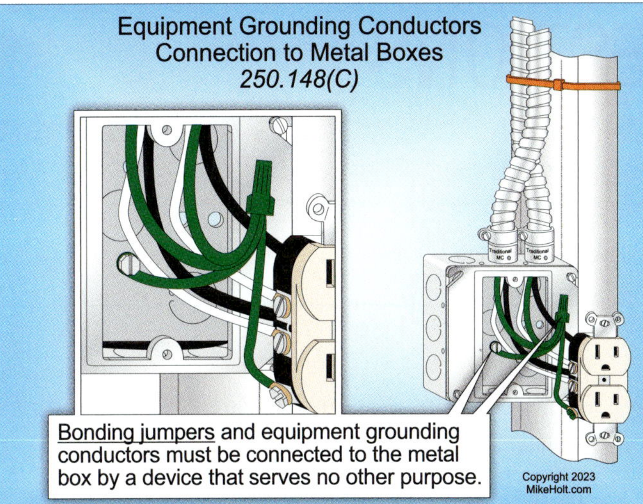
Equipment Grounding Conductors
Connection to Metal Boxes
250.148(C)
Bonding jumpers and equipment grounding conductors must be connected to the metal box by a device that serves no other purpose.
Copyright 2023
MikeHolt.com

▶Figure 250–261

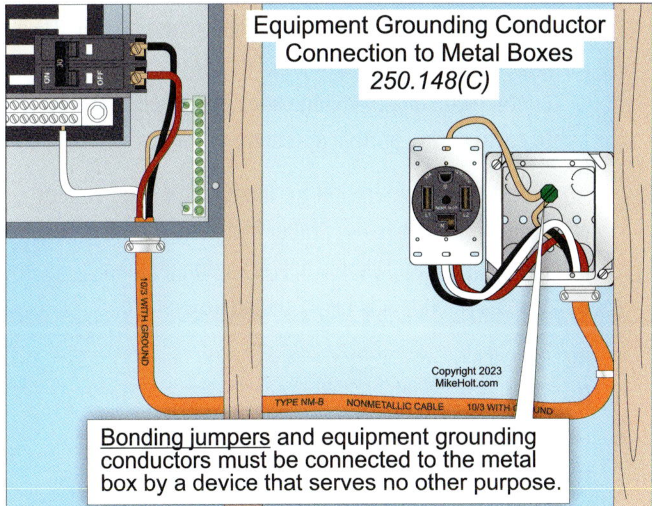
Equipment Grounding Conductor
Connection to Metal Boxes
250.148(C)
10/3 WITH GROUND
TYPE NM-B NONMETALLIC CABLE
Copyright 2023
MikeHolt.com
Bonding jumpers and equipment grounding conductors must be connected to the metal box by a device that serves no other purpose.

▶Figure 250–262

Ex: The circuit equipment grounding conductor for an isolated ground receptacle [250.146(D)] is not required to be bonded to other equipment grounding conductors or metal box. ▶Figure 250–263

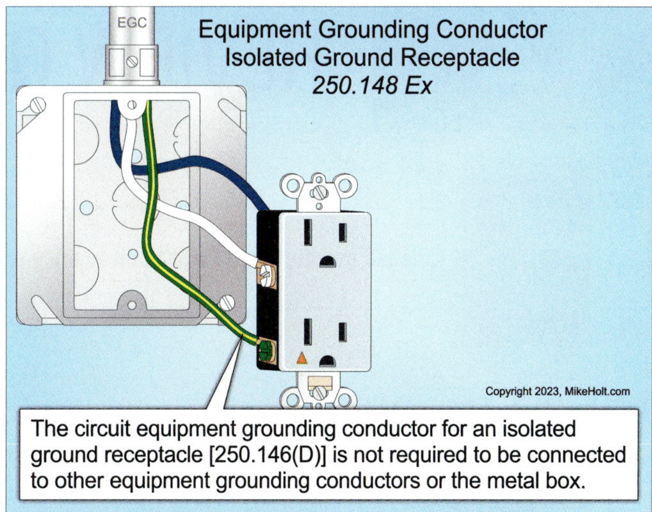
EGC
Equipment Grounding Conductor
Isolated Ground Receptacle
250.148 Ex
Copyright 2023, MikeHolt.com
The circuit equipment grounding conductor for an isolated ground receptacle [250.146(D)] is not required to be connected to other equipment grounding conductors or the metal box.

▶Figure 250–263

(D) Nonmetallic Boxes. One or more equipment grounding conductors brought into a nonmetallic outlet box shall be arranged to provide a connection to any fitting or device in that box requiring connection to an equipment grounding conductor.

CHAPTER
2

REVIEW QUESTIONS

Please use the 2023 *Code* book to answer the following questions.

Article 215—Feeders

1. Each feeder disconnect rated 1,000A or more and installed on solidly grounded wye electrical systems of more than 150V to ground, but not exceeding _____ phase-to-phase, shall be provided with ground-fault protection of equipment in accordance with 230.95.

   (a) 50V
   (b) 150V
   (c) 600V
   (d) 1,000V

2. Where a feeder supplies branch circuits in which equipment grounding conductors are required, the feeder shall include an _____, to which the equipment grounding conductors of the branch circuits shall be connected.

   (a) equipment grounding conductor
   (b) grounding conductor
   (c) bonding conductor
   (d) grounded conductor

Article 250—Grounding and Bonding

1. General requirements for grounding and bonding of electrical installations and the location of grounding connections are within the scope of _____.

   (a) Article 110
   (b) Article 200
   (c) Article 250
   (d) Article 680

2. Grounded electrical systems shall be connected to earth in a manner that will _____.

   (a) limit voltages due to lightning, line surges, or unintentional contact with higher-voltage lines
   (b) stabilize the voltage to earth during normal operation
   (c) facilitate overcurrent device operation in case of ground faults
   (d) limit voltages due to lightning, line surges, or unintentional contact with higher-voltage lines and stabilize the voltage to earth during normal operation

3. An important consideration for limiting imposed voltage on electrical systems is to remember that bonding and grounding electrode conductors should not be any longer than _____ and unnecessary bends and loops should be avoided.

   (a) necessary
   (b) 10 ft
   (c) 25 ft
   (d) 50 ft

4. For grounded systems, normally noncurrent-carrying conductive materials enclosing electrical conductors or equipment shall be connected to earth so as to limit _____ on these materials.

   (a) the voltage to ground
   (b) current
   (c) arcing
   (d) resistance

5. For grounded systems, normally noncurrent-carrying conductive materials enclosing electrical conductors shall be connected together and to the _____ to establish an effective ground-fault current path.

   (a) ground
   (b) earth
   (c) electrical supply source
   (d) enclosure

6. In grounded systems, normally noncurrent-carrying electrically conductive materials that are likely to become energized shall be connected _____ in a manner that establishes an effective ground-fault current path.

   (a) together
   (b) to the electrical supply source
   (c) to the closest grounded conductor
   (d) together and to the electrical supply source

7. For grounded systems, electrical equipment, and other electrically conductive material likely to become energized shall be installed in a manner that creates a _____ from any point on the wiring system where a ground fault occurs to the electrical supply source.

   (a) circuit facilitating the operation of the overcurrent device
   (b) low-impedance circuit
   (c) circuit capable of safely carrying the ground-fault current likely to be imposed on it
   (d) all of these

8. For grounded systems, the earth _____ considered an effective ground-fault current path.

   (a) shall be
   (b) shall not be
   (c) is
   (d) is not

9. The grounding and bonding of electrical systems, circuit conductors, surge arresters, surge-protective devices, and conductive normally noncurrent-carrying metal parts of equipment shall be installed and arranged in a manner that will prevent _____.

   (a) objectionable current
   (b) voltage transients
   (c) neutral to earth voltage
   (d) an arc flash

10. Equipment grounding conductors, grounding electrode conductors, and bonding jumpers shall be connected by _____.

    (a) listed pressure connectors
    (b) terminal bars
    (c) exothermic welding
    (d) any of these

11. Ground clamps and fittings that are exposed to physical damage shall be enclosed in _____ or equivalent protective covering.

    (a) metal or wood
    (b) wood or rubber
    (c) concrete
    (d) metal or plastic

12. _____ on equipment to be grounded shall be removed from contact surfaces to ensure electrical continuity.

    (a) Paint
    (b) Lacquer
    (c) Enamel
    (d) any of these

13. Alternating-current circuits of less than 50V shall be grounded if supplied by a transformer whose supply system exceeds _____.

    (a) 150V to ground
    (b) 300V to ground
    (c) 600V to ground
    (d) 1,000V to ground

14. _____ alternating-current systems operating at 480V shall have ground detectors installed on the system.

    (a) Grounded
    (b) Solidly grounded
    (c) Effectively grounded
    (d) Ungrounded

15. Ungrounded alternating-current systems from 50V to 1,000V or less that are not required to be grounded in accordance with 250.21(B) shall have _____.

    (a) ground detectors installed for ac systems operating at not less than 100V and at 1,000V or less
    (b) the ground detection sensing equipment connected as far as practicable to where the system receives its supply
    (c) ground detectors installed for ac systems operating at not less than 120V and at 1,000V or less, and have the ground detection sensing equipment connected as close as practicable to where the system receives its supply
    (d) ground-fault protection for equipment

16. Ungrounded alternating-current systems from 50V to less than 1,000V shall be legibly marked "CAUTION: UNGROUNDED SYSTEM—OPERATING _____ VOLTS BETWEEN CONDUCTORS" at the _____ of the system, with sufficient durability to withstand the environment involved.

    (a) source
    (b) first disconnecting means
    (c) every junction box
    (d) the source or the first disconnecting means

17. The grounding electrode conductor connection shall be made at any accessible point from the load end of the overhead service conductors, _____ to the terminal or bus to which the grounded service conductor is connected at the service disconnecting means.

    (a) service drop
    (b) underground service conductors
    (c) service lateral
    (d) any of these

18. If the main bonding jumper is a wire or busbar and is installed from the grounded conductor terminal bar to the equipment grounding terminal bar in the service equipment, the _____ is permitted to be connected to the equipment grounding terminal bar to which the main bonding jumper is connected.

    (a) equipment grounding conductor
    (b) grounded service conductor
    (c) grounding electrode conductor
    (d) system bonding jumper

19. A grounded conductor shall not be connected to normally noncurrent-carrying metal parts of equipment, to equipment grounding conductor(s), or be reconnected to ground on the load side of the _____ except as otherwise permitted.

    (a) service disconnecting means
    (b) distribution panel
    (c) switchgear
    (d) switchboard

20. For a grounded system, an unspliced _____ shall be used to connect the equipment grounding conductor(s) and the service disconnect enclosure to the grounded conductor of the system within the enclosure for each service disconnect.

    (a) grounding electrode
    (b) main bonding jumper
    (c) busbar
    (d) insulated copper conductor

21. If an ac system operating at 1,000V or less is grounded at any point, the _____ shall be routed with the ungrounded conductors to each service disconnecting means and shall be connected to each disconnecting means grounded conductor(s) terminal or bus.

    (a) system bonding jumper
    (b) supply-side bonding jumper
    (c) grounded conductor
    (d) equipment grounding conductor

22. The grounded conductor brought to service equipment shall be routed with the phase conductors and shall not be smaller than specified in Table _____ when the service-entrance conductors are 1,100 kcmil copper and smaller.

    (a) 250.102(C)(1)
    (b) 250.122
    (c) 310.16
    (d) 430.52

23. If ungrounded service-entrance conductors are connected in parallel, the size of the grounded conductors in each raceway shall be based on the total circular mil area of the parallel ungrounded service-entrance conductors in the raceway, sized in accordance with 250.24(D)(1), but not smaller than _____.

    (a) 1/0 AWG
    (b) 2/0 AWG
    (c) 3/0 AWG
    (d) 4/0 AWG

24. A grounding electrode conductor, sized in accordance with _____, shall be used to connect the equipment grounding conductors, the service-equipment enclosures, and, if the system is grounded, the grounded service conductor to the grounding electrode(s).

    (a) 250.66
    (b) 250.102(C)(1)
    (c) 250.122
    (d) 310.16

25. A main bonding jumper shall be a _____ or similar suitable conductor.

    (a) wire
    (b) bus
    (c) screw
    (d) any of these

26. If a main bonding jumper is a screw only, the screw shall be identified with a(an) _____ that shall be visible with the screw installed.

(a) silver or white finish
(b) etched ground symbol
(c) hexagonal head
(d) green finish

27. Main bonding jumpers and system bonding jumpers shall not be smaller than specified in _____.

(a) Table 250.102(C)(1)
(b) Table 250.122
(c) Table 310.16
(d) Chapter 9, Table 8

28. Where the supply conductors are larger than 1,100 kcmil copper or 1,750 kcmil aluminum, the main bonding jumper shall have an area that is _____ the area of the largest phase conductor when of the same material.

(a) at least equal to
(b) at least 50 percent of
(c) not less than 12½ percent of
(d) not more than 12½ percent of

29. A grounded conductor shall not be connected to normally noncurrent-carrying metal parts of equipment on the _____ side of the system bonding jumper of a separately derived system except as otherwise permitted.

(a) supply
(b) grounded
(c) high-voltage
(d) load

30. The connection of the system bonding jumper for a separately derived system shall be made _____ on the separately derived system from the source to the first system disconnecting means or overcurrent device.

(a) in at least two locations
(b) in every location that the grounded conductor is present
(c) at any single point
(d) effectively

31. If a building or structure is supplied by a feeder from an outdoor separately derived system, a system bonding jumper at both the source and the first disconnecting means shall be permitted if doing so does not establish a(an) _____ path for the grounded conductor.

(a) series
(b) parallel
(c) conductive
(d) effective

32. A separately derived ac system supply-side bonding jumper shall be installed to the first disconnecting means enclosure, and it is not required to be larger than the _____.

(a) neutral conductor
(b) derived ungrounded conductors
(c) equipment grounding conductor
(d) main service grounding electrode conductor

33. If the source of a separately derived system and the first disconnecting means are located in separate enclosures, a supply-side bonding jumper of the wire type shall comply with 250.102(C), based on _____.

(a) the size of the primary conductors
(b) the size of the secondary overcurrent protection
(c) the size of the derived ungrounded conductors
(d) one-third the size of the primary grounded conductor

34. The building or structure grounding electrode system shall be used as the _____ electrode for the separately derived system.

(a) grounding
(b) bonding
(c) grounded
(d) bonded

35. For a single separately derived system, the grounding electrode conductor connects the grounded conductor of the derived system to the grounding electrode at the same point on the separately derived system where the _____ is connected.

(a) metering equipment
(b) transfer switch
(c) system bonding jumper
(d) largest circuit breaker

36. Grounding electrode conductor taps from a separately derived system to a common grounding electrode conductor are permitted when a building or structure has multiple separately derived systems, provided that the taps terminate at the same point as the _____.

(a) system bonding jumper
(b) main bonding jumper
(c) supply-side bonding jumper
(d) neutral conductor

37. The common grounding electrode conductor installed for multiple separately derived systems shall not be smaller than _____ copper when using a wire-type conductor.

(a) 1/0 AWG
(b) 2/0 AWG
(c) 3/0 AWG
(d) 4/0 AWG

38. The common grounding electrode conductor installed for multiple separately derived systems shall be permitted to be a _____ pipe in accordance with 250.68(C)(1).

(a) metal gas
(b) metal water
(c) PVC water
(d) any of these

39. The common grounding electrode conductor installed for multiple separately derived systems shall be permitted to be the metal structural frame of the building or structure in accordance with 250.68(C)(2) or connected to the grounding electrode system by a conductor not smaller than _____.

(a) 6 AWG copper
(b) 1/0 AWG copper
(c) 3/0 AWG copper or 250 kcmil aluminum
(d) 4/0 AWG aluminum

40. Each tap conductor to a common grounding electrode conductor for multiple separately derived systems shall be sized in accordance with _____, based on the derived ungrounded conductors of the separately derived system it serves.

(a) 250.66
(b) 250.118
(c) 250.122
(d) 310.15

41. Tap connections to a common grounding electrode conductor for multiple separately derived systems may be made to a copper or aluminum busbar that is _____ and of sufficient length to accommodate the number of terminations necessary for the installation.

(a) smaller than ¼ in. thick × 4 in. wide
(b) not smaller than ¼ in. thick × 2 in. wide
(c) not smaller than ½ in. thick × 2 in. wide
(d) not smaller than ¼ in. thick × 2½ in. wide

42. Tap connections to a common grounding electrode conductor for multiple separately derived systems shall be made at an accessible location by _____.

(a) a connector listed as grounding and bonding equipment
(b) listed connections to aluminum or copper busbars
(c) the exothermic welding process
(d) any of these

43. A grounding electrode system and grounding electrode conductor at a building or structure shall not be required if only a _____ supplies the building or structure.

(a) 4-wire service
(b) single or multiwire branch circuit
(c) 3-wire service
(d) any of these

44. An equipment grounding conductor shall be run with the supply conductors and be connected to the building or structure _____ and to the grounding electrode.

(a) rebar
(b) disconnecting means
(c) structural steel
(d) ground rod

45. The size of the grounding electrode conductor for a building or structure supplied by a feeder shall not be smaller than that identified in _____, based on the largest ungrounded supply conductor.

(a) 250.66
(b) 250.102
(c) 250.122
(d) Table 310.16

46. Impedance grounded systems in which a grounding impedance device, typically a resistor, limits the ground-fault current for a 480V up to 1,000V three-phase system are permitted where _____.

(a) the conditions of maintenance and supervision ensure that only qualified persons service the installation
(b) ground detectors are installed on the system
(c) line-to-neutral loads are not served
(d) all of these

47. Concrete-encased electrodes _____ shall not be required to be part of the grounding electrode system if the rebar is not accessible for use without disturbing the concrete.

(a) in hazardous (classified) locations
(b) in health care facilities
(c) of existing buildings or structures
(d) in agricultural buildings with equipotential planes

48. In order for a metal underground water pipe to be used as a grounding electrode, it shall be in direct contact with the earth for _____.

(a) 5 ft
(b) 10 ft or more
(c) less than 10 ft
(d) 20 ft or more

49. One or more metal in-ground support structure(s) in direct contact with the earth vertically for _____ or more, with or without concrete encasement, is permitted to be a grounding electrode in accordance with 250.52.

(a) 4 ft
(b) 6 ft
(c) 8 ft
(d) 10 ft

50. The minimum length of a 4 AWG concrete-encased electrode is at least _____.

(a) 10 ft
(b) 20 ft
(c) 25 ft
(d) 50 ft

51. Rebar in multiple pieces used as a concrete-encased electrode shall be connected together by _____ tie wires or other effective means.

(a) steel
(b) plastic
(c) aluminum
(d) fiber glass

52. An electrode encased by at least 2 in. of concrete, located horizontally near the bottom or vertically and within that portion of a concrete foundation or footing that is in direct contact with the earth, is permitted as a grounding electrode when it consists of a bare copper conductor not smaller than _____.

(a) 8 AWG
(b) 6 AWG
(c) 4 AWG
(d) 1/0 AWG

53. If multiple concrete-encased electrodes are present at a building or structure, it shall be permissible to bond only _____ into the grounding electrode system.

(a) one
(b) two
(c) three
(d) four

54. Concrete-encased grounding electrodes that are installed where the concrete is installed with _____ is not considered to be in direct contact with the earth.

(a) insulation
(b) vapor barriers
(c) films
(d) any of these

55. A ground ring encircling the building or structure can be used as a grounding electrode when the _____.

(a) ring is in direct contact with the earth
(b) ring consists of at least 20 ft of bare copper conductor
(c) bare copper conductor is not smaller than 2 AWG
(d) all of these

56. Rod and pipe grounding electrodes shall not be less than _____ in length.

(a) 6 ft
(b) 8 ft
(c) 10 ft
(d) 20 ft

57. Grounding electrodes of the rod type less than _____ in diameter shall be listed.

(a) ½ in.
(b) ⅝ in.
(c) ¾ in.
(d) 1 in.

58. A buried iron or steel plate used as a grounding electrode shall expose not less than _____ of surface area to exterior soil.

(a) 2 sq ft
(b) 4 sq ft
(c) 9 sq ft
(d) 10 sq ft

59. Grounding electrodes of bare or electrically conductive coated iron or steel plates shall be at least _____ thick.

(a) ⅛ in.
(b) ¼ in.
(c) ½ in.
(d) ¾ in.

60. Metal underground systems or structures such as piping systems, underground tanks, and underground metal well casings that are not bonded to a metal _____ are permitted as grounding electrodes.

(a) gas pipe
(b) fire-sprinkler pipe
(c) water pipe
(d) none of these

61. _____ shall not be used as a grounding electrode(s).

(a) Metal underground gas piping systems
(b) Aluminum
(c) Swimming pool structures and structural rebar
(d) all of these

62. _____ electrodes shall be free from nonconductive coatings such as paint or enamel.

(a) Rod
(b) Pipe
(c) Plate
(d) all of these

63. If practicable, rod, pipe, and plate electrodes shall be embedded _____.

(a) directly below the electrical meter
(b) on the north side of the building
(c) below permanent moisture level
(d) all of these

64. The grounding electrode conductor to a ground rod that serves as a supplemental electrode for the metal water pipe electrode is not required to be larger than _____ copper wire.

(a) 8 AWG
(b) 6 AWG
(c) 4 AWG
(d) 3 AWG

65. Where the resistance-to-ground of 25Ω or less is not achieved for a single rod electrode, _____.

(a) other means besides electrodes shall be used in order to provide grounding
(b) the single rod electrode shall be supplemented by one additional electrode
(c) additional electrodes shall be added until 25Ω is achieved
(d) any of these

66. If multiple rod, pipe, or plate electrodes are installed to supplement the water pipe electrode, they shall not be less than _____ apart.

(a) 3 ft
(b) 4 ft
(c) 5 ft
(d) 6 ft

67. A rod or pipe electrode shall be installed such that at least _____ of length is in contact with the soil.

(a) 30 in.
(b) 6 ft
(c) 8 ft
(d) 10 ft

68. Where rock bottom is encountered, a rod or pipe electrode shall be driven at an angle not to exceed _____ from the vertical.

(a) 15 degrees
(b) 30 degrees
(c) 45 degrees
(d) 60 degrees

69. The upper end of the rod electrode shall be _____ ground level unless the aboveground end and the grounding electrode conductor attachment are protected against physical damage as specified in 250.10.

(a) no more than 1 in. above
(b) no more than 2 in. above
(c) no more than 3 in. above
(d) flush with or below ground level

70. Plate electrodes shall be installed not less than _____ below the surface of the earth.

(a) 30 in.
(b) 4 ft
(c) 5 ft
(d) 6 ft

71. Where bonding jumper(s) are used to connect the grounding electrodes together to form the grounding electrode system, _____ is not permitted to be used as a conductor to interconnect the electrodes.

(a) rebar
(b) structural steel
(c) a grounding plate
(d) none of these

72. Where a metal underground water pipe is used as a grounding electrode, the continuity of the grounding path or the bonding connection to interior piping shall not rely on _____ and similar equipment.

(a) bonding jumpers
(b) water meters or filtering devices
(c) grounding clamps
(d) all of these

73. If the supplemental electrode is a rod, pipe, or plate electrode, that portion of the bonding jumper that is the sole connection to the supplemental grounding electrode is not required to be larger than _____ copper.

(a) 8 AWG
(b) 6 AWG
(c) 4 AWG
(d) 1 AWG

74. When a ground ring is used as a grounding electrode, it shall be installed at a depth below the earth's surface of not less than _____.

(a) 18 in.
(b) 24 in.
(c) 30 in.
(d) 8 ft

75. When installing _____ electrodes, the earth shall not be used as an effective ground-fault current path.

(a) auxiliary
(b) supplemental
(c) oversized
(d) aluminum

76. Bare or covered aluminum or copper-clad aluminum grounding electrode conductors without an extruded polymeric covering shall not be installed where subject to corrosive conditions or be installed in direct contact with _____.

(a) concrete
(b) bare copper conductors
(c) wooden framing members
(d) all of these

77. Aluminum or copper-clad aluminum grounding electrode conductors external to buildings or equipment enclosures shall not terminate within _____ of the earth.

(a) 12 in.
(b) 18 in.
(c) 20 in.
(d) 24 in.

78. If _____, a grounding electrode conductor or its enclosure shall be securely fastened to the surface on which it is carried.

(a) concealed
(b) exposed
(c) accessible
(d) none of these

79. Grounding electrode conductors _____ and larger that are not exposed to physical damage can be run along the surface of the building construction without metal covering or protection.

(a) 10 AWG
(b) 8 AWG
(c) 6 AWG
(d) 4 AWG

80. A(An) _____ or larger grounding electrode conductor exposed to physical damage shall be protected in rigid metal conduit, IMC, Schedule 80 PVC conduit, reinforced thermosetting resin conduit Type XW (RTRC-XW), EMT, or cable armor.

(a) 10 AWG
(b) 8 AWG
(c) 6 AWG
(d) 4 AWG

81. Grounding electrode conductors smaller than _____ shall be protected in rigid metal conduit, IMC, PVC conduit, electrical metallic tubing, or cable armor.

(a) 10 AWG
(b) 8 AWG
(c) 6 AWG
(d) 4 AWG

82. Grounding electrode conductors in contact with _____ shall not be required to comply with 300.5 but shall be protected if subject to physical damage.

(a) water
(b) the earth
(c) metal
(d) all of these

83. Grounding electrode conductors shall be installed in one continuous length without a splice or joint, unless spliced by _____.

(a) connecting together sections of a busbar
(b) irreversible compression-type connectors listed as grounding and bonding equipment
(c) the exothermic welding process
(d) any of these

84. The common grounding electrode conductor shall be sized in accordance with 250.66, based on the sum of the circular mil area of the _____ ungrounded conductor(s) of each set of conductors that supplies the disconnecting means.

(a) smallest
(b) largest
(c) color of the
(d) material of the

85. Ferrous metal raceways for grounding electrode conductors shall be _____ continuous from the point of attachment to cabinets or equipment to the grounding electrode.

(a) electrically
(b) physically
(c) mechanically
(d) integrally

86. Ferrous metal raceways for grounding electrode conductors shall be bonded at each end of the raceway or enclosure to the grounding electrode or grounding electrode conductor to create a(an) _____ parallel path.

(a) mechanically
(b) electrically
(c) physically
(d) effective

87. The grounding electrode conductor is permitted to be run to any _____ available in the grounding electrode system.

(a) panelboards
(b) bonding jumper
(c) switchgear
(d) convenient grounding electrode

88. Grounding electrode conductors shall not be installed through a ventilation opening of a(an) _____.

(a) enclosure
(b) cabinet
(c) motor control center
(d) environmental air system

89. A metal water pipe grounding electrode conductor sized at _____ is required for a 400A service supplied with 500 kcmil conductors.

(a) 1 AWG
(b) 1/0 AWG
(c) 2/0 AWG
(d) 3/0 AWG

90. The minimum grounding electrode conductor to a rod, pipe, or plate electrode for a 30A service with 10 AWG conductors is _____.

(a) 8 AWG
(b) 6 AWG
(c) 1/0 AWG
(d) 4/0 AWG

91. A metal water pipe grounding electrode conductor sized at _____ is required for a service supplied with 350 kcmil conductors.

    (a) 6 AWG
    (b) 3 AWG
    (c) 2 AWG
    (d) 1/0 AWG

92. A(An) _____ is the smallest size grounding electrode conductor permitted for a solidly grounded ac system.

    (a) 8 AWG
    (b) 6 AWG
    (c) 1/0 AWG
    (d) 4/0 AWG

93. A service consisting of 12 AWG service-entrance conductors requires a grounding electrode conductor sized no less than _____.

    (a) 10 AWG
    (b) 8 AWG
    (c) 6 AWG
    (d) 4 AWG

94. The largest size copper grounding electrode conductor required based on Table 250.66 is _____.

    (a) 6 AWG
    (b) 1/0 AWG
    (c) 3/0 AWG
    (d) 250 kcmil

95. A grounding electrode conductor sized at _____ is required for a service supplied with 400 kcmil parallel conductors in three raceways.

    (a) 1 AWG
    (b) 1/0 AWG
    (c) 2/0 AWG
    (d) 3/0 AWG

96. A grounding electrode conductor sized at _____ is required for a service supplied with 250 kcmil conductors paralleled in two raceways.

    (a) 1 AWG
    (b) 1/0 AWG
    (c) 2/0 AWG
    (d) 3/0 AWG

97. The largest sized grounding electrode conductor to a rod, pipe, or plate electrode required for a 400A service with 500 kcmil conductors is _____.

    (a) 8 AWG
    (b) 6 AWG
    (c) 1/0 AWG
    (d) 4/0 AWG aluminum

98. If the grounding electrode conductor to a ground rod does not extend on to other types of electrodes, the grounding electrode conductor shall not be required to be larger than _____ copper wire.

    (a) 10 AWG
    (b) 8 AWG
    (c) 6 AWG
    (d) 4 AWG

99. If the grounding electrode conductor to a concrete-encased electrode does not extend on to other types of electrodes, the grounding electrode conductor shall not be required to be larger than _____ copper wire.

    (a) 10 AWG
    (b) 8 AWG
    (c) 6 AWG
    (d) 4 AWG

100. All mechanical elements used to terminate a grounding electrode conductor or bonding jumper to a grounding electrode shall be _____.

    (a) accessible
    (b) concealed
    (c) exposed
    (d) protected

101. An encased or buried grounding electrode conductor or bonding jumper connection to a concrete-encased, driven, or buried grounding electrode shall not be required to be _____.

    (a) readily accessible
    (b) accessible
    (c) available
    (d) any of these

102. When an underground metal _____ piping system is used as a grounding electrode, bonding shall be provided around insulated joints and around any equipment that is likely to be disconnected for repairs or replacement.

(a) water
(b) gas
(c) fire-sprinkled
(d) none of these

103. Interior metal water piping that is electrically continuous with a metal underground water pipe electrode and is located not more than _____ from the point of entrance to the building, as measured along the water piping, is permitted to extend the connection to an electrode(s).

(a) 2 ft
(b) 3 ft
(c) 4 ft
(d) 5 ft

104. The metal structural frame of a building is permitted to be used as a conductor to _____ electrodes that are part of the grounding electrode system, or as a grounding electrode conductor.

(a) interconnect
(b) identify
(c) separate
(d) none of these

105. A rebar-type concrete-encased electrode with an additional rebar section extended from its location within the concrete foundation or footing to an accessible location that is not subject to _____ is permitted for connection of grounding electrode conductors.

(a) physical damage
(b) moisture
(c) corrosion
(d) any of these

106. Not more than _____ grounding or bonding conductor shall be connected to the grounding electrode by a single clamp or fitting unless the clamp or fitting is listed for multiple conductors.

(a) one
(b) two
(c) three
(d) four

107. The grounding conductor connection to the grounding electrode shall be made by _____.

(a) listed lugs
(b) exothermic welding
(c) listed pressure connectors
(d) any of these

108. Listed ground clamps that are identified for _____ are also suitable for concrete encasement.

(a) wet locations
(b) outdoor use
(c) direct burial
(d) corrosive environments

109. Metal enclosures and raceways containing _____ conductors shall be connected to the grounded system conductor if the electrical system is grounded.

(a) service
(b) feeder
(c) branch-circuit
(d) outside feeder or branch-circuit

110. Metal components that are installed in a run of an underground nonmetallic raceway(s) and are isolated from possible contact by a minimum cover of _____ to all parts of the metal components shall not be required to be connected to the grounded conductor, supply-side bonding jumper, or grounding electrode conductor.

(a) 12 in.
(b) 18 in.
(c) 24 in.
(d) 30 in.

111. Metal enclosures and raceways for other than service conductors shall be connected to the _____ conductor.

(a) neutral
(b) equipment grounding
(c) ungrounded
(d) grounded

112. Short sections of metal enclosures or raceways used to provide support or protection of _____ from physical damage shall not be required to be connected to the equipment grounding conductor.

(a) conduit
(b) feeders under 600V
(c) cable assemblies
(d) grounding electrode conductors

113. The normally noncurrent-carrying metal parts of service equipment, such as service _____, shall be bonded together.

(a) raceways or service cable armor
(b) equipment enclosures containing service conductors, including meter fittings, boxes, or the like, interposed in the service raceway or armor
(c) cable trays
(d) all of these

114. Bonding jumpers for service raceways shall be used around impaired connections such as _____.

(a) oversized concentric knockouts
(b) oversized eccentric knockouts
(c) reducing washers
(d) any of these

115. Electrical continuity at service equipment, service raceways, and service conductor enclosures shall be ensured by _____.

(a) bonding equipment to the grounded service conductor
(b) connections made up wrenchtight utilizing threaded couplings
(c) other listed bonding devices, such as bonding-type locknuts, bushings, or bushings with bonding jumpers
(d) any of these

116. Connections of wrenchtight threaded couplings, threaded entries, or listed threaded hubs are considered to be effectively _____ to the service metal enclosure.

(a) attached
(b) bonded
(c) grounded
(d) secured

117. Service metal raceways and metal-clad cables are considered effectively bonded when using threadless couplings and connectors that are _____.

(a) nonmetallic
(b) made up tight
(c) sealed
(d) classified

118. A means external to enclosures for connecting intersystem _____ conductors shall be provided at the service equipment or metering equipment enclosure and disconnecting means of buildings or structures supplied by a feeder or branch circuit.

(a) bonding
(b) ungrounded
(c) secondary
(d) bonding and ungrounded

119. In accordance with 250.94(A), the intersystem bonding termination device shall _____.

(a) be accessible for connection and inspection
(b) consist of a set of terminals with the capacity for connection of not less than three intersystem bonding conductors
(c) not interfere with opening the enclosure for a service, building/structure disconnecting means, or metering equipment
(d) all of these

120. In accordance with 250.94(A), the intersystem bonding termination device shall _____.

(a) be securely mounted and electrically connected to service equipment, the meter enclosure, or exposed nonflexible metallic service raceway, or be mounted at one of these enclosures and be connected to the enclosure or grounding electrode conductor with a minimum 6 AWG copper conductor
(b) be securely mounted to the building/structure disconnecting means, or be mounted at the disconnecting means and be connected to the metallic enclosure or grounding electrode conductor with a minimum 6 AWG copper conductor
(c) have terminals that are listed as grounding and bonding equipment
(d) all of these

121. At existing buildings or structures, an intersystem bonding termination is not required if other acceptable means of bonding exists. An external accessible means for bonding communications systems together can be by the use of a(an) _____.

(a) nonflexible metal raceway
(b) exposed grounding electrode conductor
(c) connection to a grounded raceway or equipment approved by the authority having jurisdiction
(d) any of these

122. Expansion, expansion-deflection, or deflection fittings and telescoping sections of metal raceways shall be made _____ continuous by equipment bonding jumpers or other means.

(a) physically
(b) mechanically
(c) electrically
(d) directly

123. The minimum size supply-side bonding jumper for a service raceway containing 4/0 AWG aluminum conductors is _____.

(a) 6 AWG aluminum
(b) 4 AWG aluminum
(c) 4 AWG copper
(d) 3 AWG copper

124. Where ungrounded supply conductors are paralleled in two or more raceways, the bonding jumper for each raceway shall be based on the size of the _____ in each raceway.

(a) overcurrent protection for conductors
(b) grounded conductors
(c) largest ungrounded supply conductors
(d) sum of all conductors

125. If service conductors are connected in parallel in three separate metal raceways, with 600 kcmil conductors per phase, the supply-side bonding jumper size for each service raceway is _____.

(a) 1/0 AWG
(b) 3/0 AWG
(c) 250 kcmil
(d) 500 kcmil

126. The minimum size copper equipment bonding jumper for a 40A-rated circuit is _____.

(a) 14 AWG
(b) 12 AWG
(c) 10 AWG
(d) 8 AWG

127. An equipment bonding jumper can be installed on the outside of a raceway, provided the length of the equipment bonding jumper is not more than _____ long and the equipment bonding jumper is routed with the raceway.

(a) 3 ft
(b) 4 ft
(c) 5 ft
(d) 6 ft

128. Metal water piping systems shall be bonded to the _____, or to one or more grounding electrodes used if the grounding electrode conductor or bonding jumper to the grounding electrode is of sufficient size.

(a) grounded conductor at the service
(b) service equipment enclosure
(c) grounding electrode conductor if of sufficient size
(d) any of these

129. Bonding jumper(s) for the metal water piping systems shall not be required to be larger than _____ copper.

(a) 1/0 AWG
(b) 2/0 AWG
(c) 3/0 AWG
(d) 4/0 AWG

130. The metal water piping system(s) installed in or attached to a building or structure [250.104(A)(3)] shall be bonded to _____.

(a) the building or structure disconnecting means enclosure where located at the building or structure
(b) the equipment grounding conductor run with the supply conductors
(c) one or more grounding electrodes
(d) any of these

131. The bonding jumper(s) required for the metal water piping system(s) installed in or attached to a building or structure supplied by a feeder(s) or branch circuit(s) shall be sized in accordance with _____.

(a) 250.66
(b) 250.102(D)
(c) 250.122
(d) 310.16

132. If installed _____ a building or structure, a metal piping system that is likely to become energized shall be bonded.

(a) in
(b) on
(c) under
(d) in or on

133. The building structural steel bonding jumper size for a 400A service supplied with 500 kcmil conductors is _____.

(a) 6 AWG
(b) 3 AWG
(c) 2 AWG
(d) 1/0 AWG

134. Exposed structural metal that is interconnected to form a metal building frame, not intentionally grounded or bonded, and is likely to become energized shall be bonded to the_____.

(a) service equipment enclosure
(b) grounded conductor at the service
(c) disconnecting means for buildings or structures supplied by a feeder or branch circuit
(d) any of these

135. A transformer supplies power to a 100A panelboard with 2 AWG THWN-2 conductors. The size of the bonding jumper in copper required to bond the building steel to the secondary grounded conductor is _____.

(a) 8 AWG
(b) 6 AWG
(c) 4 AWG
(d) 2 AWG

136. A transformer supplies power to a 200A panelboard with 2 AWG THWN-2 conductors. The size of the bonding jumper in copper required to bond the building steel to the secondary grounded conductor is _____.

(a) 8 AWG
(b) 6 AWG
(c) 4 AWG
(d) 2 AWG

137. A separate bonding jumper to the building structural metal shall not be required if the metal in-ground support structure is used as a grounding electrode or the metal frame of a building or structure is used as the _____ for the separately derived system.

(a) bonding jumper
(b) ground-fault current path
(c) grounding electrode or grounding electrode conductor
(d) lightning protection

138. Lightning protection system ground terminals _____ bonded to the building or structure grounding electrode system.

(a) shall be
(b) shall not be
(c) shall be permitted to be
(d) shall be effectively

139. Metal enclosures shall be permitted to be used to connect bonding jumpers or _____ conductors, or both, together to become a part of an effective ground-fault current path.

(a) grounded
(b) neutral
(c) equipment grounding
(d) grounded phase

140. Exposed, normally noncurrent-carrying metal parts of cord-and-plug-connected equipment shall be connected to the equipment grounding conductor if operated at over _____ to ground.

(a) 24V
(b) 50V
(c) 120V
(d) 150V

141. An equipment grounding conductor of the wire type is required in _____.

(a) rigid metal conduit
(b) intermediate metal conduit
(c) electrical metallic tubing
(d) none of these

142. Flexible metal conduit used as an EGC where flexibility for movement of equipment is required after installation shall _____.

(a) be provided with a wire type equipment grounding conductor or bonding jumper
(b) not require a wire-type EGC if less than 6 ft
(c) not require a wire-type EGC if protected by 20A or less
(d) none of these

143. FMC can be used as the equipment grounding conductor if the length in any ground return path does not exceed 6 ft and the circuit conductors contained in the conduit are protected by overcurrent devices rated at _____ or less.

(a) 15A
(b) 20A
(c) 30A
(d) 60A

144. LFMC is acceptable as an equipment grounding conductor when it terminates in _____ and is protected by an overcurrent device rated 20A or less for trade sizes ⅜ through ½.

(a) labeled fittings
(b) identified fittings
(c) approved fittings
(d) listed fittings

145. The _____ of Type AC cable is recognized as an equipment grounding conductor.

(a) armor
(b) cover
(c) sheath
(d) any of these

146. Type MC cable is recognized as an equipment grounding conductor when _____.

(a) it contains an insulated or uninsulated equipment grounding conductor in compliance with 250.118(1)
(b) the cable assembly contains a bare copper conductor
(c) it is only hospital grade Type MC cable
(d) it is terminated with bonding bushings

147. A wire-type equipment grounding conductor can be identified by _____.

(a) a continuous outer finish that is green
(b) being bare
(c) a continuous outer finish that is green with one or more yellow stripes
(d) any of these

148. An insulated or covered conductor _____ and larger is permitted, at the time of installation, to be permanently identified as an equipment grounding conductor at each end and at every point where the conductor is accessible.

(a) 8 AWG
(b) 6 AWG
(c) 4 AWG
(d) 1/0 AWG

149. One or more insulated conductors in a multiconductor cable, at the time of installation, shall be permitted to be permanently identified as equipment grounding conductors at each end and at every point where the conductors are accessible by coloring the insulation _____.

(a) green
(b) grey
(c) green with a yellow stripe
(d) white or silver

150. Unless part of an applicable cable wiring method, bare or covered conductors shall not be installed if subject to _____ conditions or be installed in direct contact with concrete, masonry, or the earth.

(a) corrosive
(b) wet
(c) damp
(d) dry

151. Equipment grounding conductors are not required to be _____ than the circuit conductors.

(a) larger
(b) smaller
(c) less
(d) none of these

152. If the ungrounded conductors are increased in size for any reason other than as required in 310.15(B) or 310.15(C), wire-type equipment grounding conductors shall be increased in size proportionately to the increase in _____ of the ungrounded conductors.

(a) ampacity
(b) circular mil area
(c) diameter
(d) temperature rating

153. When a single equipment grounding conductor is used for multiple circuits in the same raceway, cable, or cable tray, the single equipment grounding conductor shall be sized according to the _____.

(a) combined rating of all the overcurrent devices
(b) largest overcurrent device protecting the circuit conductors
(c) combined rating of all the loads
(d) any of these

154. Equipment grounding conductors for motor branch circuits shall be sized in accordance with Table 250.122(A), based on the rating of the _____ device.

(a) motor overload
(b) motor over-temperature
(c) branch-circuit short-circuit and ground-fault protective
(d) feeder overcurrent protection

155. If circuit conductors are connected in parallel in the same raceway, a single wire-type conductor shall be permitted as the equipment grounding conductor and shall be sized in accordance with 250.122 based on the _____ for the feeder or branch circuit.

(a) fuse
(b) circuit breaker
(c) overcurrent protective device
(d) any of these

156. If conductors are installed in multiple raceways and are connected in _____, a wire-type equipment grounding conductor, if used, shall be installed in each raceway and shall be connected in parallel. The equipment grounding conductor installed in each raceway shall be sized in accordance with 250.122 based on the rating of the overcurrent protective device for the feeder or branch circuit.

(a) parallel
(b) series
(c) combination
(d) none of these

157. Except as provided in 250.122(F)(2)(c) for raceway or cable tray installations, the equipment grounding conductor in each multiconductor cable shall be sized in accordance with 250.122 based on the _____.

(a) largest circuit conductor
(b) overcurrent protective device for the feeder or branch circuit
(c) smallest branch-circuit conductor
(d) overcurrent protective device for the service

158. Equipment grounding conductors for feeder taps are not required to be _____ than the tap conductors.

(a) larger
(b) smaller
(c) less
(d) none of these

159. In accordance with 250.134, non-current-carrying metal parts of fastened in place equipment, raceways, and other enclosures, shall be connected to an _____.

(a) grounded conductor
(b) equipment grounding conductor
(c) ungrounded conductor
(d) none of these

160. Metal parts of cord-and-plug-connected equipment, shall be connected to an _____ run with the power supply conductors in a cable assembly or flexible cord properly terminated in a grounding-type attachment plug with one fixed grounding contact.

(a) grounded conductor
(b) equipment grounding conductor
(c) ungrounded conductor
(d) none of these

161. Frames of electric ranges, wall-mounted ovens, counter-mounted cooking units, _____, and outlet or junction boxes that are part of the circuit shall be connected to the equipment grounding conductor in accordance with 250.140(A) or the grounded conductor in accordance with 250.140(B).

(a) washing machines
(b) dishwashers
(c) microwaves
(d) clothes dryers

162. The circuit supplying _____ shall include an equipment grounding conductor. The frame of the appliance shall be connected to the equipment grounding conductor in the manner specified by 250.134 or 250.138.

(a) electric ranges or clothes dryers
(b) electric wall mounted ovens
(c) electric counter-mounted cooking units
(d) any of these

163. A(An) _____ shall be used to connect the grounding terminal of a grounding-type receptacle to a metal box that is connected to an equipment grounding conductor.

(a) equipment bonding jumper
(b) grounded conductor jumper
(c) equipment bonding jumper or grounded conductor jumper
(d) equipment bonding jumper and grounded conductor jumper

164. Where the metal box for a receptacle is surface mounted, direct metal-to-metal contact between the device yoke and the box shall be permitted to ground the receptacle to the box if at least _____ of the insulating washers of the receptacle is (are) removed.

(a) one
(b) two
(c) three
(d) four

165. A listed exposed work cover can be the grounding and bonding means for a surface-mounted metal box when the device is attached to the cover with at least _____ permanent fastener(s) and the exposed work cover mounting holes are located on a non-raised portion of the cover.

(a) one
(b) two
(c) three
(d) four

166. Receptacle yokes or contact devices designed and _____ as self-grounding can, in conjunction with the supporting screws, establish the equipment bonding between the device yoke and a flush-type box.

(a) approved
(b) advertised
(c) listed
(d) installed

167. The receptacle grounding terminal of an isolated ground receptacle shall be connected to a(an) _____ equipment grounding conductor run with the circuit conductors.

(a) insulated
(b) covered
(c) bare
(d) solid

168. All _____ that are spliced or terminated within the box shall be connected together. Connections and splices shall be made in accordance with 110.14(B) and 250.8 except that insulation shall not be required.

(a) neutral conductors
(b) equipment grounding conductors
(c) phase conductors
(d) switch-legs

169. The arrangement of grounding connections shall ensure that the disconnection or the removal of a luminaire, receptacle, or other device fed from the box does not interrupt the electrical continuity of the _____ conductor(s) providing an effective ground-fault current path.

(a) grounded
(b) ungrounded
(c) equipment grounding
(d) all of these

170. For the continuity of equipment grounding conductors and attachment in boxes, a connection used for _____ shall be made between the metal box and the equipment grounding conductor(s).

(a) bonding
(b) connections and splices
(c) extending the length of the circuit
(d) no other purpose

171. A connection used for no other purpose shall be made between the metal box and the equipment grounding conductor(s). The equipment bonding jumper or equipment grounding conductor shall be sized from Table 250.122 based on the largest _____ conductors in the box.

(a) overcurrent device protecting circuit
(b) ungrounded
(c) grounded
(d) neutral

172. One or more equipment grounding conductors brought into a nonmetallic outlet box shall be arranged to provide a connection to _____ in that box requiring connection to an equipment grounding conductor.

(a) any fitting or device
(b) a ground clip
(c) a clamp(s)
(d) the grounded conductor

CHAPTER

3 WIRING METHODS AND MATERIALS

Introduction to Chapter 3—Wiring Methods and Materials

Chapter 3 of the *Code* is divided into fifty-one articles containing the general rules for wiring and sizing circuits, overcurrent protection of conductors, overvoltage protection of equipment, and bonding and grounding. The rules in this chapter apply to all electrical installations covered by the *NEC*—except as modified in Chapters 5, 6, 7, or specifically referenced in Chapter 8 [90.3].

This chapter can be thought of as the rough in phase of a job because it is primarily focused on the wiring methods and materials used to rough out an installation. Every article in this chapter deals with a different method or material used to get wiring from point “A” to point “B” in a system. The Chapter 3 articles covered by this material are:

Wiring Method Articles

- **Article 300—General Requirements for Wiring Methods and Materials.** Article 300 contains the general requirements for all wiring methods included in the *Code*, except for Class 2 power-limited, fire alarm and coaxial cables, which are covered in Chapters 7 and 8.
- **Article 314—Outlet, Device, Pull, and Junction Boxes; Conduit Bodies; Fittings; and Handhole Enclosures.** Installation requirements for outlet boxes, pull and junction boxes, as well as conduit bodies and handhole enclosures are contained in this article.

Cable Articles

Articles 320 through 340 address specific types of cables. If you take the time to become familiar with the various types of cables, you will be able to:

- Understand what is available for doing the work.
- Recognize cable types having special *NEC* requirements.
- Avoid buying cable you cannot install due to *Code* requirements you cannot meet with that wiring method.

Here is a brief overview of the cable articles covered in this material:

- **Article 320—Armored Cable (Type AC).** Armored cable is an assembly of insulated conductors, 14 AWG through 1 AWG, individually wrapped with waxed paper. The conductors are contained within a flexible metal (steel or aluminum) spiral sheath that interlocks at the edges. Armored cable looks like flexible metal conduit. Many electricians call this metal cable “BX®.”

• • •

- **Article 330—Metal-Clad Cable (Type MC).** Metal-clad cable encloses insulated conductors in a metal sheath of corrugated, smooth copper or aluminum tubing, or spiral interlocked steel or aluminum. The physical characteristics of Type MC cable make it a versatile wiring method permitted in almost any location and for almost any application. The most used Type MC cable is the interlocking kind, which looks like armored cable or flexible metal conduit.
- **Article 334—Nonmetallic-Sheathed Cable (Type NM).** Nonmetallic-sheathed cable is commonly referred to by its trade name "Romex®." It encloses two, three, or four insulated conductors, 14 AWG through 2 AWG, within a nonmetallic outer jacket. Because this cable is manufactured in this manner, it contains a separate (usually bare) equipment grounding conductor. Nonmetallic-sheathed cable is commonly used for residential wiring applications but may sometimes be permitted for use in commercial occupancies.
- **Article 340—Underground Feeder and Branch-Circuit Cable (Type UF).** Underground feeder cable is a moisture-, fungus-, and corrosion-resistant cable suitable for direct burial in the Earth and is available in sizes 14 AWG through 4/0 AWG [340.104]. Multiconductor UF cable is covered in molded plastic that surrounds the insulated conductors.

Raceway Articles

Articles 342 through 390 address specific types of raceways. Refer to Article 100 for the definition of a raceway. If you take the time to become familiar with the various types of raceways, you will be able to:

- Understand what is available for doing the work.
- Recognize raceway types having special *Code* requirements.
- Avoid buying a raceway you cannot install due to *NEC* requirements you cannot meet with that wiring method.

Here is a brief overview of the raceway articles included in this material:

- **Article 342—Intermediate Metal Conduit (IMC).** Intermediate metal conduit is a circular metal raceway with the same outside diameter as rigid metal conduit. The wall thickness of this type of conduit is less than that of rigid metal conduit, so it has a larger interior cross-sectional area for holding conductors. Intermediate metal conduit is lighter and less expensive than rigid metal conduit and is approved by the *Code* for use in the same applications as rigid metal conduit. This type of conduit also uses a different steel alloy, which makes it stronger than rigid metal conduit, even though the walls are thinner.
- **Article 344—Rigid Metal Conduit (RMC).** Rigid metal conduit is like intermediate metal conduit, except the wall thickness is larger, so it has a smaller interior cross-sectional area. This type of conduit is heavier than intermediate metal conduit and is permitted for use in the same applications as intermediate metal conduit (IMC).
- **Article 348—Flexible Metal Conduit (FMC).** Flexible metal conduit is a raceway of circular cross section made of a helically wound, interlocked metal strip of either steel or aluminum. It is commonly called "Greenfield" (after its inventor) or "Flex."
- **Article 350—Liquidtight Flexible Metal Conduit (LFMC).** Liquidtight flexible metal conduit is a raceway of circular cross section with an outer liquidtight, nonmetallic, sunlight-resistant jacket over an inner flexible metal core, with associated couplings, connectors, and fittings. It is listed for the installation of electrical conductors. This type of conduit is commonly called "Sealtite®" or simply "liquidtight." Liquidtight flexible metal conduit is similar in construction to flexible metal conduit, but it has an outer thermoplastic covering.
- **Article 352—Rigid Polyvinyl Chloride Conduit (PVC).** Rigid polyvinyl chloride conduit is a nonmetallic raceway of circular cross section with integral or associated couplings, connectors, and fittings. It is listed for the installation of electrical conductors.
- **Article 356—Liquidtight Flexible Nonmetallic Conduit (LFNC).** Liquidtight flexible nonmetallic conduit (commonly referred to as "Carflex®") is a raceway of circular cross section with an outer liquidtight, nonmetallic, sunlight-resistant jacket over an inner flexible core, with associated couplings, connectors, and fittings.

- **Article 358—Electrical Metallic Tubing (EMT).** Electrical metallic tubing is a nonthreaded thinwall raceway of circular cross section designed for the physical protection and routing of conductors and cables. Compared to rigid metal conduit and intermediate metal conduit, electrical metallic tubing is relatively easy to bend, cut, and ream. EMT is not threaded, so all connectors and couplings are of the threadless type. It is available in a range of colors, such as red and blue.
- **Article 362—Electrical Nonmetallic Tubing (ENT).** Electrical nonmetallic tubing is a pliable, corrugated, circular raceway made of PVC. It is often referred to as "Smurf Pipe" or "Smurf Tube," because it was only available in blue when it was first available. The nickname is a reference to the children's cartoon characters "The Smurfs." It is now available in many other colors.
- **Article 376—Metal Wireways.** A metal wireway is a sheet metal trough with hinged or removable covers making the electrical conductors and cables housed and protected inside accessible. Metal wireways must be installed as complete and contiguous systems.
- **Article 386—Surface Metal Raceways.** A surface metal raceway is a metal raceway intended to be mounted to a surface with associated accessories, in which conductors are placed after the raceway has been installed as a complete system.

Cable Trays

- **Article 392—Cable Trays.** A cable tray system is a unit or assembly of units or sections with associated fittings forming a structural system used to securely fasten or support cables and raceways. A cable tray is not a raceway. It is a support system for raceways, cables, and enclosures.

Notice as you read through the various wiring methods that the *NEC* attempts to use similar section numbering for similar topics from one article to the next. It uses the same digits after the decimal point in the section numbers for the same topic. This makes it easier to locate the specific requirements of a particular article. For example, the rules for securing and supporting can be found in the section ending with ".30" of each article.

ARTICLE
300

GENERAL REQUIREMENTS FOR WIRING METHODS AND MATERIALS

Introduction to Article 300—General Requirements for Wiring Methods and Materials

Article 300 contains the general requirements for all installed wiring methods included in the *NEC.* Because the Code is an installation standard this article does not apply where these wiring methods are integral parts of electrical equipment.

Because Article 300 contains the general requirements for wiring methods and materials, you must have a solid understanding of these rules to correctly and safely install the wiring methods included in Chapter 3. Topics covered in this material for Article 300 include:

- Scope
- Electrical and Mechanical Continuity of Raceways and Cables
- Induced Currents in Steel Enclosures

Part I. General Requirements

300.1 Scope

(A) All Wiring Installations. Article 300 contains the general requirements for wiring methods and materials for power and lighting. ▶Figure 300–1

Author's Comment:

- The requirements contained in Article 300 do not apply to Class 2 power-limited circuits, fire alarm circuits, optical fiber cables, or coaxial cable, unless they are specifically reference in the appropriate article.

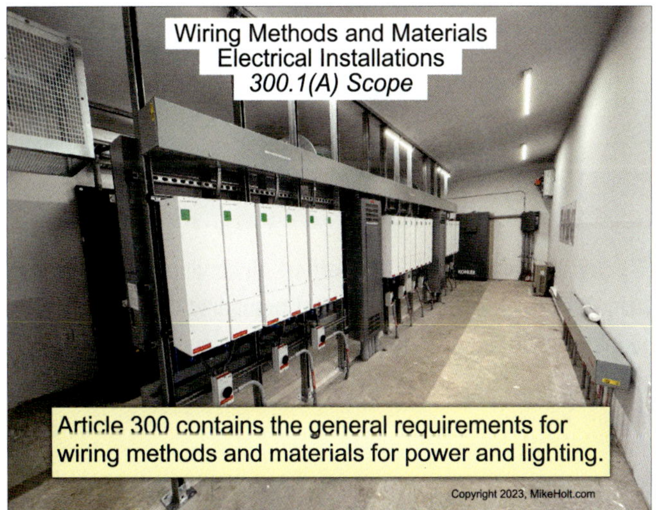
Wiring Methods and Materials
Electrical Installations
300.1(A) Scope
Article 300 contains the general requirements for wiring methods and materials for power and lighting.
Copyright 2023, MikeHolt.com

▶Figure 300–1

(B) Integral Parts of Equipment. The requirements contained in Article 300 do not apply to the integral parts of electrical equipment. ▸Figure 300–2

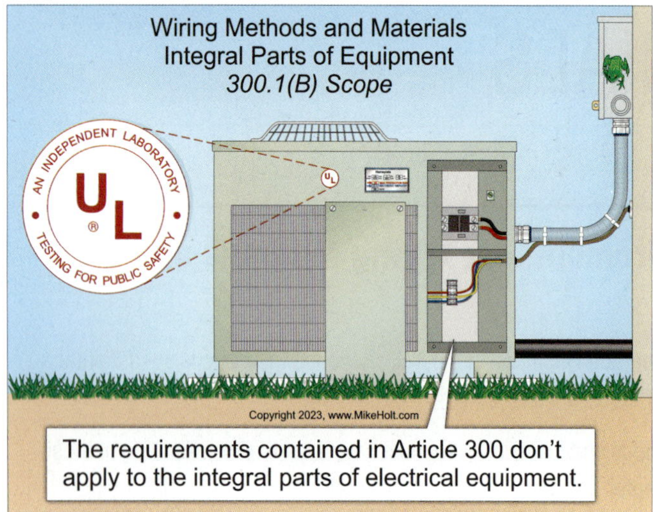
Wiring Methods and Materials
Integral Parts of Equipment
300.1(B) Scope
AN INDEPENDENT LABORATORY
UL
TESTING FOR PUBLIC SAFETY
Copyright 2023, www.MikeHolt.com
The requirements contained in Article 300 don't apply to the integral parts of electrical equipment.

▸Figure 300–2

Author's Comment:

- Integral wiring of equipment is covered by various product standards and not the *NEC*. It is the intent of this *Code* that the factory-installed internal wiring of equipment processed by a qualified testing laboratory does not need to be inspected [90.7].

300.3 Conductors

(B) Conductors Grouped Together. All conductors of a circuit, including the neutral and equipment grounding conductors, must be installed together in the same raceway, <u>conduit body,</u> cable, trench, or cable tray except as permitted by 330.3(B)(1) through (4). ▸Figure 300–3

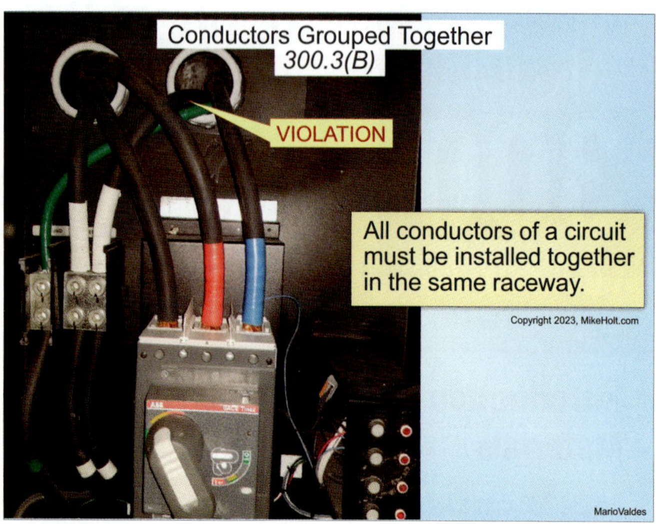
Conductors Grouped Together
300.3(B)
VIOLATION
All conductors of a circuit must be installed together in the same raceway.
Copyright 2023, MikeHolt.com
MarioValdes

▸Figure 300–3

Author's Comment:

- The equipment grounding conductor must be grouped together with the circuit conductors to provide a low impedance path during a short-circuit or ground-fault event. ▸Figure 300–4

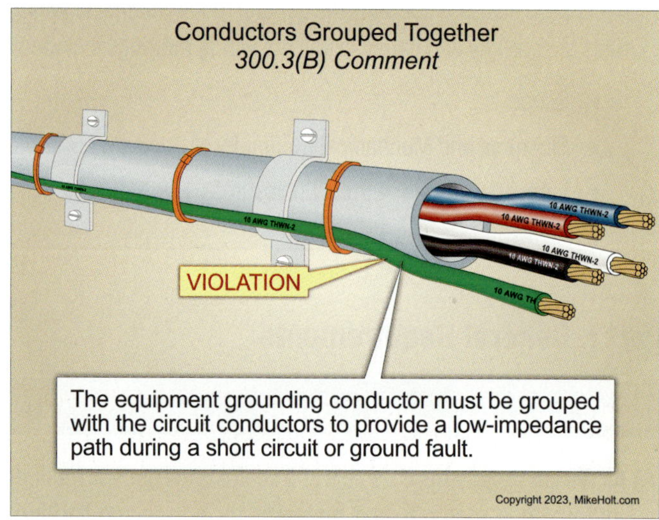
Conductors Grouped Together
300.3(B) Comment
VIOLATION
The equipment grounding conductor must be grouped with the circuit conductors to provide a low-impedance path during a short circuit or ground fault.
Copyright 2023, MikeHolt.com

▸Figure 300–4

(1) Paralleled Installations. All conductors of a parallel set must be installed within the same raceway, cable, or cable tray in accordance with 310.10(G). ▸Figure 300–5

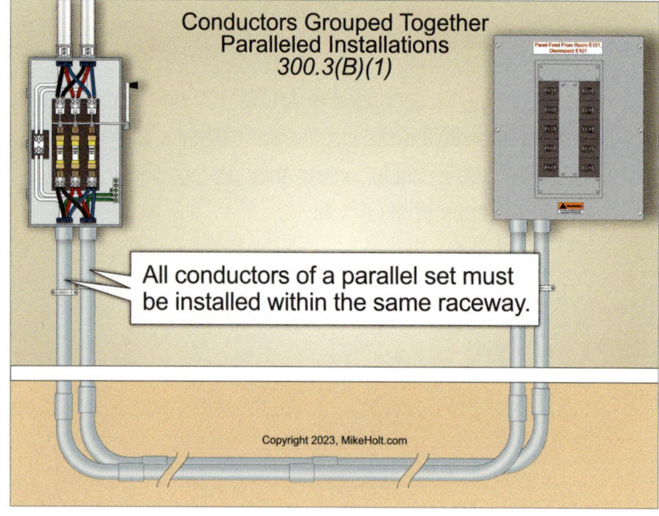
Conductors Grouped Together
Paralleled Installations
300.3(B)(1)
All conductors of a parallel set must be installed within the same raceway.
Copyright 2023, MikeHolt.com

▸Figure 300–5

Connections, taps, or extensions made from paralleled conductors must connect to all conductors of the paralleled set.

Author's Comment:

- Grouping all phase, neutral, and equipment grounding and bonding conductors of the circuit helps minimize the inductive heating of the surrounding steel raceways and enclosures for alternating-current circuits. See 300.20(A). ▸**Figure 300-6**

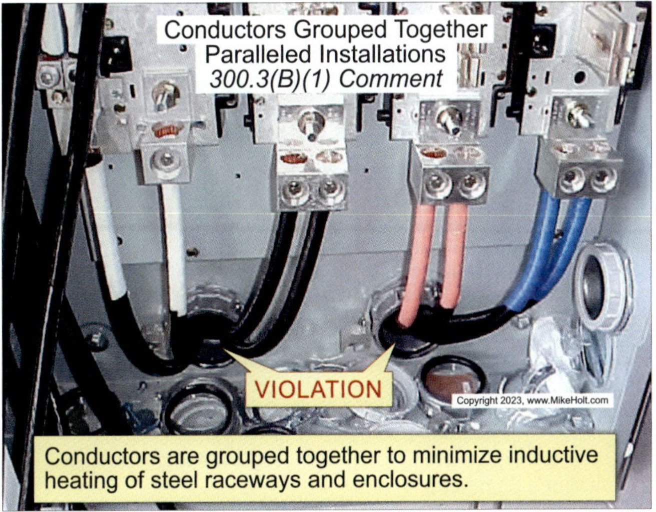
Conductors Grouped Together
Paralleled Installations
300.3(B)(1) Comment
VIOLATION
Copyright 2023, www.MikeHolt.com
Conductors are grouped together to minimize inductive heating of steel raceways and enclosures.

▸**Figure 300-6**

Ex: Isolated parallel phase and neutral conductors can be installed in individual underground nonmetallic raceways (Phase A in raceway 1, Phase B in raceway 2, and so forth) as permitted by 300.5(I) Ex 2, if the installation complies with 300.20(B). ▸**Figure 300-7**

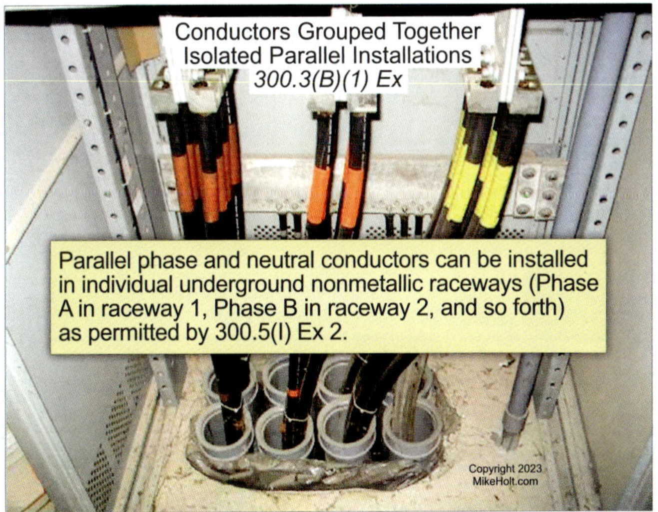
Conductors Grouped Together
Isolated Parallel Installations
300.3(B)(1) Ex
Parallel phase and neutral conductors can be installed in individual underground nonmetallic raceways (Phase A in raceway 1, Phase B in raceway 2, and so forth) as permitted by 300.5(I) Ex 2.
Copyright 2023
MikeHolt.com

▸**Figure 300-7**

(2) Bonding Jumpers Outside the Raceway. Equipment bonding jumpers for dc circuits can be run separately from the circuit conductors in accordance with 250.134(2) Ex 2. ▸**Figure 300-8**

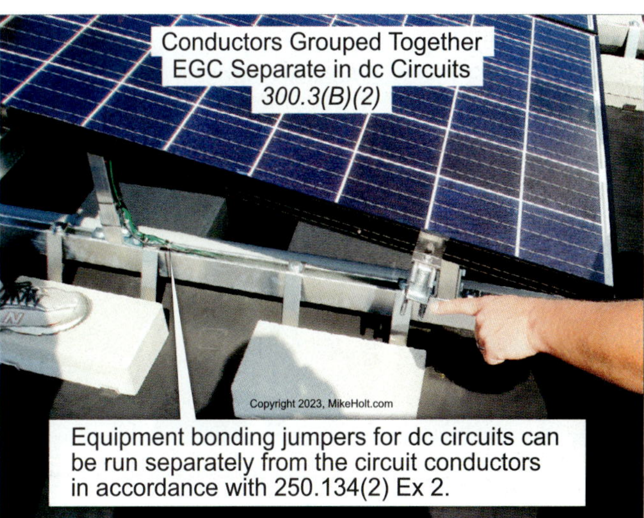
Conductors Grouped Together
EGC Separate in dc Circuits
300.3(B)(2)
Copyright 2023, MikeHolt.com
Equipment bonding jumpers for dc circuits can be run separately from the circuit conductors in accordance with 250.134(2) Ex 2.

▸**Figure 300-8**

Equipment bonding jumpers can be run outside the circuit raceway in accordance with 250.102(E)(2). ▸**Figure 300-9**

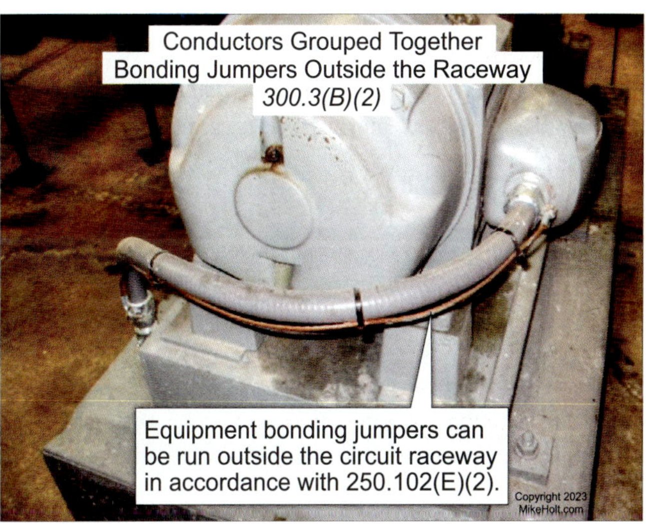
Conductors Grouped Together
Bonding Jumpers Outside the Raceway
300.3(B)(2)
Equipment bonding jumpers can be run outside the circuit raceway in accordance with 250.102(E)(2).
Copyright 2023
MikeHolt.com

▸**Figure 300-9**

300.6 Protection Against Corrosion

Raceways, cable trays, cable armor, boxes, cable sheathing, cabinets, enclosures, elbows, couplings, fittings, supports, and support hardware must be suitable for the environment.

(A) Steel Equipment. Steel raceways, cables, cable trays, cabinets, enclosures, fittings, and support hardware must be protected against corrosion by a coating of approved corrosion-resistant material. ▸Figure 300–10

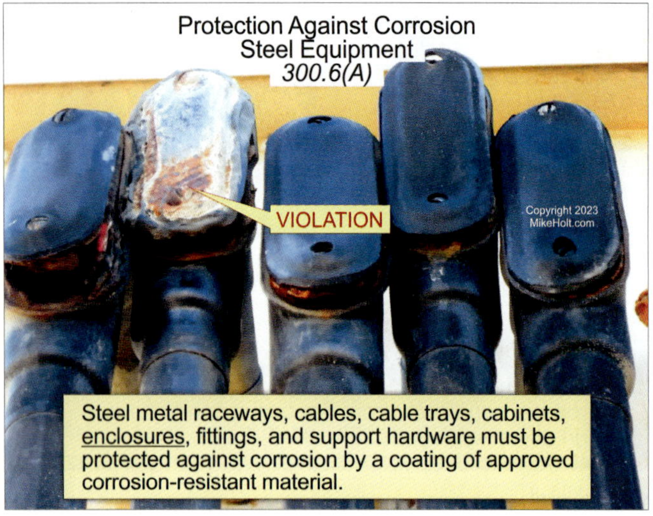
Protection Against Corrosion
Steel Equipment
300.6(A)
VIOLATION
Copyright 2023
MikeHolt.com
Steel metal raceways, cables, cable trays, cabinets, enclosures, fittings, and support hardware must be protected against corrosion by a coating of approved corrosion-resistant material.

▸Figure 300–10

Author's Comment:

- In accordance with *"UL Guide Information DYIX,"* supplementary corrosion protection is required when a steel raceway transitions from concrete encasement to the soil. ▸Figure 300–11

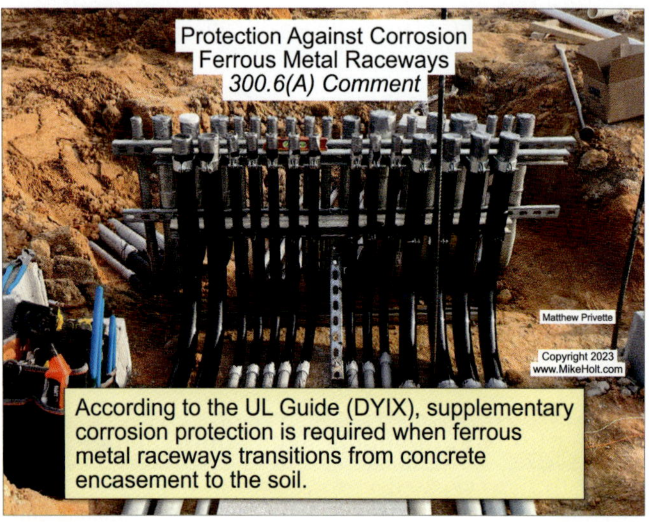
Protection Against Corrosion
Ferrous Metal Raceways
300.6(A) Comment
Matthew Privette
Copyright 2023
www.MikeHolt.com
According to the UL Guide (DYIX), supplementary corrosion protection is required when ferrous metal raceways transitions from concrete encasement to the soil.

▸Figure 300–11

Where corrosion protection is required and IMC or RMC is threaded in the field, the threads must be coated with an approved electrically conductive, corrosion-resistant compound.

300.10 Electrical Continuity

Metal raceways, cable armor, and metal enclosures must be metallically joined together to provide electrical continuity [250.4(A)(3)]. ▸Figure 300–12

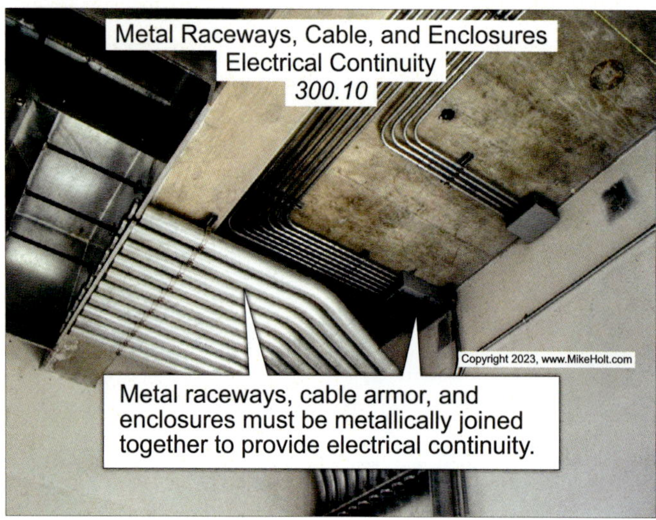
Metal Raceways, Cable, and Enclosures
Electrical Continuity
300.10
Copyright 2023, www.MikeHolt.com
Metal raceways, cable armor, and enclosures must be metallically joined together to provide electrical continuity.

▸Figure 300–12

Author's Comment:

- The purpose of electrical continuity between metal parts is to establish the effective ground-fault current path necessary to open the circuit overcurrent protective device in the event of a ground fault [250.4(A)(5)]. ▸Figure 300–13

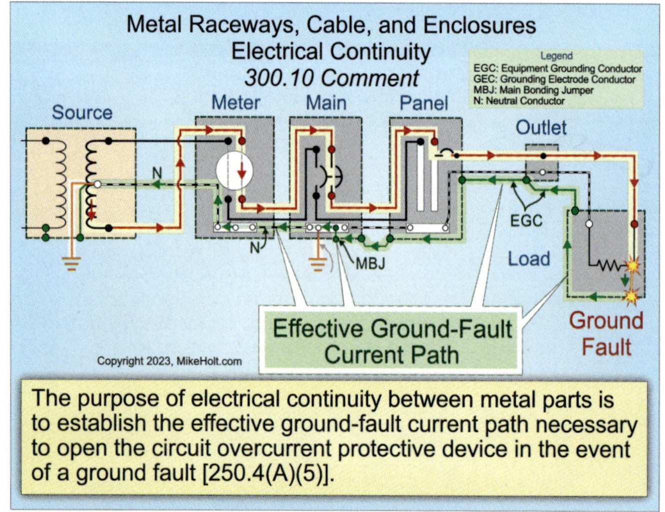
Metal Raceways, Cable, and Enclosures
Electrical Continuity
300.10 Comment
Legend
EGC: Equipment Grounding Conductor
GEC: Grounding Electrode Conductor
MBJ: Main Bonding Jumper
N: Neutral Conductor
Source
Meter
Main
Panel
Outlet
N
N
MBJ
EGC
Load
Effective Ground-Fault Current Path
Ground Fault
Copyright 2023, MikeHolt.com
The purpose of electrical continuity between metal parts is to establish the effective ground-fault current path necessary to open the circuit overcurrent protective device in the event of a ground fault [250.4(A)(5)].

▸Figure 300–13

1st Printing

Ex 1: Short lengths of metal raceways used for the support or protection of cables are not required to be electrically continuous or connected to the circuit equipment grounding conductor [250.86 Ex 2 and 300.12 Ex 1]. ▸Figure 300–14

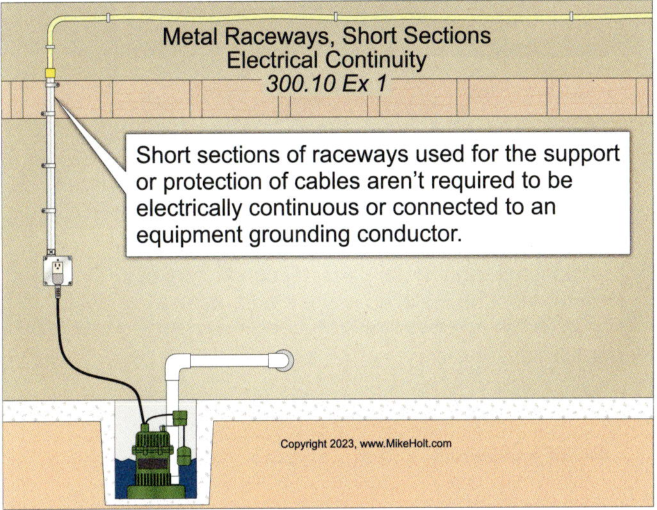
Metal Raceways, Short Sections
Electrical Continuity
300.10 Ex 1
Short sections of raceways used for the support or protection of cables aren't required to be electrically continuous or connected to an equipment grounding conductor.
Copyright 2023, www.MikeHolt.com

▸Figure 300–14

300.12 Mechanical Continuity

Raceways and cable sheaths must be mechanically continuous between boxes, cabinets, conduit bodies, fittings, or other enclosures. ▸Figure 300–15 and ▸Figure 300–16

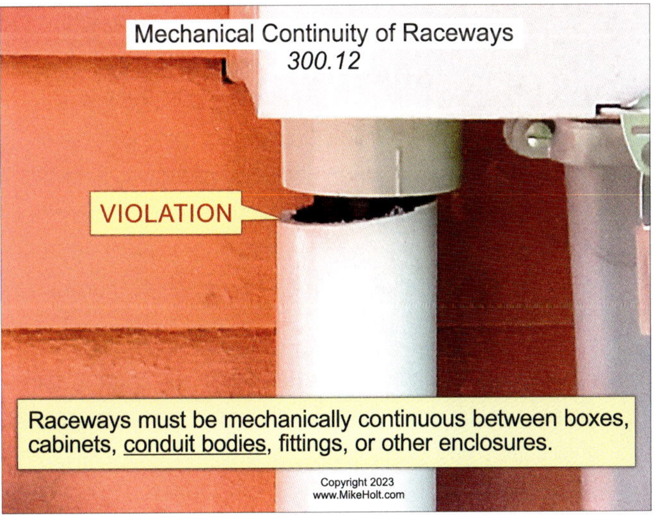
Mechanical Continuity of Raceways
300.12
VIOLATION
Raceways must be mechanically continuous between boxes, cabinets, conduit bodies, fittings, or other enclosures.
Copyright 2023
www.MikeHolt.com

▸Figure 300–15

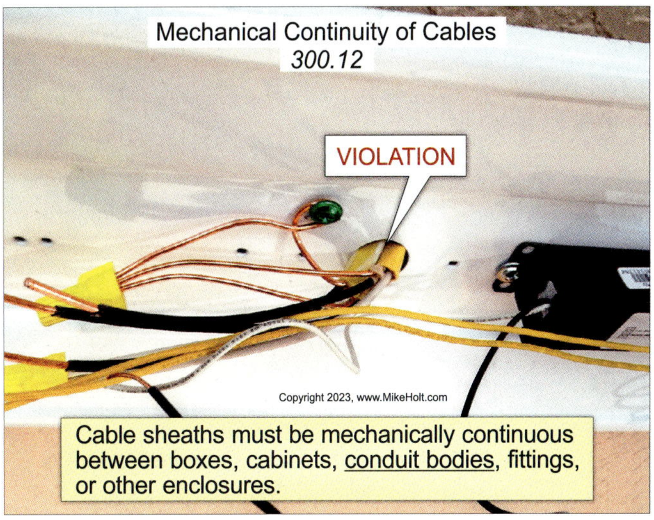
Mechanical Continuity of Cables
300.12
VIOLATION
Copyright 2023, www.MikeHolt.com
Cable sheaths must be mechanically continuous between boxes, cabinets, conduit bodies, fittings, or other enclosures.

▸Figure 300–16

Ex 1: Short sections of raceways used to provide support or protection of cables from physical damage aren't required to be mechanically continuous [250.86 Ex 2 and 300.10 Ex 1]. ▸Figure 300–17

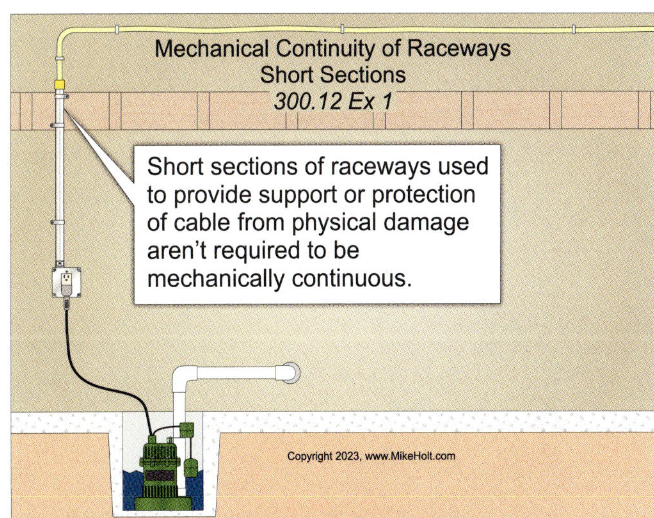
Mechanical Continuity of Raceways
Short Sections
300.12 Ex 1
Short sections of raceways used to provide support or protection of cable from physical damage aren't required to be mechanically continuous.
Copyright 2023, www.MikeHolt.com

▸Figure 300–17

Ex 2: Raceways and cables installed into the bottom of open-bottom equipment such as switchboards, motor control centers, floor- or pad-mounted transformers aren't required to be mechanically secured to the equipment. ▸Figure 300–18

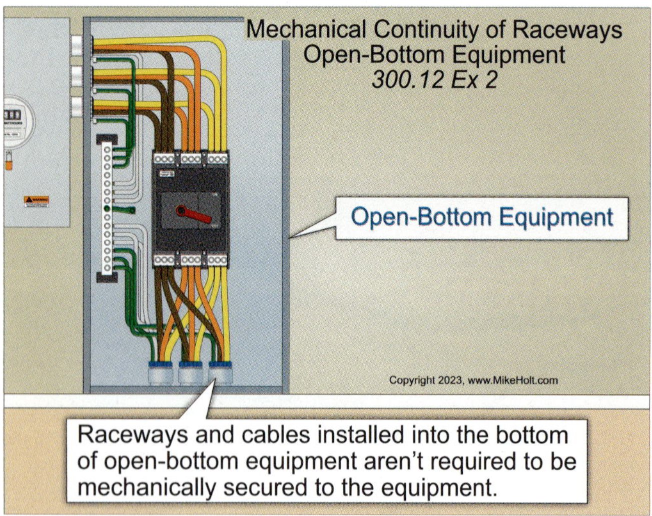
Mechanical Continuity of Raceways
Open-Bottom Equipment
300.12 Ex 2
Open-Bottom Equipment
Copyright 2023, www.MikeHolt.com
Raceways and cables installed into the bottom of open-bottom equipment aren't required to be mechanically secured to the equipment.

▸Figure 300–18

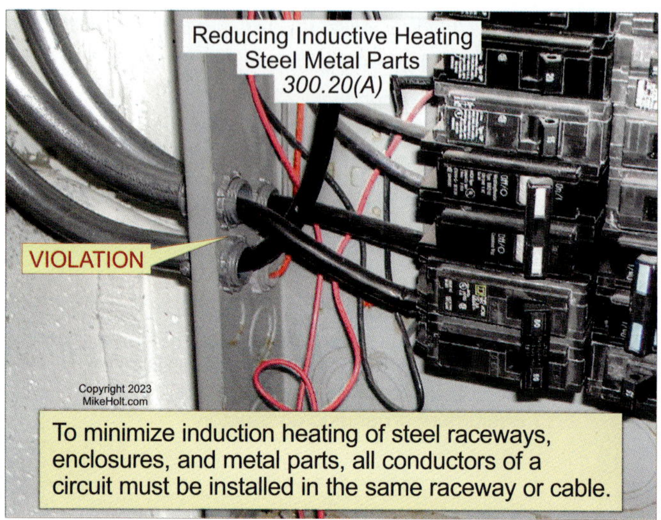
Reducing Inductive Heating
Steel Metal Parts
300.20(A)
VIOLATION
Copyright 2023
MikeHolt.com
To minimize induction heating of steel raceways, enclosures, and metal parts, all conductors of a circuit must be installed in the same raceway or cable.

▸Figure 300–20

300.20 Reducing Inductive Heating

(A) Conductors Grouped Together. To minimize the induction heating of steel raceways, enclosures, and metal parts, all conductors of a circuit (including any neutral and equipment grounding conductors) must be installed in the same raceway or cable. See 250.102(E), 300.3(B), 300.5(I), and 392. 20(C). ▸Figure 300–19 and ▸Figure 300–20

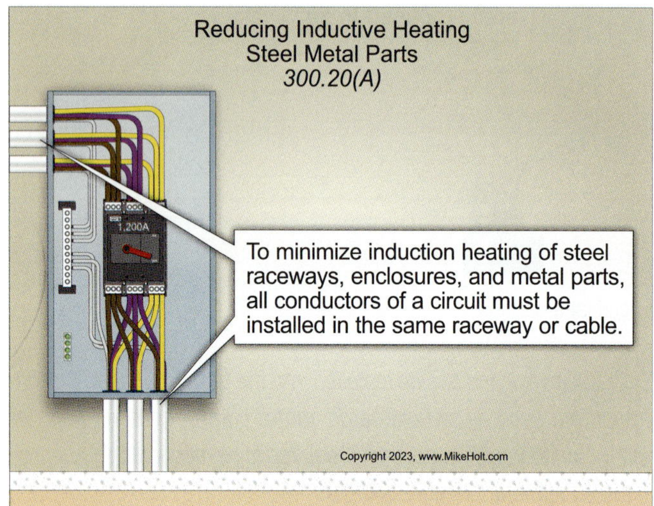
Reducing Inductive Heating
Steel Metal Parts
300.20(A)
1,200A
To minimize induction heating of steel raceways, enclosures, and metal parts, all conductors of a circuit must be installed in the same raceway or cable.
Copyright 2023, www.MikeHolt.com

▸Figure 300–19

Author's Comment:

- When alternating current flows through a conductor, a pulsating or varying magnetic field is created around the conductor. This magnetic field is constantly expanding and contracting with the amplitude of the alternating current. In the United States, the frequency is 60 cycles per second (Hz). Since alternating current reverses polarity 120 times per second, the magnetic field that surrounds the conductor also reverses direction 120 times per second. This expanding and collapsing magnetic field induces eddy currents in the steel parts that surround the conductors, causing them to heat up due to hysteresis heating.
- Magnetic materials naturally resist rapidly changing magnetic fields. The resulting friction produces its own heat (hysteresis heating), in addition to eddy current heating. A metal which offers high resistance is said to have high magnetic "permeability." Permeability can vary on a scale of 100 to 500 for magnetic materials, while nonmagnetic materials have a permeability of one.
- Simply put, the molecules of steel and iron align to the polarity of the magnetic field, and when it reverses, the molecules reverse their polarity as well. This back-and-forth alignment of the molecules heats up the metal. The more the current flows, the more the heat increases in steel parts. ▸Figure 300–21

1st Printing

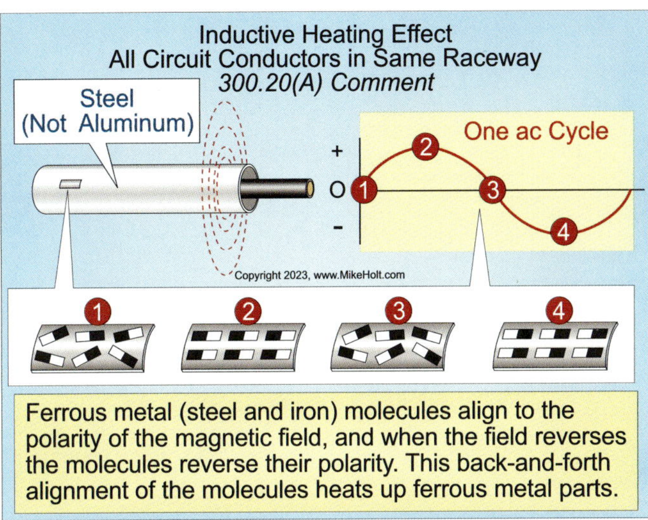
Inductive Heating Effect
All Circuit Conductors in Same Raceway
300.20(A) Comment
Steel (Not Aluminum)
One ac Cycle
+
O
-
1
2
3
4
Copyright 2023, www.MikeHolt.com
Ferrous metal (steel and iron) molecules align to the polarity of the magnetic field, and when the field reverses the molecules reverse their polarity. This back-and-forth alignment of the molecules heats up ferrous metal parts.

▶Figure 300–21

Author's Comment:

- When conductors of the same circuit are grouped together, the magnetic fields of the different conductors tend to cancel each other out, resulting in a reduced magnetic field around them. The smaller magnetic field reduces induced currents in steel raceways or enclosures, which reduces the hysteresis heating of the surrounding metal enclosure.

(B) Single Conductors. Where a single conductor or a parallel set of a conductors enter an enclosure, the inductive heating effects on the metal enclosure must be minimized by cutting slots between the individual holes through which the conductors pass, or by passing the conductors through the same wall opening. ▶Figure 300–22 and ▶Figure 300–23

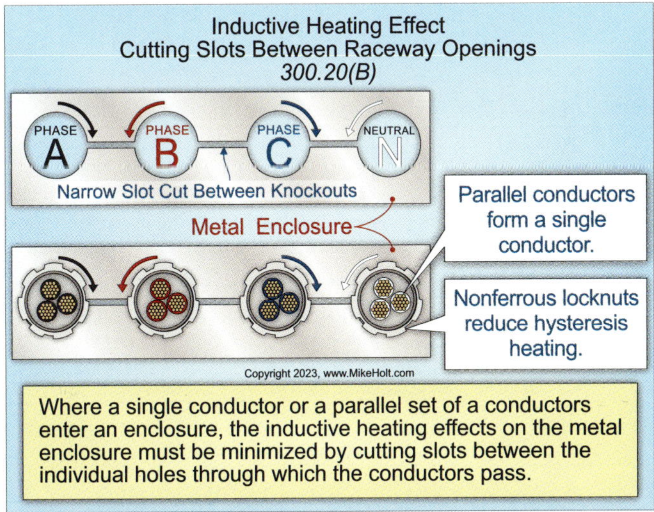
Inductive Heating Effect
Cutting Slots Between Raceway Openings
300.20(B)
PHASE A
PHASE B
PHASE C
NEUTRAL N
Narrow Slot Cut Between Knockouts
Metal Enclosure
Parallel conductors form a single conductor.
Nonferrous locknuts reduce hysteresis heating.
Copyright 2023, www.MikeHolt.com
Where a single conductor or a parallel set of a conductors enter an enclosure, the inductive heating effects on the metal enclosure must be minimized by cutting slots between the individual holes through which the conductors pass.

▶Figure 300–22

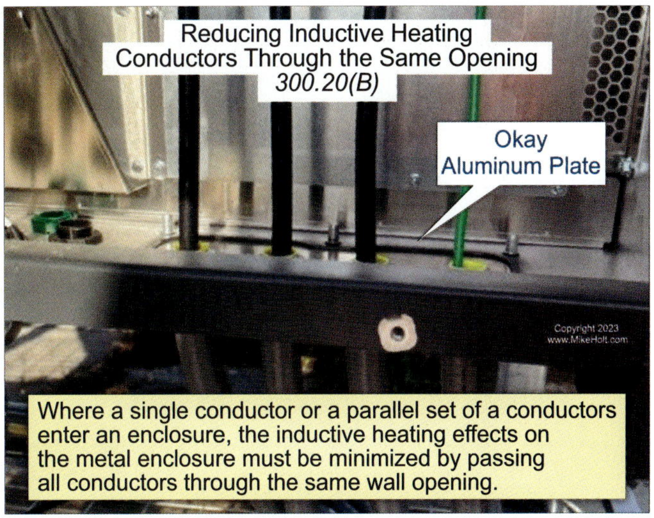
Reducing Inductive Heating
Conductors Through the Same Opening
300.20(B)
Okay
Aluminum Plate
Copyright 2023
www.MikeHolt.com
Where a single conductor or a parallel set of a conductors enter an enclosure, the inductive heating effects on the metal enclosure must be minimized by passing all conductors through the same wall opening.

▶Figure 300–23

Author's Comment:

- When single conductors are installed in nonmetallic raceways as permitted in 300.5(I) Ex 2, the inductive heating of the metal enclosure can be minimized by using aluminum locknuts and by cutting a slot between the individual holes through which the conductors pass.

Note: Because aluminum is a nonmagnetic metal, aluminum parts do not heat up due to hysteresis heating.

ARTICLE 314 BOXES, CONDUIT BODIES, AND HANDHOLE ENCLOSURES

Introduction to Article 314—Boxes, Conduit Bodies, and Handhole Enclosures

This article contains the installation requirements for outlet and device boxes, pull and junction boxes, conduit bodies, and handhole enclosures. Topics covered in this material for Article 314 include:

- Scope
- Round, Nonmetallic, and Metal boxes
- Handhole Enclosures

Part I. General

314.1 Scope

Article 314 contains the installation requirements for outlet boxes, pull and junction boxes, conduit bodies, and handhole enclosures. This article also includes installation requirements for fittings used to connect raceways and cables to boxes or conduit bodies. ▶Figure 314–1

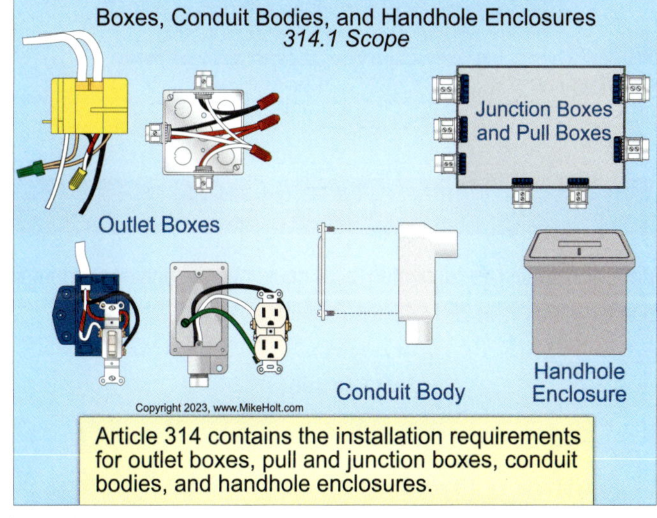
Boxes, Conduit Bodies, and Handhole Enclosures
314.1 Scope
Junction Boxes and Pull Boxes
Outlet Boxes
Conduit Body
Handhole Enclosure
Copyright 2023, www.MikeHolt.com
Article 314 contains the installation requirements for outlet boxes, pull and junction boxes, conduit bodies, and handhole enclosures.

▶Figure 314–1

314.3 Nonmetallic Boxes

Nonmetallic boxes can only be used with nonmetallic cables and raceways.

Ex 1: Metal raceways and metal cables entering nonmetallic boxes must be bonded to the circuit equipment grounding conductor. ▶Figure 314–2

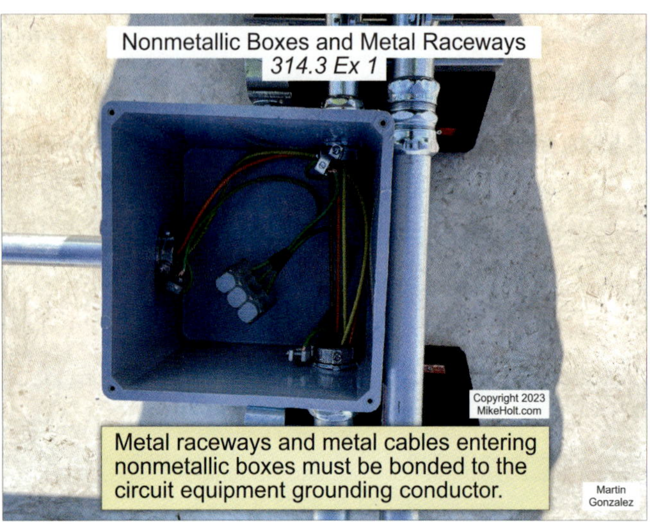
Nonmetallic Boxes and Metal Raceways
314.3 Ex 1
Copyright 2023 MikeHolt.com
Metal raceways and metal cables entering nonmetallic boxes must be bonded to the circuit equipment grounding conductor.
Martin Gonzalez

▶Figure 314–2

314.4 Metal Boxes

Metal boxes must be connected to the equipment grounding conductor in accordance with 250.148(C). ▶Figure 314–3

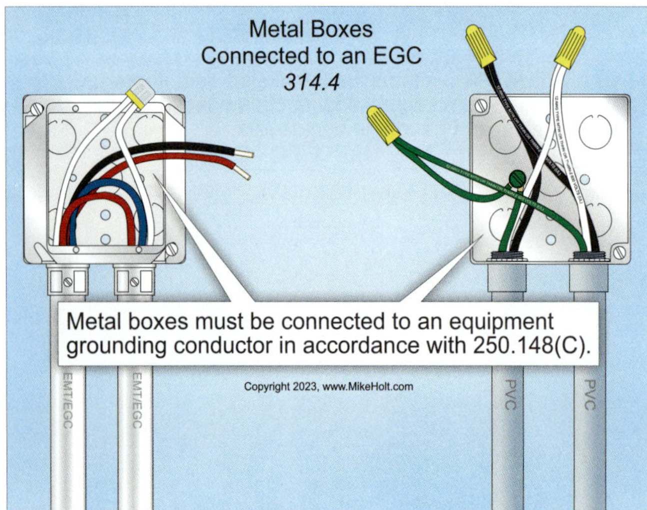
Metal Boxes
Connected to an EGC
314.4
Metal boxes must be connected to an equipment grounding conductor in accordance with 250.148(C).
Copyright 2023, www.MikeHolt.com
EMT/EGC
EMT/EGC
PVC
PVC

▶Figure 314–3

314.30 Handhole Enclosures

(D) Covers. Handhole covers must have an identifying mark or logo that prominently identifies the function of the handhole, such as "electric." Handhole covers must require the use of tools to open, or they must weigh over 100 lb. ▶Figure 314–4

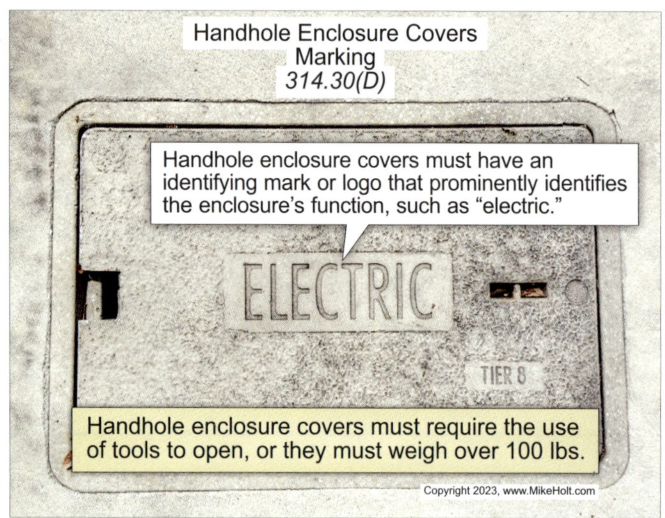
Handhole Enclosure Covers
Marking
314.30(D)
Handhole enclosure covers must have an identifying mark or logo that prominently identifies the enclosure's function, such as "electric."
ELECTRIC
TIER 8
Handhole enclosure covers must require the use of tools to open, or they must weigh over 100 lbs.
Copyright 2023, www.MikeHolt.com

▶Figure 314–4

Metal covers and exposed conductive surfaces of handhole enclosures must be connected to the circuit equipment conductor in accordance with 250.96(A). ▶Figure 314–5

1st Printing

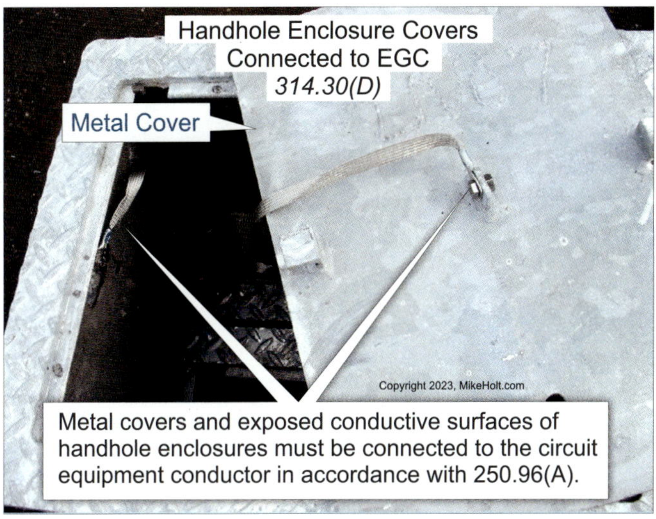
Handhole Enclosure Covers
Connected to EGC
314.30(D)
Metal Cover
Copyright 2023, MikeHolt.com
Metal covers and exposed conductive surfaces of handhole enclosures must be connected to the circuit equipment conductor in accordance with 250.96(A).

▸Figure 314–5

ARTICLE 320 ARMORED CABLE (TYPE AC)

Introduction to Article 320—Armored Cable (Type AC)

Article 320 covers the use, installation, and construction specifications of armored cable (Type AC). AC cable is an assembly of up to four phase conductors and one neutral insulated conductor, sizes 14 AWG through 1 AWG, individually wrapped in a moisture-resistant, fire-retardant paper contained within a flexible spiral metal sheath. Topics covered in this material for Article 320 include:

- Scope
- Equipment Grounding Conductor

According to Article 100, "Type AC" is a fabricated assembly of conductors in a flexible interlocked metallic armor with an internal bonding strip in intimate contact with the armor for its entire length. ▶Figure 320–1

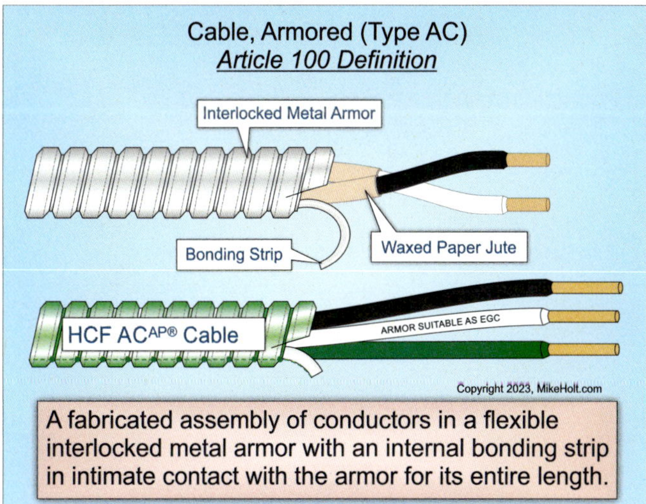
Cable, Armored (Type AC)
Article 100 Definition
Interlocked Metal Armor
Bonding Strip
Waxed Paper Jute
HCF AC$^{AP®}$ Cable
ARMOR SUITABLE AS EGC
Copyright 2023, MikeHolt.com
A fabricated assembly of conductors in a flexible interlocked metal armor with an internal bonding strip in intimate contact with the armor for its entire length.

▶Figure 320–1

320.1 Scope

This article covers the use, installation, and construction specifications of armored cable, Type AC. ▶Figure 320–2

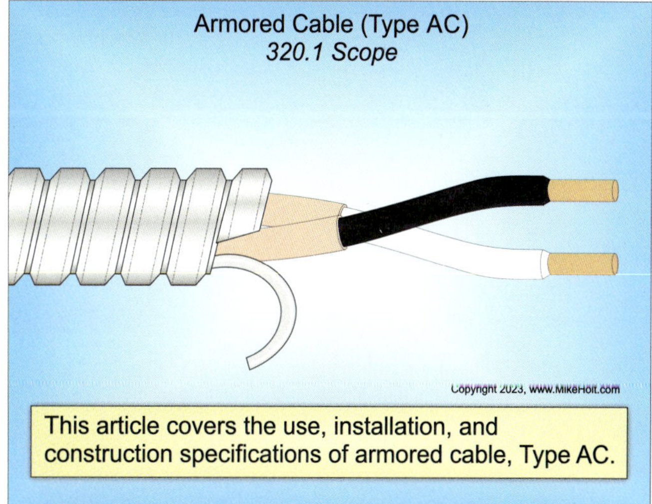
Armored Cable (Type AC)
320.1 Scope
Copyright 2023, www.MikeHolt.com
This article covers the use, installation, and construction specifications of armored cable, Type AC.

▶Figure 320–2

320.108 Equipment Grounding Conductor

Type AC cable can serve as an equipment grounding conductor [250.118(A)(8)]. ▸Figure 320–3

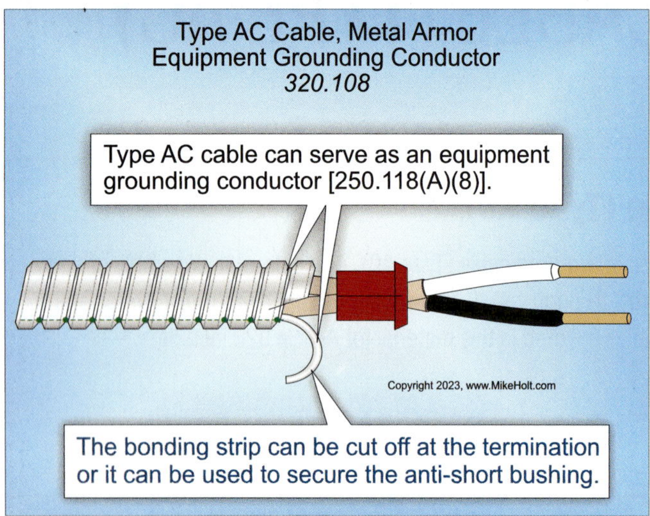
Type AC Cable, Metal Armor
Equipment Grounding Conductor
320.108
Type AC cable can serve as an equipment grounding conductor [250.118(A)(8)].
Copyright 2023, www.MikeHolt.com
The bonding strip can be cut off at the termination or it can be used to secure the anti-short bushing.

▸Figure 320–3

Author's Comment:

- The internal aluminum bonding strip is not an equipment grounding conductor, but it allows the interlocked armor to serve as one because it reduces the impedance of the armored spirals to ensure a ground fault will be cleared. It is the combination of the aluminum bonding strip and the cable armor that creates the equipment grounding conductor. Once the bonding strip exits the cable, it can be cut off because it no longer serves any purpose. The effective ground-fault current path must be maintained by using fittings specifically listed for Type AC cable [320.40]. See 300.12, 300.15, and 300.10.

ARTICLE 330 METAL-CLAD CABLE (TYPE MC)

Introduction to Article 330—Metal-Clad Cable (Type MC)

This article covers the use, installation, and construction specifications of metal-clad cable (Type MC). Type MC cable is an assembly of any number of insulated conductors, 18 AWG through 2000 kcmil, with an overall polypropylene wrap enclosed in a metal sheath of either corrugated or smooth copper or aluminum tubing, or in spiral interlocked steel or aluminum. Topics covered in this material for Article 330 include:

- Scope
- Equipment Grounding Conductor

According to Article 100, "Type MC" is a factory assembly of one or more insulated circuit conductors, with or without optical fiber members, enclosed in an armor of interlocking metal tape, or a smooth or corrugated metallic sheath. ▸**Figure 330–1**

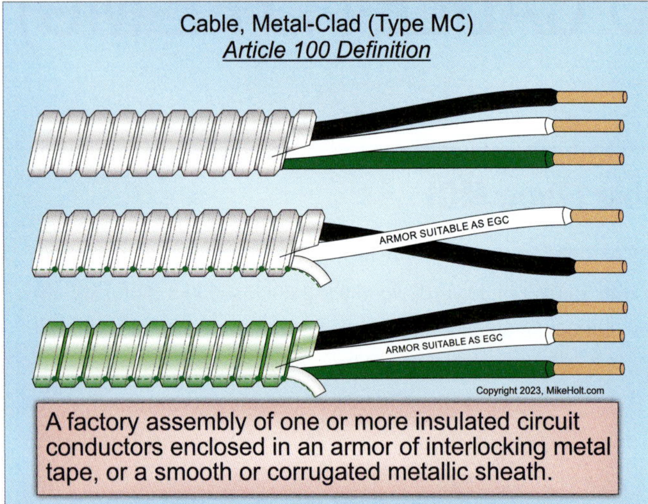
Cable, Metal-Clad (Type MC)
Article 100 Definition
ARMOR SUITABLE AS EGC
ARMOR SUITABLE AS EGC
Copyright 2023, MikeHolt.com
A factory assembly of one or more insulated circuit conductors enclosed in an armor of interlocking metal tape, or a smooth or corrugated metallic sheath.

▸**Figure 330–1**

330.1 Scope

Article 330 covers the use, installation, and construction specifications of metal-clad cable, Type MC. ▸**Figure 330–2**

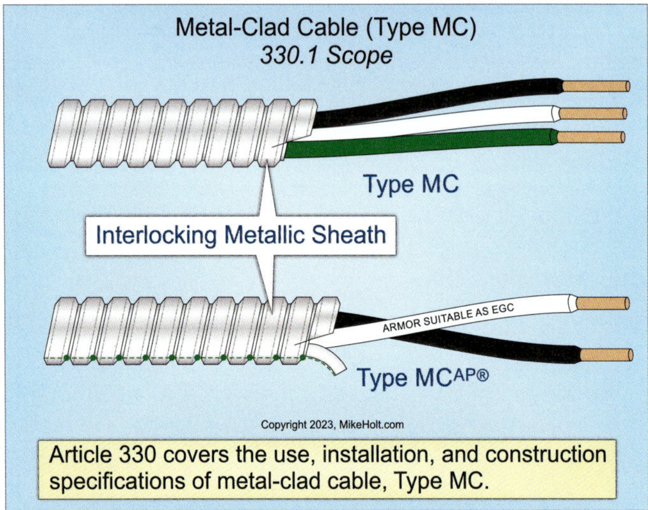
Metal-Clad Cable (Type MC)
330.1 Scope
Type MC
Interlocking Metallic Sheath
ARMOR SUITABLE AS EGC
Type MCAP®
Copyright 2023, MikeHolt.com
Article 330 covers the use, installation, and construction specifications of metal-clad cable, Type MC.

▸**Figure 330–2**

330.108 Equipment Grounding Conductor

If Type MC cable is to serve as an equipment grounding conductor, it must comply with 250.118(A)(10) and 250.122.

Author's Comment:

- The outer metal sheath of traditional interlocked Type MC cable is not permitted to serve as an equipment grounding conductor, so this cable must contain an equipment grounding conductor of the wire type in accordance with 250.118(A)(10)a. ▸**Figure 330–3**

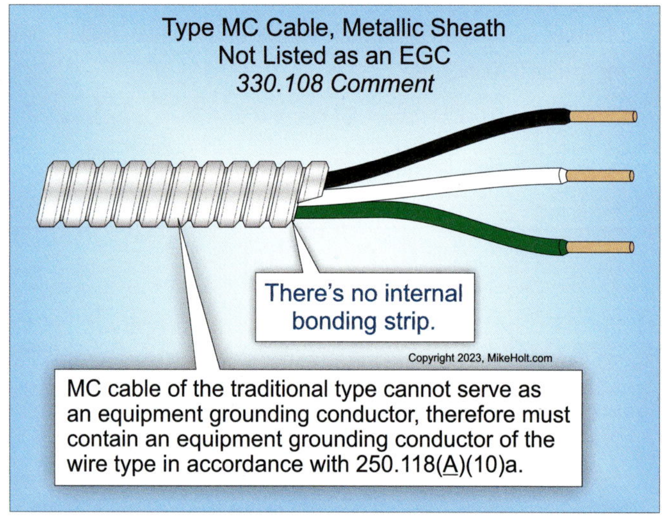
Type MC Cable, Metallic Sheath
Not Listed as an EGC
330.108 Comment
There's no internal bonding strip.
Copyright 2023, MikeHolt.com
MC cable of the traditional type cannot serve as an equipment grounding conductor, therefore must contain an equipment grounding conductor of the wire type in accordance with 250.118(A)(10)a.

▸**Figure 330–3**

- The outer metal sheath of all-purpose Type MC cable with an uninsulated aluminum grounding/bonding conductor can serve as an equipment grounding conductor in accordance with 250.118(A)(10)b. ▸**Figure 330–4**

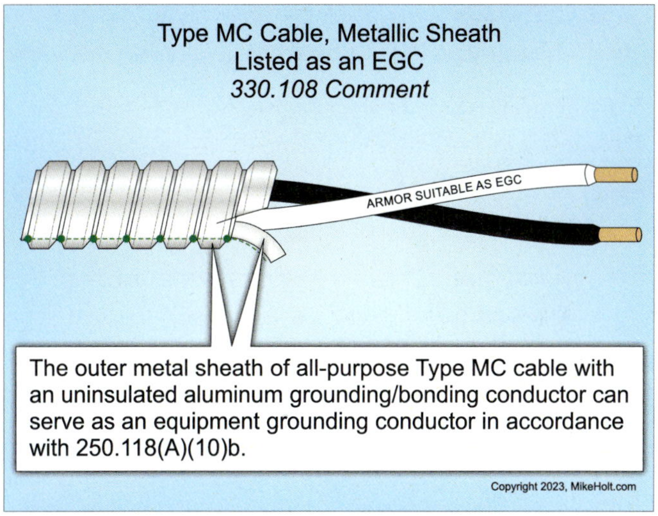
Type MC Cable, Metallic Sheath
Listed as an EGC
330.108 Comment
ARMOR SUITABLE AS EGC
The outer metal sheath of all-purpose Type MC cable with an uninsulated aluminum grounding/bonding conductor can serve as an equipment grounding conductor in accordance with 250.118(A)(10)b.
Copyright 2023, MikeHolt.com

▸Figure 330–4

Notes

NONMETALLIC-SHEATHED CABLE (TYPE NM)

Introduction to Article 334—Nonmetallic-Sheathed Cable (Type NM)

Article 334 covers the use, installation, and construction specifications of nonmetallic-sheathed cable (Type NM). Type NM cable is an assembly of insulated conductors and an insulated or bare equipment grounding conductor, 14 AWG through 2AWG, with an overall nonmetallic flame-retardant sheath. This type of cable provides limited physical protection for the conductors inside the sheath, so its uses are limited by the building construction type. Its low cost and relative ease of installation makes it a common wiring method for residential and light commercial applications. Topics covered in this material for Article 334 include:

- Scope
- Equipment Grounding Conductor

According to Article 100, "Type NM" is a wiring method that encloses two or more insulated conductors within an outer nonmetallic jacket. ▶Figure 334-1

Cable, Nonmetallic-Sheathed (Type NM)
Article 100 Definition
NON-METALLIC SHEATHED CABLE
CME
NM-B AWG 12/2 W/GROUND
1000 ft
300722
A wiring method that encloses two or more insulated conductors within an outer nonmetallic jacket.
Copyright 2023, MikeHolt.com

▶Figure 334-1

Author's Comment:

- It is the generally accepted practice in the electrical industry to call Type NM cable "Romex®," a registered trademark of the Southwire Company.

334.1 Scope

Article 334 covers the use, installation, and construction specifications of nonmetallic-sheathed cable, Type NM. ▶Figure 334-2

334.108 Equipment Grounding Conductor

Type NM cable must have an equipment grounding conductor of the wire-type. ▶Figure 334-3

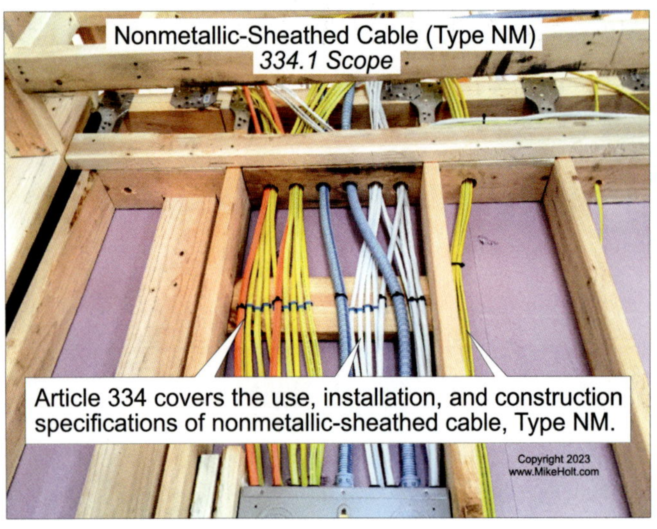
Nonmetallic-Sheathed Cable (Type NM)
334.1 Scope
Article 334 covers the use, installation, and construction specifications of nonmetallic-sheathed cable, Type NM.
Copyright 2023
www.MikeHolt.com

▸Figure 334-2

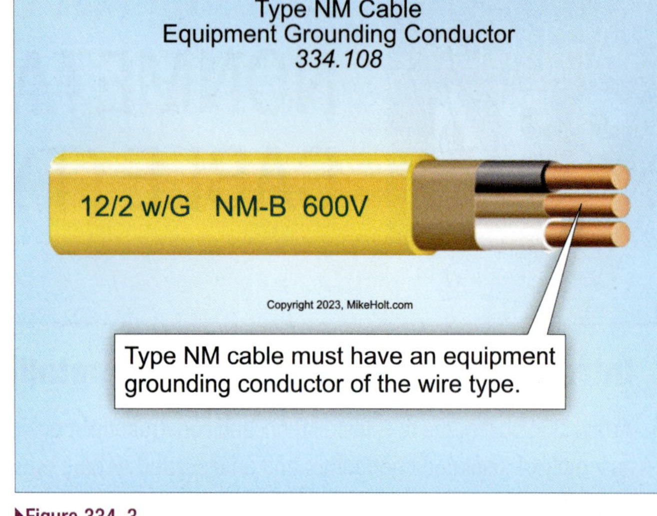
Type NM Cable
Equipment Grounding Conductor
334.108
12/2 w/G NM-B 600V
Copyright 2023, MikeHolt.com
Type NM cable must have an equipment grounding conductor of the wire type.

▸Figure 334-3

ARTICLE 340 UNDERGROUND FEEDER AND BRANCH-CIRCUIT CABLE (TYPE UF)

Introduction to Article 340—Underground Feeder and Branch-Circuit Cable (Type UF)

This article covers the use, installation, and construction specifications of underground feeder and branch-circuit cable (Type UF). Type UF cable is an assembly of conductors in sizes 14 AWG through 4/0 AWG [340.104] covered in a moisture-, fungus-, and corrosion-resistant sheath suitable for direct burial in the Earth. The sheath of multiconductor Type UF cable is a molded plastic that encases the insulated conductors. It can be difficult to strip off the sheath without damaging the conductor insulation or cutting yourself, so be careful. Topics covered in this material for Article 340 include:

- Scope
- Equipment Grounding Conductor

According to Article 100, "Underground Feeder Cable (Type UF)" is a factory assembly of insulated conductors with an integral or an overall covering of nonmetallic material suitable for direct burial in the Earth. ▶Figure 340–1

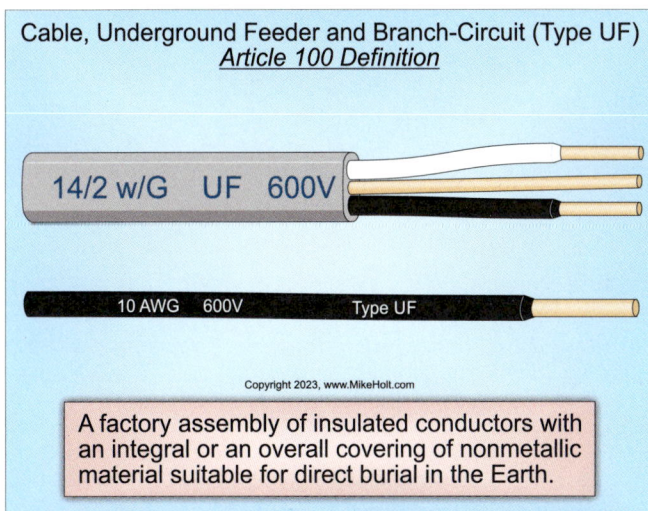

Cable, Underground Feeder and Branch-Circuit (Type UF)
Article 100 Definition
14/2 w/G UF 600V
10 AWG 600V Type UF
Copyright 2023, www.MikeHolt.com
A factory assembly of insulated conductors with an integral or an overall covering of nonmetallic material suitable for direct burial in the Earth.

▶Figure 340–1

340.1 Scope

Article 340 covers the use, installation, and construction specifications of underground feeder and branch-circuit cable, Type UF. ▶Figure 340–2

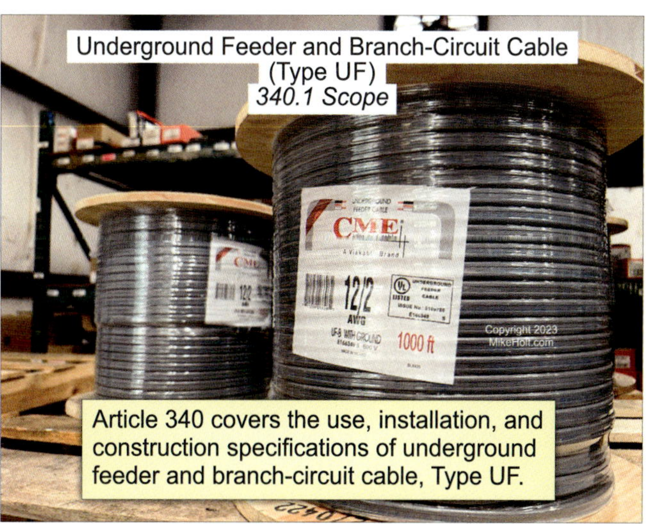

Underground Feeder and Branch-Circuit Cable (Type UF)
340.1 Scope
CME
12/2
AWG
1000 ft
Copyright 2023 MikeHolt.com
Article 340 covers the use, installation, and construction specifications of underground feeder and branch-circuit cable, Type UF.

▶Figure 340–2

340.108 Equipment Grounding Conductor

Type UF cable is permitted to have an insulated or bare equipment grounding conductor.

ARTICLE
342

INTERMEDIATE METAL CONDUIT (IMC)

Introduction to Article 342—Intermediate Metal Conduit (IMC)

Article 342 covers the use, installation, and construction specifications of intermediate metal conduit (IMC) and associated fittings. IMC is a circular metal raceway that can be threaded and is available in trade sizes from ½ to 6. It has the same outside diameter as rigid metal conduit (RMC) [Article 344] but is made of a stronger metal which allows a thinner wall, making it lighter and providing a larger interior cross-sectional area for holding conductors. Topics covered in this material for Article 342 include:

- Scope
- Equipment Grounding Conductor

According to Article 100, "IMC" is a steel raceway of circular cross section that can be threaded with integral or associated couplings, listed for the installation of electrical conductors. ▶Figure 342–1

Conduit, Intermediate Metal (IMC)
Article 100 Definition
Trade Size 1/2"
Atkore
INTERMEDIATE METAL CONDUIT
MADE IN USA
A listed steel circular raceway that can be threaded with integral or associated couplings.
Copyright 2023, MikeHolt.com

▶Figure 342–1

Author's Comment:

- The type of steel from which intermediate metal conduit is manufactured, the process by which it is made, and the corrosion protection applied are all equal (or superior) to that of rigid metal conduit.

342.1 Scope

Article 342 covers the use, installation, and construction specifications of intermediate metal conduit (IMC) and associated fittings. ▶Figure 342–2

342.60 Equipment Grounding Conductor

IMC can serve an equipment grounding conductor in accordance with 250.118(A)(3). ▶Figure 342–3

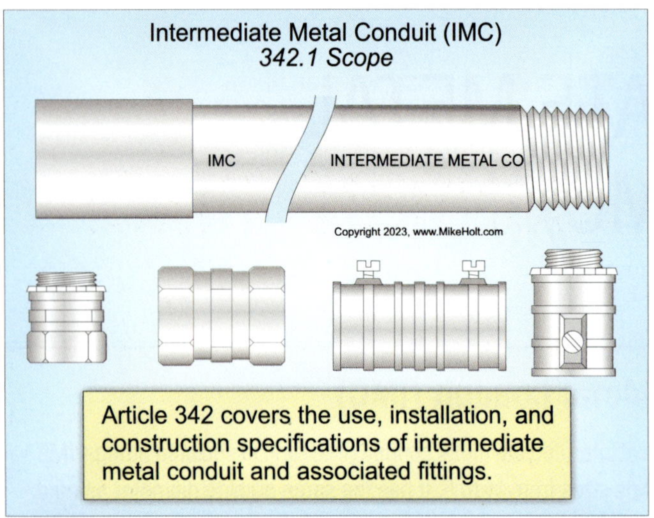
Intermediate Metal Conduit (IMC)
342.1 Scope
IMC
INTERMEDIATE METAL CO
Copyright 2023, www.MikeHolt.com
Article 342 covers the use, installation, and construction specifications of intermediate metal conduit and associated fittings.

▶Figure 342–2

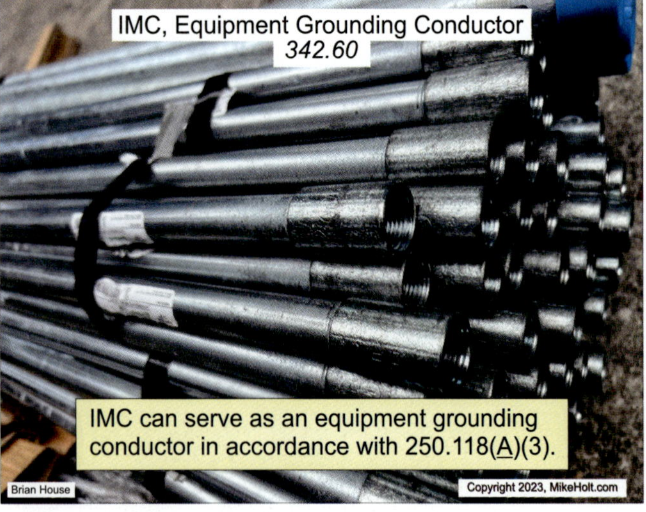
IMC, Equipment Grounding Conductor
342.60
IMC can serve as an equipment grounding conductor in accordance with 250.118(A)(3).
Brian House
Copyright 2023, MikeHolt.com

▶Figure 342–3

Author's Comment:

- The Steel Tube Institute and Georgia Tech provided studies that show ground-fault current paths travel effectively on metal raceways rather than on equipment grounding conductors. This is due to the eddy current and skin effect electrical characteristics of alternating current. Visit https://steeltubeinstitute.org for more information.

ARTICLE 344 RIGID METAL CONDUIT (RMC)

Introduction to Article 344—Rigid Metal Conduit (RMC)

This article covers the use, installation, and construction specifications of rigid metal conduit (RMC) and associated fittings. RMC, commonly called "rigid," has long been the standard raceway used to protect conductors from physical damage and from difficult environments. This type of conduit is available in trade sizes up to 6, can be threaded, and has the same outside diameter as intermediate metal conduit but has a thicker wall. It can be made of a variety of metals including steel, aluminum, red brass, and stainless steel. Topics covered in this material for Article 344 include:

- Scope
- Equipment Grounding Conductor

According to Article 100, "Rigid Metal Conduit (RMC)" is a listed metal raceway of circular cross section with integral or associated couplings listed for the installation of electrical conductors. ▶**Figure 344–1**

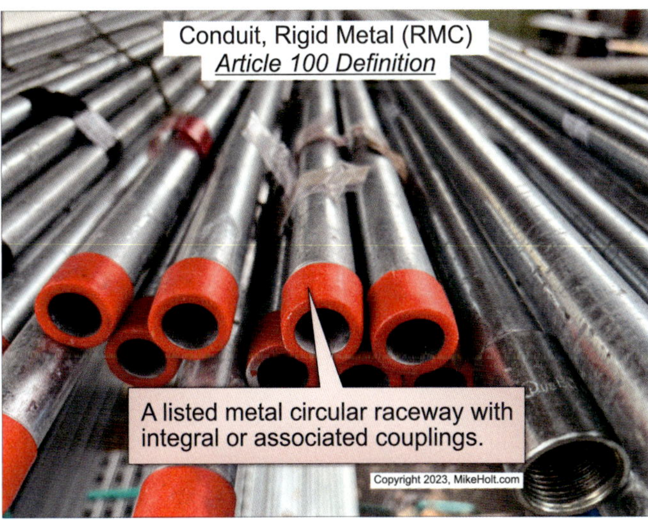
Conduit, Rigid Metal (RMC)
Article 100 Definition
A listed metal circular raceway with integral or associated couplings.
Copyright 2023, MikeHolt.com

▶**Figure 344–1**

344.1 Scope

Article 344 covers the use, installation, and construction specifications of rigid metal conduit (RMC) and associated fittings. ▶**Figure 344–2**

Rigid Metal Conduit (RMC)
344.1 Scope
Article 344 covers the use, installation, and construction specifications of rigid metal conduit and associated fittings.
Copyright 2023, MikeHolt.com

▶**Figure 344–2**

344.60 Equipment Grounding Conductor

RMC can serve an equipment grounding conductor in accordance with 250.118(A)(2). ▸Figure 344–3

RMC, Equipment Grounding Conductor
344.60
RMC can serve as an equipment grounding conductor in accordance with 250.118(A)(2).
Brian House
Copyright 2023, MikeHolt.com

▸Figure 344–3

Author's Comment:

- The Steel Tube Institute and Georgia Tech provided studies that show ground-fault current paths travel effectively on metal raceways rather than on equipment grounding conductors. This is due to the eddy current and skin effect electrical characteristics of alternating current. Visit https://steeltubeinstitute.org for more information.

ARTICLE 348 FLEXIBLE METAL CONDUIT (FMC)

Introduction to Article 348—Flexible Metal Conduit (FMC)

Article 348 covers the use, installation, and construction specifications for flexible metal conduit (FMC) and associated fittings. FMC, commonly called "flex" or sometimes "Greenfield" (after its inventor), is a raceway made a spiral interlocked steel or aluminum strip. It is primarily used where flexibility is necessary or where equipment moves, shakes, or vibrates. Topics covered in this material for Article 348 include:

- Scope
- Equipment Grounding Conductor

According to Article 100, "Flexible Metal Conduit (FMC)" is a raceway of circular cross section made of a helically wound, formed, interlocked metal strip, and listed for the installation of electrical conductors. ▸Figure 348–1

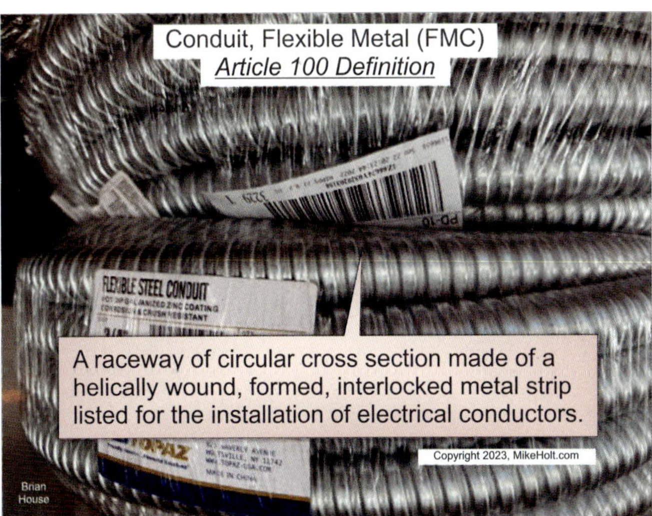
Conduit, Flexible Metal (FMC)
Article 100 Definition
FLEXIBLE STEEL CONDUIT
A raceway of circular cross section made of a helically wound, formed, interlocked metal strip listed for the installation of electrical conductors.
Copyright 2023, MikeHolt.com
Brian House

▸Figure 348–1

348.1 Scope

Article 348 covers the use, installation, and construction specifications for flexible metal conduit (FMC) and associated fittings. ▸Figure 348–2

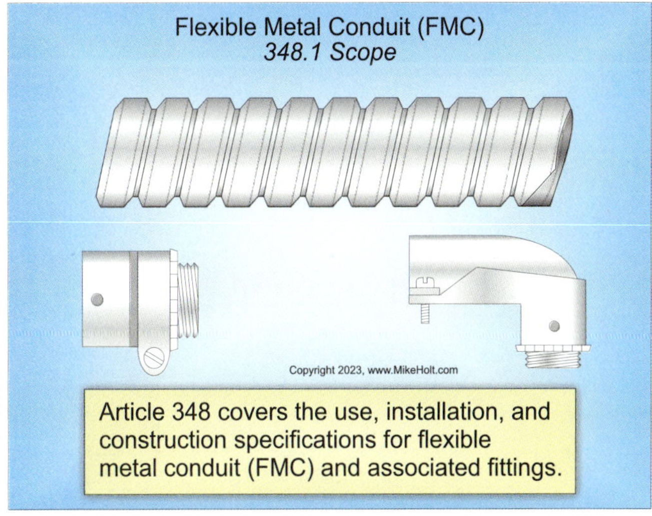
Flexible Metal Conduit (FMC)
348.1 Scope
Copyright 2023, www.MikeHolt.com
Article 348 covers the use, installation, and construction specifications for flexible metal conduit (FMC) and associated fittings.

▸Figure 348–2

A ½ FMC has a bending radius of 4 in. from the curve of the inner edge [Chapter 9 Table 2]. If the bending radius is exceeded, the conduit will be compromised and a new section will be required to be installed.

348.60 Equipment Grounding and Bonding Conductors

(A) Fixed Installation. If flexibility is not necessary after installation or vibration is not a concern, the metal armor of FMC can serve as an equipment grounding conductor in accordance with 250.118(A)(5). ▶Figure 348–3

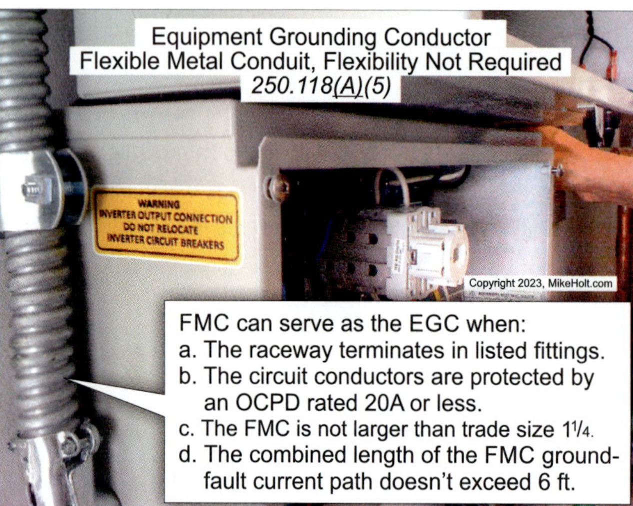
Equipment Grounding Conductor
Flexible Metal Conduit, Flexibility Not Required
250.118(A)(5)
WARNING
INVERTER OUTPUT CONNECTION
DO NOT RELOCATE
INVERTER CIRCUIT BREAKERS
Copyright 2023, MikeHolt.com
FMC can serve as the EGC when:
a. The raceway terminates in listed fittings.
b. The circuit conductors are protected by an OCPD rated 20A or less.
c. The FMC is not larger than trade size 1¼.
d. The combined length of the FMC ground-fault current path doesn't exceed 6 ft.

▶Figure 348–3

(B) Flexible Installation. If flexibility is necessary to minimize the transmission of vibration from equipment, or to provide flexibility for equipment that requires movement after installation, an equipment grounding conductor of the wire type must be installed with the circuit conductors. ▶Figure 348–4

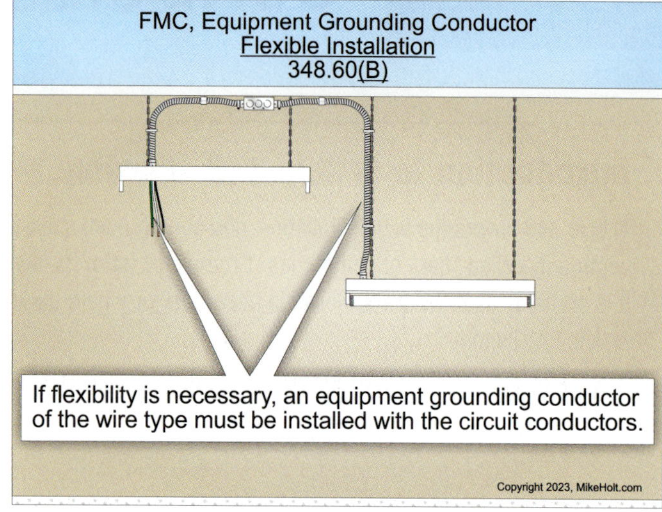
FMC, Equipment Grounding Conductor
Flexible Installation
348.60(B)
If flexibility is necessary, an equipment grounding conductor of the wire type must be installed with the circuit conductors.
Copyright 2023, MikeHolt.com

▶Figure 348–4

(D) Equipment Bonding Jumpers. The equipment bonding jumper can be installed inside or outside the flexible metal conduit. Where installed outside the FMC, the length of the equipment bonding jumper is not permitted to exceed 6 ft and must be routed with the flexible metal conduit in accordance with 250.102(E)(2).

ARTICLE 350 LIQUIDTIGHT FLEXIBLE METAL CONDUIT (LFMC)

Introduction to Article 350—Liquidtight Flexible Metal Conduit (LFMC)

This article covers the use, installation, and construction specifications of liquidtight flexible metal conduit (LFMC) and associated fittings. LFMC, with its associated connectors and fittings, is a flexible raceway commonly available in trade size ½ and larger. It is used for connections to equipment that vibrates or must be occasionally moved. LFMC is commonly called "Sealtight®" or "liquidtight." It is similar in use and construction to flexible metal conduit but has an outer liquidtight thermoplastic covering that provides protection from liquids and some corrosive effects. Topics covered in this material for Article 350 include:

- Scope
- Equipment Grounding Conductor

According to Article 100, "Liquidtight Flexible Metal Conduit (LFMC)" is a raceway of circular cross section, having an outer liquidtight, nonmetallic, sunlight-resistant jacket over an inner flexible metal core, with associated connectors and fittings, listed for the installation of electrical conductors. ▸Figure 350–1

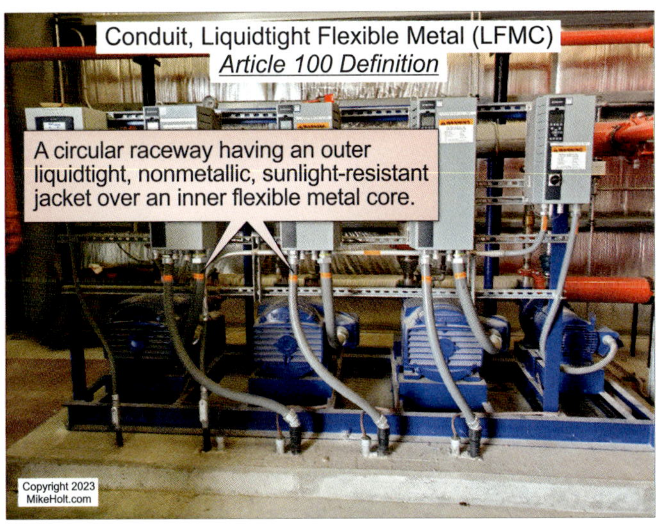
Conduit, Liquidtight Flexible Metal (LFMC)
Article 100 Definition
A circular raceway having an outer liquidtight, nonmetallic, sunlight-resistant jacket over an inner flexible metal core.
Copyright 2023 MikeHolt.com

▸Figure 350–1

350.1 Scope

Article 350 covers the use, installation, and construction specifications of liquidtight flexible metal conduit (LFMC) and associated fittings. ▸Figure 350–2

Liquidtight Flexible Metal Conduit (LFMC)
350.1 Scope
Article 350 covers the use, installation, and construction specifications of liquidtight flexible metal conduit and associated fittings.
Mario Valdez
Copyright 2023, www.MikeHolt.com

▸Figure 350–2

350.60 Equipment Grounding and Bonding Conductors

(A) Fixed Installations. If flexibility is not necessary after installation, and vibration is not a concern, the metal armor of liquidtight flexible metal conduit can serve as an equipment grounding conductor in accordance with 250.118(A)(6). ▸Figure 350-3

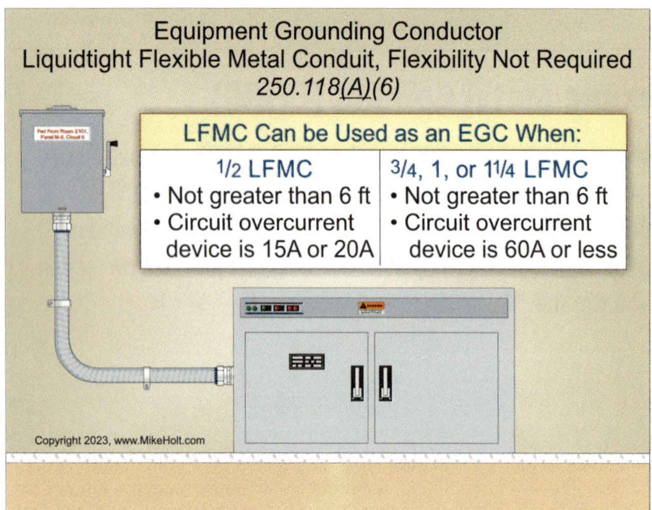
Equipment Grounding Conductor
Liquidtight Flexible Metal Conduit, Flexibility Not Required
250.118(A)(6)
LFMC Can be Used as an EGC When:
1/2 LFMC
• Not greater than 6 ft
• Circuit overcurrent device is 15A or 20A
3/4, 1, or 11/4 LFMC
• Not greater than 6 ft
• Circuit overcurrent device is 60A or less
Copyright 2023, www.MikeHolt.com

▸Figure 350-3

(B) Flexible Installations. If flexibility is necessary to minimize the transmission of vibration from equipment, or to provide flexibility for equipment that requires movement after installation, an equipment grounding conductor of the wire type must be installed with the circuit conductors. ▸Figure 350-4

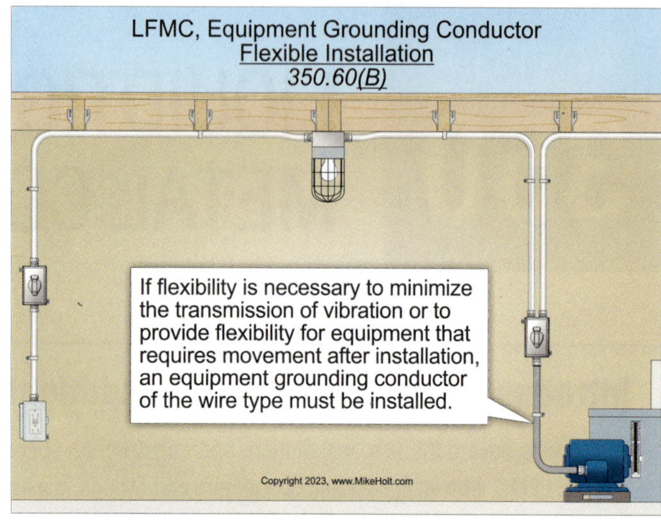
LFMC, Equipment Grounding Conductor
Flexible Installation
350.60(B)
If flexibility is necessary to minimize the transmission of vibration or to provide flexibility for equipment that requires movement after installation, an equipment grounding conductor of the wire type must be installed.
Copyright 2023, www.MikeHolt.com

▸Figure 350-4

(D) Equipment Bonding Jumper. The equipment bonding jumper can be installed inside or outside the liquidtight flexible metal conduit. Where the bonding jumper is installed outside the LFMC, the length of the equipment bonding jumper cannot exceed 6 ft, and it must be routed with the liquidtight flexible metal conduit in accordance with 250.102(E)(2).

ARTICLE 352 RIGID POLYVINYL CHLORIDE CONDUIT (PVC)

Introduction to Article 352—Rigid Polyvinyl Chloride Conduit (PVC)

Article 352 covers the use, installation, and construction specifications of polyvinyl chloride conduit (PVC) and associated fittings. PVC is a rigid nonmetallic conduit that is available in trade sizes ½ to 6. Two wall thicknesses ("schedules") are available. Schedule 40 PVC is used in most applications that are not subject to physical damage. Schedule 80 PVC, which has the same outside diameter but a thicker wall, is used where resistance to physical damage is required. This type of conduit is inexpensive, lightweight, and easily installed. It is permitted in concrete, corrosive areas, underground, and in wet locations. Topics covered in this material for Article 352 include:

- Scope
- Equipment Grounding Conductor

According to Article 100, "Polyvinyl Chloride Conduit (PVC)" is a rigid nonmetallic raceway of circular cross section with integral or associated couplings, connectors, and fittings listed for the installation of electrical conductors. ▸**Figure 352–1**

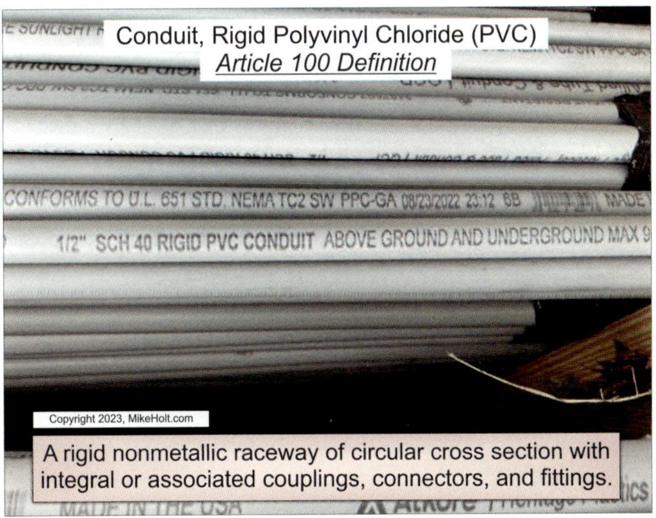
Conduit, Rigid Polyvinyl Chloride (PVC)
Article 100 Definition
CONFORMS TO U.L. 651 STD. NEMA TC2 SW PPC-GA 08/23/2022 23:12 6B
1/2" SCH 40 RIGID PVC CONDUIT ABOVE GROUND AND UNDERGROUND MAX 9
Copyright 2023, MikeHolt.com
A rigid nonmetallic raceway of circular cross section with integral or associated couplings, connectors, and fittings.

▸**Figure 352–1**

352.1 Scope

Article 352 covers the use, installation, and construction specifications of polyvinyl chloride conduit (PVC) and associated fittings. ▸**Figure 352–2**

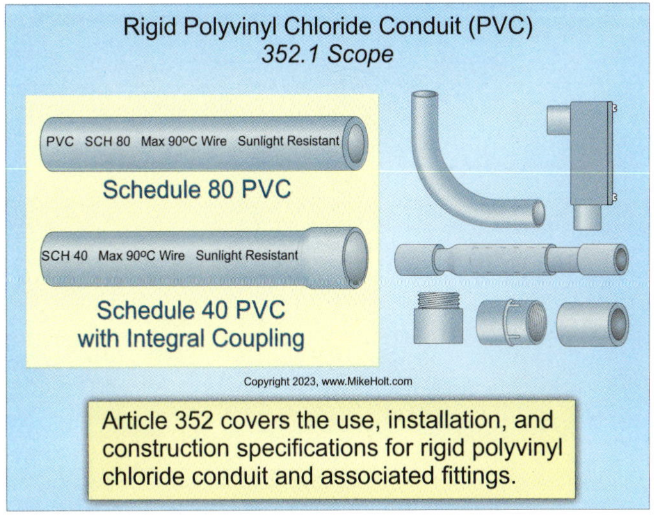
Rigid Polyvinyl Chloride Conduit (PVC)
352.1 Scope
PVC SCH 80 Max 90ºC Wire Sunlight Resistant
Schedule 80 PVC
SCH 40 Max 90ºC Wire Sunlight Resistant
Schedule 40 PVC with Integral Coupling
Copyright 2023, www.MikeHolt.com
Article 352 covers the use, installation, and construction specifications for rigid polyvinyl chloride conduit and associated fittings.

▸**Figure 352–2**

352.60 Equipment Grounding Conductor

An equipment grounding conductor must be installed within PVC when metal parts equipment require a connection to an equipment grounding conductor. ▶Figure 352-3

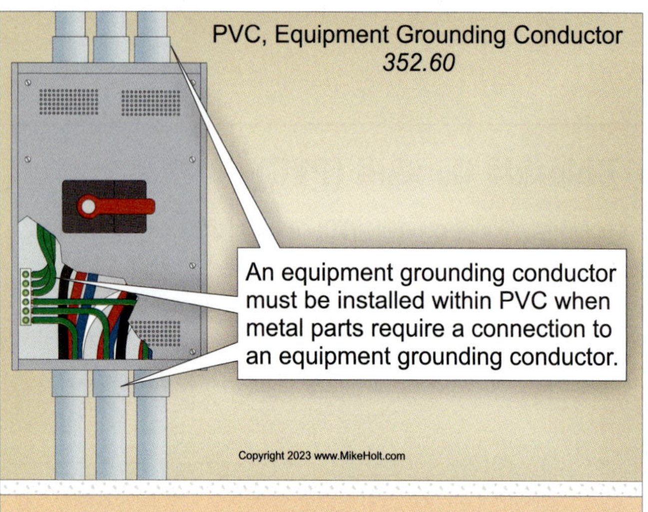
PVC, Equipment Grounding Conductor
352.60
An equipment grounding conductor must be installed within PVC when metal parts require a connection to an equipment grounding conductor.
Copyright 2023 www.MikeHolt.com

▶Figure 352-3

Ex 2: An equipment grounding conductor is not required in PVC conduit where the service neutral conductor is bonded to service equipment in accordance with 250.142(A). ▶Figure 352-4

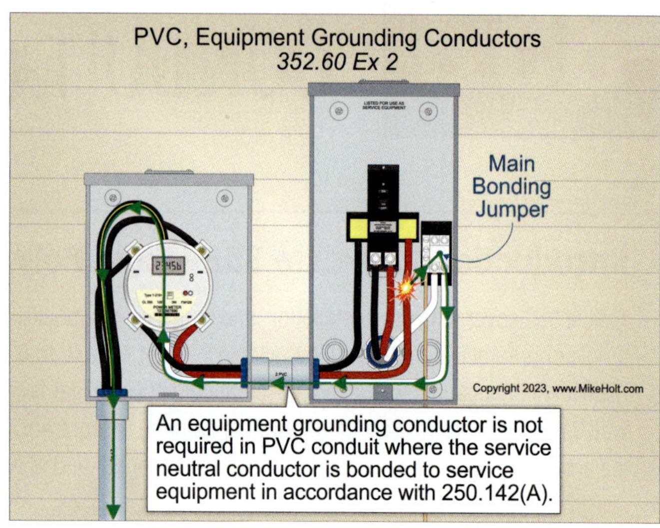
PVC, Equipment Grounding Conductors
352.60 Ex 2
Main Bonding Jumper
Copyright 2023, www.MikeHolt.com
An equipment grounding conductor is not required in PVC conduit where the service neutral conductor is bonded to service equipment in accordance with 250.142(A).

▶Figure 352-4

ARTICLE 356 LIQUIDTIGHT FLEXIBLE NONMETALLIC CONDUIT (LFNC)

Introduction to Article 356—Liquidtight Flexible Nonmetallic Conduit (LFNC)

This article covers the use, installation, and construction specifications of liquidtight flexible nonmetallic conduit (LFNC) and associated fittings. LFNC has an inner flexible core with an outer liquidtight, nonmetallic, sunlight-resistant jacket. It is available in trade sizes ½ to 4 and is sometimes referred to as "Carflex®." Topics covered in this material for Article 356 include:

- Scope
- Equipment Grounding Conductor

According to Article 100, "Liquidtight flexible nonmetallic conduit (LFNC)" is a raceway of circular cross section with an outer liquidtight, nonmetallic, sunlight-resistant jacket over a flexible inner core, with associated couplings, connectors, and fittings, listed for the installation of electrical conductors. ▶Figure 356–1

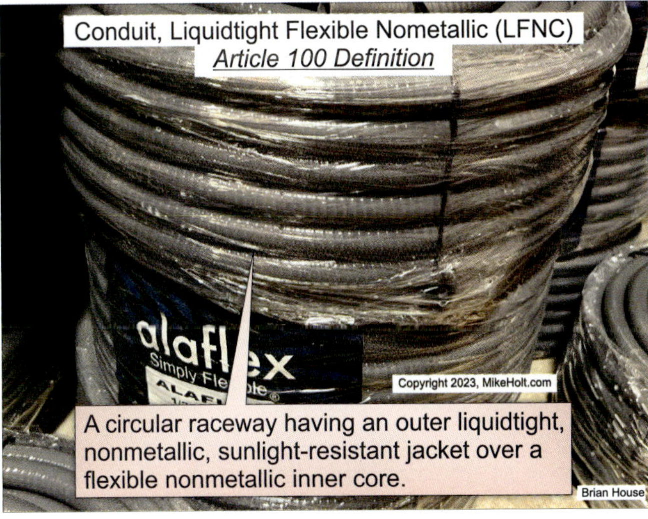
Conduit, Liquidtight Flexible Nometallic (LFNC)
Article 100 Definition
alaflex
Simply Flexible
Copyright 2023, MikeHolt.com
A circular raceway having an outer liquidtight, nonmetallic, sunlight-resistant jacket over a flexible nonmetallic inner core.
Brian House

▶Figure 356–1

356.1 Scope

Article 356 covers the use, installation, and construction specifications of liquidtight flexible nonmetallic conduit (LFNC) and associated fittings. ▶Figure 356–2

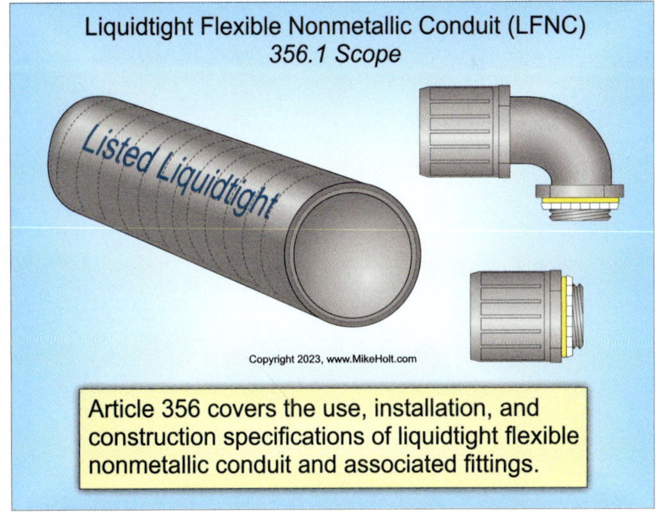
Liquidtight Flexible Nonmetallic Conduit (LFNC)
356.1 Scope
Listed Liquidtight
Copyright 2023, www.MikeHolt.com
Article 356 covers the use, installation, and construction specifications of liquidtight flexible nonmetallic conduit and associated fittings.

▶Figure 356–2

356.60 Equipment Grounding Conductor

An equipment grounding conductor must be installed within LFNC when metal parts equipment require a connection to an equipment grounding conductor. ▶Figure 356-3

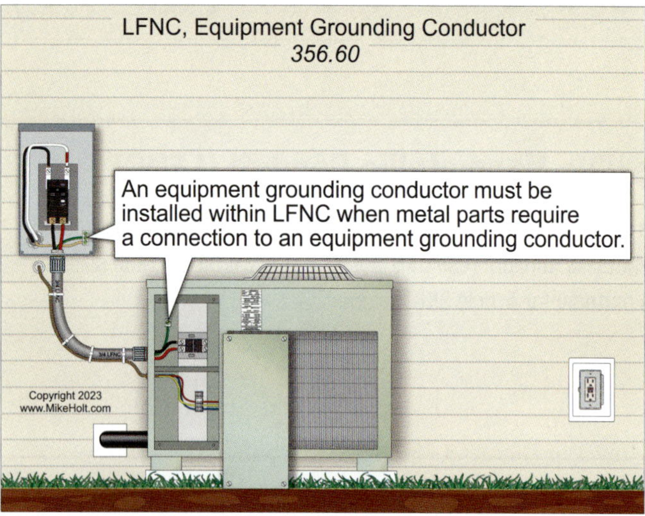
LFNC, Equipment Grounding Conductor
356.60
An equipment grounding conductor must be installed within LFNC when metal parts require a connection to an equipment grounding conductor.
Copyright 2023
www.MikeHolt.com

▶Figure 356-3

Author's Comment:

- An equipment grounding conductor is not required to be installed in a nonmetallic raceway supplying nonmetallic equipment because there is nothing in the nonmetallic box that requires a connection to an equipment grounding conductor. ▶Figure 356-4

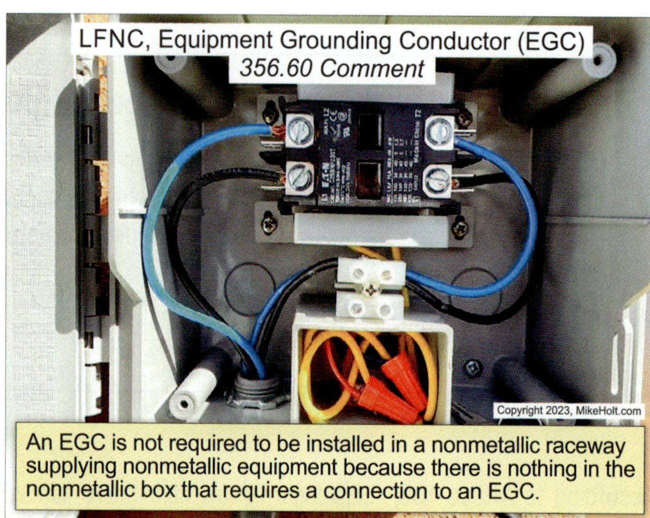
LFNC, Equipment Grounding Conductor (EGC)
356.60 Comment
Copyright 2023, MikeHolt.com
An EGC is not required to be installed in a nonmetallic raceway supplying nonmetallic equipment because there is nothing in the nonmetallic box that requires a connection to an EGC.

▶Figure 356-4

ARTICLE 358 ELECTRICAL METALLIC TUBING (EMT)

Introduction to Article 358—Electrical Metallic Tubing (EMT)

Article 358 covers the use, installation, and construction specifications of electrical metallic tubing (EMT) and associated fittings. EMT is a lightweight metal tubing that is easy to bend, cut, and ream but it cannot be threaded. It is the most common raceway used in commercial and industrial installations. Topics covered in this material for Article 358 include:

- Scope
- Equipment Grounding Conductor

According to Article 100, "Electrical Metallic Tubing (EMT)" is an unthreaded thinwall circular metallic raceway used for the installation of electrical conductors. When joined together with listed fittings and enclosures as a complete system, it is a reliable wiring method providing both physical protection for conductors as well an effective ground-fault current path. ▸Figure 358–1

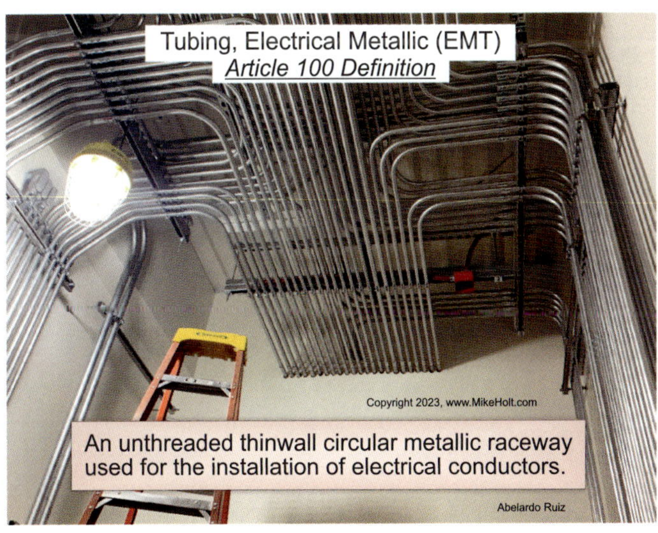
Tubing, Electrical Metallic (EMT)
Article 100 Definition
Copyright 2023, www.MikeHolt.com
An unthreaded thinwall circular metallic raceway used for the installation of electrical conductors.
Abelardo Ruiz

▸Figure 358–1

358.1 Scope

Article 358 covers the use, installation, and construction specifications of electrical metallic tubing (EMT) and associated fittings. ▸Figure 358–2

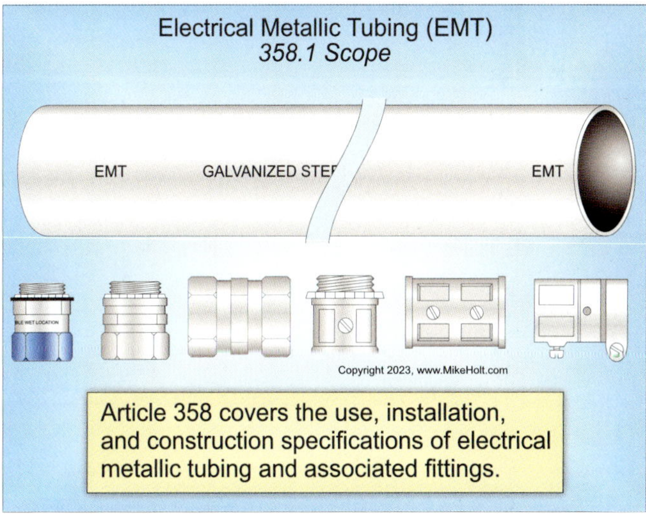
Electrical Metallic Tubing (EMT)
358.1 Scope
EMT
GALVANIZED STE
EMT
Copyright 2023, www.MikeHolt.com
Article 358 covers the use, installation, and construction specifications of electrical metallic tubing and associated fittings.

▸Figure 358–2

358.60 Equipment Grounding Conductor

EMT can serve as an equipment grounding conductor [250.118(A)(4)]. ▸Figure 358–3

EMT, Equipment Grounding Conductor
358.60
EMT can serve as an equipment grounding conductor in accordance with 250.118(A)(4).
Brian House
Copyright 2023, MikeHolt.com

▸Figure 358–3

ARTICLE 362 ELECTRICAL NONMETALLIC TUBING (ENT)

Introduction to Article 362—Electrical Nonmetallic Tubing (ENT)

This article covers the use, installation, and construction specifications of electrical nonmetallic tubing (ENT) and associated fittings. ENT is a nonmetallic, pliable, corrugated, circular raceway. It is often referred to as "Smurf Pipe" or "Smurf Tube" after the cartoon characters by the same name because it was only available in blue when it was first available, but now comes in additional colors. This type of tubing is fragile and is not sunlight resistant, so it has limited uses. Topics covered in this material for Article 362 include:

- Scope
- Equipment Grounding Conductor

According to Article 100, "Electrical Nonmetallic Tubing (ENT)" is a pliable, corrugated, circular raceway of circular cross section with integral or associated couplings, connectors, and fittings that are listed for the installation of electrical conductors. It is composed of a material that is resistant to moisture and chemical atmospheres, and it is also flame retardant. ▸**Figure 362–1**

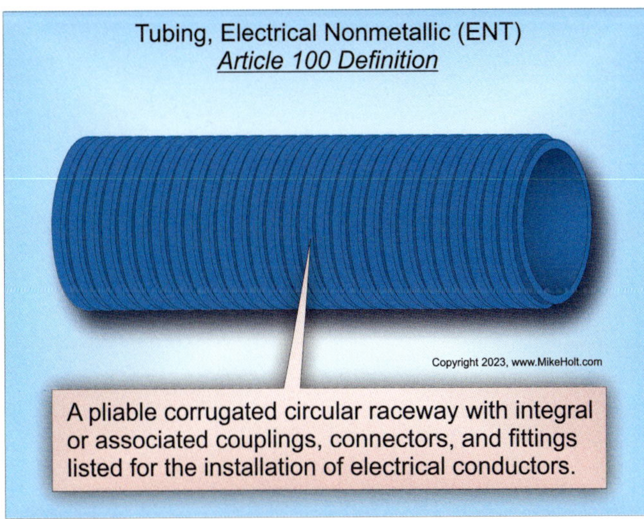
Tubing, Electrical Nonmetallic (ENT)
Article 100 Definition
Copyright 2023, www.MikeHolt.com
A pliable corrugated circular raceway with integral or associated couplings, connectors, and fittings listed for the installation of electrical conductors.

▸**Figure 362–1**

362.1 Scope

Article 362 covers the use, installation, and construction specifications of electrical nonmetallic tubing (ENT) and associated fittings. ▸**Figure 362–2**

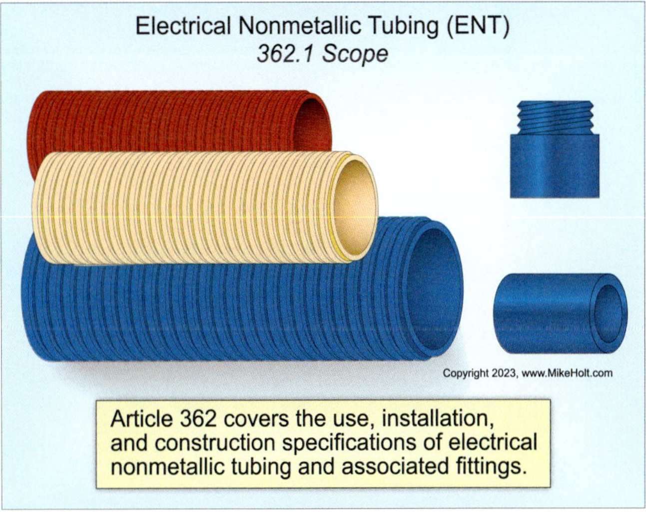
Electrical Nonmetallic Tubing (ENT)
362.1 Scope
Copyright 2023, www.MikeHolt.com
Article 362 covers the use, installation, and construction specifications of electrical nonmetallic tubing and associated fittings.

▸**Figure 362–2**

362.60 Equipment Grounding Conductor

An equipment grounding conductor must be installed within ENT when metal parts of equipment require a connection to an equipment grounding conductor. ▶Figure 362-3

Ex 2: The equipment grounding conductor is not required where the neutral conductor is used as part of the effective ground-fault current path as permitted in 250.142.

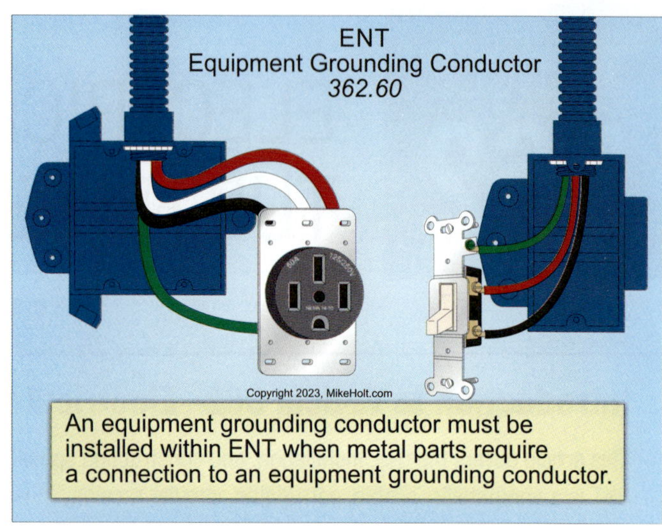
ENT
Equipment Grounding Conductor
362.60
Copyright 2023, MikeHolt.com
An equipment grounding conductor must be installed within ENT when metal parts require a connection to an equipment grounding conductor.

▶Figure 362-3

ARTICLE 376 METAL WIREWAYS

Introduction to Article 376—Metal Wireways

Article 376 covers the use, installation, and construction specifications of metal wireways and associated fittings. Metal wireways are commonly used where access to conductors inside a raceway is required to make terminations, splices, or taps to several devices at a single location. They are often incorrectly called "auxiliary gutters" or "gutters" in the field. Wireways and auxiliary gutters are similar in design but a wireway is a raceway [Article 100] while an auxiliary gutter [Article 366] is not—it is a supplemental enclosure for wiring. Topics covered in this material for Article 376 include:

- Scope
- Equipment Grounding Conductor

According to Article 100, "Metal Wireway" is a sheet metal trough with hinged or removable covers for housing and protecting electrical conductors and cable, and in which conductors are placed after the raceway has been installed. ▸Figure 376–1

Wireway, Metal
Article 100 Definition
Copyright 2023, MikeHolt.com
A sheet metal trough with hinged or removable covers for housing and protecting electric wires and cable, and in which conductors are placed after the raceway has been installed.

▸Figure 376–1

376.1 Scope

Article 376 covers the use, installation, and construction specifications of metal wireways and associated fittings. ▸Figure 376–2

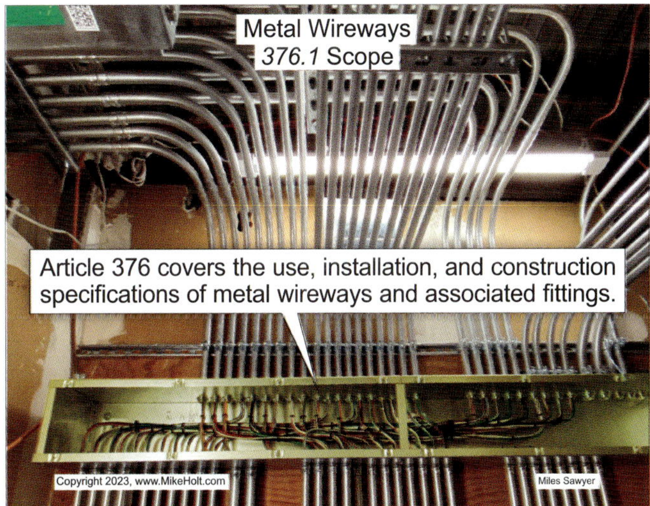
Metal Wireways
376.1 Scope
Article 376 covers the use, installation, and construction specifications of metal wireways and associated fittings.
Copyright 2023, www.MikeHolt.com
Miles Sawyer

▸Figure 376–2

376.60 Equipment Grounding Conductor

Listed metal wireways are permitted to serve as an equipment grounding conductor in accordance with 250.118(A)(13). ▸Figure 376-3

Metal Wireways
Equipment Grounding Conductor
376.60
Listed metal wireways are permitted to serve as an equipment grounding conductor in accordance with 250.118(A)(13).
Copyright 2023
www.MikeHolt.com

▸Figure 376-3

ARTICLE 386 SURFACE METAL RACEWAYS

Introduction to Article 386—Surface Metal Raceways

Article 386 covers the use, installation, and construction specifications of surface metal raceways and associated fittings. Surface metal raceways are often used where exposed traditional raceway systems are not aesthetically pleasing and raceway concealment is not economically feasible. They come in several colors and shapes and may be referred to as "Wiremold®" in the field. Topics covered in this material for Article 386 include:

- Scope
- Equipment Grounding Conductor

According to Article 100, "Surface Metal Raceway" is a raceway with associated fittings in which conductors are placed after the raceway has been installed as a complete system. ▸**Figure 386–1**

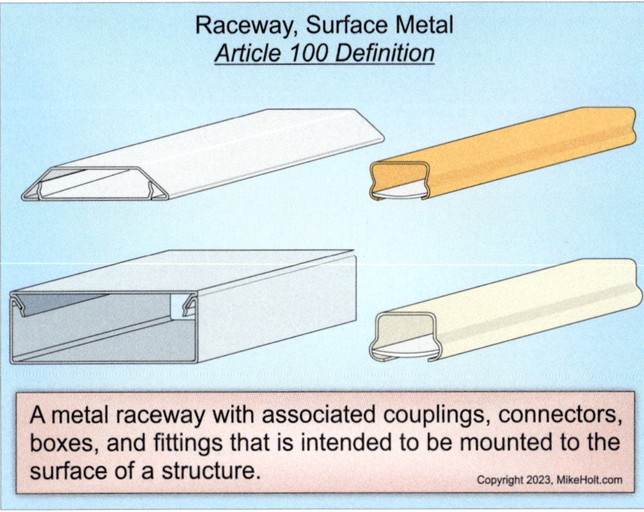

Raceway, Surface Metal
Article 100 Definition
A metal raceway with associated couplings, connectors, boxes, and fittings that is intended to be mounted to the surface of a structure.
Copyright 2023, MikeHolt.com

▸**Figure 386–1**

386.1 Scope

Article 386 covers the use, installation, and construction specifications of surface metal raceways and associated fittings. ▸**Figure 386–2**

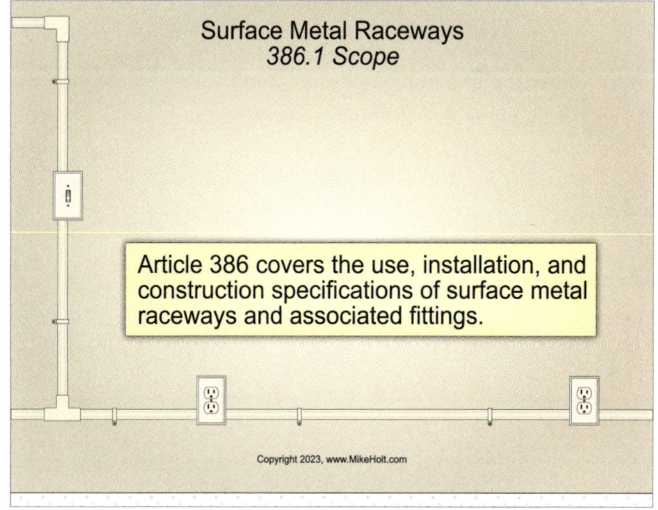

Surface Metal Raceways
386.1 Scope
Article 386 covers the use, installation, and construction specifications of surface metal raceways and associated fittings.
Copyright 2023, www.MikeHolt.com

▸**Figure 386–2**

Author's Comment:

- Surface metal raceways are available in different shapes and sizes and can be mounted on walls, ceilings, or floors.

386.60 Equipment Grounding Conductor

Surface metal raceway fittings must be mechanically and electrically joined together in a manner that does not subject the conductors to abrasion. Surface metal raceways that allow a transition to another wiring method (such as knockouts for connecting raceways) must have a means for the termination of an equipment grounding conductor.

A surface metal raceway is suitable as an equipment grounding conductor in accordance with 250.118(A)(14). ▶Figure 386-3

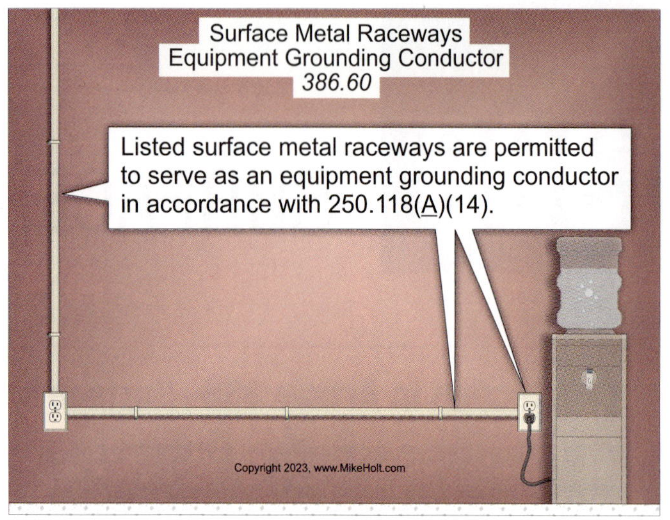
Surface Metal Raceways
Equipment Grounding Conductor
386.60
Listed surface metal raceways are permitted to serve as an equipment grounding conductor in accordance with 250.118(A)(14).
Copyright 2023, www.MikeHolt.com

▶Figure 386-3

ARTICLE 392 CABLE TRAYS

Introduction to Article 392—Cable Trays

This article covers cable tray systems including ladder, ventilated trough, ventilated channel, solid bottom, and other similar structures. A cable tray system is a unit or an assembly of units or sections with associated fittings forming a structural system used to securely fasten or support cables and raceways. Topics covered in this material for Article 392 include:

- Scope
- Equipment Grounding Conductor

According to Article 100, "Cable Tray System" is a unit, assembly of units, or sections with associated fittings forming a rigid structural system used to securely fasten or support cables and raceways. ▸Figure 392–1

Cable Tray System
Article 100 Definition
An assembly with associated fittings used to support cables and raceways.
Copyright 2023 MikeHolt.com

▸Figure 392–1

392.1 Scope

Article 392 covers cable tray systems, ladder, ventilated trough, ventilated channel, solid bottom, and other similar structures. ▸Figure 392–2

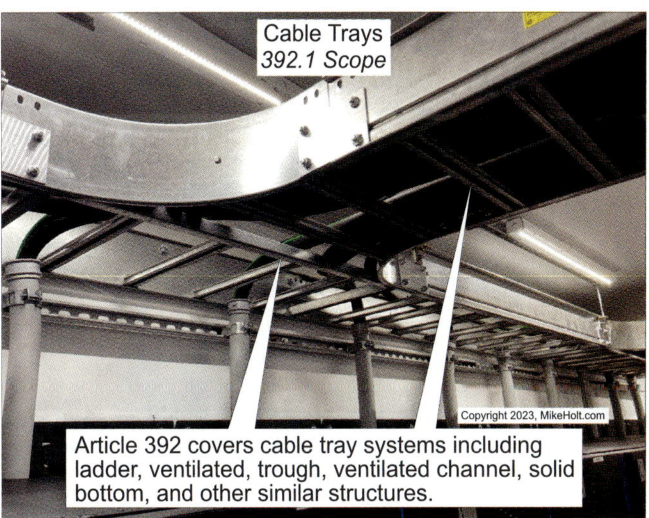

Cable Trays
392.1 Scope
Copyright 2023, MikeHolt.com
Article 392 covers cable tray systems including ladder, ventilated, trough, ventilated channel, solid bottom, and other similar structures.

▸Figure 392–2

392.60 Equipment Grounding Conductor

(A) Used as an Equipment Grounding Conductor. Metal cable trays can be used as equipment grounding conductors where continuous maintenance and supervision ensure that only qualified persons will service the cable tray system. ▸Figure 392–3

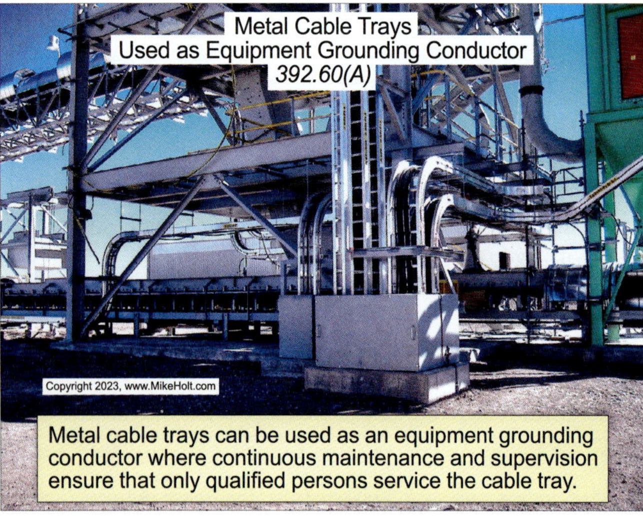
Metal Cable Trays
Used as Equipment Grounding Conductor
392.60(A)
Copyright 2023, www.MikeHolt.com
Metal cable trays can be used as an equipment grounding conductor where continuous maintenance and supervision ensure that only qualified persons service the cable tray.

▸Figure 392–3

According to Article 100, a "Qualified Person" is a person with skills and knowledge related to the construction and operation of electrical equipment and installations. This person must have received safety training to recognize and avoid the hazards involved with electrical systems. ▸Figure 392–4

Qualified Person
Article 100 Definition
70E
Copyright 2023
MikeHolt.com
A person with skills and knowledge related to the construction and operation of electrical equipment and installations. This person must have received safety training to recognize and avoid the hazards involved with electrical systems.

▸Figure 392–4

Metal cable trays containing single conductors must be bonded together to ensure they have the capacity to conduct safely any fault current likely to be imposed on them in accordance with 250.96(A).

(B) Serve as an Equipment Grounding Conductor. Metal cable trays can serve as equipment grounding conductors where the following requirements have been met:

(1) Identified as Equipment Grounding Conductor. Where metal cable trays and fittings are identified as an equipment grounding conductor. ▸Figure 392–5

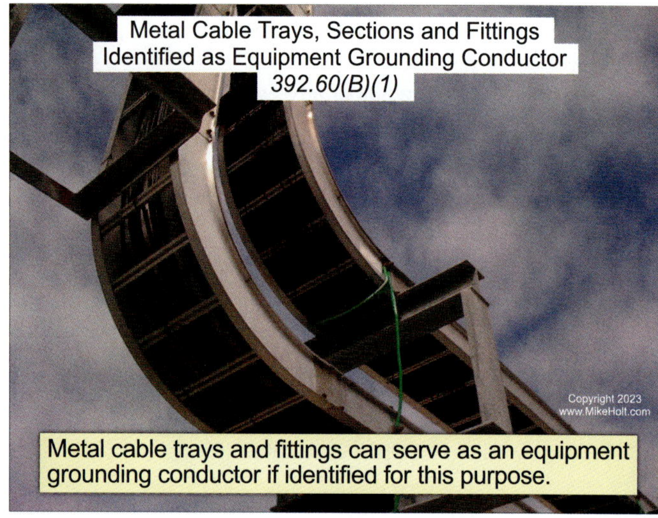
Metal Cable Trays, Sections and Fittings
Identified as Equipment Grounding Conductor
392.60(B)(1)
Copyright 2023
www.MikeHolt.com
Metal cable trays and fittings can serve as an equipment grounding conductor if identified for this purpose.

▸Figure 392–5

(4) Bonding. Cable tray sections, fittings, and connected raceways must be bonded to each other to ensure electrical continuity and the capacity to conduct safely any fault current likely to be imposed on them [250.96(A)]. This is accomplished by using bolted mechanical connectors or bonding jumpers sized in accordance with 250.102. ▸Figure 392–6

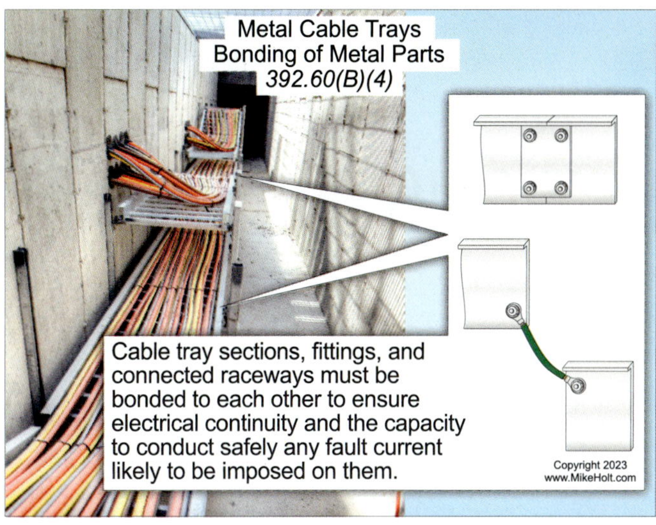
Metal Cable Trays
Bonding of Metal Parts
392.60(B)(4)
Cable tray sections, fittings, and connected raceways must be bonded to each other to ensure electrical continuity and the capacity to conduct safely any fault current likely to be imposed on them.
Copyright 2023
www.MikeHolt.com

▶Figure 392–6

CHAPTER
3 REVIEW QUESTIONS

Please use the 2023 *Code* book to answer the following questions.

Article 300—General Requirements For Wiring Methods And Materials

1. The requirements of Article 300 are not intended to apply to the conductors that form an _____ part of equipment or listed utilization equipment.

   (a) exterior
   (b) integral
   (c) interior
   (d) none of these

2. All conductors of the same circuit, including the grounded and equipment grounding conductors and bonding conductors shall be contained within the same _____, unless otherwise permitted elsewhere in the *Code*.

   (a) raceway
   (b) conduit body
   (c) trench
   (d) all of these

3. The requirement to run all paralleled circuit conductors within the same _____ applies separately to each portion of the paralleled installation.

   (a) raceway or auxiliary gutter
   (b) cable tray or trench
   (c) cable or cord
   (d) all of these

4. Conductors installed in nonmetallic raceways run underground shall be permitted to be arranged as isolated _____ installations. The raceways shall be installed in close proximity, and the conductors shall comply with 300.20(B).

   (a) neutral
   (b) grounded conductor
   (c) phase
   (d) all of these

5. Raceways, cable trays, cablebus, auxiliary gutters, cable armor, boxes, cable sheathing, cabinets, enclosures (other than surrounding fences and walls), elbows, couplings, fittings, supports, and support hardware shall be of materials suitable for _____.

   (a) corrosive locations
   (b) wet locations
   (c) the environment in which they are to be installed
   (d) damp locations

6. Where corrosion protection is necessary and the conduit is threaded anywhere other than at the factory where the product is listed, the threads shall be coated with a(an) _____ electrically conductive, corrosion-resistant compound.

   (a) marked
   (b) listed
   (c) labeled
   (d) approved

7. Metal raceways, cable armor, and other metal enclosures shall be _____ joined together into a continuous electric conductor so as to provide effective electrical continuity.

(a) electrically
(b) permanently
(c) metallically
(d) physically

8. Raceways, cable armors, and cable sheaths shall be _____ between cabinets, boxes, conduit bodies, fittings, or other enclosures or outlets.

(a) continuous
(b) protected
(c) buried
(d) encased in concrete

9. Mechanical continuity of raceways, cable armors, and cable sheaths as required by 300.12 does not apply to _____.

(a) Type MI Cable
(b) Type MC Cable
(c) short sections of raceways used for support or protection of cable assemblies
(d) any of these

10. Conductors carrying alternating current installed in ferrous metal raceways or enclosures shall be arranged so as to avoid heating the surrounding ferrous metal by induction. To accomplish this, the _____ conductor(s) shall be grouped together.

(a) phase
(b) grounded
(c) equipment grounding
(d) all of these

11. _____ is(are) a nonferrous, nonmagnetic metal that has no heating due to hysteresis heating.

(a) Steel
(b) Iron
(c) Aluminum
(d) all of these

Article 314—Boxes, Conduit Bodies, And Handhole Enclosures

1. The installation and use of all boxes and conduit bodies used as outlet, device, junction, or pull boxes, depending on their use, and handhole enclosures, are covered within _____.

(a) Article 110
(b) Article 200
(c) Article 300
(d) Article 314

2. Nonmetallic boxes can be used with _____.

(a) nonmetallic sheaths
(b) nonmetallic raceways
(c) flexible cords
(d) all of these

3. Where internal _____ means are provided between all entries, nonmetallic boxes shall be permitted to be used with metal raceways or metal-armored cables.

(a) grounding
(b) bonding
(c) connecting
(d) splicing

4. Metal boxes shall be _____ in accordance with Article 250.

(a) grounded
(b) bonded
(c) secured
(d) grounded and bonded

5. Handhole enclosure covers shall have an identifying mark or logo that prominently identifies the function of the enclosure, such as "_____."

(a) danger
(b) utility
(c) high voltage
(d) electric

6. Handhole enclosure covers shall require the use of tools to open, or they shall weigh over _____.

(a) 45 lb
(b) 70 lb
(c) 100 lb
(d) 200 lb

Article 320—Armored Cable (Type AC)

1. Article _____ covers the use, installation, and construction specifications for armored cable, Type AC.

   (a) 300
   (b) 310
   (c) 320
   (d) 334

2. Type AC cable shall provide an adequate path for _____ to act as an equipment grounding conductor.

   (a) fault current
   (b) short-circuit current
   (c) overcurrent
   (d) arcing current

Article 330—Metal-Clad Cable (Type MC)

1. Article _____ covers the use, installation, and construction specifications of metal-clad cable, Type MC.

   (a) 300
   (b) 310
   (c) 320
   (d) 330

Article 334—Nonmetallic-Sheathed Cable (Type NM)

1. In addition to the insulated conductors, Type NM cable shall have a(an) _____ equipment grounding conductor.

   (a) insulated
   (b) bare
   (c) covered
   (d) any of these

Article 340—Underground Feeder and Branch-Circuit Cable (Type UF)

1. Article 340 covers the use, installation, and construction specifications for underground feeder and branch-circuit cable, Type _____.

   (a) USE
   (b) UF
   (c) UFC
   (d) NMC

Article 342—Intermediate Metal Conduit (IMC)

1. Article _____ covers the use, installation, and construction specifications for intermediate metal conduit (IMC) and associated fittings.

   (a) 342
   (b) 348
   (c) 352
   (d) 356

Article 344—Rigid Metal Conduit (RMC)

1. Article 344 covers the use, installation, and construction specifications for _____ conduit and associated fittings.

   (a) intermediate metal
   (b) rigid metal
   (c) electrical metallic
   (d) aluminum metal

Article 348—Flexible Metal Conduit (FMC)

1. Article 348 covers the use, installation, and construction specifications for flexible metal conduit (FMC) and associated _____.

   (a) fittings
   (b) connections
   (c) terminations
   (d) devices

2. FMC shall be permitted to be used as _____ when installed in accordance with 250.118(5) where flexibility is not required after installation.

   (a) an equipment grounding conductor
   (b) an expansion fitting
   (c) flexible nonmetallic connectors
   (d) adjustable supports

3. For FMC, _____ shall be installed where flexibility is necessary to minimize the transmission of vibration from equipment or to provide flexibility for equipment that requires movement after installation.

   (a) an equipment grounding conductor
   (b) an expansion fitting
   (c) flexible nonmetallic connectors
   (d) adjustable supports

Article 350—Liquidtight Flexible Metal Conduit (LFMC)

1. The use, installation, and construction specifications for liquidtight flexible metal conduit (LFMC) and associated fittings are covered within Article _____.

   (a) 300
   (b) 334
   (c) 350
   (d) 410

2. Where flexibility is not required after installation, liquidtight flexible metal conduit shall be permitted to be used as an equipment grounding conductor when installed in accordance with _____.

   (a) 250.102
   (b) 250.118(A)(5)
   (c) 250.118(A)(6)
   (d) 348.6

3. When LFMC is used to connect equipment where flexibility is necessary to minimize the transmission of vibration from equipment or for equipment requiring movement after installation, a(an) _____ conductor shall be installed.

   (a) main bonding
   (b) grounded
   (c) equipment grounding
   (d) grounding electrode

Article 352—Rigid Polyvinyl Chloride Conduit (PVC)

1. Article 352 covers the use, installation, and construction specifications for _____ and associated fittings.

   (a) ENT
   (b) RMC
   (c) IMC
   (d) PVC

2. Where equipment grounding is required, a separate grounding conductor shall be installed in Type PVC conduit except where the _____ is used to ground equipment as permitted in 250.142.

   (a) grounding jumper
   (b) grounded conductor
   (c) bonding jumper
   (d) bonded conductor

Article 356—Liquidtight Flexible Nonmetallic Conduit (LFNC)

1. Article _____ covers the use, installation, and construction specifications for liquidtight flexible nonmetallic conduit (LFNC) and associated fittings.

   (a) 300
   (b) 334
   (c) 350
   (d) 356

2. When LFNC is used, and equipment grounding is required, a separate _____ shall be installed in the conduit.

   (a) grounding conductor
   (b) expansion fitting
   (c) flexible nonmetallic connector
   (d) grounded conductor

Article 358—Electrical Metallic Tubing (EMT)

1. Article _____ covers the use, installation, and construction specifications for electrical metallic tubing (EMT) and associated fittings.

   (a) 334
   (b) 350
   (c) 356
   (d) 358

2. EMT shall not be permitted as an equipment grounding conductor.

   (a) True
   (b) False

Article 362—Electrical Nonmetallic Tubing (ENT)

1. Article _____ covers the use, installation, and construction specifications for electrical nonmetallic tubing (ENT) and associated fittings.

   (a) 358
   (b) 362
   (c) 366
   (d) 392

2. Where ENT is the wiring method and equipment grounding is required, a _____ equipment grounding conductor shall be installed in the raceway.

(a) separate
(b) additional
(c) supplemental
(d) none of these

3. Where ENT is the wiring method and equipment grounding is required, the equipment grounding conductor shall not be required where the _____ conductor is used as part of the effective ground-fault path as permitted.

(a) grounded
(b) equipment grounding
(c) ungrounded
(d) none of these

Article 376—Metal Wireways

1. Listed metal wireway shall be permitted _____ in accordance with 250.118(A)(13).

(a) as an equipment grounding conductor
(b) where subject to physical damage
(c) for use in corrosive environments
(d) to be installed through walls

Article 386—Surface Metal Raceways

1. Article 386 covers the use, installation, and construction specifications for surface _____ and associated fittings.

(a) nonmetallic raceways
(b) metal raceways
(c) metal wireways
(d) enclosures

2. Surface metal raceway enclosures providing a transition from other wiring methods shall have a means for connecting a(an) _____ conductor.

(a) grounded
(b) ungrounded
(c) equipment grounding
(d) all of these

Article 392—Cable Trays

1. Cable tray systems, including ladder, ventilated trough, ventilated channel, solid bottom, and other similar structures are covered within Article _____.

(a) 358
(b) 362
(c) 366
(d) 392

2. Steel or aluminum cable tray systems are permitted to be used as an equipment grounding conductor, provided the cable tray sections and fittings are identified as _____, among other requirements.

(a) an equipment grounding conductor
(b) special equipment
(c) industrial grade
(d) all of these

CHAPTER

4

EQUIPMENT FOR GENERAL USE

Introduction to Chapter 4—Equipment for General Use

With the first three chapters of the *NEC* behind you, this fourth one is necessary for building a solid foundation in general equipment installations. Some examples of general equipment include but are not limited to luminaires, heaters, motors, air-conditioning units, generators, and transformers. The articles in Chapter 4 help you apply the first three chapters to installations involving general equipment. You must understand the first four chapters of the *Code* to properly apply these requirements to Chapters 5, 6, and 7, and at times to Chapter 8.

Chapter 4 is arranged in the following manner:

- **Article 404—Switches.** The requirements of Article 404 apply to switches of all types. These include snap (toggle) switches, dimmer switches, fan switches, knife switches, circuit breakers, and automatic switches such as time clocks, timers, and switches and circuit breakers used for disconnects.
- **Article 406—Receptacles and Attachment Plugs (Caps).** This article covers the rating, type, and installation of receptacles and attachment plugs. It also covers flanged surface inlets.
- **Article 408—Switchboards and Panelboards.** Article 408 covers specific requirements for switchboards, panelboards, and distribution boards that supply lighting and power circuits.

Author's Comment:

- See Article 100 for the definitions of "Panelboard" and "Switchboard."

- **Article 410—Luminaires and Lamps.** This article contains the requirements for luminaires, lampholders, and lamps. Because of the many types and applications of luminaires, manufacturer's instructions are very important and helpful for proper installation.
- **Article 440—Air-Conditioning Equipment.** Article 440 applies to electrically driven air-conditioning equipment with a motorized hermetic compressor. The requirements in this article are in addition to, or amend, those in Article 430 and others.
- **Article 450—Transformers.** This article covers the installation of transformers. Understanding the overcurrent protection requirements in Table 450.3(B) and the disconnect location is important to provide protection properly.

ARTICLE 404 SWITCHES

Introduction to Article 404—Switches

Article 404 covers all types of switches, switching devices, and circuit breakers such as snap (toggle) switches, dimmer switches, fan switches, disconnect switches, circuit breakers, and automatic switches such as those used for time clocks and timers. Topics covered in this material for Article 404 include:

- Scope
- General-Use Snap Switches, Dimmers, and Control Switches
- Bonding Enclosures

404.1 Scope

The requirements of Article 404 apply to all types of switches, switching devices, and circuit breakers. **Figure 404–1**

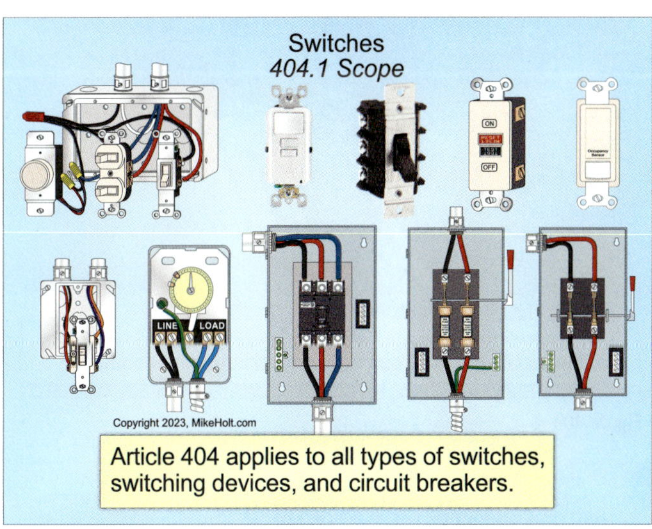
Switches
404.1 Scope
LINE
LOAD
Copyright 2023, MikeHolt.com
Article 404 applies to all types of switches, switching devices, and circuit breakers.

Figure 404–1

Article 404 does not cover wireless control equipment to which circuit conductors are not connected. **Figure 404–2**

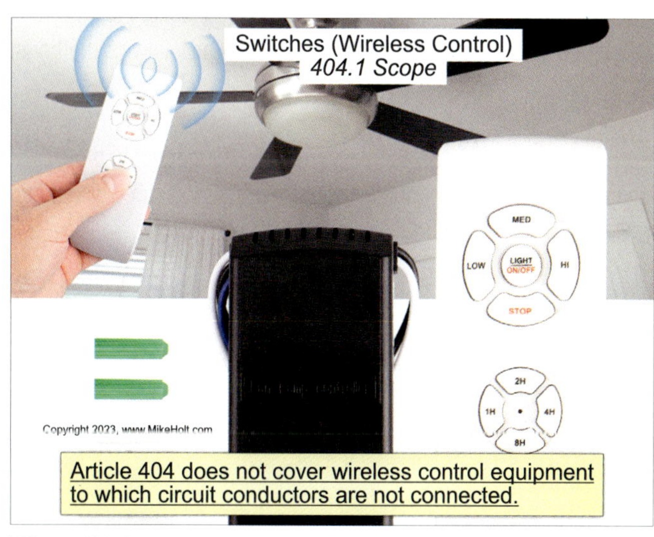
Switches (Wireless Control)
404.1 Scope
MED
LOW
LIGHT ON/OFF
HI
STOP
2H
1H
4H
8H
Copyright 2023, www.MikeHolt.com
Article 404 does not cover wireless control equipment to which circuit conductors are not connected.

Figure 404–2

Note: See 210.70 for additional information related to branch circuits that include switches or listed wall-mounted control devices.

404.9 General-Use Snap Switches, Dimmers, and Control Switches

(A) Faceplates. Faceplates for switches, dimmers, and control switches must completely cover the outlet box opening. Where flush mounted, the faceplate must seat against the wall surface. ▶**Figure 404-3**

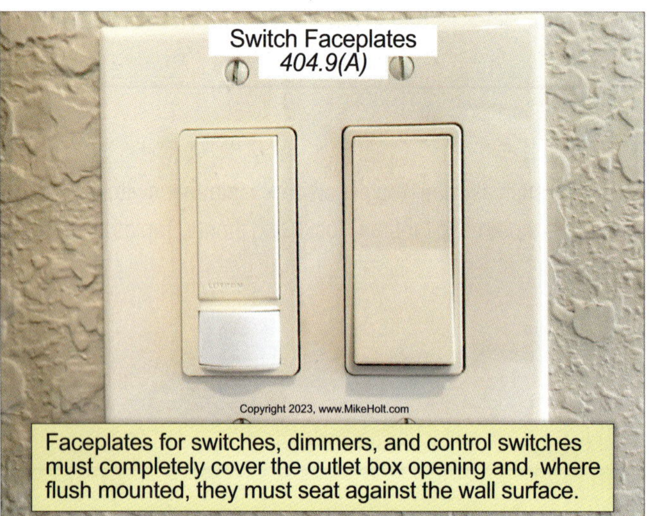
Switch Faceplates
404.9(A)
Copyright 2023, www.MikeHolt.com
Faceplates for switches, dimmers, and control switches must completely cover the outlet box opening and, where flush mounted, they must seat against the wall surface.

▶**Figure 404-3**

(B) Equipment Grounding Conductor. Switches, dimmers, and control switches and metal faceplates must be connected to the circuit equipment grounding conductor using either of the following methods:

(1) Metal Boxes.

Metal Faceplates. Metal faceplates must be connected to the circuit equipment grounding conductor (metal faceplates secured with metal screws to the switch). ▶**Figure 404-4**

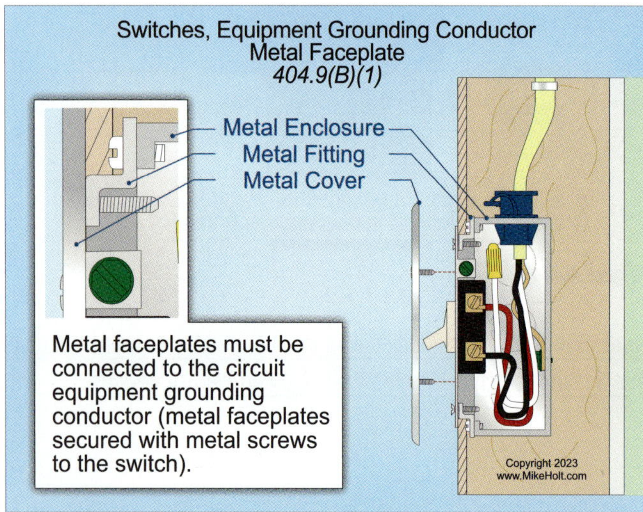
Switches, Equipment Grounding Conductor
Metal Faceplate
404.9(B)(1)
Metal Enclosure
Metal Fitting
Metal Cover
Metal faceplates must be connected to the circuit equipment grounding conductor (metal faceplates secured with metal screws to the switch).
Copyright 2023 www.MikeHolt.com

▶**Figure 404-4**

Switch. Switches in metal boxes or metal covers are connected to the equipment grounding conductor using metal screws [250.109]. ▶**Figure 404-5**

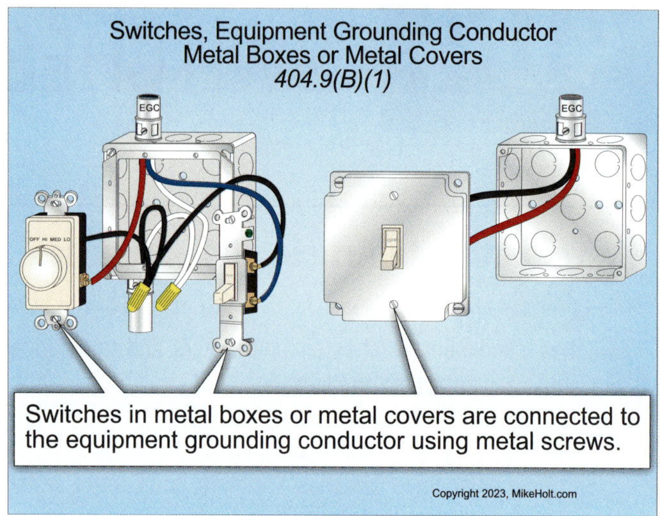
Switches, Equipment Grounding Conductor
Metal Boxes or Metal Covers
404.9(B)(1)
EGC
EGC
Switches in metal boxes or metal covers are connected to the equipment grounding conductor using metal screws.
Copyright 2023, MikeHolt.com

▶**Figure 404-5**

(2) Nonmetallic Boxes. The grounding terminal of a switch in nonmetallic boxes must be connected to the circuit equipment grounding conductor. ▶**Figure 404-6**

Switches, Equipment Grounding Conductor
Nonmetallic Boxes
404.9(B)(2)
Copyright 2023 www.MikeHolt.com
The grounding terminal of a switch in nonmetallic boxes must be connected to the circuit equipment grounding conductor.

▶**Figure 404-6**

Author's Comment:

- A switch with a metal faceplate installed in a nonmetallic box poses a shock hazard if it becomes energized. An effective ground-fault current path must be provided by connecting the metal faceplate with metal screws to a switch that is connected to an equipment grounding conductor [250.109].

Ex 1: Where no means exists within the box for bonding to an equipment grounding conductor, or if the wiring method at the existing switch does not contain an equipment grounding conductor, a switch without such a connection to the equipment grounding conductor is permitted for replacement purposes only. A switch installed under this exception must have a faceplate that is nonmetallic and noncombustible with nonmetallic screws, or the replacement switch must be GFCI protected.

Ex 2: Listed assemblies are not required to be bonded to an equipment grounding conductor if all the following conditions are met:

(1) The device is provided with a nonmetallic faceplate and designed such that no metallic faceplate replaces the one provided.

(2) The device does not have a mounting means to accept other configurations of faceplates.

(3) The device is equipped with a nonmetallic yoke.

(4) Parts of the device that are accessible after the faceplate is installed are manufactured of nonmetallic material.

Ex 3: An equipment grounding conductor is not required for bonding a snap switch with an integral nonmetallic enclosure complying with 300.15(E).

404.12 Bonding of Enclosures

Metal enclosures for switches and circuit breakers must be connected to an equipment grounding conductor of a type recognized in 250.118(A) [250.4(A)(3)].

Metal enclosures for switches and circuit breakers used as service equipment must be bonded to the service neutral conductor via the main bonding jumper to provide an effective ground-fault current path [250.92(A)].

Where nonmetallic enclosures are used with metal raceways or metal-armored cables, they must comply with 314.3 Ex 1 or Ex 2.

ARTICLE
406

RECEPTACLES, ATTACHMENT PLUGS, AND FLANGED INLETS

Introduction to Article 406—Receptacles, Attachment Plugs, and Flanged Inlets

This article covers the rating, type, and installation of receptacles, attachment plugs, and flanged inlets. There are many types of receptacles such as self-grounding, isolated ground, tamper resistant, weather resistant, GFCIs and AFCIs, energy controlled, work surface and countertop assemblies, USBs, surge protectors, and so on. Topics covered in this material for Article 406 include:

- Scope
- Receptacle Types and Ratings
- Equipment Grounding Conductor Terminals

According to Article 100, "Receptacle" is a contact device installed at an outlet for the connection of an attachment plug or equipment designed to mate with the contact device. ▸**Figure 406–1**

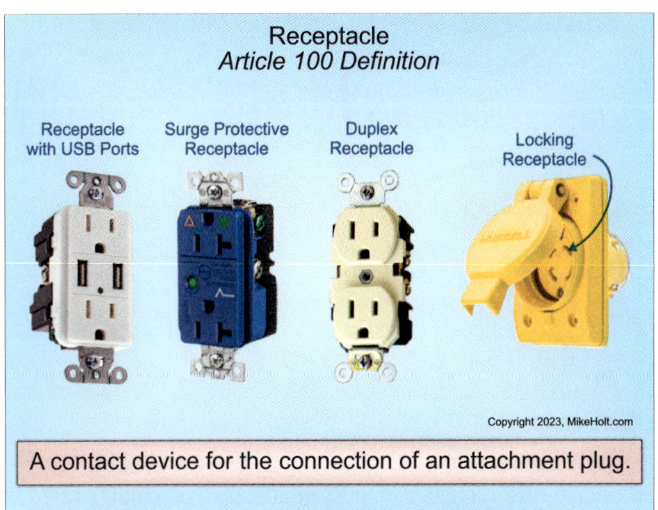
Receptacle
Article 100 Definition
Receptacle with USB Ports
Surge Protective Receptacle
Duplex Receptacle
Locking Receptacle
Copyright 2023, MikeHolt.com
A contact device for the connection of an attachment plug.

▸**Figure 406–1**

A single receptacle contains one contact device on the same yoke or strap. A multiple receptacle has more than one contact device on the same yoke or strap. ▸**Figure 406–2**

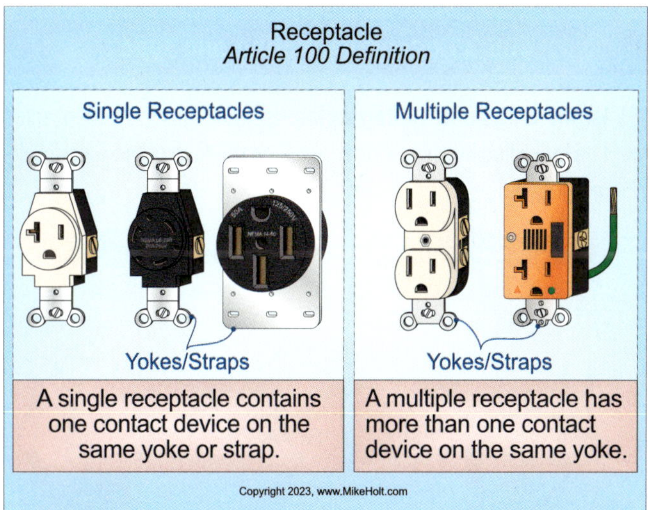
Receptacle
Article 100 Definition
Single Receptacles
Multiple Receptacles
Yokes/Straps
Yokes/Straps
A single receptacle contains one contact device on the same yoke or strap.
A multiple receptacle has more than one contact device on the same yoke.
Copyright 2023, www.MikeHolt.com

▸**Figure 406–2**

Author's Comment:

- A yoke (also called a "strap") is the metal mounting structure for such items as receptacles, switches, switches with pilot lights, and switch/receptacles to name a few.

Note: A duplex receptacle is an example of a multiple receptacle with two receptacles on the same yoke or strap.

406.1 Scope

Article 406 covers the rating, type, and installation of receptacles, attachment plugs, and flanged inlets. ▶Figure 406-3

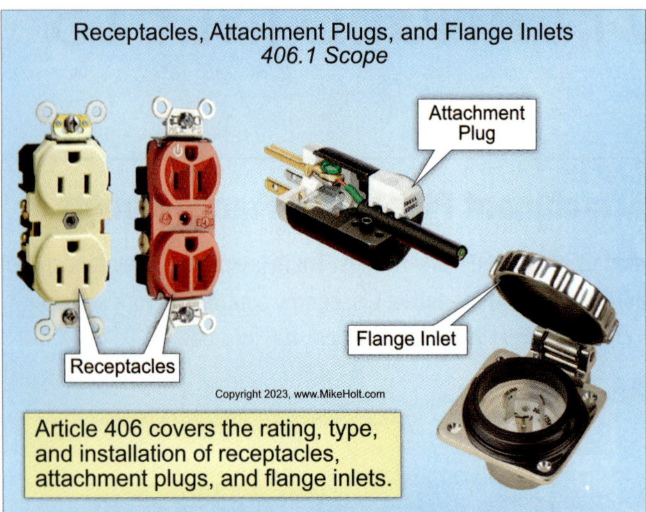
Receptacles, Attachment Plugs, and Flange Inlets
406.1 Scope
Attachment Plug
Flange Inlet
Receptacles
Copyright 2023, www.MikeHolt.com
Article 406 covers the rating, type, and installation of receptacles, attachment plugs, and flange inlets.

▶Figure 406-3

406.3 Receptacle Rating and Type

(E) Isolated Ground Receptacles. Isolated ground receptacles must be identified by an orange triangle on the face of the receptacle. ▶Figure 406-4

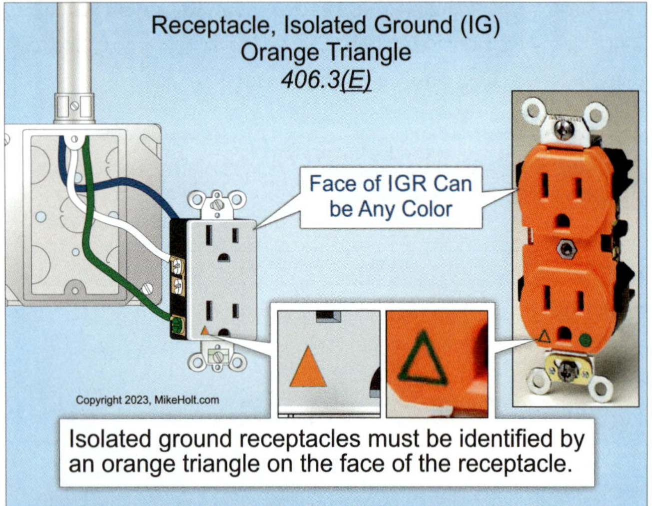
Receptacle, Isolated Ground (IG)
Orange Triangle
406.3(E)
Face of IGR Can be Any Color
Copyright 2023, MikeHolt.com
Isolated ground receptacles must be identified by an orange triangle on the face of the receptacle.

▶Figure 406-4

(1) Isolated ground receptacles must have their grounding terminals connected to an insulated equipment grounding conductor in accordance with 250.146(D). ▶Figure 406-5

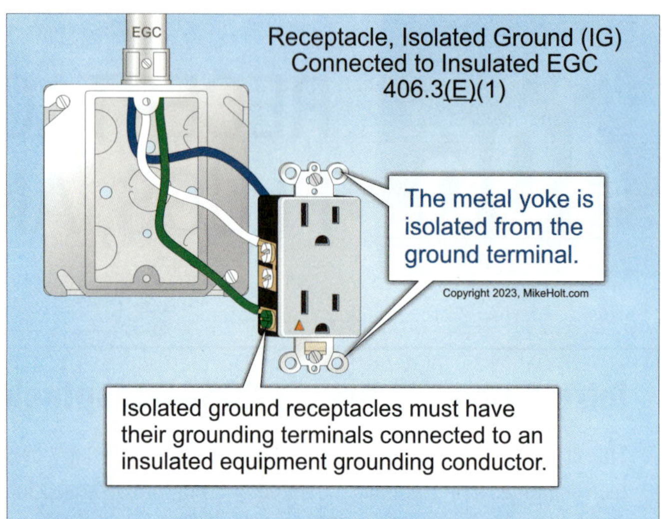
EGC
Receptacle, Isolated Ground (IG)
Connected to Insulated EGC
406.3(E)(1)
The metal yoke is isolated from the ground terminal.
Copyright 2023, MikeHolt.com
Isolated ground receptacles must have their grounding terminals connected to an insulated equipment grounding conductor.

▶Figure 406-5

406.4 General Installation Requirements

(A) Grounding Type. Receptacles installed on 15A and 20A branch circuits must be of the grounding type, except as permitted for 2-wire receptacle replacements in 406.4(D)(2). ▶Figure 406-6

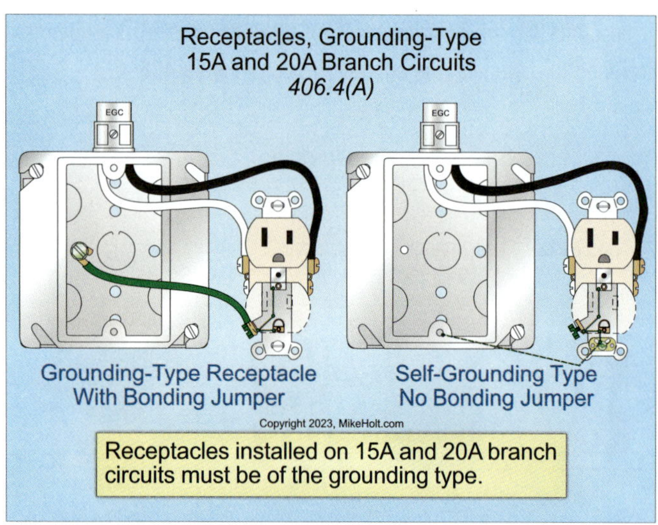
Receptacles, Grounding-Type
15A and 20A Branch Circuits
406.4(A)
EGC
EGC
Grounding-Type Receptacle
With Bonding Jumper
Self-Grounding Type
No Bonding Jumper
Copyright 2023, MikeHolt.com
Receptacles installed on 15A and 20A branch circuits must be of the grounding type.

▶Figure 406-6

Grounding-type receptacles must be installed on circuits rated in accordance with Table 210.21(B)(1) for single receptacles and Table 210.21(B)(2) or Table 210.21(B)(3) for two or more receptacles.

Table 210.21(B)(3) Receptacle Ratings

Circuit Rating	Receptacle Rating
15A	15A
20A	15A or 20A
30A	30A
40A	40A or 50A
50A	50A

(C) Methods of Connection to Equipment Grounding Conductor. The receptacle grounding terminal must be connected to the equipment grounding conductor of the circuit supplying the receptacle in accordance with 250.146. ▸**Figure 406-7**

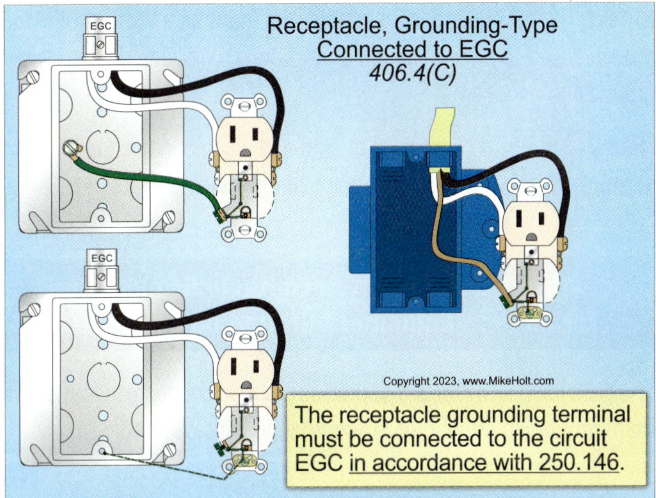
EGC
EGC
Receptacle, Grounding-Type
Connected to EGC
406.4(C)
Copyright 2023, www.MikeHolt.com
The receptacle grounding terminal must be connected to the circuit EGC in accordance with 250.146.

▸**Figure 406-7**

Cord connectors must be connected to the circuit equipment grounding conductor.

Note 1: For acceptable types of equipment grounding conductors see 250.118(A).

Note 2: See 250.130 for extensions of existing branch circuits.

(D) Receptacle Replacement. If the receptacle to be replaced is in a location that requires AFCI- and/or GFCI-type receptacles, the replacement receptacle must be installed at a readily accessible location and comply with 406.4(D)(1) though (D)(8).

(1) Equipment Grounding Conductor in Outlet Box. If an equipment grounding conductor exists in an outlet box, replacement receptacles must be of the grounding type and the receptacle's grounding terminal must be connected to the circuit equipment grounding conductor in accordance with 406.11.

(2) No Equipment Grounding Conductor in Box. If an equipment grounding conductor does not exist in the outlet box, replacement receptacles can be a:

(a) Nongrounding-type receptacle. ▸**Figure 406-8**

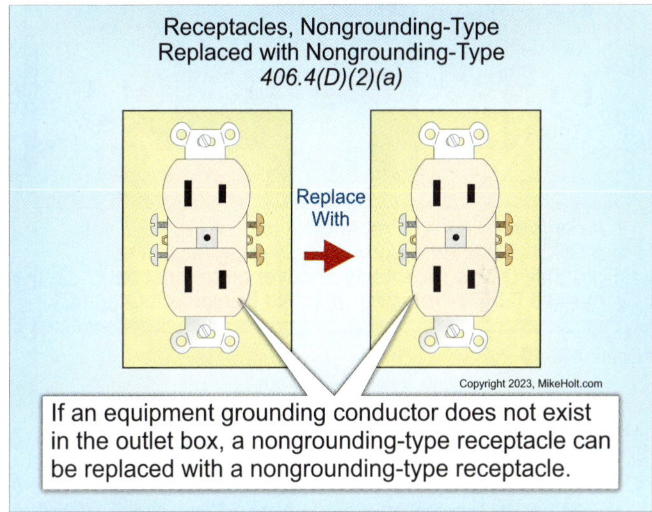
Receptacles, Nongrounding-Type
Replaced with Nongrounding-Type
406.4(D)(2)(a)
Replace
With
Copyright 2023, MikeHolt.com
If an equipment grounding conductor does not exist in the outlet box, a nongrounding-type receptacle can be replaced with a nongrounding-type receptacle.

▸**Figure 406-8**

(b) GFCI-type receptacle. The GFCI receptacle or cover plate must be marked "No Equipment Ground." An equipment grounding conductor is not required from the GFCI-type receptacle to any receptacle outlets downstream. ▸**Figure 406-9**

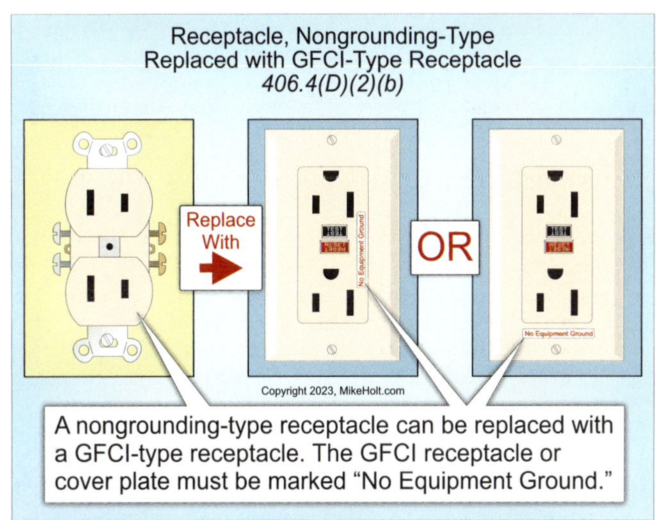
Receptacle, Nongrounding-Type
Replaced with GFCI-Type Receptacle
406.4(D)(2)(b)
Replace
With
OR
Copyright 2023, MikeHolt.com
A nongrounding-type receptacle can be replaced with a GFCI-type receptacle. The GFCI receptacle or cover plate must be marked "No Equipment Ground."

▸**Figure 406-9**

(c) Grounding-type receptacle where it is GFCI protected. The grounding-type receptacle or cover plate must be marked "GFCI Protected" and "No Equipment Ground." An equipment grounding conductor is not required from the GFCI-protected grounding-type receptacle to any receptacle outlets downstream. ▸**Figure 406-10**

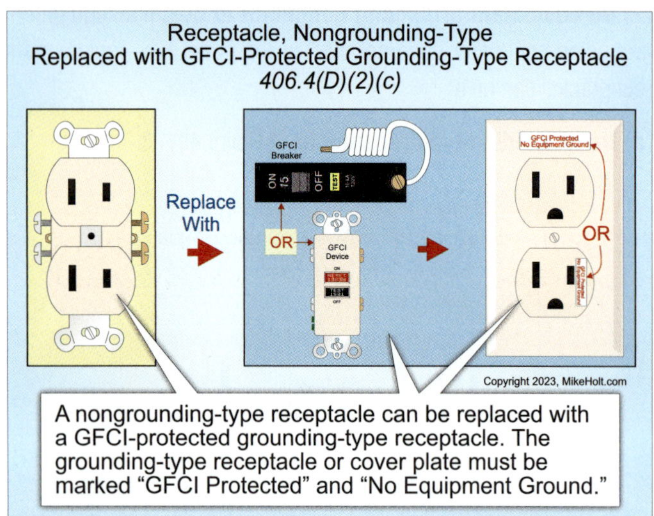
Receptacle, Nongrounding-Type
Replaced with GFCI-Protected Grounding-Type Receptacle
406.4(D)(2)(c)
Replace With
OR
GFCI Breaker
GFCI Device
GFCI Protected No Equipment Ground
OR
A nongrounding-type receptacle can be replaced with a GFCI-protected grounding-type receptacle. The grounding-type receptacle or cover plate must be marked "GFCI Protected" and "No Equipment Ground."
Copyright 2023, MikeHolt.com

▸**Figure 406-10**

Author's Comment:

- GFCI protection functions properly on a 2-wire circuit without an equipment grounding conductor because the circuit's equipment grounding conductor serves no role in the operation of a GFCI device.

According to Article 100, "Ground-Fault Circuit Interrupter" is a device intended to protect people by de-energizing a circuit when ground-fault current exceeds the value established for a Class A device. ▸**Figure 406-11**

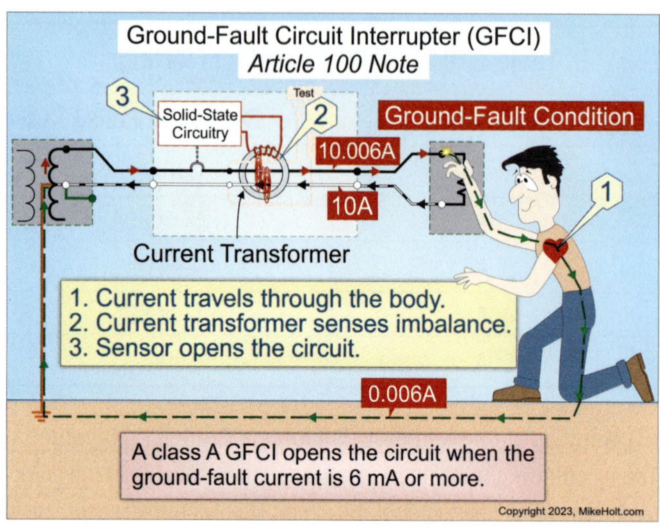
Ground-Fault Circuit Interrupter (GFCI)
Article 100 Note
3
Solid-State Circuitry
Test
2
Ground-Fault Condition
10.006A
10A
1
Current Transformer
1. Current travels through the body.
2. Current transformer senses imbalance.
3. Sensor opens the circuit.
0.006A
A class A GFCI opens the circuit when the ground-fault current is 6 mA or more.
Copyright 2023, MikeHolt.com

▸**Figure 406-11**

Note 1: Some equipment or appliance manufacturers require the branch circuit to the equipment or appliance to include an equipment grounding conductor.

Note 2: See 250.114 for a list of cord-and-plug-connected equipment or appliances that require an equipment grounding conductor.

406.11 Connecting Receptacle Grounding Terminal to Equipment Grounding Conductor

The grounding terminal of receptacles must be connected to an equipment grounding conductor in accordance with 250.146.

ARTICLE 408 SWITCHBOARDS AND PANELBOARDS

Introduction to Article 408—Switchboards and Panelboards

Article 408 covers the specific requirements for switchboards and panelboards that control power and lighting circuits. Since these rules address the equipment at the heart of the premises electrical system, take some time to become familiar with them. Topics covered in this material for Article 408 include:

- Scope
- Equipment Grounding Conductor

Author's Comment:

- The slang term in the electrical field for a panelboard is "the guts." The requirements for panelboards are contained in Article 408.

408.1 Scope

Article 408 covers the requirements for switchboards and panelboards that control power and lighting circuits. ▶**Figure 408–1**

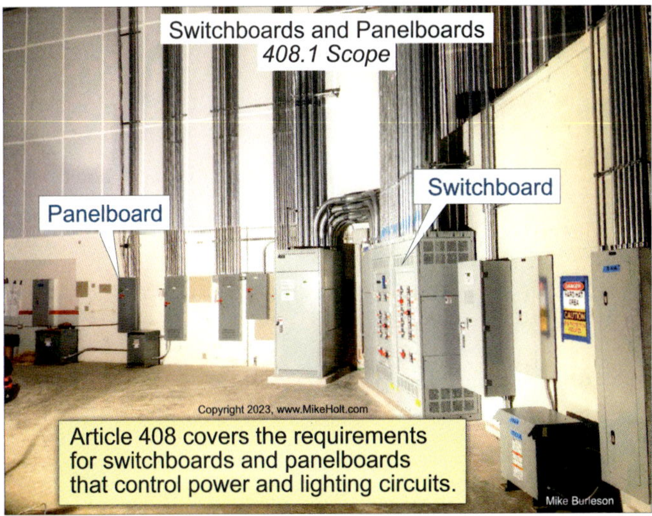
Switchboards and Panelboards
408.1 Scope
Panelboard
Switchboard
Copyright 2023, www.MikeHolt.com
Article 408 covers the requirements for switchboards and panelboards that control power and lighting circuits.
Mike Burleson

▶**Figure 408–1**

408.40 Equipment Grounding Conductor

Where equipment grounding conductors of the wire-type enter an enclosed panelboard, they must terminate to a grounding terminal bar within the enclosed panelboard. ▶**Figure 408–2**

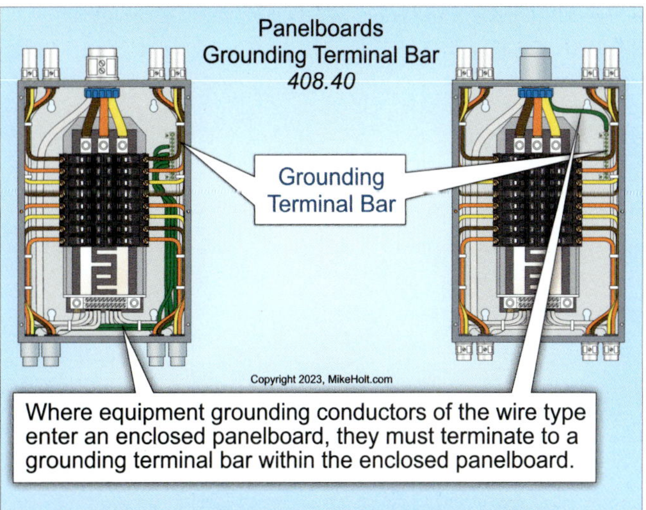
Panelboards
Grounding Terminal Bar
408.40
Grounding
Terminal Bar
Copyright 2023, MikeHolt.com
Where equipment grounding conductors of the wire type enter an enclosed panelboard, they must terminate to a grounding terminal bar within the enclosed panelboard.

▶**Figure 408–2**

Equipment grounding conductors are not permitted to terminate on the neutral terminal bar except as permitted by 250.24(D) for services and 250.30(A) for separately derived systems. ▶Figure 408–3

Panelboards, EGC Connected to Neutral Terminal Bar
408.40
Copyright 2023, MikeHolt.com
Equipment grounding conductors are not permitted to terminate on the neutral terminal bar except as permitted by 250.24(D) for services and 250.30(A) for separately derived systems.

▶Figure 408–3

Caution

CAUTION: Many panelboards are rated for use as service disconnects, which means they are supplied with a main bonding jumper [250.28]. This screw or strap is not permitted to be installed except when the panelboard is used for a service disconnect [250.24(B)] or separately derived system [250.30(A)(1)].

ARTICLE 410 LUMINAIRES

Introduction to Article 410—Luminaires

This article covers luminaires, lampholders, lamps, decorative lighting products, lighting accessories for temporary seasonal and holiday use, portable flexible lighting products, and the wiring and equipment of such products and lighting installations. Article 410 is massive. It contains 84 sections divided into 17 parts. Several of these parts and their corresponding sections are not within the scope of this material. Topics covered in this material for Article 410 include:

- Scope
- Supports
- Equipment Grounding Conductor

According to Article 100, "Luminaire" is a complete lighting unit consisting of a light source with parts designed to position the light source and connect it to the power supply. It may also include parts to protect and distribute the light. **▶Figure 410–1**

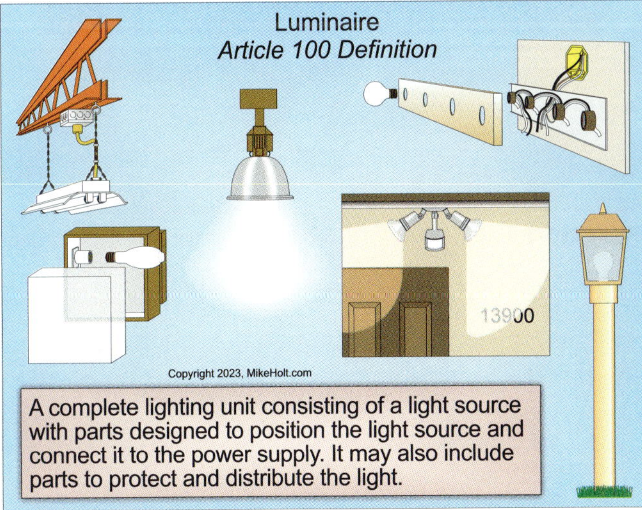
Luminaire
Article 100 Definition
13900
Copyright 2023, MikeHolt.com
A complete lighting unit consisting of a light source with parts designed to position the light source and connect it to the power supply. It may also include parts to protect and distribute the light.

▶Figure 410–1

410.1 Scope

Article 410 covers luminaires, lampholders, lamps, decorative lighting products, lighting accessories for temporary seasonal and holiday use, portable flexible lighting products, and the wiring and equipment of such products and lighting installations. **▶Figure 410–2**

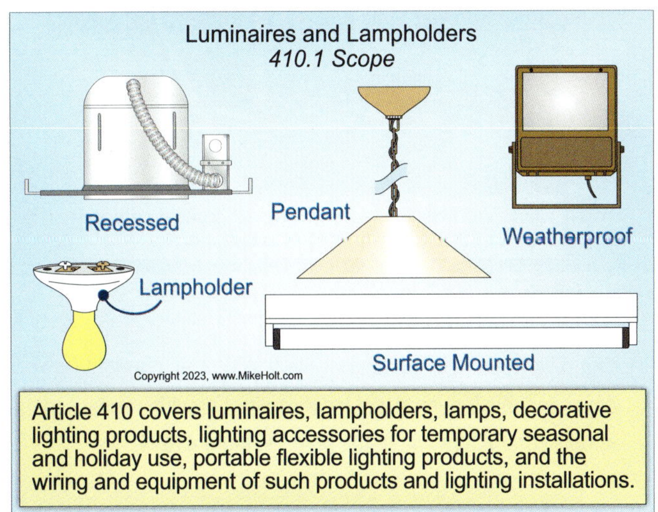
Luminaires and Lampholders
410.1 Scope
Recessed
Pendant
Weatherproof
Lampholder
Surface Mounted
Copyright 2023, www.MikeHolt.com
Article 410 covers luminaires, lampholders, lamps, decorative lighting products, lighting accessories for temporary seasonal and holiday use, portable flexible lighting products, and the wiring and equipment of such products and lighting installations.

▶Figure 410–2

Author's Comment:

- Because of the many types and applications of luminaires, manufacturers' instructions are very important and helpful for proper installation. UL produces a pamphlet called the *Luminaire Marking Guide*, which provides information for properly installing common types of incandescent, fluorescent, and high-intensity discharge (HID) luminaires.

410.30 Supports

(B) Poles. Poles used to support luminaires can be used as a raceway to enclose supply conductors where the following conditions are met:

Author's Comment:

- With security being a high priority, many property owners want to install security cameras on existing parking lot poles. Sections 725.136 and 800.133 prohibit mixing power, Class 2 power-limited circuits, and coaxial cables in the same raceway. ▶**Figure 410–3**

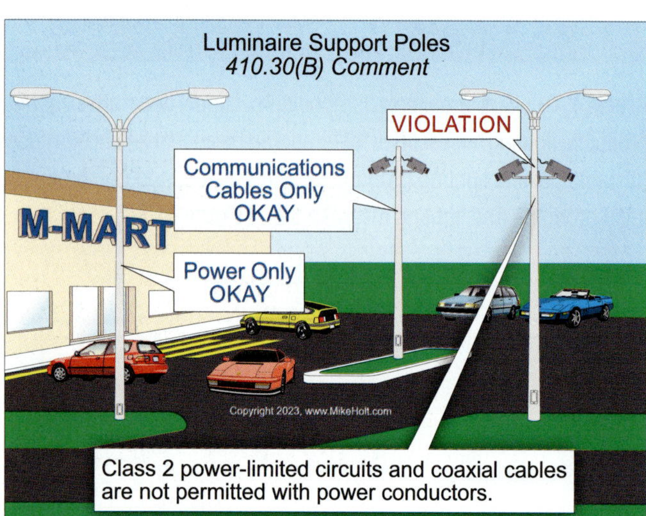
Luminaire Support Poles
410.30(B) Comment
VIOLATION
Communications Cables Only OKAY
M-MART
Power Only OKAY
Copyright 2023, www.MikeHolt.com
Class 2 power-limited circuits and coaxial cables are not permitted with power conductors.

▶**Figure 410–3**

(1) The pole must have an accessible 2 in. × 4 in. handhole with a cover suitable for use in wet locations that provides access to the supply conductors within the pole. ▶**Figure 410–4**

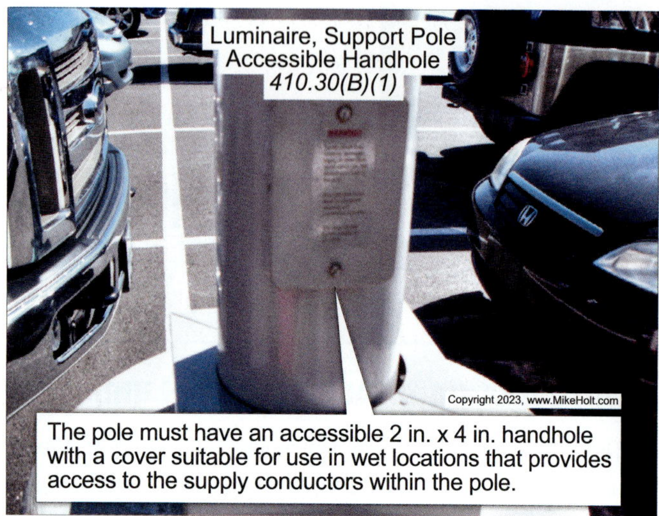
Luminaire, Support Pole
Accessible Handhole
410.30(B)(1)
Copyright 2023, www.MikeHolt.com
The pole must have an accessible 2 in. x 4 in. handhole with a cover suitable for use in wet locations that provides access to the supply conductors within the pole.

▶**Figure 410–4**

Ex 1: The handhole is not required for a pole 8 ft or less in height if the supply conductors for the luminaire are accessible by removing the luminaire. ▶**Figure 410–5**

Luminaire, Support Pole
Handhole Not Required
410.30(B)(1) Ex 1
A handhole isn't required if the pole is 8 ft or less, and the supply conductors are accessible by removing the luminaire.
Copyright 2023, www.MikeHolt.com

▶**Figure 410–5**

Ex 2: The handhole can be omitted on poles that are 20 ft or less in height if the pole is provided with a hinged base.

(3) A metal pole must have an equipment grounding terminal accessible from the handhole.

Ex: A grounding terminal is not required in a pole 8 ft or less in height above grade if the splices are accessible by removing the luminaire.

(5) Metal poles used for the support of luminaires must be connected to the circuit equipment grounding conductor. ▸**Figure 410–6**

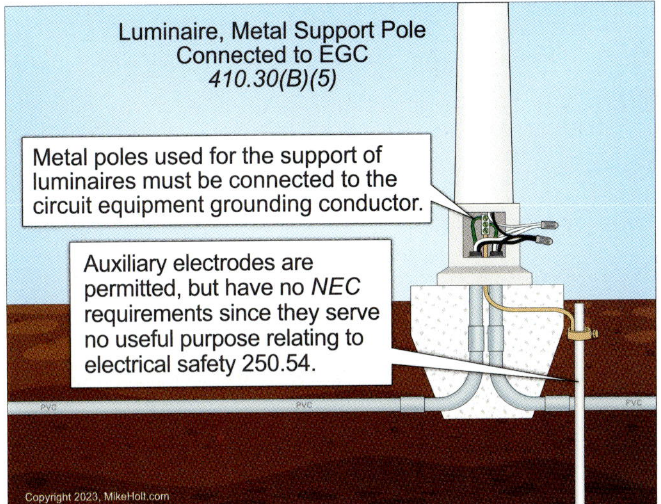
Luminaire, Metal Support Pole
Connected to EGC
410.30(B)(5)
Metal poles used for the support of luminaires must be connected to the circuit equipment grounding conductor.
Auxiliary electrodes are permitted, but have no NEC requirements since they serve no useful purpose relating to electrical safety 250.54.
Copyright 2023, MikeHolt.com

▸**Figure 410–6**

Danger

DANGER: Because the contact resistance of an electrode to the Earth is so high, very little fault current returns to the power supply if it is the only fault current return path. As a result, the circuit overcurrent protective device will not open and clear the ground fault, and the metal pole will become and remain energized by the circuit voltage. ▸**Figure 410–7**

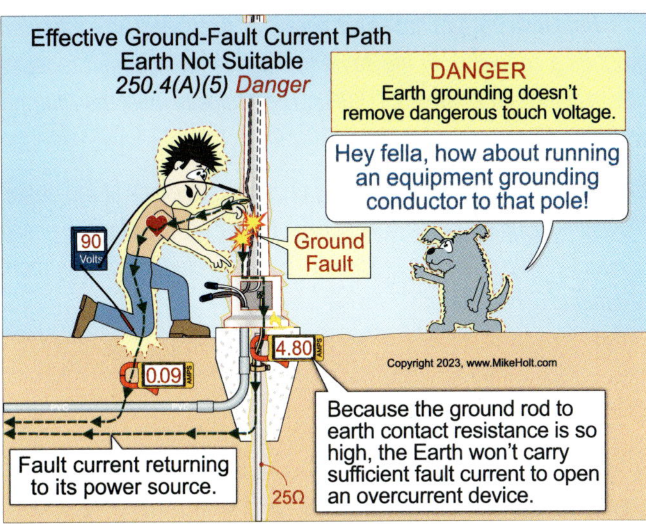
Effective Ground-Fault Current Path
Earth Not Suitable
250.4(A)(5) Danger
DANGER
Earth grounding doesn't remove dangerous touch voltage.
Hey fella, how about running an equipment grounding conductor to that pole!
90 Volts
Ground Fault
0.09
4.80
Copyright 2023, www.MikeHolt.com
Fault current returning to its power source.
25Ω
Because the ground rod to earth contact resistance is so high, the Earth won't carry sufficient fault current to open an overcurrent device.

▸**Figure 410–7**

410.44 Connection to the Equipment Grounding Conductor

Metal surfaces of luminaires must be connected to the circuit equipment grounding conductor. ▸**Figure 410–8**

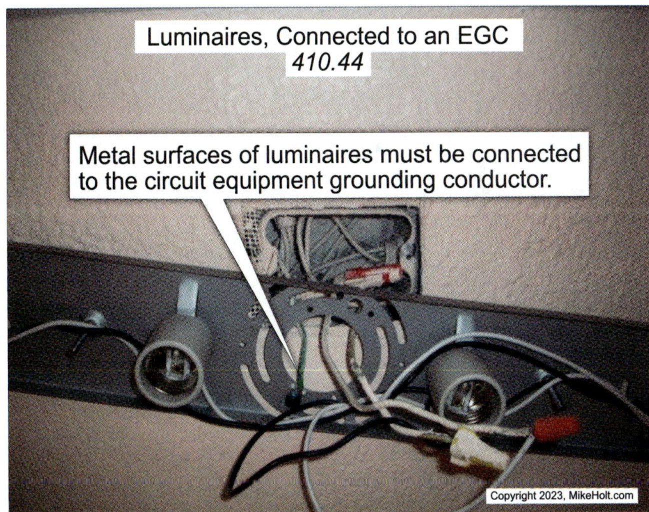
Luminaires, Connected to an EGC
410.44
Metal surfaces of luminaires must be connected to the circuit equipment grounding conductor.
Copyright 2023, MikeHolt.com

▸**Figure 410–8**

Ex 1: Replacement luminaires are permitted to connect an equipment grounding conductor in the same manner as replacement receptacles in compliance with 250.130(C). The luminaire must then comply with 410.42.

Ex 2: Where no equipment grounding conductor exists at the outlet, replacement luminaires that are GFCI protected, or do not have exposed conductive parts, are not required to be connected to an equipment grounding conductor.

410.182 Equipment Grounding Conductor

Lighting equipment identified for horticultural use must be connected to the circuit equipment grounding conductor of the type described in 250.118(A) [250.4(A)(5)].

ARTICLE
440

AIR-CONDITIONING EQUIPMENT

Introduction to Article 440—Air-Conditioning Equipment

Article 440 applies to hermetic refrigerant motor-compressors, such as those used for pool heat pumps and HVAC equipment. In most cases the manufacturer has worked out all the details and identifies the minimum conductor ampacity, maximum overcurrent protective device rating, and other information (such as running-load amperes) on the nameplate, so the rules covered in this material deal with what the installer needs to know. Topics covered in this material for Article 440 include:

- Scope
- Equipment Grounding Conductor

According to Article 100, "Hermetic Refrigerant Motor-Compressor" is a compressor and motor enclosed in the same housing and operating in refrigerant. ▸**Figure 440–1**

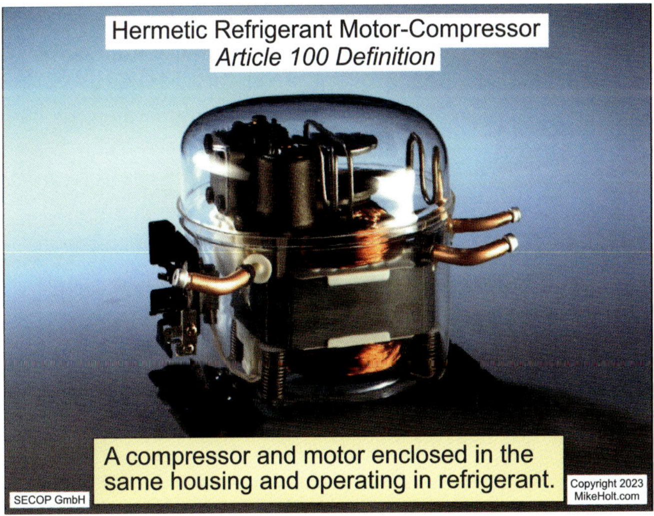
Hermetic Refrigerant Motor-Compressor
Article 100 Definition
A compressor and motor enclosed in the same housing and operating in refrigerant.
SECOP GmbH
Copyright 2023
MikeHolt.com

▸**Figure 440–1**

440.1 Scope

Article 440 applies to hermetic refrigerant motor-compressors, such as those used for pool heat pumps and air-conditioning equipment. ▸**Figure 440–2**

Air-Conditioning Equipment
440.1 Scope
6 FLAVORS
CHOCOLATE
CHIP
COOKIE
MONSTER
Copyright 2023, www.MikeHolt.com
Article 440 applies to hermetic refrigerant motor-compressors, such as pool heat pumps and air-conditioning equipment.

▸**Figure 440–2**

440.9 Equipment Grounding Conductor

Outdoor portions of metal raceways on a roof using unthreaded fittings must contain an equipment grounding conductor of the wire type. ▶Figure 440-3

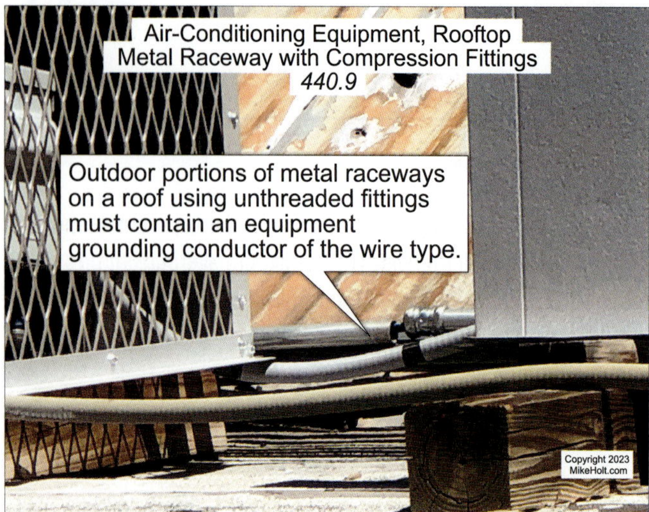
Air-Conditioning Equipment, Rooftop
Metal Raceway with Compression Fittings
440.9
Outdoor portions of metal raceways on a roof using unthreaded fittings must contain an equipment grounding conductor of the wire type.
Copyright 2023 MikeHolt.com

▶Figure 440-3

Author's Comment:

- The outdoor portions of rooftop metal raceways with compression fittings are exposed to a higher likelihood of physical damage and are often stepped on and broken from roof activities such as snow removal or roof repair/replacement. The installation of an equipment grounding conductor of the wire type within outdoor portions of metal raceways ensures an effective ground-fault current path.

ARTICLE
450

TRANSFORMERS

Introduction to Article 450—Transformers

Article 450 covers the installation requirements for transformers supplying power and lighting loads. Those types of transformers not covered by these rules are listed in the "Scope" section of this article. While the *NEC* does not provide design criteria for transformers, it does give an extensive set of rules to ensure a properly selected transformer can be installed and perform as intended by the designer. Several sections of this article fall outside the scope of this material and will not be covered. Topics covered in this material for Article 450 include:

- Scope
- Grounding and Bonding

450.1 Scope

Article 450 covers the installation requirements of all transformers other than the following: ▶**Figure 450–1**

Transformers
450.1 Scope
Mario Valdes
Transformer
Copyright 2023,MikeHolt.com
Article 450 covers the installation of transformers.

▶**Figure 450–1**

1. Current transformers
2. Transformers that constitute a component part of another apparatus
3. Transformers that are an integral part of an X-ray, high-frequency, or electrostatic-coating apparatus
4. Transformers for Class 2 and Class 3 power-limited circuits
5. Transformers for signs
6. Transformers for electric-discharge lighting
7. Transformers for power-limited fire alarm circuits
8. Transformers used for research, development, or testing

According to Article 100, a "Transformer" uses electromagnetic induction to convert current and voltage in a primary circuit into current and voltage in a secondary circuit. ▶**Figure 450–2**

Transformer
Article 100 Definition
Equipment that uses electromagnetic induction to convert current and voltage in a primary circuit into current and voltage in a secondary circuit.
Copyright 2023, www.MikeHolt.com

▸Figure 450–2

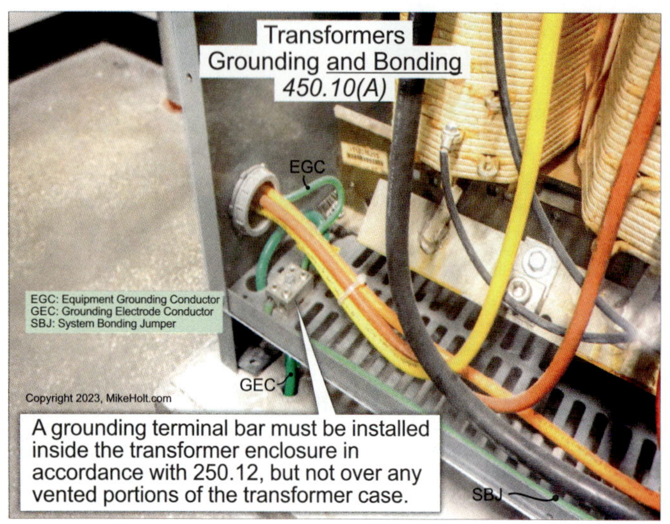
Transformers
Grounding and Bonding
450.10(A)
EGC
EGC: Equipment Grounding Conductor
GEC: Grounding Electrode Conductor
SBJ: System Bonding Jumper
GEC
Copyright 2023, MikeHolt.com
A grounding terminal bar must be installed inside the transformer enclosure in accordance with 250.12, but not over any vented portions of the transformer case.
SBJ

▸Figure 450–3

450.10 Grounding and Bonding

(A) Dry-Type Transformer Enclosures. A grounding terminal bar must be installed inside the transformer enclosure in accordance with 250.12, but not on or over any vented portions of the transformer case. **▸Figure 450–3**

CHAPTER
4

REVIEW QUESTIONS

NFPA
70
nec

Please use the 2023 *Code* book to answer the following questions.

Article 404—Switches

1. Article 404 covers all _____ used as switches operating at 1,000V and below, unless specifically referenced elsewhere in this *Code* for higher voltages.

   (a) switches
   (b) switching devices
   (c) circuit breakers
   (d) all of these

2. Metal faceplates for snap switches, including dimmer and similar control switches, shall be connected _____ whether or not a metal faceplate is installed.

   (a) to the grounded electrode
   (b) to the equipment grounding conductor
   (c) to the grounded conductor
   (d) to the ungrounded conductor

3. A snap switch wired under the provisions of 404.9(B) Ex 1 and located within 8 ft vertically, or _____ horizontally, of ground or exposed grounded metal objects shall be provided with a faceplate of nonconducting noncombustible material with nonmetallic attachment screws, unless the switch mounting strap or yoke is nonmetallic or the circuit is protected by a ground-fault circuit interrupter.

   (a) 3 ft
   (b) 5 ft
   (c) 7 ft
   (d) 9 ft

4. Snap switches in listed assemblies are not required to be connected to an equipment grounding conductor if _____.

   (a) the device is provided with a nonmetallic faceplate and the device is designed such that no metallic faceplate replaces the one provided
   (b) the device is equipped with a nonmetallic yoke
   (c) all parts of the device that are accessible after installation of the faceplate are manufactured of nonmetallic material
   (d) all of these

5. A snap switch with an integral nonmetallic enclosure complying with 300.15(E) shall be permitted without a _____ connection to an equipment grounding conductor.

   (a) grounding
   (b) bonding
   (c) earth
   (d) none of these

6. Metal enclosures for switches or circuit breakers shall be connected to a(an) _____ conductor.

   (a) grounded
   (b) grounding
   (c) equipment grounding
   (d) any of these

Article 406—Receptacles, Attachment Plugs, and Flanged Inlets

1. Article _____ covers the rating, type, and installation of receptacles, cord connectors, and attachment plugs (cord caps).

   (a) 400
   (b) 404
   (c) 406
   (d) 408

2. Receptacles incorporating an isolated grounding conductor connection intended for the reduction of electromagnetic interference shall be identified by _____ located on the face of the receptacle.

   (a) the letters "IG"
   (b) a green circle
   (c) a green square
   (d) an orange triangle

3. Except as permitted for two-wire replacements as provided in 406.4(D), receptacles installed on _____ branch circuits shall be of the grounding type.

   (a) 15A and 20A
   (b) up to 30A
   (c) 125V
   (d) 250V

4. Receptacles and cord connectors that have equipment grounding conductor contacts shall have those contacts connected to _____.

   (a) the enclosure
   (b) a bonding bushing
   (c) an equipment grounding conductor
   (d) any of these

5. Where a grounding means exists in the receptacle enclosure a(an) _____ receptacle shall be used.

   (a) isolated ground-type
   (b) grounding-type
   (c) GFCI-type
   (d) dedicated-type

6. When replacing a nongrounding-type receptacle where attachment to an equipment grounding conductor does not exist in the receptacle enclosure, a _____ can be used as the replacement.

   (a) nongrounding-type receptacle
   (b) grounding receptacle
   (c) AFCI-type receptacle
   (d) Tamper-resistant receptacle

7. When nongrounding-type receptacles are replaced by GFCI-type receptacles where attachment to an equipment grounding conductor does not exist in the receptacle enclosure, _____ shall be marked "No Equipment Ground."

   (a) the receptacle
   (b) the protective device
   (c) the branch circuit
   (d) these receptacles or their cover plates

8. Where attachment to an equipment grounding conductor does not exist in the receptacle enclosure, a nongrounding-type receptacle(s) shall be permitted to be replaced with a grounding-type receptacle(s) where supplied through a ground-fault circuit interrupter and _____ shall be marked "GFCI Protected" and "No Equipment Ground," visible after installation.

   (a) the receptacle(s)
   (b) their cover plates
   (c) the branch circuit
   (d) the receptacle(s) or their cover plates

9. Where attachment to an equipment grounding conductor does not exist in the receptacle enclosure, a nongrounding-type receptacle shall be permitted to be replaced with a GFCI-type receptacle; however, some equipment or appliance manufacturers require that the _____ to the equipment or appliance includes an equipment grounding conductor.

   (a) feeder
   (b) branch circuit
   (c) small-appliance circuit
   (d) power cord

Article 408—Switchboards and Panelboards

1. Article 408 covers _____.

   (a) switchboards
   (b) switchgear
   (c) panelboards
   (d) all of these

2. Panelboard cabinets and panelboard frames, if of metal, shall be in physical contact with each other and shall be connected to a(an) _____.

(a) equipment grounding conductor
(b) grounding electrode conductor
(c) steel building structure
(d) separate ground rod

3. When separate equipment grounding conductors are provided in panelboards, a _____ shall be secured inside the cabinet.

(a) grounded conductor
(b) terminal lug
(c) terminal bar
(d) bonding jumper

Article 410—Luminaires

1. Article 410 covers luminaires, portable luminaires, lampholders, pendants, incandescent filament lamps, arc lamps, electric-discharge lamps, and _____, and the wiring and equipment forming part of such products and lighting installations.

(a) decorative lighting products
(b) lighting accessories for temporary seasonal and holiday use
(c) portable flexible lighting products
(d) all of these

2. A pole supporting luminaires shall have a handhole not less than _____ with a cover suitable for use in wet locations to provide access to the supply terminations within the pole or pole base.

(a) 2 in. × 2 in.
(b) 2 in. × 4 in.
(c) 4 in. × 4 in.
(d) 4 in. × 6 in.

3. Metal raceways shall be bonded to the metal pole supporting luminaires with a(an) _____.

(a) grounding electrode
(b) grounded conductor
(c) equipment grounding conductor
(d) any of these

4. Luminaires shall be _____ to an equipment grounding conductor.

(a) securely connected
(b) clamped
(c) mechanically connected
(d) none of these

5. Replacement luminaires are not required to be connected to an equipment grounding conductor if no equipment grounding conductor exists at the outlet box and the luminaire is _____.

(a) more than 20 years old
(b) mounted to the box using nonmetallic fittings and screws
(c) mounted more than 6 ft above the floor
(d) GFCI protected

Article 440—Air-Conditioning Equipment

1. Article _____ applies to electric motor-driven air-conditioning and refrigerating equipment that has a hermetic refrigerant motor-compressor.

(a) 440
(b) 442
(c) 450
(d) 460

2. Where air-conditioning and refrigeration equipment is installed outdoors on a roof, a(an) _____ conductor of the wire type shall be installed in outdoor portions of metallic raceway systems that use compression-type fittings.

(a) equipment grounding
(b) grounding
(c) equipment bonding
(d) bonding

Article 450—Transformers

1. Article 450 covers the installation of all _____.

(a) motors and motor control centers
(b) refrigeration and air-conditioning equipment
(c) transformers
(d) generators

2. The equipment grounding conductor terminal bar of a dry-type transformer shall be bonded to the enclosure in accordance with 250.12 and shall not be installed on or over any _____.

   (a) ungrounded conductor terminations
   (b) transformer coils or windings
   (c) vented portion of the enclosure
   (d) all of these

CHAPTER

5 SPECIAL OCCUPANCIES

Introduction to Chapter 5—Special Occupancies

Chapter 5, which covers special occupancies, is the first of three *NEC* chapters that deal with special requirements. A "Special Occupancy" is a location where a facility, or its use, creates conditions that require additional measures to ensure the "practical safeguarding of people and property." Chapter 5 contains 27 articles that address occupancies from aircraft hangers to recreational vehicles. While many of these articles are outside the scope of this material, the following are included:

- **Article 501—Class I Locations.** A Class I location is an area where flammable or combustible liquid-produced vapors or flammable gases may present the hazard of a fire or explosion.
- **Article 502—Class II Locations.** A Class II location is an area where the possibility of fire or explosion may exist due to the presence of combustible dust.
- **Article 517—Health Care Facilities.** This article applies to electrical wiring in human health care facilities such as hospitals, nursing homes, limited care facilities, clinics, medical and dental offices, and ambulatory care—whether permanent or movable. It does not apply to animal veterinary facilities.
- **Article 547—Agricultural Buildings.** Article 547 covers agricultural buildings or those parts of buildings (or adjacent areas) where excessive dust or dust with water may accumulate. It also includes buildings where a corrosive atmosphere exists.
- **Article 555—Marinas, Boatyards, and Docking Facilities.** This article covers the installation of wiring and equipment in the areas comprised of fixed or floating piers, wharves, docks, and other areas in marinas, boatyards, boat basins, boathouses, and similar locations. These areas are used for the repair, berthing, launching, storing, or fueling of small craft and the mooring of floating buildings.

Notes

ARTICLE 501

CLASS I HAZARDOUS (CLASSIFIED) LOCATIONS

Introduction to Article 501—Class I Hazardous (Classified) Locations

Article 501 contains the requirements for electrical equipment and wiring in Class I, Division 1 and Division 2 locations. These are locations where flammable gases, flammable liquid-produced vapors, or combustible liquid-produced vapors are (or might be) present in the air in quantities sufficient to produce explosive or ignitable mixtures. Examples of such locations include some fuel storage areas, certain solvent storage areas, grain processing facilities (where hexane is used), plastic extrusion areas (where oil removal is part of the process), refineries, and paint storage areas. Many of these rules are outside of the scope of this material, however we do cover the following topics in this article:

- Wiring Methods
- Sealing and Drainage
- Grounding and Bonding
- Surge Protection
- Luminaires
- Receptacles and Attachment Plugs

Article 501 consists of three parts:

- Part I. General
- Part II. Wiring
- Part III. Equipment

501.1 Scope

This article covers the electrical equipment and wiring for Class I, Division 1 and Division 2 locations where flammable gases, flammable liquid-produced vapors, or combustible liquid-produced vapors are (or might be, present in the air in quantities sufficient to produce explosive or ignitable mixtures. ▸Figure 501–1

501.30 Grounding and Bonding

Because of the explosive conditions associated with electrical installations in hazardous (classified) locations [500.5], electrical continuity of metal parts of equipment and raceways must be ensured, regardless of the voltage of the circuit.

(B) Bonding. Bonding must comply with 501.30(B)(1) and (B)(2).

(1) Specific Bonding Means. Bonding in a Class 1 hazardous (classified) location must comply with the following:

Class I Hazardous (Classified) Locations
501.1 Scope
Copyright 2023, www.MikeHolt.com
Article 501 covers the electrical equipment and wiring for Class I, Division 1 and Division 2 locations where flammable gases, flammable liquid-produced vapors, or combustible liquid-produced vapors are, or might be, present in the air in quantities sufficient to produce explosive or ignitable mixtures.

▶Figure 501-1

(a) Locknuts are not suitable for bonding purposes in hazardous (classified) locations. Bonding jumpers with identified fittings or other approved means of bonding must be used. Such means of bonding apply to all metal raceways between Class I locations and service disconnects or a separately derived system. ▶Figure 501-2

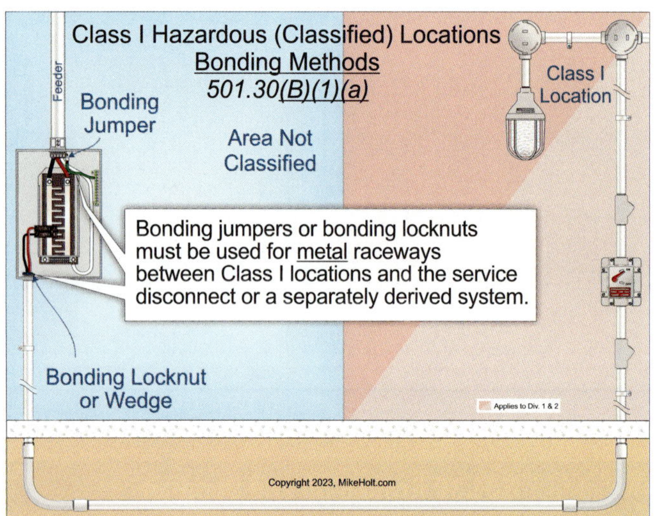
Class I Hazardous (Classified) Locations
Bonding Methods
501.30(B)(1)(a)
Feeder
Bonding Jumper
Area Not Classified
Class I Location
Bonding jumpers or bonding locknuts must be used for metal raceways between Class I locations and the service disconnect or a separately derived system.
Bonding Locknut or Wedge
Applies to Div. 1 & 2
Copyright 2023, MikeHolt.com

▶Figure 501-2

Author's Comment:

- Regardless of the circuit voltage, the electrical continuity of metal parts of equipment and raceways in hazardous (classified) locations must be ensured by using bonding-type locknuts, wedges, or bushings with bonding jumpers [250.92(B)(4)], whether or not equipment grounding conductors of the wire type are installed in the raceway [250.100]. Threaded couplings and hubs made up wrenchtight provide a suitable low-impedance fault current path [250. 92(B)(2)]. Locknuts alone are not sufficient to serve this purpose.

(2) Flexible Metal Conduit and Liquidtight Flexible Metal Conduit.

(a) Where flexible metal conduit and liquidtight flexible metal conduit is installed as permitted by 501.10(B)(2)(a), the raceway must have an internal or external equipment bonding jumper of the wire type installed in accordance with 250.102(E). ▶Figure 501-3

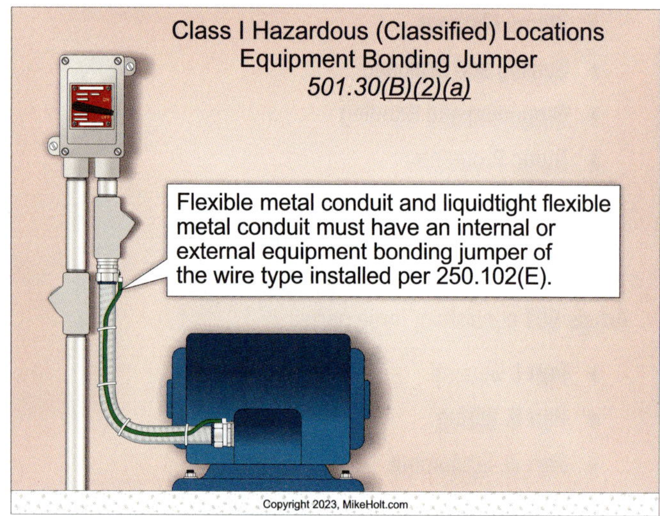
Class I Hazardous (Classified) Locations
Equipment Bonding Jumper
501.30(B)(2)(a)
Flexible metal conduit and liquidtight flexible metal conduit must have an internal or external equipment bonding jumper of the wire type installed per 250.102(E).
Copyright 2023, MikeHolt.com

▶Figure 501-3

Author's Comment:

- Load-side bonding jumpers are sized in accordance with Table 250.122 based on the rating of the overcurrent protective device [250.102(D)]. Where installed outside a raceway, the length of bonding jumpers is not permitted to exceed 6 ft and must be routed with the raceway [250.102(E)(2)]. ▶Figure 501-4

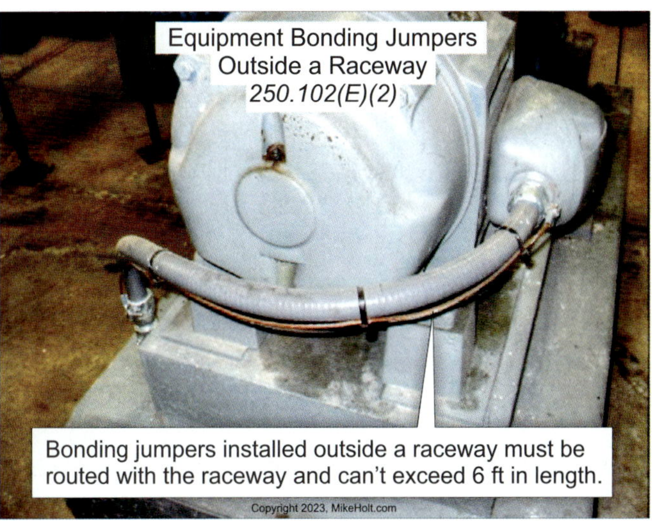
Equipment Bonding Jumpers
Outside a Raceway
250.102(E)(2)
Bonding jumpers installed outside a raceway must be
routed with the raceway and can't exceed 6 ft in length.
Copyright 2023, MikeHolt.com

▸Figure 501-4

ARTICLE 502 CLASS II HAZARDOUS (CLASSIFIED) LOCATIONS

Introduction to Article 502—Class II Hazardous (Classified) Locations

This article covers the requirements for electrical equipment and wiring in Class II, Division 1 and 2 locations where fire or explosion hazards might exist due to the presence of combustible dust. Examples of such locations include flour mills, grain silos, coal bins, wood pulp storage areas, and munitions plants. Many of these rules are outside of the scope of this material, however we do cover the following topics in this article:

- Wiring Methods
- Grounding and Bonding
- Surge Protection
- Luminaires
- Receptacles and Attachment Plugs

Article 502 consists of three parts:

- Part I. General
- Part II. Wiring
- Part III. Equipment

502.1 Scope

This article covers the requirements for electrical equipment and wiring in Class II, Division 1 and 2 locations where fire or explosion hazards might exist due to the presence of combustible dust. ▸Figure 502–1

Author's Comment:

- Examples of combustible dust include combustible metal dusts, coal, carbon black, charcoal, coke, flour, grain, wood, plastic, and chemicals in the air in quantities sufficient to produce explosive or ignitible mixtures [500.5(C) and 500.8].

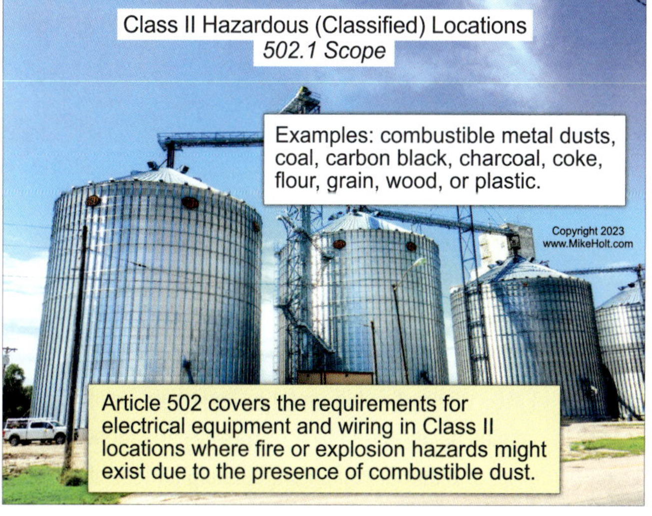
Class II Hazardous (Classified) Locations
502.1 Scope
Examples: combustible metal dusts, coal, carbon black, charcoal, coke, flour, grain, wood, or plastic.
Copyright 2023
www.MikeHolt.com
Article 502 covers the requirements for electrical equipment and wiring in Class II locations where fire or explosion hazards might exist due to the presence of combustible dust.

▸Figure 502–1

502.30 Grounding and Bonding

Because of the explosive conditions associated with electrical installations in hazardous (classified) locations [500.5], electrical continuity of the metal parts of equipment and raceways must be ensured regardless of the voltage of the circuit.

(B) Bonding.

(1) Specific Bonding Means.

(a) Locknuts are not suitable for bonding purposes in hazardous (classified) locations. Bonding jumpers with identified fittings or other approved means of bonding must be used. Such means of bonding apply to all metal raceways between Class II locations and service disconnects or a separately derived system. ▶Figure 502–2

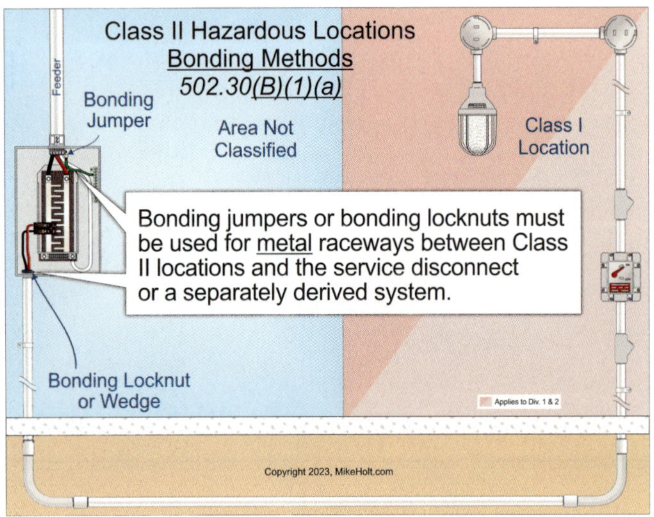
Class II Hazardous Locations
Bonding Methods
502.30(B)(1)(a)
Feeder
Bonding Jumper
Area Not Classified
Class I Location
Bonding jumpers or bonding locknuts must be used for metal raceways between Class II locations and the service disconnect or a separately derived system.
Bonding Locknut or Wedge
Applies to Div. 1 & 2
Copyright 2023, MikeHolt.com

▶Figure 502–2

Author's Comment:

- The special bonding requirements for Class II locations are the same as those for 501.30(A) Class 1 locations [250.94(B)(4)]. Threaded couplings and hubs made up wrenchtight provide a suitable low-impedance fault current path [250. 92(B)(2)].

(2) Flexible Metal Conduit and Liquidtight Flexible Metal Conduit.

(a) Type LFMC. Where flexible metal or liquidtight flexible metal conduit is installed as permitted by 502.10(A)(2), the raceway must have an internal or external equipment bonding jumper of the wire type installed in accordance with 250.102(E). ▶Figure 502–3

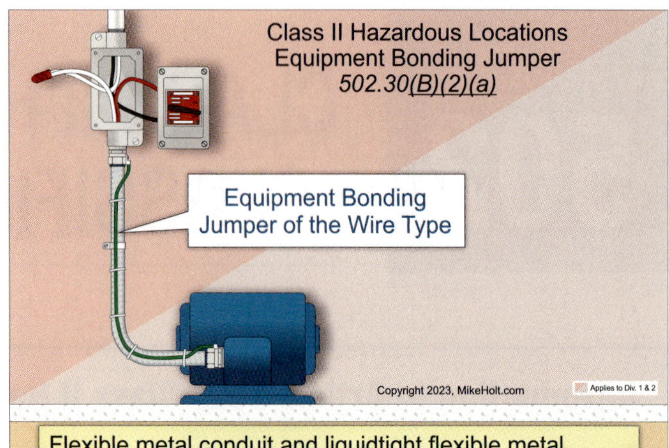
Class II Hazardous Locations
Equipment Bonding Jumper
502.30(B)(2)(a)
Equipment Bonding Jumper of the Wire Type
Copyright 2023, MikeHolt.com
Applies to Div. 1 & 2
Flexible metal conduit and liquidtight flexible metal conduit must have an internal or external equipment bonding jumper of the wire type installed per 250.102(E).

▶Figure 502–3

Author's Comment:

- Load-side bonding jumpers must be sized in accordance with 250.122 based on the rating of the overcurrent protective device [250.102(D)]. Where the bonding jumper is installed outside a raceway, the length of the bonding jumpers is not permitted to exceed 6 ft and they must be routed with the raceway [250.102(E)(2)]. ▶Figure 502–4

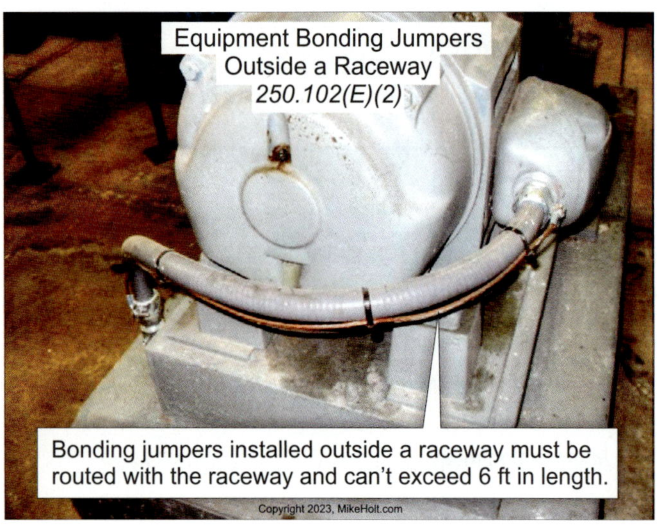
Equipment Bonding Jumpers
Outside a Raceway
250.102(E)(2)
Bonding jumpers installed outside a raceway must be routed with the raceway and can't exceed 6 ft in length.
Copyright 2023, MikeHolt.com

▶Figure 502–4

ARTICLE 517 HEALTH CARE FACILITIES

Introduction to Article 517—Health Care Facilities

Article 517 applies to electrical wiring in health care facilities such as hospitals, nursing homes, limited care and supervisory care facilities, clinics, medical and dental offices, and ambulatory care facilities that provide services to human beings. The requirements of Article 517 do not apply to business offices or waiting rooms, or to animal veterinary facilities. Many of these rules are outside of the scope of this material, however we do cover the following topics in this article:

- Wiring Methods
- Equipment Grounding Conductor for Receptacles and Fixed Electrical Equipment in Patient Care Spaces
- Isolated Ground Receptacles

Article 517 consists of seven parts:

- Part I. General
- Part II. Wiring and Protection
- Part III. Essential Electrical Systems (not covered)
- Part IV. Inhalation Anesthetizing Locations (not covered)
- Part V. Diagnostic Imaging and Treatment Equipment (not covered)
- Part VI. Communications, Signaling Systems, Data Systems, Fire Alarm Systems, and Systems Less than 120V, Nominal (not covered)
- Part VII. Isolated Power Systems (not covered)

517.1 Scope

This article applies to electrical wiring in health care facilities such as hospitals, nursing homes, limited care and supervisory care facilities, clinics, medical and dental offices, and ambulatory care facilities that provide services to human beings. ▸Figure 517–1

According to Article 100, "Health Care Facilities" are buildings (or portions of buildings) or mobile enclosures in which medical, dental, psychiatric, nursing, obstetrical, or surgical care is provided for humans.

Note: Examples of health care facilities include, but are not limited to, hospitals, nursing homes, limited care facilities, supervisory care facilities, clinics, medical and dental offices, and ambulatory care facilities.

According to Article 100, a "Limited Care Facility" is a building (or area of a building) used for the housing, on a 24-hour basis, of four or more persons. These are persons incapable of self-preservation because of age, physical limitations (due to accident or illness), or limitations such as intellectual disability, developmental disability, mental illness, or chemical dependency (Article 517).

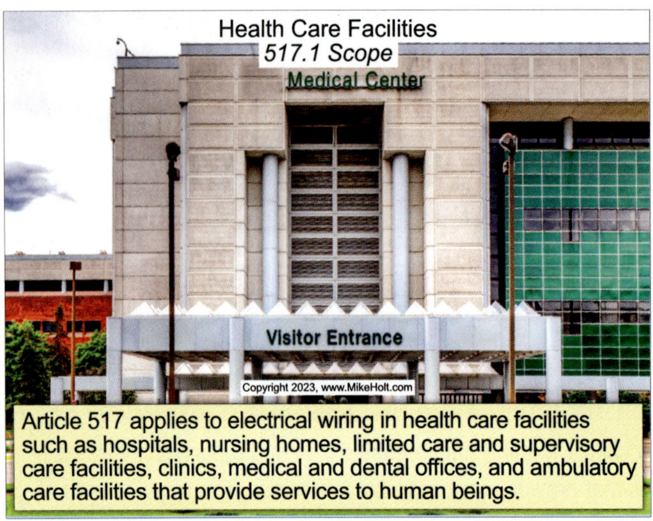
Health Care Facilities
517.1 Scope
Medical Center
Visitor Entrance
Copyright 2023, www.MikeHolt.com
Article 517 applies to electrical wiring in health care facilities such as hospitals, nursing homes, limited care and supervisory care facilities, clinics, medical and dental offices, and ambulatory care facilities that provide services to human beings.

▶Figure 517–1

Author's Comment:

- This article does not apply to animal veterinary facilities.
- Areas of health care facilities not used for the treatment of patients (such as business offices and waiting rooms) are not required to comply with the provisions contained in Article 517.

Article 517 requirements specify the installation criteria and wiring methods that minimize electrical hazards by adequate low-potential differences only between exposed conductive surfaces that are likely to become energized and those that could be contacted by a patient.

Note 1: In a health care facility, it is difficult to prevent the occurrence of a conductive or capacitive path from the patient's body to some grounded object, because that path might be established accidentally or through instrumentation directly connected to the patient. Other electrically conductive surfaces that might make an additional contact with the patient, or instruments that might be connected to the patient, become possible sources of electric currents that can traverse the patient's body.

517.13 Equipment Grounding Conductor for Receptacles and Fixed Electrical Equipment in Patient Care Spaces

Wiring serving patient care spaces, including the circuit from the patient care space to the panelboard, must comply with the requirements of 517.13(A) and (B).

(A) Wiring Methods. Branch-circuits serving patient care spaces must be in a metal raceway or metal cable having an armor or sheath that qualifies as an equipment grounding conductor in accordance with 250.118(A). ▶Figure 517–2

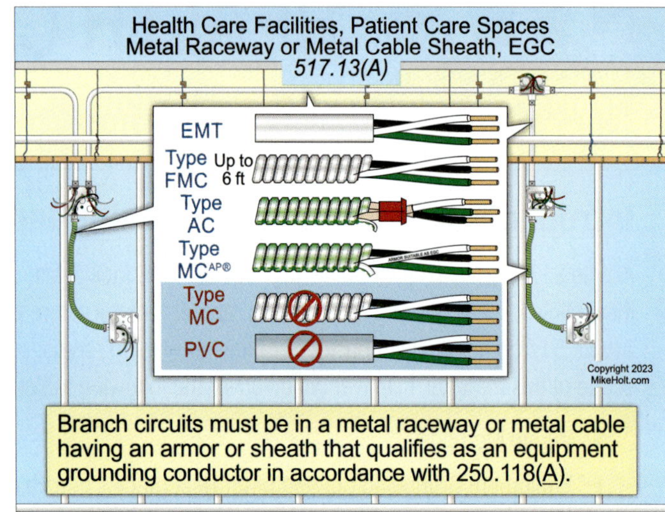
Health Care Facilities, Patient Care Spaces
Metal Raceway or Metal Cable Sheath, EGC
517.13(A)
EMT
Type FMC Up to 6 ft
Type AC
Type MC^AP®
Type MC
PVC
Copyright 2023 MikeHolt.com
Branch circuits must be in a metal raceway or metal cable having an armor or sheath that qualifies as an equipment grounding conductor in accordance with 250.118(A).

▶Figure 517–2

Author's Comment:

- The metal sheath of traditional Type MC interlocked cable does not qualify as an equipment grounding conductor [250.118(A)(10)(a)]. Therefore, this wiring method cannot be used for circuits in patient care spaces. ▶Figure 517–3

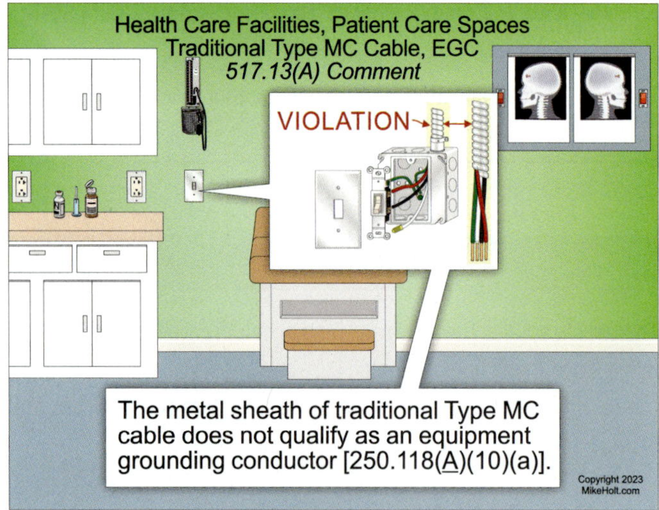
Health Care Facilities, Patient Care Spaces
Traditional Type MC Cable, EGC
517.13(A) Comment
VIOLATION
The metal sheath of traditional Type MC cable does not qualify as an equipment grounding conductor [250.118(A)(10)(a)].
Copyright 2023 MikeHolt.com

▶Figure 517–3

- The metal armor of Type AC cable listed as an equipment grounding conductor because it contains an internal bonding strip that is in direct contact with the metal armor of the interlock cable. ▸Figure 517-4

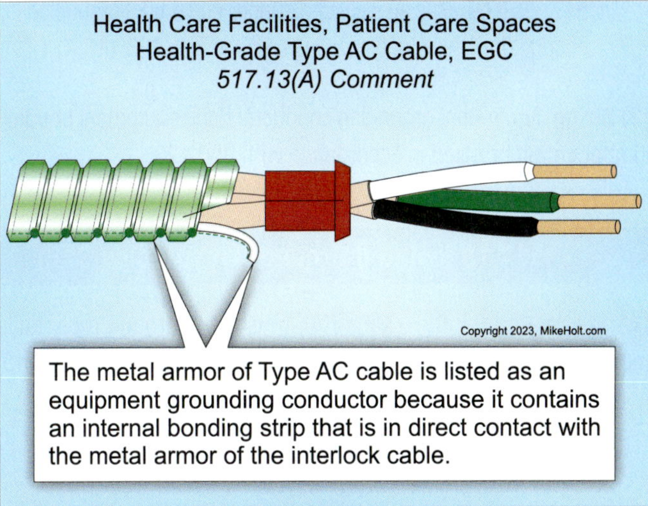
Health Care Facilities, Patient Care Spaces
Health-Grade Type AC Cable, EGC
517.13(A) Comment
Copyright 2023, MikeHolt.com
The metal armor of Type AC cable is listed as an equipment grounding conductor because it contains an internal bonding strip that is in direct contact with the metal armor of the interlock cable.

▸Figure 517-4

- The metal sheath of all-purpose Type MC[AP®] cable listed as an equipment grounding conductor because it contains an internal bonding/grounding conductor that is in direct contact with the metal sheath of the interlock cable. ▸Figure 517-5

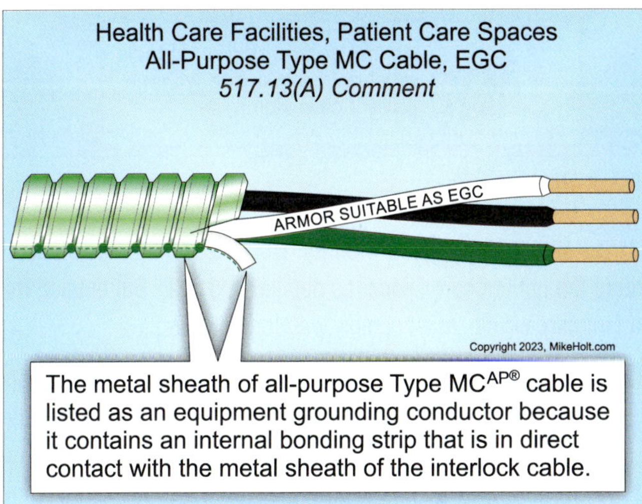
Health Care Facilities, Patient Care Spaces
All-Purpose Type MC Cable, EGC
517.13(A) Comment
ARMOR SUITABLE AS EGC
Copyright 2023, MikeHolt.com
The metal sheath of all-purpose Type MC[AP®] cable is listed as an equipment grounding conductor because it contains an internal bonding strip that is in direct contact with the metal sheath of the interlock cable.

▸Figure 517-5

(B) Insulated Equipment Grounding Conductor.

(1) General. An insulated copper equipment grounding conductor with green insulation along its entire length, installed within a suitable wiring method as required in 517.13(A), must be connected to the following:

(1) Grounding terminals of receptacles, other than isolated ground receptacles, must be connected to a green insulated copper equipment grounding conductor. ▸Figure 517-6

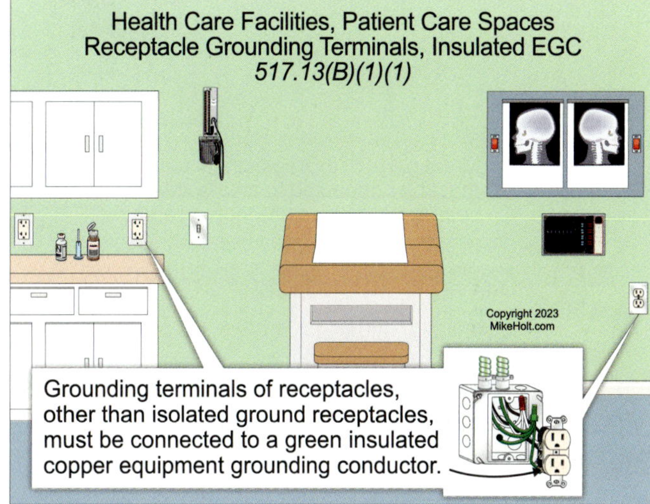
Health Care Facilities, Patient Care Spaces
Receptacle Grounding Terminals, Insulated EGC
517.13(B)(1)(1)
Copyright 2023 MikeHolt.com
Grounding terminals of receptacles, other than isolated ground receptacles, must be connected to a green insulated copper equipment grounding conductor.

▸Figure 517-6

(2) Metal boxes and enclosures containing circuit conductors must be connected to a green insulated copper equipment grounding conductor. ▸Figure 517-7

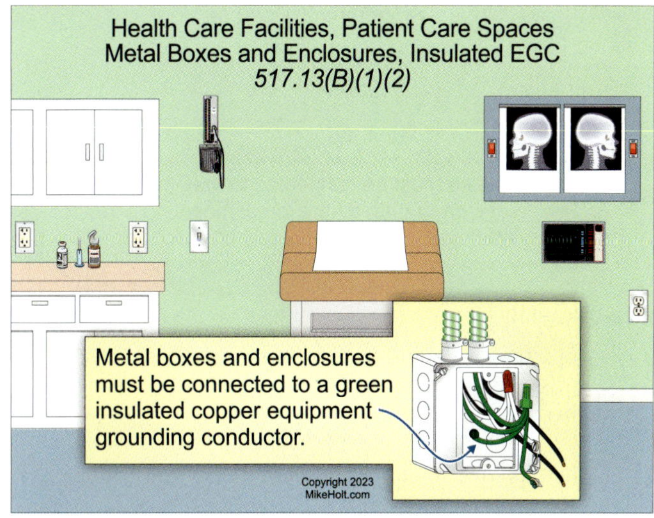
Health Care Facilities, Patient Care Spaces
Metal Boxes and Enclosures, Insulated EGC
517.13(B)(1)(2)
Metal boxes and enclosures must be connected to a green insulated copper equipment grounding conductor.
Copyright 2023 MikeHolt.com

▸Figure 517-7

(3) Metal parts of fixed electrical equipment operating at over 100V must be connected to an insulated copper equipment grounding conductor. ▸Figure 517-8

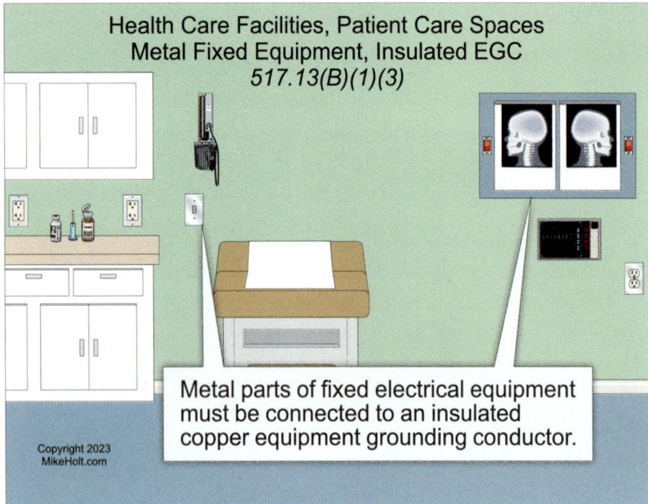
Health Care Facilities, Patient Care Spaces
Metal Fixed Equipment, Insulated EGC
517.13(B)(1)(3)
Metal parts of fixed electrical equipment must be connected to an insulated copper equipment grounding conductor.
Copyright 2023 MikeHolt.com

▸Figure 517-8

Ex 2: Metal faceplates must be connected to the effective ground-fault current path by the metal mounting screw(s) securing the faceplate to a receptacle or metal box. ▸Figure 517-9

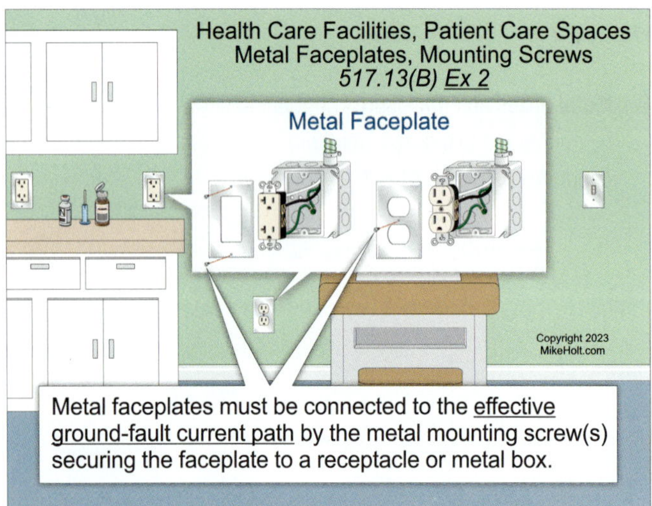
Health Care Facilities, Patient Care Spaces
Metal Faceplates, Mounting Screws
517.13(B) Ex 2
Metal Faceplate
Metal faceplates must be connected to the effective ground-fault current path by the metal mounting screw(s) securing the faceplate to a receptacle or metal box.
Copyright 2023 MikeHolt.com

▸Figure 517-9

Author's Comment:

- Often referred to as "redundancy," equipment grounding requirements in patient care spaces are based on the concept of two different types of equipment grounding conductors. This way if there is an installation error, the effective ground-fault current paths are not lost. One effective ground-fault current path is "mechanical" (the wiring method) and the other is of the "wire type." Section 517.13(A) requires the wiring method to be a metal raceway or metal cable that qualifies as an equipment grounding conductor in accordance with 250.118(A)(8) and 250.118(A)(10)(b). Section 517.13(B) requires an insulated copper equipment grounding conductor of the wire type in accordance with 250.118(A)(1).

(2) Sizing. Equipment grounding conductors and equipment bonding jumpers must be sized in accordance with 250.122.

517.16 Isolated Ground Receptacles

(A) Inside Patient Care Vicinity. An isolated ground receptacle must not be installed within a patient care vicinity. ▸Figure 517-10

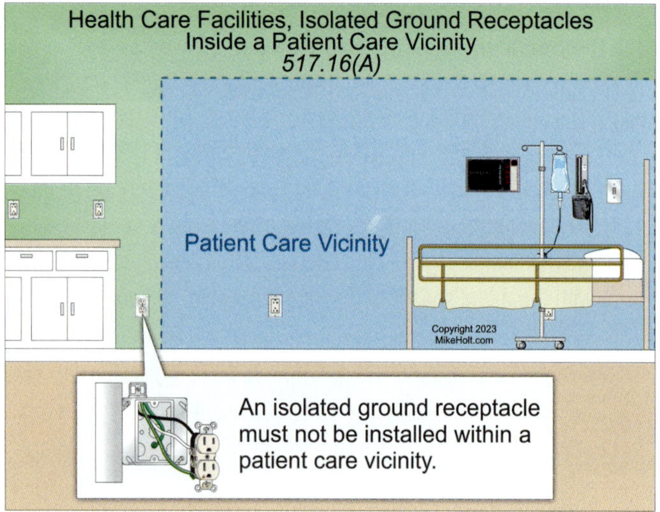
Health Care Facilities, Isolated Ground Receptacles
Inside a Patient Care Vicinity
517.16(A)
Patient Care Vicinity
An isolated ground receptacle must not be installed within a patient care vicinity.
Copyright 2023 MikeHolt.com

▸Figure 517-10

(B) Outside Patient Care Vicinity. Isolated ground receptacle(s) within the patient care space (as defined in 517.2), but outside the patient care vicinity must comply with the following:

(1) The equipment grounding terminal of isolated grounding receptacles must be connected to an insulated equipment grounding conductor in accordance with 250.146(D) and installed in a wiring method described in 517.13(A). The equipment grounding conductor connected to the equipment grounding terminals of the isolated grounding receptacle must have green insulation with one or more yellow stripes along its entire length. ▸Figure 517-11

(2) The insulated equipment grounding conductor required by 517.13(B)(1) must be connected to the metal enclosure containing the isolated ground receptacle in accordance with 517.13(B)(1)(2).

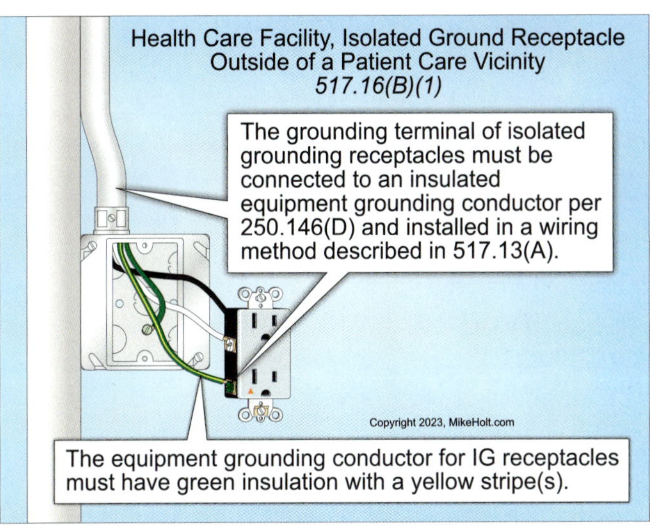
Health Care Facility, Isolated Ground Receptacle
Outside of a Patient Care Vicinity
517.16(B)(1)
The grounding terminal of isolated grounding receptacles must be connected to an insulated equipment grounding conductor per 250.146(D) and installed in a wiring method described in 517.13(A).
Copyright 2023, MikeHolt.com
The equipment grounding conductor for IG receptacles must have green insulation with a yellow stripe(s).

▶Figure 517–11

Note 2: Care should be taken in specifying a system containing isolated ground receptacles because the impedance of the effective ground-fault current path is dependent on the equipment grounding conductor(s). It does not benefit from any conduit or building structure in parallel with the equipment grounding conductor.

Author's Comment:

- Use of an isolated equipment grounding conductor does not relieve the requirement for connecting the raceway system and outlet box to an equipment grounding conductor to establish a low-impedance fault current path back to the supply source.
- The equipment grounding conductor of isolated ground receptacles does not provide the benefits of the multiple equipment grounding paths required in 517.13. For that reason, isolated ground receptacles cannot be installed in a patient care vicinity, but are allowed in a patient care space where the installation complies with 517.13(A) and (B), if the isolated equipment grounding conductor is identified by green insulation with one or more yellow stripes.

ARTICLE
547

AGRICULTURAL BUILDINGS

Introduction to Article 547—Agricultural Buildings

This article applies to buildings, parts of a buildings, or buildings adjacent to areas with accumulations of excessive dust, dust with water, or a corrosive environment. These areas may include poultry, livestock, and fish confinement areas where litter or feed dust may accumulate or where animal excrement may cause corrosive conditions. It also applies to areas where livestock with low tolerances to small voltage differences require an equipotential plane. Many of these rules are outside of the scope of this material, however we do cover the following topics in this article:

- Equipotential Planes

Article 547 consists of three parts:

- Part I. General
- Part II. Installations
- Part III. Distribution (not covered)

547.1 Scope

Article 547 applies to buildings, parts of a building, or buildings' adjacent to areas specified in 547.1(A) or (B): ▸Figure 547–1

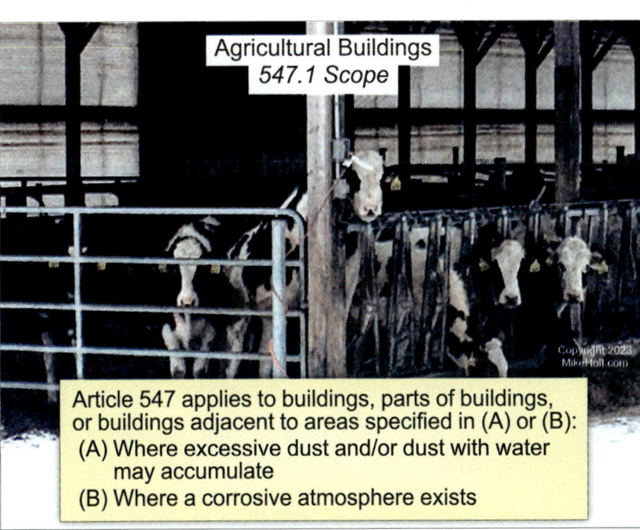
Agricultural Buildings
547.1 Scope
Copyright 2023
MikeHolt.com
Article 547 applies to buildings, parts of buildings, or buildings adjacent to areas specified in (A) or (B):
(A) Where excessive dust and/or dust with water may accumulate
(B) Where a corrosive atmosphere exists

▸Figure 547–1

(A) Excessive Dust and Dust with Water. Buildings or areas where excessive dust, or dust with water, may accumulate. These include areas with poultry, livestock, and fish confinement systems where litter or feed dust may accumulate.

(B) Corrosive Atmosphere. Buildings or areas where a corrosive atmosphere exists, and where the presence of the following conditions exist:

(1) Poultry and animal excrement

(2) Corrosive particles that may combine with water

(3) Areas made damp or wet by periodic washing

547.44 Equipotential Planes

According to Article 100, an "Equipotential Plane (as applied to agricultural buildings)" is an area where conductive elements are embedded in or placed under concrete, bonded to all metal structures and nonelectrical equipment that could become energized, and connected to the electrical system to minimize voltage differences within the plane. ▶Figure 547-2

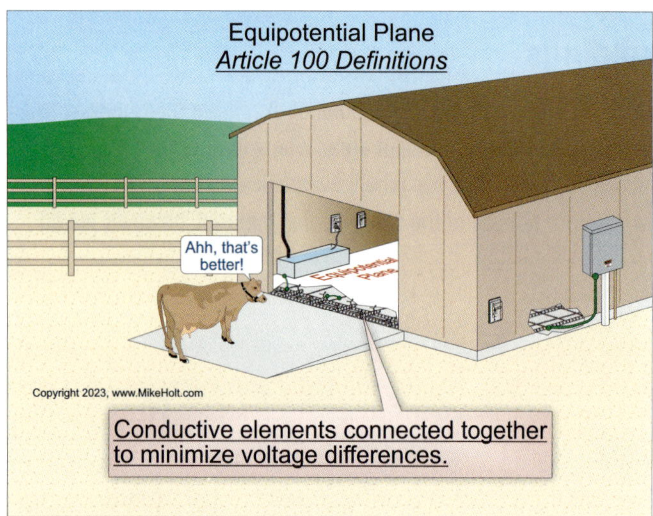
Equipotential Plane
Article 100 Definitions
Ahh, that's better!
Equipotential Plane
Copyright 2023, www.MikeHolt.com
Conductive elements connected together to minimize voltage differences.

▶Figure 547-2

(A) Where Required. Equipotential planes must be installed as follows:

(1) Indoor Concrete Livestock Confinement Areas. An equipotential plane must be installed in indoor concrete floors where metal equipment is accessible to livestock. ▶Figure 547-3

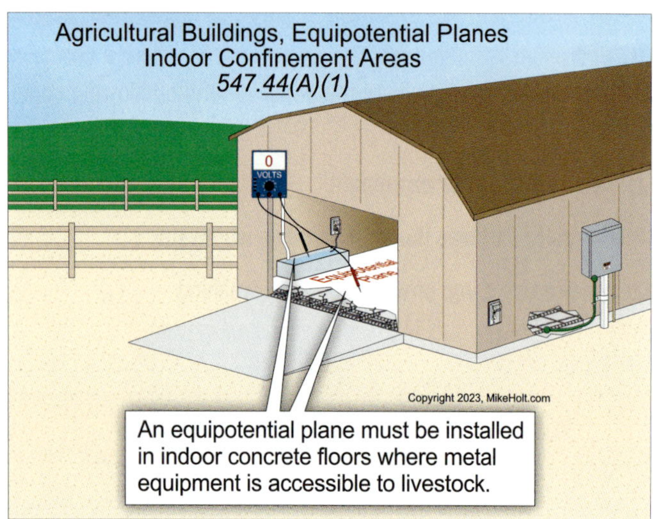
Agricultural Buildings, Equipotential Planes
Indoor Confinement Areas
547.44(A)(1)
0
VOLTS
Copyright 2023, MikeHolt.com
An equipotential plane must be installed in indoor concrete floors where metal equipment is accessible to livestock.

▶Figure 547-3

(2) Outdoor Concrete Livestock Confinement Areas. An equipotential plane must be installed in outdoor concrete slabs where metal equipment is accessible to livestock. ▶Figure 547-4

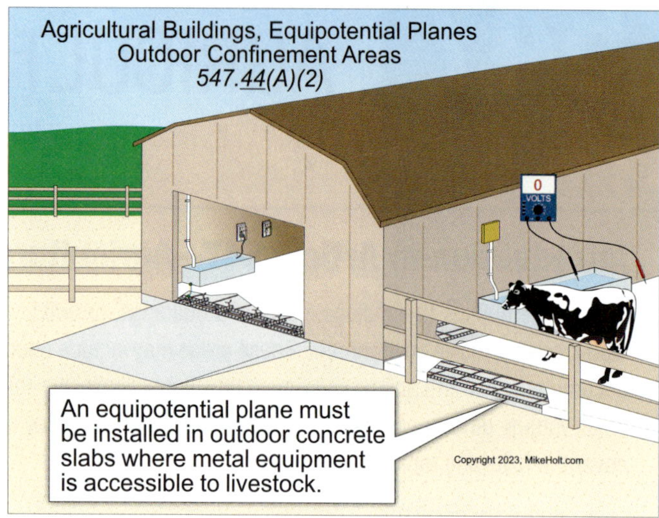
Agricultural Buildings, Equipotential Planes
Outdoor Confinement Areas
547.44(A)(2)
0
VOLTS
An equipotential plane must be installed in outdoor concrete slabs where metal equipment is accessible to livestock.
Copyright 2023, MikeHolt.com

▶Figure 547-4

(B) Bonding. The equipotential plane must be bonded to the grounding electrode system or an equipment grounding terminal in any panelboard of the building's electrical grounding system associated with the equipotential plane by using a solid copper conductor not smaller than 8 AWG. ▶Figure 547-5

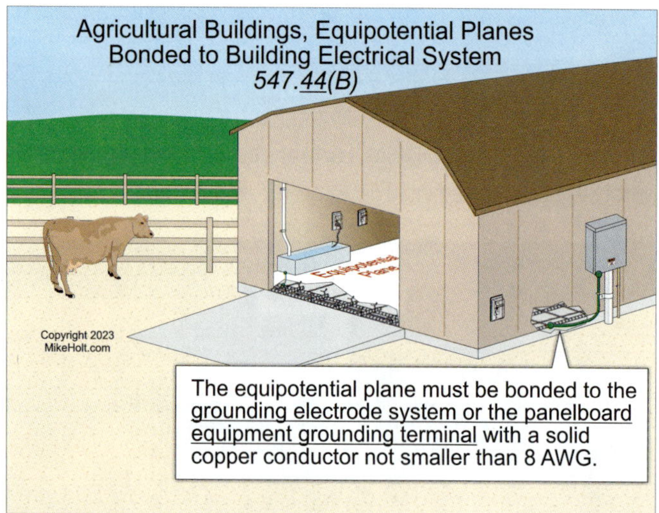
Agricultural Buildings, Equipotential Planes
Bonded to Building Electrical System
547.44(B)
Copyright 2023
MikeHolt.com
The equipotential plane must be bonded to the grounding electrode system or the panelboard equipment grounding terminal with a solid copper conductor not smaller than 8 AWG.

▶Figure 547-5

Note 1: ASABE Standard EP473.2, *Equipotential Planes in Animal Containment Areas*, provides the recommendation of a voltage gradient ramp at the entrances of agricultural buildings.

Note 2: See the American Society of Agricultural and Biological Engineers (ASABE) EP342.2, *Safety for Electrically Heated Livestock Waterers*.

Author's Comment:

- The bonding requirements contained in Article 547 are unique because of the sensitivity of livestock to small voltage differences, especially in wet or damp concrete animal confinement areas.
- In most instances the voltage difference between metal parts and the Earth will be too low to present a shock hazard to people. However, livestock might detect the voltage difference if they come into contact with the metal parts. Although voltage differences may not be life threatening to the livestock, it has been reported that as little as 0.50V RMS can adversely affect milk production.

Notes

ARTICLE 555 MARINAS, BOATYARDS, AND DOCKING FACILITIES

Introduction to Article 555—Marinas, Boatyards, and Docking Facilities

Article 555 covers the installation of wiring and equipment for fixed or floating piers, wharfs, docking facilities, marinas, and boatyards. Fluctuating water levels and the hazard of electric shock drowning (ESD) require special rules to protect the users of these facilities from the hazards that arise from the use of electricity. Many of these rules are outside of the scope of this material, however we do cover the following topics in this article:

- Equipment Grounding Conductor

Article 555 consists of three parts:

- Part I. General
- Part II. Marinas, Boatyards, and Docking Facilities
- Part III. Floating Buildings (not covered)

555.1 Scope

Article 555 covers the installation of wiring and equipment for fixed or floating piers, wharfs, docking facilities, marinas, and boatyards. ▸Figure 555–1

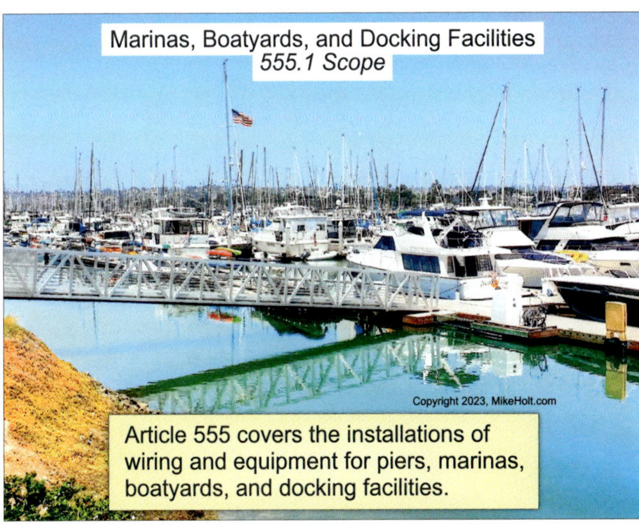
Marinas, Boatyards, and Docking Facilities
555.1 Scope
Copyright 2023, MikeHolt.com
Article 555 covers the installations of wiring and equipment for piers, marinas, boatyards, and docking facilities.

▸Figure 555–1

555.37 Equipment Grounding Conductor

(A) Equipment to be Connected to the Equipment Grounding Conductor. The following items in a marina, boatyard, or docking facility must be connected to an equipment grounding conductor run with the circuit conductors:

(1) Metal boxes, metal cabinets, and all other metal enclosures

(2) Metal frames of utilization equipment

(3) Grounding terminals of grounding-type receptacles

(B) Type of Equipment Grounding Conductor. An insulated equipment grounding conductor, sized in accordance with 250.122 but not smaller than 12 AWG, must be provided for all circuits in a marina, boatyard, or docking facility. ▸Figure 555–2

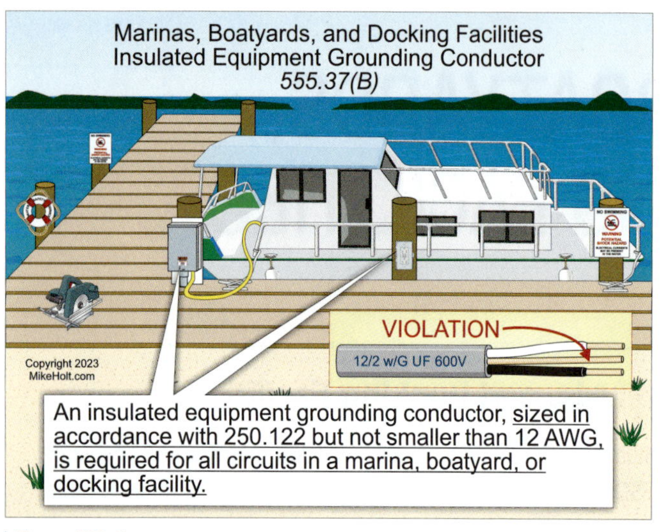

Marinas, Boatyards, and Docking Facilities
Insulated Equipment Grounding Conductor
555.37(B)
VIOLATION
12/2 w/G UF 600V
Copyright 2023
MikeHolt.com
An insulated equipment grounding conductor, sized in accordance with 250.122 but not smaller than 12 AWG, is required for all circuits in a marina, boatyard, or docking facility.

▶Figure 555–2

(C) Feeder Equipment Grounding Conductor. A feeder to a panelboard or distribution equipment must have an insulated equipment grounding conductor [555.37(B)] run from the service to the panelboard or distribution equipment.

(D) Branch-Circuit Equipment Grounding Conductor. The required branch-circuit insulated equipment grounding conductor [555.37(B)] must terminate at a grounding terminal in a panelboard, distribution equipment, or service equipment.

CHAPTER

5

REVIEW QUESTIONS

Please use the 2023 *Code* book to answer the following questions.

Article 501—Class I Hazardous (Classified) Locations

1. Article 501 covers the requirements for electrical and electronic equipment and wiring for all voltages in Class I, Division 1 and 2 locations, where _____ are or might be present in the air in quantities sufficient to produce explosive or ignitible mixtures.

   (a) flammable gases
   (b) flammable liquid-produced vapors
   (c) combustible liquid-produced vapors
   (d) any of these

2. In Class I locations, the locknut-bushing and double-locknut types of contacts shall not be depended on for _____ purposes.

   (a) bonding
   (b) grounding
   (c) securing
   (d) supporting

3. When FMC or LFMC is used as permitted in Class I, Division 2 locations, it shall include an equipment bonding jumper of the _____ type in compliance with 250.102.

   (a) wire
   (b) raceway
   (c) steel
   (d) none of these

Article 502—Class II Hazardous (Classified) Locations

1. Article 502 covers the requirements for electrical and electronic equipment and wiring in Class II, Division 1 and 2 locations where fire or explosion hazards may exist due to _____.

   (a) ignitible gases or vapors
   (b) ignitible fibers/flyings
   (c) combustible dust
   (d) all of these

2. In Class II Locations the locknut-bushing and double-locknut types of contacts shall not be depended on for _____ purposes, but bonding jumpers with identified fittings or other approved means of bonding shall be used.

   (a) bonding
   (b) grounding
   (c) continuity
   (d) any of these

3. Where LFMC is used in a Class II, Division 1 location as permitted in 502.10, It shall _____.

   (a) not be unsupported
   (b) not exceed 6 ft in length
   (c) include an equipment bonding jumper of the wire type
   (d) be listed for use in Class I locations

Article 517—Health Care Facilities

1. Article 517 applies to electrical construction and installation criteria in health care facilities that provide services to _____.

   (a) human beings
   (b) animals
   (c) children only
   (d) intellectually challenged persons

2. Branch circuits serving fixed electrical equipment in patient care spaces shall be provided with a(an) _____ by installation in a metal raceway system or a cable having a metallic armor or sheath assembly.

   (a) effective ground-fault current path
   (b) ground-fault current path
   (c) effective current path
   (d) none of these

3. In patient care spaces, metal faceplates shall be connected to an effective ground-fault current path by means of _____ securing the faceplate to a metal yoke or strap of a receptacle or to a metal outlet box.

   (a) ground clips
   (b) rivets
   (c) metal mounting screws
   (d) spot welds

4. In health care facilities, isolated ground receptacles shall be installed in a patient care vicinity.

   (a) True
   (b) False

5. In health care facilities, _____ ground receptacle(s) installed in patient care spaces outside of a patient care vicinity(s) shall comply with 517.16(B)(1) and (2).

   (a) AFCI-protected
   (b) GFCI-protected
   (c) isolated
   (d) all of these

6. Outside of patient care vicinities, the equipment grounding terminals of isolated ground receptacles installed in branch circuits for patient care _____ shall be connected to an insulated equipment grounding conductor in accordance with 250.146(D) installed in a wiring method described in 517.13(A).

   (a) vicinities
   (b) spaces
   (c) bathrooms
   (d) vicinities or spaces

7. Outside of patient care vicinities, the insulated equipment grounding conductor required in 517.13(B)(1) for health care facilities shall be clearly _____ along its entire length by green insulation, with no yellow stripes, and shall not be connected to the grounding terminals of isolated ground receptacles but shall be connected to the box or enclosure indicated in 517.13(B)(1)(2) and to noncurrent-carrying conductive surfaces of fixed electrical equipment indicated in 517.13(B)(1)(3).

   (a) listed
   (b) labeled
   (c) identified
   (d) approved

8. Outside of patient care vicinities, care should be taken in specifying a system containing isolated ground receptacles in health care facilities because the _____ of the effective ground-fault current path is dependent upon the equipment grounding conductor(s) and does not benefit from any conduit or building structure in parallel with the equipment grounding conductor.

   (a) ampacity
   (b) resistance
   (c) effectiveness
   (d) impedance

Article 547—Agricultural Buildings

1. Agricultural buildings where excessive dust and dust with water may accumulate, including all areas of _____ confinement systems where litter dust or feed dust may accumulate shall comply with Article 547.

   (a) poultry
   (b) livestock
   (c) fish
   (d) all of these

2. Agricultural buildings where corrosive atmospheres exist include areas where the following condition(s) exist(s) _____.

(a) poultry and animal excrement
(b) corrosive particles which may combine with water
(c) areas of periodic washing with water and cleansing agents
(d) all of these

3. A(An) _____ plane shall be installed in all concrete floor confinement areas of livestock buildings, and all outdoor confinement areas with a concrete slab that contains metallic equipment accessible to livestock and that may become energized.

(a) equipotential
(b) electrical datum
(c) neutral-to-earth voltage
(d) elevated

Article 555—Marinas, Boatyards, and Docking Facilities

1. Article 555 covers the installation of wiring and equipment in the areas comprising of _____ and other areas in marinas and boatyards.

(a) fixed or floating piers
(b) floating buildings
(c) wharves and docks
(d) all of these

2. Marina equipment grounding conductors shall be of the wire-type, insulated, and sized in accordance with 250.122 but not smaller than _____.

(a) 14 AWG
(b) 12 AWG
(c) 10 AWG
(d) 8 AWG

3. Where a marina shore power feeder supplies a remote panelboard, an insulated _____ shall extend from a grounding terminal in the service equipment to a grounding terminal in the remote panelboard.

(a) bonding jumper
(b) equipment grounding conductor
(c) grounding electrode conductor
(d) copper conductor

Notes

CHAPTER

6 SPECIAL EQUIPMENT

Introduction to Chapter 6—Special Equipment

Chapter 6, which covers special equipment, is the second of the three *NEC* chapters dealing with special equipment requirements. Special equipment is that, by the nature of its use, construction, or unique nature, have special installation requirements to safeguard people and property from the hazards of electricity arising from its use. This chapter contains 27 articles addressing special equipment used for things like electric signs, swimming pools, and solar PV systems. Many of the Chapter 6 articles are outside of the scope of this material, however, we do cover the following:

- **Article 600—Electric Signs.** This article covers the installation of conductors and equipment for electric signs as defined in Article 100. All products and installations that utilize neon tubing, such as signs, decorative elements, skeleton tubing, or art forms are included.
- **Article 645—Information Technology Equipment.** Article 645 applies to equipment, power-supply wiring, equipment interconnecting wiring, and grounding of information technology equipment and systems including terminal units in an information technology equipment room.
- **Article 680—Swimming Pools, Spas, Hot Tubs, Fountains, and Similar Installations.** This article covers the electrical installation requirements for equipment used for swimming, wading, therapeutic and decorative pools, fountains, hot tubs, spas, and hydromassage bathtubs.
- **Article 690—Solar Photovoltaic (PV) Systems.** Article 690 contains the special installation requirements for equipment used for solar PV systems.

ARTICLE
600

ELECTRIC SIGNS

Introduction to Article 600—Electric Signs

Article 600 covers the special requirements for the installation of conductors, equipment, and field wiring for electric signs. These signs come in many forms and may utilize neon tubing such as decorative elements, skeleton tubing, or art forms. Commercial occupancies often leverage electric signs for aesthetics, identification, or advertising and this article provides the rules governing the installation of this equipment. Many of these rules are outside of the scope of this material, however we do cover the following topics in this article:

- Branch Circuits
- Disconnects
- Grounding and Bonding
- PV Powered Signs
- Retrofit Kits

Article 600 consists of two parts:

- Part I. General
- Part II. Field-Installed Skeleton Tubing, Outline Lighting, and Secondary Wiring (not covered)

600.1 Scope

Article 600 covers the installation of conductors, equipment, and field wiring for electric signs. It also covers installations and equipment using neon tubing such as signs, decorative elements, skeleton tubing, or art forms. ▸Figure 600–1

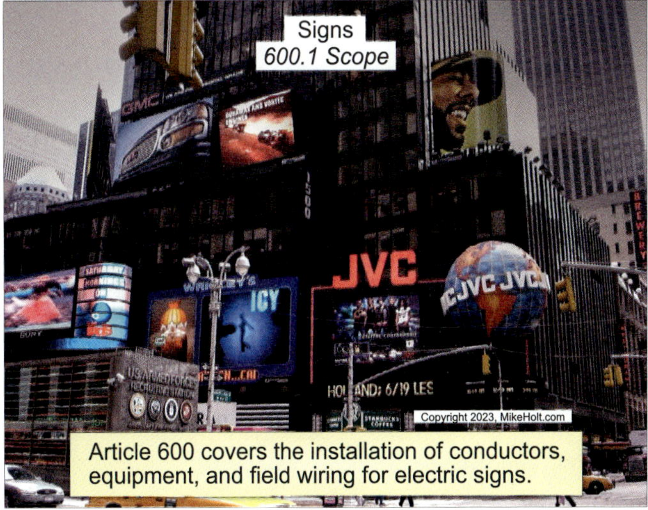
Signs
600.1 Scope
JVC
ICY
Copyright 2023, MikeHolt.com
Article 600 covers the installation of conductors, equipment, and field wiring for electric signs.

▸Figure 600–1

According to Article 100, an "Electric Sign" is any fixed, stationary, or portable self-contained, electrically illuminated utilization equipment with words or symbols designed to convey information or attract attention. ▸Figure 600–2

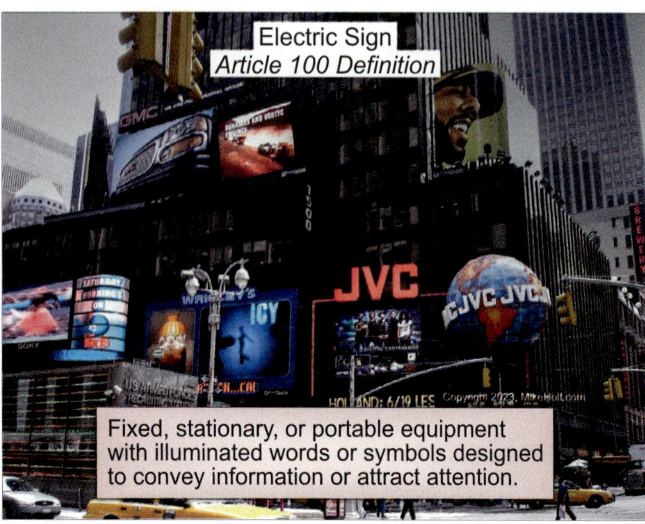
Electric Sign
Article 100 Definition
Fixed, stationary, or portable equipment with illuminated words or symbols designed to convey information or attract attention.
JVC
Copyright 2023, MikeHolt.com

▶Figure 600–2

600.7 Grounding and Bonding

(A) Equipment Grounding Conductor and Grounding.

(1) Equipment Grounding Conductor. Metal parts of signs must be connected to the circuit equipment grounding conductor. ▶Figure 600–3

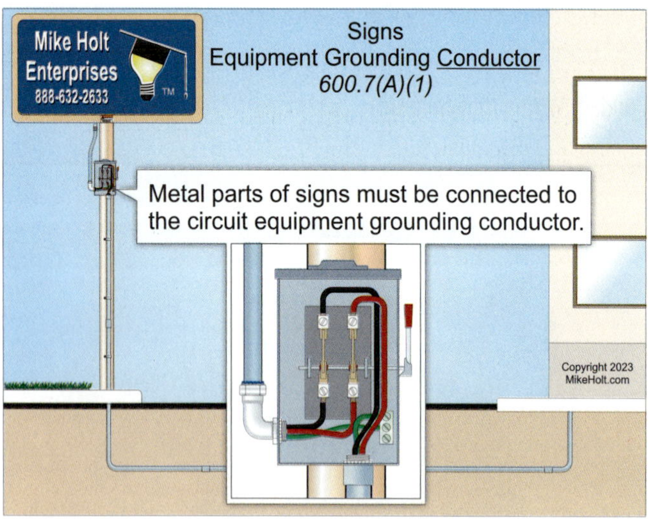
Mike Holt Enterprises 888-632-2633
Signs
Equipment Grounding Conductor
600.7(A)(1)
Metal parts of signs must be connected to the circuit equipment grounding conductor.
Copyright 2023 MikeHolt.com

▶Figure 600–3

(2) Size of Equipment Grounding Conductor. If the equipment grounding conductor is of the wire type, it must be sized in accordance with 250.122.

(3) Connections of Equipment Grounding Conductor. Equipment grounding conductor connections must be made in accordance with 250.130 in a method specified in 250.8.

Author's Comment:

- According to 250.8, equipment grounding conductors of the wire type must terminate in any of the following methods:

  (1) Listed pressure connectors
  (2) Terminal bars
  (3) Pressure connectors listed for grounding and bonding
  (4) Exothermic welding
  (5) Machine screws that engage at least two threads or are secured with a nut
  (6) Self-tapping machine screws that engage at least two threads
  (7) Connections that are part of a listed assembly
  (8) Other listed means

(4) Auxiliary Grounding Electrode. Auxiliary grounding electrodes are not required for signs, but if installed they must comply with 250.54. ▶Figure 600–4

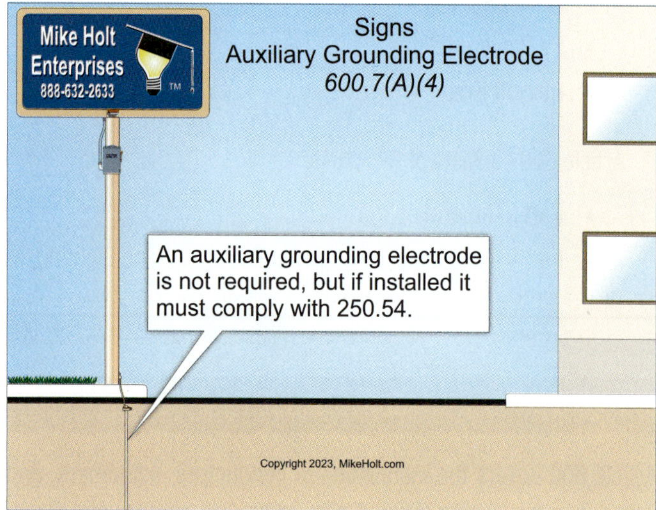
Mike Holt Enterprises 888-632-2633
Signs
Auxiliary Grounding Electrode
600.7(A)(4)
An auxiliary grounding electrode is not required, but if installed it must comply with 250.54.
Copyright 2023, MikeHolt.com

▶Figure 600–4

Author's Comment:

- According to 250.54, auxiliary electrodes need not be bonded to the building grounding electrode system, the grounding conductor to the electrode need not be sized in accordance with 250.66, and the contact resistance of the electrode to the Earth is not required to comply with the 25Ω requirement of 250.53(A)(2) Ex.

- The Earth must not be used as the effective ground-fault current path required by 250.4(A)(4) and(A)(5). This is because the contact resistance of a grounding electrode to the Earth is high, and very little ground-fault current returns to the electrical supply source via the Earth. The result is the circuit overcurrent protective device will not open and clear a ground fault, so metal parts will remain energized with dangerous step and touch voltage. ▸Figure 600–5

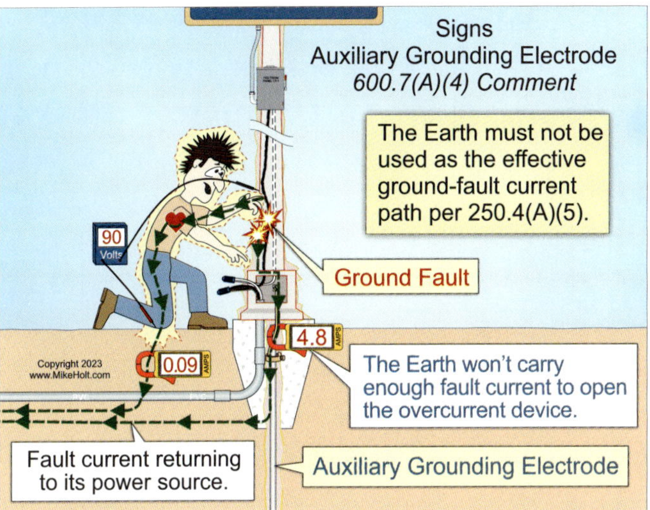
Signs
Auxiliary Grounding Electrode
600.7(A)(4) Comment
The Earth must not be used as the effective ground-fault current path per 250.4(A)(5).
90 Volts
Ground Fault
4.8
0.09
Copyright 2023 www.MikeHolt.com
The Earth won't carry enough fault current to open the overcurrent device.
Fault current returning to its power source.
Auxiliary Grounding Electrode

▸Figure 600–5

(B) Bonding.

(1) Metal Parts. Metal parts of sign systems must be bonded together and to the transformer or power-supply equipment grounding conductor.

Ex: Remote metal parts of a section sign system supplied by a Class 2 power-limited power supply are not required to be connected to an equipment grounding conductor.

(2) Bonding Connections. Bonding connections must be made in accordance with 250.8.

Author's Comment:

- According to 250.8, bonding conductors must terminate in any of the following methods:

  (1) Listed pressure connectors
  (2) Terminal bars
  (3) Pressure connectors listed for grounding and bonding
  (4) Exothermic welding
  (5) Machine screws that engage at least two threads or are secured with a nut
  (6) Self-tapping machine screws that engage at least two threads
  (7) Connections that are part of a listed assembly
  (8) Other listed means

(4) Flexible Metal Conduit Length. Listed flexible metal conduit or listed liquidtight flexible metal conduit for secondary circuit conductors for neon tubing can be used as a bonding means if the total length of the flexible metal conduit does not exceed 100 ft.

(7) Bonding Conductors. Bonding conductors installed outside a sign or raceway must be protected from physical damage, installed in accordance with 250.120, sized in accordance with 250.122, and comply with one of the following:

(1) Bonding conductors must be copper and not smaller than 14 AWG.

(2) Bonding conductors must be copper-clad aluminum and not smaller than 12 AWG.

ARTICLE 645 INFORMATION TECHNOLOGY EQUIPMENT (ITE)

Introduction to Article 645—Information Technology Equipment (ITE)

This article provides optional wiring methods and materials for information technology equipment (ITE) and systems in an information technology equipment room as an alternative to those required in other chapters of this *Code*. Information technology rooms often contain huge racks of equipment, raised floors, massive numbers of data and fiber optic cables, and exposed power cords creating special challenges needing special rules to protect those who use these areas. Many of these rules are outside of the scope of this material, however we do cover the following topics in this article:

- Equipment Grounding Conductor

645.1 Scope

Article 645 provides optional wiring methods and materials for information technology equipment (ITE) and systems in an information technology equipment room as an alternative to those required in other chapters of this *Code*. ▸Figure 645-1

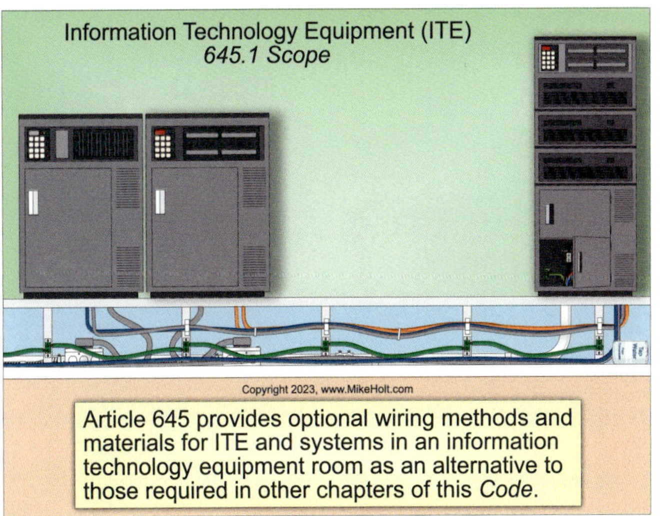
Information Technology Equipment (ITE)
645.1 Scope
Copyright 2023, www.MikeHolt.com
Article 645 provides optional wiring methods and materials for ITE and systems in an information technology equipment room as an alternative to those required in other chapters of this *Code*.

▸Figure 645-1

Note 1: An information technology equipment room is an enclosed area specifically designed to comply with the construction and fire protection provisions of NFPA 75, *Standard for the Fire Protection of Information Technology Equipment*.

645.15 Equipment Grounding and Bonding

Exposed metal parts of an information technology system must be connected to the circuit equipment grounding conductor or be double insulated. ▸Figure 645-2

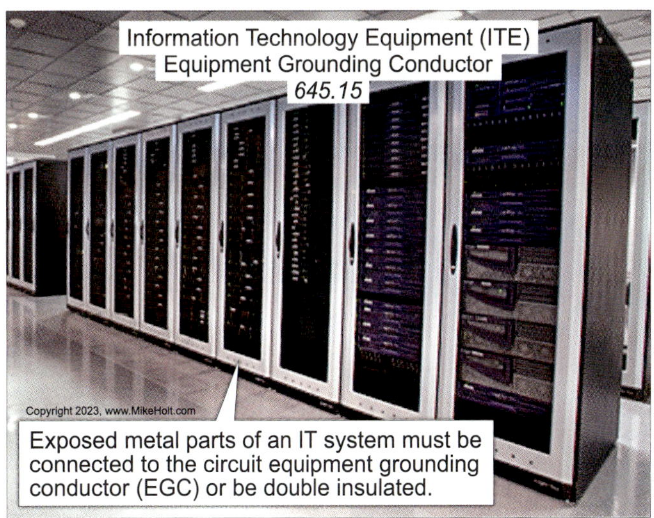
Information Technology Equipment (ITE)
Equipment Grounding Conductor
645.15
Copyright 2023, www.MikeHolt.com
Exposed metal parts of an IT system must be connected to the circuit equipment grounding conductor (EGC) or be double insulated.

▸Figure 645-2

Where signal reference structures are installed, they must be connected to the circuit equipment grounding conductor for the information technology equipment. ▸Figure 645-3

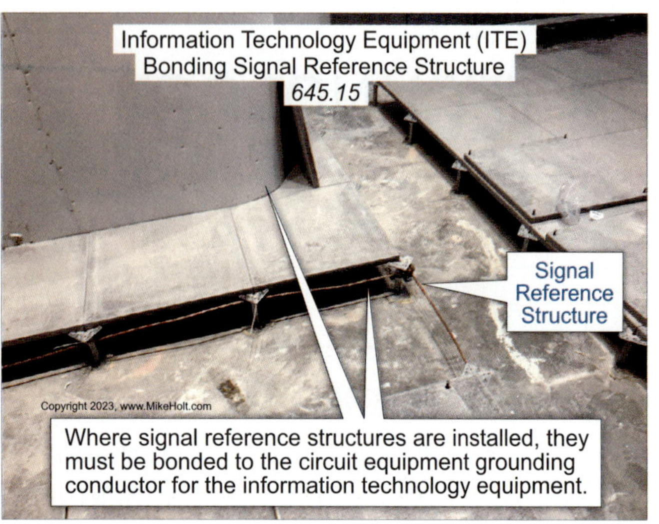
Information Technology Equipment (ITE)
Bonding Signal Reference Structure
645.15
Signal Reference Structure
Copyright 2023, www.MikeHolt.com
Where signal reference structures are installed, they must be bonded to the circuit equipment grounding conductor for the information technology equipment.

▶Figure 645-3

If isolated ground receptacles are installed, they must be connected to an insulated equipment grounding conductor in accordance with 250.146(D) and 406.3(E).

ARTICLE 680 SWIMMING POOLS, SPAS, HOT TUBS, FOUNTAINS, AND SIMILAR INSTALLATIONS

Introduction to Article 680—Swimming Pools, Spas, Hot Tubs, Fountains, and Similar Installations

Article 680 applies to the installation of electrical wiring and equipment for swimming pools, hot tubs, spas, fountains, and hydromassage bathtubs.

This article is divided into eight parts which apply to certain types of installations. Be very careful to determine which part(s) of this article apply to what and where. For instance, Part I and Part II apply to hot tubs installed outdoors, except as modified in Part IV. In contrast, hydromassage bathtubs are only covered by Part VII. Read the details of Article 680 carefully so you will be able to provide a safe installation. Many of these rules are outside of the scope of this material, but we do cover these topics:

- Bonding and Grounding
- Underwater Pool Luminaires
- Pool Light Junction Boxes, Transformers, or GFCI Enclosures
- Equipotential Bonding
- Hot Tubs
- Fountains

Article 680 consists of eight parts:

- Part I. General Requirements for Pools, Spas, Hot Tubs, and Fountains
- Part II. Permanently Installed Pools
- Part III. Storable Pools, Hot Tubs, and Immersion Pools (not covered)
- Part IV. Hot Tubs
- Part V. Fountains
- Part VI. Therapeutic Pools and Tubs (not covered)
- Part VII. Hydromassage Bathtubs
- Part VIII. Electrically Powered Pool Lifts (not covered)

Part I. General Requirements for Pools, Spas, Hot Tubs, and Fountains

680.1 Scope

Article 680 applies to the installation of electric wiring and equipment for swimming pools, hot tubs, spas, fountains, and hydromassage bathtubs. ▶Figure 680-1

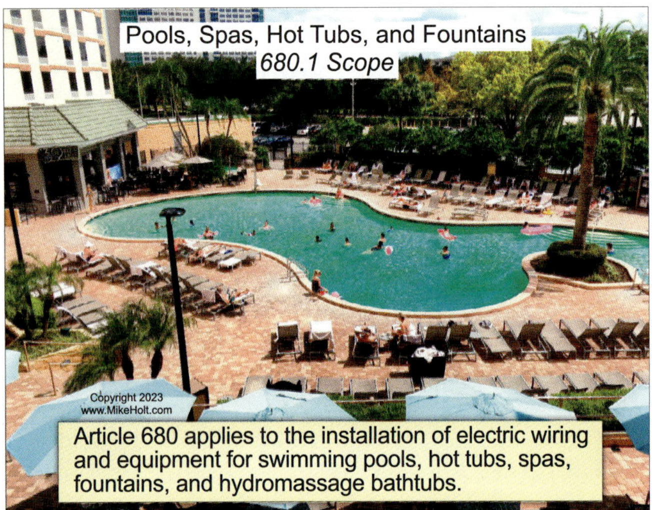
Pools, Spas, Hot Tubs, and Fountains
680.1 Scope
Copyright 2023
www.MikeHolt.com
Article 680 applies to the installation of electric wiring and equipment for swimming pools, hot tubs, spas, fountains, and hydromassage bathtubs.

▶Figure 680-1

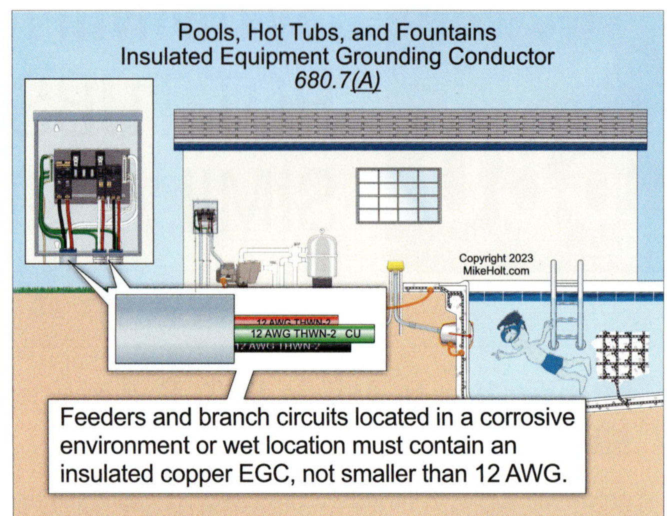
Pools, Hot Tubs, and Fountains
Insulated Equipment Grounding Conductor
680.7(A)
Copyright 2023
MikeHolt.com
12 AWG THWN-2
12 AWG THWN-2 CU
12 AWG THWN-2
Feeders and branch circuits located in a corrosive environment or wet location must contain an insulated copper EGC, not smaller than 12 AWG.

▶Figure 680-2

680.7 Grounding and Bonding

(A) Insulated Equipment Grounding Conductor. Feeders and branch circuits located in a corrosive environment or wet location must contain an insulated copper equipment grounding conductor sized in accordance with Table 250.122, but not smaller than 12 AWG. ▶Figure 680-2

According to Article 100, "Corrosive Environment" are areas or enclosures without adequate ventilation where electrical equipment is located and pool sanitation chemicals are stored, handled, or dispensed (Article 680). ▶Figure 680-3

Corrosive Environment
Article 100 Definition
Copyright 2023, MikeHolt.com
Areas or enclosures without adequate ventilation where electrical equipment is located and pool sanitation chemicals are stored, handled, or dispensed (680).

▶Figure 680-3

Note 1: Sanitation chemicals and pool water pose a risk of corrosion (gradually damaging or destroying materials) due to the presence of oxidizers (for example, calcium hypochlorite, sodium hypochlorite, bromine, and chlorinated isocyanurates) and chlorinating agents that release chlorine when dissolved in water.

(B) Cord-and-Plug Connections. Flexible cords must contain an equipment grounding conductor that is an insulated copper conductor sized in accordance with Table 250.122, but not smaller than 12 AWG. The flexible cord must terminate in a grounding-type attachment plug having a fixed grounding contact member.

(C) Terminals. Field-installed terminals in damp or wet locations or corrosive environments must be listed for direct burial use. ▶Figure 680-4

Pools, Hot Tubs, and Fountains
Equipment Grounding/Bonding Terminals
680.7(C)
VIOLATION
Field-installed terminals in damp or wet locations, or corrosive environments, must be listed for direct burial use.
Copyright 2023, www.MikeHolt.com

▸Figure 680–4

Part II. Permanently Installed Pools

According to Article 100, "Permanently Installed Pools" are pools constructed or installed in the ground (or partially in the ground), and pools installed inside of a building (680). ▸**Figure 680–5**

Pool, Permanently Installed
Article 100 Definition
A pool constructed or installed in the ground or partially in the ground, and all pools installed inside of a building (680).
Copyright 2023 MikeHolt.com

▸Figure 680–5

680.23 Underwater Pool Luminaires

This section covers all luminaires installed below the maximum water level of the pool.

(A) General.

(2) Transformers and Power Supplies for Underwater Pool Luminaires. Transformers and power supplies for underwater pool luminaires must be listed, labeled, and identified for swimming pool use.

(3) GFCI Protection. Branch circuits supplying underwater pool luminaires at 120V must be GFCI protected. ▸**Figure 680–6**

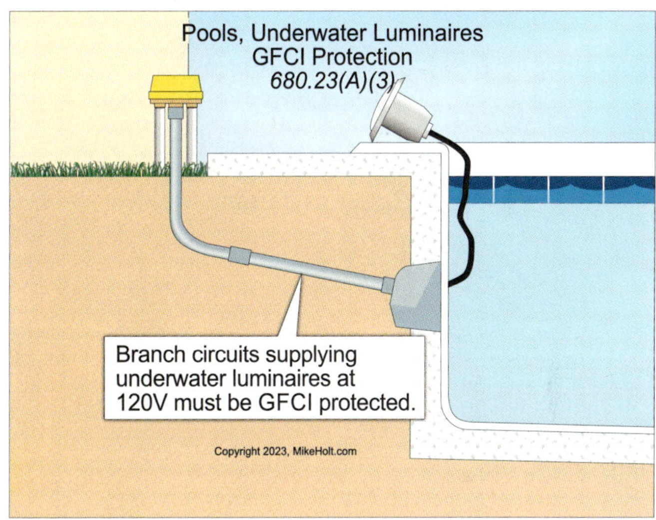
Pools, Underwater Luminaires
GFCI Protection
680.23(A)(3)
Branch circuits supplying underwater luminaires at 120V must be GFCI protected.
Copyright 2023, MikeHolt.com

▸Figure 680–6

(5) Wall-Mounted Luminaires. Underwater wall-mounted luminaires must be installed so the top of the luminaire lens is not less than 18 in. below the normal water level. ▸**Figure 680–7**

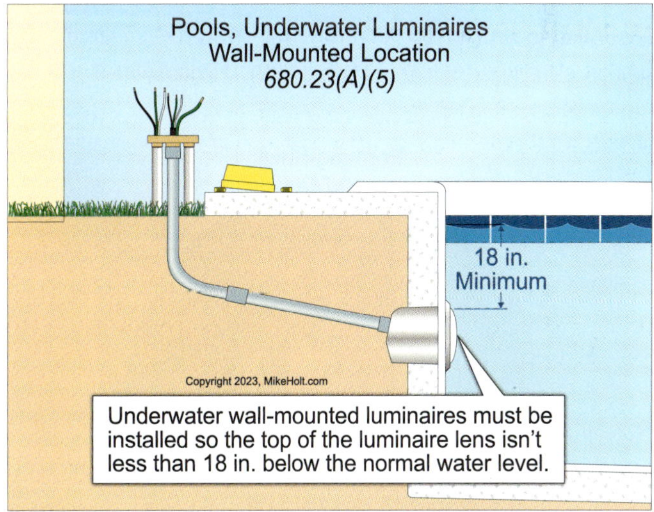
Pools, Underwater Luminaires
Wall-Mounted Location
680.23(A)(5)
18 in.
Minimum
Underwater wall-mounted luminaires must be installed so the top of the luminaire lens isn't less than 18 in. below the normal water level.
Copyright 2023, MikeHolt.com

▸Figure 680–7

(B) Wet-Niche Luminaires.

According to Article 100, "Wet-Niche Luminaire" is a luminaire intended to be installed in a forming shell where it will be completely surrounded by water (Article 680). ▸**Figure 680–8**

Luminaire, Wet-Niche
Article 100 Definition
A luminaire intended to be installed in a forming shell where it will be completely surrounded by water (680).

▸**Figure 680–8**

(1) Wet-Niche Forming Shells. Forming shells must be installed for the mounting of all wet-niche underwater luminaires. Forming shells must include provisions for terminating an 8 AWG copper conductor unless the forming shell is part of a listed low-voltage lighting system.

(2) Wiring to the Wet-Niche Forming Shell.

According to Article 100, "Forming Shell" is a structure designed to support a wet-niche luminaire (Article 680). ▸**Figure 680–9**

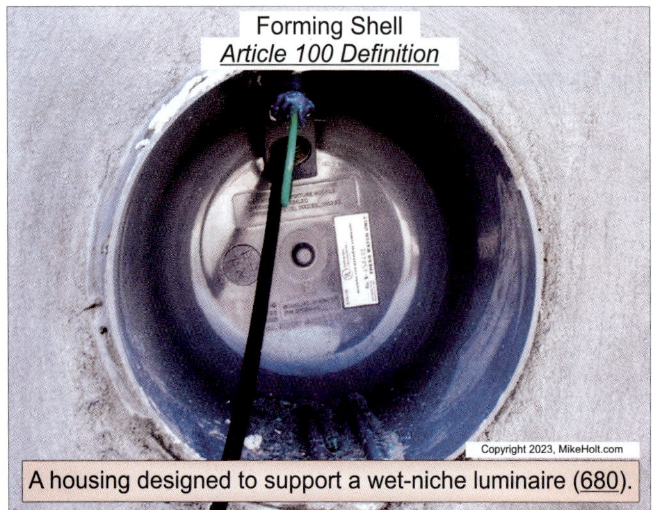
Forming Shell
Article 100 Definition
A housing designed to support a wet-niche luminaire (680).

▸**Figure 680–9**

(b) Nonmetallic Raceway. A nonmetallic raceway run to the forming shell of a wet-niche luminaire must contain an 8 AWG insulated copper conductor that terminates to the forming shell. ▸**Figure 680–10**

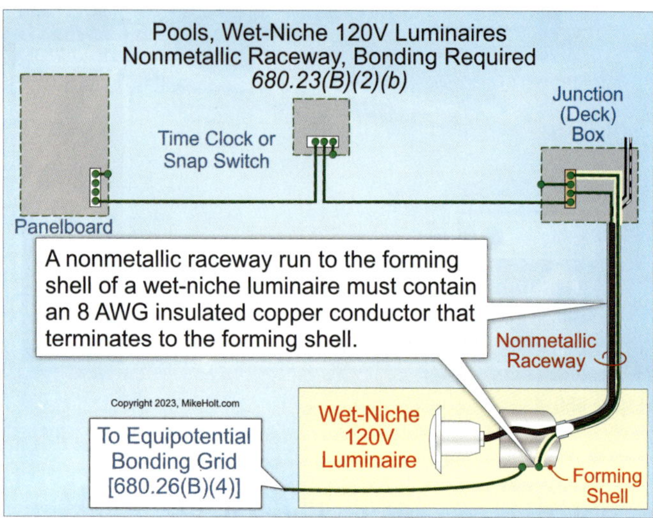
Pools, Wet-Niche 120V Luminaires
Nonmetallic Raceway, Bonding Required
680.23(B)(2)(b)
Time Clock or Snap Switch
Junction (Deck) Box
Panelboard
A nonmetallic raceway run to the forming shell of a wet-niche luminaire must contain an 8 AWG insulated copper conductor that terminates to the forming shell.
Nonmetallic Raceway
To Equipotential Bonding Grid [680.26(B)(4)]
Wet-Niche 120V Luminaire
Forming Shell

▸**Figure 680–10**

Low-Voltage Lighting System. A nonmetallic raceway run to the forming shell of a listed low-voltage lighting system that does not require grounding does not require an 8 AWG insulated copper conductor to the forming shell. ▸**Figure 680–11**

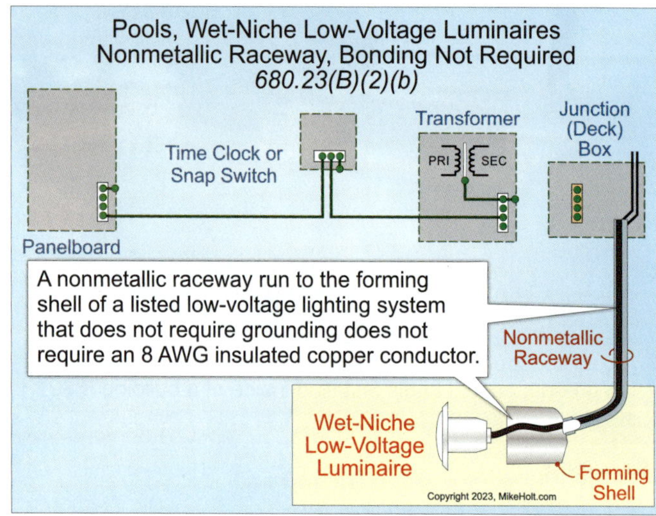
Pools, Wet-Niche Low-Voltage Luminaires
Nonmetallic Raceway, Bonding Not Required
680.23(B)(2)(b)
Time Clock or Snap Switch
Transformer
PRI
SEC
Junction (Deck) Box
Panelboard
A nonmetallic raceway run to the forming shell of a listed low-voltage lighting system that does not require grounding does not require an 8 AWG insulated copper conductor.
Nonmetallic Raceway
Wet-Niche Low-Voltage Luminaire
Forming Shell

▸**Figure 680–11**

The termination of the 8 AWG bonding jumper in the forming shell must be covered with a listed potting compound to protect the connection from the possible deteriorating effects of pool water.

(3) Equipment Grounding Provisions for Cords. The cord or cable supplying a low-voltage underwater luminaire that does not require grounding does not require an insulated copper equipment grounding conductor. ▸Figure 680–12

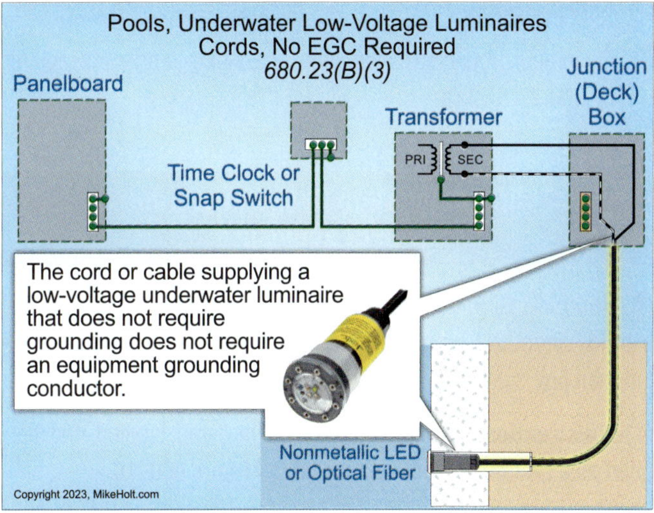
Pools, Underwater Low-Voltage Luminaires
Cords, No EGC Required
680.23(B)(3)
Panelboard
Time Clock or
Snap Switch
Transformer
PRI
SEC
Junction
(Deck)
Box
The cord or cable supplying a low-voltage underwater luminaire that does not require grounding does not require an equipment grounding conductor.
Nonmetallic LED
or Optical Fiber
Copyright 2023, MikeHolt.com

▸Figure 680–12

(6) Luminaire Servicing. The location of the forming shell and length of flexible cord for wet-niche pool luminaires must allow for personnel to place the luminaire on the deck or other dry location for maintenance. ▸Figure 680–13

Wet-Niche Luminaires, Servicing, Spa
680.23(B)(6)
Copyright 2023, www.MikeHolt.com
Where wet-niche luminaires are installed in the foot well of the spa, the location of the forming shell and length of flexible cord for the underwater spa luminaire must allow for personnel to place the luminaire on the bench where the spa can be drained to make the bench location dry.

▸Figure 680–13

(F) Branch-Circuit Wiring to Underwater Luminaires.

(1) Wiring Methods. Branch-circuit wiring for underwater luminaires run in corrosive environments must be in rigid metal conduit, intermediate metal conduit, rigid polyvinyl chloride conduit, reinforced thermosetting resin conduit, or liquidtight flexible nonmetallic conduit [680.14]. ▸Figure 680–14

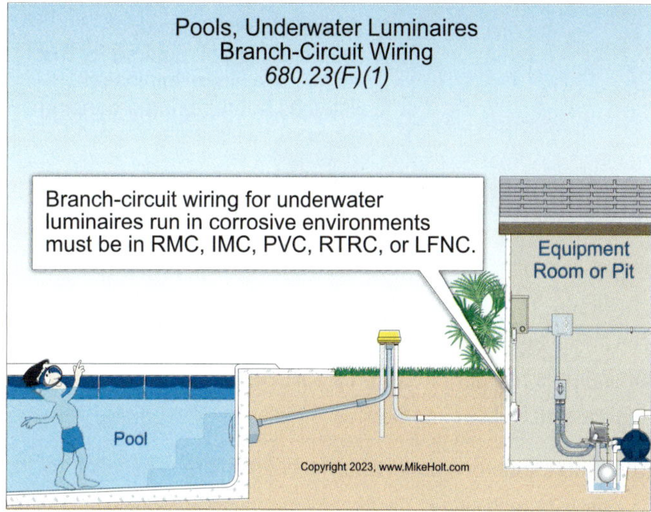
Pools, Underwater Luminaires
Branch-Circuit Wiring
680.23(F)(1)
Branch-circuit wiring for underwater luminaires run in corrosive environments must be in RMC, IMC, PVC, RTRC, or LFNC.
Equipment
Room or Pit
Pool
Copyright 2023, www.MikeHolt.com

▸Figure 680–14

(2) Branch-Circuit Equipment Grounding Conductor.

Wet-Niche 120V Luminaires. An insulated copper equipment grounding conductor not smaller than 12 AWG is required for a wet-niche 120V luminaires. ▸Figure 680–15

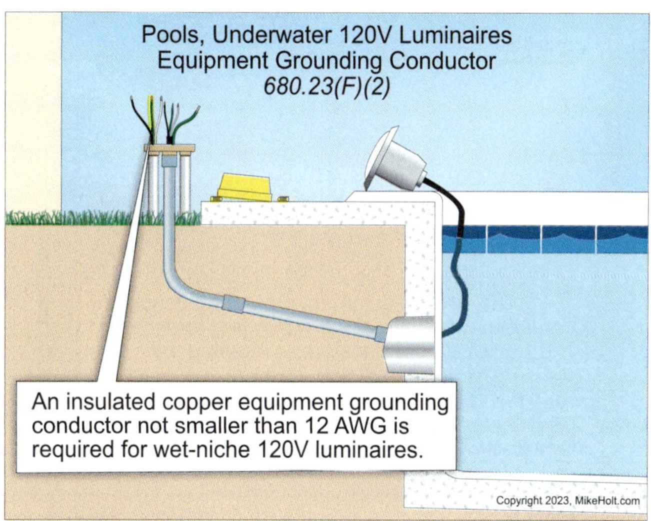
Pools, Underwater 120V Luminaires
Equipment Grounding Conductor
680.23(F)(2)
An insulated copper equipment grounding conductor not smaller than 12 AWG is required for wet-niche 120V luminaires.
Copyright 2023, MikeHolt.com

▸Figure 680–15

Low-Voltage Luminaires. An equipment grounding conductor is not required for a low-voltage luminaires listed as not requiring grounding. ▸Figure 680–16

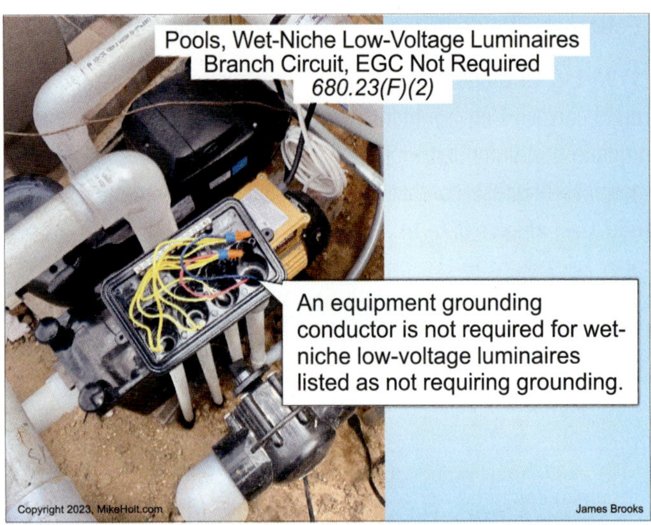
Pools, Wet-Niche Low-Voltage Luminaires
Branch Circuit, EGC Not Required
680.23(F)(2)
An equipment grounding conductor is not required for wet-niche low-voltage luminaires listed as not requiring grounding.
Copyright 2023, MikeHolt.com
James Brooks

▸Figure 680–16

The circuit equipment grounding conductor for the underwater pool luminaire is not permitted to be spliced, except for the following applications:

(a) If more than one underwater pool luminaire is supplied by the same branch circuit, the circuit equipment grounding conductor can terminate at a listed pool junction box meeting the requirements of 680.24(A).

(b) The circuit equipment grounding conductor can terminate at the grounding terminal of a listed pool transformer meeting the requirements of 680.23(A)(2). ▸Figure 680–17

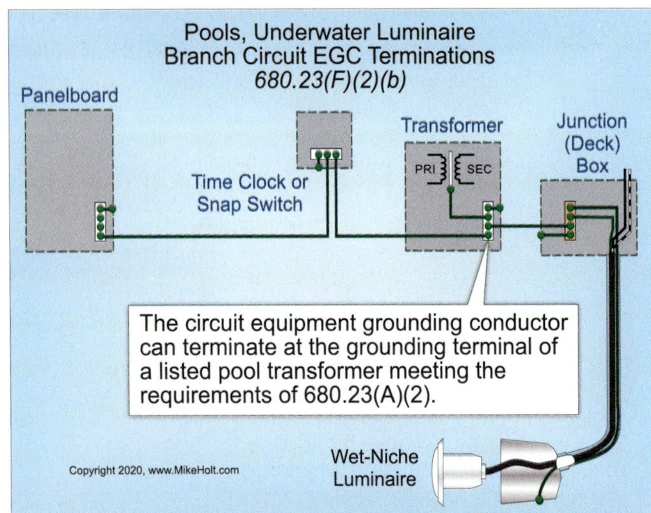
Pools, Underwater Luminaire
Branch Circuit EGC Terminations
680.23(F)(2)(b)
Panelboard
Time Clock or Snap Switch
Transformer
PRI
SEC
Junction (Deck) Box
The circuit equipment grounding conductor can terminate at the grounding terminal of a listed pool transformer meeting the requirements of 680.23(A)(2).
Wet-Niche Luminaire
Copyright 2020, www.MikeHolt.com

▸Figure 680–17

(3) Conductors. The branch-circuit conductors for the underwater pool luminaire on the load side of a GFCI or transformer used to comply with 680.23(A)(8) are not permitted to occupy raceways or enclosures with other conductors unless the other conductors are:

(1) GFCI protected

(2) Equipment grounding conductors and bonding jumpers as required by 680.23(B)(2)(b)

680.24 Junction Box, Transformer, or GFCI Enclosure

(A) Junction Box. If a junction box is connected to a raceway that extends directly to an underwater pool luminaire forming shell, the junction box must comply with the following:

(1) Construction. The junction box must be listed, labeled, and identified as a swimming pool junction box. ▸Figure 680–18

Pools, Listed Junction Box
680.24(A)(1)
Copyright 2023 www.MikeHolt.com
The junction box for an underwater pool luminaire must be listed as a swimming pool junction box.

▸Figure 680–18

(2) Installation.

(a) Vertical Spacing. If the underwater pool luminaire operates at 120V, the junction box must be not less than 4 in. above the ground or pool, or not less than 8 in. above the maximum water level, whichever provides the greater elevation. ▸Figure 680–19

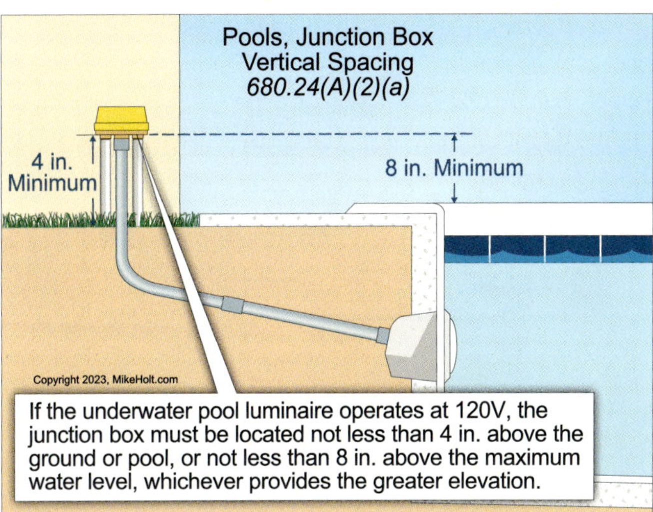
Pools, Junction Box
Vertical Spacing
680.24(A)(2)(a)
4 in. Minimum
8 in. Minimum
Copyright 2023, MikeHolt.com
If the underwater pool luminaire operates at 120V, the junction box must be located not less than 4 in. above the ground or pool, or not less than 8 in. above the maximum water level, whichever provides the greater elevation.

▸Figure 680-19

(b) Horizontal Spacing. If the underwater pool luminaire operates at 120V, the junction box must be not less than 4 ft from the inside wall of the pool unless separated by a solid fence, wall, or other permanent barrier. ▸Figure 680-20

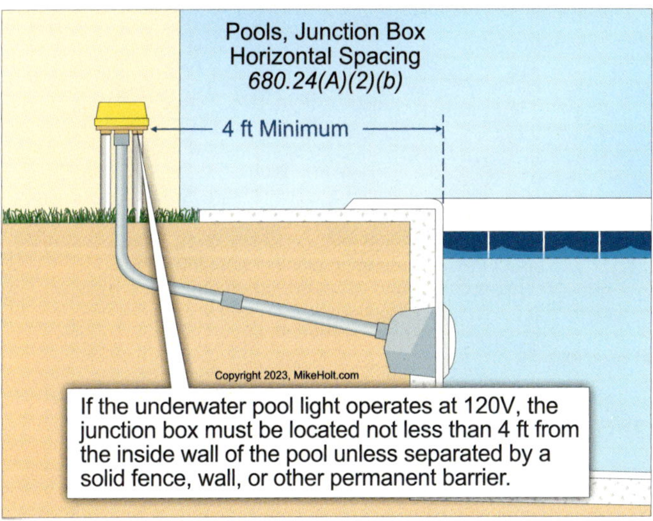
Pools, Junction Box
Horizontal Spacing
680.24(A)(2)(b)
4 ft Minimum
Copyright 2023, MikeHolt.com
If the underwater pool light operates at 120V, the junction box must be located not less than 4 ft from the inside wall of the pool unless separated by a solid fence, wall, or other permanent barrier.

▸Figure 680-20

Author's Comment:

- If conduits are used to support the junction box, the junction box must be supported by two metal conduits threaded wrenchtight into the enclosure according to 314.23(E).

(B) Transformer or GFCI Enclosure. If the enclosure for a transformer or GFCI is connected to a raceway that extends directly to an underwater luminaire forming shell, the enclosure must be listed for this purpose.

(C) Physical Protection. Junction boxes for underwater luminaires are not permitted to be in a walkway unless afforded protection by being under diving boards or adjacent to fixed structures.

(F) Equipment Grounding Conductor Termination. The equipment grounding of the wire type required for a junction box, transformer enclosure, or GFCI enclosure for the connection of an underground pool luminaire must terminate to the panelboard enclosure. ▸Figure 680-21

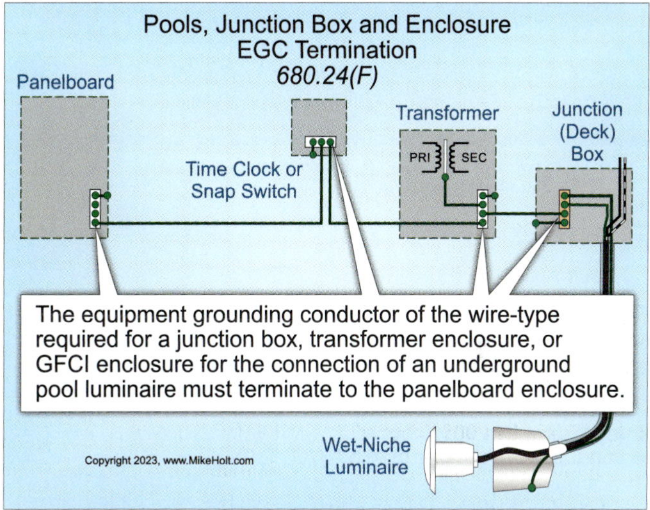
Pools, Junction Box and Enclosure
EGC Termination
680.24(F)
Panelboard
Transformer
Junction (Deck) Box
PRI
SEC
Time Clock or Snap Switch
The equipment grounding conductor of the wire-type required for a junction box, transformer enclosure, or GFCI enclosure for the connection of an underground pool luminaire must terminate to the panelboard enclosure.
Copyright 2023, www.MikeHolt.com
Wet-Niche Luminaire

▸Figure 680-21

680.26 Equipotential Bonding

(A) Voltage Gradients. Equipotential bonding is intended to reduce voltage gradients in the area around a permanently installed pool. ▸Figure 680-22

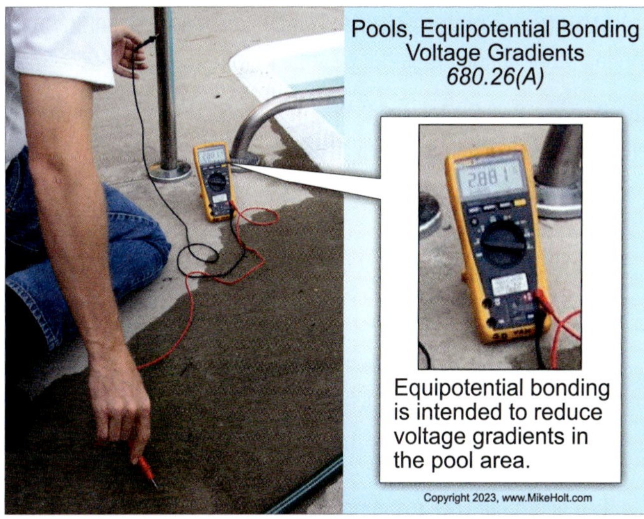
Pools, Equipotential Bonding
Voltage Gradients
680.26(A)
Equipotential bonding is intended to reduce voltage gradients in the pool area.
Copyright 2023, www.MikeHolt.com

▸Figure 680-22

Equipotential bonding must be installed for pools with or without associated electrical equipment related to the pool.

(B) Equipotential Bonded. The parts of a permanently installed pool listed in 680.26(B)(1) through (B)(7) must be bonded together with a solid insulated or bare copper conductor not smaller than 8 AWG using a listed pressure connector, terminal bar, or other listed means in accordance with 250.8(A) and 680.7. ▸Figure 680–23

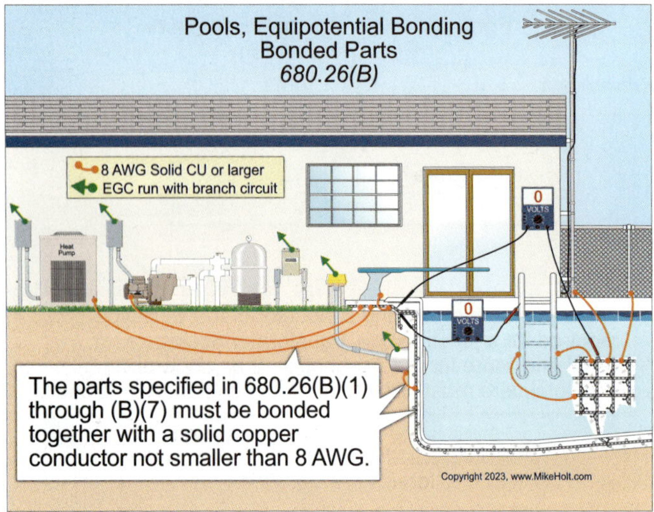
Pools, Equipotential Bonding
Bonded Parts
680.26(B)
8 AWG Solid CU or larger
EGC run with branch circuit
The parts specified in 680.26(B)(1) through (B)(7) must be bonded together with a solid copper conductor not smaller than 8 AWG.
Copyright 2023, www.MikeHolt.com

▸Figure 680–23

The 8 AWG equipotential bonding conductor is not required to extend to any panelboard, service disconnect, or grounding electrode.

(1) Conductive Pool Shells. Cast-in-place concrete, pneumatically applied or sprayed concrete, and concrete block with painted or plastered coatings must be bonded. Reconstructed conductive pool shells must be bonded.

(a) Structural Reinforcing Steel. Unencapsulated structural reinforcing rebar bonded together by steel tie wires. ▸Figure 680–24

(b) Copper Conductor Grid. Where structural reinforcing steel is encapsulated in a nonconductive compound, a copper conductor grid must be installed as follows: ▸Figure 680–25

Author's Comment:

- Encapsulated structural reinforcing steel is used to prevent rebar corrosion and (if used) will make the pool shell insulated, therefore a conductive copper grid is required to bond the pool shell.

(1) Be constructed of a minimum of 8 AWG bare solid copper conductors bonded to each other at all points of crossing in accordance with 250.8 and 680.7, or other approved means

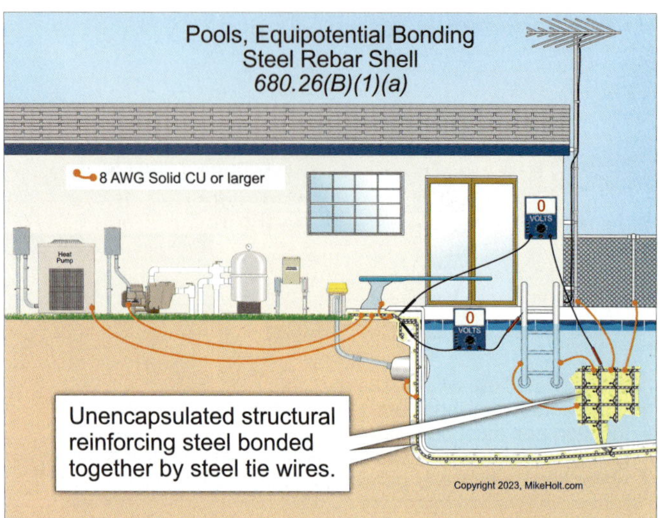
Pools, Equipotential Bonding
Steel Rebar Shell
680.26(B)(1)(a)
8 AWG Solid CU or larger
Unencapsulated structural reinforcing steel bonded together by steel tie wires.
Copyright 2023, MikeHolt.com

▸Figure 680–24

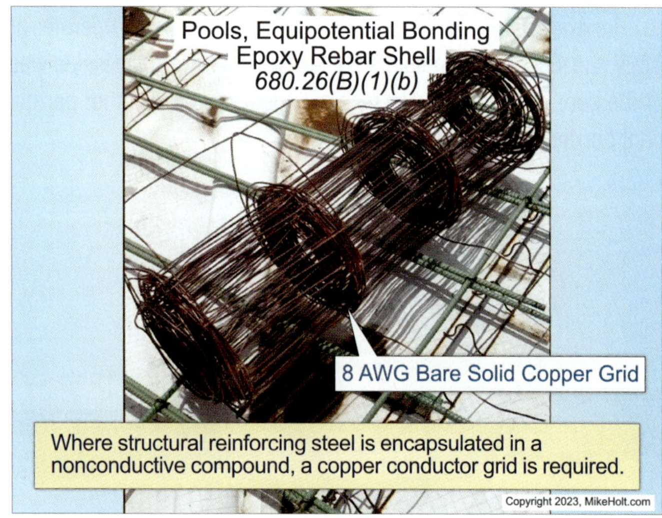
Pools, Equipotential Bonding
Epoxy Rebar Shell
680.26(B)(1)(b)
8 AWG Bare Solid Copper Grid
Where structural reinforcing steel is encapsulated in a nonconductive compound, a copper conductor grid is required.
Copyright 2023, MikeHolt.com

▸Figure 680–25

(2) Conform to the contour of the pool

(3) Be arranged in a 12-in. by 12-in. network of conductors in a uniformly spaced perpendicular grid pattern with a tolerance of 4 in.

(4) Be secured within or under the pool no more than 6 in. from the outer contour of the pool shell

(2) Perimeter Surfaces. Equipotential perimeter bonding must extend a minimum of 3 ft horizontally from the inside walls of a pool where not separated by a building or permanent wall 5 ft in height. ▸Figure 680–26

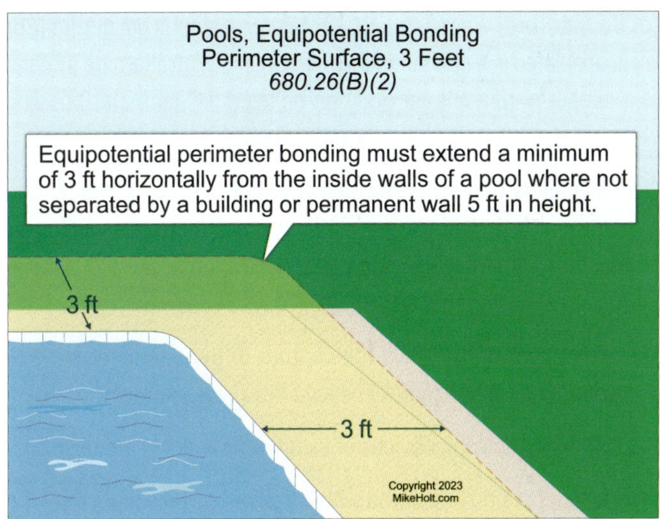
Pools, Equipotential Bonding
Perimeter Surface, 3 Feet
680.26(B)(2)
Equipotential perimeter bonding must extend a minimum of 3 ft horizontally from the inside walls of a pool where not separated by a building or permanent wall 5 ft in height.
3 ft
3 ft
Copyright 2023 MikeHolt.com

▸Figure 680–26

Perimeter surfaces less than 3 ft separated by a permanent wall or building 5 ft or more in height require equipotential bonding only on the pool side of the wall or building. ▸Figure 680–27

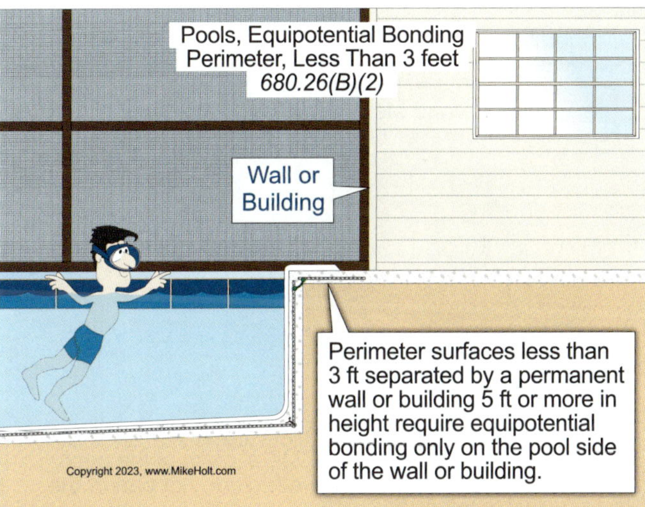
Pools, Equipotential Bonding
Perimeter, Less Than 3 feet
680.26(B)(2)
Wall or Building
Perimeter surfaces less than 3 ft separated by a permanent wall or building 5 ft or more in height require equipotential bonding only on the pool side of the wall or building.
Copyright 2023, www.MikeHolt.com

▸Figure 680–27

For conductive pool shells, equipotential bonding for perimeter surfaces must be attached to the concrete pool reinforcing steel rebar or copper conductor grid at a minimum of four points uniformly spaced around the perimeter of the pool and be one of the following: ▸Figure 680–28

(a) Structural Reinforcing Steel Rebar. Unencapsulated structural reinforcing steel bonded together by steel tie wires in accordance with 680.26(B)(1)(a). ▸Figure 680–29

Pools, Equipotential Bonding
Perimeter, Bond Four Points
680.26(B)(2)
For conductive (concrete or metal) pool shells, equipotential bonding for perimeter surfaces must be attached to the pool shell rebar in at least four points uniformly spaced around the pool.
Copyright 2023 MikeHolt.com

▸Figure 680–28

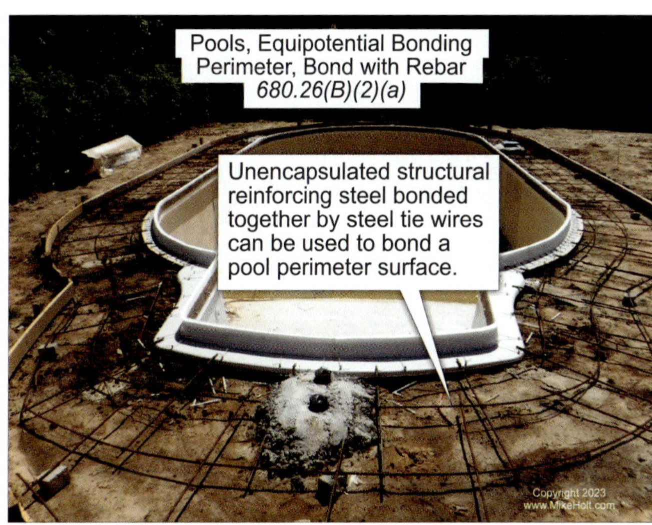
Pools, Equipotential Bonding
Perimeter, Bond with Rebar
680.26(B)(2)(a)
Unencapsulated structural reinforcing steel bonded together by steel tie wires can be used to bond a pool perimeter surface.
Copyright 2023 www.MikeHolt.com

▸Figure 680–29

Author's Comment:

- The *NEC* does not provide a layout requirement for conductive structural steel when used as a perimeter surface equipotential bonding method. ▸Figure 680–30

(b) Copper Ring. Where structural reinforcing steel is not available or is encapsulated in a nonconductive compound, a copper conductor can be used for equipotential perimeter bonding where the following requirements are met: ▸Figure 680–31

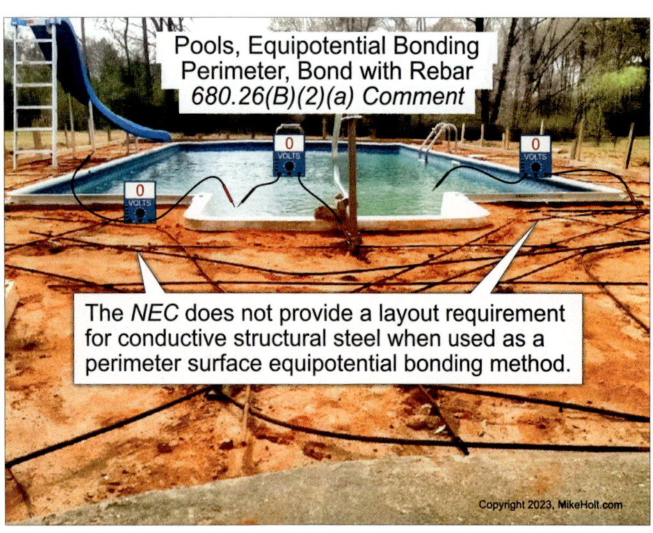
Pools, Equipotential Bonding
Perimeter, Bond with Rebar
680.26(B)(2)(a) Comment
The NEC does not provide a layout requirement for conductive structural steel when used as a perimeter surface equipotential bonding method.
Copyright 2023, MikeHolt.com

▸Figure 680–30

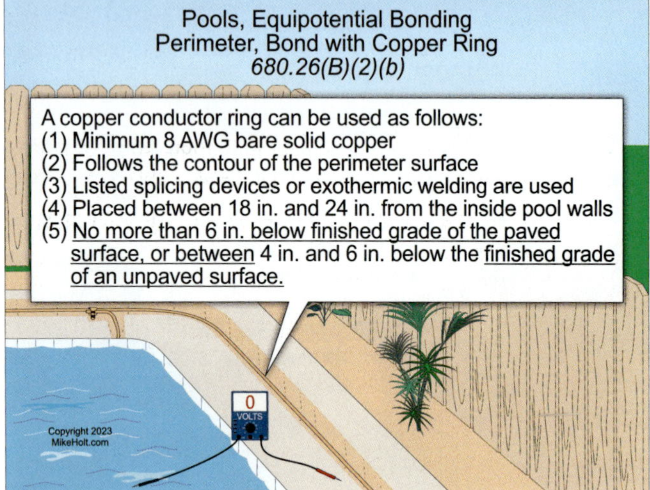
Pools, Equipotential Bonding
Perimeter, Bond with Copper Ring
680.26(B)(2)(b)
A copper conductor ring can be used as follows:
(1) Minimum 8 AWG bare solid copper
(2) Follows the contour of the perimeter surface
(3) Listed splicing devices or exothermic welding are used
(4) Placed between 18 in. and 24 in. from the inside pool walls
(5) No more than 6 in. below finished grade of the paved surface, or between 4 in. and 6 in. below the finished grade of an unpaved surface.
Copyright 2023 MikeHolt.com

▸Figure 680–31

(1) The copper ring is constructed of 8 AWG bare solid copper or larger.

(2) The copper ring conductor follows the contour of the perimeter surface.

(3) Only listed splicing devices or exothermic welding are used.

(4) The copper ring conductor is placed between 18 in. and 24 in. from the inside walls of the pool.

(5) The copper ring conductor is secured within a paved surface (concrete), no more than 6 in. below finished grade of the paved surface (pavers or concrete), or between 4 in. and 6 in. below the finished grade of an unpaved surface (dirt).

(c) Copper Grid. Where structural reinforcing steel is not available or is encapsulated in a nonconductive compound as an alternate method to a copper ring, a copper grid can be used for perimeter bonding where all the following requirements are met:

(1) The copper grid is constructed of 8 AWG solid bare copper and arranged in a 12-in. × 12-in. network of conductors in a uniformly spaced perpendicular grid pattern with a tolerance of 4 in. in accordance with 680.26(B)(1)(b)(3).

(2) The copper grid follows the contour of the perimeter surface extending 3 ft horizontally beyond the inside walls of the pool.

(3) Only listed splicing devices or exothermic welding are used.

(4) The copper grid is secured within a paved surface (concrete), no more than 6 in. below finished grade of the paved surface (pavers or concrete), or between 4 in. and 6 in. below the finished grade of an unpaved surface (dirt).

(3) Metal Parts of Pool Structure. Metal parts of the pool structure, not part of the pool shell [680.26(B)(1)(a)] must be bonded. ▸Figure 680–32

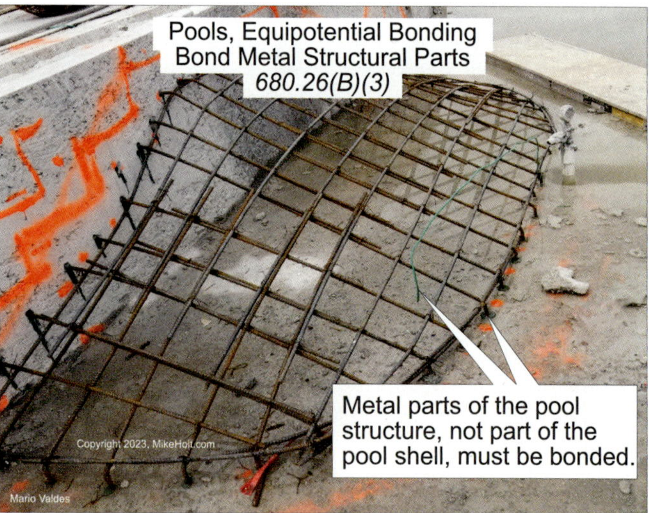
Pools, Equipotential Bonding
Bond Metal Structural Parts
680.26(B)(3)
Metal parts of the pool structure, not part of the pool shell, must be bonded.
Copyright 2023, MikeHolt.com
Mario Valdes

▸Figure 680–32

(4) Metal Forming Shells. All metal forming shells for underwater luminaires must be bonded. ▸Figure 680–33

Ex: Listed low-voltage lighting are not required to be bonded.

(5) Metal Pool Fittings. Metal fittings attached to the pool structure such as ladders and handrails must be bonded. ▸Figure 680–34

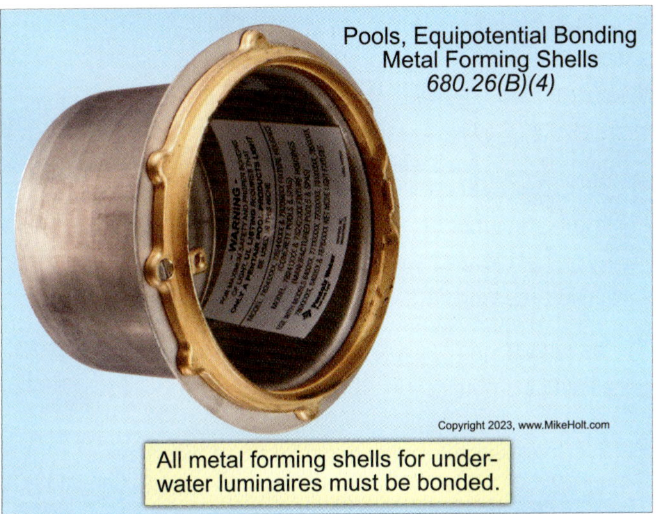
Pools, Equipotential Bonding
Metal Forming Shells
680.26(B)(4)
Copyright 2023, www.MikeHolt.com
All metal forming shells for underwater luminaires must be bonded.

▸Figure 680–33

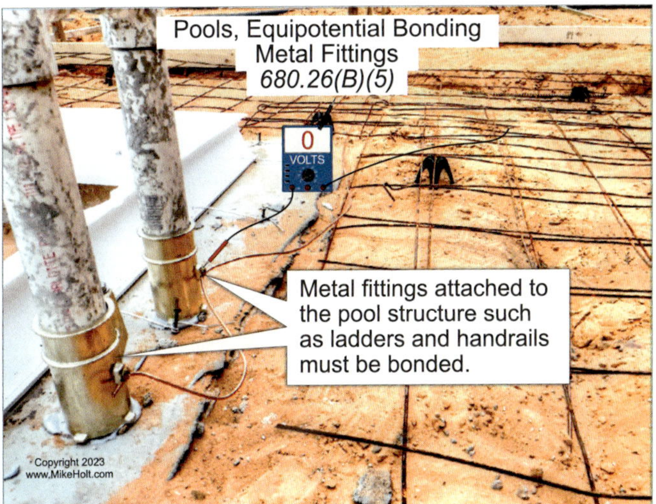
Pools, Equipotential Bonding
Metal Fittings
680.26(B)(5)
0
VOLTS
Metal fittings attached to the pool structure such as ladders and handrails must be bonded.
Copyright 2023
www.MikeHolt.com

▸Figure 680–34

Ex: The following are not required to be bonded:

(1) Isolated parts not over 4 in. in any dimension and not penetrating the pool structure more than1 in.

(2) Metallic pool cover anchors in a concrete or masonry deck, 1 in. or less in any dimension and 2 in. or less in length.

(3) Metallic pool cover anchors in a wood or composite deck, 2 in. or less in any dimension and 2 in. or less in length.

(6) Electrical Pool Equipment. Metal parts of the following electrical equipment must be bonded.

(1) Electrically powered pool cover(s)

(2) Pool water circulation, treatment, heating, cooling, or dehumidification equipment ▸Figure 680–35

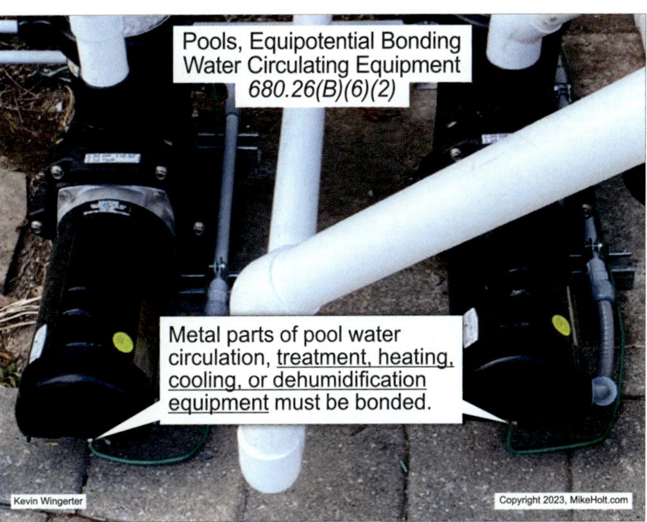
Pools, Equipotential Bonding
Water Circulating Equipment
680.26(B)(6)(2)
Metal parts of pool water circulation, treatment, heating, cooling, or dehumidification equipment must be bonded.
Kevin Wingerter
Copyright 2023, MikeHolt.com

▸Figure 680–35

(3) Other electrical equipment within 5 ft horizontally and 12 ft vertically from the inside walls of the pool, unless separated from the pool by a permanent barrier

(7) Fixed Metal Parts. Fixed metal parts of metal awnings, metal fences, metal doors, and metal window frames within 5 ft horizontally and 12 ft vertically from the inside walls of the pool must be bonded. ▸Figure 680–36

Pools, Equipotential Bonding
Fixed Metal Parts
680.26(B)(7)
0
Volts
Fixed metal parts of metal awnings, metal fences, metal doors, and metal window frames within 5 ft horizontally and 12 ft vertically from the inside walls of the pool must be bonded.
Copyright 2023, www.MikeHolt.com

▸Figure 680–36

Ex: Fixed metal parts separated from the pool by a permanent barrier that prevents contact by a person are not required to be bonded.

(C) Nonconductive Pool Shell. If the water in a vinyl or fiberglass pool shell does not make contact to one of the bonded parts in 680.26(B), a minimum 9 sq in. corrosion-resistant conductive surface in contact with the water must be bonded with a solid copper conductor not smaller than 8 AWG. ▸Figure 680–37

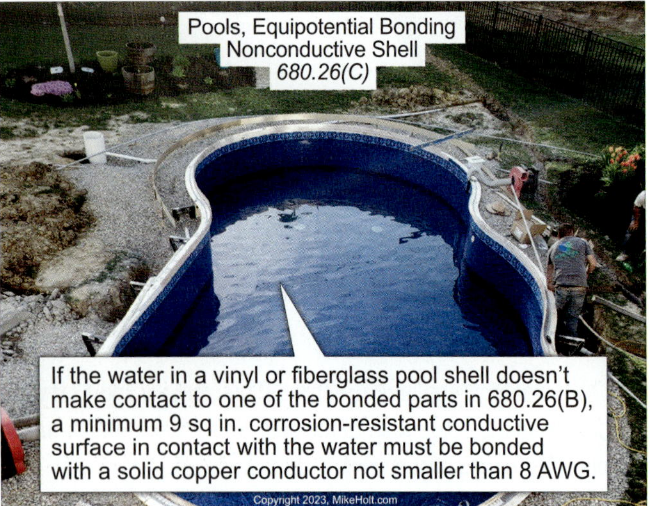
Pools, Equipotential Bonding
Nonconductive Shell
680.26(C)
If the water in a vinyl or fiberglass pool shell doesn't make contact to one of the bonded parts in 680.26(B), a minimum 9 sq in. corrosion-resistant conductive surface in contact with the water must be bonded with a solid copper conductor not smaller than 8 AWG.
Copyright 2023, MikeHolt.com

▸Figure 680–37

Author's Comment:

- Where bonded items such as a conductive pool shell, metal ladders, metal rails, or underwater luminaires are in direct contact with the pool water and provide the required surface area, it is not necessary to install a corrosion-resistant conductive device.

Part IV. Hot Tubs

According to Article 100, "Spa or Hot Tub" is a hydromassage tub designed for recreational or therapeutic use typically not drained after each use (Article 680). ▸Figure 680–38

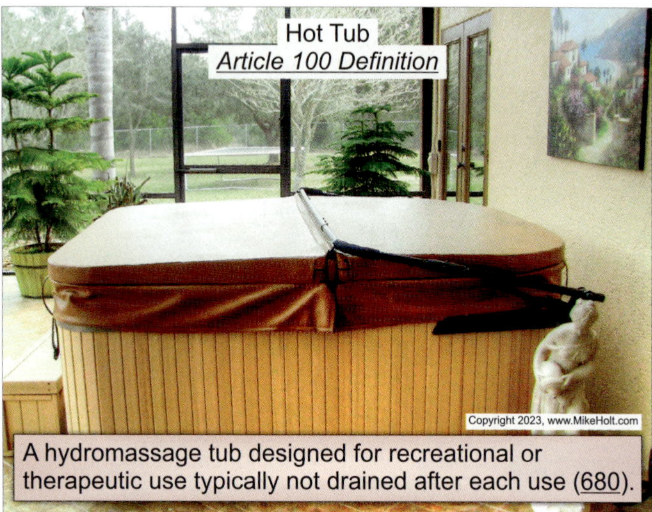
Hot Tub
Article 100 Definition
Copyright 2023, www.MikeHolt.com
A hydromassage tub designed for recreational or therapeutic use typically not drained after each use (680).

▸Figure 680–38

680.40 General

Electrical installations for permanently installed self-contained hot tubs must comply with Part I as well as Part IV of Article 680.

680.42 Outdoor Installations

(B) Equipotential Bonding. Equipotential bonding of perimeter surfaces for hot tubs is not required if all the following conditions apply:

(1) The hot tub is listed, labeled, and identified as a self-contained hot tub for aboveground use. ▸Figure 680–39

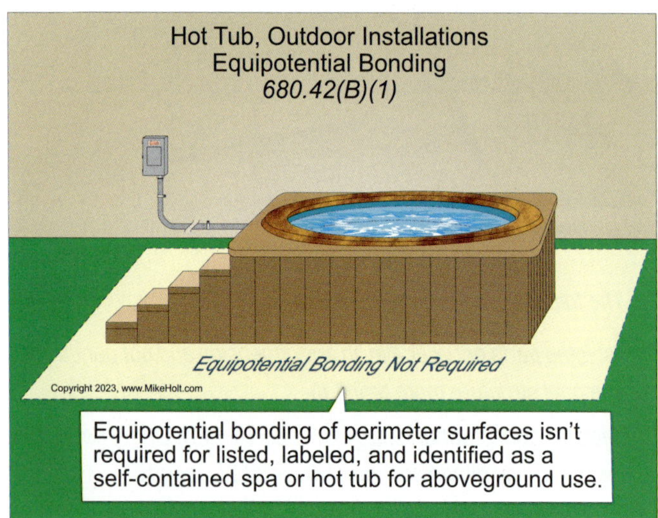
Hot Tub, Outdoor Installations
Equipotential Bonding
680.42(B)(1)
Equipotential Bonding Not Required
Copyright 2023, www.MikeHolt.com
Equipotential bonding of perimeter surfaces isn't required for listed, labeled, and identified as a self-contained spa or hot tub for aboveground use.

▸Figure 680–39

(2) The hot tub is not identified as suitable only for indoor use.

(3) The hot tub is on or above grade.

(4) The top rim of the hot tub is at least 28 in. above any perimeter surface within 30 in. of the hot tub. Nonconductive external steps do not apply to the rim height measurement. ▸Figure 680–40

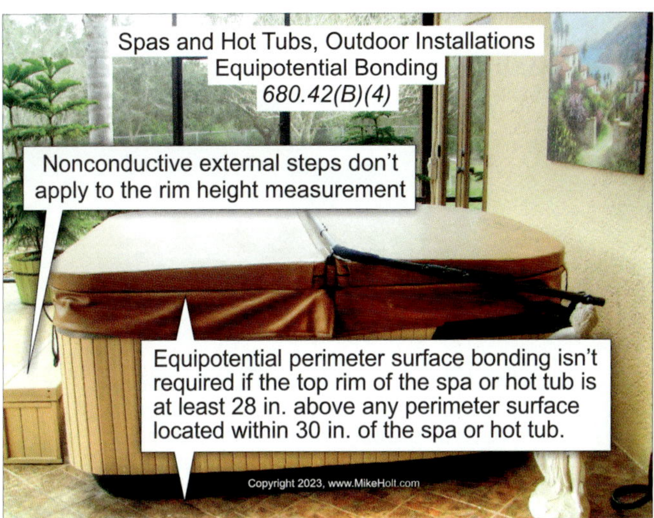
Spas and Hot Tubs, Outdoor Installations
Equipotential Bonding
680.42(B)(4)
Nonconductive external steps don't apply to the rim height measurement
Equipotential perimeter surface bonding isn't required if the top rim of the spa or hot tub is at least 28 in. above any perimeter surface located within 30 in. of the spa or hot tub.
Copyright 2023, www.MikeHolt.com

▸Figure 680–40

(C) Underwater Luminaires. Wiring to an underwater luminaire in a hot tub must comply with 680.23 or 680.33.

Part V. Fountains

According to Article 100, "Fountain" is an ornamental structure or recreational water feature from which one or more jets or streams of water are discharged into the air including splash pads, ornamental pools, display pools, and reflection pools. This definition does not include drinking water fountains or water coolers (Article 680). ▸Figure 680–41

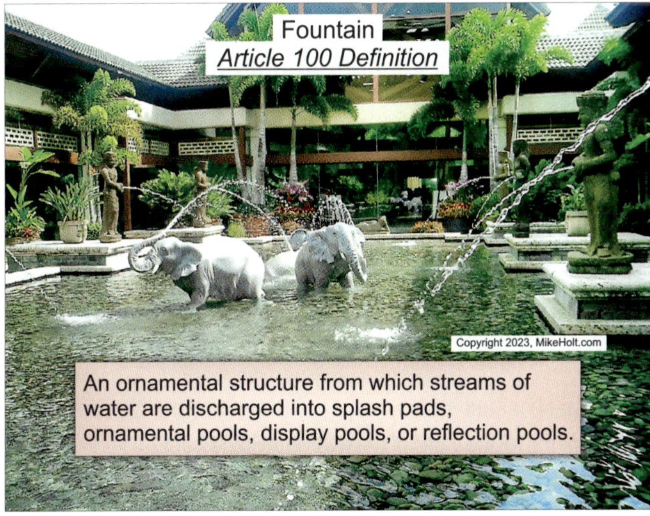
Fountain
Article 100 Definition
Copyright 2023, MikeHolt.com
An ornamental structure from which streams of water are discharged into splash pads, ornamental pools, display pools, or reflection pools.

▸Figure 680–41

680.50 General

The general installation requirements contained in Part I apply to fountains and splash pads intended for recreational use, in addition to those requirements contained in Part V.

Part II of Article 680 applies to fountains that have water common to pools.

(A) Additional Requirements.

(1) Fountains that have water common to a pool must comply with Part II of Article 680.

(2) Splash pads must have equipotential bonding in accordance with 680.26.

(B) Equipment Exceeding the Low-Voltage Contact Limit. Fountain equipment with ratings exceeding the low-voltage contact limit must be located at least 5 ft horizontally from the inside walls of a fountain, unless separated from the fountain by a solid fence, wall, or other permanent barrier.

680.54 Connection to an Equipment Grounding Conductor

(A) Connection to Equipment Grounding Conductor. The following must be connected to the circuit equipment grounding conductor:

(1) Electrical equipment within the fountain or within 5 ft of the inside wall of the fountain

(2) Electrical equipment associated with the recirculating system of the fountain

(3) Panelboards that supply electrical equipment associated with the fountain

(B) Bonding, General. The following parts must be bonded together with a minimum 8 AWG solid copper conductor and connected to an equipment grounding conductor for a branch circuit supplying fountain equipment:

(1) Metal piping systems associated with the fountain

(2) Metal fittings within or attached to the fountain

(3) Metal parts of electrical equipment associated with the fountain water-circulating system

(4) Metal raceways within 5 ft of the inside wall or perimeter of the fountain and not separated from it by a permanent barrier

(5) Metal surfaces within 5 ft of the inside wall or perimeter of the fountain and not separated from it by a permanent barrier

(6) Electrical equipment within 5 ft from the fountain's inside wall or perimeter

(C) Equipotential Bonding of Splash Pad. For the purpose of equipotential bonding, the shell of a splash pad comprised of the area where pedestrians walk, bounded by the extent of footing of the splash pad that rises to its exposed surface and its collection basin area.

According to Article 100, "Splash Pad" is a fountain intended for recreational use by pedestrians with a water depth of 1 in. or less. This definition does not include showers intended for hygienic rinsing prior to use of a pool, spa, or other water feature (Article 680). ▸**Figure 680–42**

Splash Pad
Article 100 Definition
Copyright 2023, www.MikeHolt.com
A fountain intended for recreational use by pedestrians with a water depth of 1 in. or less (680).

▸**Figure 680–42**

680.55 Methods of Equipment Grounding

(A) Other Requirements. The requirements of 680.7(A), 680.21(A), 680.23(B)(3), 680.23(F)(1) and (2), and 680.24(F) apply to fountains.

(B) Supplied by Flexible Cord. Fountain equipment supplied by a flexible cord must have all exposed metal parts connected to an insulated copper equipment grounding conductor that is an integral part of the cord. ▸**Figure 680–43**

Fountains, Supplied by a Flexible Cord
Connected to EGC
680.55(B)
Copyright 2020, www.MikeHolt.com
Fountain equipment supplied by a flexible cord must have all exposed metal parts connected to an insulated copper equipment grounding conductor that is an integral part of the cord.

▸**Figure 680–43**

680.56 Cord-and-Plug-Connected Equipment

(A) GFCI Protection. All electrical equipment, including power-supply cords, must be GFCI protected.

Part VII. Hydromassage Bathtubs

680.70 General

A hydromassage bathtub must only comply with the requirements of Part VII. It is not required to comply with the other parts of this article.

According to Article 100, "Hydromassage Bathtub" is defined as a permanently installed bathtub with a recirculating piping system designed to accept, circulate, and discharge water after each use.

680.74 Equipotential Bonding

(A) General. The following parts must be bonded together.

(1) Metal fittings within, or attached to, the hydromassage bathtub structure that are in contact with the circulating water

(2) Metal parts of electrical equipment associated with the hydromassage bathtub water circulating system, including pump and blower motors

(3) Metal-sheathed cables, metal raceways, and metal piping within 5 ft of the inside walls of the hydromassage bathtub and not separated from its area by a permanent barrier

(4) Exposed metal surfaces within 5 ft of the inside walls of the hydromassage bathtub and not separated from it by a permanent barrier

(5) Metal parts of electrical devices not associated with the hydromassage bathtub within 5 ft from the hydromassage bathtub

1st Printing

Ex 1: Small conductive surfaces not likely to become energized such as air and water jets, supply valve assemblies, drain fittings not connected to metallic piping, towel bars, mirror frames, and similar nonelectrical equipment not connected to metal framing are not required to be bonded.

Ex 2: Double-insulated motors and blowers are not required to be bonded.

Ex 3: Small conductive surfaces of electrical equipment not likely to become energized, such as the mounting strap or yoke of a listed light switch or receptacle is not required to be bonded.

(B) Bonding Conductor. Metal parts required to be bonded by 680.74(A) must be bonded together using an insulated or bare solid copper conductor not smaller than 8 AWG. Bonding jumpers are not required to be extended or attached to any remote panelboard, service disconnect, or any electrode.

A bonding jumper long enough to terminate on a replacement nondouble-insulated pump or blower motor must be provided, and it must terminate to the equipment grounding conductor of the branch circuit of the motor when a double-insulated circulating pump or blower motor is used.

ARTICLE 690 SOLAR PHOTOVOLTAIC (PV) SYSTEMS

Introduction to Article 690—Solar Photovoltaic (PV) Systems

This article applies to solar PV systems that are interactive with other electric power production sources, stand-alone systems, or both—other than those covered by Article 691. These PV systems may have ac or dc output for utilization and require expert knowledge in the special electrical requirements contained in this article as well as in general construction. Many of these rules are outside of the scope of this material, however we do cover the following topics in this article:

- Equipment Grounding Conductor
- Grounding Electrode System

Article 690 consists of six parts:

- Part I. General
- Part II. Circuit Requirements (not covered)
- Part III. Disconnecting Means (not covered)
- Part IV. Wiring Methods and Materials (not covered)
- Part V. Grounding and Bonding
- Part VI. Source Connections (not covered)

Part I. General

690.1 Scope

The requirements contained in Article 690 apply to solar photovoltaic (PV) systems other than those covered by Article 691. ▸Figure 690–1

According to Article 100, "Photovoltaic (PV) System" is the combination of components, circuits, and equipment up to and including the PV system disconnect. ▸Figure 690–2

PV Systems
690.1 Scope
Copyright 2023
MikeHolt.com
Article 690 applies to solar photovoltaic (PV) systems other than those covered by Article 691.

▸Figure 690–1

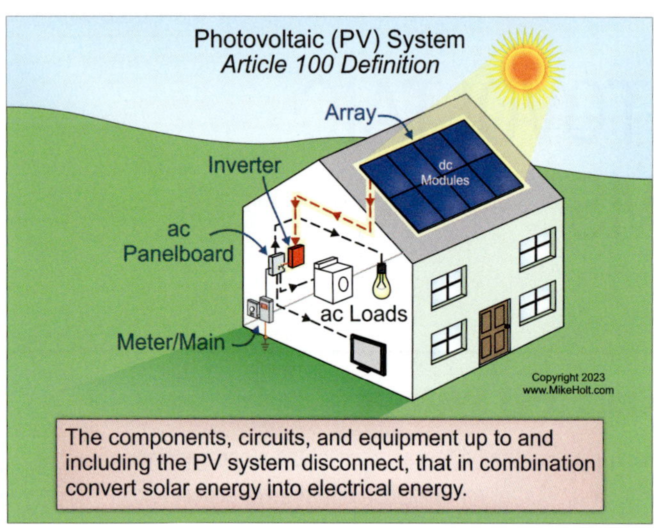
Photovoltaic (PV) System
Article 100 Definition
Array
Inverter
dc Modules
ac Panelboard
ac Loads
Meter/Main
Copyright 2023 www.MikeHolt.com
The components, circuits, and equipment up to and including the PV system disconnect, that in combination convert solar energy into electrical energy.

▸Figure 690–2

690.43 Equipment Grounding Conductor

Metal parts of PV module frames, electrical equipment, and enclosures containing PV system conductors must be connected to the PV system circuit equipment grounding conductor in accordance with 690.43(A) through (D). ▸Figure 690–3

PV Systems
Equipment Grounding Conductor
690.43
Copyright 2023, www.MikeHolt.com
Metal parts of PV module frames, electrical equipment, and enclosures containing PV system conductors must be connected to the PV system circuit equipment grounding conductor.

▸Figure 690–3

(A) Photovoltaic Module Mounting Systems and Devices. Devices used to secure and bond PV module frames to metal support structures and adjacent PV modules must be listed for bonding PV modules. ▸Figure 690–4

PV System, Bonding
PV Modules and Frames
690.43(A)
Devices used to secure and bond PV module frames to metal support structures and adjacent PV modules must be listed for bonding PV modules.
Copyright 2023, MikeHolt.com

▸Figure 690–4

(B) Bonding Equipment to Metal Support Structure. Metal support structures listed, labeled, and identified for bonding and grounding metal parts of PV systems can be used to bond PV equipment to the metal support structure. ▸Figure 690–5

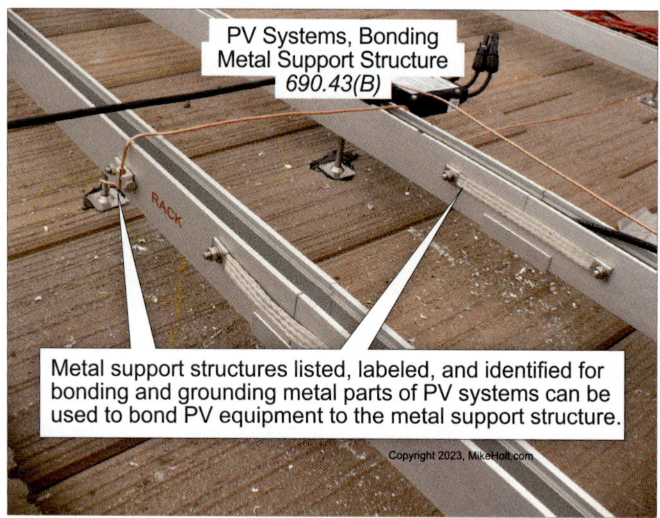
PV Systems, Bonding
Metal Support Structure
690.43(B)
Metal support structures listed, labeled, and identified for bonding and grounding metal parts of PV systems can be used to bond PV equipment to the metal support structure.
Copyright 2023, MikeHolt.com

▸Figure 690–5

(C) Equipment Grounding Conductor Location. Equipment grounding conductors are permitted to be run separately from the PV circuit conductor within the PV array. ▸Figure 690–6

(D) Bonding Over 250V. The bonding requirements contained in 250.97 for circuits over 250V to ground do not apply to metal raceways and metal cables with PV dc conductors. ▸Figure 690–7

1st Printing

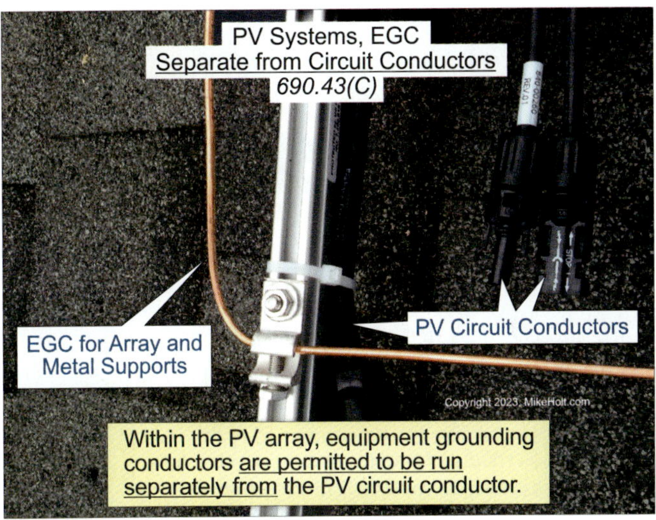
PV Systems, EGC
Separate from Circuit Conductors
690.43(C)
EGC for Array and Metal Supports
PV Circuit Conductors
Within the PV array, equipment grounding conductors are permitted to be run separately from the PV circuit conductor.
Copyright 2023, MikeHolt.com

▸Figure 690–6

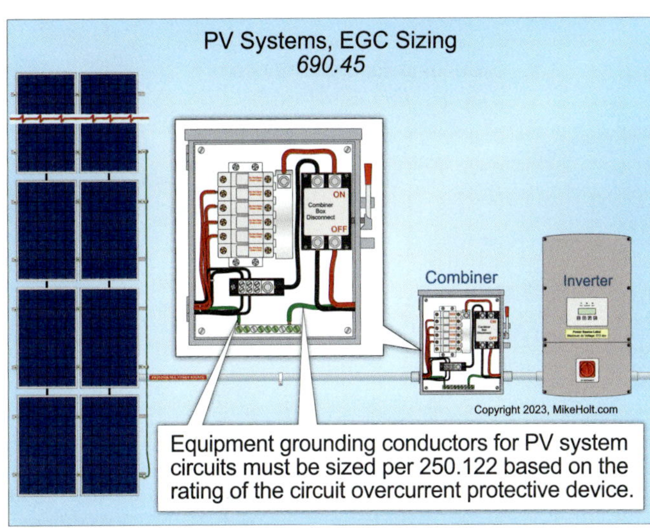
PV Systems, EGC Sizing
690.45
Combiner
Inverter
Equipment grounding conductors for PV system circuits must be sized per 250.122 based on the rating of the circuit overcurrent protective device.
Copyright 2023, MikeHolt.com

▸Figure 690–8

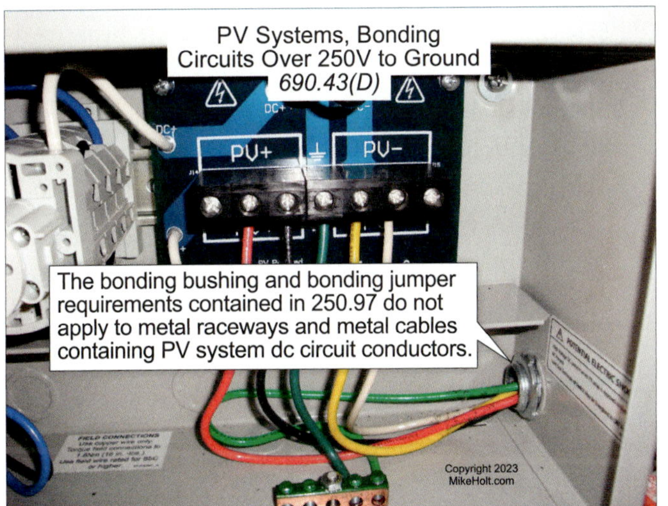
PV Systems, Bonding
Circuits Over 250V to Ground
690.43(D)
PV+
PV–
The bonding bushing and bonding jumper requirements contained in 250.97 do not apply to metal raceways and metal cables containing PV system dc circuit conductors.
Copyright 2023
MikeHolt.com

▸Figure 690–7

PV Systems, EGC Sizing
Voltage Drop
690.45
Copyright 2023
www.MikeHolt.com
Equipment grounding conductors for PV system circuits are not required to be increased in size to address voltage drop.

▸Figure 690–9

690.45 Size of Equipment Grounding Conductors

Equipment grounding conductors for PV system circuits must be sized in accordance with 250.122 based on the rating of the circuit overcurrent protective device. ▸Figure 690–8

Where no overcurrent protective device is required [690.9(A)(1)], the equipment grounding conductor for the PV system dc circuit must be sized in accordance with Table 250.122 based on an assumed overcurrent protective device for the circuit sized in accordance with 690.9(B).

Equipment grounding conductors are not required to be increased in size to address voltage-drop considerations. ▸Figure 690–9

690.47 Grounding Electrode System

(A) Required Grounding Electrode System. A building or structure supporting a PV system must have a grounding electrode system installed. ▸Figure 690–10

(1) Functionally Grounded PV Systems. PV systems are grounded when the PV output ac circuit equipment grounding conductor terminates to the distribution equipment grounding conductor terminal. ▸Figure 690–11

Most PV systems are functionally grounded rather than solidly grounded.

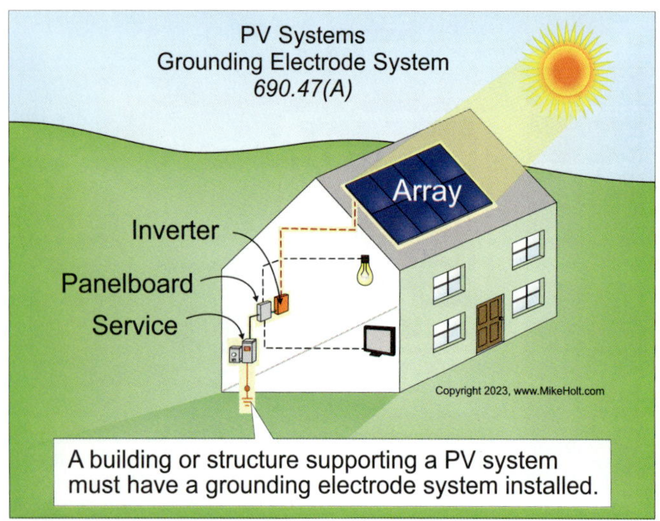
PV Systems
Grounding Electrode System
690.47(A)
Array
Inverter
Panelboard
Service
Copyright 2023, www.MikeHolt.com
A building or structure supporting a PV system must have a grounding electrode system installed.

▸Figure 690–10

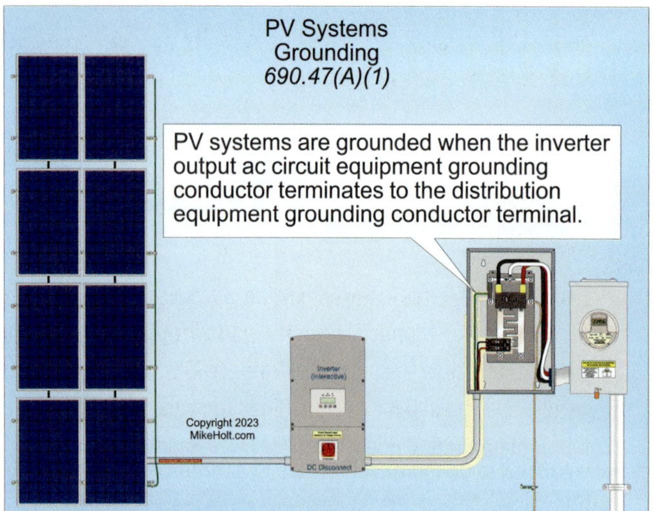
PV Systems
Grounding
690.47(A)(1)
PV systems are grounded when the inverter output ac circuit equipment grounding conductor terminates to the distribution equipment grounding conductor terminal.
Copyright 2023
MikeHolt.com

▸Figure 690–11

Author's Comment:

- A functionally grounded system is one that has an electrical ground reference for operational purposes that is not solidly grounded. It is often connected to ground through an electronic means that is internal to an inverter or charge controller that provides ground-fault protection.

(B) Auxiliary Grounding Electrode. Auxiliary grounding electrodes, in accordance with 250.54 are permitted to be connected to the PV module frame(s) or support structure. ▸**Figure 690–12**

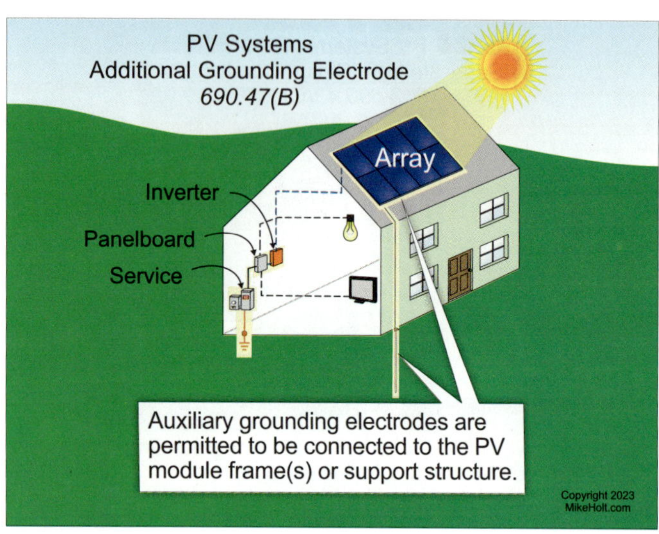
PV Systems
Additional Grounding Electrode
690.47(B)
Array
Inverter
Panelboard
Service
Auxiliary grounding electrodes are permitted to be connected to the PV module frame(s) or support structure.
Copyright 2023
MikeHolt.com

▸Figure 690–12

Author's Comment:

- According to 250.54, if an auxiliary electrode is installed, it is not required to be bonded to the building grounding electrode system, to have the grounding conductor sized to 250.66, nor must it comply with the 25Ω single ground rod requirement of 250.53(A)(2) Ex.

Caution

CAUTION: An auxiliary electrode may cause PV system equipment failures by providing a path for lightning to travel through electronic equipment. ▸**Figure 690–13**

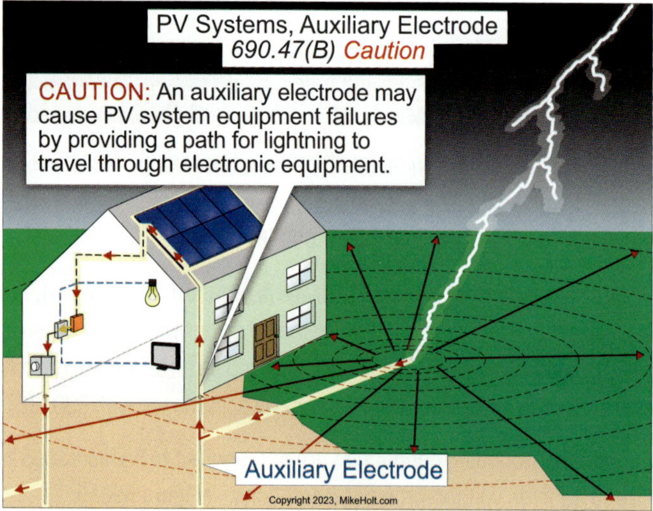
PV Systems, Auxiliary Electrode
690.47(B) Caution
CAUTION: An auxiliary electrode may cause PV system equipment failures by providing a path for lightning to travel through electronic equipment.
Auxiliary Electrode
Copyright 2023, MikeHolt.com

▸Figure 690–13

CHAPTER
6

REVIEW QUESTIONS

NFPA
70
nec

Please use the 2023 *Code* book to answer the following questions.

Article 600—Electric Signs

1. Article 600 covers the installation of conductors, equipment, and field wiring for _____, and outline lighting, regardless of voltage.

   (a) electric signs
   (b) retrofit kits
   (c) neon tubing
   (d) all of these

2. Metal equipment of signs, outline lighting, and skeleton tubing systems shall be grounded by connection to the _____ of the supply branch circuit(s) or feeder using the types of equipment grounding conductors specified in 250.118.

   (a) grounding electrode conductor
   (b) equipment grounding conductor
   (c) neutral conductor
   (d) ground rod

3. Listed flexible metal conduit or listed liquidtight flexible metal conduit that encloses the secondary sign circuit conductor from a transformer or power supply for use with neon tubing is permitted as a bonding means if the total accumulative length of the conduit in the secondary sign circuit does not exceed _____.

   (a) 10 ft
   (b) 25 ft
   (c) 50 ft
   (d) 100 ft

4. Bonding conductors installed outside of a sign or raceway used for the bonding connections of the noncurrent-carrying metal parts of signs shall be protected from physical damage and shall be copper not smaller than _____.

   (a) 14 AWG
   (b) 12 AWG
   (c) 8 AWG
   (d) 6 AWG

5. Bonding conductors installed outside of a sign or raceway used for the bonding connections of the noncurrent-carrying metal parts of signs, shall be protected from physical damage and are permitted to be copper-clad aluminum not smaller than _____.

   (a) 14 AWG
   (b) 12 AWG
   (c) 8 AWG
   (d) 6 AWG

Article 645—Information Technology Equipment (ITE)

1. Article 645 covers _____ and grounding of information technology equipment and systems in an information technology equipment room.

   (a) equipment
   (b) power-supply wiring
   (c) interconnecting wiring
   (d) all of these

2. Exposed noncurrent-carrying metal parts of an information technology system shall be _____.

(a) GFPE protected
(b) inaccessible to unqualified personnel
(c) GFCI protected
(d) bonded to an equipment grounding conductor or double insulated

Article 680—Swimming Pools, Spas, Hot Tubs, Fountains, and Similar Installations

1. The construction and installation requirements of electrical wiring for, and equipment in or adjacent to, all swimming, wading, therapeutic, and decorative pools are covered in Article _____.

(a) 555
(b) 600
(c) 680
(d) 690

2. Feeders and branch circuits installed in a corrosive environment or wet location near swimming pools shall contain an insulated copper EGC sized in accordance with Table 250.122, but not smaller than _____.

(a) 12 AWG
(b) 10 AWG
(c) 8 AWG
(d) 6 AWG

3. Field-installed terminals for swimming pools in damp or wet locations or corrosive environments shall be composed of copper, copper alloy, or stainless steel and shall be _____ for direct burial use.

(a) identified
(b) labeled
(c) listed
(d) approved

4. Transformers and power supplies used for the supply of underwater luminaires for swimming pools, together with the transformer or power-supply enclosure, shall be listed, labeled, and identified for _____ use.

(a) damp location
(b) wet location
(c) outdoor location
(d) swimming pool and spa

5. For permanently installed pools, a GFCI shall be installed in the branch circuit supplying luminaires operating at more than the low-voltage _____.

(a) setting
(b) listing
(c) contact limit
(d) trip limit

6. Wet-niche luminaires shall be installed with the top of the luminaire lens not less than _____ below the normal water level of the pool.

(a) 6 in.
(b) 12 in.
(c) 18 in.
(d) 24 in.

7. When PVC is run from a pool light forming shell to a pool junction box, an 8 AWG _____ bonding jumper shall be installed in the raceway.

(a) solid bare
(b) solid insulated copper
(c) stranded insulated copper
(d) solid or stranded insulated copper

8. Wet-niche luminaires installed in swimming pools shall be removable from the water for inspection, relamping, or other maintenance. The luminaire maintenance location shall be accessible _____.

(a) while the pool is drained
(b) without entering the pool water
(c) during construction
(d) all of these

9. Where branch-circuit wiring on the supply side of enclosures and junction boxes connected to conduits run to underwater luminaires are installed in _____ environments, the wiring method of that portion of the branch circuit shall be in accordance with 680.14.

(a) dry
(b) damp
(c) wet
(d) corrosive

10. A pool light junction box connected to a conduit that extends directly to a forming shell shall be _____ for this use.

    (a) listed
    (b) identified
    (c) labeled
    (d) all of these

11. The pool light junction box shall be located not less than _____, measured from the inside of the bottom of the box, above the ground level or pool deck, or not less than 8 in. above the maximum pool water level, whichever provides the greater elevation.

    (a) 4 in.
    (b) 6 in.
    (c) 8 in.
    (d) 12 in.

12. The pool light junction box shall be located not less than _____ from the inside wall of the pool, unless separated from the pool by a solid fence, wall, or other permanent barrier

    (a) 2 ft
    (b) 3 ft
    (c) 4 ft
    (d) 6 ft

13. The _____ of a pool light junction box, transformer enclosure, or other enclosure in the supply circuit to a wet-niche or no-niche luminaire and the field-wiring chamber of a dry-niche luminaire shall be connected to the equipment grounding terminal of the panelboard.

    (a) equipment grounding jumper
    (b) grounded conductors
    (c) grounding terminals
    (d) ungrounded conductors

14. The equipotential bonding required by 680.26(B)and (C) to reduce _____ gradients in the pool area shall be installed only for pools with associated electrical equipment related to the pool.

    (a) current
    (b) voltage
    (c) resistance
    (d) power

15. The parts specified in 680.26(B)(1) through (B)(7) shall be bonded together using solid copper conductors, insulated, covered, or bare, not smaller than _____.

    (a) 12 AWG
    (b) 10 AWG
    (c) 8 AWG
    (d) 6 AWG

16. Reconstructed pool shells shall meet the equipotential bonding requirements of section 680.26.

    (a) True
    (b) False

17. For equipotential bonding of permanently installed pools, the perimeter surface to be bonded shall be considered to extend for _____ horizontally beyond the inside walls of the pool and shall include unpaved surfaces and other types of paving.

    (a) 3 ft
    (b) 5 ft
    (c) 10 ft
    (d) 12 ft

18. Where a copper grid is used for the purposes of equipotential bonding around pool perimeter surfaces, the copper grid shall be secured within or below a paved surface, but no more than _____ below finished grade.

    (a) 2 in.
    (b) 4 in.
    (c) 6 in.
    (d) 8 in.

19. For perimeter equipotential bonding of permanently installed pools, where conductive pool shell structural reinforcing steel is not available or is encapsulated in a nonconductive compound, a copper ring shall be utilized where _____.

    (a) a minimum 8 AWG bare solid copper conductor is provided and follows the contour of the perimeter surface
    (b) only listed splicing devices or exothermic welding are used
    (c) the conductor is 18 in. to 24 in from the inside wall of the pool and 4 to 6 in. below the finished grade
    (d) all of these

20. All fixed metal parts where located no greater than _____ horizontally of the inside walls of the pool shall be bonded unless separated by a permanent barrier.

    (a) 4 ft
    (b) 5 ft
    (c) 8 ft
    (d) 10 ft

21. All fixed metal parts where located no greater than _____ vertically above the maximum water level of the pool, observation stands, towers, or platforms, or any diving structures, shall be bonded.

    (a) 6 ft
    (b) 8 ft
    (c) 10 ft
    (d) 12 ft

22. Permanently installed fountains shall comply with Part(s) I and V of Article 680. Fountains that have water common to a pool shall also comply with Part(s) _____ of Article 680.

    (a) II
    (b) III
    (c) IV
    (d) all of these

23. Permanently installed fountains intended for recreational use by pedestrians, including _____, shall also comply with the requirements in 680.26.

    (a) splash pads
    (b) hot tubs
    (c) spas
    (d) all of these

24. Permanently installed fountain equipment with ratings exceeding the low-voltage contact limit shall be located at least _____ horizontally from the inside walls of a spa or hot tub, unless separated from the spa or hot tub by a solid fence, wall, or other permanent barrier.

    (a) 3 ft
    (b) 5 ft
    (c) 6 ft
    (d) 10 ft

25. Metal piping systems associated with a fountain shall be bonded to the equipment grounding conductor of the _____.

    (a) branch circuit supplying the fountain
    (b) bonding grid
    (c) fountain's equipotential plane
    (d) grounding electrode system

26. For the purpose of _____, the shell of a splash pad is bounded by the extent of the footing of the splash pad and rising to its exposed surface(s) and its collection basin area. The boundary of this area shall be considered to be the inside wall for the purpose of perimeter bonding.

    (a) lightning protection
    (b) equipotential bonding
    (c) ground-fault protection
    (d) current leakage prevention

27. Electrical equipment for fountains that is supplied by a flexible cord shall have all exposed noncurrent-carrying metal parts grounded by an insulated copper equipment grounding conductor that is an integral part of the _____.

    (a) cord
    (b) feeder circuit
    (c) branch circuit
    (d) fountain

28. All electrical equipment for fountains, including power-supply cords, shall be _____ protected.

    (a) AFCI
    (b) GFCI
    (c) current-limiting
    (d) GFPE

29. For hydromassage bathtubs, small conductive surfaces not likely to become energized, such as air and water jets, supply valve assemblies, and drain fittings not connected to metallic piping, and towel bars, mirror frames, and similar nonelectrical equipment not connected to _____ shall not be required to be bonded.

    (a) metal framing
    (b) nonmetallic framing
    (c) metal gas piping
    (d) any of these

30. Where installed for hydromassage bathtubs, double-insulated _____ shall not be bonded.

    (a) motors and blowers
    (b) cords
    (c) cables
    (d) fittings

31. Where installed for hydromassage bathtubs, small conductive surfaces of electrical equipment not likely to become energized, such as the mounting strap or yoke of a listed light switch or receptacle that is grounded, shall not be required to be bonded.

    (a) True
    (b) False

32. Where installed for hydromassage bathtubs, _____ shall be bonded together.

    (a) all exposed metal surfaces that are within 5 ft of the inside walls of the tub and not separated from the tub area by a permanent barrier
    (b) small conductive surfaces such as towel bars and mirror frames
    (c) double-insulated motors
    (d) mounting straps or yokes of listed light switches or receptacles

33. The 8 AWG solid bonding jumper required for equipotential bonding in the area of hydromassage bathtubs shall not be required to be extended to any _____.

    (a) remote panelboard
    (b) service equipment
    (c) electrode
    (d) any of these

Article 690—Solar Photovoltaic (PV) Systems

1. Article 690 applies to solar _____ systems, including the array circuit(s), inverter(s), and controller(s) for such systems.

    (a) photoconductive
    (b) PV
    (c) photogenic
    (d) photosynthesis

2. Exposed noncurrent-carrying metal parts of PV module frames, electrical equipment, and conductor enclosures of PV systems shall be connected to a(an) _____.

    (a) grounding jumper
    (b) bonding jumper
    (c) equipment grounding conductor
    (d) grounding jumper or bonding jumper

3. Devices and systems used for mounting PV modules that are also used for bonding module frames shall be _____ for bonding PV modules.

    (a) listed
    (b) labeled
    (c) identified
    (d) all of these

4. _____ conductors shall be permitted to be run separately from the PV system conductors within the PV array.

    (a) Bonding
    (b) Alternating-current
    (c) Surge protective
    (d) Equipment grounding

5. The bonding requirements contained in 250.97 shall apply only to solidly grounded PV system circuits operating over _____ to ground.

    (a) 30V
    (b) 60V
    (c) 120V
    (d) 250V

6. Equipment grounding conductors for PV system circuits shall be sized in accordance with _____.

    (a) 250.4
    (b) 250.66
    (c) 250.102
    (d) 250.122

7. For PV systems that are not solidly grounded, the _____ for the output of the PV system, where connected to associated distribution equipment connected to a grounding electrode system, shall be permitted to be the only connection to ground for the system.

    (a) equipment grounding conductor
    (b) grounding conductor
    (c) grounded conductor
    (d) any of these

CHAPTER

8

COMMUNICATIONS SYSTEMS

Introduction to Chapter 8—Communications Systems

Chapter 8 covers the wiring requirements for hard-wired telephones [805], radio and television antennas, satellite dishes [810], and CATV systems [820]. ▸Figure 8–1

Communications systems are not subject to the general requirements contained in Chapters 1 through 4 or the special requirements of Chapters 5 through 7, except where a Chapter 8 rule specifically refers to one of those article or chapters [90.3]. This chapter contains six articles addressing communications systems. Most of these rules are outside the scope of this material since the communications utility handles most of these connections instead of electricians. Our material only covers the Chapter 8, Article 810:

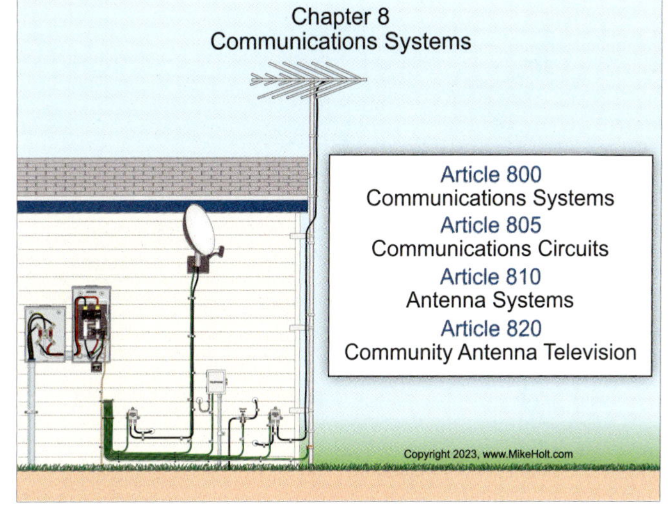
Chapter 8
Communications Systems
Article 800
Communications Systems
Article 805
Communications Circuits
Article 810
Antenna Systems
Article 820
Community Antenna Television
Copyright 2023, www.MikeHolt.com

▸Figure 8–1

- **Article 810—Radio and Television Antenna Equipment.** This article covers antenna systems for radio and television receiving equipment, amateur radio transmitting and receiving equipment, and certain features of transmitter safety. It also addresses antennas such as multi-element, vertical rod and dish, and the wiring and cabling connecting them to the equipment.

1st Printing

ARTICLE 810 ANTENNA SYSTEMS

Introduction to Article 810—Antenna Systems

Article 810 covers antenna systems for radio and television receiving equipment, and amateur and citizen band radio transmitting and receiving equipment. It also covers wire-strung, multi-element, vertical rod, flat, or parabolic antennas. Unlike other articles in this chapter, this one is not covered by the general rules in Article 800 and stands completely alone, unless a specific rule here is referenced as a requirement. Many of these rules are outside of the scope of this material, however we do cover the following topics in this article:

- Bonding Metal Antenna Supports
- Antenna Discharge Units
- Bonding Conductors and Grounding Electrode Conductors

Article 810 consists of four parts:

- Part I. General
- Part II. Receiving Equipment—Antenna Systems
- Part III. Amateur and Citizen Band—Antenna Systems (not covered)
- Part IV. Interior Installation—Transmitting Stations (not covered)

Part I. General

810.1 Scope

Article 810 covers antenna systems for radio and television receiving equipment, and amateur and citizen band radio transmitting and receiving equipment. It also covers antennas such as wire-strung, multi-element, vertical rod, flat, or parabolic. ▸Figure 810–1

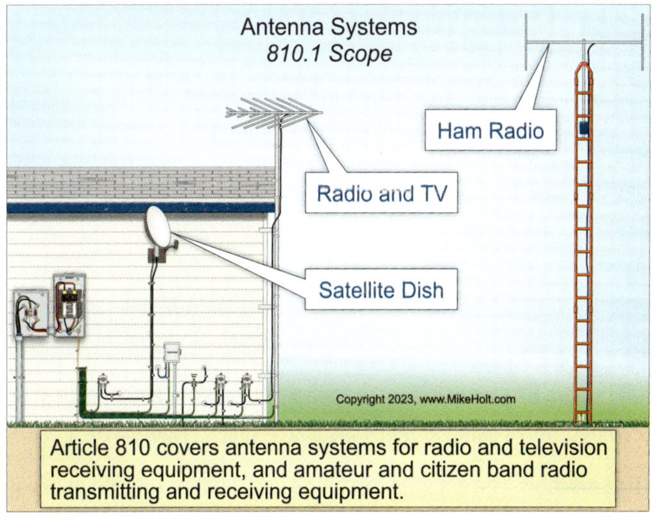
Antenna Systems
810.1 Scope
Ham Radio
Radio and TV
Satellite Dish
Copyright 2023, www.MikeHolt.com
Article 810 covers antenna systems for radio and television receiving equipment, and amateur and citizen band radio transmitting and receiving equipment.

▸Figure 810–1

Author's Comment:

- Article 810 covers:
  - Antennas that receive local television signals
  - Satellite antennas often referred to as satellite dishes
  - Roof-mounted antennas for AM/FM/XM radio reception
  - Amateur radio transmitting and receiving equipment, including HAM radio equipment which is a noncommercial (amateur) communications system ▶Figure 810–2

Antenna Systems
810.1 Scope Comment
Copyright 2023, www.MikeHolt.com
Article 810 covers amateur radio transmitting and receiving equipment, including HAM radio equipment.

▶Figure 810–2

Part II. Receiving Equipment—Antenna Systems

810.15 Metal Antenna Supports—Bonding

Outdoor masts and metal structures that support antennas must be bonded in accordance with 810.21. ▶Figure 810–3

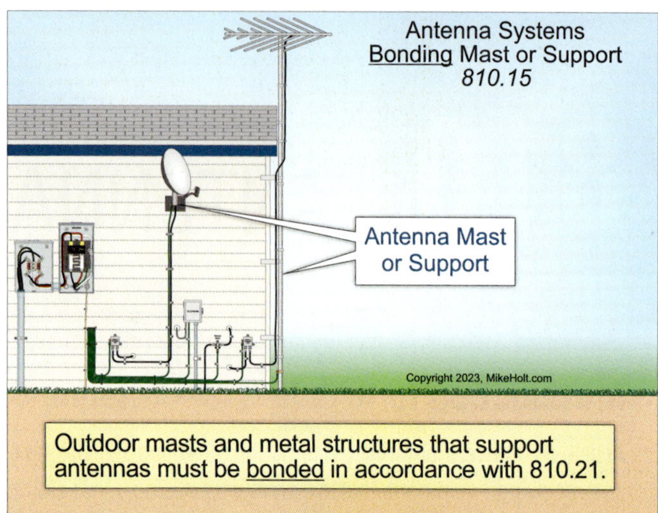
Antenna Systems
Bonding Mast or Support
810.15
Antenna Mast or Support
Copyright 2023, MikeHolt.com
Outdoor masts and metal structures that support antennas must be bonded in accordance with 810.21.

▶Figure 810–3

Note: See NFPA 780, *Standard for the Installation of Lightning Protection Systems*, for the application of the term "Rolling Sphere."

810.20 Antenna Discharge Unit

(A) Listed. Each lead-in conductor from an outdoor antenna must be provided with a listed antenna discharge unit. ▶Figure 810–4

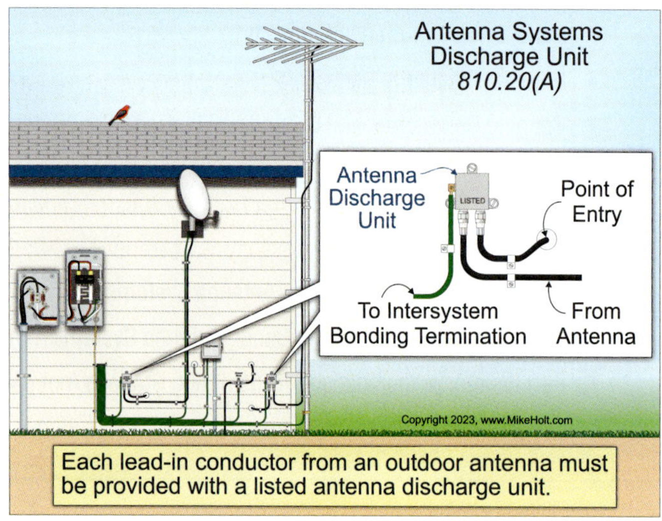
Antenna Systems
Discharge Unit
810.20(A)
Antenna Discharge Unit
Point of Entry
To Intersystem Bonding Termination
From Antenna
Copyright 2023, www.MikeHolt.com
Each lead-in conductor from an outdoor antenna must be provided with a listed antenna discharge unit.

▶Figure 810–4

(B) Location. The antenna discharge unit must be outside or inside the building, nearest the point of entrance, but not near combustible material.

(C) Bonding. The antenna discharge unit must be bonded in accordance with 810.21.

810.21 Bonding Conductors and Grounding Electrode Conductors

Bonding conductors must meet the following requirements:

(A) Material. The bonding conductor to the intersystem bonding termination must be copper, copper-clad aluminum, copper-clad steel, aluminum, bronze, or other corrosion-resistant conductive material. ▶Figure 810–5

If aluminum or copper-clad aluminum is used, the bonding conductor must not be installed outside within 18 in. from the Earth, or if subject to corrosive conditions.

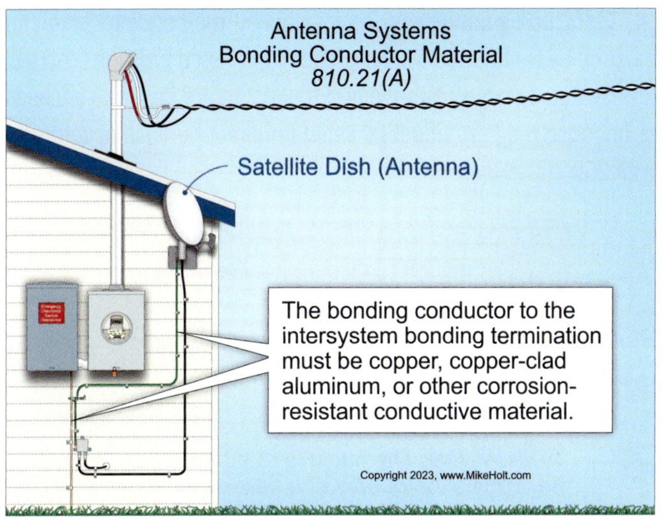
Antenna Systems
Bonding Conductor Material
810.21(A)
Satellite Dish (Antenna)
The bonding conductor to the intersystem bonding termination must be copper, copper-clad aluminum, or other corrosion-resistant conductive material.
Copyright 2023, www.MikeHolt.com

▸Figure 810–5

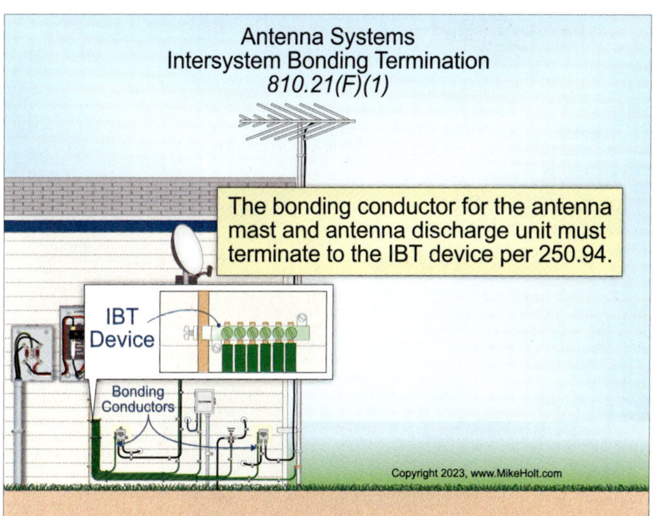
Antenna Systems
Intersystem Bonding Termination
810.21(F)(1)
The bonding conductor for the antenna mast and antenna discharge unit must terminate to the IBT device per 250.94.
IBT Device
Bonding Conductors
Copyright 2023, www.MikeHolt.com

▸Figure 810–6

(B) Insulation. Insulation on bonding conductors is not required.

(C) Supports. The bonding conductor must be securely fastened in place.

(D) Physical Protection. Bonding conductors must be mechanically protected where subject to physical damage. Where installed in a metal raceway, both ends of the raceway must be bonded to the contained conductor.

Author's Comment:

- Installing the bonding conductor in PVC conduit is a better practice.

(E) Run in Straight Line. The bonding conductor must be run in as straight a line as practicable.

Author's Comment:

- Lightning does not like to travel around corners or through loops, which is why the bonding conductor must be run as straight as practicable.

(F) Bonding Terminations. The bonding conductor must terminate in accordance with the following:

(1) Buildings or Structures with an Intersystem Bonding Termination. The bonding conductor for the antenna mast and antenna discharge unit must terminate to the intersystem bonding termination [100] as required by 250.94. ▸Figure 810–6

(2) Buildings or Structures without an Intersystem Bonding Termination. If the building or structure has no intersystem bonding termination, the bonding conductor must be connected to the nearest accessible grounding location on one of the following:

(1) The grounding electrode system as covered in 250.50

(2) The service accessible means external to the building as covered in 250.94

(4) The service disconnect enclosure

(5) The grounding electrode conductor or the grounding electrode conductor metal enclosures of the service disconnect

(6) The grounded interior metal water piping systems, within 5 ft from its point of entrance to the building, as covered in 250.68(C)(1)

Author's Comment:

- Section 250.68(C)(1) permits interior metal water piping within 5 ft from the point of entrance to a building to extend or interconnect bonding jumpers to grounding electrodes.

An intersystem bonding termination device must not interfere with the opening of an equipment enclosure and must be mounted on nonremovable parts. An intersystem bonding termination device cannot be mounted on a door or cover even if the door or cover is nonremovable.

(G) Inside or Outside Building. The bonding conductor can be installed either inside or outside the building.

(H) Size. The bonding conductor is not permitted to be smaller than 10 AWG copper, 8 AWG aluminum, or 17 AWG copper-clad steel or bronze. ▸Figure 810–7

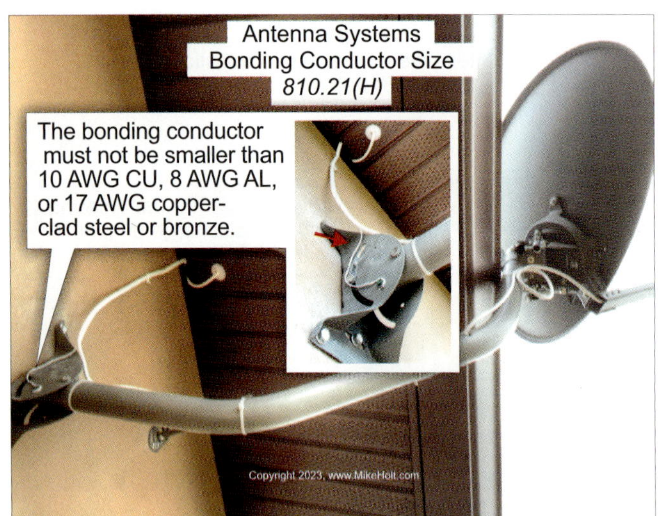
Antenna Systems
Bonding Conductor Size
810.21(H)
The bonding conductor must not be smaller than 10 AWG CU, 8 AWG AL, or 17 AWG copper-clad steel or bronze.
Copyright 2023, www.MikeHolt.com

▸Figure 810-7

(J) Bonding of Electrodes. A ground rod installed for the antenna system must be bonded to the building's power grounding electrode system with a minimum 6 AWG copper conductor. ▸Figure 810-8

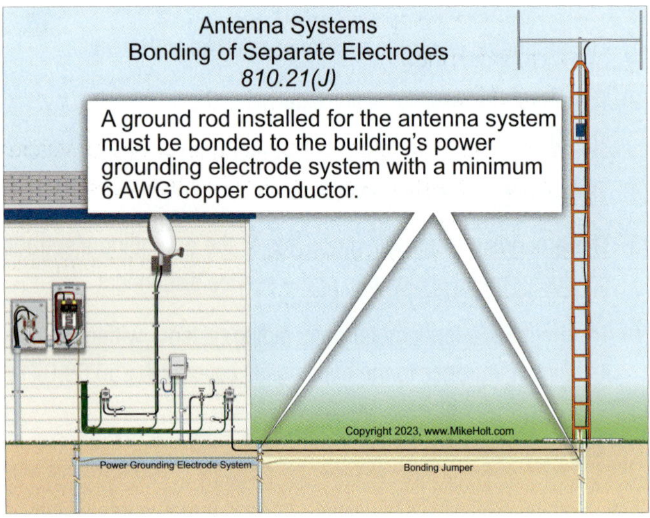
Antenna Systems
Bonding of Separate Electrodes
810.21(J)
A ground rod installed for the antenna system must be bonded to the building's power grounding electrode system with a minimum 6 AWG copper conductor.
Copyright 2023, www.MikeHolt.com
Power Grounding Electrode System
Bonding Jumper

▸Figure 810-8

Author's Comment:

- A separate grounding electrode is not required for radio and TV equipment, but if it is installed, then it must be bonded to the building's power grounding electrode system with a minimum 6 AWG copper conductor.
- Bonding of electrodes helps reduce induced voltage differences between the power and communications systems during lightning events.

(K) Electrode Connection. Termination of the bonding conductor must be by exothermic welding, listed lugs, listed pressure connectors, or listed clamps. Grounding fittings that are concrete-encased or buried in the Earth must be listed for direct burial in accordance with 250.70. ▸Figure 810-9

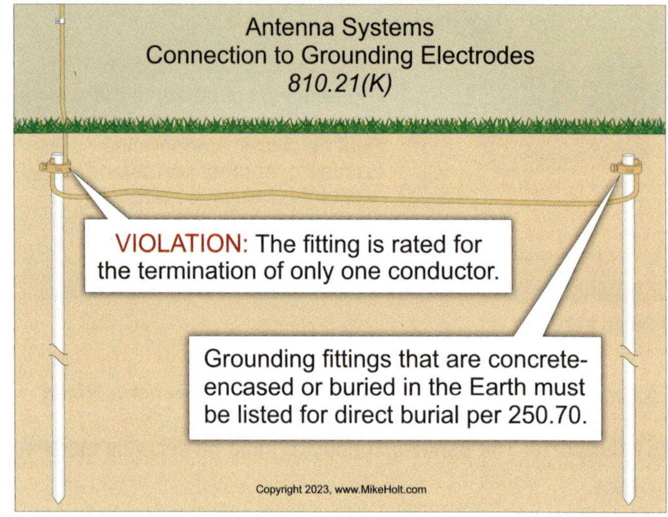
Antenna Systems
Connection to Grounding Electrodes
810.21(K)
VIOLATION: The fitting is rated for the termination of only one conductor.
Grounding fittings that are concrete-encased or buried in the Earth must be listed for direct burial per 250.70.
Copyright 2023, www.MikeHolt.com

▸Figure 810-9

Author's Comment:

- Grounding the lead-in antenna coaxial cables and the mast helps prevent voltage surges caused by static discharge or nearby lightning strikes from reaching the center conductor of the lead-in coaxial cable. Because the satellite dish sits outdoors, wind creates a static charge on the antenna as well as on the cable to which it is attached. This charge can build up on both the antenna and the cable until it jumps across an air space, often passing through the electronics inside the low noise block down converter feedhorn (LNBF) or receiver. Connecting the antenna and/or satellite dish to the building's grounding electrode system (grounding) helps dissipate this static charge.

Nothing can prevent damage from a direct lightning strike, but grounding with proper surge protection can help reduce damage to the satellite dish and other equipment from nearby lightning strikes.

CHAPTER 8

REVIEW QUESTIONS

Please use the 2023 *Code* book to answer the following questions.

Article 810—Antenna Systems

1. Article _____ covers antenna systems for radio and television receiving equipment, amateur and citizen band radio transmitting and receiving equipment, and certain features of transmitter safety.

   (a) 680
   (b) 700
   (c) 810
   (d) 840

2. Masts and metal structures supporting antennas shall be grounded or bonded in accordance with 810.21, unless the antenna and its related supporting mast or structure are within a zone of protection defined by a _____ radius rolling sphere.

   (a) 75-ft
   (b) 100-ft
   (c) 125-ft
   (d) 150-ft

3. NFPA 780, *Standard for the Installation of Lightning Protection Systems*, provides information for the application of the term "_____" as used in 810.15.

   (a) air terminals
   (b) zone protection
   (c) rolling sphere
   (d) copper rod

4. Receiving station antenna discharge units shall be located outside the building or inside the building between the point of entrance of the lead-in and the radio set or transformers and as near as practicable to the _____.

   (a) entrance of the conductors to the building
   (b) intersystem bonding termination
   (c) grounding electrode system
   (d) any of these

5. The bonding conductor or grounding electrode conductor for a radio/television receiving station antenna system shall be protected where subject to physical damage, and where installed in a metal raceway, both ends of the raceway shall be bonded to the _____ conductor.

   (a) contained
   (b) grounded
   (c) ungrounded
   (d) largest

6. The bonding conductor or grounding electrode conductor for an antenna mast or antenna discharge unit for radio and television equipment shall be run to the _____ in as straight a linc as practicable.

   (a) lightning arrester
   (b) surge-protective device
   (c) grounding electrode
   (d) main electrical disconnect enclosure

7. If the building or structure served has an intersystem bonding termination, the bonding conductor for the radio and television equipment antenna mast or antenna discharge unit, shall be connected to the _____.

(a) main electrical disconnect enclosure
(b) grounding electrode
(c) surge protective device
(d) intersystem bonding termination

8. For antenna systems, an intersystem bonding termination device shall not be mounted on a door or cover even if the door or cover is _____.

(a) plastic
(b) removable
(c) nonremovable
(d) fiberglass

9. The bonding conductor or grounding electrode conductor for radio and television receiving station antenna discharge units shall not be smaller than _____.

(a) 10 AWG copper
(b) 8 AWG aluminum
(c) 17 AWG copper-clad steel or bronze
(d) any of these

10. If a separate grounding electrode is installed for the radio and television receiving station equipment, it shall be bonded to the building's electrical power grounding electrode system with a bonding jumper not smaller than _____.

(a) 10 AWG
(b) 8 AWG
(c) 6 AWG
(d) 1/0 AWG

FINAL EXAM A

NEC FINAL EXAM A— STRAIGHT ORDER

Please use the 2023 *Code* book to answer the following questions.

Article 90—Introduction to the *National Electrical Code*

1. The *NEC* covers the installation and removal of _____.

   (a) electrical conductors, equipment, and raceways
   (b) signaling and communications conductors, equipment, and raceways
   (c) optical fiber cables
   (d) all of these

2. Installations used to export electric power from vehicles to premises wiring or for _____ current flow is covered by the *NEC*.

   (a) emergency
   (b) primary
   (c) bidirectional
   (d) secondary

3. The *NEC* does not cover installations in _____.

   (a) ships and watercraft
   (b) mobile homes
   (c) recreational vehicles
   (d) any of these

4. The *Code* does not cover installations under the exclusive control of an electric utility such as _____.

   (a) service drops or service laterals
   (b) electric utility office buildings
   (c) electric utility warehouses
   (d) electric utility garages

5. The enforcement of the *NEC* is the responsibility of the authority having jurisdiction, who is responsible for _____.

   (a) making interpretations of rules
   (b) approval of equipment and materials
   (c) granting special permission
   (d) all of these

CHAPTER 1—GENERAL RULES

Article 100—Definitions

6. Type _____ cable is a fabricated assembly of insulated conductors in a flexible interlocked metallic armor.

   (a) AC
   (b) TC
   (c) NM
   (d) MA

7. Type _____ cable is a factory assembly of two or more insulated conductors, with or without associated bare or covered grounding conductors, under a nonmetallic jacket.

   (a) NM
   (b) TC
   (c) SE
   (d) UF

8. Type _____ cable is a factory assembly of one or more insulated conductors with an integral or an overall covering of nonmetallic material suitable for direct burial in the earth.

(a) NM
(b) UF
(c) SE
(d) TC

9. _____ is a raceway of circular cross section having an outer liquidtight, nonmetallic, sunlight-resistant jacket over an inner flexible metal core.

(a) FMC
(b) LFNMC
(c) LFMC
(d) Vinyl-Clad Type MC

10. A fixed, stationary, or portable self-contained, electrically operated and/or electrically illuminated utilization equipment with words or symbols designed to convey information or attract attention is the definition of _____.

(a) an electric sign
(b) equipment
(c) appliances
(d) exit lighting

11. "Exposed (as applied to _____)," is defined as on or attached to the surface, or behind access panels designed to allow access.

(a) equipment
(b) luminaires
(c) wiring methods
(d) motors

12. A(An) _____ grounded system is an electrical system that is grounded by intentionally connecting the system neutral point to ground through an impedance device.

(a) impedance
(b) solidly
(c) isolated
(d) separately

13. Connected to ground without the insertion of any resistor or impedance device is referred to as "_____."

(a) grounded
(b) solidly grounded
(c) effectively grounded
(d) a grounding conductor

14. A(An) _____ is a conductive path(s) that is part of an effective ground-fault current path and connects normally noncurrent-carrying metal parts of equipment together and to the system grounded conductor or to the grounding electrode conductor, or both.

(a) grounding electrode conductor
(b) main bonding jumper
(c) system bonding jumper
(d) equipment grounding conductor

15. A conducting object through which a direct connection to earth is established is a "_____."

(a) bonding conductor
(b) grounding conductor
(c) grounding electrode
(d) grounded conductor

16. A handhole enclosure is an enclosure for use in underground systems, provided with an open or closed bottom, and sized to allow personnel to _____.

(a) enter and exit freely
(b) reach into but not enter
(c) have full working space
(d) visually examine the interior

17. Recognized as suitable for the specific purpose, function, use, environment, and application is the definition of "_____."

(a) labeled
(b) identified (as applied to equipment)
(c) listed
(d) approved

18. A "limited care facility" is defined as a building or portion thereof used on a(an) _____ basis for the housing of four or more persons who are incapable of self-preservation because of age; physical limitation due to accident or illness; or limitations such as intellectual disability/developmental disability, mental illness, or chemical dependency.

(a) occasional
(b) 10-hour or less per day
(c) 24-hour
(d) temporary

1st Printing

19. The _____ is the "neutral point."

    (a) common point on a wye-connection in a polyphase system
    (b) midpoint on a single-phase, 3-wire system
    (c) midpoint of a single-phase portion of a 3-phase delta system
    (d) any of these

20. Permanently installed pools are those that are constructed or installed in the ground or partially in the ground, and all pools installed inside of a building, whether or not served by electrical circuits of any nature.

    (a) in the ground
    (b) partially in the ground
    (c) inside of a building
    (d) any of these

21. A "PV dc circuit" is any dc conductor in PV source circuits, PV string circuits, and PV _____ converter circuits.

    (a) ac-to-dc
    (b) dc-to-ac
    (c) dc-to-dc
    (d) any of these

22. A "PV _____" is a complete, environmentally protected unit consisting of solar cells and other components, designed to produce dc power.

    (a) interface
    (b) battery
    (c) module
    (d) cell bank

23. A "_____ system" is an electrical power supply output, other than a service, having no direct connection(s) to circuit conductors of any other electrical source other than those established by grounding and bonding connections.

    (a) separately derived
    (b) classified
    (c) direct
    (d) emergency

24. "Service conductors" are the conductors from the service point to the _____.

    (a) service disconnecting means
    (b) panelboard
    (c) switchgear
    (d) fire switch

25. A "structure" is that which is _____, other than equipment.

    (a) built
    (b) constructed
    (c) built or constructed
    (d) none of these

26. A switch constructed so that it can be installed in device boxes or on box covers, or otherwise used in conjunction with wiring systems recognized by this *Code* is called a "_____ switch."

    (a) transfer
    (b) motor-circuit
    (c) general-use snap
    (d) bypass isolation

Article 110 General Requirements for Electrical Installations

27. Product testing, evaluation, and listing (product certification) shall be performed by _____.

    (a) recognized qualified electrical testing laboratories
    (b) the manufacturer
    (c) a qualified person
    (d) an electrical engineer

28. Internal parts of electrical equipment, including busbars, wiring terminals, insulators, and other surfaces, shall not be damaged or contaminated by foreign materials such as _____, or corrosive residues.

    (a) paint, plaster
    (b) cleaners
    (c) abrasives
    (d) any of these

29. Conductors of dissimilar metals shall not be intermixed in a terminal or splicing connector where physical contact occurs between dissimilar conductors unless the device is _____ for the purpose and conditions of use.

    (a) identified
    (b) listed
    (c) approved
    (d) designed

CHAPTER 2—WIRING AND PROTECTION

Article 250—Grounding and Bonding

30. General requirements for grounding and bonding of electrical installations and the location of grounding connections are within the scope of _____.

    (a) Article 110
    (b) Article 200
    (c) Article 250
    (d) Article 680

31. For grounded systems, normally noncurrent-carrying conductive materials enclosing electrical conductors or equipment shall be connected to earth so as to limit _____ on these materials.

    (a) the voltage to ground
    (b) current
    (c) arcing
    (d) resistance

32. For grounded systems, normally noncurrent-carrying conductive materials enclosing electrical conductors shall be connected together and to the _____ to establish an effective ground-fault current path.

    (a) ground
    (b) earth
    (c) electrical supply source
    (d) enclosure

33. For grounded systems, the earth _____ considered an effective ground-fault current path.

    (a) shall be
    (b) shall not be
    (c) is
    (d) is not

34. _____ alternating-current systems operating at 480V shall have ground detectors installed on the system.

    (a) Grounded
    (b) Solidly grounded
    (c) Effectively grounded
    (d) Ungrounded

35. A grounding electrode conductor, sized in accordance with _____, shall be used to connect the equipment grounding conductors, the service-equipment enclosures, and, if the system is grounded, the grounded service conductor to the grounding electrode(s).

    (a) 250.66
    (b) 250.102(C)(1)
    (c) 250.122
    (d) 310.16

36. If a main bonding jumper is a screw only, the screw shall be identified with a(an) _____ that shall be visible with the screw installed.

    (a) silver or white finish
    (b) etched ground symbol
    (c) hexagonal head
    (d) green finish

37. A grounded conductor shall not be connected to normally noncurrent-carrying metal parts of equipment on the _____ side of the system bonding jumper of a separately derived system except as otherwise permitted.

    (a) supply
    (b) grounded
    (c) high-voltage
    (d) load

38. If the source of a separately derived system and the first disconnecting means are located in separate enclosures, a supply-side bonding jumper of the wire type shall comply with 250.102(C), based on _____.

    (a) the size of the primary conductors
    (b) the size of the secondary overcurrent protection
    (c) the size of the derived ungrounded conductors
    (d) one-third the size of the primary grounded conductor

39. The building or structure grounding electrode system shall be used as the _____ electrode for the separately derived system.

    (a) grounding
    (b) bonding
    (c) grounded
    (d) bonded

40. The common grounding electrode conductor installed for multiple separately derived systems shall be permitted to be the metal structural frame of the building or structure in accordance with 250.68(C)(2) or connected to the grounding electrode system by a conductor not smaller than _____.

    (a) 6 AWG copper
    (b) 1/0 AWG copper
    (c) 3/0 AWG copper or 250 kcmil aluminum
    (d) 4/0 AWG aluminum

41. An equipment grounding conductor shall be run with the supply conductors and be connected to the building or structure _____ and to the grounding electrode.

    (a) rebar
    (b) disconnecting means
    (c) structural steel
    (d) ground rod

42. In order for a metal underground water pipe to be used as a grounding electrode, it shall be in direct contact with the earth for _____.

    (a) 5 ft
    (b) 10 ft or more
    (c) less than 10 ft
    (d) 20 ft or more

43. Rod and pipe grounding electrodes shall not be less than _____ in length.

    (a) 6 ft
    (b) 8 ft
    (c) 10 ft
    (d) 20 ft

44. Where the resistance-to-ground of 25 ohms or less is not achieved for a single rod electrode, _____.

    (a) other means besides electrodes shall be used in order to provide grounding
    (b) the single rod electrode shall be supplemented by one additional electrode
    (c) additional electrodes shall be added until 25 ohms is achieved
    (d) any of these

45. The upper end of the rod electrode shall be _____ ground level unless the aboveground end and the grounding electrode conductor attachment are protected against physical damage as specified in 250.10.

    (a) no more than 1 in. above
    (b) no more than 2 in. above
    (c) no more than 3 in. above
    (d) flush with or below ground level

46. If _____, a grounding electrode conductor or its enclosure shall be securely fastened to the surface on which it is carried.

    (a) concealed
    (b) exposed
    (c) accessible
    (d) none of these

47. Grounding electrode conductors in contact with _____ shall not be required to comply with 300.5 but shall be protected if subject to physical damage.

    (a) water
    (b) the earth
    (c) metal
    (d) all of these

48. The common grounding electrode conductor shall be sized in accordance with 250.66, based on the sum of the circular mil area of the _____ ungrounded conductor(s) of each set of conductors that supplies the disconnecting means.

    (a) smallest
    (b) largest
    (c) color of the
    (d) material of the

49. A metal water pipe grounding electrode conductor sized at _____ is required for a 400A service supplied with 500 kcmil conductors.

    (a) 1 AWG
    (b) 1/0 AWG
    (c) 2/0 AWG
    (d) 3/0 AWG

50. A metal water pipe grounding electrode conductor sized at _____ is required for a service supplied with 350 kcmil conductors.

    (a) 6 AWG
    (b) 3 AWG
    (c) 2 AWG
    (d) 1/0 AWG

51. A grounding electrode conductor sized at _____ is required for a service supplied with 400 kcmil parallel conductors in three raceways.

    (a) 1 AWG
    (b) 1/0 AWG
    (c) 2/0 AWG
    (d) 3/0 AWG

52. The largest sized grounding electrode conductor to a rod, pipe, or plate electrode required for a 400A service with 500 kcmil conductors is _____.

    (a) 8 AWG
    (b) 6 AWG
    (c) 1/0 AWG
    (d) 4/0 AWG aluminum

53. A rebar-type concrete-encased electrode with an additional rebar section extended from its location within the concrete foundation or footing to an accessible location that is not subject to _____ is permitted for connection of grounding electrode conductors.

    (a) physical damage
    (b) moisture
    (c) corrosion
    (d) any of these

54. Bonding jumpers for service raceways shall be used around impaired connections such as _____.

    (a) oversized concentric knockouts
    (b) oversized eccentric knockouts
    (c) reducing washers
    (d) any of these

55. In accordance with 250.94(A), the intersystem bonding termination device shall _____.

    (a) be securely mounted and electrically connected to service equipment, the meter enclosure, or exposed nonflexible metallic service raceway, or be mounted at one of these enclosures and be connected to the enclosure or grounding electrode conductor with a minimum 6 AWG copper conductor
    (b) be securely mounted to the building/structure disconnecting means, or be mounted at the disconnecting means and be connected to the metallic enclosure or grounding electrode conductor with a minimum 6 AWG copper conductor
    (c) have terminals that are listed as grounding and bonding equipment
    (d) all of these

56. Where ungrounded supply conductors are paralleled in two or more raceways, the bonding jumper for each raceway shall be based on the size of the _____ in each raceway.

    (a) overcurrent protection for conductors
    (b) grounded conductors
    (c) largest ungrounded supply conductors
    (d) sum of all conductors

57. The metal water piping system(s) installed in or attached to a building or structure [250.104(A)(3)] shall be bonded to _____.

    (a) the building or structure disconnecting means enclosure where located at the building or structure
    (b) the equipment grounding conductor run with the supply conductors
    (c) one or more grounding electrodes
    (d) any of these

58. The bonding jumper(s) required for the metal water piping system(s) installed in or attached to a building or structure supplied by a feeder(s) or branch circuit(s) shall be sized in accordance with _____.

    (a) 250.66
    (b) 250.102(D)
    (c) 250.122
    (d) 310.16

59. If installed _____ a building or structure, a metal piping system that is likely to become energized shall be bonded.

    (a) in
    (b) on
    (c) under
    (d) in or on

60. The building structural steel bonding jumper size for a 400A service supplied with 500 kcmil conductors is _____.

    (a) 6 AWG
    (b) 3 AWG
    (c) 2 AWG
    (d) 1/0 AWG

61. Exposed structural metal that is interconnected to form a metal building frame, not intentionally grounded or bonded, and is likely to become energized shall be bonded to the_____.

    (a) service equipment enclosure
    (b) grounded conductor at the service
    (c) disconnecting means for buildings or structures supplied by a feeder or branch circuit
    (d) any of these

62. Lightning protection system ground terminals _____ bonded to the building or structure grounding electrode system.

    (a) shall be
    (b) shall not be
    (c) shall be permitted to be
    (d) shall be effectively

63. Metal enclosures shall be permitted to be used to connect bonding jumpers or _____ conductors, or both, together to become a part of an effective ground-fault current path.

    (a) grounded
    (b) neutral
    (c) equipment grounding
    (d) grounded phase

64. LFMC is acceptable as an equipment grounding conductor when it terminates in _____ and is protected by an overcurrent device rated 20A or less for trade sizes ⅜ through ½.

    (a) labeled fittings
    (b) identified fittings
    (c) approved fittings
    (d) listed fittings

65. The circuit supplying _____ shall include an equipment grounding conductor. The frame of the appliance shall be connected to the equipment grounding conductor in the manner specified by 250.134 or 250.138.

    (a) electric ranges or clothes dryers
    (b) electric wall mounted ovens
    (c) electric counter-mounted cooking units
    (d) any of these

CHAPTER 3—WIRING METHODS AND MATERIALS

Article 300—General Requirements for Wiring Methods and Materials

66. Conductors installed in nonmetallic raceways run underground shall be permitted to be arranged as isolated _____ installations. The raceways shall be installed in close proximity, and the conductors shall comply with 300.20(B).

    (a) neutral
    (b) grounded conductor
    (c) phase
    (d) all of these

67. Raceways, cable armors, and cable sheaths shall be _____ between cabinets, boxes, conduit bodies, fittings, or other enclosures or outlets.

    (a) continuous
    (b) protected
    (c) buried
    (d) encased in concrete

Article 340—Underground Feeder and Branch-Circuit Cable (Type UF)

68. Article 340 covers the use, installation, and construction specifications for underground feeder and branch-circuit cable, Type _____.

    (a) USE
    (b) UF
    (c) UFC
    (d) NMC

Article 344—Rigid Metal Conduit (RMC)

69. Article 344 covers the use, installation, and construction specifications for _____ conduit and associated fittings.

    (a) intermediate metal
    (b) rigid metal
    (c) electrical metallic
    (d) aluminum metal

Article 348—Flexible Metal Conduit (FMC)

70. Article 348 covers the use, installation, and construction specifications for flexible metal conduit (FMC) and associated _____.

    (a) fittings
    (b) connections
    (c) terminations
    (d) devices

Article 358—Electrical Metallic Tubing (EMT)

71. EMT shall not be permitted as an equipment grounding conductor.

    (a) True
    (b) False

Article 386—Surface Metal Raceways

72. Surface metal raceway enclosures providing a transition from other wiring methods shall have a means for connecting a(an) _____ conductor.

    (a) grounded
    (b) ungrounded
    (c) equipment grounding
    (d) all of these

CHAPTER 4—EQUIPMENT FOR GENERAL USE

Article 406—Receptacles, Attachment Plugs, and Flanged Inlets

73. Except as permitted for two-wire replacements as provided in 406.4(D), receptacles installed on _____ branch circuits shall be of the grounding type.

    (a) 15A and 20A
    (b) up to 30A
    (c) 125V
    (d) 250V

74. Receptacles and cord connectors that have equipment grounding conductor contacts shall have those contacts connected to _____.

    (a) the enclosure
    (b) a bonding bushing
    (c) an equipment grounding conductor
    (d) any of these

75. Where a grounding means exists in the receptacle enclosure a(an) _____ receptacle shall be used.

    (a) isolated ground-type
    (b) grounding-type
    (c) GFCI-type
    (d) dedicated-type

76. When replacing a nongrounding-type receptacle where attachment to an equipment grounding conductor does not exist in the receptacle enclosure, a _____ can be used as the replacement.

    (a) nongrounding-type receptacle
    (b) grounding receptacle
    (c) AFCI-type receptacle
    (d) Tamper-resistant receptacle

77. Where attachment to an equipment grounding conductor does not exist in the receptacle enclosure, a nongrounding-type receptacle(s) shall be permitted to be replaced with a grounding-type receptacle(s) where supplied through a ground-fault circuit interrupter and _____ shall be marked "GFCI Protected" and "No Equipment Ground," visible after installation.

    (a) the receptacle(s)
    (b) their cover plates
    (c) the branch circuit
    (d) the receptacle(s) or their cover plates

Article 410—Luminaires

78. A pole supporting luminaires shall have a handhole not less than _____ with a cover suitable for use in wet locations to provide access to the supply terminations within the pole or pole base.

    (a) 2 in. × 2 in.
    (b) 2 in. × 4 in.
    (c) 4 in. × 4 in.
    (d) 4 in. × 6 in.

Article 440—Air-Conditioning Equipment

79. Article _____ applies to electric motor-driven air-conditioning and refrigerating equipment that has a hermetic refrigerant motor-compressor.

    (a) 440
    (b) 442
    (c) 450
    (d) 460

80. Where air-conditioning and refrigeration equipment is installed outdoors on a roof, a(an) _____ conductor of the wire type shall be installed in outdoor portions of metallic raceway systems that use compression-type fittings.

    (a) equipment grounding
    (b) grounding
    (c) equipment bonding
    (d) bonding

Article 450—Transformers

81. Article 450 covers the installation of all _____.

    (a) motors and motor control centers
    (b) refrigeration and air-conditioning equipment
    (c) transformers
    (d) generators

CHAPTER 5—SPECIAL OCCUPANCIES

Article 517—Health Care Facilities

82. Branch circuits serving fixed electrical equipment in patient care spaces shall be provided with a(an) _____ by installation in a metal raceway system or a cable having a metallic armor or sheath assembly.

    (a) effective ground-fault current path
    (b) ground-fault current path
    (c) effective current path
    (d) none of these

83. Outside of patient care vicinities, care should be taken in specifying a system containing isolated ground receptacles in health care facilities because the _____ of the effective ground-fault current path is dependent upon the equipment grounding conductor(s) and does not benefit from any conduit or building structure in parallel with the equipment grounding conductor.

    (a) ampacity
    (b) resistance
    (c) effectiveness
    (d) impedance

CHAPTER 6—SPECIAL EQUIPMENT

Article 600—Electric Signs

84. Article 600 covers the installation of conductors, equipment, and field wiring for _____, and outline lighting, regardless of voltage.

    (a) electric signs
    (b) retrofit kits
    (c) neon tubing
    (d) all of these

85. Listed flexible metal conduit or listed liquidtight flexible metal conduit that encloses the secondary sign circuit conductor from a transformer or power supply for use with neon tubing is permitted as a bonding means if the total accumulative length of the conduit in the secondary sign circuit does not exceed _____.

    (a) 10 ft
    (b) 25 ft
    (c) 50 ft
    (d) 100 ft

Article 645—Information Technology Equipment (ITE)

86. Article 645 covers _____ and grounding of information technology equipment and systems in an information technology equipment room.

    (a) equipment
    (b) power-supply wiring
    (c) interconnecting wiring
    (d) all of these

Article 680—Swimming Pools, Spas, Hot Tubs, Fountains, and Similar Installations

87. Transformers and power supplies used for the supply of underwater luminaires for swimming pools, together with the transformer or power-supply enclosure, shall be listed, labeled, and identified for _____ use.

    (a) damp location
    (b) wet location
    (c) outdoor location
    (d) swimming pool and spa

88. For perimeter equipotential bonding of permanently installed pools, where conductive pool shell structural reinforcing steel is not available or is encapsulated in a nonconductive compound, a copper ring shall be utilized where _____.

(a) a minimum 8 AWG bare solid copper conductor is provided and follows the contour of the perimeter surface
(b) only listed splicing devices or exothermic welding are used
(c) the conductor is 18 in. to 24 in from the inside wall of the pool and 4 to 6 in. below the finished grade
(d) all of these

89. All fixed metal parts where located no greater than _____ horizontally of the inside walls of the pool shall be bonded unless separated by a permanent barrier.

(a) 4 ft
(b) 5 ft
(c) 8 ft
(d) 10 ft

90. Permanently installed fountain equipment with ratings exceeding the low-voltage contact limit shall be located at least _____ horizontally from the inside walls of a spa or hot tub, unless separated from the spa or hot tub by a solid fence, wall, or other permanent barrier.

(a) 3 ft
(b) 5 ft
(c) 6 ft
(d) 10 ft

91. For the purpose of _____, the shell of a splash pad is bounded by the extent of the footing of the splash pad and rising to its exposed surface(s) and its collection basin area. The boundary of this area shall be considered to be the inside wall for the purpose of perimeter bonding.

(a) lightning protection
(b) equipotential bonding
(c) ground-fault protection
(d) current leakage prevention

92. Where installed for hydromassage bathtubs, small conductive surfaces of electrical equipment not likely to become energized, such as the mounting strap or yoke of a listed light switch or receptacle that is grounded, shall not be required to be bonded.

(a) True
(b) False

Article 690—Solar Photovoltaic (PV) Systems

93. Article 690 applies to solar _____ systems, including the array circuit(s), inverter(s), and controller(s) for such systems.

(a) photoconductive
(b) PV
(c) photogenic
(d) photosynthesis

94. Exposed noncurrent-carrying metal parts of PV module frames, electrical equipment, and conductor enclosures of PV systems shall be connected to a(an) _____.

(a) grounding jumper
(b) bonding jumper
(c) equipment grounding conductor
(d) grounding jumper or bonding jumper

95. For PV systems that are not solidly grounded, the _____ for the output of the PV system, where connected to associated distribution equipment connected to a grounding electrode system, shall be permitted to be the only connection to ground for the system.

(a) equipment grounding conductor
(b) grounding conductor
(c) grounded conductor
(d) any of these

CHAPTER 8—COMMUNICATIONS SYSTEMS

Article 810—Antenna Systems

96. Masts and metal structures supporting antennas shall be grounded or bonded in accordance with 810.21, unless the antenna and its related supporting mast or structure are within a zone of protection defined by a _____ radius rolling sphere.

(a) 75-ft
(b) 100-ft
(c) 125-ft
(d) 150-ft

97. NFPA 780, Standard for the Installation of Lightning Protection Systems, provides information for the application of the term "_____" as used in 810.15.

(a) air terminals
(b) zone protection
(c) rolling sphere
(d) copper rod

98. The bonding conductor or grounding electrode conductor for an antenna mast or antenna discharge unit for radio and television equipment shall be run to the _____ in as straight a line as practicable.

    (a) lightning arrester
    (b) surge-protective device
    (c) grounding electrode
    (d) main electrical disconnect enclosure

99. For antenna systems, an intersystem bonding termination device shall not be mounted on a door or cover even if the door or cover is _____.

    (a) plastic
    (b) removable
    (c) nonremovable
    (d) fiberglass

100. The bonding conductor or grounding electrode conductor for radio and television receiving station antenna discharge units shall not be smaller than _____.

    (a) 10 AWG copper
    (b) 8 AWG aluminum
    (c) 17 AWG copper-clad steel or bronze
    (d) any of these

FINAL EXAM

B

NEC FINAL EXAM B—RANDOM ORDER

Please use the 2023 *Code* book to answer the following questions.

1. A(An) _____ or larger grounding electrode conductor exposed to physical damage shall be protected in rigid metal conduit, IMC, Schedule 80 PVC conduit, reinforced thermosetting resin conduit Type XW (RTRC-XW), EMT, or cable armor.

   (a) 10 AWG
   (b) 8 AWG
   (c) 6 AWG
   (d) 4 AWG

2. If the building or structure served has an intersystem bonding termination, the bonding conductor for the radio and television equipment antenna mast or antenna discharge unit, shall be connected to the _____.

   (a) main electrical disconnect enclosure
   (b) grounding electrode
   (c) surge protective device
   (d) intersystem bonding termination

3. Metal piping systems associated with a fountain shall be bonded to the equipment grounding conductor of the _____.

   (a) branch circuit supplying the fountain
   (b) bonding grid
   (c) fountain's equipotential plane
   (d) grounding electrode system

4. Equipment grounding conductors for motor branch circuits shall be sized in accordance with Table 250.122(A), based on the rating of the _____ device.

   (a) motor overload
   (b) motor over-temperature
   (c) branch-circuit short-circuit and ground-fault protective
   (d) feeder overcurrent protection

5. Article 410 covers luminaires, portable luminaires, lampholders, pendants, incandescent filament lamps, arc lamps, electric-discharge lamps, and _____, and the wiring and equipment forming part of such products and lighting installations.

   (a) decorative lighting products
   (b) lighting accessories for temporary seasonal and holiday use
   (c) portable flexible lighting products
   (d) all of these

6. Article _____ covers the use, installation, and construction specifications for electrical metallic tubing (EMT) and associated fittings.

   (a) 334
   (b) 350
   (c) 356
   (d) 358

7. Capable of being removed or exposed without damaging the building structure or finish or not permanently closed in or blocked by the structure, other electrical equipment, other building systems, or finish of the building refers to _____.

(a) wiring methods that are accessible
(b) equipment that is accessible
(c) being readily accessible
(d) being serviceable

8. A panel, including buses and automatic overcurrent devices, designed to be placed in a cabinet, enclosure, or cutout box and accessible only from the front is known as a "_____."

(a) switchboard
(b) disconnect
(c) panelboard
(d) switchgear

9. The connection between two or more portions of the equipment grounding conductor is the definition of a(an) "_____."

(a) system bonding jumper
(b) main bonding jumper
(c) equipment ground-fault jumper
(d) equipment bonding jumper

10. Not more than _____ grounding or bonding conductor shall be connected to the grounding electrode by a single clamp or fitting unless the clamp or fitting is listed for multiple conductors.

(a) one
(b) two
(c) three
(d) four

11. Article _____ covers the use, installation, and construction specifications for electrical nonmetallic tubing (ENT) and associated fittings.

(a) 358
(b) 362
(c) 366
(d) 392

12. A conductor installed on the supply side of a service or within a service equipment enclosure, or for a separately derived system, to ensure the required electrical conductivity between metal parts required to be electrically connected is known as the "_____."

(a) supply-side bonding jumper
(b) ungrounded conductor
(c) electrical supply source
(d) grounding electrode conductor

13. Ungrounded alternating-current systems from 50V to less than 1,000V shall be legibly marked "CAUTION: UNGROUNDED SYSTEM—OPERATING _____ VOLTS BETWEEN CONDUCTORS" at the _____ of the system, with sufficient durability to withstand the environment involved.

(a) source
(b) first disconnecting means
(c) every junction box
(d) the source or the first disconnecting means

14. When LFNC is used, and equipment grounding is required, a separate _____ shall be installed in the conduit.

(a) grounding conductor
(b) expansion fitting
(c) flexible nonmetallic connector
(d) grounded conductor

15. In health care facilities, _____ ground receptacle(s) installed in patient care spaces outside of a patient care vicinity(s) shall comply with 517.16(B)(1) and (2).

(a) AFCI-protected
(b) GFCI-protected
(c) isolated
(d) all of these

16. Feeders and branch circuits installed in a corrosive environment or wet location near swimming pools shall contain an insulated copper EGC sized in accordance with Table 250.122, but not smaller than _____.

(a) 12 AWG
(b) 10 AWG
(c) 8 AWG
(d) 6 AWG

17. Article 404 covers all _____ used as switches operating at 1,000V and below, unless specifically referenced elsewhere in this *Code* for higher voltages.

(a) switches
(b) switching devices
(c) circuit breakers
(d) all of these

18. The equipotential bonding required by 680.26(B)and (C) to reduce _____ gradients in the pool area shall be installed only for pools with associated electrical equipment related to the pool.

(a) current
(b) voltage
(c) resistance
(d) power

19. The grounding conductor connection to the grounding electrode shall be made by _____.

(a) listed lugs
(b) exothermic welding
(c) listed pressure connectors
(d) any of these

20. Tap connections to a common grounding electrode conductor for multiple separately derived systems shall be made at an accessible location by _____.

(a) a connector listed as grounding and bonding equipment
(b) listed connections to aluminum or copper busbars
(c) the exothermic welding process
(d) any of these

21. If the main bonding jumper is a wire or busbar and is installed from the grounded conductor terminal bar to the equipment grounding terminal bar in the service equipment, the _____ is permitted to be connected to the equipment grounding terminal bar to which the main bonding jumper is connected.

(a) equipment grounding conductor
(b) grounded service conductor
(c) grounding electrode conductor
(d) system bonding jumper

22. At existing buildings or structures, an intersystem bonding termination is not required if other acceptable means of bonding exists. An external accessible means for bonding communications systems together can be by the use of a(an) _____.

(a) nonflexible metal raceway
(b) exposed grounding electrode conductor
(c) connection to a grounded raceway or equipment approved by the authority having jurisdiction
(d) any of these

23. When a single equipment grounding conductor is used for multiple circuits in the same raceway, cable, or cable tray, the single equipment grounding conductor shall be sized according to the _____.

(a) combined rating of all the overcurrent devices
(b) largest overcurrent device protecting the circuit conductors
(c) combined rating of all the loads
(d) any of these

24. One or more insulated conductors in a multiconductor cable, at the time of installation, shall be permitted to be permanently identified as equipment grounding conductors at each end and at every point where the conductors are accessible by coloring the insulation _____.

(a) green
(b) grey
(c) green with a yellow stripe
(d) white or silver

25. The grounding electrode conductor to a ground rod that serves as a supplemental electrode for the metal water pipe electrode is not required to be larger than _____ copper wire.

(a) 8 AWG
(b) 6 AWG
(c) 4 AWG
(d) 3 AWG

26. Short sections of metal enclosures or raceways used to provide support or protection of _____ from physical damage shall not be required to be connected to the equipment grounding conductor.

(a) conduit
(b) feeders under 600V
(c) cable assemblies
(d) grounding electrode conductors

27. The normally noncurrent-carrying metal parts of service equipment, such as service _____, shall be bonded together.

    (a) raceways or service cable armor
    (b) equipment enclosures containing service conductors, including meter fittings, boxes, or the like, interposed in the service raceway or armor
    (c) cable trays
    (d) all of these

28. The "patient care space category" is any space of a health care facility where patients are intended to be _____.

    (a) admitted
    (b) evaluated
    (c) registered
    (d) examined or treated

29. The minimum length of a 4 AWG concrete-encased electrode is at least _____.

    (a) 10 ft
    (b) 20 ft
    (c) 25 ft
    (d) 50 ft

30. The arrangement of grounding connections shall ensure that the disconnection or the removal of a luminaire, receptacle, or other device fed from the box does not interrupt the electrical continuity of the _____ conductor(s) providing an effective ground-fault current path.

    (a) grounded
    (b) ungrounded
    (c) equipment grounding
    (d) all of these

31. Bare or covered aluminum or copper-clad aluminum grounding electrode conductors without an extruded polymeric covering shall not be installed where subject to corrosive conditions or be installed in direct contact with _____.

    (a) concrete
    (b) bare copper conductors
    (c) wooden framing members
    (d) all of these

32. Mechanical continuity of raceways, cable armors, and cable sheaths as required by 300.12 does not apply to _____.

    (a) Type MI Cable
    (b) Type MC Cable
    (c) short sections of raceways used for support or protection of cable assemblies
    (d) any of these

33. For the continuity of equipment grounding conductors and attachment in boxes, a connection used for _____ shall be made between the metal box and the equipment grounding conductor(s).

    (a) bonding
    (b) connections and splices
    (c) extending the length of the circuit
    (d) no other purpose

34. Where a metal underground water pipe is used as a grounding electrode, the continuity of the grounding path or the bonding connection to interior piping shall not rely on _____ and similar equipment.

    (a) bonding jumpers
    (b) water meters or filtering devices
    (c) grounding clamps
    (d) all of these

35. In many circumstances, the _____ or his or her designated agent assumes the role of the authority having jurisdiction.

    (a) property owner
    (b) developer
    (c) general contractor
    (d) insurance underwriter

36. Article 517 applies to electrical construction and installation criteria in health care facilities that provide services to _____.

    (a) human beings
    (b) animals
    (c) children only
    (d) intellectually challenged persons

37. Type _____ cable is a factory assembly of insulated circuit conductors in an armor of interlocking metal tape, or a smooth or corrugated metallic sheath.

    (a) AC
    (b) MC
    (c) NM
    (d) CMS

38. Handhole enclosure covers shall have an identifying mark or logo that prominently identifies the function of the enclosure, such as "_____."

    (a) danger
    (b) utility
    (c) high voltage
    (d) electric

39. Article _____ covers the rating, type, and installation of receptacles, cord connectors, and attachment plugs (cord caps).

    (a) 400
    (b) 404
    (c) 406
    (d) 408

40. Equipment grounding conductors for PV system circuits shall be sized in accordance with _____.

    (a) 250.4
    (b) 250.66
    (c) 250.102
    (d) 250.122

41. Type MC cable is recognized as an equipment grounding conductor when _____.

    (a) it contains an insulated or uninsulated equipment grounding conductor in compliance with 250.118(1)
    (b) the cable assembly contains a bare copper conductor
    (c) it is only hospital grade Type MC cable
    (d) it is terminated with bonding bushings

42. Where rock bottom is encountered, a rod or pipe electrode shall be driven at an angle not to exceed _____ from the vertical.

    (a) 15 degrees
    (b) 30 degrees
    (c) 45 degrees
    (d) 60 degrees

43. For hydromassage bathtubs, small conductive surfaces not likely to become energized, such as air and water jets, supply valve assemblies, and drain fittings not connected to metallic piping, and towel bars, mirror frames, and similar nonelectrical equipment not connected to _____ shall not be required to be bonded.

    (a) metal framing
    (b) nonmetallic framing
    (c) metal gas piping
    (d) any of these

44. The grounding electrode conductor connection shall be made at any accessible point from the load end of the overhead service conductors, _____ to the terminal or bus to which the grounded service conductor is connected at the service disconnecting means.

    (a) service drop
    (b) underground service conductors
    (c) service lateral
    (d) any of these

45. Chapter 8 covers _____ systems and is not subject to the requirements of Chapters 1 through 7 unless specifically referenced in Chapter 8.

    (a) communications
    (b) fire alarm
    (c) emergency standby
    (d) sustainable energy

46. Equipment grounding conductors are not required to be _____ than the circuit conductors.

    (a) larger
    (b) smaller
    (c) less
    (d) none of these

47. For permanently installed pools, a GFCI shall be installed in the branch circuit supplying luminaires operating at more than the low-voltage _____.

    (a) setting
    (b) listing
    (c) contact limit
    (d) trip limit

48. "_____" means acceptable to the authority having jurisdiction.

    (a) Identified
    (b) Listed
    (c) Approved
    (d) Labeled

49. When LFMC is used to connect equipment where flexibility is necessary to minimize the transmission of vibration from equipment or for equipment requiring movement after installation, a(an) _____ conductor shall be installed.

    (a) main bonding
    (b) grounded
    (c) equipment grounding
    (d) grounding electrode

50. A transformer supplies power to a 100A panelboard with 2 AWG THWN-2 conductors. The size of the bonding jumper in copper required to bond the building steel to the secondary grounded conductor is _____.

(a) 8 AWG
(b) 6 AWG
(c) 4 AWG
(d) 2 AWG

51. An encased or buried grounding electrode conductor or bonding jumper connection to a concrete-encased, driven, or buried grounding electrode shall not be required to be _____.

(a) readily accessible
(b) accessible
(c) available
(d) any of these

52. Where branch-circuit wiring on the supply side of enclosures and junction boxes connected to conduits run to underwater luminaires are installed in _____ environments, the wiring method of that portion of the branch circuit shall be in accordance with 680.14.

(a) dry
(b) damp
(c) wet
(d) corrosive

53. A generator is a machine that converts mechanical energy into electrical energy by means of a _____ and alternator and/or inverter.

(a) converter
(b) rectifier
(c) prime mover
(d) turbine

54. Alternating-current circuits of less than 50V shall be grounded if supplied by a transformer whose supply system exceeds _____.

(a) 150V to ground
(b) 300V to ground
(c) 600V to ground
(d) 1,000V to ground

55. Each tap conductor to a common grounding electrode conductor for multiple separately derived systems shall be sized in accordance with _____, based on the derived ungrounded conductors of the separately derived system it serves.

(a) 250.66
(b) 250.118
(c) 250.122
(d) 310.15

56. For FMC, _____ shall be installed where flexibility is necessary to minimize the transmission of vibration from equipment or to provide flexibility for equipment that requires movement after installation.

(a) an equipment grounding conductor
(b) an expansion fitting
(c) flexible nonmetallic connectors
(d) adjustable supports

57. When separate equipment grounding conductors are provided in panelboards, a _____ shall be secured inside the cabinet.

(a) grounded conductor
(b) terminal lug
(c) terminal bar
(d) bonding jumper

58. Tap connections to a common grounding electrode conductor for multiple separately derived systems may be made to a copper or aluminum busbar that is _____ and of sufficient length to accommodate the number of terminations necessary for the installation.

(a) smaller than ¼ in. thick × 4 in. wide
(b) not smaller than ¼ in. thick × 2 in. wide
(c) not smaller than ½ in. thick × 2 in. wide
(d) not smaller than ¼ in. thick × 2½ in. wide

59. Annexes are not part of the requirements of this *Code* but are included for _____ purposes only.

(a) informational
(b) reference
(c) supplemental enforcement
(d) educational

60. If the grounding electrode conductor to a ground rod does not extend on to other types of electrodes, the grounding electrode conductor shall not be required to be larger than _____ copper wire.

    (a) 10 AWG
    (b) 8 AWG
    (c) 6 AWG
    (d) 4 AWG

61. FMC shall be permitted to be used as _____ when installed in accordance with 250.118(5) where flexibility is not required after installation.

    (a) an equipment grounding conductor
    (b) an expansion fitting
    (c) flexible nonmetallic connectors
    (d) adjustable supports

62. If the supplemental electrode is a rod, pipe, or plate electrode, that portion of the bonding jumper that is the sole connection to the supplemental grounding electrode is not required to be larger than _____ copper.

    (a) 8 AWG
    (b) 6 AWG
    (c) 4 AWG
    (d) 1 AWG

63. Frames of electric ranges, wall-mounted ovens, counter-mounted cooking units, _____, and outlet or junction boxes that are part of the circuit shall be connected to the equipment grounding conductor in accordance with 250.140(A) or the grounded conductor in accordance with 250.140(B).

    (a) washing machines
    (b) dishwashers
    (c) microwaves
    (d) clothes dryers

64. The minimum grounding electrode conductor to a rod, pipe, or plate electrode for a 30A service with 10 AWG conductors is _____.

    (a) 8 AWG
    (b) 6 AWG
    (c) 1/0 AWG
    (d) 4/0 AWG

65. A contact device installed at an outlet for the connection of an attachment plug is known as a(an) "_____."

    (a) attachment point
    (b) tap
    (c) receptacle
    (d) wall plug

66. Interior metal water piping that is electrically continuous with a metal underground water pipe electrode and is located not more than _____ from the point of entrance to the building, as measured along the water piping, is permitted to extend the connection to an electrode(s).

    (a) 2 ft
    (b) 3 ft
    (c) 4 ft
    (d) 5 ft

67. Information and technology equipment and systems are used for creation and manipulation of _____.

    (a) data
    (b) voice
    (c) video
    (d) all of these

68. If multiple concrete-encased electrodes are present at a building or structure, it shall be permissible to bond only _____ into the grounding electrode system.

    (a) one
    (b) two
    (c) three
    (d) four

69. The receptacle grounding terminal of an isolated ground receptacle shall be connected to a(an) _____ equipment grounding conductor run with the circuit conductors.

    (a) insulated
    (b) covered
    (c) bare
    (d) solid

70. Bonding conductors installed outside of a sign or raceway used for the bonding connections of the noncurrent-carrying metal parts of signs shall be protected from physical damage and shall be copper not smaller than _____.

(a) 14 AWG
(b) 12 AWG
(c) 8 AWG
(d) 6 AWG

71. A "wet-niche luminaire" is intended to be installed in a _____ surrounded by water.

(a) transformer
(b) forming shell
(c) hydromassage bathtub
(d) all of these

72. A Class A GFCI trips when the ground-fault current is _____ or higher.

(a) 4 mA
(b) 5 mA
(c) 6 mA
(d) 7 mA

73. The *NEC* defines a "_____" as all circuit conductors between the service equipment, the source of a separately derived system, or other power supply source, and the final branch-circuit overcurrent device.

(a) service
(b) feeder
(c) branch circuit
(d) all of these

74. All _____ that are spliced or terminated within the box shall be connected together. Connections and splices shall be made in accordance with 110.14(B) and 250.8 except that insulation shall not be required.

(a) neutral conductors
(b) equipment grounding conductors
(c) phase conductors
(d) switch-legs

75. Only wiring methods recognized as _____ are included in this *Code*.

(a) expensive
(b) efficient
(c) suitable
(d) cost effective

76. If the *Code* requires new products that may not yet be available at the time the *NEC* is adopted, the _____ can allow products that comply with the most recent previous edition of the *Code* adopted by the jurisdiction.

(a) electrical engineer
(b) master electrician
(c) authority having jurisdiction
(d) none of these

77. _____ conductors shall be permitted to be run separately from the PV system conductors within the PV array.

(a) Bonding
(b) Alternating-current
(c) Surge protective
(d) Equipment grounding

78. Equipment not _____ for outdoor use and equipment identified only for indoor use such as "dry locations" or "indoor use only," shall be protected against damage from the weather during construction.

(a) listed
(b) identified
(c) suitable
(d) marked

79. When FMC or LFMC is used as permitted in Class I, Division 2 locations, it shall include an equipment bonding jumper of the _____ type in compliance with 250.102.

(a) wire
(b) raceway
(c) steel
(d) none of these

80. Exposed, normally noncurrent-carrying metal parts of cord-and-plug-connected equipment shall be connected to the equipment grounding conductor if operated at over _____ to ground.

(a) 24V
(b) 50V
(c) 120V
(d) 150V

81. A system or circuit conductor that is intentionally grounded is called a(an) "_____."

(a) grounding conductor
(b) unidentified conductor
(c) grounded conductor
(d) grounding electrode conductor

82. A rigid nonmetallic raceway of circular cross section, with integral or associated couplings, connectors, and fittings for the installation of electrical conductors and cables describes _____.

    (a) ENT
    (b) RMC
    (c) IMC
    (d) PVC

83. If ungrounded service-entrance conductors are connected in parallel, the size of the grounded conductors in each raceway shall be based on the total circular mil area of the parallel ungrounded service-entrance conductors in the raceway, sized in accordance with 250.24(D)(1), but not smaller than _____.

    (a) 1/0 AWG
    (b) 2/0 AWG
    (c) 3/0 AWG
    (d) 4/0 AWG

84. Equipment that is _____ or identified for a use shall be installed and used in accordance with any instructions included in the listing, labeling, or identification.

    (a) listed, labeled, or both
    (b) listed
    (c) marked
    (d) suitable

85. Where equipment grounding is required, a separate grounding conductor shall be installed in Type PVC conduit except where the _____ is used to ground equipment as permitted in 250.142.

    (a) grounding jumper
    (b) grounded conductor
    (c) bonding jumper
    (d) bonded conductor

86. The bonding requirements contained in 250.97 shall apply only to solidly grounded PV system circuits operating over _____ to ground.

    (a) 30V
    (b) 60V
    (c) 120V
    (d) 250V

87. For grounded systems, electrical equipment, and other electrically conductive material likely to become energized shall be installed in a manner that creates a _____ from any point on the wiring system where a ground fault occurs to the electrical supply source.

    (a) circuit facilitating the operation of the overcurrent device
    (b) low-impedance circuit
    (c) circuit capable of safely carrying the ground-fault current likely to be imposed on it
    (d) all of these

88. A grounding electrode system and grounding electrode conductor at a building or structure shall not be required if only a _____ supplies the building or structure.

    (a) 4-wire service
    (b) single or multiwire branch circuit
    (c) 3-wire service
    (d) any of these

89. Where a copper grid is used for the purposes of equipotential bonding around pool perimeter surfaces, the copper grid shall be secured within or below a paved surface, but no more than _____ below finished grade.

    (a) 2 in.
    (b) 4 in.
    (c) 6 in.
    (d) 8 in.

90. Wet-niche luminaires shall be installed with the top of the luminaire lens not less than _____ below the normal water level of the pool.

    (a) 6 in.
    (b) 12 in.
    (c) 18 in.
    (d) 24 in.

91. The conductors and equipment connecting the serving utility to the wiring system of the premises served is called a "_____."

    (a) branch circuit
    (b) feeder
    (c) service
    (d) service attachment

92. The installation and use of all boxes and conduit bodies used as outlet, device, junction, or pull boxes, depending on their use, and handhole enclosures, are covered within _____.

(a) Article 110
(b) Article 200
(c) Article 300
(d) Article 314

93. Chapters 5, 6, and 7 of the *NEC* apply to _____ and may supplement or modify the requirements contained in Chapters 1 through 7.

(a) special occupancies
(b) special equipment
(c) special conditions
(d) all of these

94. A "neutral conductor" is the conductor connected to the _____ of a system, which is intended to carry current under normal conditions.

(a) grounding electrode
(b) neutral point
(c) intersystem bonding termination
(d) electrical grid

95. "_____" is an unthreaded thinwall raceway of circular cross section designed for the physical protection and routing of conductors and cables and for use as an equipment grounding conductor when installed utilizing appropriate fittings.

(a) LFNC
(b) EMT
(c) NUCC
(d) RTRC

96. Nonmandatory information relative to the use of the *NEC* is provided in informative annexes and are _____.

(a) included for information purposes only
(b) not enforceable requirements of the *Code*
(c) enforceable as a requirement of the *Code*
(d) included for information purposes only and are not enforceable requirements of the *Code*

97. Except to detect alterations or damage, qualified electrical testing laboratory listed factory-installed _____ wiring of equipment does not need to be inspected for *NEC* compliance at the time of installation.

(a) external
(b) associated
(c) internal
(d) all of these

98. An impedance grounding conductor is a conductor that connects the system _____ to the impedance device in an impedance grounded system.

(a) main bonding jumper
(b) neutral point
(c) supply-side bonding jumper
(d) load-side bonding jumper

99. Equipment, materials, or services included in a list published by an organization that is acceptable to the authority having jurisdiction defines the term "_____."

(a) booked
(b) a digest
(c) a manifest
(d) listed

100. Compliance with the *Code* and proper maintenance result in an installation that is _____.

(a) essentially free from hazard
(b) not necessarily efficient or convenient
(c) not necessarily adequate for good service or future expansion
(d) all of these

INDEX

*The sections for **Electrical Theory** reference those same sections found in our *Understanding Electrical Theory for NEC Applications* book. For more information about this product visit Mikeholt.com/Theory.

ABOUT THE AUTHOR

Mike Holt
Founder and President
Mike Holt Enterprises
Groveland, Florida

Mike Holt is an author, businessman, educator, speaker, publisher and *National Electrical Code* expert. He has written hundreds of electrical training books and articles, founded three successful businesses, and has taught thousands of electrical *Code* seminars across the U.S. and internationally. His dynamic presentation style, deep understanding of the trade, and ability to connect with students are some of the reasons that he is one of the most sought-after speakers in the industry.

His company, Mike Holt Enterprises, has been serving the electrical industry for almost 50 years, with a commitment to creating and publishing books, videos, online training, and curriculum support for electrical trainers, students, organizations, and electrical professionals. His devotion to the trade, coupled with the lessons he learned at the University of Miami's MBA program, have helped him build one of the largest electrical training and publishing companies in the United States.

Mike is committed to changing lives and helping people take their careers to the next level. He has always felt a responsibility to provide education beyond the scope of just passing an exam. He draws on his previous experience as an electrician, inspector, contractor and instructor, to guide him in developing powerful training solutions that electricians understand and enjoy. He is always mindful of how hard learning can be for students who are intimidated by school, by their feelings towards learning, or by the complexity of the *NEC*. He's mastered the art of simplifying and clarifying complicated technical concepts and his extensive use of illustrations helps students apply the content and relate the material to their work in the field. His ability to take the intimidation out of learning is reflected in the successful careers of his students.

Mike's commitment to pushing boundaries and setting high standards extends into his personal life as well. He's an eight-time Overall National Barefoot Waterski Champion. Mike has more than 20 gold medals, many national records, and has competed in three World Barefoot Tournaments. In 2015, at the tender age of 64, he started a new adventure—competitive mountain bike racing and at 65 began downhill mountain biking. Every day he continues to find ways to motivate himself, both mentally and physically.

Mike and his wife, Linda, reside in New Mexico and Florida, and are the parents of seven children and seven grandchildren. As his life has changed over the years, a few things have remained constant: his commitment to God, his love for his family, and doing what he can to change the lives of others through his products and seminars.

Special Acknowledgments

My Family. First, I want to thank God for my godly wife who's always by my side and for my children.

My Staff. A personal thank you goes to my team at Mike Holt Enterprises for all the work they do to help me with my mission of changing peoples' lives through education. They work tirelessly to ensure that, in addition to our products meeting and exceeding the educational needs of our customers, we stay committed to building life-long relationships throughout their electrical careers.

The National Fire Protection Association. A special thank you must be given to the staff at the National Fire Protection Association (NFPA), publishers of the *NEC*—in particular, Jeff Sargent for his assistance in answering my many *Code* questions over the years. Jeff, you're a "first class" guy, and I admire your dedication and commitment to helping others understand the *NEC*.

ABOUT THE ILLUSTRATOR

Mike Culbreath—Illustrator

Mike Culbreath
Graphic Illustrator
Alden, Michigan

Mike Culbreath has devoted his career to the electrical industry and worked his way up from apprentice electrician to master electrician. He started working in the electrical field doing residential and light commercial construction, and later did service work and custom electrical installations. While working as a journeyman electrician, he suffered a serious on-the-job knee injury. As part of his rehabilitation, Mike completed courses at Mike Holt Enterprises, and then passed the exam to receive his Master Electrician's license. In 1986, with a keen interest in continuing education for electricians, he joined the staff to update material and began illustrating Mike Holt's textbooks and magazine articles.

Mike started with simple hand-drawn diagrams and cut-and-paste graphics. Frustrated by the limitations of that style of illustrating, he took a company computer home to learn how to operate some basic computer graphics software. Realizing that computer graphics offered a lot of flexibility for creating illustrations, Mike took every computer graphics class and seminar he could to help develop his skills. He's worked as an illustrator and editor with the company for over 30 years and, as Mike Holt has proudly acknowledged, has helped to transform his words and visions into lifelike graphics.

Originally from South Florida, Mike now lives in northern lower Michigan where he enjoys hiking, kayaking, photography, gardening, and cooking; but his real passion is his horses. He also loves spending time with his children Dawn and Mac and his grandchildren Jonah, Kieley, and Scarlet.

ABOUT THE MIKE HOLT TEAM

There are many people who played a role in the production of this textbook. Their efforts are reflected in the quality and organization of the information contained in this textbook, and in its technical accuracy, completeness, and usability.

Technical Writing

Mario Valdes is the Technical Content Editor and works directly with Mike to ensure the content is technically accurate, relatable, and valuable to all electrical professionals. He played an important role in gathering research, analyzing data, and assisting Mike in the writing of this book. He reworked content into different formats to improve the flow of information and assure the expectations were being met in terms of message, tone, and quality. He edited illustrations and proofread content to 'fact-check' each sentence, title, and image structure. Mario enjoys working in collaboration with Mike and Brian to enhance the company's brand image, training products, and technical publications.

Editorial and Production

Brian House is part of the content team that reviews our material to make sure it's ready for our customers. He also coordinates the team that constructs and reviews this textbook and its supporting resources to ensure its accuracy, clarity, and quality.

Toni Culbreath worked tirelessly to proofread and edit this publication. Her attention to detail and her dedication is irreplaceable. A very special thank you goes out to Toni (Mary Poppins) Culbreath for her many years of dedicated service.

Cathleen Kwas handled the design, layout, and typesetting of this book. Her desire to create the best possible product for our customers is greatly appreciated, and she constantly pushes the design envelope to make the product experience just a little bit better.

Vinny Perez and **Eddie Anacleto** have been a dynamic team. They have taken the best instructional graphics in the industry to the next level. Both Eddie and Vinny bring years of graphic art experience to the pages of this book and have been a huge help updating and improving the content, look, and style our graphics.

Dan Haruch is an integral part of the video recording process and spends much of his time making sure that the instructor resources created from this product are the best in the business. His dedication to the instructor and student experience is much appreciated.

Video Team

Special thank you to **Jon Dyer** for attending this video recording as a guest and contributing his time and energy to help us. Jon hails from Massachusetts and is a Master Electrician, Instructor, Business Owner and Senior Master Electrician for Momentum Solar.

The following special people provided technical advice in the development of this textbook as they served on the video team along with author **Mike Holt**.

Vince Della Croce
Business Development Manager, Licensed Electrical Inspector, Plans Examiner, Master Electrician
vincent.della_croce@siemens.com
Port Saint Lucie, Florida

Vince Della Croce began his career in IBEW Local Union #3, New York City as a helper, and progressed to journeyman and foreman electrician, before relocating to Florida. He's licensed by the State of Florida as a Master Electrician and Electrical Inspector and Plans Examiner.

He holds an Associate of Science degree in Electronic Engineering and Electrical Maintenance Technology from Penn Foster College and represents Siemens in the role of Business Development Manager with a focus on supporting electrical inspectors throughout the country.

Vince serves the IAEI Florida Chapter and IAEI Southern Section as Education Chairman. He was an alternate member of Code-Making Panels 7 and 12 for the 2017 *NEC*. He is an alternate member of Code-Making Panel 17 for the 2023 *NEC*. Vince is also a principal technical committee member of NFPA 73, 78, 99, and 1078.

Vince has two sons. The oldest is serving the community as a police sergeant and holds a Master's Degree in Business Administration. The youngest is working as a business developer and holds a Bachelor's Degree in Marketing.

Daniel Brian House

Vice President of Digital and Technical Training Mike Holt Enterprises, Instructor, Master Electrician
Brian@MikeHolt.com
Ocala, Florida

Brian House is Vice President of Digital and Technical Training at Mike Holt Enterprises, and a Certified Mike Holt Instructor. He is a permanent member of the video teams, on which he has served since the 2011 *Code* cycle. Brian has worked in the trade since the 1990s in residential, commercial and industrial settings. He opened a contracting firm in 2003 that designed energy-efficient lighting retrofits, explored "green" biomass generators, and partnered with residential PV companies in addition to traditional electrical installation and service.

In 2007, Brian was personally selected by Mike for development and began teaching seminars for Mike Holt Enterprises after being named a "Top Gun Presenter" in Mike's Train the Trainer boot camp. Brian travels around the country teaching electricians, instructors, military personnel, and engineers. His experience in the trenches as an electrical contractor, along with Mike Holt's instructor training, gives him a teaching style that is practical, straightforward, and refreshing.

Today, as Vice President of Digital and Technical Training at Mike Holt Enterprises, Brian leads the apprenticeship and digital product teams. They create cutting-edge training tools, and partner with in-house and apprenticeship training programs nationwide to help them reach the next level. He is also part of the content team that helps Mike bring his products to market, assisting in the editing of the textbooks, coordinating the content and illustrations, and assuring the technical accuracy and flow of the information.

Brian is high energy, with a passion for doing business the right way. He expresses his commitment to the industry and his love for its people in his teaching, working on books, and developing instructional programs and software tools.

Brian and his wife Carissa have shared the joy of their four children and many foster children during 25 years of marriage. When not mentoring youth at work or church, he can be found racing mountain bikes or SCUBA diving with his kids. He's passionate about helping others and regularly engages with the youth of his community to motivate them into exploring their future.

Eric Stromberg, P.E.

Electrical Engineer, Instructor
Eric@MikeHolt.com
Los Alamos, New Mexico

Eric Stromberg has a bachelor's degree in Electrical Engineering and is a professional engineer. He started in the electrical industry when he was a teenager helping the neighborhood electrician. After high school, and a year of college, Eric worked for a couple of different audio companies, installing sound systems in a variety of locations from small buildings to baseball stadiums. After returning to college, he worked as a journeyman wireman for an electrical contractor.

After graduating from the University of Houston, Eric took a job as an electronic technician and installed and serviced life safety systems in high-rise buildings. After seven years he went to work for Dow Chemical as a power distribution engineer. His work with audio systems had made him very sensitive to grounding issues and he took this experience with him into power distribution. Because of this expertise, Eric became one of Dow's grounding subject matter experts. This is also how Eric met Mike Holt, as Mike was looking for grounding experts for his 2002 Grounding vs. Bonding video.

Eric taught the *National Electrical Code* for professional engineering exam preparation for over 20 years, and has held continuing education teacher certificates for the states of Texas and New Mexico. He was on the electrical licensing and advisory board for the State of Texas, as well as on their electrician licensing exam board. Eric now consults for a Department of Energy research laboratory in New Mexico, where he's responsible for the electrical standards as well as assisting the laboratory's AHJ.

Eric's oldest daughter lives with her husband in Zurich, Switzerland, where she teaches for an international school. His son served in the Air Force, has a degree in Aviation logistics, and is a pilot and owner of an aerial photography business. His youngest daughter is a singer/songwriter in Los Angeles.

1st Printing

Mario Valdes, Jr.
Technical Content Editor Mike Holt Enterprises, Electrical Inspector, Electrical Plans Examiner, Master Electrician
Mario@MikeHolt.com
Ocala, Florida

Mario Valdes, Jr. is a member of the technical team at Mike Holt Enterprises, working directly with Mike Holt in researching, re-writing, and coordinating content, to assure the technical accuracy of the information in the products. He is a permanent member of the video teams, on which he has served since the 2017 *Code* cycle.

Mario is licensed as an Electrical Contractor, most recently having worked as an electrical inspector and plans examiner for an engineering firm in South Florida. Additionally, he was an Electrical Instructor for a technical college, teaching students pursuing an associate degree in electricity. He taught subjects such as ac/dc fundamentals, residential and commercial wiring, blueprint reading, and electrical estimating. He brings to the Mike Holt team a wealth of knowledge and devotion for the *NEC*.

He started his career at 16 years old in his father's electrical contracting company. Once he got his Florida State contractor's license, he ran the company as project manager and estimator. Mario's passion for the *NEC* prompted him to get his inspector and plans review certifications and embark on a new journey in electrical *Code* compliance. He's worked on complex projects such as hospitals, casinos, hotels and multi-family high rise buildings. Mario is very passionate about educating electrical professionals about electrical safety and the *National Electrical Code*.

Mario's a member of the IAEI, NFPA, and ICC, and enjoys participating in the meetings; he believes that by staying active in these organizations he'll be ahead of the game, with cutting-edge knowledge pertaining to safety codes.

When not immersed in the electrical world Mario enjoys fitness training. He resides in Pembroke Pines, Florida with his beautiful family, which includes his wife and his two sons. They enjoy family trip getaways to Disney World and other amusement parks.

Mike Holt Enterprises

TAKE IT UP A NOTCH

Upgrade your learning tool box...

Do you have the digital products that accompany this book?

Videos

Adding videos to your studies will have a huge impact on your understanding of this topic. Mike's video recordings are dynamic, and feature a panel of industry experts that discuss the rules, explain why they are important, and provide insight as to how to apply them in the field. Whether you're a visual or an auditory learner, watching the videos will not only help you process the information, but will also help you remember content later on. Watch on your computer, tablet or phone!

Digital Book

Take your product on the road! The digital version of the textbook will allow you to use it on the job site or on the move!

SCAN NOW TO UPGRADE THIS BOOK

MikeHolt.com/Upgrade23BG

Have multiple Mike Holt Products?
Contact the office for the best pricing on upgrades.

Digital Answer Key

Wherever you've chosen to work on your program, you'll have access to the answer key readily available at your fingertips.

Did you buy the book from another seller?
To get your copy of the answer key, scan the QR Code to the right or visit: MikeHolt.com/MyAK23BG

Did you purchase your product directly from Mike Holt Enterprises?
The digital answer key that comes with your product can be accessed in your account at: MikeHolt.com/MyAccount

Have questions? Call our team at 888.632.2633

Mike Holt Enterprises